JESUS AND THE EYEWITNESSES

JESUS AND THE EYEWITNESSES

The Gospels as Eyewitness Testimony

Richard Bauckham

WILLIAM B. EERDMANS PUBLISHING COMPANY

GRAND RAPIDS, MICHIGAN / CAMBRIDGE, U.K.

Published 2006 by

Wm. B. Eerdmans Publishing Co.

2140 Oak Industrial Drive N.E., Grand Rapids, Michigan 49505 /

P.O. Box 163, Cambridge CB3 9PU U.K.

Printed in the United States of America

12 11 10 09 08 07   8 7 6 5 4 3 2

Library of Congress Cataloging-in-Publication Data

Bauckham, Richard.

    Jesus and the eyewitnesses: the Gospels as eyewitness testimony / Richard Bauckham.

        p.   cm.

      ISBN 978-0-8028-3162-0 (cloth: alk. paper)

      1. Jesus Christ — Historicity. 2. Bible. N.T. Gospels — Evidences,

      authority, etc.   I. Title.

    BT303.2.B36   2006

    226′.067 — dc22

                                    2006016806

www.eerdmans.com

To all my colleagues,
past and present,
in St Mary's College,
University of St Andrews

Contents

CONTENTS

Tables

Preface

Some of the material in this book was first presented as lectures that I was invited to give in three institutions in the U.S.: the fourteenth Annual Biblical Studies Lectures, 2003, at Beeson Divinity School, Samford University, Birmingham, Alabama; the Payton Lectures, 2003, at Fuller Theological Seminary, Pasadena, California; and the Derward W. Deere Lectures, 2004, at Golden Gate Baptist Theological Seminary, Mill Valley, California. I am grateful to these institutions for inviting me and to many people, staff and students, who made valuable comments on the lectures and who helped to make my visits a great pleasure.

Much of this book was written during a gradual recuperation from prolonged illness. I believe it could not have been written without the prayers of many who supported me during that period, or without — to use Paul's phrase (2 Cor 12:9) — God's grace working as power in weakness.

RICHARD BAUCKHAM

Abbreviations

AB	Anchor Bible
ABD	*Anchor Bible Dictionary*
Adv. Haer.	*Adversus Haereses* (Irenaeus)
AnBib	Analectia Biblica
Ant.	*Antiquities* (Josephus)
ASNU	Acta Seminarii Neotestamentici Upsaliensis
b.	Babylonian Talmud
BeO	*Bibbia e oriente*
BETL	Bibliotheca ephemeridum theologicarum lovaniensium
Bib	*Biblica*
BIS	Biblical Interpretation Series
BJRL	*Bulletin of the John Rylands Library*
BNTC	Black's (Harper's) New Testament Commentaries
BZ	*Biblische Zeitschrift*
BZNW	Beihefte zur Zeitschrift für die neutestamentliche Wissenschaft
C. Ap.	*Contra Apionem* (Josephus)
C. Cels.	*Contra Celsum* (Origen)
CB[NT]	Coniectanea biblica: New Testament Series, Coniectanea neotestamentica
CBQ	*Catholic Biblical Quarterly*
CCSA	Corpus Christianorum Series Apocryphorum
CG	Corpus Gnosticum (Nag Hammadi Library)
CGTC	Cambridge Greek Testament Commentary

CSCO	Corpus Scriptorum Christianorum Orientalium
De vir. ill.	*De viris illustribus* (Jerome)
DJD	Discoveries in the Judean Desert
Ep.	*Epistulae* (Pliny, Seneca)
ETL	*Ephemerides theologicae lovanienses*
ExpT	*Expository Times*
FRLANT	Forschungen zur Religion und Literatur des Alten und Neuen Testaments
HDR	Harvard Dissertations in Religion
Hist. Conscr.	*Quomodo historia conscribenda sit* (Lucian of Samosata)
Hist. Eccl.	*Historia ecclesiastica* (Eusebius)
HTKNT	Herders theologischer Kommentar zum Neuen Testament
HTR	*Harvard Theological Review*
ICC	International Critical Commentary
IEJ	*Israel Exploration Journal*
Inst.	*Institutio oratoria* (Quintilian)
Int	*Interpretation*
JBL	*Journal of Biblical Literature*
JECS	*Journal of Early Christian Studies*
JEH	*Journal of Ecclesiastical History*
JHS	*Journal of Hellenic Studies*
JJS	*Journal of Jewish Studies*
JR	*Journal of Religion*
JSHJ	*Journal for the Study of the Historical Jesus*
JSJ	*Journal for the Study of Judaism in the Persian, Hellenistic, and Roman Periods*
JSNT	*Journal for the Study of the New Testament*
JSNTSup	Journal for the Study of the New Testament Supplement Series
JSOTSup	Journal for the Study of the Old Testament Supplement Series
JSS	*Journal of Semitic Studies*
JTS	*Journal of Theological Studies*
m.	Mishnah
NICNT	New International Commentary on the New Testament
NIGTC	New International Greek Testament Commentary
NovT	*Novum Testamentum*
NovTSup	Novum Testamentum Supplements
NRSV	New Revised Standard Version
NTS	*New Testament Studies*

Pap. Oxy.	Oxyrhynchus Papyri/us
PEQ	*Palestine Exploration Quarterly*
RB	*Revue biblique*
SBLDS	Society of Biblical Literature Dissertation Series
SC	Sources chrétiennes
SNTSMS	Society for New Testament Studies Monograph Series
SPAW	Sitzungsberichte der Preußischen Akademie der Wissenschaften
ST	*Studia Theologica*
STAR	Studies in Theology and Religion
TSAJ	Texte und Studien zum antiken Judentum
TU	Texte und Untersuchungen
TynB	*Tyndale Bulletin*
WBC	Word Biblical Commentary
WTJ	*Westminster Theological Journal*
WUNT	Wissenschaftliche Untersuchungen zum Neuen Testament
y.	Jerusalem Talmud
ZAC	*Zeitschrift für Antikes Christentum*
ZNW	*Zeitschrift für die neutestamentliche Wissenschaft*

1. From the Historical Jesus to the Jesus of Testimony

The Historical Quest and Christian Faith

For two centuries scholars have been in quest of the historical Jesus. The quest began with the beginnings of modern historical critical study of the New Testament. It has often seemed the most significant task that critical study of the New Testament could pursue. Thousands of scholars have been drawn into the pursuit, and hundreds, perhaps thousands, of books, scholarly and popular, have been products of the quest. Interest and activity have waxed and waned over the years. Many have pronounced the quest misguided, fruitless, and finished. Others have castigated their predecessors but put their faith in new methods and approaches that they claim will succeed where others failed. Whole eras of western cultural, as well as religious, history have been reflected in the various stages of the quest. Attitudes to the quest, positive, negative, or qualified, have distinguished whole schools of theology.

At the beginning of the twenty-first century the quest of the historical Jesus flourishes as never before, especially in North America. The unprecedented size of the industry of New Testament scholarship and the character of the American media both play a part in this. But the fact that the figure of Jesus retains its supremely iconic significance in American culture,[1] as compared with the more secularized societies of Europe and the British isles, is what makes the continuing efforts of historians — rather than theologians or

---

1. See S. Prothero, *American Jesus: How the Son of God Became a National Icon* (New York: Farrar, Straus and Giroux, 2003).

spiritual leaders — to reconstruct the historical reality of Jesus a matter of seemingly endless interest to believers, half-believers, ex-believers, and would-be believers in the Jesus of Christian faith. Is the so-called "historical Jesus" — the Jesus historians may reconstruct as they do any other part of history — the same Jesus as the figure at the center of the Christian religion? This is the question that both excites and disturbs the scholars and the readers of their books alike.

From the beginning of the quest the whole enterprise of attempting to reconstruct the historical figure of Jesus in a way that is allegedly purely historical, free of the concerns of faith and dogma, has been highly problematic for Christian faith and theology. What, after all, does the phrase "the historical Jesus" mean? It is a seriously ambiguous phrase, with at least three meanings. It could mean Jesus as he really was in his earthly life, in that sense distinguishing the earthly Jesus from the Jesus who, according to Christian faith, now lives and reigns exalted in heaven and will come to bring history to its end. In that sense the historical Jesus is by no means all of the Jesus Christians know and worship, but as a usage that distinguishes Jesus in his earthly life from the exalted Christ the phrase could be unproblematic.

However, the full reality of Jesus as he historically was is not, of course, accessible to us. The world itself could not contain the books that would be needed to record even all that was empirically observable about Jesus, as the closing verse of the Gospel of John puts it. Like any other part of history, the Jesus who lived in first-century Palestine is knowable only through the evidence that has survived. We could therefore use the phrase "the historical Jesus" to mean, not all that Jesus was, but Jesus insofar as his historical reality is accessible to us. But here we reach the crucial methodological problem. For Christian faith this Jesus, the earthly Jesus as we can know him, is the Jesus of the canonical Gospels, Jesus as Matthew, Mark, Luke, and John recount and portray him. There are difficulties, of course, in the fact that these four accounts of Jesus differ, but there is no doubt that the Jesus of the church's faith through the centuries has been a Jesus found in these Gospels. That means that Christian faith has trusted these texts. Christian faith has trusted that in these texts we encounter the real Jesus, and it is hard to see how Christian faith and theology can work with a radically distrusting attitude to the Gospels.

Yet everything changes when historians suspect that these texts may be hiding the real Jesus from us, at best because they give us the historical Jesus filtered through the spectacles of early Christian faith, at worst because much of what they tell us is a Jesus constructed by the needs and interests of various groups in the early church. Then that phrase "the historical Jesus" comes to mean, not the Jesus of the Gospels, but the allegedly real Jesus behind the

Gospels, the Jesus the historian must reconstruct by subjecting the Gospels to ruthlessly objective (so it is claimed) scrutiny. It is essential to realize that this is not just treating the Gospels as historical evidence. It is the application of a methodological skepticism that must test every aspect of the evidence so that what the historian establishes is not believable because the Gospels tell us it is, but because the historian has independently verified it. The result of such work is inevitably not one historical Jesus, but many. Among current historical Jesuses on offer there is the Jesus of Dominic Crossan, the Jesus of Marcus Borg, the Jesus of N. T. (Tom) Wright, the Jesus of Dale Allison, the Jesus of Gerd Theissen, and many others.[2] The historian's judgment of the historical value of the Gospels may be minimal, as in some of these cases, or maximal, as in others, but in all cases the result is a Jesus reconstructed by the historian, a Jesus attained by the attempt to go back behind the Gospels and, in effect, to provide an alternative to the Gospels' constructions of Jesus.

There is a very serious problem here that is obscured by the naive historical positivism that popular media presentations of these matters promote, not always innocently. All history — meaning all that historians write, all historiography — is an inextricable combination of fact and interpretation, the empirically observable and the intuited or constructed meaning. In the Gospels we have, of course, unambiguously such a combination, and it is this above all that motivates the quest for the Jesus one might find if one

2. J. D. Crossan, *The Historical Jesus: The Life of a Mediterranean Jewish Peasant* (Edinburgh: Clark, 1991); M. J. Borg, *Jesus: A New Vision* (2nd edition; San Francisco: HarperSanFrancisco, 1991); N. T. Wright, *Jesus and the Victory of God* (London: SPCK, 1996); D. C. Allison, *Jesus of Nazareth: Millenarian Prophet* (Minneapolis: Fortress, 1998); G. Theissen and A. Merz, *The Historical Jesus: A Comprehensive Guide* (tr. J. Bowden; London: SCM, 1998). These examples are selected to represent the wide variety of current accounts of the historical Jesus. Other notable recent books include: J. P. Meier, *A Marginal Jew: Rethinking the Historical Jesus*, 3 vols. (New York: Doubleday, 1991-2001); E. P. Sanders, *The Historical Figure of Jesus* (London: Allen Lane [Penguin], 1993); S. McKnight, *A New Vision for Israel: The Teachings of Jesus in National Context* (Grand Rapids: Eerdmans, 1999); M. Bockmuehl, *This Jesus: Martyr, Lord, Messiah* (Edinburgh: Clark, 1994); B. Chilton, *Rabbi Jesus: An Intimate Biography* (New York: Doubleday, 2000); R. W. Funk, *A Credible Jesus: Fragments of a Vision* (Santa Rosa: Polebridge, 2002); J. D. G. Dunn, *Jesus Remembered* (Grand Rapids: Eerdmans, 2003); E. Schüssler Fiorenza, *Jesus and the Politics of Interpretation* (New York: Continuum, 2000); G. Vermes, *The Authentic Gospel of Jesus* (London: Penguin, 2004). Surveys include: J. H. Charlesworth and W. P. Weaver, eds., *Images of Jesus Today* (Valley Forge: Trinity, 1994); M. J. Borg, *Jesus in Contemporary Scholarship* (Valley Forge: Trinity, 1994); D. Marguerat, E. Norelli, and J.-M. Poffet, eds., *Jésus de Nazareth. Nouvelles Approches d'une Énigme* (Geneva: Labor et Fides, 1998); B. Witherington, *The Jesus Quest: The Third Search for the Jew of Nazareth* (2nd edition; Downers Grove: InterVarsity, 1997); J. Schröter and R. Brucker, eds., *Der historische Jesu. Tendenzen und Perspektiven der gegenwärtigen Forschung* (BZNW 114; Berlin: de Gruyter, 2002).

could leave aside all the meaning that inheres in each Gospel's story of Jesus. One might, of course, acquire from a skeptical study of the Gospels a meager collection of extremely probable but mere facts that would be of very little interest. That Jesus was crucified may be indubitable but in itself it is of no more significance than the fact that undoubtedly so were thousands of others in his time. The historical Jesus of any of the scholars of the quest is no mere collection of facts, but a figure of significance. Why? If the enterprise is really about going back behind the Evangelists' and the early church's interpretation of Jesus, where does a different interpretation come from? It comes not merely from deconstructing the Gospels but also from reconstructing a Jesus who, as a portrayal of who Jesus really was, can rival the Jesus of the Gospels. We should be under no illusions that, however minimal a Jesus results from the quest, such a historical Jesus is no less a construction than the Jesus of each of the Gospels. Historical work, by its very nature, is always putting two and two together and making five — or twelve or seventeen.

From the perspective of Christian faith and theology we must ask whether the enterprise of reconstructing a historical Jesus behind the Gospels, as it has been pursued through all phases of the quest, can ever substitute for the Gospels themselves as a way of access to the reality of Jesus the man who lived in first-century Palestine. It cannot be said that historical study of Jesus and the Gospels is illegitimate or that it cannot assist our understanding of Jesus. To say that would be, as Wright points out, a modern sort of docetism.[3] It would be tantamount to denying that Jesus really lived in history that must be, in some degree, accessible to historical study. We need not question that historical study can be relevant to our understanding of Jesus in significant ways. What is in question is whether the reconstruction of a Jesus other than the Jesus of the Gospels, the attempt, in other words, to do all over again what the Evangelists did, though with different methods, critical historical methods, can ever provide the kind of access to the reality of Jesus that Christian faith and theology have always trusted we have in the Gospels. By comparison with the Gospels, any Jesus reconstructed by the quest cannot fail to be reductionist from the perspective of Christian faith and theology.

Here, then, is the dilemma that has always faced Christian theology in the light of the quest of the historical Jesus. Must history and theology part company at this point where Christian faith's investment in history is at its most vital? Must we settle for trusting the Gospels for our access to the Jesus in whom Christians believe, while leaving the historians to construct a historical Jesus based only on what they can verify for themselves by critical histori-

3. N. T. Wright, *The Challenge of Jesus* (London: SPCK, 2000) 3-10.

cal methods? I think there is a better way forward, a way in which theology and history may meet in the historical Jesus instead of parting company there. In this book I am making a first attempt to lay out some of the evidence and methods for it. Its key category is testimony.

Introducing the Key Category: Eyewitness Testimony

I suggest that we need to recover the sense in which the Gospels are testimony. This does not mean that they are testimony *rather than* history. It means that the kind of historiography they are is testimony. An irreducible feature of testimony as a form of human utterance is that it asks to be trusted. This need not mean that it asks to be trusted uncritically, but it does mean that testimony should not be treated as credible only to the extent that it can be independently verified. There can be good reasons for trusting or distrusting a witness, but these are precisely reasons for *trusting or distrusting*. Trusting testimony is not an irrational act of faith that leaves critical rationality aside; it is, on the contrary, the rationally appropriate way of responding to authentic testimony. Gospels understood as testimony are the entirely appropriate means of access to the historical reality of Jesus. It is true that a powerful trend in the modern development of critical historical philosophy and method finds trusting testimony a stumbling-block in the way of the historian's autonomous access to truth that she or he can verify independently. But it is also a rather neglected fact that all history, like all knowledge, relies on testimony. In the case of some kinds of historical event this is especially true, indeed obvious. In the last chapter we shall consider a remarkable modern instance, the Holocaust, where testimony is indispensable for adequate historical access to the events. We need to recognize that, historically speaking, testimony is a unique and uniquely valuable means of access to historical reality.

Testimony offers us, I wish to suggest, both a reputable historiographic category for reading the Gospels as history, and also a theological model for understanding the Gospels as the entirely appropriate means of access to the historical reality of Jesus. Theologically speaking, the category of testimony enables us to read the Gospels as precisely the kind of text we need in order to recognize the disclosure of God in the history of Jesus. Understanding the Gospels as testimony, we can recognize this theological meaning of the history not as an arbitrary imposition on the objective facts, but as the way the witnesses perceived the history, in an inextricable coinherence of observable event and perceptible meaning. Testimony is the category that enables us to read the Gospels in a properly historical way and a properly theological way. It is where history and theology meet.

In order to pursue this agenda, we need to give fresh attention to the eyewitnesses of the history of Jesus and their relationship to the Gospel traditions and to the Gospels themselves. In general, I shall be arguing in this book that the Gospel texts are much closer to the form in which the eyewitnesses told their stories or passed on their traditions than is commonly envisaged in current scholarship. This is what gives the Gospels their character as testimony. They embody the testimony of the eyewitnesses, not of course without editing and interpretation, but in a way that is substantially faithful to how the eyewitnesses themselves told it, since the Evangelists were in more or less direct contact with eyewitnesses, not removed from them by a long process of anonymous transmission of the traditions. In the case of one of the Gospels, that of John, I conclude, very unfashionably, that an eyewitness wrote it.

This directness of relationship between the eyewitnesses and the Gospel texts requires a quite different picture of the way the Gospel traditions were transmitted from that which most New Testament scholars and students have inherited from the early-twentieth-century movement in New Testament scholarship known as form criticism. Although the methods of form criticism are no longer at the center of the way most scholars approach the issue of the historical Jesus, it has bequeathed one enormously influential legacy. This is the assumption that the traditions about Jesus, his acts and his words, passed through a long process of oral tradition in the early Christian communities and reached the writers of the Gospels only at a late stage of this process. Various different models of the way oral tradition happens — or can be supposed to have happened in those communities — have been canvassed as alternatives to the way the form critics envisaged this. They will be discussed later in this book (see chapter 10). But the assumption remains firmly in place that, whatever the form in which the eyewitnesses of the history of Jesus first told their stories or repeated Jesus' teachings, a long process of anonymous transmission in the communities intervened between their testimony and the writing of the Gospels. The Gospels embody their testimony only in a rather remote way. Some scholars would stress the conservatism of the process of oral tradition, which preserved the traditions of the eyewitnesses rather faithfully; others would stress the creativity of the communities, which adapted the traditions to their needs and purposes and frequently augmented the traditions with freshly invented ones. But, however conservative or creative the tradition may have been, the eyewitnesses from whom it originated appear to have nothing significantly to do with it once they have set it going.

There is a very simple and obvious objection to this picture that has often been made but rarely taken very seriously. It was put memorably in 1933 by Vincent Taylor, the scholar who did most to introduce the methods of German form criticism into English-speaking New Testament scholarship. In an often-quoted comment, he wrote that "[i]f the Form-Critics are right, the disciples must have been translated to heaven immediately after the Resurrection."[4] He went on to point out that many eyewitness participants in the events of the Gospel narratives "did not go into permanent retreat; for at least a generation they moved among the young Palestinian communities, and through preaching and fellowship their recollections were at the disposal of those who sought information."[5] More recently Martin Hengel has insisted, against the form-critical approach, that the "personal link of the Jesus tradition with particular tradents, or more precisely their memory and missionary preaching . . . is historically undeniable," but was completely neglected by the form-critical notion that "the tradition 'circulated' quite anonymously . . . in the communities, which are viewed as pure collectives."[6] Part of my intention in this book is to present evidence, much of it not hitherto noticed at all, that makes the "personal link of the Jesus tradition with particular tradents," throughout the period of the transmission of the tradition down to the writing of the Gospels, if not "historically undeniable," then at least historically very probable.

The Gospels were written within living memory of the events they recount. Mark's Gospel was written well within the lifetime of many of the eyewitnesses, while the other three canonical Gospels were written in the period when living eyewitnesses were becoming scarce, exactly at the point in time when their testimony would perish with them were it not put in writing. This is a highly significant fact, entailed not by unusually early datings of the Gospels but by the generally accepted ones. One lasting effect of form criticism, with its model of anonymous community transmission, has been to give most Gospels scholars an unexamined impression of the period between the events of the Gospel story and the writing of the Gospels as much longer than it realistically was. We have been accustomed to working with models of oral tradition as it is passed down through the generations in traditional communities. We imagine the traditions passing through many minds and mouths before they reached the writers of the Gospels. But the period in question is actually that of a relatively (for that period) long lifetime.

---

4. V. Taylor, *The Formation of the Gospel Tradition* (2nd edition; London: Macmillan, 1935) 41.

5. Taylor, *Formation*, 42.

6. M. Hengel, *The Four Gospels and the One Gospel of Jesus Christ* (tr. J. Bowden; London: SCM, 2000) 143.

Birger Gerhardsson makes this point about the influence of form criticism, which often worked with folklore as a model for the kind of oral tradition that lies behind the Gospels:

> It seems as though parallels from folklore — that is, material extending over centuries and widely different geographical areas — have tempted scholars unconsciously to stretch out the chronological and geographical dimensions of the formation of the early Christian tradition in an unreasonable manner. What is needed here is a more sober approach to history. In the New Testament period the church was not nearly as widespread or as large in numbers as we usually imagine.[7]

If, as I shall argue in this book, the period between the "historical" Jesus and the Gospels was actually spanned, not by anonymous community transmission, but by the continuing presence and testimony of the eyewitnesses, who remained the authoritative sources of their traditions until their deaths, then the usual ways of thinking of oral tradition are not appropriate at all. Gospel traditions did not, for the most part, circulate anonymously but in the name of the eyewitnesses to whom they were due. Throughout the lifetime of the eyewitnesses, Christians remained interested in and aware of the ways the eyewitnesses themselves told their stories. So, in imagining how the traditions reached the Gospel writers, not oral tradition but eyewitness testimony should be our principal model.

Samuel Byrskog and the Eyewitnesses

An important contribution to putting the eyewitnesses back into our understanding of the transmission of Gospel traditions in the early Christian movement has recently been made by the Swedish scholar Samuel Byrskog. His book *Story as History — History as Story,* published in 2000, carries the illuminating subtitle: *The Gospel Tradition in the Context of Ancient Oral History.*[8] Byrskog compares the practice of Greco-Roman historians with the fairly recent discipline of "oral history" and finds the role of eyewitness-informants very similar in both. The ancient historians — such as Thucydides, Polybius, Josephus, and Tacitus — were convinced that true history could be written only while events were still within living memory, and

7. B. Gerhardsson, *The Reliability of the Gospel Tradition* (Peabody: Hendrickson, 2001) 40.

8. WUNT 123; Tübingen: Mohr, 2000; reprinted Leiden: Brill, 2002.

they valued as their sources the oral reports of direct experience of the events by involved participants in them. Ideally, the historian himself should have been a participant in the events he narrates — as, for example, Xenophon, Thucydides, and Josephus were — but, since he could not have been at all the events he recounts or in all the places he describes, the historian had also to rely on eyewitnesses whose living voices he could hear and whom he could question himself: "Autopsy [eyewitness testimony] was the essential means to reach back into the past."[9]

Of course, not all historians lived up to these ideals, and most employed oral traditions and written sources at least to supplement their own knowledge of the events and the reports of other eyewitnesses. But the standards set by Thucydides and Polybius were historiographic best practice, to which other historians aspired or at least paid lip-service. Good historians were highly critical of those who relied largely on written sources. That some historians pretended to firsthand knowledge they did not really have[10] is backhanded support for the acknowledged necessity of eyewitness testimony in historiography.

A very important point that Byrskog stresses is that, for Greek and Roman historians, the ideal eyewitness was not the dispassionate observer but one who, as a participant, had been closest to the events and whose direct experience enabled him to understand and interpret the significance of what he had seen. The historians "preferred the eyewitness who was socially involved or, even better, had been actively participating in the events."[11] "Involvement was not an obstacle to a correct understanding of what they perceived as historical truth. It was rather the essential means to a correct understanding of what had really happened."[12]

The coinherence of fact and meaning, empirical report and engaged interpretation, was not a problem for these historians. Eyewitnesses were "as much interpreters as observers."[13] Their accounts became essential parts of the historians' writings. In this way, these ancient historians' approach bears quite close comparison with modern oral history. The latter recognizes, on the one hand, that bare facts do not make history and the subjective aspects of an eyewitness's experience and memory are themselves evidence that the historian should not discard, while, on the other hand, it is also important to realize that a "person involved remembers better than a disinterested ob-

9. Byrskog, *Story*, 64.
10. Byrskog, *Story*, 214-20.
11. Byrskog, *Story*, 167.
12. Byrskog, *Story*, 154.
13. Byrskog, *Story*, 149.

server."[14] Of course, the interpretative, as well as evidential, role of the eyewitnesses whose testimony a Greek or Roman historian took into his work is by no means incompatible with the historian's own interpretative task, which involved selectivity as well as the shaping of the overall narrative into a coherent story. In the best practice, advocated, for example, by Polybius, the historian tells an interpretative story, but "only history in its factual pastness" was allowed "to be part of his interpretative story."[15]

Having established the key role of eyewitness testimony in ancient historiography, Byrskog argues that a similar role must have been played in the formation of the Gospel traditions and the Gospels themselves by individuals who were qualified to be both eyewitnesses and informants about the history of Jesus. He attempts to identify such eyewitnesses and to find the traces of their testimony in the Gospels, stressing that they, like the historians and their informants, would have been involved participants who not only remembered facts but naturally also interpreted in the process of experiencing and remembering. "The gospel narratives . . . are thus syntheses of history and story, of the oral history of an eyewitness and the interpretative and narrativizing procedures of an author."[16] In Byrskog's account the eyewitnesses do not disappear behind a long process of anonymous transmission and formation of traditions by communities, but remain an influential presence in the communities, people who could be consulted, who told their stories and whose oral accounts lay at no great distance from the textualized form the Gospels gave them.

The relevance of Byrskog's work to our own concern in this book for understanding the Gospels as embodying eyewitness testimony is obvious. Byrskog has shown that testimony — the stories told by involved participants in the events — was not alien to ancient historiography but essential to it. Oral testimony was preferable to written sources, and witnesses who could contribute the insider perspective only available from those who had participated in the events were preferred to detached observers. This goes against the instincts of much modern historiography because it seems to compromise objectivity, putting the historian at the mercy of the subjective perspectives of those who had axes to grind and interpretations of their own to pass on, but there is much to be said for ancient historiographic practice as at least an important element in historical research and writing: the ancient historians knew that firsthand insider testimony gave access to truth

14. Byrskog, *Story*, 28, 165-66.
15. Byrskog, *Story*, 264.
16. Byrskog, *Story*, 304-5.

that could not be had otherwise. Though not uncritical, they were willing to trust their eyewitness-informants for the sake of the unique access they gave to the truth of the events. In this respect, we can see that the Gospels are much closer to the methods and aims of ancient historiography than they are to typical modern historiography, though Byrskog importantly draws attention to the quite recent development of oral history, which values the perspective and experience of oral informants, not just mining their evidence for discrete facts.[17]

Byrskog's work is a major contribution with which all Gospel scholars should feel obliged to come to terms. Some criticisms have already been voiced. It has been charged that Byrskog assumes, rather than demonstrates, that the Gospels are comparable with the practice of oral history in ancient Greek and Roman historiography.[18] Another reviewer is disappointed that Byrskog provides little in the way of criteria either to identify eyewitnesses or to identify eyewitness testimony in the tradition.[19] These are important observations and show at least that Byrskog's work, impressive as it is, cannot yet stand as a completed case, but requires further testing and development. We shall attempt this in the following chapters.

17. Byrskog, *Story*, 26-33; and especially P. Thompson, *The Voice of the Past: Oral History* (2nd edition; Oxford: Oxford University Press, 1988).

18. C. R. Matthews, review in *JBL* 121 (2002) 175-77; cf. P. M. Head, "The Role of Eyewitnesses in the Formation of the Gospel Tradition," *TynB* 52 (2001) 294, who thinks Byrskog should have taken more seriously the distinction between ancient historiography and ancient biography.

19. W. Carter, review in *CBQ* 63 (2001) 545-46.

2. Papias on the Eyewitnesses

Papias and His Book

Papias[1] was bishop of Hierapolis, a city in the Lycus valley in the Roman province of Asia, not far from Laodicea and Colossae. He completed his major work, *Exposition of the Logia*[2] *of the Lord,* in five books, sometime near the beginning of the second century, but sadly it has not survived. It is one of those lost works that historians of early Christianity could most wish to see recovered from a forgotten library or the sands of Egypt. It might well solve many of our problems about the origins of the Gospels. As it is, we have no more than two dozen fragments surviving as quotations in later writers.[3] The best-known and, from the point of view of Gospels studies most interesting, of the fragments are those preserved by Eusebius of Caesarea. Eusebius thought Papias stupid ("a man of very little intelligence," *Hist. Eccl.* 3.39.13[4]) because he was a millenarian who expected a paradise on earth at the second coming of Christ and probably also be-

---

1. For a good brief account of scholarship on Papias, see W. R. Schoedel, "Papias," in *ABD* 5.140-42.

2. Because the meaning of Greek *logia* here is disputed I have left it untranslated. It probably means something like "accounts of what Jesus said and did." See the discussion in chapter 9 below.

3. A collection of the fragments in English translation is in J. B. Lightfoot, J. R. Harmer, and M. W. Holmes, *The Apostolic Fathers* (Leicester: Apollos, 1990) 307-29. A slightly less complete collection is in W. R. Schoedel, *The Apostolic Fathers,* vol. 5: *Polycarp, Martyrdom of Polycarp, Fragments of Papias* (Camden: Nelson, 1967) 89-127.

4. The phrase may have been Papias's own self-deprecating usage; cf. Schoedel, *Polycarp,* 104.

cause Eusebius did not agree with some of what Papias wrote about the origins of New Testament writings. There is no reason why we should adopt this prejudiced attitude to Papias, who seems to have been in a good position to know some interesting facts about the origins of the Gospels. But what Papias says about such matters, in the quotations from the Prologue to his book that Eusebius has rather carefully selected, does not easily cohere with the scholarly views about the Gospels that have been most prevalent in the last few decades. At one time, these passages from Papias were often discussed and debated at length, but more recently they have been more often ignored.

Papias belonged, roughly speaking, to the third Christian generation, and therefore to a generation that had been in touch with the first Christian generation, the generation of the apostles. He was personally acquainted with the daughters of Philip the evangelist, the Philip who was one of the Seven (though later writers assimilated him with the Philip who was one of the Twelve). This Philip spent the last years of his life in Hierapolis, and two of his daughters, who were well known as prophets (Acts 21:8-9), also lived out the rest of their lives there, unmarried.[5] Perhaps Papias knew Philip himself in his childhood, but it was from Philip's daughters that he learned some stories about the apostles (Eusebius, *Hist. Eccl.* 3.39.9).

We do not know exactly when Papias wrote (or rather completed) his book. The date commonly given — c. 130 — is based on very unreliable evidence: the claim made by the early-fifth-century writer Philip of Side that Papias said that those who were raised from the dead by Jesus survived to the reign of Hadrian (117-38 CE).[6] This statement should probably not be trusted,[7] since Eusebius attributes a statement of this kind to another second-century Christian writer, Quadratus (*Hist. Eccl.* 4.3.2-3), and Philip of Side's statement may well be no more than a mistaken reminiscence of this. (William Schoedel comments that Philip of Side "is a bungler and cannot be trusted."[8]) Eusebius,

---

5. A third daughter died in Ephesus, having presumably married. The information is from Polycrates of Ephesus, writing c. 190, quoted in Eusebius, *Hist. Eccl.* 5.24.2. Polycrates identifies the two Philips, calling the Philip who died in Hierapolis and had daughters who were prophets one of the Twelve; cf. R. Bauckham, "Papias and Polycrates on the Origin of the Fourth Gospel," *JTS* 44 (1993) 30-31. The Montanist writer Proclus also knew the tradition that Philip and his daughters settled in Hierapolis, but speaks of four daughters, as in Acts 21:8-9, and claims that all four died in Hierapolis (Eusebius, *Hist. Eccl.* 3.31.4).

6. Fragment 16 in J. Kürzinger, *Papias von Hierapolis und die Evangelien des Neuen Testaments* (Regensburg: Pustet, 1983) 116-17 = fragment 5 in Lightfoot, Harmer, and Holmes, *The Apostolic Fathers*, 317-18.

7. Hengel, *Die johanneische Frage. Ein Lösungsversuch* (Tübingen: Mohr, 1993), 77, is one who thinks it can be trusted and therefore dates Papias's work between 120 and 135.

8. Schoedel, *Polycarp*, 120.

on the other hand, by the point at which he introduces Papias in his chronologically sequential narrative and his association of Papias with Clement of Rome and Ignatius of Antioch (*Hist. Eccl.* 3.36.1-2), implies that Papias was active during the reign of Trajan (98-117 CE) and presumably before Ignatius suffered martyrdom (c. 107 CE). Since Eusebius was motivated to discredit Papias and a later dating of Papias's work would serve this purpose, Eusebius can probably be trusted for an approximate date of Papias's work. We also know that Papias quoted 1 Peter and 1 John (*Hist. Eccl.* 3.39.17) and that he knew the Book of Revelation,[9] probably, as some other scholars and I[10] have argued, the Gospel of John (see chapter 9 below), and quite possibly the Gospel of Luke.[11] We cannot therefore date his writing before the very end of the first century, but it could be as early as the turn of the century. Several scholars have argued for a date around 110 CE or even earlier.[12]

For our purposes it is much more important that, whenever Papias actually wrote, in the passage we shall study he speaks *about* an earlier period in his life, the time during which he was collecting oral reports of the words and deeds of Jesus. As we shall see the period of which he is speaking must be c. 80 CE. It is the period in which the Gospels of Matthew, Luke, and John were most likely all being written. This makes this particular passage from Papias very precious evidence of the way in which Gospel traditions were understood to be related to the eyewitnesses at the very time when three of our canonical Gospels were being written. Its evidence on this point has rarely been sufficiently appreciated because few scholars have taken seriously the difference between the time at which Papias wrote (or completed his writing) and the time about which he reminisces in this passage. Even Samuel Byrskog, who takes Papias's statement about the Gospel of Mark very seriously,[13] gives little attention to this passage.[14]

---

9. See fragments 10 and 11 in Lightfoot, Harmer, and Holmes, *The Apostolic Fathers*, 320-21.

10. Bauckham, "Papias and Polycrates," 44-63.

11. Luke 10:18 is quoted in the fragment of Papias in the Armenian version of Andrew of Caesarea: fragment 23 in J. Kürzinger, *Papias von Hierapolis und die Evangelien des Neuen Testaments*, 128-33 = fragment 24 in Lightfoot, Harmer, and Holmes, *The Apostolic Fathers*, 326-27.

12. V. Bartlet, "Papias's 'Exposition': Its Date and Contents," in H. G. Wood, ed., *Amicitiae Corolla* (J. R. Harris FS; London: University of London Press, 1933) 16-17, 20-22; Schoedel, *Polycarp*, 51-52; U. H. J. Körtner, *Papias von Hierapolis* (FRLANT 133; Göttingen, 1983) 89-94, 167-72, 225-26. R. H. Gundry, *Matthew: A Commentary on His Handbook for a Mixed Church under Persecution* (2nd edition; Grand Rapids: Eerdmans, 1994) 610-11; *Mark: A Commentary on His Apology for the Cross* (Grand Rapids: Eerdmans, 1993) 1027-29, argues for a date between 101 and 108 CE.

13. S. Byrskog, *Story as History — History as Story* (WUNT 123; Tübingen: Mohr, 2000; reprinted Leiden: Brill, 2002) 272-92.

14. Byrskog, *Story*, 244-45.

As well as the period about which Papias speaks in this passage, we should also note the relevance of his geographical location in Hierapolis. Vernon Bartlet explains:

> Hierapolis, of which he became "bishop" or chief local pastor, stood at the meeting-point of two great roads: one running east and west, between Antioch in Syria and Ephesus, the chief city of "Asia," the other south-east to Attalia in Pamphylia and north-west to Smyrna. There Papias was almost uniquely placed for collecting traditions coming direct from the original home of the Gospel both before his own day and during it, as well as from Palestinian [Christian] leaders settled in Asia (a great centre of the Jewish Dispersion).[15]

Papias on the Eyewitnesses

The passage is from the Prologue to Papias's work. Like Luke's Gospel, Papias's work was dedicated to a named individual, though the name has not survived, and in the Prologue addressed this dedicatee directly:

> I shall not hesitate also to put into properly ordered form for you [singular] everything I learned carefully in the past from the elders and noted down well, for the truth of which I vouch.[16] For unlike most people I did not enjoy those who have a great deal to say, but those who teach the truth. Nor did I enjoy those who recall someone else's commandments, but those who remember the commandments given by the Lord to the faith and proceeding from the truth itself. And if by chance anyone who had been in attendance on[17] *(parēkolouthēkōs tis)* the elders should come my way, I inquired about the words of the elders — [that is,] what [ac-

---

15. Bartlet, "Papias's 'Exposition,'" 17.

16. The translation of this first sentence follows the suggestions of Kürzinger, *Papias,* 77-82. Kürzinger proposes this German version: "Ich will die Mühe nicht scheuen, dir auch alles, was ich ehedem von den Alten (Presbytern) gut in Erfahrung gebracht und gut aufgezeichnet habe, in den Ausführungen geordnet darzustellen, wobei ich mich für deren Wahrheit verbürge" (77-78).

17. The usual translation is "anyone who had been a follower of," but this is potentially misleading, especially in contemporary English. The meaning of the verb *parakoloutheō* is not so much "come after" as "go closely with, attend." Moreover, the rendering of *parēkolouthēkōs* by the English noun "follower" suggests that the person was no longer in the relationship of disciple to the elders, whereas all that is meant is that the person had been present at their teaching (and might well be again). Schoedel, *Polycarp,* 99, rightly but awkwardly, translates: "someone . . . who had actually attended the elders."

cording to the elders] Andrew or Peter said *(eipen),* or Philip, or Thomas or James, or John or Matthew or any other of the Lord's disciples, and whatever Aristion and the elder John, the Lord's disciples, were saying *(legousin).* For I did not think that information from books would profit me as much as information from a living and surviving voice (Eusebius, *Hist. Eccl.* 3.39.3-4).[18]

In order to understand this passage correctly, we must first sort out the four categories of people Papias mentions:[19] (1) those who "had been in attendance on the elders," i.e. people who had been present at their teaching; (2) the elders themselves; (3) the Lord's disciples, consisting of Andrew, Peter, Philip, Thomas, James, John, Matthew, and others; (4) Aristion and John the Elder, who are also called "the Lord's disciples."

In the first place, category (1), those who "had been in attendance on the elders," are not to be understood as another generation following that of the elders. Some have supposed that Papias refers to three generations: the disciples of Jesus, the elders, and the elders' disciples,[20] and that he locates himself therefore in the third generation. That the disciples of the elders "had been in attendance on" (often, rather misleadingly translated "had been a follower of") the elders does not mean that the elders were, at the time about which Papias was writing, dead. It simply means that these people, before their travels took them through Hierapolis, had sat at the feet of the elders, attending to their teaching. The elders themselves were still alive, still teaching, when Papias spoke to these people who had recently heard them and could report their teaching to him.

Some scholars, including apparently Eusebius himself (*Hist. Eccl.* 3.39.7), have understood categories (2) and (3), the elders and the Lord's disciples, as one and the same,[21] but in that case it is hard to understand why Papias uses the word "elders" so emphatically and does not simply label this group "the Lord's disciples." It is much more satisfactory to read the text in the sense indicated by the words I have added in square brackets in the trans-

18. Apart from the first sentence and the translation of *parēkolouthēkōs tis* as "anyone who had been in attendance on," this translation is from Lightfoot, Harmer, and Holmes, *The Apostolic Fathers,* 314, with the words in square brackets added.

19. Schoedel, *Polycarp,* 98-100, provides a good brief account of the rival interpretations and supports the interpretation offered here.

20. E.g., C. E. Hill, *The Johannine Corpus in the Early Church* (Oxford: Oxford University Press, 2004) 384.

21. E.g., B. Orchard in B. Orchard and H. Riley, *The Order of the Synoptics: Why Three Synoptic Gospels?* (Macon: Mercer University Press, 1987) 176.

lation just given.[22] The elders are the senior Christian teachers in various cities of Asia at the time to which Papias refers in this passage. This is the sense in which Irenaeus, who knew Papias's work well and several times quoted traditions of "the elders" (*Adv. Haer.* 2.22.5; 4.28.1; 5.5.1; 5.30.1; 5.36.1, 2; 6.33.3), probably from Papias, understood the term.[23] Papias, living in Hierapolis, did not normally have the opportunity to hear these Asiatic elders himself, but when any of their disciples visited Hierapolis he asked what they were saying. In particular, of course, he wanted to hear of any traditions that the elders had from the Lord's disciples: Andrew, Peter, and the others. The apparent ambiguity in Papias's words really derives from the fact that he takes it for granted that the words of the elders in which he would be interested are those that transmit traditions from Andrew, Peter, and other disciples of the Lord.

As well as the debatable relationship between categories (2) and (3), interpreters have puzzled over category (4). Why are these two named disciples, called "the Lord's disciples" just as those in category (3) are, separated from the others? As many scholars have recognized, the key to Papias's distinction between categories (3) and (4) lies in the distinction between the aorist verb *eipen* ("said") and the present tense verb *legousin* ("were saying"). At the time of which Papias is speaking, those in category (3) were already dead and Papias could learn only what they had said, reported by the elders, whereas Aristion and John the Elder were still teaching — somewhere other than Hierapolis — and Papias could learn from their disciples what they were (still) saying. These two had been personal disciples of Jesus but at the time of which Papias speaks were prominent Christian teachers in the province of Asia. He calls the second of them "John the Elder" to distinguish him from the John he includes in category (3).[24] Both Johns were "disciples of the Lord" but only "John the Elder" was also a prominent teacher in the churches of Asia.[25]

Many scholars have been unable to believe that Aristion and John the Elder had been personal disciples of Jesus, usually either because these scholars have understood Papias to be speaking of a time after the death of "the el-

22. The interpretation of Papias's statement argued by J. Chapman, *John the Presbyter and the Fourth Gospel* (Oxford: Clarendon, 1911) 9-27, is in this respect convincing. Others who accept this interpretation include Körtner, *Papias,* 114-22 (but his view that the elders were itinerant teachers is much more questionable); B. Reicke, *The Roots of the Synoptic Gospels* (Philadelphia: Fortress, 1986) 155; M. Hengel, *Die johanneische Frage,* 79.

23. Chapman, *John the Presbyter,* 13-16.

24. For the significance of this title used of John, see chapter 16.

25. Chapman, *John the Presbyter,* made the best case for identifying the two Johns in this passage of Papias, but it is hard to believe that Papias would have included the same John in both categories (3) and (4).

ders" and so presumably beyond the lifetime of Jesus' contemporaries, or because they have not sufficiently distinguished the time *about* which Papias is writing from the time *at* which he is writing. Once we recognize that, at the time to which he refers, most of the disciples of Jesus had died but two were still alive and were among the prominent Christian teachers in Asia, we can see that the time about which he writes must be late in the first century. There is nothing in the least improbable about this. Papias was doubtless himself a young man at the time. He himself was of the next generation, but young enough for his adult life to overlap with that of the longest-lived of Jesus' young contemporaries. Even if we accept the date often given for Papias's completion of his book, 130 CE (in my opinion too late), there is still nothing improbable about the situation. He could have been, say, twenty years of age in 90 CE, when the very elderly Aristion and John the Elder were still alive, and thus sixty in 130 when he finally completed his book, which we could understand to have been his life's work. (Papias's contemporary Polycarp, bishop of Smyrna, was martyred at the age of eighty-six in c. 156 CE at the earliest or c. 167 at the latest.[26] He would have been between eleven and twenty in 90 CE.[27]) Papias also seems to have had direct contact with the daughters of Philip the evangelist (cf. Acts 21:9), who had settled in Hierapolis.[28] This is also entirely credible if Papias were twenty years of age in 90 CE. However, since the evidence for dating his book as late as 130 is, as we have noted, suspect, he could easily have been born as early as 50 CE.[29]

Since Aristion and John the Elder were disciples of the Lord who were still alive at the time about which Papias is writing, as well as relatively close to him geographically (probably in Smyrna[30] and Ephesus respectively) and easily accessible on major routes, he was able to collect their sayings mediated

26. For these dates, see Lightfoot, Harmer, and Holmes, *The Apostolic Fathers*, 131-32.

27. Thus, what Irenaeus wrote about Polycarp is entirely credible, if we take the "John" to whom he refers to be John the Elder: "how he would tell of his conversation with John and with others who had seen the Lord, how he would relate their words from memory; and what the things were which he had heard from them concerning the Lord, his mighty works and his teaching" (*apud* Eusebius, *Hist. Eccl.* 5.20.6; translation from R. M. Grant, *Second-Century Christianity* [London: SPCK, 1946] 116). See chapter 17 below.

28. Eusebius, *Hist. Eccl.* 3.39.9. Eusebius, like others before him, confused this Philip with Philip the Apostle, one of the Twelve, whom Papias mentions in the passage we are discussing. Had Philip the Apostle lived in Hierapolis, Papias would not have had to ask people visiting Hierapolis what he had said.

29. Cf. Bartlet, "Papias's 'Exposition,'" 17: "not later than A.D. 60, and possibly even earlier."

30. Aristion is probably the same person as Ariston, whom the *Apostolic Constitutions* (7.46) considers first bishop of Smyrna. For the historical value of this connection of Aristion with Smyrna, see B. H. Streeter, *The Primitive Church* (London: Macmillan, 1929) 92-97.

by only one transmitter — any of their disciples who visited Hierapolis. So it is not surprising that he valued their traditions especially and quoted them often in his work (Eusebius, *Hist. Eccl.* 3.39.7). Sayings from other disciples of the Lord he mentions were at least one more link in the chain of tradition removed from him. Eusebius understood Papias to have actually himself heard Aristion and John the Elder (*Hist. Eccl.* 3.39.7), and Irenaeus says the same of Papias's relation to John (*Adv. Haer.* 5.33.4 and *apud* Eusebius, *Hist. Eccl.* 3.39.1). It is conceivable that Papias went on from the words Eusebius quoted from the Prologue to say that at a later date he was able to travel and to hear Aristion and John the Elder for himself. (If Papias heard them himself, he could hardly have failed to say so in his Prologue, where he is explaining the sources of the traditions he reports and interprets in the rest of his work.) But it is also possible that both Eusebius and Irenaeus supposed the first sentence of Eusebius's extract from the Prologue ("everything I learned carefully in the past from the elders") to mean that Papias had *personally* heard Aristion and John the Elder teaching. It is more likely that this sentence actually means that he learned from these two elders in the way in which he goes on to explain — by inquiring of any of their disciples he met.[31] In that case we must assume that at the time of his life when Aristion and John the Elder were still living, Papias was not in a position to travel to hear them[32] but relied on visitors to Hierapolis to report what they were saying. This relationship would sufficiently account for the high value he set on traditions from these two disciples of the Lord elsewhere in his work.

As we have already noted, Papias in this passage speaks of a time before the time at which he is writing. The time when he collected oral traditions deriving from disciples of Jesus was in the past. At that time most of the disciples of Jesus had died, but at least two such disciples, Aristion and John the Elder, were still alive.[33] This must be during or close to the decade 80-90 CE. According to most scholars, this is the time at which the Gospels of

31. This seems more likely than the view of Chapman, *John the Presbyter*, 30-31, that Papias first gives his principal source (he learned directly from the elders) and then his secondary sources (he asked disciples of the elders when they visited Hierapolis).

32. Chapman, *John the Presbyter*, 31, says: "Unless they lived at an extraordinary distance, it would be inexplicable that he should not have taken the trouble to make their personal acquaintance. It appears that John lived at Ephesus, Aristion at Smyrna, great cities to which Hierapolis was linked by an important road." But we do not know what particular personal circumstances might have prevented Papias from traveling, and the period in which he was collecting traditions and they were still living may not have been long.

33. Reicke, *The Roots*, 154-55, fails to recognize that two personal disciples of the Lord were still alive at this time and so concludes that Papias was collecting traditions from around 100 CE onward.

Matthew[34] and Luke were written, and a little earlier than the time at which the Fourth Gospel was written. Thus what Papias says in this passage can be placed alongside Luke's reference to the eyewitnesses (Luke 1:2) as evidence for the way the relationship of the eyewitnesses to Gospel traditions was understood at the time when the Gospels were being written.

There is no reason at all to regard Papias's claims in this passage as apologetic exaggeration, for they are strikingly modest. To traditions from members of the Twelve he claims at best to have had access only at second hand, while, as we have seen, he probably did not even claim to have heard Aristion and John the Elder himself but only to have received their teaching, during their lifetimes, from those who did hear them. We may therefore trust the most significant implication of what Papias says: that oral traditions of the words and deeds of Jesus were attached to specific named eyewitnesses. This speaks decisively against the old form-critical assumption that sight of the eyewitness origins of the Gospel traditions would, by the time the Gospels were written, have long been lost in the anonymity of collective transmission. Not only from Luke 1:2, but even more clearly from Papias, we can see that this was not the case. Papias expected to hear specifically what Andrew or Peter or another named disciple had said or specifically what Aristion or John the Elder was still saying.[35] We can probably deduce that, just as these last two, long surviving disciples continued to repeat their oral witness in their teaching as long as they lived, so the other disciples were not just originators of oral traditions in the earliest period but authoritative living sources of the traditions up to their deaths. The oral traditions had not evolved away from them but continued to be attached to them, so that people like Papias wanted to hear specifically what any one of them said.

Not too much weight should be placed on the particular names in Papias's list of seven disciples. Like other Jewish and early Christian writers, he doubtless uses the number seven as indicating completeness, so that a list of seven can stand representatively for all (cf. the seven disciples in John 21:2). As has often been noticed, the order of the list is striking Johannine, reflecting the order in John 1:40-44 and 21:2. From these Johannine lists Papias has omitted the peculiarly Johannine disciple Nathanael, no doubt because he

34. If Papias's statement about Matthew's Gospel comes, like his statement about Mark's Gospel, from "the Elder" (i.e., probably John the Elder), then he would have known (or come to know) Matthew's Gospel in the period when he was collecting traditions. But it is not entirely clear from Eusebius whether Papias's comment on Matthew did come from the Elder.

35. This point is made by B. Gerhardsson, *Memory and Manuscript: Oral Tradition and Written Transmission in Rabbinic Judaism and Early Christianity* (ASNU 22; Uppsala: Almqvist and Wiksells, 1961) 206-7.

wished to add instead the non-Johannine Matthew, important to Papias as a well-known source of Gospel traditions.[36] This dependence on the Gospel of John doubtless belongs to Papias's composition of the passage, not to his thinking at the time about which he is writing. There is a somewhat Johannine flavor to the whole passage. The use of "disciples" rather than "apostles" recalls the Gospel of John (which never uses the word "apostle" in the technical sense), but may also be a usage designed to emphasize eyewitness testimony to the words and deeds of Jesus in a way that "apostle," a term applied to Paul in Asia in Papias's time, need not. But the references to "the truth" in the second sentence of the passage, including the apparent reference to Jesus himself as "the truth" (cf. John 14:6), have Johannine resonances, while a further possible Johanninism occurs in the final phrase of the passage: "a living and surviving voice" *(zōēs phōnēs kai menousēs).* Is Papias recalling the Fourth Gospel's concluding discussion of how long the beloved disciple would "remain" or "survive" (*menein;* cf. also 1 Cor 15:6)?

"A Living and Surviving Voice"

Papias's denial that "information from books would profit me as much as information from a living and surviving voice" has been often remarked and much misunderstood. Many have taken it to mean that he preferred oral tradition in general to books in general. Such a prejudice against books and in favor of the spoken word would make the fact that Papias recorded in writing the Gospel traditions he collected, as well as the fact that he himself later wrote a book that bore some relationship to these traditions, paradoxical to say the least. We also know that by the time he was writing his own book Papias knew written Gospels, at least those of Mark and Matthew, and, even though he seems conscious of some deficiencies in these two Gospels, by no means disparages them (see chapter 9 below).

In order to understand Papias's preference for the "living voice" over written sources we must first recognize that it was an ancient topos or commonplace. Loveday Alexander has pointed out the close parallel in the prologue to one of the works of the medical writer Galen, where he quotes a "saying current among most craftsmen" to the effect that "gathering information

---

36. Papias's list would be even more Johannine if we supposed that he identified Matthew with Nathanael (the two names have a similar meaning) and that he took the two anonymous disciples in John 21:2 to be Aristion and John the Elder; cf. Hengel, *Die johanneische Frage,* 80-83.

out of a book is not the same thing, nor even comparable to learning from the living voice."[37] The phrase "from the living voice" *(para zōēs phōnēs)* here is precisely that used by Papias, though Papias adds "and surviving" *(kai menousēs)*. Two other known sources refer to the assertion that "the living voice" (in these Latin texts: *viva vox*) is preferable to writing as a common saying (Quintilian, *Inst.* 2.2.8; Pliny, *Ep.* 2.3).[38] So it seems certain that Papias is alluding to a proverb. In the context of scientific and technical treatises such as Galen's, this proverb expresses the easily understandable attitude that learning a craft by oral instruction from a practitioner was preferable to learning from a book.[39] But even if it originated in the craft traditions, the saying was certainly not confined to them. Seneca applied it to philosophy, meaning that personal experience of a teacher made for much more effective teaching than writing: "you will gain more from the living voice *(viva vox)* and sharing someone's daily life than from any treatise" (*Ep.* 6.5).[40] In all such cases, what is preferable to writing is not a lengthy chain of oral tradition, but direct personal experience of a teacher. In discussion of rhetoric, the phrase was used by Quintilian (*Inst.* 2.2.8) and Pliny (*Ep.* 2.3) to express a preference for the communicative power of oral performance by an orator, which cannot be adequately conveyed in written texts.[41]

Alexander sums up her study of this topos:

> We have seen that the "living voice" had a wide currency as a proverb of general import, but also that it is possible to identify three cultural worlds in which it has a more specific application. In rhetoric, it reinforces the centrality of live performance. Among craftsmen, it expresses the widely-felt difficulty of learning practical skills without live demonstration. And in the schools generally it serves as a reminder of the primacy of person-to-person oral instruction over the study (or the production) of manuals and handbooks.[42]

37. Galen, *De comp. med. sec. loc.* 6 pref. (Kühn XII.894.1-4), quoted in L. A. Alexander, "The Living Voice: Scepticism towards the Written Word in Early Christian and in Graeco-Roman Texts," in D. J. A. Clines, S. E. Fowl, S. E. Porter, eds., *The Bible in Three Dimensions* (JSOTSup 87; Sheffield: Sheffield Academic, 1990) 224-25; L. A. Alexander, *The Preface to Luke's Gospel* (SNTSMS 78; Cambridge: Cambridge University Press, 1993) 83. (The translation given is Alexander's in the latter place.)

38. Alexander, "The Living Voice," 227.

39. Alexander, *The Preface*, 83.

40. Alexander, "The Living Voice," 232.

41. Alexander, "The Living Voice," 226-27; Byrskog, *Story*, 106-7.

42. Alexander, "The Living Voice," 242.

In all these cases, the proverb refers to firsthand experience of a speaker, whether an instructor or an orator, not to transmission of tradition through a chain of traditioners across generations. In the context of the schools, it seems sometimes to have been brought into connection with oral tradition,[43] but even in this usage the "living voice" of the proverb does not *refer* to oral tradition, but to the actual voice of the teacher from whose oral instruction one learns directly. It follows that in the case of Papias's use of the proverb, as Harry Gamble points out, "it is not oral tradition as such that Papias esteemed, but first-hand information. To the extent that he was able to get information directly, he did so and preferred to do so."[44]

Alexander does not mention historiography, and the saying about the living voice itself does not seem to appear in the extant works of the historians. There is, however, an equivalent proverb, also cited by Galen, who says it is "better to be an eyewitness *(autoptēs)* by the side of the master himself and not to be like those who navigate out of books."[45] Galen applies this proverb, like the saying about the living voice, to learning a craft directly from an instructor rather than from a book, but it was also cited by the historian Polybius (writing three centuries before Galen) when he compared historiography to medical practice (12.15d.6). This is part of Polybius's savage criticism of the work of the historian Timaeus, who relied entirely on written sources. It is notable that Polybius was also fond of the word *autoptēs* ("eyewitness"),[46] which Alexander has shown was characteristic of medical literature, as in the quotation from Galen just given.[47] Though this word is not common in the historians generally, Polybius uses it to refer to a concept that was central to the method of ancient historiography: reliance on direct personal experience of the subject matter, either by the historian himself or at least by his informant. Continuing his attack on Timaeus, Polybius writes that there are three modes of historical — as of other — inquiry, one by sight and two by hearing. Sight refers to the historian's personal experience of the places or events of which he writes, which was so highly prized by ancient historians and which Polybius, like Thucydides and others, considered of first importance. One of the two forms of hearing is the reading of memoirs *(hypomnēmata)* (in the ancient world written texts were

43. Alexander, "The Living Voice," 232-33.

44. H. Y. Gamble, *Books and Readers in the Early Church* (New Haven: Yale University Press, 1995) 30-31.

45. Galen, *Temp. med.* 6 pref. (Kühn XI.796-97), also cited in Galen, *De libr. propr.* 5 (Kühn XIX.33), both quoted in translation in Alexander, "The Living Voice," 228; cf. Alexander, *The Preface*, 83.

46. For Polybius's use, see Alexander, *The Preface*, 35-36.

47. Alexander, *The Preface*, 121-22.

"heard" even when a reader read them for him/herself[48]): this was Timaeus's exclusive method of historical research but was put by Polybius third in order of importance. More important for Polybius was the other form of hearing: the interrogation *(anakriseis)* of living witnesses (12.27.3).

As Samuel Byrskog has reminded us and as we noted in the previous chapter, ancient historians, considering that only the history of times within living memory could be adequately researched and recounted, valued above all the historian's own direct participation in the events about which he wrote (what Byrskog calls autopsy), but also, as second best, the reminiscences of living witnesses who could be questioned in person by the historian (what Byrskog calls indirect autopsy).[49] The latter might sometimes be stretched to include reports received by the historian from others who had questioned the eyewitnesses, but since the principle at stake was personal contact with eyewitnesses it cannot be understood as a general preference for oral tradition over books. It did not, of course, prevent the historians themselves from writing books, since their purpose was, among other things, to give permanence to memories that would otherwise cease to be available, to provide, in Thucydides' famous phrase, "a possession for all time" (1.22.4).[50]

This historiographic context is the one in which Papias's use of the proverb about the living voice most appropriately belongs. It would have been easy for this common saying, used as we have seen in a variety of contexts, to be applied also to the well-known preference among the best historians for eyewitness testimony rather than written accounts. It expresses that as aptly as it does the practice of learning directly from master craftsmen or philosophers. Against a historiographic background, what Papias thinks preferable to books is not oral tradition as such but access, while they are still alive, to those who were direct participants in the historical events — in this case "disciples of the Lord." He is portraying his inquiries on the model of those made by historians, appealing to historiographic "best practice"(even if many historians actually made much more use of written sources than their theory professed).[51] That

48. Cf. B. Gerhardsson, *The Reliability of the Gospel Tradition* (Peabody: Hendrickson, 2001) 113-14.

49. Byrskog, *Story,* 48-65; cf. also Alexander, *The Preface,* 33-34.

50. This is quoted in Lucian, *Hist. Conscr.* 42. Herodotus also said he wrote "so that [the memory] of past things may not be blotted out from among mankind by time" (1.1). Cf. Byrskog, *Story,* 122-23.

51. D. Aune, "Prolegomena to the Study of Oral Traditions in the Hellenistic World," in H. Wansbrough, ed., *Jesus and the Oral Gospel Tradition* (JSNTSup 64; Sheffield: Sheffield Academic, 1991) 81, also thinks that Papias "thought of himself as a historian"; cf. D. Aune, *The New Testament in Its Literary Environment* (Philadelphia: Westminster, 1988) 67.

he himself wrote down the traditions he collected is not at all, as some scholars have thought, paradoxical. It was precisely what historians did. Papias, who in spite of Eusebius's prejudiced jibe at his stupidity was well-educated,[52] may well have read Polybius. This historian's strict principles of historiography were, like those of Thucydides, something of an ideal for later historians at least to claim to practice. Alexander suggests that Josephus was dependent on Polybius when he insisted on his qualifications, as a participant and eyewitness (*autoptēs*), for writing the history of the Jewish War.[53]

That Papias claims to have conducted inquiries in the manner of a good historian may also be suggested by his use of the verb *anakrinein* for his inquiries about the words of the elders, which he made when disciples of the elders visited Hierapolis ("I inquired [*anekrinon*] about the words of the elders"). This verb and its cognate noun *anakrisis* were most often used in judicial contexts to refer to the examination of magistrates and parties. But we have noticed that Polybius uses the noun for the historian's interrogation of eyewitnesses (12.27.3). At another point in his criticism of Timaeus, Polybius calls *anakriseis* the most important part of history (12.4c.3). The way he continues indicates that again he is thinking of the interrogation of eyewitnesses (i.e., direct observers both of events and of places):

> For since many events occur at the same time in different places, and one man cannot be in several places at one time, nor is it possible for a single man to have seen with his own eyes every place in the world and all the peculiar features of different places, the only thing left for a historian is to inquire from as many people as possible, to believe those worthy of belief and to be an adequate critic of the reports that reach him (12.4c.4-5).

The verb *anakrinein* also occurs in the advice given by Lucian of Samosata in his book about writing history. The context is similar:

> As to the facts themselves, [the historian] should not assemble them at random, but only after much laborious and painstaking investigation (*peri tōn autōn anakrinanta*). He should for preference be an eyewitness (*paronta kai ephorōnta*), but, if not, listen to those who tell the more impartial story . . . (*Hist. Conscr.* 47).

This suggestion that Papias deliberately uses the terminology of historiographic practice can be further supported from the first sentence of

---

52. On his knowledge of rhetoric, see Kürzinger, *Papias*, 43-67.
53. Alexander, *The Preface*, 38-39, citing Polybius 3.4.13 and Josephus, *C. Ap.* 1.55.

the passage from his Prologue that we are studying. This has conventionally been translated in this way:

> I will not hesitate to set down for you, along with my interpretations *(synkatataxai tais hermēneiais)*, everything I carefully learned from the elders and carefully remembered *(emnēmoneusa)*, guaranteeing their truth.[54]

In favor of this translation is the fact that it is the way in which Rufinus translated the Greek text of Eusebius into Latin. But Kürzinger has proposed a considerably different translation that is very attractive.[55] I have incorporated Kürzinger's suggestions into the translation of the passage I gave above, translating the opening sentence thus:

> I shall not hesitate also to put into properly ordered form *(synkatataxai tais hermēneiais)* for you everything I learned carefully in the past from the elders and noted down *(emnēmoneusa)* well, for the truth of which I vouch.

According to this interpretation, Papias is describing the stages of producing a historical work precisely as Lucian, in his book on how to write history, describes them (immediately after the passage just quoted from him):

> When he has collected all or most of the facts let him first make them into a series of notes *(hypomnēma)*, a body of material as yet with no beauty or continuity. Then, after arranging them into order *(epitheis tēn taxin)*, let him give it beauty and enhance it with the charms of expression, figure and rhythm *(Hist. Conscr. 48)*.

Papias's use of the verb *mnēmoneuein* refers, on this interpretation, not to remembering but to recording, that is, making the notes *(hypomnēmata)* — the memoranda or aids to memory — which are often mentioned in references to the practice of historians in antiquity.[56] The collection of notes constituted a rough draft that then needed to be artistically arranged to make an acceptable literary work. This latter stage of the writing process is what, according to this interpretation, Papias meant by the words *synkatataxai* (or *syntaxai*, the vari-

---

54. This translation is from Lightfoot, Harmer, and Holmes, *The Apostolic Fathers*, 314.
55. Kürzinger, *Papias*, 77-82.
56. G. Avenarius, *Lukians Schrift zur Geschichtsschreibung* (Meisenheim am Glan: Hain, 1956) 85-104; C. B. R. Pelling, "Plutarch's Method of Work in the Roman Lives," *JHS* 99 (1979) 94-95.

ant reading that Kürzinger prefers) *tais hermēneiais* (usually translated "set down together with my interpretations").[57] There is much to be said for this understanding of Papias's statement. That he vouches for the truth of what he reports is also, of course, a conventional part of the historian's practice (cf. Lucian, *Hist. Conscr.* 39-40, 42).

So we may see Papias's Prologue as claiming that he followed the best practice of historians: he made careful inquiries, collected the testimonies of eyewitnesses, set them down in a series of notes, and finally arranged his material artistically to form a work of literature. His preference for the testimony of eyewitnesses, obtained at second or third hand, is therefore that of the historian, for whom, if direct autopsy was not available (i.e., the historian himself was not present at the events), indirect autopsy was more or less essential.

What is most important for our purposes is that, when Papias speaks of "a living and surviving voice," he is not speaking metaphorically of the "voice" of oral tradition, as many scholars have supposed. He speaks quite literally of the voice of an informant — someone who has personal memories of the words and deeds of Jesus and who is still alive. In fact, even if the suggestion that he alludes specifically to historiographic practice is rejected, this must be his meaning. As we have seen, the saying about the superiority of the "living voice" to books refers not to oral tradition as superior to books, but to direct experience of an instructor, informant, or orator as superior to written sources.[58] But Papias, uniquely, expands the usual cliché "living voice" to "living and surviving voice,"[59] thereby making it even more appropriate to the context in which he uses it — the situation in which what he seeks are the reminiscences of those who knew Jesus and in which the passage of time has now been such that few of those people are still alive.

It is worth noting that Jerome, who translated this section of Papias's prologue into Latin in his brief life of Papias, evidently understood the phrase "living voice" in this way. He translates the whole sentence thus:

57. Lucian, *Hist. conscr.* 24, 43 (cf. 34) uses *hermēneia* in the common sense of "literary expression," but the plural in Papias cannot be quite comparable with Lucian's use. It must refer to instances of literary expression.

58. This seems to me true of all the instances Alexander cites and even of the somewhat different language used in Plato's famous preference for orality over literature in *Phaedo* 276a6-10 (cited in Alexander, "The Living Voice," 237-38).

59. Papias may be remembering 1 Pet 1:23, where the word of God is described as *logou zōntos theou kai menontos,* but if so he is adapting the phraseology for a different purpose. He does not consider the voices of the eyewitnesses to be in this sense the word of God which endures forever (cf. 1 Pet 1:25) because of its inherent divine quality.

> For books to be read are not so profitable for me as the living voice that
> even until the present day resounds on the lips of their authors (*viva vox
> et usque hodie in suis auctoribus personans*) (*De vir. ill.* 18).

Jerome here seems to take Papias to mean that he preferred the oral communication of eyewitnesses to the written records of their testimony in the Gospels.

The whole concluding sentence of the passage from Papias, including "a
living and surviving voice," refers most properly to the immediately preceding words: "what Aristion and John the Elder, the Lord's disciples, were saying." The words of these surviving witnesses are the most valuable to Papias.
What the elders reported of the words of the disciples now dead he collected,
but, however illustrious these disciples, the additional distance from direct
contact with living witnesses made these traditions less valuable than reports
of what still living witnesses were still saying. Papias's account of what he inquired of the visitors to Hierapolis therefore lists the disciples who were no
longer alive first but climaxes with the most valuable information he obtained. Though this came from only two disciples still alive and geographically proximate enough for Papias's visitors to have sat at their feet and to
have much to report from their words, it may well be that, just as the number
of the seven named disciples is symbolic, so also Papias evokes the symbolism
of the number two, the number required for adequate witness. Though only
two, Aristion and John the Elder are sufficient for their witness to be valid.

Therefore Papias's use of the verb *menein* ("to remain, to survive") in
the phrase "a living and surviving voice" *(zōēs phōnēs kai menousēs)* can be
compared with Paul's when he writes that, of the more than five hundred
who saw the Lord, "most are still alive *(menousin heōs arti)*, though some
have died" (1 Cor 15:6), or, as we have already suggested, with the words of Jesus about the Beloved Disciple at the end of the Gospel of John: "If it is my
will that he remain *(menein)* until I come" (John 21:22, 23). These texts refer
to the survival of those who had seen the Lord. If, as I have argued elsewhere[60]
and will argue again in chapter 16 of this book, Papias considered John the Elder to be the Beloved Disciple and the author of the Fourth Gospel, the resemblance to John 21:22, 23, would be especially apt, and an actual allusion to
this text would seem rather probable. But nothing in our present argument
depends on this possibility.

Once again, we should notice a key implication of Papias's words: he
does not regard the Gospel traditions as having by this date long lost a living
connection with the eyewitnesses who originated them. Whether these eye-

---

60. Bauckham, "Papias and Polycrates."

witnesses were still living would not matter if the oral tradition were essentially independent of them. Papias assumes that the value of oral traditions depends on their derivation from still living witnesses who are still themselves repeating their testimony.[61] Now that these are few, secondhand reports of what eyewitnesses now dead used to say are valuable, but Papias's whole statement implies that the value of oral tradition decreases with distance from the personal testimony of the eyewitnesses themselves. In fact, the period he writes about, when he collected his traditions, was virtually the last time at which such collecting would be worth doing, and this, of course, is why Papias collected the traditions at that time, wrote them down, and eventually made a book of them. It is surely not accidental that this was also the period in which the Gospels of Matthew, Luke, and John were being written.

Of the traditions of the words and deeds of Jesus that Papias collected very few have come down to us in the extant fragments of his work. From Eusebius's remarks it is clear that he recorded many Gospel traditions especially from Aristion and John the Elder, and that more than the few that have survived were without parallels in our canonical Gospels (Eusebius, *Hist. Eccl.* 3.39. 7, 12, 14). But we should probably assume that the majority were simply versions of stories and sayings to be found in the Gospels, of which, by the time he wrote his book, Papias knew at least those of Matthew, Mark, and John. (Papias's book probably consisted of collections of Gospel traditions along with commentary on them. It belonged, then, to the familiar ancient genre of authoritative text [often oral teachings committed to writing] along with commentary thought necessary for students to fully appreciate the text. In Papias's case he seems to have offered not so much his own commentary [at least, little of that survives], but rather the comments offered by the Elders he so revered.)

This passage from Papias's Prologue can usefully be compared with the Prologue to Luke's Gospel, probably written around the time when Papias was engaged in the collecting of traditions that he describes in the passage. In his relationship to the eyewitnesses Luke is comparable with those Papias calls "the elders" (though this terminology was probably confined to Asia). That is, Luke received traditions directly from the eyewitnesses. As Martin Hengel puts it:

> As the emphatic "just as they were delivered *to us*"[Luke 1:2] shows, between Jesus and the earliest "literary sources" about him (including Luke, the author himself) stand only those who had been direct eye-witnesses

---

61. Cf. Byrskog, *Story,* 252: "the need to account for the source became urgent as soon as an ancient author felt distanced by time to [*sic*] the events of interest."

of the activity of Jesus from the beginning. . . . Luke was an author at the end of the second generation.[62]

It is particularly significant that Luke refers to the eyewitnesses, those whom Papias calls "disciples of the Lord," as "those who from the beginning were eyewitnesses *(autoptai)* and ministers of the word."[63] These are certainly a single group of people, not two.[64] They are disciples who accompanied Jesus throughout his ministry (cf. Acts 1:21) and who were prominent teachers in the early church. They certainly include the Twelve (cf. Acts 6:4) but also others, since Luke's Gospel and Acts make it particularly clear that Jesus had many disciples besides the Twelve (Luke 6:17; 8:1-3; 10:1-20; 19:37; 23:27; 24:9, 33; Acts 1:15, 21-23), and the possibility that Luke's informants included such disciples must be taken seriously. The fact that these informants — whether the Twelve or other disciples — were not only eyewitnesses but also prominent teachers in the early Christian movement shows, in coherence with what we have learned from Papias, that they did not merely start the traditions going and then withdraw from view but remained for many years the known sources and guarantors of traditions of the deeds and words of Jesus. Like Papias, Luke will have inquired and learned what Peter or Cleopas or Joanna or James had said or was saying.

Oral Tradition or Oral History?

The passage of Papias we have studied has been routinely used to show that there was a preference among early Christians for oral tradition rather than written forms of the Gospel traditions and that this preference continued even after written Gospels were widely used. From our study of the passage we should emphasize, first, that Papias's statements do not show a preference that continued after written Gospels were widely known. The time to which he refers was probably prior to the availability of the Gospels of Matthew, Luke, and John. There is no paradox entailed by the fact that Papias himself wrote a collection of Gospel traditions that he had acquired by oral transmission. His preference for oral materials belonged only to the period during which he was collecting the materials. He wrote them down as he heard them because the value of orally transmitted traditions would soon decline considerably once there were no longer any living eyewitnesses.

62. M. Hengel, *The Four Gospels and the One Gospel of Jesus Christ* (London: SCM, 2000) 141-42.
63. This phrase will be discussed in much more detail in chapter 6.
64. Alexander, *The Preface*, 119; against Reicke, *The Roots*, 51.

Secondly, we should question whether it may not be rather misleading to refer to "oral tradition" in this context. Jan Vansina, in his authoritative study of oral tradition as historical source, distinguishes clearly and sharply between oral tradition and oral history. Of the former he says that "to a historian the truly distinctive characteristic of oral tradition is its transmission by word of mouth over a period longer than the contemporary generation."[65] He emphasizes that "all oral sources are not oral traditions. There must be transmission by word of mouth over at least a generation. Sources for oral history are therefore not included."[66] The reason for making such a sharp distinction is that the historian treats oral tradition and oral history quite differently:

> The sources of oral historians are reminiscences, hearsay, or eyewitness accounts about events and situations which are contemporary, that is, which occurred during the lifetime of the informants. This differs from oral tradition in that oral traditions are no longer contemporary. They have passed from mouth to mouth, for a period beyond the lifetime of the informants. The two situations typically are very different with regard to the collection of sources as well as with regard to their analysis; oral historians typically interview participants in recent or very recent events, often of a dramatic nature, when historical consciousness in the communities involved is still in flux.[67]

Firsthand contact with the participants was also, as we have noted, the way in which ancient historians went about their task in the best circumstances. Papias, who clearly aspired to best historical practice, though he was unable to interview participants directly, attached most importance to the reports given by people who had recently heard the eyewitness testimony of participants who were still alive and still giving their testimony. The Evangelists who were writing their Gospels at the time of which Papias speaks were probably in a better position than Papias to practice what Vansina defines as oral history.

Papias defines two ways in which traditions about Jesus came to him, distinguished by their particular eyewitness sources but therefore also correspondingly by the number of stages of transmission between the eyewitness sources and Papias:

65. J. Vansina, *Oral Tradition as History* (Madison: University of Wisconsin Press, 1985) 29.
66. Vansina, *Oral Tradition*, 28.
67. Vansina, *Oral Tradition*, 12; cf. also Ø. Andersen, "Oral Tradition," in H. Wansbrough, ed., *Jesus and the Oral Gospel Tradition* (JSNTSup 64; Sheffield: Sheffield Academic, 1991) 26-27: he notes the distinction, along with Henige's distinction between "oral tradition" and "oral testimony," but he prefers not to make a terminological distinction himself.

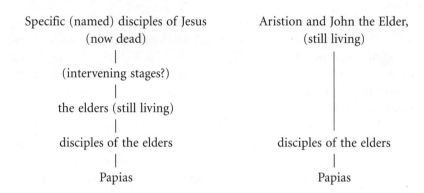

Specific (named) disciples of Jesus (now dead)	Aristion and John the Elder, (still living)
(intervening stages?)	
the elders (still living)	
disciples of the elders	disciples of the elders
Papias	Papias

The second of these tables clearly outlines a case of oral history. We should stress that in this case the stages of transmission are geographical rather than temporal. Only the smallest lapse in time — the time taken by those who had been listening to Aristion or John the Elder to travel the hundred and twenty miles or so from Smyrna or Ephesus to Hierapolis — need have elapsed between these two disciples of Jesus giving their testimony and Papias receiving it. Scholars who read Papias with an inappropriate model of oral *tradition* in mind tend to miss this point.

But Papias is speaking of the period in which oral history was becoming no longer possible. The two living eyewitnesses to whom he had access were very old. All the more famous disciples of Jesus were dead. So the traditions that came to Papias by way of the chain of transmission represented in the first table have become oral tradition, in the sense that they have been transmitted beyond the lifetime of the original informants. We cannot be sure how many stages of transmission were involved in this case, but we can certainly suppose that Papias, with his aspirations to the best historical practice, would have valued particularly those traditions that the elders had received directly from named disciples of Jesus. The elders were the leaders of Asiatic Christianity and lived in major cities on the routes of travel. It is not at all unlikely that disciples of Jesus had passed through their cities and taught. Polycrates, bishop of Ephesus a century later, claimed at the age of sixty-five that he had "conversed with the brethren from all parts of the world" (Eusebius, *Hist. Eccl.* 5.24.7), presumably mainly as a result of his strategic position in Ephesus. But also, in view of the general mobility of early Christian leaders,[68] we can easily suppose that some of the elders had traveled. Melito, bishop of Sardis and a contemporary of Polycrates, visited Jerusalem; it is even more

68. See R. Bauckham, "For Whom Were Gospels Written?" in R. Bauckham, ed., *The Gospels for All Christians: Rethinking the Gospel Audiences* (Grand Rapids: Eerdmans, 1998) 33-38.

likely that Jewish Christian leaders in the province of Asia before 70 would have gone on pilgrimage to Jerusalem and met remaining disciples of Jesus in the Jerusalem church. These perfectly real possibilities of personal contact rarely make an appearance in scholarly discussion of the transmission of Gospel traditions because the latter are dominated by a model of oral tradition that thinks of collective rather than individual transmission and *presupposes* that the origins of the traditions were far removed, by many stages of transmission, from the form the traditions took by the later first century. But this model neglects — while Papias takes for granted — the importance of individual leaders, often very mobile, whose careers in Christian leadership often spanned decades and among whom the eyewitnesses of Jesus' ministry had a special position.

It is clear that neither in the case of the second table but not even in the case of the first does Papias think of traditions belonging merely to the collectivity of a Christian community and passed down collectively and anonymously. The elders were prominent leaders. In addition to Aristion and John the Elder, whose names he gives because they were themselves disciples of Jesus, the names of the others would have been well known to him, as to all Christians in the province of Asia. He could also have named those disciples of theirs, Papias's immediate informants, who passed through Hierapolis and whom he got to know personally. He would not have valued what *the elders said* that Andrew or Peter or Thomas had said if these traditions were merely part of the collective memory of the churches to which the elders belonged. Papias would expect these traditions from the elders to be authorized by individual personal contacts.

Oral tradition is typically collective:

> The corpus is more than what a single person remembers because the information is a memory, that is, it does not go only from one person to another. Performances are held for audiences, not for single auditors, and historical gossip gets around as any other gossip does. So in practice the corpus becomes what is known to a community or to a society in the same way that culture is so defined.[69]

In this sense, there certainly was collective tradition in the early Christian communities. But the existence of a collective memory produced by frequent recitation of traditions in a communal context does not at all exclude the role of particular individuals who are especially competent to perform the tradi-

---

69. Vansina, *Oral Tradition,* 149.

tion. The roles of individuals in relation to community traditions vary in different societies.[70] We shall discuss these more general issues relating to the transmission of Gospel traditions in chapters 10-12. Here we must simply challenge the assumption that collective memory *excluded or took the place of* individual named informants and guarantors of tradition about Jesus.

Papias was clearly not interested in tapping the collective memory as such. He did not think, apparently, of recording the Gospel traditions as they were recited regularly in his own church community. Even in Hierapolis it was on his personal contact with the daughters of Philip that he set store. What mattered to Papias, as a collector and would-be recorder of Gospel traditions, was that there were eyewitnesses, some still around, and access to them through brief and verifiable channels of named informants. It is natural to suppose that those who were writing Gospels (our canonical Gospels) at the time of which Papias speaks would have gone about their task similarly, as indeed the preface to Luke's Gospel confirms. For the purpose of *recording* Gospel traditions in writing, Evangelists would have gone either to eyewitnesses or to the most reliable sources that had direct personal links with the eyewitnesses. Collective tradition as such would not have been the preferred source.[71]

The model of traditions passing from one named individual to another — as distinct from the purely communal transmission imagined by most

70. Vansina, *Oral Tradition*, 34-39.

71. J. D. G. Dunn, "On History, Memory and Eyewitnesses: In Response to Bengt Holmberg and Samuel Byrskog," *JSNT* 26 (2004) 483-84, criticizing Byrskog's use of the model of oral history for the Gospels, writes: "I simply do not believe that Peter, Mary of Magdala and the like stored up many memories of Jesus' mission, which were only jerked into remembrance by 'oral history' inquiries of a Luke or a Matthew. They had already fed those memories into the living tradition of the churches, as major contributory elements in the forming and shaping of that tradition. No doubt other memories were brought to the surface by inquiries of a Luke or a Matthew, but these would be supplementary to what was already known and performed in the various assemblies week by week. I guess the same was true of Papias and Irenaeus" (this is an expansion of the point already made in idem, *Jesus Remembered* [Grand Rapids: Eerdmans, 2003] 198-99 n. 138). Dunn here simply assumes that the Gospels were primarily the product of the community tradition, but this is not at all how Luke 1:2 represents the matter. If the eyewitness guarantors of the tradition were still accessible, would not an Evangelist prefer to depend on such a source? The point I am making in this chapter is that if the Evangelist were anything like Papias he would. Of course, Papias is not supposing that his inquiries will "jerk into remembrance" memories not already formulated by the eyewitnesses. In the case of Aristion and John the Elder, they had been telling their testimony for decades and were still doing so in their regular teaching. But this need not be decisively different from oral history, where an informant who had strong memories of important events would tell his stories countless times to friends, neighbors, and visitors before telling them to an oral historian in a form already honed by frequent retelling.

Gospels scholars — is in fact the model with which later-second-century Christian writers worked. As it happens, our best evidence comes from the same area, the province of Asia, as that in which Papias lived and worked. Toward the end of the second century Irenaeus, who spent his early life in that area, fondly (but also purposefully) recalled Papias's contemporary, Polycarp, bishop of Smyrna (who died, at the age of eighty-six, around the middle of the second century), and his transmission of Gospel traditions:

> For I distinctly recall the events of that time better than those of recent years (for what we learn in childhood keeps pace with the growing mind and becomes part of it), so that I can tell the very place where the blessed Polycarp used to sit as he discoursed, his goings out and his comings in, the character of his life, his bodily appearance, the discourses he would address to the multitude, how he would tell of his conversations with John [in my view this is Papias's John the Elder[72]] and with the others who had seen the Lord, how he would relate their words from memory; and what the things were which he had heard from them concerning the Lord, his mighty works and his teaching, Polycarp, as having received them from the eyewitnesses *(autoptōn)* of the life of the Logos, would declare in accordance with the scriptures (Irenaeus, *Letter to Florinus, apud* Eusebius, *Hist. Eccl.* 5.20.5-6).[73]

Owing to its role in Irenaeus's polemic against the heretic Florinus, scholars have been rather disinclined to trust this reminiscence, but since he claims to remember Florinus himself as also a member of Polycarp's circle, his reminiscence would not hold water as argument directed personally to Florinus unless it had some substantial truth behind it. However, what concerns us here is not the fact but the model of transmission of Gospel traditions from the eyewitnesses that Irenaeus makes so plain. This model was in fact shared with second-century Gnostic teachers who claimed that their teaching was esoteric teaching of Jesus transmitted to them orally through named intermediaries from named disciples of Jesus. (Basilides, for example, claimed to have been taught by Glaucias, a disciple and interpreter of Peter.)[74]

The fact that Papias works with this second-century model of the transmission of Gospel traditions makes many scholars suspicious of his claims. But why should this model not be the appropriate one for the early period? There is no reason simply to assume that second-century writers got it wrong.

72. See chapter 17 below.
73. Translation from Grant, *Second-Century Christianity,* 115-16.
74. See chapter 12 below.

The reason this model of personal transmission was abandoned by twentieth-century Gospels scholarship in favor of collective and anonymous transmission is that the form critics applied the latter model to the Gospels and read the evidence of the Gospels in ways that confirmed it. We shall return to the methods and findings of form criticism in chapter 10. More immediately, we must turn to the Gospels themselves. Are the conclusions we have drawn from Papias really applicable to the Gospels? We might well ask why, if Gospel traditions were known as the traditions told by specific named eyewitnesses, they are not attached to such names in the Gospels themselves. Perhaps they are. Perhaps we need to look at the names in the Gospels more carefully and with fresh questions. In the following chapters we shall pursue this approach.

A final comment on the distinction we have made between oral tradition and oral history needs to be made. As far as the use of the word "tradition" is concerned, this terminological distinction is a modern one, used for clarification by those who research oral tradition and oral history. It does not correspond to the ancient use of the word "tradition" (Greek *paradosis*). Two passages from the Jewish historian Josephus are instructive here.[75] Josephus, in his account of the *Jewish War,* strove to conform to the ancient historiographic ideal of contemporary history written by one who was himself a participant of the events and who also had firsthand information from other direct participants. His work was oral history, not the product of oral tradition in the sense we have discussed (passed down across generations as collective memory). In stating his credentials for writing the history accurately, he referred to his extensive participation in the Jewish resistance and then, after his capture by the Romans, his attendance on the Roman generals throughout the siege of Jerusalem. At that stage he already kept a written

> record of all that went on under my eyes in the Roman camp, and was alone in a position to understand the information brought by deserters. Then, in the leisure which Rome afforded me, with all my materials in readiness . . . , at last I committed to writing my narrative of the events *(epoiēsamēn tōn praxeōn tēn paradosin).* So confident was I of its veracity that I presumed to take as my witnesses, before all others, the commanders-in-chief in the war, Vespasian and Titus . . . (*C. Ap.* 1.49-50, tr. H. St. J. Thackeray).

Josephus then continues to stress the way the recipients of complimentary copies of his book confirmed its veracity. The point of interest for us here is

75. The significance of these passages was pointed out by R. O. P. Taylor, *The Groundwork of the Gospels* (Oxford: Blackwell, 1946) 68.

that he calls his written record "tradition." The phrase Thackeray here, in the Loeb edition, translates "I committed to writing my narrative of the events" could be literally rendered: "I set down [in writing] the tradition of the acts." "Tradition"*(paradosis)* here has no implication of transmission through many intermediaries. It refers rather to Josephus's largely firsthand testimony to what happened, well within the memory of those to whom he gave presentation copies of the book, set down in writing as a record that others could now read.

In a very similar passage, where Josephus again defends the accuracy of his history against detractors, he again uses the word *paradosis:*

> I presented the volumes to the Emperors themselves, when the events had hardly passed out of sight, conscious as I was that I had preserved the true story *(tetērēkoti tēn tēs alēthēias paradosin)*. I expected to receive testimony to my accuracy, and I was not disappointed (*Life* 361, tr. H. St. J. Thackeray).

Here the crucial phrase could be literally translated: "I had kept the tradition of the truth." The verb *tēreō* here, meaning "keep" or "preserve intact" or "guard," belongs, with *paradosis,* to the stereotyped language of tradition, referring to the accurate preservation of tradition (cf. the use of synonymous verbs in 1 Cor 11:2; 2 Thess 2:15[76]), but it does not refer here to the preservation of tradition through chains of traditioners but simply to Josephus's faithful rendering in writing of firsthand memories — his own and others' — that he had assembled in his work of (as we would call it) oral history.

Thus, when the New Testament uses the stereotyped language of tradition, we should resist the influence of preconceptions about the collective and cross-generational nature of oral tradition. Paul, for example, constituted the single intermediary between the eyewitnesses (especially Peter: cf. Gal 1:18) and the Corinthians when he "handed on to you . . . what I first received"(1 Cor 15:3), and even when he, just like Josephus, appeals to the confirmation of the account that could be given by many other eyewitnesses ("five hundred brothers and sisters . . . , many of whom are still alive, though some have died": 1 Cor 15:6), since the events were well within the living memory of people to whom easy access was possible. As we also learn from Josephus, the language of tradition does not require that an account be handed on orally. It can refer to the writing of recollections. So, when Luke's preface claims that "those who from the beginning were eyewitnesses and

---

76. See chapter 11 below.

ministers of the word handed on *(paredosan)* to us [the tradition of the events]" (Luke 1:2), the reference could be to or could include written accounts by the eyewitnesses. The language of tradition, as used in the New Testament and related literature, entails neither cross-generational distance nor even orality to the exclusion of written records.

3. Names in the Gospel Traditions

Names in the Gospels

There is one phenomenon in the Gospels that has never been satisfactorily explained. It concerns names. Many characters in the Gospels are unnamed, but others are named. I want to suggest now the possibility that many of these named characters were eyewitnesses who not only originated the traditions to which their names are attached but also continued to tell these stories as authoritative guarantors of their traditions. In some cases the Evangelists may well have known them.

Tables 1–4 show the relative number and the identities of both named and unnamed characters in the four Gospels. (Old Testament characters and non-human persons are excluded, as well as the persons in the two genealogies of Jesus and Luke's dedicatee Theophilus. The many references to anonymous groups — "some Pharisees," "some scribes," "the chief priests," "the guards," "John's disciples," and so on — are not included.) In all the Gospels the number of named and of unnamed characters is more or less equal.

It is easy to see that certain categories of people fall mostly into one or the other group. Public persons, that is, those who would have been known apart from the story of Jesus (John the Baptist, Herod, Herodias, Caiaphas, Pilate, presumably Barabbas) are usually named. The beneficiaries in stories of Jesus' healings and exorcisms are usually unnamed. Persons who encounter Jesus on one occasion and do not become disciples are usually unnamed. Some of the unnamed persons are so insignificant in the narratives that we would not normally expect them to be named.[1] Disciples of Jesus, including the Twelve, are usually named. These categories are readily intelligible. One would expect that the names of disciples of Jesus would be remembered in the traditions and that public persons would also appear by name, while the names of people who were healed or encountered Jesus on one occasion might not even have been known to those who first told the stories and would not seem to present any good reason for being remembered.

Especially noteworthy, therefore, are exceptions to these principles. While Matthew and John name the high priest Caiaphas, in Mark and Luke he is anonymous.[2] While disciples (other than in indefinite groups) are usually named, sometimes they are not. Why should one of the two disciples on the road to Emmaus be named (Cleopas) and the other not? While most beneficiaries of Jesus' healings and resuscitation miracles are anonymous, Jairus (whose daughter was raised) is named in Mark and Luke, Bartimaeus in Mark, Lazarus in John. Since people who encounter Jesus on one occasion are usually not named, why should the Pharisee who entertains Jesus to dinner in Luke 7 be named (Simon, 7:40)? Why should Simon of Cyrene be named? There are also cases where a person who is anonymous in one Gospel is named in another. For example, John alone identifies the woman who anoints Jesus as Mary of Bethany, the man who cut off the ear of the high priest's slave as Peter, and the slave himself as Malchus.

Several issues require separate discussion. In chapter 5 we will discuss the Twelve, and in chapter 8 we will consider cases in which the lack of a personal name in the Gospels, especially in Mark, is surprising and seems to need explanation. Here we will focus on the presence in the Gospel traditions of names other than those of the Twelve and of public persons. Table 5 is confined to these names and enables comparison of their occurrences in the four Gospels. We shall now discuss the names largely with reference to the data in Table 5.

The phenomena depicted in Table 5 have previously been discussed mostly only in the context of wider discussion of the significance of more or fewer details in Gospel narratives. For example, Rudolf Bultmann considered increasing detail a law of oral tradition. Like other such details, he considered

---

1. E.g., those in Luke 12:13; 13:23; 14:15. Luke has a tendency to attribute questions and comments to anonymous individuals in crowds or groups, where Matthew and Mark tend to have a generalized "they." This increases the number of anonymous persons in Luke rather artificially.

2. Mark's rather surprising failure to name the high priest Caiaphas is discussed in chapter 8 below. Luke 3:2 refers to "the high priesthood of Annas and Caiaphas," leaving the reader in doubt which is the high priest in 22:50, 54.

personal names, including most of those listed above, to be secondary additions to the traditions. They are an example of "novelistic interest" in the characters, which tended to individualize them in a number of ways, including giving them names.[3] However, consistent application of this view required some forced argumentation in individual cases. For example, Bultmann had to suggest that Matthew and Luke knew a text of Mark 10:46 that lacked the name Bartimaeus, despite the fact that there is no textual evidence at all for such a text.[4] He also had to consider the name of Jairus not original in Mark 5:22 but a secondary addition to the text derived from Luke 8:41.[5] In this case, there is some textual support (D and five manuscripts of the Old Latin) for omitting "named Jairus" in Mark 5:22,[6] but more recent scholars have found the case for treating these words as original compelling,[7] while Joseph Fitzmyer calls Bultmann's suggestion "preposterous"![8]

With equal confidence Henry Cadbury claimed an opposite tendency, stating (of oral transmission of narratives) that "the place, the person, the time, in so far as they are not bound up with the point of the incident, tend to disappear,"[9] and (of the Gospel miracle stories specifically): "After repeated re-tellings even the names of the persons and places disappear."[10] But Cadbury also recognized that there is evidence (for example, in apocryphal Gospels) of the late introduction of names out of novelistic interest. This means that "meeting the current toward elimination of names is the counter current of late development, which . . . gave to simplified matter the verisimilitude of

---

3. R. Bultmann, *The History of the Synoptic Tradition* (tr. J. Marsh; revised edition; Oxford: Blackwell, 1972) 68, 215, 241, 283, 310, 345, 393; cf. also R. Bultmann, "The New Approach to the Synoptic Problem," in idem, *Existence and Faith* (tr. S. M. Ogden; London: Hodder and Stoughton, 1961) 42; M. Dibelius, *From Tradition to Gospel* (tr. B. L. Woolf; London: Nicholson and Watson, 1934) 50-53.

4. Bultmann, *The History*, 213; cf. also the fuller treatment of Bartimaeus in Dibelius, *From Tradition*, 51-53.

5. Bultmann, *The History*, 215.

6. This reading was accepted, e.g., by V. Taylor, *The Gospel According to St Mark* (second edition; London: Macmillan, 1966) 287; D. E. Nineham, *The Gospel of Mark* (Pelican Gospel Commentary; revised edition: London: Black, 1968) 160.

7. R. Pesch, "Jaïrus (Mk 5,22/Lk 8,41)," *BZ* 14 (1970) 252-56; B. M. Metzger, *A Textual Commentary on the Greek New Testament* (Stuttgart: United Bible Societies, 1971) 85-86.

8. J. A. Fitzmyer, *The Gospel According to Luke (I–IX)* (AB 28A; New York: Doubleday, 1981) 744.

9. H. J. Cadbury, *The Making of Luke-Acts* (London: Macmillan, 1927) 34.

10. Cadbury, *The Making*, 94. This conclusion was also suggested to Vincent Taylor through the results of an experiment in oral transmission, one of which was the conclusion that "Personal names and place-names tend to disappear": V. Taylor, *The Formation of the Gospel Tradition* (London: Macmillan, 1933) 208.

proper names."[11] E. P. Sanders, in a chapter on "Increasing Detail as a Possible Tendency of the Tradition," attempted to assess the evidence for this alleged tendency by comparing not only the Synoptic texts but also extracanonical parallels.[12] Unfortunately for our purposes, he did not separate out the phenomena described in our Table 5 as a distinct category of evidence, and so his conclusions do not relate specifically to the cases where a character is named in one Gospel but not in another.

Table 5 enables us to make the following observations on the matter. If we assume the priority of Mark (i.e., that where Matthew, Mark and Luke have closely parallel material they are dependent on Mark), then, where Matthew and Luke have both taken over Markan material, they both retain the names in four cases (Simon of Cyrene, Joseph of Arimathea, Mary Magdalene, and Mary the mother of James and Joses[13]), Luke retains the name in one case where Matthew changes it (Levi[14]), Luke retains the name in one case where Matthew drops it (Jairus), and both drop the name in four cases (Bartimaeus, Alexander, Rufus,[15] and Salome). In no case does a character unnamed in Mark gain a new name in Matthew or Luke. There is one instance (not revealed by the data in Table 5) in which two disciples whom Mark leaves anonymous (14:13)[16] are identified as Peter and John by Luke (22:8), but this phenomenon of identifying unnamed persons in Mark with named characters already known from Mark should not be confused with giving characters anonymous in Mark new names not found at all in Mark. The material common to the three Synoptic Gospels therefore shows an unambiguous tendency toward the elimination of names, which refutes Bultmann's argument, so long as one accepts Markan priority, as Bultmann did.

It is not surprising that the Q material (non-Markan material common to Matthew and Luke) contributes no names, since it consists so predominantly of sayings of Jesus. Matthew's special material also contributes

---

11. Cadbury, *The Making*, 59.

12. E. P. Sanders, *The Tendencies of the Synoptic Tradition* (SNTSMS 9; Cambridge: Cambridge University Press, 1969) chapter 3.

13. But Luke omits the name of one of her sons, Joses.

14. But Luke omits the name of his father Alphaeus.

15. I have assumed that Mark names Alexander and Rufus not merely to identify Simon, distinguishing him from other Simons, since "of Cyrene" (retained by Matthew and Luke) would be sufficient for that purpose. The sons must in some sense be named in their own right, whereas apparently Alphaeus (Mark 2:14, omitted by Luke) and Joses (Mark 15:40, 47, omitted by Luke) are not.

16. Matthew's abbreviation of Mark here eliminates the selected two disciples and speaks only of the disciples in general (26:17-19).

no new names other than that of Jesus' father Joseph, which is also independently given in Luke and John.[17] By contrast, Luke's special material supplies eleven named characters (two of whom — Martha and her sister Mary — occur also in John) in addition to those Luke took from Mark. This evidence does not contradict the tendency toward elimination of names since there is no reason to think that Luke has added them to the traditions in which they occur.

Finally, John names four characters who do not appear at all in the Synoptics (Nathanael, Nicodemus, Lazarus, and Mary of Clopas) and also gives a name to one character who is anonymous in the other Gospels, the high priest's slave Malchus. Even if we add that John identifies who cut off Malchus's ear, anonymous in the Synoptics, with Peter, and the woman who anointed Jesus, unnamed in the other Gospels, with Mary of Bethany (12:3), herself known also in Luke, this does not provide strong evidence of a counter-tendency to invent names for characters who had been anonymous at earlier stages of the tradition. After all, John still has quite a number of unnamed characters. Why should he have been influenced by a novelistic tendency to name unnamed characters in the case of Malchus but not in the cases of the Samaritan woman, the paralyzed man, or the man born blind, all of whom are much more prominent characters than Malchus?

For a tendency to name previously unnamed characters there is a little more evidence in extracanonical Gospels and traditions, though even here it is notably scarce in the earlier texts. In the *Gospel of Peter* the centurion in charge of the guard at the grave of Jesus (cf. Matt 27:65), evidently identified with the centurion at the cross (Matt 27:54; Mark 15:39; Luke 23:47), is named Petronius (8:31). The text of Luke's Gospel in Papyrus Bodmer XVII (P75), dating from c. 200, gives the name Neves to the rich man in the parable (Luke 16:19), prompted no doubt by the fact that the other character in the parable is named. Origen (*C. Cels.* 2.62) gave the name Simon to the anonymous companion of Cleopas in Luke 24 — the first of many attempts to identify this disciple.[18] But these seem to be the only examples of invented names for anonymous characters in the Gospels before the fourth

17. If the category of named characters were extended slightly to include characters identified by their relationship to named characters, then the mother of the sons of Zebedee (Matt 20:20; 27:56) would be mentioned here. In that case, we should also include Simon Peter's mother-in-law (in all three Synoptic Gospels) and the relative of Malchus (John 18:26).

18. If Origen intended, as he probably did, an otherwise known Simon, this would not really be an example of the tendency we are discussing. He may have identified Cleopas correctly with Jesus' uncle Clopas and Cleopas's companion with Clopas's son Simeon/Simon, known from Hegesippus as the second bishop of Jerusalem.

century. In two medieval testimonies to the *Gospel of the Nazarenes* the woman with a hemorrhage (Matt 9:20; Mark 5:25; Luke 8:43) is named Mariosa, and in one of these the man with a withered hand (Matt 12:10; Mark 3:1; Luke 6:6) is called Malchus,[19] but it is improbable that these names can be reliably attributed to the Gospel used by the Nazarenes in the early centuries.[20] For other examples we must go to the Clementine Homilies (fourth century), the *Acts of Pilate* (fifth or sixth century), the *Gospel of Bartholomew* (fifth or sixth century?) and other later literature, as well as to manuscripts of the Old Latin version of the Gospels from the sixth century and later.[21] The practice of giving an invented name to a character unnamed in the canonical Gospels seems to have become increasingly popular from the fourth century on, but it is remarkable how few earlier examples are known.[22]

It was a common Jewish practice, in retelling or commenting on the biblical narratives, to give names to characters not named in Scripture. For example, in Pseudo-Philo's *Biblical Antiquities,* a first-century Jewish Palestinian example of "rewritten biblical narrative," we find names given to such characters as Cain's wife, Sisera's mother, Jephthah's daughter, Samson's mother, and the witch of Endor.[23] So it would not have been surprising to find Christians doing the same with the Gospel narratives from an early date.

19. W. Schneemelcher and R. McL. Wilson, *New Testament Apocrypha,* vol. 1 (revised edition; Louisville: Westminster John Knox, 1991) 163, cf. 160, where an actual quotation from this Gospel, preserved by Jerome, calls the man a mason (as does the medieval text) but does not give him a name.

20. But Sanders, *The Tendencies,* 132, incorrectly attributes names for the three wise men to a quotation from a *Gospel of the Hebrews.* As his own text of this quotation from Sedulius Scotus makes clear (301), Sedulius did not find these names in the Gospel he quotes, but adds that "according to some" the three foremost wise men bore these names. Names of the magi are not attested before the sixth century (B. M. Metzger, "Names for the Nameless in the New Testament," in P. Granfield and J. A. Jungmann, eds., *Kyriakon* [J. Quasten FS; Münster: Aschendorff, 1970], vol. 1, 80, 82).

21. Sanders, *The Tendencies,* 131-32; Bultmann, *The History,* 241, 310; W. Bauer, *Das Leben Jesu im Zeitalter der neutestamentlichen Apokryphen* (Tübingen: Mohr, 1909) 516-18; Metzger, "Names," 79-99. A. Barr, "The Factor of Testimony in the Gospels," *ExpT* 49 (1937-38) 401-8, is probably roughly right in proposing three stages: an early stage when actual names were remembered and used, a middle stage when some names were dropped, and a late stage when fictional names were invented.

22. This must be distinguished from the invention of new characters with names, as, e.g., probably in Pap. Oxy. 840, where a Pharisaic chief priest named Levi appears, and in the *Infancy Gospel of Thomas,* in which Jesus' school teacher is called Zacchaeus and one of his playmates Zenon.

23. *Biblical Antiquities* 2:1-2; 31:8; 40:1; 42:1; 64:3.

But the evidence suggests that this did not happen.[24] Certainly there is no ground for postulating that it occurred in the transmission of the Gospel traditions behind and in the Synoptic Gospels.

We must conclude that most of the names in Table 5 belonged originally to the Gospel traditions in which they are found. We cannot from the evidence presented here tell whether some traditions originally contained names that have not survived into our Gospels, though the tendency of Matthew and Luke in their redaction of Mark to omit names might suggest, by analogy, that other names were already omitted by Mark or were dropped by Matthew or Luke from their special traditions. What we do need to explain is that some Gospel characters bear names while others in the same categories do not, as well as the tendency to omit names that we can observe in Matthew's and Luke's redaction of Mark.

The phenomena described in Table 5 have never been satisfactorily explained as a whole, but an explanation that could account for all the names there except for Jesus' father Joseph and the names in Luke's birth and infancy narratives is that all these people joined the early Christian movement and were well known at least in the circles in which these traditions were first transmitted. This explanation has occasionally been suggested for some of the names, such as Bartimaeus,[25] Simon of Cyrene and his sons,[26] and Joseph of Arimathea,[27] though surprisingly not for Jairus.[28] It has been widely assumed

24. Note, e.g., that the man with the withered hand and the woman with a hemorrhage are both unnamed in *Epistle of the Apostles* 5, as are the wise men in *Protevangelium of James* 21:1-4.

25. See the references given in J. F. Williams, *Other Followers of Jesus: Minor Characters as Major Figures in Mark's Gospel* (JSNTSup 102; Sheffield: Sheffield Academic, 1994) 153 n. 2; and add Dibelius, *From Tradition,* 53; J. P. Meier, *A Marginal Jew,* vol. 2 (New York: Doubleday, 1994) 687-90. G. Theissen, *The Gospels in Context: Social and Political History in the Synoptic Tradition* (tr. L. M. Maloney; Minneapolis: Fortress, 1991) 101, makes the significant observation that Bartimaeus "is the only healed person the miracle story tells us became a 'follower' in the narrower sense." In form, Mark's story of Bartimaeus (Mark 10:46-52) resembles a story of the call of a disciple as much as or perhaps more than a story of a healing miracle: H. D. Betz, "The Early Christian Miracle Story: Some Observations on the Form Critical Problem," *Semeia* 11 (1978) 74-75; P. J. Achtemeier, "'And He Followed Him': Miracles and Discipleship in Mark 10:46-52," *Semeia* 11 (1978) 115-45.

26. See, e.g., Theissen, *The Gospels,* 176-77; R. E. Brown, *The Death of the Messiah,* vol. 2 (New York: Doubleday, 1994) 913-16; S. Légasse, *The Trial of Jesus* (tr. J. Bowden; London: SCM, 1997) 80-81; R. T. France, *The Gospel of Mark* (NIGTC; Grand Rapids: Eerdmans, 2002) 641.

27. See Brown, *The Death,* 1223-24.

28. It is curious that scholars who take the occurrence of the name (apart from Bartimaeus, unique in the Gospel miracle stories as the name of a petitioner for a healing or exorcism) as indicative of historicity do not go on to suggest that Jairus became well known in the early Christian movement (e.g., Meier, *A Marginal Jew,* vol. 2, 629-30, 784-85; G. H. Twelftree, *Je-*

(without much argument) for some others, such as Mary Magdalene and the sisters Martha and Mary. But these piecemeal uses of the explanation can well be superseded by the proposal that this explanation provides a comprehensive hypothesis to account for all or most of these names. We know that the four brothers of Jesus (named in Matt 13:55; Mark 6:3) were prominent leaders in the early Christian movement (1 Cor 9:5; Gal 1:19), and, when Luke in Acts 1:14 depicts some women with the Twelve and Jesus' brothers, he probably intends his readers to suppose that at least the women named in Luke 24:10 were among the first members of the Jerusalem church. There is no difficulty in supposing that the other persons named in the Gospels became members either of the Jerusalem church or of other early communities in Judea or Galilee.

In fact, they comprise just the range of people we should expect to have formed these earliest Christian groups: some who had been healed by Jesus (Bartimaeus, the women in Luke 8:2-3, perhaps Malchus[29]), some who had joined Jesus in his itinerant ministry (certainly a larger group than the Twelve, and including the named women disciples, Levi, Nathanael, and Cleopas), some of Jesus' relatives (his mother and brothers, his uncle Cleopas/Clopas and aunt Mary), and several residents of Jerusalem and its environs who had been supporters of or sympathetic to Jesus' movement (Nicodemus, Joseph of Arimathea, Simon the leper, Lazarus, Martha, and Mary). It is striking how many of these people can be localized in or near Jerusalem (including Jericho): in addition to the six just mentioned, this would also be true of Bartimaeus, Malchus, Simon of Cyrene and his sons, Zacchaeus, and (after the resurrection) Jesus' brother James and probably other relatives. So they would have been known in the Jerusalem church where stories in which they are named were first told.

The tendency of Matthew and Luke to omit some of the names we find in Mark would be explained if these people had become, by the time Matthew and Luke wrote, too obscure for them to wish to retain the names when they were engaged in abbreviating Mark's narratives. It is also worth noticing that personal names are usually the least well remembered features of remembered events,[30] and so we should not be surprised to find names dropping out. On the contrary, if the phenomenon of personal names in Gospel tradi-

---

sus: The Miracle Worker [Downers Grove: InterVarsity, 1999] 305-6), but this is the most obvious explanation of the preservation of his name, unlike the names of other characters in miracle stories. This is recognized by R. H. Gundry, Mark: A Commentary on His Apology for the Cross (Grand Rapids: Eerdmans, 1993) 267.

29. But for a different hypothesis about Malchus, see chapter 8.

30. G. Cohen, Memory in the Real World (Hove and London: Erlbaum, 1989) 100-108.

tions is due to real memories, we should expect there to be reasons why they should be remembered. The supposition that they are of persons known in the early Christian movement provides at least part of the explanation, but there is probably a further dimension to be considered.

If the names are of persons well known in the Christian communities, then it also becomes likely that many of these people were themselves the eye-witnesses who first told and doubtless continued to tell the stories in which they appear and to which their names are attached. A good example is Cleopas (Luke 24:18): the story does not require that he be named[31] and his companion remains anonymous.[32] There seems no plausible reason for naming him other than to indicate that he was the source of this tradition. He is very probably the same person as Clopas, whose wife Mary[33] appears among the women at the cross in John 19:25.[34] Clopas is a very rare Semitic form of the Greek name Cleopas, so rare that we can be certain this is the Clopas who, according to Hegesippus, was the brother of Jesus' father Joseph and the father of Simon, who succeeded his cousin James as leader of the Jerusalem church (*apud* Eusebius, *Hist. Eccl.* 3.11; 4.22.4). Cleopas/Clopas was doubtless one of those relatives of Jesus who played a prominent role in the Palestinian Jewish Christian movement.[35] The story Luke tells would have been essentially the story Cleopas himself told about his encounter with the risen Jesus. Probably it was one of many traditions of the Jerusalem church which Luke has incorporated in his work.

Three other cases are especially instructive: the women at the cross and the tomb, Simon of Cyrene and his sons, and recipients of Jesus' healing miracles. I have discussed the first of these in detail elsewhere,[36] but it is so important for the present argument that I must repeat some key points here.

31. The story is comparable with Luke 7:36-50 in that a character who first appears as anonymous is later named in the course of the narrative. This seems to be a Lukan narrative technique.

32. On the possible identity of the companion and on the eyewitness character of the story, see C. P. Tiede, *The Emmaus Mystery* (New York: Continuum, 2005) 93-98.

33. John's designation of her — "Mary of Clopas" — could mean that she was the wife, the daughter, or even the mother of Clopas. Probably she was his wife. But more important is the fact that this ambiguous designation presupposes that she was a well-known person; readers would be expected to know her relationship to Clopas.

34. See R. Bauckham, *Gospel Women: Studies of the Named Women in the Gospels* (Grand Rapids: Eerdmans, 2002) chapter 6: "Mary of Clopas."

35. See R. Bauckham, *Jude and the Relatives of Jesus in the Early Church* (Edinburgh: Clark, 1990).

36. Bauckham, *Gospel Women*, chapter 8: "The Women and the Resurrection: The Credibility of Their Stories."

The Women at the Cross and the Tomb

In the Synoptic Gospels the role of the women as eyewitnesses is crucial: they see Jesus die, they see his body being laid in the tomb, they find the tomb empty. The fact that some of the women were at all three events means that they can testify that Jesus was dead when laid in the tomb and that it was the tomb in which he was buried that they subsequently found empty. All three Synoptic Gospels repeatedly make the women the subjects of verbs of seeing: they "saw" the events as Jesus died (Matt 27:55; Mark 15:40; Luke 23:49), they "saw" where he was laid in the tomb (Mark 15:47; Luke 23:55), they went on the first day of the week to "see" the tomb (Matt 28:1), they "saw" the stone rolled away (Mark 16:4), they "saw" the young man sitting on the right side (Mark 16:5), and the angel invited them to "see" the empty place where Jesus' body had lain (Matt 28:6; Mark 16:6). It could hardly be clearer that the Gospels are appealing to their role as eyewitnesses.[37] The primacy of sight (often expressed in the well-known saying of Heraclitus: "Eyes are surer witnesses than ears"[38]) was a feature of the ancient Greek theory of cognition,[39] to which the historians' emphasis on autopsy corresponded: "they related to the past visually," Samuel Byrskog observes.[40] Of course, this does not mean that the other senses are excluded from the eyewitnesses' recollections and testimony, but the primacy of sight signifies the importance of having actually been there, as opposed to merely hearing a report of the events. The women at the cross and the tomb are important mainly for what they see, but also for their hearing of the message of the angel(s).

They are not an anonymous group: all the Gospels name some of them, also stating or implying that there were others (Matt 27:55; 28:1, 5; Mark 15:41, 47; 16:6; Luke 24:10; John 20:2). The significance of this naming and of the variations in the lists of names seems never to have been properly appreciated. Byrskog supposes that specific names are given "perhaps because as female eyewitnesses they were already from the outset somewhat suspect."[41] But it is not really clear how suspicions of women's credibility could be much

---

37. Cf. B. Gerhardsson, "Mark and the Female Witnesses," in H. Behrens, D. Loding, and M. T. Roth, eds., *Dumu-E2-Dub-Ba-A* (A. W. Sjöberg FS; Occasional Papers of the Samuel Noah Kramer Fund 11; Philadelphia: The University Museum, 1989) 219-20, 222-23; S. Byrskog, *Story as History — History as Story* (WUNT 123; Tübingen: Mohr, 2000; reprinted Leiden: Brill, 2002) 75-78.

38. Byrskog, *Story,* 52-53.

39. Byrskog, *Story,* 65.

40. Byrskog, *Story,* 64.

41. Byrskog, *Story,* 77.

allayed by naming them. The naming is surely more likely to reflect how very important for the whole story of Jesus were the events of which they were the sole witnesses, since the Synoptic Gospels agree that none of the male disciples witnessed the burial or the empty tomb.

The names are not the same in each Gospel, though Mary Magdalene appears in all, and Mary the mother of James appears in all three Synoptics:

	Cross	*Burial*	*Empty tomb*
Mark	Mary Magdalene Mary mother of James the little and Joses Salome	Mary Magdalene Mary (mother) of Joses	Mary Magdalene Mary (mother) of James Salome
Matthew	Mary Magdalene Mary (mother) of James and Joseph Mother of sons of Zebedee	Mary Magdalene the other Mary	Mary Magdalene the other Mary
Luke			Mary Magdalene Joanna Mary (mother) of James

The divergences among these lists are much more interesting and significant than is usually realized. Probably the Torah's requirement of two or three witnesses (Deut 19:15) plays a role in the accounts. As Birger Gerhardsson rightly points out, the influence of this legal ruling extended far beyond the law courts to any situations in ordinary life where evidence needed to be assured.[42] So it is certainly notable that all three Synoptic Gospels name two or three women on each occasion in the passion-resurrection narratives where they are cited as witnesses. But, of course, the requirement of two or three witnesses cannot explain the variations in the specific names given.

The divergences among the lists have often been taken as grounds for not taking them seriously as naming eyewitnesses of the events. In fact, the opposite is the case: these divergences, properly understood, demonstrate the scrupulous *care* with which the Gospels present the women as witnesses.

42. Gerhardsson, "Mark," 218.

Mark names three women at the cross and the same three women as those who go to the tomb, but only two of the three are said to observe the burial of Jesus.[43] The explanation must be that in the known testimony of these three women the two Marys were known to be witnesses of the burial but Salome was not. Similar care is perhaps even more impressive in Matthew. For Matthew Salome was evidently not a well-known witness and he omits her from the lists.[44] At the cross he substitutes the mother of the sons of Zebedee, who has appeared earlier in his narrative (Matt 20:20) and is unique to his Gospel. He does not, however, add her to the two Marys at the burial or the empty tomb, surely because she was not known as an eyewitness of these events.[45] Matthew could so easily have used her to make up the number at the tomb but instead he is scrupulously content with the only two women well known to him as witnesses. Luke, who names the women only at the end of his account of their visit to the tomb,[46] lists, besides the indispensable Mary Magdalene, Joanna, who is peculiar to his Gospel and has already been introduced at 8:3, and Mary the mother of James. This third name may be Luke's only borrowing from Mark in his narrative of the empty tomb. Like Matthew Luke omits Mark's Salome, but he does not simply reproduce the list of women fol-

43. The persistent attempts (examples are cited in E. L. Bode, *The First Easter Morning: The Gospel Accounts of the Women's Visit to the Tomb of Jesus* [AnB 45; Rome: Biblical Institute, 1970] 20-22) to explain the variations in Mark's lists of the women by postulating different sources are unconvincing and unnecessary. One theory thinks that Mark found two different women, "Mary of Joses" (Mark 15:40) and "Mary of James" (Mark 16:1), in two different sources but identified them and harmonized the sources in 15:40, where he refers to "Mary the mother of James the little and Joses." It is much easier to suppose that Mark first refers to this Mary by reference to both of her sons, including the nickname of one, in order to facilitate readers'/hearers' identification of her, and then feels free to identify her more concisely, in two different ways, in 15:47 and 16:1, just as Matthew, having introduced her as "Mary the mother of James and Joses" (Matt 27:56), can then call her "the other Mary" (Matt 27:61; 28:1). That this Mary is identified in all three Synoptic Gospels by reference to her sons need not imply, as Theissen, *The Gospels*, 178, claims, that the sons were better known than the mother. A woman called Mary, however well known, needed to be distinguished from other Marys, including Mary Magdalene. That she is identified by reference to her sons rather than, for example, by reference to her husband, implies that the sons were also well known in the Christian movement but not that they were better known than their mother.

44. On Salome, see Bauckham, *Gospel Women*, chapter 7: "The Two Salomes and the Secret Gospel of Mark."

45. That Matthew does not put the mother of the sons of Zebedee in the group who find the tomb empty is conclusive evidence against the rather common view that she is the same person as Mark's Salome.

46. This may be so that the naming of Mary Magdalene and Joanna can function as an *inclusio* with 8:2-3, reminding readers that the women have accompanied Jesus and his story from early in the Galilean ministry until the resurrection.

lowers of Jesus he has employed earlier in his Gospel (8:2-3: Mary Magdalene, Joanna, Susanna). Mary Magdalene and Joanna he knew to be witnesses of the empty tomb, Susanna he evidently did not. In this way my proposal that the Evangelists were careful to name precisely the women who were well known to them as witnesses to these crucial events in the origins of the Christian movement explains the variations among their lists of women as no other proposal has succeeded in doing.

It is natural to suppose that these women were well known not just for having once told their stories but as people who remained accessible and authoritative sources of these traditions as long as they lived. Which women were well known to each Evangelist may have depended on the circles in which that Evangelist collected traditions and the circles in which each woman moved during her lifetime. The differences among the Gospel narratives of the women's visit to the tomb may well reflect rather directly the different ways in which the story was told by the different women. These women were not all already obscure figures by the time the Synoptic Evangelists wrote. The omission of Salome by both Matthew and Luke shows that the Evangelists did not retain the names of women who had become obscure. Those named by each Evangelist were, like their stories, still fresh in the memories of that Evangelist's informants, if not in the Evangelist's own memory.

Simon of Cyrene and His Sons

Our second example is more readily understandable in the light of the first. In this case, the variation among the Gospels is that Mark names not only Simon but also his two sons Alexander and Rufus (15:21), whereas Matthew (27:32) and Luke (23:26) omit the sons. Martin Dibelius's suggestion that Simon of Cyrene was named by Mark as an eyewitness[47] is quickly dismissed by Byrskog as "no more than pure conjecture."[48] But careful consideration shows that there is more to be said for it. In the first place, readers of Mark who wondered about the sources of Mark's information would readily suppose that most of his narrative derives from the circle of the Twelve, who are almost the only disciples of Jesus mentioned by Mark before the women appear in 15:40 and who participate in most of the events until all but Peter leave Mark's narrative, never to reappear in person, at 14:50. As we shall see later, Mark's readers are also likely to have supposed that, among the Twelve, Peter

47. Dibelius, *From Tradition*, 182-83.
48. Byrskog, *Story*, 66.

especially stands behind Mark's narrative. But even he disappears after 14:72. We have already seen that Mark carefully portrays the women as eyewitnesses of the crucial events from which Peter and the Twelve were absent. But another plausible eyewitness, Simon of Cyrene, appears in 15:21, before readers hear about the women in 15:40.

Second, the way Simon is described by Mark — as "Simon of Cyrene, the father of Alexander and Rufus" — needs explanation. The case is not parallel to that of Mary the mother of James the little and Joses (Mark 15:40), where the sons serve to distinguish this Mary from others, because Simon (very common though this name was) is already sufficiently distinguished by reference to his native place, Cyrene. Matthew and Luke, by omitting the names of the sons, show that they recognize that. Nor is it really plausible that Mark names the sons *merely* because they were known to his readers. Mark is far from prodigal with names. The reference to Alexander and Rufus certainly does presuppose that Mark expected many of his readers to know them, in person or by reputation, as almost all commentators have agreed, but this cannot in itself explain why they are named. There does not seem to be a good reason available other than that Mark is appealing to Simon's eyewitness testimony, known in the early Christian movement not from his own firsthand account but through his sons. Perhaps Simon himself did not, like his sons, join the movement, or perhaps he died in the early years, while his sons remained well-known figures,[49] telling their father's story of the crucifixion of Jesus. That they were no longer such when Matthew and Luke wrote would be sufficient explanation of Matthew's and Luke's omission of their names.

Recipients of Healing

Our third example is the recipients of Jesus' healings. Only in three Gospel stories of healing, exorcism, or resuscitation are the recipients of Jesus' act

---

49. It has often been suggested that Rufus is the same person as the Rufus of Rom 16:13. In favor of this is the fact that the Rufus of Romans must have moved to Rome from the eastern Mediterranean since Paul knew his mother well. Contacts between the Jerusalem church and the church in Rome were close, as the presence in Rome of several persons originally members of the Jerusalem church shows: Andronicus and Junia (Rom 16:7) and Peter, Sylvanus, and Mark (1 Pet 5:12-13). If Mark's Gospel was written in Rome, this could also add to the plausibility of identifying Mark's Rufus with Paul's. On the other hand, Rufus was a popular name with Jews, who used it as a kind of Latin equivalent of Reuben, and so it can be only a possibility that the two Rufi are the same.

named (taking "recipient" loosely enough to include Jairus, whose daughter Jesus raised): Jairus, Bartimaeus, and Lazarus. In addition, though no stories are preserved, the three women named in Luke 8:2-3 — Mary Magdalene, Joanna, and Susanna — are among women said to have been "cured of evil spirits and infirmities," while Mary Magdalene specifically is said to have had seven demons cast out from her.[50] One more named recipient of Jesus' healing may be Simon the leper. Since he was able to entertain visitors in his house, Simon must have been cured of his leprosy, and it is possible that he had been healed by Jesus.[51] These persons said to have been healed by Jesus, but whose healing stories are not told and who are mentioned in the Gospels for other reasons, help to highlight the rarity of names in the healing stories themselves. It is quite clear that the names of the beneficiaries do not belong to the genre of gospel miracle stories.[52] So explanation of those names that do occur is certainly required.

With Jairus and Bartimaeus we encounter once again the phenomenon of a character named by Mark, presumably because he was well known in the early Christian movement, but whose name was dropped by one or both of the later Synoptic Evangelists (Jairus is named in Luke), presumably because they were not well known when or where the Evangelists wrote. Here the evidence makes interesting contact with a quotation Eusebius gives from the early-second-century Christian apologist Quadratus:

> [T]he works of our Savior were always present, for they were true: those who were healed, those who rose from the dead, those who were not only seen in the act of being healed or raised, but were also always present, not merely when the Savior was living on earth, but also for a considerable time after his departure, so that some of them survived even to our own times (Eusebius, *Hist. Eccl.* 4.3.2).

Quadratus addressed his work to the emperor Hadrian, and so was writing in or after 117 CE, but by "our own times" he presumably means not when he wrote but a time earlier in his life. Evidently he was of the same generation as Papias. The period of which it could credibly be said that some people healed

---

50. Meier, *A Marginal Jew,* vol. 2, 657-59, argues for the historicity of this tradition about Mary Magdalene.

51. This is suggested, e.g., by C. A. Evans, *Mark 8:27–16:20* (WBC 34B; Nashville: Nelson, 2001) 359.

52. The careful study of the motifs of miracle stories in G. Theissen, *Miracle Stories of the Early Christian Tradition* (tr. F. McDonagh; Edinburgh: Clark, 1983) 47-80, does not even refer to the occurrence of names.

by Jesus were still alive would be the same period toward the end of the first century in which Papias was collecting traditions, including some from two disciples of Jesus still living. This was also the time when Matthew and Luke were writing their Gospels. But the most important aspect of what Quadratus says is not his specific claim that some people healed by Jesus survived into his own time. More significant is his very explicit notion of the eyewitness function of the recipients of Jesus' healings and resuscitations during the whole of their lifetimes, however long these may have been. In this sense he views the recipients of healings in a way similar to Papias's view of the disciples of Jesus: they belonged not only to the origins of the Gospel traditions but also to the ongoing process of tradition in the early Christian movement. Just as Papias's view must date from the period in which he was collecting traditions, so Quadratus's view in this passage is not likely to have originated at the time he was writing but must rather go back to the time in his life when he doubtless heard about a few beneficiaries of Jesus' miracles who were still living. In that case it was a view current in the period when Matthew, Luke, and John produced their Gospels.

The paucity of names in healing stories even in Mark suggests that far fewer of the recipients of Jesus' healings fulfilled the function of continuing eyewitnesses than Quadratus suggests, though it is possible that even Mark has omitted some names of such people. But Quadratus's view does offer a very plausible explanation of the occurrence of the few such names that there are in the four canonical Gospels. Mark could expect his readers to know of Bartimaeus as a kind of living miracle, who made Jesus' act of healing still, so to speak, visible to all who encountered him as a well-known figure in the churches of Jerusalem and Judea. But after his death and after the fall of Jerusalem, which removed the Jewish Christians of Palestine from the usual purview of Christians outside Palestine, Bartimaeus was presumably no longer a figure of wide repute, and so Matthew and Luke omitted his name.

Vivid Detail of Eyewitness Recollections?

We might well expect a story told by an eyewitness to incorporate vivid details of visual or aural recollection not strictly necessary to the story. Such detail certainly cannot prove that we are dealing with eyewitness testimony, and too much has sometimes been made of the vivid details in Mark's narratives as indicative of eyewitness testimony (usually Peter's). An imaginative and skilled storyteller can also write with vivid detail, and so this feature of Mark's narratives may be evidence only of his own artistry. On the other hand, eyewitness testimony need not necessarily include vivid detail. Whether or not Mark's vivid detail comes from his eyewitness sources, we can observe how readily Luke and especially Matthew, in the interests of abbreviating Mark's narrative, dispense with it. This suggests that in no more than one step, from the vivid details as told by an eyewitness to the text of an author incorporating that testimony in a written work, vivid detail could easily disappear. So vivid detail has no probative force — for or against — in an argument about eyewitness testimony. (This topic will be discussed further, with reference to psychological studies, in chapter 13.)

That said, it is at least interesting that some of the stories we have suggested come from those who are named in them are among the most vividly told. This is true of the raising of Jairus's daughter (Mark 5:22-24a, 35-43), the healing of Bartimaeus (Mark 10:46-52), the story of Zacchaeus (Luke 19:1-10), and the story of Cleopas and his companion (Luke 24:13-35). The last three of these four stories are certainly told from the perspective of the named characters. In fact, if the details in these stories really are recollected, rather than the product of storytelling imagination, they can only have been recollected by, respectively, Bartimaeus, Zacchaeus, and Cleopas (or his anonymous companion). The recollection of the raising of Jairus's daughter, if that is indeed the basis of the story, could be that of Peter, James, John, or the girl's mother, but could at any rate plausibly be that of Jairus.

Table 1: Anonymous and Named Persons in Mark

	Anonymous (34)	Related to named persons (5+)	Named persons (33)
1:4			John the Baptist
1:9			Jesus
1:16			Simon (Peter)
			Andrew
1:19			James
			John
1:20			Zebedee
1:23	demoniac		
1:30		Peter's mother-in-law	
1:40	leper		
2:3	paralyzed man and four friends		
2:14			Levi son of Alphaeus
3:1	man with a withered hand		
3:18			Philip
			Bartholomew
			Matthew
			Thomas
			James son of Alphaeus
			Thaddaeus
			Simon the Cananean
3:19			Judas Iscariot
5:2	demoniac		
5:22			Jairus
5:23		Jairus's daughter	
5:25	woman with hemorrhage		
6:3			Mary, James, Joses, Judas, Simon
		sisters of Jesus	
6:14			Herod
6:17			Herodias
			Philip (Herodian)
6:22		Herodias' daughter	

	Anonymous	Related to named persons	Named persons
7:25	Syrophoenician woman and daughter		
7:32	deaf and dumb man		
8:22	blind man		
9:17	man and epileptic son		
10:17	rich man		
10:46			Bartimaeus
11:1	two disciples		
12:38	scribe		
12:42	poor widow		
14:3	woman who anoints Jesus		
14:13	two disciples		
14:14	owner of the house man with water jar		
14:47	man who draws sword slave of high priest		
14:51	young man who flees naked		
14:54	high priest		
14:66	servant girl		
15:1			Pilate
15:7			Barabbas
15:21			Simon of Cyrene father of Alexander and Rufus
15:27	two bandits		
15:39	centurion		
15:40			Mary Magdalene Mary mother of James and Joses Salome
15:43			Joseph of Arimathea

Table 2: Anonymous and Named Persons in Luke

	Anonymous (54)	Related to named persons (5+)	Named persons (44)
1:5			Herod (the Great)
			Zechariah
			Elizabeth
1:27			Joseph
			Mary
1:63			John (the Baptist)
2:1			Augustus
2:2			Quirinius
2:21			Jesus
2:25			Simeon
2:36			Anna daughter of Phanuel
3:1			Tiberius
			Pontius Pilate
			Herod (Antipas)
			Philip (Herodian)
			Lysanias
3:2			Annas
			Caiaphas
3:19			Herodias
		Herod's brother	
4:33	demoniac		
4:38			Simon (Peter)
		Simon's mother-in-law	
5:10			James
			John
5:12	leper		
5:18	paralyzed man		
5:27			Levi
6:6	man with withered hand		
6:14			Andrew
			Philip
			Bartholomew

	Anonymous	Related to named persons	Named persons
6:15			Matthew
			Thomas
			James son of Alphaeus
			Simon the Zealot
			Judas Iscariot
7:2	centurion		
	centurion's slave		
7:12	widow and son		
7:37	woman who anoints Jesus		
7:40			Simon the Pharisee
8:2			Mary Magdalene
8:3			Joanna wife of Chuza
			Susanna
8:19		Jesus' brothers	
8:27	demoniac		
8:41			Jairus
8:42		Jairus's daughter	
8:43	woman with hemorrhage		
9:38	man and epileptic son		
9:57	would-be disciple		
9:59	would-be disciple		
9:61	would-be disciple		
10:25	lawyer		
10:38			Martha
10:39			Mary her sister
11:14	dumb man		
11:27	woman in crowd		
11:37	Pharisee		
11:45	lawyer		
12:13	someone in crowd		
13:11	crippled woman		
13:14	leader of synagogue		
13:23	someone		
14:1	a Pharisaic leader		
14:15	one of guests		

Anonymous	Named persons
17:12 ten lepers	
18:18 rich ruler	
18:35 blind man	
19:2	Zacchaeus
19:29 two disciples	
21:2 poor widow	
22:10 man with water jar	
22:11 owner of house	
22:50 one who strikes with sword	
22:50 slave of high priest	
22:54 high priest[53]	
22:56 servant girl	
22:58 someone else	
22:59 someone else	
23:18	Barabbas
23:26	Simon of Cyrene
23:32 two criminals	
23:47 centurion	
23:50	Joseph of Arimathea
24:10	Mary mother of James
24:18	Cleopas
his companion	

53. I have included the high priest because, although Luke names both Annas and Caiaphas in 3:2, it is not clear which of these is intended in 22:50, 54.

Table 3: Anonymous and Named Persons in Matthew

	Anonymous (36)	Related to named persons (6+)	Named persons (33)
1:16			Joseph
			Mary
			Jesus
2:3			Herod (the Great)
2:22			Archelaus
3:1			John the Baptist
4:18			Simon (Peter)
			Andrew
4:21			James
			John
			Zebedee
8:2	leper		
8:5	centurion		
	centurion's servant		
8:14		Peter's mother-in-law	
8:19	scribe		
8:21	disciple		
8:28	two demoniacs		
9:2	paralyzed man		
9:9			Matthew
9:18	leader of synagogue		
	his daughter		
9:20	woman with hemorrhage		
9:27	two blind men		
9:32	mute demoniac		
10:3			Philip
			Bartholomew
			Thomas
			James son of Alphaeus
			Thaddaeus
			Simon the Cananean
			Judas Iscariot
12:10	man with withered hand		
12:22	blind and mute demoniac		

	Anonymous	Related to named persons	Named persons
13:55			James, Joseph, Simon, Judas
13:56		Jesus' sisters	
14:1			Herod (Antipas)
14:3			Herodias
			Philip (Herodian)
14:6		Herodias's daughter	
15:22	Canaanite woman and daughter		
17:15	man and epileptic son		
19:16	rich young man		
20:20		mother of sons of Zebedee	
20:30	two blind men		
21:1	two disciples		
26:3			Caiaphas
26:6			Simon the leper
26:7	woman who anoints Jesus		
26:18	owner of house		
26:51	one who draws sword slave of high priest		
26:60	two false witnesses		
26:69	servant girl		
26:71	another servant girl		
27:2			Pilate
27:16			Barabbas
27:19		Pilate's wife	
27:32			Simon of Cyrene
27:38	two bandits		
27:54	centurion		
27:56			Mary Magdalene
			Mary mother of James and Joseph

Table 4: Anonymous and Named Persons in John

	Anonymous (15)	Related to named persons (6+)	Named persons (20)
1:15			John (the Baptist)
1:40			Andrew
	a disciple[54]		
1:42			Simon (Peter) son of John
1:43			Philip
1:45			Nathanael
2:3		Jesus' mother	
2:8	chief steward		
2:12		Jesus' brothers	
3:1			Nicodemus
4:7	Samaritan woman		
4:46	royal official		
	his son		
5:5	paralyzed man		
6:9	boy with food		
6:71			Judas son of Simon Iscariot
9:1	blind man		
9:18	his parents		
11:1			Lazarus
			Mary
			Martha
11:16			Thomas
11:49			Caiaphas
14:22			Judas (not Iscariot)
18:10			Malchus
18:13			Annas
18:15	another disciple		
18:16	woman guard		
18:26		a relative of Malchus	
18:28			Pilate
18:40			Barabbas

54. Because I consider this disciple the same as the Beloved Disciple (13:23, etc.; see chapter 6 below), I have not listed the latter separately.

	Anonymous	Related to named persons	Named persons
19:18	two crucified with Jesus		
19:23	four soldiers		
19:25			Mary of Clopas
			Mary Magdalene
19:38			Joseph of Arimathea
21:2		sons of Zebedee	

Table 5: Names in the Four Gospels

excluding Jesus, Old Testament persons, non-human persons, names
in the two genealogies of Jesus, public persons, and the Twelve

Names in Mark	Mark	Matthew	Luke	John
Levi	2:14	[9:9 Matthew]	5:27	
son of Alphaeus	2:14			
Jairus	5:22	[9:18 unnamed]	8:41	
Mary (Jesus' mother)	6:3	13:55	cf. 1:27 etc.	
James	6:3	13:55		
Joses	6:3	13:55 (Joseph)		
Judas	6:3	13:55		
Simon	6:3	13:55		
Bartimaeus	10:46	[20:30 two	[18:35	
son of Timaeus	10:46	men unnamed]	unnamed]	
Simon the leper	14:3	26:6	(cf. 7:40, 43, 44)[55]	
Simon of Cyrene	15:21	27:32	23:26	
Alexander	15:21			
Rufus	15:21			
Joseph of Arimathea	15:43	27:57	23:50	19:38
Mary Magdalene	15:40, 47; 16:1	27:56, 61; 28:1	8:2; 24:10	19:25, etc.
Mary	15:40, 47; 16:1	27:56, 61; 28:1	24:10	
mother of James	15:40; 16:1	27:56	24:10	
and Joses	15:40, 47	27:56 (Joseph)		
Salome	15:40; 16:1			

Additional names in Matthew

Joseph (father of Jesus)		1:18, etc.	1:27, etc.	6:42

Additional names in Luke

Zechariah			1:5, etc.	
Elizabeth			1:5, etc.	
Simeon			2:25	

55. Since Luke's story of the anointing is not drawn from Mark but from another source, it seems best not to treat Luke's Simon (a Pharisee) as identical with Mark's Simon the leper.

Additional names in Luke	Mark	Matthew	Luke	John
Anna			2:36	
daughter of Phanuel			2:36	
Simon the Pharisee	(cf. 14:3)	(cf. 26:6)	7:40, 43, 44[56]	
Joanna wife of Chuza			8:3	
Susanna			8:3	
Martha			10:38, 40-41	11:1 etc.
Mary			10:39, 42	11:1 etc.
Zacchaeus			19:2, 5, 8	
Cleopas			24:18	(cf. 19:25)[57]

Names in John[58]

	Mark	Matthew	Luke	John
Nathanael				1:45 etc.
Nicodemus				3:1 etc.
Joseph		1:18 etc.	1:27 etc.	6:42
Lazarus				11:1 etc.
Mary			10:39, 42	11:1 etc.
Martha			10:38, 40-41	11:1 etc.
Malchus	[14:47 unnamed]	[26:51 unnamed]	[22:50 unnamed]	18:10
Mary Magdalene	15:40, 47; 16:1	27:56, 61; 28:1	8:2; 24:10	19:25, etc.
Mary of Clopas				19:25
Joseph of Arimathea	15:43	27:57	23:50	19:38

56. See previous note.

57. For the probability that Clopas (John 19:25) is the same person as Cleopas (Luke 24:18), see Bauckham, *Gospel Women*, 206-10.

58. Because I do not wish here to judge the question whether John knew any of the Synoptic Gospels, the list given is not limited to names that are additional to those in the other Gospels.

4. Palestinian Jewish Names

A New Resource for Study of the Gospels

In this chapter we must step temporarily aside from our investigation of the eyewitnesses of the gospel traditions and turn to a subject that will usefully inform that investigation when we resume it. This topic is the study of the names borne by Palestinian Jews in the period of Jesus and the early church.

Names are a valuable resource for ancient historians, but one of which New Testament scholars have made relatively little use. Because names are preserved not only in our literary sources but also plentifully in epigraphic sources such as burial inscriptions and in papyri such as legal documents, we know the names of large numbers of ancient people about whom we know little else besides (often approximately) where and when they lived. This is true, among many other categories, of Palestinian Jews. Such evidence enables us to know, for example, which names were the most popular or the ways in which names were combined, and such information can help to shed light on the named persons in our literary sources, such as the Gospels.

To make full use of this resource, however, we need a database of information. Such a database — invaluable for New Testament scholars — has recently been compiled by the Israeli scholar Tal Ilan and was published in 2002 as *Lexicon of Jewish Names in Late Antiquity: Part I: Palestine 330 BCE–200 CE*.[1] She describes it as "both an onomasticon and a prosopography. It is an onomasticon in as far as it is a collection of all the recorded names used by the

1. TSAJ 91; Tübingen: Mohr, 2002.

Jews of Palestine [in the period 330 BCE–200 CE]. . . . It is a prosopography, in as far as it collects not just names but also the people who bore the names. In this respect it bears the character of a modern telephone book."[2] The chronological period it covers begins at the Hellenistic conquest of Palestine and concludes at the end of the Mishnaic period. Thus its sources include the works of Josephus, the New Testament, the texts from the Judean desert and from Masada, ossuary inscriptions from Jerusalem, and the earliest (tannaitic) rabbinic sources. For the study of the Gospels this period of five centuries might seem too broad, but this possible disadvantage for the New Testament scholar in Ilan's collection of data is offset by the facts that in many respects the practices of name-giving seem to have remained fairly constant over this period and also, importantly, that a large proportion of the data actually comes from the first century CE and early second century (to 135 CE), just because the sources for this shorter period are much more plentiful than for other parts of the whole period.

It may come as a surprise to many readers that we know the names of as many as three thousand Palestinian Jews who lived during the five centuries covered by Ilan's *Lexicon*. In most cases we know at least a little more about these persons, even if it is only their relationship to another named person. This material obviously provides a very rich resource for the history of Jewish Palestine and, among other specific parts of that history, the history of the beginnings of Christianity. The availability of the information in the comprehensive and systematic form of the *Lexicon* now makes the use of this resource much more possible and accurate.

On Counting Names

I have to begin with some explanations of how the statistics about names in Tables 6-9 on pages 85-92 below have been calculated from the data in Ilan's work. While hugely indebted to Ilan's work, I have differed from her in a few aspects of the criteria used for calculating statistics. The explanations are rather technical, but necessary for those who might make their own use of Ilan's work in connection with my arguments in this chapter.

Tal Ilan's *Lexicon* classifies all the names into such categories as "Biblical Names — Male" or "Latin Names — Female." Within these categories it lists every name attested in the sources (as that of persons belonging to the period) and under each name has an entry for each person attested in the

---

2. Ilan, *Lexicon*, 1.

sources. However, some of these entries are statistically invalid. That is, they are not counted when Ilan compiles statistics about numbers of persons from the catalogue. Those that are statistically invalid have a comment in section E of the entry. Such entries indicate that the person bearing the name is ficti- tious, may not be Jewish, was not born in Palestine, was Samaritan, or was a proselyte who retained their old (Gentile) name, or that the name was a nick- name, a family name, or a second name. In these last three cases the person has another name and is listed under that name if it is known. Excluding these names from the statistics ensures that no individual is counted twice.

When entries with a comment in section E have been discounted as sta- tistically invalid, Ilan calculates that the catalogue includes 2826 persons (2509 male, 317 female) bearing 831 different names (721 male, 110 female).[3] However, these figures are seriously misleading, because whereas the number of persons (2826) counts only statistically valid entries, the number of names (831) is the total number of names in the catalogue, including those borne by statistically invalid persons. It is not true that 2826 persons bore 831 names; those 2826 bore a considerably smaller number of names.

In compiling the material presented in Tables 6-9 I have used Ilan's data, but I have differed from her in one aspect of what counts as statistically valid. I have not excluded second names in cases where an individual bore two names (usually one Semitic, the other Greek or Latin), each genuinely a name (rather than a nickname created *ad hoc* or a family name).[4] Thus the New Testament character John Mark is counted in my statistics for both his He- brew name John (Yohanan) and his Latin name Mark (Marcus), whereas in Ilan's statistics he counts only once because his entry under "Marcus" labels that name as, in his case, a second name. This means that, whereas Ilan counts persons, I count occurrences of a name. This is more useful for our present purposes, which particularly include gauging the popularity of each name. If we wish to know how popular the name Marcus was among Palestinian Jews, we need to know how many persons are known to have borne it, no matter whether they also bore another name.

I have accepted Ilan's other reasons for excluding occurrences of names from statistics (i.e., the other comments made in section E of each entry), but sometimes I differ from her judgments in particular cases. Some of the per- sons she regards as fictitious I think historical and some of those she regards

3. Ilan, *Lexicon*, 55 (Table 4).

4. It is not always easy to distinguish between nicknames and second names. I have in- cluded nicknames that seem to function as names, whereas Ilan tends to treat all singular and inexplicable names as nicknames (*Lexicon*, 46).

as historical I judge to be fictitious. Whether a person, though living in Palestine, was born in the Diaspora (and would therefore not constitute evidence for the naming practices of Palestinian Jews) is not easy to tell, and so I have, for example, excluded all the names of the Seven in Acts 6:5 from my calculations, since it is likely (though far from certain) that the Seven were all born in the Diaspora, whereas Ilan includes them in her statistics. My differences from Ilan's judgments in particular cases are often indicated in the notes to Tables 6-7, though not always.

We have noted above that Ilan excludes statistically invalid entries when counting persons but includes them when counting names. Therefore, when she provides two tables of, respectively, the twenty most common male names and the ten most popular female names,[5] she does not discount the statistically invalid entries. Her figures therefore include, for example, names given in Christian apocryphal literature of the fourth century or later to characters who are purported to belong to the first century CE. Such fictitious cases clearly should not be included in a calculation of the popularity of such names in Ilan's period. My own Tables 6 and 7 rank names in order of popularity based only on those entries in Ilan's catalogue that I judge to be statistically valid, using her own criteria with the exception of the issue of second names.[6] The scale of the differences can be seen in the following figures for the six most popular male names:

Bauckham		Ilan	
Simon	243	Simon	257
Joseph	218	Joseph	231
Eleazar	166	Judah	179
Judah	164	Eleazar	177
Yohanan	122	Yohanan	128
Joshua	99	Joshua	103

5. Ilan, *Lexicon*, 56-57.

6. R. Hachlili, "Hebrew Names, Personal Names, Family Names and Nicknames of Jews in the Second Temple Period," in J. W. van Henten and A. Brenner, eds., *Families and Family Relations as Represented in Early Judaisms and Early Christianities* (STAR 2; Leiden: Deo, 2000) 113-15, gives tables ranking the most popular male and female names. They are based on a narrower basis of data than Ilan's. In Hachlili's table the six most popular male names are:

Simeon/Simon	167
Yohanan	118
Joseph	112
Judah	96
Eleazar	85
Joshua	60

My calculations produce the following total figures: 2953 occurrences of 521 names, comprising 2625 occurrences of 447 male names and 328 occurrences of 74 female names.

With these explanations, we are now ready to move to some observations on the data I present in Tables 6 and 7, where the names are ranked in order of popularity.

The Relative Popularity of Names

It can easily be seen that among Jews of this period there were a small number of very popular names and a large number of rare ones. Of course, the larger totals are statistically more significant than the small ones. We can be pretty sure that Simon (243 occurrences) and Joseph (218 occurrences) were the most popular male names, but not really that, say, Hillel (11 occurrences) was more popular than Zebedee (5 occurrences). The accuracy of the calculations of relative popularity among the most popular names can be confirmed by observing the breakdowns of the total figures in the figures for certain identifiable sources of the data: the New Testament, Josephus, ossuaries, and the texts from the Judean desert (these figures are given in the four last columns in Tables 6 and 7). (These four sources complement each other in being of different kinds: literary, epigraphic and documentary.) We can see, for example, that Simon and Joseph are the two most popular male names in all four sources, and Simon is more popular than Joseph in three of the sources. Similarly, Mary and Salome are the two most popular female names in all of these four sources, and Mary is also more popular than Salome in all of them. In fact, the relative proportions of the first nine names in all four sources are strikingly close to the relative proportions of the overall figures for these names. It is not surprising that there are some anomalies (such as only one Eleazar [Lazarus] in the New Testament) since the figures for each of these four sources are rather small. But these facts may certainly strengthen our confidence in the reasonable accuracy of the relative popularity of the names that is indicated by the total figures for each.

Some indication of the relative popularity of the names can be gained from the following figures:

15.6% of men bore one of the two most popular male names, Simon and Joseph.

41.5% of men bore one of the nine most popular male names.

7.9% of men bore a name that is attested only once in our sources.

28.6% of women bore one of the two most popular female names, Mary and Salome.

49.7% of women bore one of the nine most popular female names.

9.6% of women bore a name that is attested only once in our sources.

We can compare these total figures with those for the Gospels and Acts (which are also, of course, included in the total figures just given):

18.2% of men bore one of the two most popular male names, Simon and Joseph.

40.3% of men bore one of the nine most popular male names.

3.9% of men bore a name that is attested only once in our sources.[7]

38.9% of women bore one of the two most popular female names, Mary and Salome.

61.1% of women bore one of the nine most popular female names.

2.5% of women bore a name that is attested only once in our sources.[8]

The percentages for men in the New Testament thus correlate remarkably closely with those for the population in general. It is not surprising that the percentages for women do not match those for the population in general nearly as closely. The statistical base for women's names is considerably smaller than that for men, both in the New Testament and in the sources in general.

Also of interest is the proportion of Greek names in the population.[9] This is a much more difficult matter, since probably considerably more Jews bore both a Semitic and a Greek name than we are able to tell from our sources. Usually only one of the two names would be used on any particular occasion, and so in most cases only one would occur in our sources. (For example, it is likely that the twelve Jews called Jason in our sources also bore one of the similar-sounding Hebrew names, Joshua or Joseph. Some of the twenty-four Jews called Alexander may also have been called Benjamin, the Hebrew name for which Alexander was treated as the Greek equivalent.) There is also the fact that the most common male name of all, Simon/Simeon, was at one and the same time the Hebrew name Simeon and the Greek name Simon, with the latter treated virtually as the spelling in Greek letters of the Hebrew name. If we treat this name as Semitic, then the proportion of occurrences of male

7. These are Agabus, Bartimaeus/Timaeus, and Caiaphas.

8. These are Drusilla and Rhoda.

9. See Ilan, *Lexicon,* 55, for her statistics on the language of names.

Greek names within the total for the whole male population (using my statistics) is 12.3%. Among Palestinian Jews in the New Testament, the proportion of occurrences of male Greek names is 22%. The proportion of occurrences of female Greek names within the total for the whole female population is 18.1%, while the corresponding proportion in the New Testament is 16.7%. In this case the match is better for female than for male names. The fact that none of the most popular names were Greek (none of the 15 most popular male names, none of the 6 most popular female) and few of the even moderately popular names are Greek must make the statistics for occurrences of Greek names less reliable than some of the other statistics we have given.

We should note that the pattern of Jewish names in the Diaspora was not at all the same as in Palestine. Although we do not yet have a database for the Jewish Diaspora comparable to Ilan's lexicon of names in Jewish Palestine, the fact that the practices of naming were very different in the two cases is clear from the evidence we do have.[10] For example, the most common male names in the Jewish inscriptions from Greco-Roman Egypt are Eleazar/Lazarus (11 occurrences), Sabbataius and variants (10), Joseph (6), Dositheus (5), Pappus and variants (5), Ptolemaius (4), and Samuel (4).[11] The extent of divergence from the Palestinian data can be seen thus:

Name	*Egypt*		*Palestine*		*NT*
	Number	*Rank*	*Number*	*Rank*	*Number*
Eleazar	11	1	166	3	1
Sabbataius	10	2	5	68 =	2 (Barsabbas)
Joseph	6	3	218	2	6
Dositheus	5	4 =	27	16	0
Pappus	5	4 =	8	39 =	0
Ptolemaius	4	6 =	7	50 =	1 (Bartholomew)
Samuel	4	6 =	20	23	0

Thus the names of Palestinian Jews in the Gospels and Acts coincide very closely with the names of the general population of Jewish Palestine in this period, but not to the names of Jews in the Diaspora. In this light it be-

10. M. Williams, "Palestinian Jewish Personal Names in Acts," in R. Bauckham, ed., *The Book of Acts in Its Palestinian Setting* (Grand Rapids: Eerdmans, 1995) 106-8.

11. Data from W. Horbury and D. Noy, *Jewish Inscriptions of Graeco-Roman Egypt* (Cambridge: Cambridge University Press, 1992). Unlike the figures calculated from Ilan's data, these do not include literary sources or papyri.

comes very unlikely that the names in the Gospels are late accretions to the traditions. Outside Palestine the appropriate names simply could not have been chosen. Even within Palestine, it would be very surprising if random accretions of names to this or that tradition would fit the actual pattern of names in the general population. In Palestine we might expect the addition of popular names like Joseph, Judas, Jonathan, or Mattathias, but not Zacchaeus, Jairus, Nathanael, Malchus, Cleopas, or Nicodemus, just to mention some of the male names that have most often been suspected of being late additions rather than original to the Gospel traditions.

Why Were Some Names So Popular?

Why were the most popular names popular? Although the question is not strictly required for our purposes in this book, we shall attend to it briefly. It is very striking that six of the nine most popular male names are those of the Hasmonean family, Mattathias and his five sons (John, Simon, Judas, Eleazar, and Jonathan), while the three most popular female names, Mary (Mariam), Salome, and Shelamzion (the longer form of Salome), were also the names of members of the Hasmonean ruling family. Since it was the Hasmoneans who won Jewish independence in the second century BCE and were the last Jewish rulers of an independent Jewish state, the popularity of their names into the period of Roman rule was no doubt patriotic.[12] Rather paradoxically, however, the unequalled popularity of the name Simon may well be partly due to the fact that the Hebrew name Simeon and the Greek name Simon were nearly identical. They were the perfect instance of the practice of those Jews in this period who adopted a Greek or Latin name that sounded similar to their Semitic name. In the case of Simeon and Simon the match was nearly exact and the latter was treated virtually as the former in Greek letters.[13]

The popularity of the names of the Hasmoneans illustrates the fact that biblical names, though widely used by Palestinian Jews in this period, seem mostly not to have been used for the purpose of recalling the biblical characters who bore these names (a purpose which seems to have been more commonly operative in the Diaspora). The names of the Hasmoneans were all bib-

12. Williams, "Palestinian Jewish Personal Names," 106-7; Ilan, *Lexicon,* 6-9, 56.

13. N. G. Cohen, "Jewish Names as Cultural Indicators in Antiquity," *JSJ* 7 (1967) 112-17. An ossuary inscription (L. Y. Rahmani, *A Catalogue of Jewish Ossuaries in the Collections of the State of Israel* [Jerusalem: Israel Antiquities Authority/Israel Academy of Sciences and Humanities, 1994], number 651), gives the same person the names Simôn and Shim'ôn, both in Hebrew letters, the latter the Hebrew name, the former a Hebrew transliteration of the Greek name.

lical, two of them patriarchal (Simeon, Judah),[14] but it was because of their Hasmonean use that they were popular.[15] There may be some exceptions, such as the fact that Jacob (James) was the eleventh most popular male name.[16] But most striking are that Joseph is the second most popular male name, very close to Simon in frequency, and that Joshua (Jesus) is the sixth most popular. Ilan has suggested that, as well as the five Hasmonean brothers known to us from 1 Maccabees, there was also a sixth brother called Joseph, mentioned in 2 Macc 8:22,[17] where most scholars have considered the name a mistake for John.[18] It

14. The names of the twelve tribes of Israel appear in Ilan's data as follows:

Tribe	Number of occurrences	Rank (in popularity)
Simeon	243	1
Judah	164	4
Levi	25	17=
Manasseh	13	26
Reuben	8	39=
Benjamin	5	68=
Ephraim	2	not ranked
Issachar	0	
Zebulon	0	
Dan	0	
Asher	0	
Gad	0	
Naphtali	0	

These figures show very clearly that the tribal names were not used because they were tribal names.

15. Therefore J. P. Meier, *A Marginal Jew,* vol. 1 (New York: Doubleday, 1991) 206, and vol. 3 (New York: Doubleday, 2001) 616, is wrong to suppose that "every name in Jesus' family harks back to the beginnings of Israel's history: the patriarch Jacob (= James), who received the name Israel; the twelve sons (and tribes) of Israel (including Judah, Joseph, and Simeon); Miriam, the sister of Moses; and finally Joshua/Jesus, the successor of Moses and leader of Israel into the promised land" (616; cf. also S. McKnight, *A New Vision for Israel* [Grand Rapids: Eerdmans, 1999] 2 n. 3). This is probably true only of the names Jacob and Joshua, so that the associations of the names in Jesus' family would mix the origins of Israel and the conquest of the land with, even more prominently, the Maccabean revolt. But might not this family have used these names for no other reason than that they were very popular?

16. The occurrences listed in Ilan's catalogue show that both Williams, "Palestinian Jewish Personal Names," 107 ("hardly used" in Palestine), and R. Hachlili, "Hebrew Names," 85 ("rarely used"), were mistaken in denying that it was popular, though Hachlili was correct in saying that Abraham and Isaac were not.

17. Ilan, *Lexicon,* 7.

18. However, Ilan's suggestion is supported by J. A. Goldstein, *II Maccabees* (AB41A; New York: Doubleday, 1984) 299-300, 334-35, who also finds a seventh Hasmonean brother in the variant reading Ezra, for Eleazar, in 2 Macc 8:23.

is an attractive suggestion and would make all five of the five most popular male names Hasmonean, but Ilan does not explain the popularity of the names Joshua and Hananiah, that intervene as sixth and seventh most popular before two Hasmonean names, Jonathan and Mattathiah.

Joshua would seem most readily explicable as a patriotic usage inspired by the hope of a reconquest of the land from Roman rule, comparable with the conquest of the land by the famous Joshua of the Hebrew Bible. But the name's popularity could have been enhanced by the fact that it is a theophoric name that begins with the divine name (most obviously in its full form Yehoshua). The name Joseph, which is not really theophoric, was in this period frequently spelled Yehosef, making it theophoric, and the name Judah (Yehudah) was probably also thought to incorporate the divine name YHWH.[19] They would be the only patriarchal names including the divine name, a fact that might well have helped to make them popular. Moreover, the names John (Yehohanan, Yohanan) and Jonathan (Yehonatan, Yonatan) are genuinely theophoric. So it seems likely that five of the eight most popular male names were understood as beginning with the divine name: Joseph (second), Judah (fourth), John (fifth), Joshua (sixth), Jonathan (eighth). It may be that even the names Jacob, in eleventh place, and Ishmael, in thirteenth place, had their popularity assisted by the fact that both begin with the letter Y.[20]

Some names must have been popular primarily because of their meaning. A related group of three very popular names are John, in fifth place, Hananiah, in seventh place, and Hanan, the shortened form of Hananiah, in twelfth place. As well as being one of the names of the Hasmoneans, John (Yehohanan) has exactly the same meaning as Hananiah. They both mean "YHWH has been gracious" and differ only in putting the divine element (YH) in first or last place. Hanan ("he has been gracious") has the same meaning while not explicitly referring to God. Such names could have had a very personal meaning, expressing God's grace to the parents in giving them a child. But they might also have had a more national significance as expressions of the hope for God's gracious favor to his people when he delivers them from the pagan oppressors and restores Israel as he has promised to do. It is notable that names with this meaning (Hananiah, Hananiel, Hannah) are prominent in the book of Tobit, where they symbolize that book's expectation of God's gracious restoration of the exiles of Israel.[21]

19. See b. Sota 10b and 36b, where Judah and Joseph are both explained with reference to YHWH.

20. In y. Ta'anith 65d the name Israel is related to YHWH by the fact that it begins with the letter Y.

21. Bauckham, *Gospel Women* (Grand Rapids: Eerdmans, 2002) 97.

Ishmael ("God has listened"),[22] which occurs in thirteenth place in the order of popularity, might similarly have had either a personal — God has heard our prayers for a child — or a more national significance. But in the case of Menahem ("comforter"), which ranks tenth in popularity, it is impossible to avoid the conclusion that it was understood as carrying messianic or eschatological significance. The verb "comfort" was closely associated with the hope of Israel's restoration, especially through its reiteration as the first two words of Isaiah 40 and recurrence throughout the following prophecies (Isa 49:13; 51:3, 12; 52:9; 61:2; 66:13; cf. Jer 31:13; Zech 1:17), and so it is probable that the popularity of Menahem expressed, like the Hasmonean names and Joshua, the Jewish hope of God's intervention and deliverance of his people from pagan domination. It can hardly be accidental that the most famous Menahem of this period[23] was the messianic pretender, son of Judas the Galilean, who in 66 CE, early in the Jewish revolt, marched into Jerusalem like a king with an army of Sicarii (Josephus, *War* 2.433-34). Could it have been his name that inspired him and his followers to think he was the Messiah?[24]

It is therefore rather clear that, not only the names of the Hasmoneans, but also several of the other most popular male names were popular because of their association with the nationalistic religious expectations of national deliverance and restoration by God. Of course, this does not mean that such associations were in the minds of every parent who chose a name for their child. Once names become popular for some reason, they are also popular just because they are popular. Moreover, there were also family traditions, especially in aristocratic families, of repeating the same names from one generation to another. But these are secondary factors that do not nullify the rather clear general reasons for the really rather extraordinary popularity of a rather small number of names.

In most cases, as we have seen, the popularity of names had nothing to do with the biblical persons who bore the names. Most of the popular names were biblical but were popular regardless of their biblical bearers. Only the cases of Jacob and Joshua seem to be exceptions. But it is also worth noting that among some famous biblical names that were not used at all by Palestin-

22. This is a clear case in which the ability of a name to recall a famous character who bore it in the Hebrew Bible is obviously not operative. Jews who called their children Ishmael in this period were certainly not thinking of Abraham's son Ishmael, ancestor of Arab nations.

23. He is number 1 in Ilan's list: *Lexicon*, 185.

24. A later rabbinic tradition (b. Sanhedrin 98b) maintained that the Messiah would be called Menahem son of Hezekiah (doubtless king Hezekiah).

ian Jews in this period were Moses,[25] David, and Elijah.[26] This conspicuous avoidance must also relate to the eschatological hope, in which three eschatological figures were required to lead the new theocracy: the royal Messiah (the son of David), the eschatological high priest (the returning Elijah), and the prophet like Moses. It may have been thought that to use these names for one's own children would be a presumptuous expectation that these children were actually the expected eschatological deliverers. So the non-use of these names is itself a kind of negative form of evidence for the messianic hopes of the period.

How to Tell Simon from Simon

That about half the population of Jewish Palestine were called by only about a dozen personal names had one very important effect. It meant that a single personal name was not sufficient to distinguish them. Their neighbors, sometimes even their own family members, needed other ways of distinguishing them from others who bore the same very common names. There were a considerable variety of ways of doing this, all highly characteristic of Palestinian Jewish appellations, but not, for the most part, of the Diaspora.[27]

Virtually all these ways of distinguishing people who bore the same common names can be illustrated from the Gospels and Acts. In what follows I will give such illustrations, but I will not refer to the Twelve, who are a special case that I reserve for the next chapter.

(1) *Variant forms of a name.* Many names had different forms and these could sometimes be used to distinguish one bearer of the name from another. For example, Jesus' brother Joseph (Matt 13:55) was evidently known by the abbreviated form Yoses (Greek *Iōsēs*: Mark 6:3) in order to distinguish him within the family from his father Joseph. This is exactly like a modern family within which the father is known as James and the son as Jim. It is possible that other persons known by abbreviated forms of a name were first so called to distinguish them from close relatives of the same name. Perhaps Zacchaeus (Luke 19:2, i.e., Zakkai, the short form of Zachariah) was first so called to distinguish him from his father or an uncle or grandfather called Zachariah.[28]

25. Ilan, *Lexicon*, 190, gives one instance, but the reading is dubious.

26. The only instance in Ilan, *Lexicon*, 63, is Samaritan.

27. Patronymics were common in the Diaspora (as throughout the ancient world), as was the use of two names in different languages for the same individual.

28. For examples of both the full and the contracted name of the same person on ossuaries, see Rahmani, *A Catalogue*, numbers 9, 42, 270, 370, and 468.

(2) *Patronymic added.* A simple and very common means of distinguishing a man was to add a patronymic (reference to his father's name) to
his personal name, thus: "X son of (Aramaic *bar* or Hebrew *ben*) Y." Examples
abound. Within the New Testament, there is Levi son of Alphaeus (Mark
2:14), John son of Zachariah (Luke 3:2), and Jesus son of Joseph (John 1:45).
Patronymics were also used for women,[29] but less frequently, because a married woman would often be called the wife of her husband rather than the
daughter of her father.

(3) *Patronymic substituted.* A patronymic could also simply take the
place of the personal name. This was a common phenomenon.[30] For example, among the Masada ostraca we find Bar Simon, Bar Hilqai, Bar Yeshua',
Bar Qesa', Bar Hanun, Bar Harsha', Bar Benaiah, Bar Haggai, Bar Halafta',
Bar Jason, Bar Pinhi, Bar Levi, and others.[31] It is notable that in many such
cases, though by no means all, the name is relatively or very unusual. In such
cases, especially if the person's proper name were common (and especially if
he had no brothers known in the context), the patronymic could be more
useful than the proper name for distinguishing an individual.

In the Gospels we find this phenomenon in the cases of Barabbas (= son
of Abba) and Bartimaeus (= son of Timaeus). Mark calls the latter "Bartimaeus son of Timaeus" (Mark 10:46), thus explaining "Bartimaeus" for his
Greek readers. He could never have been called "Bartimaeus son of Timaeus"
(= Bar Timaeus bar Timaeus!). Timaeus is a Greek name occurring only in this
case as a Palestinian Jewish name.[32] This is no reason to question its authenticity or to treat Bartimaeus as a nickname rather than a real patronymic, since
there are many other cases of Greek names occurring only once as the name of
a Palestinian Jew. In this case, it is precisely the rarity of the name that makes
the patronymic entirely sufficient for naming Timaeus's son.

Barabbas and Bartimaeus are examples of what Ilan calls a "unique
phenomenon in N[ew] T[estament] transliteration," in which the Aramaic
bar (son of) forms an integral part of the name.[33] Other examples are

29. E.g., Rahmani, *A Catalogue,* number 342.

30. For other examples and a discussion of the phenomenon of patronymics used without personal names, see J. Naveh, "Nameless People," *IEJ* 40 (1990) 108-23.

31. Y. Yadin and J. Naveh, eds., *Masada I: The Aramaic and Hebrew Ostraca and Jar Inscriptions from Masada* (Jerusalem: Israel Exploration Society/Hebrew University of Jerusalem,
1989) 23-56, numbers 415, 420, 421, 422, 425, 480, 481, 482, 483, 502, and 577. The only example on
an ossuary in Rahmani, *A Catalogue,* is number 571: Bar Nahum.

32. Nor is this name found in inscriptions from the Jewish Diaspora.

33. Ilan, *Lexicon,* 18. In fact, as she points out, the phenomenon is also found in a few
other cases of Greek transliterations of Aramaic — in Eusebius, Epiphanius, and Cassius Dio.

Bartholomew, Bar-jesus, Bar-jonah, Barnabas, and Barsabbas. It looks as though this form is used when the patronymic (whether a true patronymic or a nickname, as in the cases of Barnabas and Barsabbas) functions as a personal name and could stand alone to designate the person without his personal name. In other cases, the Aramaic *bar* is translated. This is a striking instance of the closeness of the names in the Gospels and Acts to Palestinian Jewish usage.

(4) *Names of husband or sons added.* Married or widowed women could be identified by reference to their husband[34] or children.[35] In the Greek of the New Testament we find the abbreviated "Mary of Clopas" (John 19:25) and "Mary of James" (Luke 24:10), which could specify the relationship (in fact, probably wife in the former case, certainly mother in the latter) only for those who knew them. One character in the Gospels is known only by her relationship to her husband and sons: "the mother of the sons of Zebedee" (Matt 20:20; 27:56). There are women who are similarly nameless even on their ossuaries.[36]

(5) *Nickname added.* Nicknames were of many kinds. For example, they might refer to physical characteristics or defects, or they could be terms of endearment. Gospel examples of nicknames used with personal names are "James the little *(tou mikrou)*" (Mark 15:40), "Simon the leper" (Matt 26:6; Mark 14:3), and "John the baptizer." "James the little" has often been understood in a comparative sense ("James the less"), designating him "lesser" or "younger" than some other James, and many translations have followed this misinterpretation. In fact, the nickname probably just means that he was short. A contemporary parallel is the ossuary inscription that reads, in Greek script, *Salōna katana,* where the first word is a version of the very common female name Salome and the second a transliteration of the Hebrew for "small."[37] Another ossuary inscription refers, in Hebrew script, to "Gaius the small," where the word for "small" is probably a version of the Greek word *nanos,* meaning "dwarf."[38] Later examples include "Yose the little" (Greek *ho mikkos* [*sic*]) and "Domnica the little (Greek *hē mikra)*" from Bet She'arim.[39] (It is possible that the nickname "small" could have been given to especially large people, as with Robin Hood's Little John.)

34. E.g., Rahmani, *A Catalogue,* number 559.

35. E.g., Rahmani, *A Catalogue,* numbers 822 and 868.

36. E.g., Rahmani, *A Catalogue,* number 150: "Simeon and (his) wife."

37. Rahmani, *A Catalogue,* number 552; cf. Ilan, *Lexicon,* 443. She was evidently an adult, not a child.

38. Rahmani, *A Catalogue,* number 421; cf. Ilan, *Lexicon,* 300.

39. M. Schwabe and B. Lifshitz, *Beth Shearim,* vol. 2: *The Greek Inscriptions* (Jerusalem: Massada, 1974) nos. 28, 198. For similar examples, see Hachlili, "Hebrew Names," 104.

"Simon the leper" (Mark 14:3) presumably had had a skin disease and been cured of it, perhaps by Jesus. Had he been a leper[40] at the time of Mark's story he would not have been able to entertain people in his home. It seems likely that the description "the leper" stuck with him as a useful nickname, or perhaps it was never meant literally but used because, while not diseased, he resembled a leper in some way. We might compare the nicknames of two of Josephus's ancestors: "Simon the stammerer" and "Matthias the hunchback" (presumably so called in part to distinguish him from his father, also called Matthias; *Vita* 3.4).

Nicknames could look like patronymics.[41] Two persons in Acts have the second name Barsabbas: "Joseph called Barsabbas, who was also known as Justus" (1:23) and "Judas called Barsabbas" (15:22). This could be a real patronymic referring to a father named Sabba,[42] or it could mean "son of the old man" (Aramaic *Sabba,* elderly), used as a nickname because the son was a child of his father's old age, or it could perhaps mean "son of the Sabbath,"[43] a nickname given to someone born on the Sabbath. More certainly a nickname is Barnabas, since this name was given by the apostles to Joseph of Cyprus (Acts 4:36); its derivation is debatable.[44]

(6) *Nickname substituted.* Like patronymics, nicknames could be used alone without a personal name. Joseph Barnabas is usually called just Barnabas, just as Simon Peter could be called either Cephas or Peter, the Aramaic and Greek versions of the nickname Jesus gave him.

(7) *Place of origin or dwelling added.* Gospel examples are Jesus the Nazarene (= of Nazareth), Jesus the Galilean (Matt 26:69), Mary Magdalene (= of Magdala), Simon the Cyrenian (= of Cyrene), Joseph of Arimathea, and Nathanael of Cana (John 21:2). Of course, people could be distinguished in this way only when they were elsewhere than in their place of origin or dwelling. This is why Nathanael is called "from Cana of Galilee" in John 21:2, but not in 1:45. Joseph of Arimathea doubtless had estates near a town called

40. The Hebrew and Greek terms usually translated "leprosy" in English translations of the Bible (*ṣāraʿat, lepra*) do not refer to what has been called "leprosy" in modern times (Hansen's disease), but to a variety of serious skin diseases, possibly including true leprosy in the New Testament usage.

41. For nicknames with *ben* or *bar,* see especially Naveh, "Nameless People."

42. Ilan, *Lexicon,* 395-96; but it is not really clear that in any of these six examples Sabba is a real name.

43. Names referring to the Sabbath (Sabbatius and variants) were quite commonly used by Jews in the Diaspora, where Sabbath observance was what most prominently marked Jews out from Gentiles.

44. C. K. Barrett, *A Critical and Exegetical Commentary on the Acts of the Apostles,* vol. 1 (ICC; Edinburgh: Clark, 1994) 258-59.

Ramathaim, but lived mostly in Jerusalem, where he was naturally called Joseph of Ramathaim. Such designations were common. Examples from ossuaries and ostraca are Philo the Cyrenian, Hillel the Cyrenian,[45] Sara the Ptolemaican (from Ptolemais in Cyrenaica),[46] Nicanor the Alexandrian,[47] Simon the Babylonian,[48] Salome the Galilean,[49] and Yehoʿezer the Ezobite (= from Bet Ezob).[50] The best-known example from Josephus is the rebel leader Judas the Galilean (*Ant.* 18.23, etc.), which is doubtless what he was called outside Galilee. Within Galilee he may have been known as Judas "the Gaulanite" or "man from the Golan" (cf. *Ant.* 18.4).

(8) *Place of origin or dwelling substituted.* It cannot have been common to refer to someone purely by their place of origin, but there are some cases. An ossuary inscription reads in Aramaic: "Imma, daughter of Hananiah, mother of the Sokhite" (i.e., the man from Sokho).[51] The popular prophet who led his followers into the desert seems to have been known only as "the Egyptian" (Acts 21:38; Josephus, *Ant.* 20.171-72).

(9) *Family name.* So far as we know only some socially important families had family names, which could take the form of a nickname carried by more than one family member or of an apparent patronymic referring to an ancestor of the family rather than to a person's immediate parent.[52] This ancestral name might itself have been originally a nickname. The nickname Goliath, originally borne by members of a Jericho family because of their huge stature, became a family name.[53] An example from the Gospels is the high priest Caiaphas, whose personal name, we know from Josephus (*Ant.* 18.35) as well as from what is probably his ossuary, was the very common Joseph. On

45. Ilam, *Lexicon,* 337-38, takes the Greek *Kyrēnaios* in these two cases to be the Latin name Quirinius (which in the Greek of Josephus and the New Testament is *Kurēnios*), but it is hard to see why. *Kurēnaios* is exactly paralleled in Mark 15:21 with reference to Simon of Cyrene, as well as in Acts 6:9; 11:20, where the reference is undoubtedly to people from Cyrene. Philo and Hillel were no doubt Jews from the Diaspora who, like Simon of Cyrene, had come to live in Jerusalem.

46. Rahmani, *A Catalogue,* number 99. It is possible that the ossuaries of this Sara, daughter of Simon, and of Alexander the Cyrenian, son of Simon, found in the same tomb in the Kidron Valley, actually belonged to members of the family of Simon of Cyrene (J. P. Kane, "The Ossuary Inscriptions of Jerusalem," *JSS* 23 [1978] 278-79).

47. Kane, "The Ossuary Inscriptions," 279.

48. Ilan, *Lexicon,* 221, number 98.

49. Yadin and J. Naveh, eds., *Masada I,* 22, number 404.

50. Rahmani, *A Catalogue,* numbers 797 and 803. For other examples, see Hachlili, "Hebrew Names," 98-99; Ilan, *Lexicon,* 34.

51. Rahmani, *A Catalogue,* number 257.

52. Ilan, *Lexicon,* 46; Hachlili, "Hebrew Names," 92-95.

53. Ilan, *Lexicon,* 84; Hachlili, "Hebrew Names," 94, 103.

his ossuary he is called Joseph bar Caiaphas (Yehosef bar Qayyafa or Qafa).[54] The New Testament references show how he could be known by his family name alone — not even bar Caiaphas, but just Caiaphas. The name must originally have been a nickname of an ancestor (in Aramaic it means "coagulation, jelly sediments of boiled meat").[55]

(10) *Two names in two languages.* It was not uncommon for Palestinian Jews to have both Semitic and Greek (or, much less commonly, Latin) names. Using both names together could solve the problem of distinguishing people with very common names. The two Salomes who feature in the legal documents of the Babatha archive are called Salome Grapte and Salome Komaise, while Simon Bar Kokhba's steward is called Simon Dositheus. But it was also possible to use the two names as alternatives in different contexts. Silas, as he was known in the Jerusalem church (Acts 15:22), used the Latin name Silvanus, as he is called in the letters of Paul, when he traveled in the Diaspora. Joseph Barsabbas, who already bore this nickname or patronymic to distinguish him from other Josephs, also used the Latin name Justus, surely not at the same time, but as an alternative. Both these are cases where the Semitic and non-Semitic names have been chosen because they sound somewhat alike (Silas–Silvanus, Joseph–Justus). We might suspect that a Jew with a very unusual Greek name such as Andrew (Greek Andreas), of which there are only three occurrences in our database, also had a Semitic name that was very common and chose, for pragmatic reasons, to be known usually by his much rarer Greek name. In fact, most of the Greek and Latin names used by Palestinian Jews are quite rare in Palestinian Jewish usage.

(11) *Occupation.* A person's occupation could be used to distinguish him in such a way as to become a form of nickname. In the case of a person's profession or occupation recorded on their ossuaries, it is not easy to tell whether this had been used as a nickname during their lifetimes or was put on their ossuary simply as an honorific record. But in cases such as "Joseph son of Hananiah the scribe" or "Shelamzion daughter of Simeon the priest"[56] it is clear that the term serves to distinguish the father from others of the name. Some of the ostraca from Masada even use the occupation of the father

---

54. The identification of this man as the high priest Caiaphas has been widely accepted, but for doubts see W. Horbury, "The 'Caiaphas' Ossuaries and Joseph Caiaphas," *PEQ* 126 (1994) 32-48. The objections are discussed and answered by H. K. Bond, *Caiaphas: Friend of Rome and Judge of Jesus?* (Louisville: Westminster John Knox, 2004) 1-8, though she thinks it impossible to be sure of the identity, a position also taken by J. C. VanderKam, *From Joshua to Caiaphas: High Priests after the Exile* (Minneapolis: Fortress, 2004) 435-36.

55. Ilan, *Lexicon*, 408.

56. Hachlili, "Hebrew Names," 100.

without the father's name to distinguish the son: "Judah son of the druggist" or just "son of the baker" or "son of the builder" (though this may be "son of Benaiah").[57] A New Testament example is Simon the tanner (Acts 9:43; 10:6), once again a bearer of the most common of all Jewish names and here distinguished from his namesake and guest "Simon called Peter" (10:5-6, 32).

Conclusion

Onomastics (the study of names) is a significant resource for assessing the origins of Gospel traditions. The evidence in this chapter shows that the relative frequency of the various personal names in the Gospels corresponds well to the relative frequency in the full database of three thousand individual instances of names in the Palestinian Jewish sources of the period. This correspondence is very unlikely to have resulted from addition of names to the traditions, even within Palestinian Jewish Christianity, and could not possibly have resulted from the addition of names to the traditions outside Jewish Palestine, since the pattern of Jewish name usage in the Diaspora was very different. The usages of the Gospels also correspond closely to the variety of ways in which persons bearing the same very popular names could be distinguished in Palestinian Jewish usage. Again these features of the New Testament data would be difficult to explain as the result of random invention of names within Palestinian Jewish Christianity and impossible to explain as the result of such invention outside Jewish Palestine. All the evidence indicates the general authenticity of the personal names in the Gospels. This underlines the plausibility of the suggestion made in chapter 3 as to the significance of many of these names: that they indicate the eyewitness sources of the individual stories in which they occur.

---

57. These and other examples are in Hachlili, "Hebrew Names," 102.

Table 6: The 99 Most Popular Male Names among Palestinian Jews, 330 BCE–200 CE[58]

Rank	Name as in English NT	English form used by Ilan	Total valid	Total in Gospels and Acts	Total in Josephus	Total on ossuaries	Total in Judean Desert texts
1	Simon/ Simeon	Simon	243	8[59]	29	59	72
2	Joseph/ Joses	Joseph	218	6	21	45	78
3	Lazarus	Eleazar	166	1[60]	20	29	52
4	Judas	Judah	164	5[61]	14	44	35
5	John	Yohanan	122	5[62]	13	25	40
6	Jesus	Joshua	99[63]	2[64]	14	22	38
7	Ananias	Hananiah	82	2[65]	10	18	13
8	Jonathan	Jonathan	71[66]	(1)[67]	14[68]	14	21
9	Matthew/ Matthias	Mattathias	62	2	12	17	15
10	Manaen	Menahem	42	1	2	4	23
11	James	Jacob	40	5[69]	4	5	10

58. These statistics are compiled from the data in Ilan, *Lexicon*.

59. This figure excludes Simon Magus (a Samaritan) and Simon of Cyrene (born in the Diaspora).

60. This is Lazarus in John 11–12. Lazarus in the parable (Luke 16:20) is excluded as patently fictitious.

61. Ilan takes the Judas of Luke 6:16 and the Judas of John 14:22 to be different persons, but in my figures they are considered identical. Like Ilan, I exclude the Judas of Acts 9:11 as Syrian, not Palestinian.

62. This figure includes the John of Acts 4:6 (where there is a variant reading: Jonathan) and the John who was Simon Peter's father according to John 1:42; 21:15. Ilan does not list the latter, including Peter's father only under Jonah, the name given him in Matt 16:17.

63. I differ from Ilan in thinking the Jeshua of 4Q551 is probably a fictional character.

64. With Ilan I include Jesus the father of Elymas Bar-Jesus (Acts 13:6-8). Though the latter appears in Cyprus in the Acts narrative, the Aramaic form of his patronymic makes it likely, though not certain, that he came from Palestine. Since Ilan does not list the name Elymas, it seems she regards the father, but not the son, as Palestinian by birth.

65. I exclude the Ananias of Acts 9:10 as presumably Syrian rather than Palestinian. Ilan fails to note this in her category E for this person, although she does so for the Judas of Acts 9:11. Probably this is because Ananias was a Christian (and so may have come to Damascus from Palestine) whereas Judas was not. There does not seem to me sufficient reason to doubt that Ananias was a native of Damascus.

66. I differ from Ilan in regarding the Jonathan of 4Q551 as probably a fictional character.

67. Variant reading at Acts 4:6, not included in Ilan's list.

68. Ilan's list also includes a Jonathan who appears only in the Slavonic version of *War* 1.364.

69. I exclude Jacob the grandfather of Jesus according to the Matthean genealogy (Matt

12	Annas	Hanan	35	1	5[70]	6	12
13		Ishmael	30[71]		3	8	9
14 =		Saul	29[72]		2	9	9
14 =		Honi	29		6	5	8
16		Dositheus	27		3	6	4
17 =	Zechariah/Zacchaeus	Zachariah	25	2	4	5	4
17 =	Levi	Levi	25	1	4[73]	5	6
19 =		Yoezer	24		3	14	1
19 =	Alexander	Alexander	24	2	14	4	3
21 =		Hezekiah	21		4	6	5
21 =	Barabbas	Abba	21	1	1	5	
23		Samuel	20		3	2	8
24 =		Phineas	14		3	2	1
24 =	Herod	Herod	14	3	11		
26		Manaseh	13[74]		2	1	6
27 =		Antipatrus	12		11		
27 =		Jason	12		5	2	
29 =		Aqub	11		2	2	
29 =		Tehinah	11			5	2
29 =		Hyrcanus	11		5	1	
32 =		Abshalom	10		4	1	2
32 =		Benaiah	10		1	1	1
34 =		Isaiah	9		1	1	
34 =		Dorotheus	9		3	3	
34 =	Theudas	Theodorus	9	1	3	2	3
34 =	Gamaliel	Gamaliel	9	1	3	1	
34 =		Aristobulus	9		8		
39 =	Jairus	Yair	8	1	4		
39 =	Thaddaeus	Thaddaius	8	1	3	3	
39 =		Helkiah	8		4	1	
39 =		Tobiah	8		1	1	
39 =		Nathan	8			2	
39 =		Azariah	8		1	4	
39 =		Reuben	8			2	1
39 =		Pappus	8		1	3	
39 =		Halafta	8			1	
39 =		Rabba	8			1	5
39 =	Agrippa	Agrippa	8	1	6		
50 =		Hillel	7				3

1:15-16), who is listed by Ilan. This is the only name from either of the two Gospel genealogies that she includes. In view of the special problem of the genealogies, it seems best to exclude all the names. In my view Luke's genealogy is more likely than Matthew's to preserve Jesus' family's tradition of their ancestry.

70. Ilan's list also includes an Ananus who appears only in the Slavonic version of *War* 1.364.

71. I differ from Ilan in thinking the Ishmael of 4Q551 is probably a fictional character.

72. Saul of Tarsus is excluded as born in the Diaspora.

73. Ilan's list also includes a Levi who appears only in the Slavonic version of *War* 1.364.

74. Mnason (Acts 21:16) is excluded as a Cypriot. He is not listed by Ilan at all.

=							
50 =		Isaac	7			3	1
50 =		Yaqim	7		2	1	1
50 =	Nathanael	Nathanel	7	1	1	3	1
50 =		Eutolmus	7			1	1
50 =		Theodotus	7		2	3	
50 =	Bartholomew	Ptolemy	7	1	2	1	
50 =	Malchus	Malka	7	1	2		4
50 =		Elisha	7			1	2
50 =		Guria	7		3[75]		
50 =		Ahi	7			3	1
61 =		Nehemiah	6			2	
61 =		Shemayah	6				2
61 =		Tryphon	6		1	2	
61 =	Philip	Philip	6	2[76]	4		
61 =		Meir	6		2	2	1
61 =	Alphaeus	Halfai	6	2[77]	1		
61 =	Justus	Justus	6	1[78]	3		
68 =		Babi	5				1
68 =		Benjamin	5				1
68 =		Hagai	5			3	1
68 =		Shamoa	5				3
68 =		Ariston	5		1		2
68 =	Cleopas/ Clopas	Cleopas	5[79]	1		1	2
68 =		Nehonia	5				
68 =	Silas	Sheila	5	1	3		
68 =		Phasael	5		3	2	
68 =	Mark	Marcus	5	1[80]		1	
68 =	Zebedee	Zebediah	5	1			1
68 =	Barsabbas	Sabba	5	2		3	1
80 =	Jonah	Yonah	4	1[81]		2	
80 =		Yitra	4			3	1
80 =		Nahum	4			1	

75. In my view Josephus refers to three different individuals named Gurion, whereas Ilan believes he refers only to two; see R. Bauckham, "Nicodemus and the Gurion Family," *JTS* 46 (1996) 1-37.

76. Philip, one of the Seven (Acts 6:5), is not included, on the grounds that he was probably born in the Diaspora.

77. Ilan considers Alphaeus the father of Levi (Mark 2:14) and Alphaeus the father of James (Mark 3:18) to be the same person. This may be correct, but it is perhaps more likely that they are not the same.

78. Acts 1:23, where it is the Latin name adopted by Joseph Barsabbas.

79. Ilan considers the Cleopas of Luke 24:18, the Clopas of John 19:25, and the Clopas of Eusebius, *Hist. Eccl.* 3.11 to be three different individuals, but in my view they are the same person.

80. This is John Mark, who adopted the Latin name Marcus in addition to his Hebrew name John.

81. This is Simon Peter's father, according to Matt 16:17, though according to John (1:42) his name was John.

80 =		Ezra	4			2	
80 =		Shabi	4			2	1
80 =		Shlamiah	4		1		1
80 =	Archelaus	Archelaus	4	1	3		
80 =		Eros	4	4			
80 =		Zenon	4				1
80 =	Nicodemus	Nicodemus	4[82]	1	3		
80 =		Sosipatrus	4		3		
80 =		Gaius	4			2	1
80 =		Adi[83]	4				1
80 =		Marion	4			1	1
80 =		Antigonus	4		2		
80 =		Julius	4		2		
80 =	Peter	Petrus	4	1			1
80 =		Baruch	4	1			1
80 =		Harashah	4				1
80 =		Meshulam	4		2		1

Names occurring only 3 times: 34
Names occurring only twice: 80
Names occurring only once: 234[84]

Total number of names: 447
Total number of occurrences: 2625

82. In my view, the sources refer to four individuals of this name, all members of the same aristocratic family; see Bauckham, "Nicodemus and the Gurion Family."

83. In my view, this name is Addai, the abbreviated form of Adaiah. The apostle of Edessa (sometimes confused with Thaddaeus) was known in Christian tradition as Addai (the earliest reference to him is in the Nag Hammadi *First Apocalypse of James* [CG, V] 36:16) and in my view (differing from Ilan) he was a historical person and probably originally a member of the Jerusalem church.

84. Names that I judge, often in agreement with Ilan, to be probably nicknames, are not included.

Table 7: The 31 Most Popular Female Names among Palestinian Jews, 330 BCE–200 CE[85]

Rank	Name as in English NT	English form used by Ilan	Total valid	Total in Gospels and Acts	Total in Josephus	Total on ossuaries	Total in Judean Desert texts
1	Mary	Mariam	70	6	7	42	9
2	Salome	Salome	58	1	3	41	8
3		Shelamzion	24		1	19	3
4	Martha	Martha	20	1		17	
5 =	Joanna	Joanna	12	1		7	3
5 =	Sapphira	Shiphra	12	1		9	1
7	Berenice	Berenice	8	1	3	1	
8 =		Imma	7			6	
8 =		Mara[86]	7			5	
10 =		Cyprus	6		6		
10 =		Sarah	6			3	1
10 =		Alexandra	6		5	1	
13 =	Anna	Hannah	4	1		2	
13 =	Herodias	Herodias	4	1	1		
13 =		Julia	4			3	1
16 =		Judith	3			3	
16 =		Leah	3			2	
16 =		Rebekah	3				
16 =		Cyria	3			3	
16 =	Susanna	Susanna	3	1	2		
21 =	Elizabeth	Elisheba	2	1	1		
21 =		Antigona	2			2	
21 =		Demarchia	2			2	
21 =		Helene	2			1	1
21 =		Erotarion	2			2	
21 =		Heras	2			2	
21 =		Ide	2			2	
21 =		Cleopatra	2		1	1	
21 =		Verutia	2			2	
21 =	Tabitha	Tabitha	2	1			
21 =	Dorcas	Dorcas	2	1	1		

Names occurring only once: 43

Total number of names: 74
Total number of occurrences: 328

Total of names, male and female: 521
Total of occurrences, male and female: 2953

85. These statistics are compiled from the data in Ilan, *Lexicon*.
86. Probably an abbreviated form of Martha. On one ossuary the same woman is called both Martha and Mara (Ilan, number 4).

Table 8: Index of Palestinian Jewish Male Names in the Gospels and Acts

Name as in English NT	Total in Gospels and Acts	Rank in comprehensive list (Table 6)
Aeneas	1	not ranked (total 3)
Agabus	1	not ranked (total 1)
Agrippa	1	39=
Alexander	2	19 =
Alphaeus	2	61 =
Ananias	2	7
Andrew	1	not ranked (total 3)
Annas	1	12
Archelaus	1	80 =
Barabbas	1	22 =
Barsabbas	2	68 =
Bartholomew	1	50 =
Bartimaeus	1	not ranked (total 1)
Caiaphas	1	not ranked (total 1)
Cleopas/Clopas	1	68 =
Gamaliel	1	34 =
Herod	3	24 =
Jairus	1	39 =
James	5	11
Jesus	2	6
John	5	5
Jonah	1	68 =
Jonathan	(1)	8
Joseph/Joses	6	2
Judas	5	4
Justus	1	61 =
Lazarus	1	3
Levi	1	17 =
Malchus	1	50 =
Manaen	1	10
Mark	1	68 =
Matthew/Matthias	2	9
Nathanael	1	50 =
Nicodemus	1	80 =
Peter	1	80 =

Name as in English NT	Total in Gospels and Acts	Rank in comprehensive list (Table 6)
Philip	2	61=
Rufus	1	not ranked (total 2)
Silas	1	68 =
Simon/Simeon	8	1
Thaddaeus	1	39 =
Theudas	1	34 =
Thomas	1	not ranked (total 2)
Timaeus	1	not ranked (total 1)
Zebedee	1	68 =
Zechariah/Zacchaeus	2	17 =

Table 9: Index of Palestinian Jewish Female Names in the Gospels and Acts

Name as in English NT	Total in Gospels and Acts	Rank in comprehensive list (Table 7)
Anna	1	13 =
Berenice	1	7
Drusilla	1	not ranked (total 1)
Elizabeth	1	21 =
Herodias	1	13 =
Joanna	1	5 =
Martha	1	4
Mary	6	1
Rhoda	1	not ranked (total 1)
Salome	1	2
Sapphira	1	5 =
Susanna	1	16 =
Tabitha	1	21 =

5. The Twelve

The Significance of the Twelve

It is the contention of this book that, in the period up to the writing of the Gospels, gospel traditions were connected with named and known eyewitnesses, people who had heard the teaching of Jesus from his lips and committed it to memory, people who had witnessed the events of his ministry, death, and resurrection and themselves had formulated the stories about these events that they told. These eyewitnesses did not merely set going a process of oral transmission that soon went its own way without reference to them. They remained throughout their lifetimes the sources and, in some sense that may have varied for figures of central or more marginal significance, the authoritative guarantors of the stories they continued to tell.

The role of named individuals in the formulation and transmission of traditions of Jesus' words and deeds largely disappeared from the normal awareness of New Testament scholars as a result of the form-critical movement in Gospels scholarship in the early twentieth century.[1] It was not recovered as Gospels scholars moved on to redaction criticism, literary criticism, or social scientific criticism. As Birger Gerhardsson observes,

> The form critics did not think much of the information which the ancient church provides concerning the concrete persons behind the Gospels, not even of the personal references in the New Testament. The no-

1. On form criticism see chapter 10 below.

tion of the creative community makes questions of concrete traditionists uninteresting. This depersonalization has had a contagious effect right into the present. It still regularly happens that people blithely speak of "products of the church" *(Gemeindebildungen)*[2] and of traditions which "circulated in the communities," instead of asking who has formulated, reformulated, or transmitted a certain text.[3]

In attempting to restore our awareness of these concrete named persons who were responsible for the formulation and transmission of the traditions, Gerhardsson himself focused rather exclusively on the Twelve, who formed, as he rightly supposed, "an authoritative collegium"[4] in Jerusalem for some years at the beginning of the church's history. As we shall see later, I think this focus on the Twelve to the exclusion of other eyewitnesses and stress on the authoritative status of the Twelve, as those who exercised a controlling authority over the traditions, is excessive.[5] There were other eyewitnesses, and we should probably reckon with individual members of the Twelve formulating and transmitting particular traditions as individuals as well as corporately as the Twelve. The evidence of Papias, examined in chapter 2, implies that. But these qualifications do not nullify the importance of the Twelve as "an authoritative collegium." If they were close companions of Jesus throughout his ministry, as the Gospels claim they were, and if they were also, as most scholars agree, the first leaders of the mother church in Jerusalem and of its initial outreach elsewhere, we should certainly expect them to have been authoritative transmitters of the traditions of Jesus and to have had something like an official status for their formulations of those traditions.

That Jesus himself appointed twelve of his disciples for a special place in his mission of renewing or restoring God's people Israel has been doubted by some scholars (following especially the lead of Rudolf Bultmann), who have supposed that the notion of the Twelve originated only later.[6] However, a

2. The German term is more often translated "community-product" or "community formulation."

3. B. Gerhardsson, *The Reliability of the Gospel Tradition* (Peabody: Hendrickson, 2001) 74.

4. Gerhardsson, *The Reliability,* 73; B. Gerhardsson, *Memory and Manuscript* (ASNU 22; Uppsala: Almqvist and Wiksells, 1961) 329-30.

5. However, Gerhardsson does admit that the "eyewitnesses" of Luke's prologue are "first of all the twelve but hardly exclusively": B. Gerhardsson, *The Gospel Tradition* (CB[NT]15; Malmö: Gleerup, 1986) 29.

6. For one of the more recent attempts to explain the origin of the Twelve without tracing it back to Jesus, see H. O. Guenther, *The Footprints of Jesus' Twelve in Early Christian Traditions* (American University Studies 7/7; New York: Lang, 1985).

large majority of recent scholars has accepted it, especially since it coheres so well with the trend to understand Jesus in thoroughly Jewish terms.[7] John Meier has recently mounted a very extensive and thorough defense of the historicity of the Twelve as a group formed by Jesus himself,[8] and we do not need to repeat his argument here. The significance of the group is undoubtedly related to the ideal constitution of Israel as comprising twelve tribes and the Jewish hopes for the restoration of all twelve tribes in the messianic age. The Twelve appointed by Jesus, though they could not have been literally each a member of a different tribe (they contained two pairs of brothers), may nevertheless have corresponded symbolically to the twelve princes of the tribes of Israel in the wilderness (Num 1:4-16).[9] Israel in its beginnings in the wilderness was taken as prototypical for the restored Israel of the messianic age. Jesus' appointment of the Twelve symbolized the claim that in his own ministry this messianic restoration of Israel had already begun in nucleus.[10] The appointment of the Twelve constituted, as several scholars have argued, a prophetic sign of what God was doing in Jesus' ministry.[11]

This status of the Twelve in relation to the renewed people of God explains their authoritative status in the early church. But it is also for our purposes crucial to note that the Twelve were disciples of Jesus the teacher, appointed in the first place to be "with him" (Mark 3:14) and to learn from both his teaching and his company, and thereby qualified for the mission of continuing his mission. They were not the only disciples to travel with Jesus — for example, there were also the women (Luke 8:1-3) — but they were evidently his constant close companions. It is not difficult to imagine that their role in the earliest Christian community would include that of authoritative

7. E.g., R. P. Meye, *Jesus and the Twelve: Discipleship and Redaction in Mark's Gospel* (Grand Rapids: Eerdmans, 1968) chapter 8; B. F. Meyer, *The Aims of Jesus* (London: SCM, 1979) 153-54; M. Hengel, *The Charismatic Leader and His Followers* (tr. J. C. G. Grieg; Edinburgh: Clark, 1981) 68; E. P. Sanders, *Jesus and Judaism* (London: SCM, 1985) 98-106; R. A. Horsley, *Jesus and the Spiral of Violence* (Minneapolis: Fortress, 1993) 199-208; N. T. Wright, *Jesus and the Victory of God* (London: SPCK, 1996) 299-300; G. Theissen and A. Merz, *The Historical Jesus* (tr. J. Bowden; London: SCM, 1998) 216-17; M. Casey, *Aramaic Sources of Mark's Gospel* (SNTSMS 102; Cambridge: Cambridge University Press, 1998) 194-96; J. D. G. Dunn, *Jesus Remembered* (Grand Rapids: Eerdmans, 2003) 507-11.

8. J. P. Meier, *A Marginal Jew,* vol. 3 (New York: Doubleday, 2001) 128-47: this incorporates his earlier article: "The Circle of the Twelve: Did It Exist during Jesus' Public Ministry?" *JBL* 116 (1997) 635-72.

9. W. Horbury, "The Twelve and the Phylarchs," *NTS* 32 (1986) 503-27.

10. S. M. Bryan, *Jesus and Israel's Traditions of Judgement and Restoration* (SNTSMS 117; Cambridge: Cambridge University Press, 2002) 123-24.

11. E.g., Hengel, *The Charismatic Leader,* 60; Meier, *A Marginal Jew,* vol. 3, 148-54.

transmitters of the sayings of Jesus and authoritative eyewitnesses of the events of Jesus' history. If any group in the earliest community was responsible for some kind of formulation and authorization of a body of Jesus traditions, the Twelve are much the most obviously likely to have been that group.

The Lists of the Twelve

Confirmation of this hypothesis that the Twelve constituted an official body of eyewitnesses may be found in the lists of the Twelve that occur in all three of the Synoptic Gospels (though not in John, a fact that has its own significance, as we shall see later). These three lists are in Matt 10:2-4; Mark 3:16-19; and Luke 6:13-16. There is a fourth list in Acts 1:13. Of course, it is true that the Twelve play a significant role in the narrative of these Gospels, especially Matthew and Mark, and the lists could be seen as merely introducing principal characters in the story. That the lists are intended to portray the membership of Jesus' group of Twelve during his ministry is shown by the fact that they include Judas Iscariot, but at the same time the fact that Judas is placed last in all these lists with the explanation that he was the one who handed Jesus over to the authorities shows that this is a retrospective view of the Twelve from a perspective after Jesus' death. The lists look, therefore, like lists fashioned precisely to display the continuity of this group during and after Jesus' ministry, that is, with Jesus and in the early Christian community. As Davies and Allison remark, contrasting the genealogy at the beginning of Matthew's Gospel with the list of the Twelve in ch. 10,

> Unlike a genealogy in which the names outline a pre-history, a list of students indicates a post-history. In our gospel the genealogy in 1.2-17 shows Jesus' pre-history to lie in Israel, in Abraham's descendants, while the list of disciples in chapter 10 shows his post-history to be in the church which has Peter as its head.[12]

If the lists were merely introducing the characters in the Gospel narratives, it is remarkable that no less than seven of these persons are never mentioned again or appear as individuals in the Gospels of Mark and Luke, while the same is true of six of them in Matthew. In chapter 2 we posed and answered the question why it is that, along with so many anonymous characters in the Gospels, including anonymous disciples, there are also named charac-

12. W. D. Davies and D. C. Allison, *A Critical and Exegetical Commentary on the Gospel according to Saint Matthew*, vol. 2 (Edinburgh: Clark, 1991) 150.

ters in the Gospels. There we answered the question by arguing that specific traditions were associated with the persons named in them, understood as the eyewitnesses who told those stories. This explanation will hardly serve precisely in that form for the members of the Twelve who are named only in the lists. However, it could well be that the Twelve are listed as the official body of eyewitnesses who formulated and authorized the core collection of traditions in all three Synoptic Gospels. They are named, not as the authorities for this or that specific tradition, but as responsible for the overall shape of the story of Jesus and much of its content. As we shall see in chapter 8, there is much to be said for the view that much of Mark's passion narrative took form as a sequence of traditions at the hands of the Twelve. Just as they are not, by the appearance of the lists in the Gospels, credited with specific traditions, so they are not credited as individuals but as a group. Nevertheless this group was evidently so important for the transmission of gospel traditions that the Synoptic Evangelists are not content to leave them largely anonymous but preserve carefully lists of the members of the Twelve as the group was constituted during Jesus' ministry. In the case of Luke's Gospel, the list serves to identify by name an important group of those "eyewitnesses and ministers of the word" to whom he refers as his sources in the prologue (Luke 1:2).[13] The point is less explicit, but surely implicit, in Matthew and Mark.

Differences among the Lists of the Twelve

Is it true that the names of the Twelve are carefully preserved in these lists? Many scholars have thought not and have pointed to the differences among the lists as indicating that at any rate by the time the Gospels were written the membership of the Twelve was no longer accurately remembered. If true, this would count against the argument that the Twelve were the authoritative guarantors of the Gospel traditions not only at the beginning but also for as long as they lived.

The lists are presented synoptically in Table 10 below. We should notice first that the differences are not great. In each list the names are grouped into three groups of four names (except that the list in Acts omits Judas Iscariot), and the first name in each group is the same in all lists: Simon Peter always heads the first group, Philip the second, and James the son of Alphaeus the

13. F. Bovon, *Luke 1* (Hermeneia; Minneapolis: Fortress, 2002) 211. Note also the importance of the fact that Luke lists the Twelve again at the beginning of Acts (1:13) where their ministry of witness begins.

third. The order of the other three names in each group varies, with no agreement across all four lists, though Judas Iscariot takes the last place in all three lists that include him. In the second and third groups the variation in order should probably be explained as variations in the way the list was remembered either in oral tradition or by the Evangelist. It is quite intelligible that a list of this kind should be remembered as consisting of three groups, with the first name in each group a fixed point in the memory, but with the order of the other three names in each group variable. It is also easily intelligible that Judas Iscariot should always come in last place in a list of the Twelve as they were during Jesus' ministry.

In the first group of four names, it may be that the order in Matthew and Luke, which keeps the two pairs of brothers together (Peter and his brother Andrew, James and his brother John), is the standard order, which has been varied for redactional reasons in both Mark and Acts. Mark wished to place first the three disciples to whom Jesus gave nicknames: Simon, to whom he gave the name Peter, and the sons of Zebedee, whom he called Boanerges.[14] This group of three are also the three who feature as the inner circle of the Twelve elsewhere in Mark's Gospel (5:37; 9:2; 14:33). The two parallel clauses in which Mark says that Jesus gave the nicknames are grammatically very awkward intrusions into the structure of the list and were probably added by Mark to the list of the Twelve that he knew, with the first substituted for a simpler reference to Simon's nickname such as Matthew has. It should be noted that Mark always calls Peter Simon up to this point in his Gospel, but Peter from here onward. He would therefore have wished to substitute for a simple statement that Simon had the nickname Peter, as in Matthew's list, an indication that the nickname was at this point in his story given by Jesus to Simon. As for the variation in the order of the first group of four names in the list in Acts, this is readily explained by the fact that Peter and John appear to be the leading members of the Twelve in the early chapters of Acts (3:1–4:31; 8:14-25). The martyrdom of James is recorded in Acts (12:2), but Andrew never appears. Thus it seems that, while Mark has varied the order of these names in accordance with the prominence of three in his Gospel, Acts has varied the order in accordance with their prominence in Acts.

One other variation in the lists should probably be understood as redaction by an Evangelist. Matthew's is the only list to call Matthew "the tax-collector" (10:3). This is surely intended to alert readers to the connection

14. On the problem posed by this term, see most recently M. Casey, *Aramaic Sources of Mark's Gospel* (SNTSMS 102; Cambridge: Cambridge University Press, 197-98; R. T. France, *The Gospel of Mark* (NIGTC; Grand Rapids: Eerdmans, 2002) 161-62.

with the account of Matthew's call in 9:9, where the tax collector called by Jesus is called Matthew, not, as in Mark's and Luke's versions of this story, Levi. (We shall consider later whether Matthew and Levi are the same person, but it is at least clear that no reader of Mark's or Luke's Gospel could have any reason for thinking they were.)

So far we have found no differences among the lists that require us to think of more than one traditional list of the Twelve, but one remaining difference probably does require this. In the last group of four names, Mark and Matthew have Thaddaeus, but Luke and Acts have Judas (son) of James. This is the only apparent difference among the lists as to the actual membership of the Twelve.[15] It has often been taken to indicate that the lists are unreliable. According to Joseph Fitzmyer, for example, this difference shows "that the names of the Twelve were no longer accurately preserved in the early church by the time that Luke and Matthew were writing, and that the group of the Twelve, though important at the outset, gradually lost its significance, even to the extent that people no longer could recall who once constituted the Twelve."[16] This seems a rather sweeping conclusion from a variation in just one of the names, but it does constitute a challenge to our argument that the names of the Twelve were remembered in the gospel traditions primarily because they were the official eyewitnesses and guarantors of the core of the traditions. If it was for that reason that specifically the names were remembered, we should expect them all to have been remembered accurately.

There are two possible explanations of the variation between Thaddaeus and Judas of James. One is that Thaddaeus was a member of the Twelve who dropped out, for whatever reason, already during Jesus' ministry and was replaced by Judas the son of James.[17] However, it seems unlikely that a member of the Twelve who had already been replaced before Jesus' death should belong to a standard list of the Twelve reproduced by Mark. This would not really be parallel to the case of Judas Iscariot, since Judas is an essential character in Mark's story and his defection is clearly stated in the list.

The other possibility, that Thaddaeus and Judas of James are the same person, should certainly not be dismissed because, as John Meier charges, it "smacks of harmonization."[18] Harmonization is not always illegitimate, and

---

15. We need not discuss here the name Lebbaeus or Labbaeus that occurs in a few texts of Mark 3:18 and Matt 10:3 either in place of Thaddaeus or as an additional name of Thaddaeus. Whatever the origin of this name, it is unlikely to be original in either Gospel.

16. J. A. Fitzmyer, *The Gospel according to Luke I–IX* (AB 28; New York: Doubleday, 1981) 620.

17. Meier, *A Marginal Jew*, vol. 3, 131; Casey, *Aramaic Sources*, 195-96.

18. Meier, *A Marginal Jew*, vol. 3, 131.

in this case the possibility that the same individual bore both names is well supported by what we know of names in Jewish Palestine at this period. The name Thaddaeus (Greek *Thaddaios*) is an example of a Greek name (it could be *Theodosios, Theodotos,* or *Theodoros*) which has first been turned into a Semitic shortened version, *Taddai,*[19] and has then been Graecized again as *Thaddaios.*[20] Besides our Thaddaeus, seven other individuals of this period are known to have borne the name in this Semitic shortened form.[21] The Greek names Theodosios, Theodotus, and Theodorus (also shortened to Theudas) were all popular with Jews because of their theophoric character (i.e., they incorporate the Greek word for God, *theos,* and so resemble the many Hebrew names that incorporate either *El* or *YHWH*).[22] As we already noted in the last chapter, Palestinian Jews sometimes — perhaps often — bore both Semitic and Greek names. For example, on ossuary inscriptions, we find individuals called Yehudan (Judah) and Yason (Jason),[23] Mara (a female name apparently short for the Aramaic name Martha[24]) and Alexas,[25] Judas and Simon,[26] Sorra (Sara) and Aristobula,[27] and probably Nathanael and Theodotus (these are equivalent in meaning).[28] It is not at all improbable that

19. This form is found in rabbinic literature, including a reference to an individual of our period: Tal Ilan, *Lexicon of Jewish Names in Late Antiquity* (Tübingen: Mohr, 2002) 283, number 3. An ossuary has the name in both Hebrew *(Tadda)* and Greek *([Thad]da)* script: Ilan, *Lexicon,* 283, number 6.

20. This form is found on an ossuary (Rahmani number 114: *Thadaiou*) and as the name of three individuals in two papyri from the Judean desert: Ilan, *Lexicon,* 283, numbers 7-10. A differently Hellenized form is given in Hebrew script on an ossuary: *Taddiōn:* Ilan, *Lexicon,* 283, number 5. The old suggestion that Thaddaeus/Taddiai derives from Aramaic *tad* (= Hebrew *shad*), meaning "breast," is mistaken (this suggestion was already rejected by G. Dalman, *The Words of Jesus* [tr. D. M. Kay; Edinburgh: Clark, 1902] 50; E. Nestle, "Thaddaeus," in J. Hastings, ed., *A Dictionary of the Bible,* vol. 4 [Edinburgh: Clark, 1902] 741; but cf. R. Harris, *The Twelve Apostles* [Cambridge: Heffer, 1927] 28-29; W. D. Davies and D. C. Allison, *A Critical and Exegetical Commentary on the Gospel according to Saint Matthew,* vol. 2 [ICC; Edinburgh: Clark, 1991] 156 n. 52). M. J. Wilkins, "Disciples," in J. B. Green and S. McKnight, eds., *Dictionary of Jesus and the Gospels* (Downers Grove: InterVarsity, 1992) 181, is also incorrect in saying that "Thaddaeus is a nickname or place name."

21. Ilan, *Lexicon,* 283, numbers 3, 5-10.

22. See Ilan, *Lexicon,* 10-11.

23. Rahmani number 477 (both in Hebrew script).

24. Cf. Ilan, *Lexicon,* 423 n. 1.

25. Rahmani number 868. Alexas is here an Aramaized contraction of the somewhat popular female name Alexandra.

26. Rahmani number 868 (both in Greek script). Simon, though frequently used as equivalent to the Hebrew name Simeon, is a Greek name.

27. Rahmani number 95 (both in Greek script).

28. Rahmani numbers 789 and 796; cf. Ilan, *Lexicon,* 200 n. 10.

the same man should have been called both Judas *(Yehudah)* and Thaddaeus *(Taddai)*. The two names may well have been treated as sound equivalents,[29] just as Joseph (or Jesus) and Justus, Reuben and Rufus, Jesus and Jason, Saul (Hebrew *Sha'ul*) and Paul (Latin *Paulus*) evidently were.[30]

A member of the Twelve named Judas would certainly need to be distinguished in some way from the other member of the Twelve who bore this name, Judas Iscariot. In John 14:22 he is called rather awkwardly "Judas, not Iscariot," but this could hardly have been usual in practice. To distinguish him from Judas Iscariot, this Judas could have been identified by his patronymic, Judas son of James *(Yehudah bar Ya'aqov)*, or, alternatively, he could have been known by his Greek name, Thaddaeus *(Taddai)*. Both alternatives could have been used, and the two versions of the list of the Twelve, the one preserved in Mark and Matthew and the one in Luke and Acts, have adopted different alternatives. Possibly, as Jeremias suggested, after the defection of Judas Iscariot it would seem preferable to call his namesake who remained a member of the Twelve Thaddaeus rather than Judas.[31] Luke's usage, Judas son of James, was perhaps how he was styled in an official, written list of the Twelve, whereas Thaddaeus was how he was more commonly known.[32]

Names and Epithets of the Twelve

The variation between Thaddaeus and Judas son of James need therefore be no impediment to supposing that the list of members of the Twelve has been rather carefully preserved and recorded in all three Synoptic Gospels. Another striking feature of the list in all its forms will confirm that. This is the fact that virtually all the epithets attached to the names (patronymics, nicknames, and other forms of a second name) or substituted for personal names are designed to distinguish one member of the Twelve from another.

29. For other Hebrew and Greek names treated as sound equivalents, cf. Josephus, *Ant.* 12.239, 385.

30. R. Bauckham, "Paul and Other Jews with Latin Names," in A. Christophersen, C. Claussen, J. Frey, and B. Longenecker, eds., *Paul, Luke and the Graeco-Roman World: Essays in Honour of Alexander J. M. Wedderburn* (JSNTSup 217; Sheffield: Sheffield Academic, 2002) 207-10.

31. J. Jeremias, *New Testament Theology* (tr. J. Bowden; London: SCM, 1971) 232-33.

32. The later connection of Thaddaeus with the evangelization of Edessa (Eusebius, *Hist. Eccl.* 1.13; 2.1.6-8) results from confusion of this name with Addai. But Thaddaeus was probably remembered as a disciple of Jesus in the rabbinic list of five disciples of Jesus in b. Sanhedrin 43a, where the name Todah appears. Very probably the name Taddai has been adapted to Todah for the sake of the scriptural pun made here with the latter word in the quoted words from Pss 100:1 and 50:23; see R. Bauckham, "Nicodemus and the Gurion Family," *JTS* 46 (1996) 34-37.

We should note, first, that, as we would expect, many of the names are very common ones:[33] Simon (the most common of all Jewish male names: 243 occurrences), Judas (fourth most common: 164 occurrences), John (fifth most common: 122 occurrences), Matthew (ninth most common: 62 occurrences),[34] and James (eleventh most common: 40 occurrences). Others are much less common: Thaddaeus (thirty-ninth in order of popularity: 8 occurrences), Philip (sixty-first in order: 7 occurrences), Andrew (3 occurrences),[35] and Thomas (2 occurrences). Bartholomew as a patronymic is unique, though his father's name itself, Ptolemy *(Ptolemaios),* is fiftieth in order of popularity, occurring 7 times. This mixture of very common, relatively common, rare, and almost unique names is not at all surprising in view of what we have learned about the Palestinian Jewish onomasticon, which contains a small number of very common names and many very uncommon names.

However, the epithets attached to the names of the Twelve in the list are not included to distinguish those with very common names from their many namesakes in general or from disciples of Jesus other than the Twelve. For that a member of the Twelve could always be distinguished as "one of the Twelve" (cf. Mark 14:10; John 20:24).[36] The epithets seem designed more specifically to distinguish members of the Twelve from each other and so must have originated within the circle of the Twelve themselves. Thus the two members of the Twelve named Simon needed to be distinguished, as did the two named James and the two named Judas (according to Luke's list). There may be, as we shall see, other instances not immediately obvious.

In the last chapter I listed and illustrated the various ways in which Palestinian Jews distinguished persons of common names from each other. It is remarkable that most of these can be found within the lists of the Twelve. In what follows I number the categories with the numbers I gave them in the last chapter.

(2) *Patronymic added.* This, the commonest and simplest way of distinguishing individuals with the same personal name, occurs three times in the lists of the Twelve: James son of Zebedee, James son of Alphaeus, Judas son of James.

(3) *Patronymic substituted.* As we saw, it was common for a patronymic

33. For the data summarized here, see Table 6.
34. However, among the many forms of the name Mattathias, the short form Mattai, born by the Matthew (Μαθθαῖος) of the Gospels, is not very common. There are only seven occurrences: Ilan, *Lexicon,* 191-93, numbers 16 (the Gospels' *Maththaios*), 32, 40, and 43 *(Mattai),* 45 *(Mathaiō),* 52 *(Maththaios),* and 53 *(Maththaiou).*
35. Even one of these three occurrences may be a female name: Ilan, *Lexicon,* 262-63, n. 3.
36. Note how Acts 21:8 identifies "Philip, the evangelist, one of the Seven," presumably distinguishing him from the Philip who was one of the Twelve.

simply to take the place of the personal name. In all the lists of the Twelve Bartholomew *(Bartholomaios)* is known only by this patronymic. The biblical name *Talmai* (2 Sam 3:3; 13:37; 1 Chron 3:2) and the Greek name *Ptolemaios,* popular because it was a royal name of the Hellenistic rulers of Egypt, seem to have been treated as equivalent, and Bartholomew would probably have been known in Aramaic as Bar Tolmai.[37] Because this patronymic functions as a name, the Gospels do not translate the Aramaic *bar,* as they do in other cases in the lists of the Twelve, but transliterate it as part of the name, as in the cases of Bartimaeus, Barabbas, Bar-Jonah (Matt 16:17), Bar-Jesus (Acts 13:6), Barnabas, and Barsabbas.

Although patronymics of this kind were used as family names and in that usage indicated not an individual's actual father but an ancestor after which the whole family was named, such a usage only seems suitable when the patronymic appears as a second name beside a personal name. A family name used alone would not usefully distinguish an individual. So it seems that Bartholomew's patronymic probably does refer to his own father. He could have been known by his patronymic alone before becoming a disciple of Jesus, but it is also possible that his personal name was shared by other members of the Twelve (Simon, Judas, James, or perhaps John) or by Jesus, and so his patronymic became, within the circle of the Twelve, a means of distinguishing him from others in the same circle.

Bartholomew's father's name was fairly unusual (fiftieth in order of popularity: 7 occurrences), as was often, though not always, the case when a patronymic was used alone. Correspondingly, one would expect the personal name that the patronymic replaced to have been common. This makes it rather unlikely that Bartholomew was the same person as the disciple called Nathanael, who appears in John's Gospel but not in the Synoptics (John 1:45-48; 21:2). Nathanael was no more common than Tolmai/Ptolemy (fiftieth in order: 7 occurrences).

(5) *Nickname added.* The common practice of adding a nickname to the personal name is found among the Twelve in the cases of Simon Peter and Simon the Cananaean/zealot. In Peter's case, his nickname (Aramaic *Kepha',* translated in these lists as Greek *Petros*)[38] was given him by Jesus. Evidently he had previously been distinguished by his patronymic, son of John (John 1:42) or Bar-Jonah (Matt 16:17). This apparent conflict as to the name of Simon Pe-

---

37. See the various forms of the name in Ilan, *Lexicon,* 304-5.

38. See J. A. Fitzmyer, "Aramaic *Kepha'* and Peter's Name in the New Testament," in Fitzmyer, *To Advance the Gospel* (New York: Crossroad, 1981) 112-24; M. Bockmuehl, "Simon Peter's Names in Jewish Sources," *JJS* 55 (2004) 58-80.

ter's father is not strictly relevant to our discussion of the lists of the Twelve, but it can be quickly resolved. In Matt 16:17 Jesus calls Peter, in Greek, *Bariōna*. This probably represents Aramaic *Bar Yôḥana'*, where *Yôḥana'* would be, not *Yônāh*, Jonah, but an Aramaized form of *Yĕhôḥānān*, John.[39] Presumably it would still be as "son of John" that Peter would have continued to be identified by many outsiders, but within the circle of Jesus' disciples (and later, in the early church) he was known by his nickname Peter.

In the case of Simon the Cananaean/zealot, the lists of the Twelve in Mark and Matthew give a Greek transliteration *(ho Kananaios)* of the Aramaic term *(qan'ānā')*, whereas Luke translates it as "the zealot" *(ho zēlōtēs)*. (This difference may be another piece of evidence, along with the difference between Thaddaeus and Judas son of James, for the view that Luke followed a different traditional version of the list of the Twelve from that used by Mark, though it is also possible that Luke himself, who generally prefers not to use Semitic terms,[40] translated this term as *ho zēlōtēs*.) It is now widely recognized that, since a specific political party with the name Zealots does not appear in our sources until after the outbreak of the Jewish revolt in 66 CE, the term applied to Simon here must have the broader sense, current in this period, of "zealot for the law" (cf. Acts 21:20; 22:3, 19), often implying that such a person would take violent action to punish flagrant violation of the Torah. Such violence, however, would normally be aimed against fellow Jews rather than the Romans.[41] We should probably presume that Simon already bore this nickname before becoming a disciple of Jesus. Meier points out that "the only instance in prerabbinic Judaism of an individual Israelite bearing the additional name of 'the Zealot' is found in 4 Macc 18:12, where Phinehas (the grandson of Aaron) is called 'the Zealot Phinehas' *(ton zēlōtēn Phinees)*."[42] Perhaps Simon's nickname amounts to calling him "a new Phinehas." However, although Phinehas was indeed, for Jews of this period, the archetypal

---

39. Apart from Peter's father, Ilan, *Lexicon,* 143, lists three individuals called Jonah: in Hebrew script *Yônāh* (numbers 2 and 4), in Greek script *Iōna* (number 3). So it is quite possible that *Bariōna* in Matt 16:17 represents Aramaic *bar Yônāh.* But, in view of John 1:42, it more likely represents *bar Yôḥana'* where *Yôḥana'* is an Aramaic form of the Hebrew *Yôḥānān* (John). This Aramaic form is found four times among the 122 occurrences of John (Yohanan): Ilan, *Lexicon,* 135-37, numbers 44, 89, 90, and 91. Bockmuehl, "Simon Peter's Names," 66-67, argues against the quite different proposal that Hebrew *Yônāh* was used as an abbreviation for *Yôḥānān.* My argument is that the Aramaic *Yôḥana'* was transliterated in Greek as *Iōna* in Matt 16:17, whereas John (1:42), correctly regarding it as a form of the Hebrew *Yôḥānān,* used the usual Greek transliteration of the latter: *Iōannēs* (John).

40. Meier, *A Marginal Jew,* vol. 3, 132.

41. Meier, *A Marginal Jew,* vol. 3, 205-8, gives a good summary account.

42. Meier, *A Marginal Jew,* vol. 3, 206.

"zealot," the usage in 4 Maccabees 18:12 is probably a description rather than strictly a nickname. Another possible parallel that has not previously been noticed is the name of the owner inscribed on a stone jar from Masada. The two words *(yhwsp qny)* can be translated either as "Joseph (the) zealot" *(qannay)* or as "Joseph (the) silversmith" *(qēnay)*.[43]

(6) *Nickname substituted.* Like patronymics, a nickname could be used alone without a personal name. This is probably the case, in the list of the Twelve, with Thomas. Thomas is the Aramaic word for "twin" *(tĕ'ômā'),* as John indicates when he gives also the Greek *Didymos,* the Greek word for "twin" (11:16; 20:24; 21:2). Unlike Didymus, which was certainly used as a name, there is little indication that Thomas was used as a name by Palestinian Jews. But discussion of the name Thomas in the New Testament has not yet caught up with the fact that we now know of a Palestinian Jew from the early second century with the Aramaic name *Tōmah*.[44] It could have any of the meanings "simplicity," "garlic," or "fringe," but these meanings are not very likely for a personal name. It is much more likely to mean "twin," but both in this case and in the case of the Thomas of the Gospels the word is probably not a personal name but a nickname. Each of these individuals happened to be a twin, and this characteristic made the term an appropriate nickname for distinguishing them from others who bore their personal name. In the case of the Thomas of the Gospels, there is no need to speculate as to who his twin was, as though his nickname would not make sense unless he were the twin of someone better known than himself (such as Jesus). His twin may well have had nothing to do with the Jesus movement. Simply that he was a twin would be enough for him to have gained this nickname, quite possibly before becoming a disciple of Jesus.

The fact that Thomas is a nickname and that this disciple must have had another, proper name, was recognized in the East Syrian Christian tradition, where he was known as Judas Thomas. The Curetonian Syriac version of John 14:22 calls him "Judas Thomas," the *Acts of Thomas* calls him "Judas who is also Thomas," and the *Gospel of Thomas* calls him "Didymus Judas Thomas." This tradition may have preserved his true name. If he were in fact named Judas, then it is quite intelligible that within the circle of the Twelve, with its two

---

43. Y. Yadin and J. Naveh, eds., *Masada I: The Aramaic and Hebrew Ostraca and Jar Inscriptions from Masada* (Jerusalem: Israel Exploration Society/Hebrew University of Jerusalem, 1989) 41, number 474; cf. R. Hachlili, "Hebrew Names, Personal Names, Family Names and Nicknames of Jews in the Second Temple Period," in J. W. van Henten and A. Brenner, eds., *Families and Family Relations as Represented in Early Judaisms and Early Christianities* (STAR 2; Leiden: Deo, 2000) 101.

44. Ilan, *Lexicon,* 416, number 3: *Tômah* (Papyrus Yadin 10, 15).

other disciples named Judas, his nickname would be used instead of his proper name. He may, of course, have shared another name with one of the Twelve who has a distinguishing epithet (Simon, James, or perhaps John) or with Bartholomew. Finally, his proper name might have been Jesus. Since this was a common name (sixth most common: 99 occurrences) it would not be surprising if one of the Twelve bore it.

(7) *Place of origin or dwelling added,* and (9) *Family name.* Here we must consider the case of Judas Iscariot. Despite many other conjectures, the best explanation of Judas's second name remains the Hebrew phrase *'îsh qeriyyôt,* "man of Kerioth," understood to refer to a place (either a town named Kerioth, which is the plural of *qiryāh,* "city," or Jerusalem).[45] There are rabbinic parallels to this Hebrew expression used as a second name referring to the person's place of origin.[46] If we take seriously into account John's way of referring to Judas as "Judas son of Simon Iscariot" (John 6:71; 13:2, 26), reference to a place of origin seems almost the only plausible explanation of "Iscariot." Evidently the second name "man of Kerioth" passed from Simon to his son Judas, constituting therefore a family name as well as a reference to the family's place of origin. Such a sobriquet passed from father to son seems to make no sense unless they no longer lived in that place but still identified themselves as having come from that place. (If Judas alone bore the name, it could have been the second name he acquired when he left home to travel with Jesus, though in this case we should not expect the phrase to be in Hebrew rather than Aramaic. But since his father was also known by the name Iscariot, the family must have left "Kerioth" and settled elsewhere.) The many parallels to a place of origin as an identifying second name, from ossuaries and other Second Temple period sources, all seem to refer to a place from which the individual or the family came before living elsewhere.[47] In one case, three generations of a family recorded on an ossuary and an incantation bowl from Jericho are all said to be "from Jerusalem."[48] Thus the family of Ju-

45. For recent accounts of the various suggestions, see R. E. Brown, *The Death of the Messiah,* vol. 2 (New York: Doubleday, 1994) 1413-16; W. Klassen, *Judas: Betrayer or Friend of Jesus?* (London: SCM, 1996) 32-34; Meier, *A Marginal Jew,* vol. 3, 208-11. None thinks the evidence sufficient to decide the issue, though Meier sees that Johannine usage strongly favors the view that Iscariot refers to a place of origin.

46. Dalman, *The Words,* 51-52. Brown, *The Death,* 1414, is mistaken in dismissing these rabbinic examples as irrelevant just because of their date. Note also that Josephus, *Ant.* 18.4 refers to *Ioudas Gaulanitēs anēr,* which could well render *Yehûdah 'îsh ha-gôlan* (Hachlili, "Hebrew Names," 99).

47. Hachlili, "Hebrew Names," 98-99.

48. Hachlili, "Hebrew Names," 98; Ilan, *Lexicon,* 177 (number 20), 205 (Pelatyah), 222 (number 129).

das may well have been settled in Galilee: the reference to his place of origin need not, as many have thought,[49] indicate that he personally came from outside Galilee. The use of a Hebrew family name may indicate a socially important family, though we cannot be sure of this.

(10) *Two names in two languages.* In the list of the Twelve there are no examples of the use of both names (Semitic and Greek or Latin) together, but I have argued that in Matthew's and Mark's list Thaddaeus is the Greek name of the Judas son of James listed by Luke. Luke distinguishes him from Judas Iscariot by adding his patronymic, Matthew and Mark do so by using his Greek name. There are two other Greek names in the lists (besides Simon): Philip and Andrew. It could be that these men also bore Semitic names that were common and so were usually known by their more distinctive Greek names. Philip is rather uncommon (sixty-first in order of popularity: 6 occurrences), Andrew very uncommon (3 occurrences only).

(11) *Occupation.* Only in the list in Matthew's Gospel does an epithet accompany the name Matthew: "the tax collector" *(ho telōnēs)*. As we have already noted, this is most probably a redactional addition designed to make a connection with Matt 9:9, but it would not be inconsistent with this to suppose that the author of this Gospel knew "the tax collector" as an epithet regularly attached to Matthew's name. If so, it would have been not strictly an indication of his occupation but a nickname derived from the fact that he had once been a tax collector. Of course, among the Twelve during Jesus' ministry there would be no need to distinguish one Matthew from another, but when Matthias was chosen to replace Judas Iscariot (Acts 1:23-26), there were two members of the Twelve with names that, though distinct, were both abbreviated forms of the name Mattathias. The form Matthias (in Greek *Maththias* [Acts 1:23] or, more usually, *Matthias* or *Mathias*, in Aramaic/Hebrew usually *Mattiya'* or *Mattiyah*)[50] is the commonest form of the name (32 occurrences), whereas Matthew *(Mattaios, Mattai)* is relatively rare (7 occurrences, out of a total of 62 for all forms of the name). It might well be that these different forms of the name were sufficient to distinguish Matthew and Matthias. Still, it is possible that the occupational nickname "the tax collector" was sometimes used to avoid possible confusion.

49. E.g., Davies and Allison, *A Critical and Exegetical Commentary,* vol. 2, 157 n. 59: "If Judas was from Kerioth he would be the only disciple not from Galilee." But, in any case, how do we know that all the other disciples were from Galilee? We have no information as to where Bartholomew, Thaddaeus/Judas son of James, or Simon the zealot came from.

50. Ilan, *Lexicon,* 191-93, numbers 3, 6, 7, 8, 9, 10, 11, 13, 14, 15 (Greek *Matthias*), 17 *(Maththias,* Acts 1:23), 18 *(Matthias),* 19, 20, 21, 22, 23 (Aramaic *Mattiya'*), 24, 26, 27 (Hebrew *Mattiyah*), 28 (Greek *Mathiou*), 30, 31, 33, 35, 36 (Hebrew *Mattiyah*), 39, 47 (Greek *Mathiou*), 49, 55 (Hebrew *Mattiyah*), 62 (Greek *Mathia*), and 63 (Hebrew *Mattiyah*).

The conclusion we can draw from this study of the epithets in the lists of the Twelve is that these lists have preserved very accurately not just the names but also the epithets that were used to distinguish members of the Twelve among themselves and in their circle.[51] The lists show, not carelessness about the precise membership of the Twelve, but quite the opposite: great care to preserve precisely the way they were known in their own milieu during the ministry of Jesus and in the early Jerusalem church. It is difficult to account for this phenomenon except by the hypothesis that the Twelve were the official eyewitnesses and guarantors of the core of the gospel traditions. It is not true that many of them were forgotten; as essential members of this official group of eyewitnesses all twelve were remembered.

A Note on Matthew and Levi

I have argued that the identification of Thaddaeus and Judas the son of James as the same man is a very plausible harmonization, in the light of plentiful onomastic evidence. But the identification of Matthew with Levi the son of Alphaeus[52] — a traditional case of harmonizing the Gospels in view of the parallel passages Matt 9:9 (about Matthew) and Mark 2:14 (about Levi) — must, on the same grounds of the onomastic evidence available to us, be judged implausible.

Mark tells the story of the call of Levi son of Alphaeus to be a disciple of Jesus in 2:14 (followed by Luke 5:27, where the man is called simply Levi) and lists Matthew, with no further qualification, in his list of the Twelve. It is clear that Mark did not himself consider these two the same person. In view of the other details Mark does include in his list of the Twelve, he would surely have pointed out Matthew's identity with Levi there had he known it.[53] However, this may not be entirely decisive, since Mark may have drawn his story about Levi and his list of the Twelve from different sources and not known that Levi and Matthew were the same person.

Secondly, however, if Matthew and Levi were the same person, we

---

51. The list of temple officials in m. Sheqalim 5:1 is somewhat similar in its mixture of personal names alone, names with patronymics, patronymics alone, nicknames alone: see J. Naveh, "Nameless People," *IEJ* 40 (1990) 109-11, who argues, from comparison with similar lists, that this is a list of the temple officials in one particular generation.

52. This position is still taken by, e.g., D. A. Hagner, *Matthew 1–13* (WBC 33A; Dallas: Word, 1993) 237-38.

53. The point is well made by E. Best, *Following Jesus: Discipleship in the Gospel of Mark* (JSNTSup 4; Sheffield: Sheffield Academic, 1981) 176-77.

should be confronted with the virtually unparalleled phenomenon of a Palestinian Jew bearing two common Semitic personal names (Matthew: ninth most popular, 62 occurrences; Levi: seventeenth most common, 25 occurrences). This is a quite different case from that of an individual having both a Semitic and a Greek or Latin name, as well as from that of an individual having a Semitic name and also a nickname or family name.[54]

Among Palestinian Jews of this period the only possibly comparable examples of the same individual having two Semitic names appear to be these: (1) on an ostracon from Masada, Simon (in Hebrew script *Sîmô*)[55] with the additional name Benaiah;[56] (2) on a legal document in the Babatha archive, Joseph with the additional name Zaboud (in Greek script *Zaboudo[u]*);[57] (3) from Epiphanius (*Panarion* 42), a leader of a Jewish sect called Judah with the additional name Addan or Annan;[58] (4) a temple official in a list of officials in the Mishna (Sheqalim 5:1), called Petahiah and said to be also Mordecai; and (5) Tehina son of Perisha, identified in Sifre Deuteronomy 240 as the same person as Eleazar ben Dinai.[59] About these examples we may first observe that all except one of these individuals bear one very common Semitic name (Simon, Joseph, Judah, or Eleazar) along with a relatively unusual one (unless we prefer Annan to Addan in the third case). This is what we should expect if this phenomenon occurred at all: the unusual second name would help to distinguish the individual from others bearing his common name. In this respect, they are not really comparable with the case of a person bearing the two common names Matthew and Levi.

54. So the parallels cited by Davies and Allison, *A Critical and Exegetical Commentary*, vol. 2, 98, n. 85; R. H. Gundry, *Matthew: A Commentary on His Handbook for a Mixed Church under Persecution* (second edition; Grand Rapids: Eerdmans, 1994) 166, are not relevant. W. L. Lane, *The Gospel of Mark* (NICNT; Grand Rapids: Eerdmans, 1974) 100-101, n. 29, offers three Nabatean examples from inscriptions, but these hardly constitute, without argument, evidence for Jewish practice.

55. Note that this form is unambiguously a Hebrew rendering of the Greek name Simon, not the Hebrew Simeon.

56. Ilan, *Lexicon*, 226 (Simon 250), 81 (Benaiah 11).

57. Ilan, *Lexicon*, 155 (Joseph 167), 89 (Zebediah 3).

58. Ilan, *Lexicon*, 113 (Judah 26), 360 (Adi 2).

59. Ilan, *Lexicon*, 237 (Tehina 1), 65 (Eleazar 7). A woman named on her ossuary both Martha and Mara (Ilan, *Lexicon*, 422-23) is not an example of this phenomenon, because Mara is probably a short form of Martha. Similarly, in the case of a woman named on her ossuary both Mariamne and Mara (Rahmani, *A Catalogue*, number 701; but Ilan does not list this instance of Mara; cf. *Lexicon*, 244 [Mariam 52], 422-23), Mara may be used as a short form of Mariamne. In the cases of Rahmani, numbers 31 and 552, the two names could be those of the same woman, but more probably refer to two different women. Rahmani, 14, refers to two or three later instances in rabbinic literature (b. Pesiqta 113b-14a; b. Gittin 34b).

However, it is by no means clear that any of the five examples just given are valid. (3) and (5) are from late and unreliable sources. While the Mishnaic list of temple officials from which (4) comes is probably reliable, the information that Petahiah was also called Mordecai is an added note, and this note itself explains the (very unusual) name Petahiah as a nickname. Not much confidence can be placed in this example. In example (2), the name Zaboud, while certainly Semitic and occurring in the Bible (Ezra 8:8), was popular with other Semitic peoples and found in Palmyran, Nabatean, Idumean, and Egyptian use. In this instance, as the second name of Babatha's first husband's grandfather, it may well be treated as a Nabatean and non-Jewish name, which a Jew living in Nabatea might adopt in the same way as other Jews adopted a Greek or Latin second name. Finally, in (1) *bny'* may be not the name Benaiah but a nickname given Simon because of his occupation: "the builder."[60] Alternatively, since it was the name of David's famous general, it might be a nickname.

We must conclude that the evidence makes it very unlikely indeed that a disciple of Jesus was called both Matthew and Levi the son of Alphaeus.[61] So, assuming the priority of Mark's Gospel to Matthew's, why did the author of the latter change the name in the story he took from Mark? Apart from the name, the two stories, very briefly told, are virtually identical in wording. Davies and Allison conveniently list the explanations that have been offered (apart from the one we have just eliminated).[62] It has been suggested that the author of the Gospel of Matthew limited the disciples of Jesus to the Twelve and needed therefore to make this disciple one of the Twelve,[63] or that the name Matthew was chosen because, through assonance with the word

---

60. So Yadin and Naveh, eds., *Masada I*, 57.

61. The same argument applies to the proposal of C. E. Hill, "The Identity of John's Nathanael," *JSNT* 67 (1997) 45-61, that Nathanael (John 1:45) is the same person as James son of Alphaeus in the lists of the Twelve. The examples he gives to show that a Palestinian Jew might bear two Hebrew names (57) are not comparable. In the case of Judas Maccabeus, the second name is a nickname, as is Thomas in the double name Judas Thomas (given to Thomas the member of the Twelve in Syrian Christian tradition), while in the case of Joseph Caiaphas, the second name is a family name that must have originated as a nickname. These are not cases of two Hebrew personal names both in ordinary use, as Nathanael and James would be. In fact, though from as early as the mid-second century attempts were made to identify Nathanael with one of the Twelve (Hill argues that the *Epistula Apostolorum* identifies him with James son of Alphaeus), there is no reason that Nathanael in the Gospel of John should be considered a member of the Twelve.

62. Davies and Allison, *A Critical and Exegetical Commentary*, vol. 2, 98-99.

63. R. Pesch, "Levi-Matthäus (Mc 2 ₁₄/Mt 9₉ 10₃). Ein Beitrag zur Lösung eines alten Problems," *ZNW* 59 (1968) 347-51; Meier, *A Marginal Jew*, vol. 3, 165 n. 3.

mathētēs ("disciple"), which occurs twice in the following verses (Matt 9:10-11), and the verb *mathete* ("learn") in v. 13, it emphasized the theme of discipleship.[64] Both ideas are unpersuasive because they make no connection between the occurrence of the name Matthew and the fact that the Gospel is called "according to Matthew."

Surely this Gospel's change of Mark's "Levi son of Alphaeus" to "Matthew" and its addition "the tax collector" to the name "Matthew" in the list of the Twelve are connected in some way with the title of the Gospel, which, like all the Gospel titles, was probably already attached to it when copies were first circulated.[65] It is hardly likely that these two references to the apostle Matthew within the Gospel led to the Gospel later being attributed to Matthew. As G. D. Kilpatrick observed, "Even after the changes of Matt. ix.9, x.3, Matthew is a much less important figure than Peter and if an apostolic name was to be sought from the contents of the book, it would be expected that Peter would be chosen. The fact that this is not so makes against the possibility that the title of the book was subsequent to its production and arose out of Matt. ix.9, x.3."[66]

The most plausible explanation of the occurrence of the name Matthew in 9:9 is that the author of this Gospel, knowing that Matthew was a tax collector and wishing to narrate the call of Matthew in the Gospel that was associated with him, but not knowing a story of Matthew's call, transferred Mark's story from Levi to Matthew. The story, after all, is so brief and general it might well be thought appropriate to any tax collector called by Jesus to follow him as a disciple. There is one feature of Matthew's text that helps to make this explanation probable. In Mark, the story of Levi's call is followed by a scene in which Jesus dines with tax collectors (Mark 2:15-17). Mark sets this scene in "his house," which some scholars take to mean Jesus' house, but could certainly appropriately refer to Levi's house. In Matthew's Gospel, the same passage follows the narrative of the call of Matthew, but the scene is set simply in "the house" (Matt 9:10). Thus this Evangelist has appropriated Mark's story of the call of Levi, making it a story of Matthew's call instead, but has not continued this appropriation by setting the following story in Matthew's house. He has appropriated for Matthew only as much as Mark's story of Levi as he needed.

64. M. Kiley, "Why 'Matthew' in Matt 9,9-13?" *Bib* 65 (1984) 347-51.

65. M. Hengel, *Studies in the Gospel of Mark* (tr. J. Bowden; London: SCM, 1985) chapter 3; idem, *The Four Gospels and the One Gospel of Jesus Christ* (tr. J. Bowden; London: SCM, 2000) 48-56. See also chapter 12 below.

66. G. D. Kilpatrick, *The Origins of the Gospel according to St. Matthew* (Oxford: Oxford University Press, 1946) 138.

If this explanation of the name Matthew in Matt 9:9 is correct, it has one significant implication: that the author of Matthew's Gospel intended to associate the Gospel with the apostle Matthew but was not himself the apostle Matthew. Matthew himself could have described his own call without having to take over the way Mark described Levi's call.

Table 10: The Names of the Twelve

Matthew	*Mark*	*Luke*	*Acts*
first Simon, who was called Peter,	and he gave Simon the name Peter,	Simon who was also named Peter,	Peter
and Andrew his brother	and James the son of Zebedee	and Andrew his brother,	and John
and James the son of Zebedee	and John the brother of James, and he gave them the name Boanerges, that is, Sons of Thunder,	and James	and James
and John his brother,	and Andrew	and John	and Andrew,
Philip	and Philip	and Philip	Philip
and Bartholomew,	and Bartholomew	and Bartholomew	and Thomas,
Thomas,	and Matthew	and Matthew	Bartholomew
Matthew the tax-collector,	and Thomas	and Thomas	and Matthew,
James the son of Alphaeus	and James the son of Alphaeus	and James [the son] of Alphaeus	and James [the son] of Alphaeus
and Thaddaeus,	and Thaddaeus	and Simon who was called the zealot	and Simon the zealot,
Simon the Cananaean	and Simon the Cananaean	and Judas [the son] of James	and Judas [the son] of James
and Judas Iscariot who also betrayed him	and Judas Iscariot who betrayed him	and Judas Iscariot, who became a traitor	

6. Eyewitnesses "from the Beginning"

"From the Beginning"

If the Gospels embody eyewitness testimony, then some at least of the eyewitnesses must have been able to testify not just to particular episodes or particular sayings of Jesus but to the whole course of Jesus' story. Broadly the four Gospels agree on the scope of this story: it begins with John the Baptist and it ends with the resurrection appearances. (Matthew's and Luke's infancy narratives, like John's prologue, are prologues to the story as traditionally told, and while Mark's Gospel narrates no resurrection appearances it ends by anticipating them.)

An important reference to this acknowledged scope of the story of Jesus occurs in the first chapter of the Acts of the Apostles. The context is the selection of a successor to Judas Iscariot to make up the number of the Twelve. Peter states that a candidate for this vacancy must be someone who has

> accompanied us [i.e., the eleven remaining members of the Twelve] during all the time that the Lord Jesus went in and out among us,[1] beginning *(arxamenos)* from the baptism of John[2] until the day that he was taken up from us — one of these must become a witness *(martyra)* with us to his resurrection (Acts 1:21-22 NRSV).

---

1. The expression "went in and out" is a Semitism or Septuagintalism (e.g., Ps 121[120]:8), with the sense of the English phrase "comings and goings."

2. This may mean not specifically Jesus' baptism by John but more generally John's ministry of baptizing.

This qualification is evidently necessary for the task of witness to Jesus, which has already appeared in this first chapter of Acts as the role of the Twelve in the future (1:8). Although the notion of witness is here attached specifically to the resurrection ("one of these must become a witness with us to his resurrection"), having known Jesus from the beginning was also required for the role of the Twelve. It is worth noticing that, in this story of the replacement of Judas, two disciples are proposed for the vacant place (1:23). Thus there were certainly more disciples who met this qualification than just the Twelve. But in Luke's depiction of the early church the Twelve evidently had a specially authoritative role.

Later in Acts Luke depicts Peter preaching a summary of the gospel story with precisely the same parameters and with the claim to witness linked specifically to the resurrection appearances:

> You know the message [God] sent to the people of Israel, preaching peace by Jesus Christ — he is Lord of all. That message spread throughout Judea, beginning *(arxamenos)* in Galilee after the baptism that John announced: how God anointed Jesus of Nazareth with the Holy Spirit and with power; how he went about doing good and healing all who were oppressed by the devil, for God was with him. We are witnesses to all that he did both in Judea and in Jerusalem. They put him to death by hanging him on a tree; but God raised him on the third day and allowed him to appear, not to all the people but to us who were chosen by God as witnesses, and who ate and drank with him after he rose from the dead. He commanded us to preach to the people and to testify that he is the one ordained by God as judge of the living and the dead (Acts 10:36-42 NRSV).

Significantly, "beginning" *(arxamenos)* occurs again, here referring to the message preached by Jesus, which began from Galilee after the baptism preached by John (10:37). Luke elsewhere uses the same verb *(archein)* to draw attention to the beginning of Jesus' ministry in Galilee (Luke 3:23; 23:5; Acts 1:1).

This concept of disciples especially qualified to tell the Gospel story because they themselves had participated in it from beginning to end is not peculiarly Lukan. Although it has rarely been given much attention by scholars,[3] there is a striking parallel to it in John's Gospel. In the farewell discourse after the last supper, Jesus addresses his disciples (not here confined to the Twelve):

3. R. Riesner, *Jesus als Lehrer* (WUNT 2/7; Tübingen: Mohr Siebeck, 1981) 486, draws attention to it.

> When the Advocate comes, whom I will send to you from the Father, the Spirit of truth who comes from the Father, he will testify on my behalf. You also are to testify because you have been with me from the beginning *(ap' archēs)* (John 15:26-27 NRSV).

The courtroom metaphor is characteristic of John's Gospel. The motif of a trial runs through the whole of this Gospel. But in this particular usage it is equally characteristic of Luke's writings. Luke and John agree that the qualification to be witnesses to Jesus is to have been with Jesus "from the beginning" of his ministry. (In passing we should note that in John's Gospel "witness" is not the calling of Christian believers in general, as is often supposed, but the specific task of the personal disciples of Jesus who had been with him "from the beginning." This will be discussed further in chapter 15.) John 15:27 may well refer back to the way the beginning of Jesus' ministry is represented in John. After the miracle at Cana, John comments:

> Jesus did this, the first of his signs [literally: "beginning *(archēn)* of signs"], in Cana of Galilee, and revealed his glory; and his disciples believed in him (2:11 NRSV).

An idea on which Luke and John agree in this way is likely also to have been more widespread in the early Christian movement, not confined to these two authors. Evidently in the early Christian movement a special importance attached to the testimony of disciples who had been eyewitnesses of the whole ministry of Jesus, from its beginning when John was baptizing to Jesus' resurrection appearances. This was a necessary qualification for membership of the Twelve, but there were also other disciples who fulfilled the qualification and whose witness would have been especially valuable for that reason. We must now consider whether the Gospels themselves show indications of embodying the testimony of disciples who fulfilled this maximum qualification. The easiest case to answer, at least in part, is Luke's.

The Preface to Luke's Gospel

Luke's Gospel is alone among the Gospels in having a preface in which the author addresses the dedicatee of his work:

> Since many have undertaken to set down an orderly account of the events that have been fulfilled among us, just as they were handed on to us by those who from the beginning were eyewitnesses and servants of the

word *(kathōs paredosan hēmin hoi ap' archēs autoptai kai hupēretai genomenoi tou logou)*, I too decided, after investigating *(parēkolouthēkoti)*[4] everything carefully from the very first *(anōthen)*, to write an orderly account for you, most excellent Theophilus, so that you may know the truth concerning the things about which you have been instructed (Luke 1:1-4 NRSV).

This preface has been the object of extensive and intensive scholarly discussion. We must confine ourselves here to what is relevant to the question of the eyewitness sources of Luke's traditions and his own relationship to these eyewitnesses.

We should note that the Greek word used in v. 2 for "eyewitnesses" *(autoptai)* does not have a forensic meaning, and in that sense the English word "eyewitnesses," with its suggestion of a metaphor from the law courts, is a little misleading. The *autoptai* are simply firsthand observers of the events. (Loveday Alexander offers the translations: "those with personal/firsthand experience: those who know the facts at first hand."[5]) But the concept expressed in the words "those who from the beginning were eyewitnesses" is clearly the same as in Acts 1:21-22 and John 15:27, while the phrase *ap' archēs* is common to Luke and John. Moreover, the occurrence of this phrase in Luke's preface enables us to recognize that it has a historiographic background, as we shall see.

Most scholars have taken the view that Luke's preface as a whole belongs within the tradition of Greek historiography and for its first readers would serve to identify the genre of Luke's work as some kind of history. But Loveday Alexander has offered a significant challenge to this view, arguing from an exhaustive examination of prefaces in ancient Greek literature that the form and rhetoric of Luke's preface much more closely resemble those of prefaces to technical or professional[6] treatises (for example, handbooks on medicine, mathematics, engineering, or rhetorical theory) than those of prefaces to historical works. (She is not denying that Luke-Acts may, on grounds of content,

---

4. The meaning of this verb will be discussed below.

5. L. Alexander, *The Preface to Luke's Gospel* (SNTSMS 78; Cambridge: Cambridge University Press, 1993) 120.

6. In *The Preface*, she used the term "scientific," but in her essay "Formal Elements and Genre: Which Greco-Roman Prologues Most Closely Parallel the Lukan Prologues?" in D. P. Moessner, ed., *Jesus and the Heritage of Israel* (Harrisburg: Trinity, 1999) 9-26, she substitutes the term "technical," which probably better conveys the range of subject matter of the literature in question. V. K. Robbins, "The Claims of the Prologues and Greco-Roman Rhetoric: The Prefaces to Luke and Acts in Light of Greco-Roman Rhetorical Strategies," in Moessner, ed., *Jesus,* 66, suggests the term "profession-oriented writings."

have to be classified as some kind of historiography, only that the prefaces to Luke and Acts do not themselves indicate this.[7]) Other scholars, responding to Alexander's work, have considered that her evidence and argument are revealing as to the socio-literary level and context of Luke's work but do not render the resemblances to the terminology and concepts of Greek historiography irrelevant.[8]

David Aune rightly points out that "only a fraction of Greek historical works have survived," while "of those that have survived, most are written by authors with a social status to which Luke could never have aspired and in an elevated style that he could never have emulated."[9] He presents some, admittedly small, evidence that Luke's preface may have resembled those of "the hundreds of lost mediocre histories"[10] more than it does those of the best Hellenistic historiography, which are the ones that have survived. He also comments that "it begins to appear increasingly plausible that the distinction between historical and scientific [technical or professional] *prooimia* [prefaces] is in reality a false dichotomy."[11] Daryl Schmidt, reviewing once again the rhetoric of Hellenistic historiography, points out that "the conventions of Hellenistic historiography inspired a wide range of narrative writings, with varying degrees of verisimilitude and styles," and concludes that Luke's preface suggests obvious influences from the rhetorical conventions of Hellenistic historiography. That makes Luke a writer of "historical" narrative, but not necessarily a "historian." Luke-Acts appropriately belongs within the rather wide spectrum of "Hellenistic historiography."[12]

What is of first importance for our present purposes is the historiographic significance of the phrase "eyewitnesses from the beginning" (*ap' archēs autoptai*). Alexander has undoubtedly shown that the word *autoptēs* is by no means limited to historiographic use, while among extant historians

7. L. C. A. Alexander, "The Preface to Acts and the Historians," in B. Witherington III, ed., *History, Literature and Society in the Book of Acts* (Cambridge: Cambridge University Press, 1996) 100-101; idem, "Formal Elements," 23.

8. See especially D. D. Schmidt, "Rhetorical Influences and Genre: Luke's Preface and the Rhetoric of Hellenistic Historiography," in Moessner, ed., *Jesus,* 27-60.

9. D. E. Aune, "Luke 1:1-4: Historical or Scientific *Prooimion?*" in A. Christopherson, C. Claussen, J. Frey, and B. Longenecker eds., *Paul, Luke and the Graeco-Roman World: Essays in Honour of Alexander J. M. Wedderburn* (JSNTSup 217 (Sheffield: Sheffield Academic, 2002) 142.

10. Aune, "Luke 1:1-4," 148. Alexander, "Formal Elements," 23, comes close to agreeing: "At most, such a reader [i.e., an informed ancient reader] might regard Luke's work as potential 'raw material' for a real historian to polish and refine, as Lucian regards the 'soldier's diary' produced by an army surgeon in the Parthian War." The reference is to Lucian, *Hist. Conscr.* 16.

11. Aune, "Luke 1:1-4," 148.

12. Schmidt, "Rhetorical Influences," 59.

only Polybius (3.4.3) and Josephus (*C. Ap.* 1.55) use it with reference to the observation of events narrated in a history in a preface or other methodological passage.[13] She therefore claims that "there is no need to go to the historians at all" and that prefaces in the technical or professional tradition provide more appropriate parallels to the usage in Luke's preface.[14] But this claim is convincing only within her overall argument for dissociating Luke's preface from historiographic parallels, whereas a different view of the preface as a whole would make the usage of Polybius and Josephus the most obviously relevant parallels to Luke's usage. Samuel Byrskog criticizes Alexander's narrow focus on the terminology of the *autoptein* word-group, insisting that the concept which Polybius and Josephus use it to describe is much more widespread in ancient historiography than the word itself.[15] Moreover, if Josephus could imitate Polybius's use of *autoptēs,* as Alexander thinks he probably did,[16] so could other historians. Polybius was widely admired as defining and exemplifying the best principles of Hellenistic historiography, and it would not be unnatural for later writers who aspired to be historians to echo his terminology, whether or not they succeeded in coming anywhere near him in their own historiographic practice. In any case, whether or not *autoptai* would have been recognized as a technical historiographical term in Luke's preface, there is no doubt, from its total context in Luke-Acts, that it carries the historiographic meaning of people who witnessed firsthand the events of Luke's gospel story.

Of particular interest, however, is that the phrase "from the beginning" (*ap' archēs*) can now also be seen as belonging to the same historiographic complex of ideas. This phrase is not, as has been claimed, an evocation of the authority of antiquity in Hellenistic culture or a reference to the authoritative ancient sources of an oral tradition,[17] but a claim that the eyewitnesses had been present throughout the events from the appropriate commencement of the author's history onward.

There is one rather general use of such a phrase in a preface to a historiographic work contemporary with Luke's Gospel: Philo of Byblos writes "Sanchuniathon, truly a man of great learning and curiosity, who desired to learn from everyone about what happened from the first (*ex archēs*) . . . quite carefully searched out the works of Taautos."[18] Closer to Luke's us-

13. Alexander, *The Preface,* 34-41, 80-82, 120-22.
14. Alexander, *The Preface,* 122-23, 124-25.
15. S. Byrskog, *Story as History — History as Story* (Tübingen: Mohr, 2000) 48-49.
16. Alexander, *The Preface,* 38-39.
17. So Alexander, *The Preface,* 120; idem, "Formal Elements," 20-21.
18. Quoted in Schmidt, "Rhetorical Influences," 52 n. 91.

age, however, is the example David Aune gives. This is a pseudonymous preface to a work actually written by Plutarch. It purports to have been written by a man who was present at the famous symposium of the Seven Sages in the sixth century BCE and can therefore offer his dedicatee a true account of that event. The account is fictional and the preface is intended to lend verisimilitude to it, but this does not diminish its value as evidence for our purposes, since Plutarch would certainly have written the preface in accordance with the conventions of historiographic writing known in his time. Aune points out a series of parallels with Luke's preface, as well as with the prefaces to technical treatises,[19] and bases on these his suggestion that the prefaces to more popular historical works may well have been more similar to those of technical treatises than to the prefaces of the more distinguished works of history that have come down to us.[20] The section of this pseudepigraphal preface that concerns us just now is the last sentence. The author has informed his dedicatee that other accounts of the event were unreliable because, unlike himself, their authors had not actually been present. He concludes: "Since I now have a lot of free time, and old age is not trustworthy enough to delay telling my story, I will recount everything from the beginning *(ap' archēs hapanta diēgēsomai),* since you are eager to listen."[21] Here the phrase "from the beginning" is the assurance that the author, having been an eyewitness, was able to give a comprehensive account, not the misleadingly partial account that writers who had merely heard something about what happened might be able to give.

The claim is functionally equivalent to that of Josephus when, contrasting his own history of the Jewish war with that of other writers who had had only a few hearsay reports to go by, he claims that his is a genuinely adequate history because he was present at all the events: "I, on the contrary, have written a veracious account, at once comprehensive and detailed, of the war, having been present in person at all the events" (*C. Ap.* 1:47). One of the letters Josephus received from King Agrippa, to whom he sent copies of his work, congratulated him on instructing his readers about everything "from the beginning" *(archēthen)* (*Vita* 366).[22]

It was considered important for a historian to choose the right beginning, as well as the right conclusion, to the story he told. In his preface to his

19. Aune, "Luke 1:1-4," 145-47.

20. Aune, "Luke 1:1-4," 148.

21. Plutarch, *Septem sapientium convivium,* quoted in Aune, "Luke 1:1-4," 145.

22. For this kind of eyewitness qualification, see also Polybius's choice of Gaius Laelius as a reliable source of information on Scipio Africanus because "from youth [he] participated with him in every word and deed until death" (Polybius 10.3.2).

Histories Polybius stated precisely his starting point and justified his choice of it as the appropriate place to begin *(archēn)* (1.3.1-5; 1.5.1; 1.12.5). Dionysius of Halicarnassus, writing in the first century BCE, criticized no less than Thucydides on this score:

> Some critics also find fault with the order of his history, complaining that he neither chose the right beginning *(archēn)* for it nor a fitting place to end it. They say that by no means the least important aspect of good arrangement is that a work should begin *(archēn)* where nothing can be imagined as preceding it, and end where nothing further is felt to be required.[23]

Interestingly, Polybius, while determining the most natural starting point for his narrative in the usual way, also decided to narrate some events prior to this starting point so as to be able to elucidate fully some aspects of his history:

> Such then was the occasion and motive of this the first crossing of the Romans from Italy with an armed force, an event which I take to be the most natural starting-point *(archēn)* of this whole work. I have therefore made it my serious base, but went also somewhat further back in order to leave no possible obscurity in my statements of general causes. To follow out this previous history . . . seems to me necessary for anyone who hopes to gain a proper general survey of their present supremacy (1.12.5-7).[24]

We may compare the fact that Luke's narrative based on the accounts of those who were eyewitnesses "from the beginning" properly begins with the ministry of John the Baptist, but that he also has a kind of historical prologue narrating the birth and youth of John and Jesus. It is not plausible, as has recently been suggested,[25] that the "beginning" to which Luke refers is the events of chs. 1-2 of his Gospel and that the "eyewitnesses" include the characters in these preliminary stories. Rather Luke abides by the starting point for the history of Jesus that in his time was generally agreed and which the oral testi-

---

23. Dionysius of Halicarnassus, *De Veterum Censura* 11, quoted in D. Moessner, "The Appeal and Power of Poetics (Luke 1:1-4): Luke's Superior Credentials (παρηκολουθηκότι), Narrative Sequence (καθεξῆς), and Firmness of Understanding (ἡ ἀσφάλεια) for the Reader," in Moessner, ed., *Jesus*, 111.

24. Quoted in Moessner, "The Appeal," 120.

25. K. A. Kuhn, "Beginning the Witness: The αὐτόπται καὶ ὑπηρέται of Luke's Infancy Narrative," *NTS* 49 (2003) 237-55. Kuhn says nothing about how Luke could have received traditions from these persons, who include the shepherds, as well as the named adults in the stories.

mony of the eyewitnesses observed, but added a preliminary account of events that would give his main story an appropriate background and context.

Josephus followed a somewhat similar course in his *Jewish War*. In his preface he explains that, in order to fill in the background to the events of his own time, he did not need to recount the early history of his people because this was adequately done in the Jewish Scriptures and by other Jewish authors. He did need, however, to continue the history of the Jewish people from the point where those records left off. Therefore he gave a summary account of events prior to his own lifetime but reserved his full treatment for the events immediately leading up to the war and of the war itself. We should note that he considered this distinction justified, not only by the fact that the war is the real subject of his work, but also by the fact that it was these events in which he himself had participated:

> I shall therefore begin *(archēn)* my work at the point where the historians of these events [the ancient history of the Jews] and our prophets [the writers of Scripture] conclude. Of the subsequent history, I shall describe the incidents of the war through which I lived with all the detail and elaboration at my command; for the events preceding my lifetime I shall be content with a brief summary (*War* 1.18).

The notion that the principal witnesses to the events of Jesus' life, death, and resurrection had to be those who had been with him "from the beginning" — a notion we have seen to be common at least to Luke and John and therefore likely to go back in early Christian tradition behind those two authors — was presumably at first a common-sense notion rather than a precisely historiographic one. But Luke certainly appreciated the way it coincided with the historiographic principle of choosing the appropriate starting point for a history and also with the historiographic importance of "autopsy," the testimony of those who could speak from firsthand experience of the events. The principal eyewitness sources of his work were qualified to provide a comprehensive account of the events "from the beginning."

Luke's full phrase, "those who were from the beginning eyewitnesses and ministers of the word" (1:2), almost certainly refers to a single group of people, not two groups.[26] Probably it should not be pressed to state that those who were eyewitnesses from the beginning subsequently became ministers of the

---

26. Alexander, *The Preface*, 119; J. A. Fitzmyer, *The Gospel according to Luke I–IX* (AB 28; New York: Doubleday, 1981) 294. This is usually thought to be grammatically necessary, though Kuhn, "Beginning the Witness," 239 n. 8, registers a caution about this.

word,[27] though this is a possible translation (taking *genomenoi* with *hupēretai* only and translating it as "became"). Nevertheless it is clear that "from the beginning" qualifies only "eyewitnesses," and it must be assumed that these eyewitnesses became also ministers of the word only at a later stage. The full phrase corresponds rather precisely to Acts 1:21-22, referring to disciples who, because they had been eyewitnesses of the whole course of Jesus' ministry, were qualified thereafter to be servants of the word (terminology similar to the way Luke speaks of the ministry of the Twelve in Acts 6:4), telling the gospel message, which included the whole story of Jesus. What Christopher Evans finds a "strange combination" of eyewitnesses and servants of the word[28] is explicated by Acts 1:21-22: in the case of *these* eyewitnesses their account of what they saw was not merely delivered to a historian but formed an indispensable part of their own communication of the Christian message. In Luke's preface they may not be limited to the Twelve — we shall return to this point — but surely include the Twelve prominently among them.

Before leaving Luke's preface, we need to attend briefly to another phrase, rendered in the NRSV as "after investigating *(parēkolouthēkoti)* everything carefully from the very first *(anōthen)*" (1:3). The meaning of *parēkolouthēkoti* (literally "followed") here has been much discussed,[29] but David Moessner has recently argued very thoroughly and persuasively that the verb does not here (or in Josephus, *C. Ap.* 1:53, which is often cited as a parallel) mean "investigate," which he argues is not an otherwise attested meaning, but "to follow with the mind."[30] Luke means that he has thoroughly understood everything that the eyewitnesses have passed on to him. His "informed familiarity" (Moessner's phrase) is his qualification for writing a history based on these eyewitness accounts and, probably, for doing so more satisfactorily than his predecessors who have already done so.

As for *anōthen*, which could mean merely "thoroughly,"[31] it is surely used here with the temporal meaning "from way back" and as a parallel to "from the beginning" *(ap' archēs)*. Luke himself uses the two phrases as

---

27. This is argued, for example, by R. J. Dillon, *From Eye-Witnesses to Ministers of the Word* (AnBib 82; Rome: Biblical Institute Press, 1978) 270-72, especially n. 114 (and is embodied in the title of the book).

28. C. A. Evans, *Saint Luke* (Philadelphia: Trinity, 1990) 126.

29. See especially Alexander, *The Preface*, 128-30.

30. Moessner, "The Appeal," 84-123. I cannot agree fully with all of Moessner's further conclusions. Moessner's earlier article, "'Eyewitnesses,' 'Informed Contemporaries,' and 'Unknowing Inquirers': Josephus' Criteria for Authentic Historiography and the Meaning of ΠΑΡΑΚΟΛΟΥΘΕΩ," *NovT* 38 (1996) 105-22, discusses the evidence of Josephus in more detail.

31. Alexander, *The Preface*, 130.

roughly equivalent elsewhere (Acts 26:4-5).[32] Here as there, the variation between the two phrases is for stylistic reasons. The point in Luke's preface is
that, just as the scope of the eyewitness testimony was comprehensive, cover-
ing the whole story Luke's Gospel had to tell ("from the beginning"), so
Luke's thorough familiarity with and understanding of this testimony were
equally comprehensive. Luke can tell the story "from the beginning" because
he is familiar with the traditions of those who were eyewitnesses "from the
beginning." It seems that the principle of eyewitness testimony "from the beginning" was remarkably important for the way that the traditions about Jesus were transmitted and understood in early Christianity.

The *Inclusio* of Eyewitness Testimony in Mark

Now that we have discovered how important was the notion of an eyewitness
who was qualified to tell the whole gospel story by virtue of participation in it
from beginning to end, we are in a position to recognize that the Gospels employ a literary device, hardly noticed by modern scholars, to indicate precisely
this qualification on the part of their eyewitness sources. We find it first in the
Gospel of Mark.

The first disciple named in Mark's Gospel, immediately following the
outset of Jesus' ministry, is Peter (or rather Simon, as Mark consistently calls
him until Jesus changes his name at 3:16):

> As Jesus passed along the Sea of Galilee, he saw Simon and Simon's[33]
> brother Andrew casting a net into the sea — for they were fishermen. And
> Jesus said to them, "Follow me and I will make you fish for people." And
> immediately they left their nets and followed him (Mark 1:16-18 NRSV al-
> tered).

There is a particular emphasis here on Simon's name.[34] Mark could have
written "Simon and his brother Andrew,"[35] just as in the following verse he
refers to "James the son of Zebedee and his brother John" (1:19). Elsewhere
Mark does indeed say, "James and John the brother of James" (5:37; cf. 3:17),

---

32. Cf. also the reference to Aelian in Alexander, *The Preface*, 130.

33. NRSV here has "his," but this is making better English out of the Greek "Simon's."

34. One of the few commentators to remark on this at all is R. A. Guelich, *Mark 1–8:26*
(WBC 34A; Dallas: Word, 1989) 50: "The double reference to Simon most likely indicates his relative stature in Mark's Gospel."

35. Note that the parallel in Matthew has: "Simon who is called Peter and Andrew his
brother" (Matt 4:18).

and so the repetition of the first brother's name seems to be an aspect of Markan style. But he does not always follow this practice, and in 1:16 it helps to give particular prominence to Simon.

In Mark's narrative all the male disciples desert Jesus in Gethsemane, and Peter, of course, goes on to deny Jesus. None of the Twelve therefore witness the events of Mark's story after Jesus is taken to Pilate, but nevertheless Peter is named again right at the end of the Gospel, when the women at the empty tomb are told to tell Jesus' "disciples and Peter that he is going ahead of you to Galilee: there you will see him" (16:7). The rather surprisingly specific mention of Peter (who after all was one of the disciples)[36] surely points ahead to the resurrection appearance of Jesus to Peter individually. Both Paul (1 Cor 15:5) and Luke (Luke 24:34) refer to such an appearance, so that its presence very early in the traditions is certain, but oddly it is nowhere narrated. Mark's reference to it, in the penultimate verse of his Gospel, pointing beyond the end of his own narrative, is designed to place Peter as prominently at the end of the story as at the beginning. The two references form an *inclusio* around the whole story, suggesting that Peter is the witness whose testimony includes the whole.[37] This is striking confirmation of the much disputed testimony of Papias (to be discussed in chapter 9 below) to the effect that Peter was the source of the Gospel traditions in Mark's Gospel.

If this device of *inclusio* is intended to indicate that Peter was the main eyewitness source behind Mark's Gospel, then it is coherent with the evidence (to be found in Table 11) of the remarkable frequency with which his name occurs in Mark.[38] The name Simon occurs seven times with reference to Simon Peter[39] and the name Peter nineteen times.[40] This frequency, relative to the length of the Gospels, is considerably higher in Mark than in the other Gospels. Matthew's much longer Gospel has the name Simon (with reference to Simon Peter) five times and the name Peter twenty-four times. Luke has

36. Cf. M. Hengel, *The Four Gospels and the One Gospel of Jesus Christ* (tr. J. Bowden; London: SCM, 2000) 82: "The 'and Peter' disrupts the narrative and is completely superfluous. Peter is one of 'the disciples.'"

37. M. Hengel, *Studies in the Gospel of Mark* (tr. J. Bowden; London: SCM, 1985) 61; idem, *The Four Gospels*, 82.

38. My calculations are made in a somewhat different way than those for the Synoptics given by R. Feldmeier, "The Portrayal of Peter in the Synoptic Gospels," in Hengel, *Studies in the Gospel of Mark*, 59.

39. This number — the Jewish symbolic number of completeness — might be deliberate.

40. Hengel, *Studies*, 155 n. 72, also claims that references to Peter "occur more frequently at the key points of the Gospel: at the beginning, in the *peripateia* and then at the beginning of the passion narrative." I am not sure this is very significant, especially since most of the references in ch. 14 are in connection with Peter's denials.

the name Simon (with reference to Simon Peter) twelve times and the name Peter eighteen times. John has the name Simon (with reference to Simon Peter) twenty-two times and the name Peter thirty-four times, but these very high figures conceal the fact that John uses the combination "Simon Peter" much more frequently than the other Gospels (seventeen times, whereas Mark never uses this double name, Matthew has it once, Luke once). But even taking this factor into account and counting the double name Simon Peter only once, John's Gospel has comparatively the highest frequency (once for each 395 words), while Mark has the second (once for each 432 words), with Matthew (once for each 654 words) and Luke (once for each 670 words) coming close together in third and fourth place. Since Matthew's Gospel has a special interest in Peter (cf. Matt 14:28-29; 16:17-18) it is very noteworthy that Mark mentions Peter by name considerably more frequently than Matthew does. Furthermore — a point of considerable importance for our argument that Mark's Gospel claims Peter as its principal eyewitness source — Peter is actually present through a large proportion of the narrative from 1:16 to 14:72 (the only exceptions are 6:14-29; 10:35-40; 14:1-2, 10-11, 55-65). It is certainly not the case, as Joel Marcus claims, that "were it not for Papias, one would never suspect that the Second Gospel were particularly Petrine."[41]

Strong confirmation that Mark's references to Simon Peter at the beginning and the end of his story form a deliberate *inclusio* comes from Luke's Gospel. Luke has not, in his use of Mark and other sources, preserved these two Markan references to Peter in their Markan positions. Luke's story of the call of Peter occurs later in Luke's Gospel (5:1-11), after Peter has already appeared in the narrative (4:38), but Luke nevertheless insures that Peter is the first disciple to be individually named in his Gospel. Moreover, he contrives an equivalent to Mark's emphatic reiteration of the name Simon on first appearance in the story: "After leaving the synagogue he [Jesus] entered Simon's house. Now Simon's mother-in-law was suffering from a high fever . . ." (4:38).[42] Similarly, at the end of his story, Luke does not name Peter in the words of the angels at the empty tomb (Luke 24:6-7), as Mark does. Since Luke's narrative continues with narration of resurrection appearances, such an occurrence of Peter's name would not in Luke's Gospel make him the last disciple to be named. Instead, Luke refers retrospectively to the resurrection appearance of Jesus to Peter. When the two disciples return from Emmaus to

41. J. Marcus, *Mark 1–8* (AB 27; New York: Doubleday, 1999) 24.

42. The proximity of the two occurrences of the name Simon here results from Luke's abbreviation of Mark's text, which has: "As soon as they left the synagogue, they entered the house of Simon and Andrew, with James and John. Now Simon's mother-in-law was in bed with a fever . . ." (1:29-30).

Jerusalem, the others tell them: "The Lord is risen indeed, and he has appeared to Simon!" (24:34). This reference makes Simon the last personal name other than Jesus and Moses to appear in Luke's Gospel. In thus imitating Mark's *inclusio* of eyewitness testimony with reference to Peter, Luke has acknowledged the extent to which his own Gospel is indebted to the Petrine testimony he recognized in Mark.

The *Inclusio* of Eyewitness Testimony in John

In my view, the author of the Gospel of John knew Mark's Gospel and expected many of his readers to know it,[43] although this is not the same as claiming that he used Mark as a source. It is intriguing to observe what in the Fourth Gospel corresponds to Mark's references to Peter at the beginning and the end of Jesus' ministry. In John the first disciples of Jesus, who appear initially as disciples of John the Baptist (1:35), are two who remain anonymous until one of them is named as Andrew (1:40). But Andrew's companion is not, as we might expect, his brother Peter, as in Mark's story of the call of the first disciples, for Andrew subsequently goes to find his brother and introduces him to Jesus (1:41-42). For readers who know Mark, it will seem that John displaces Peter from the priority he has in Mark, not only by his brother Andrew but also by the other of the first two disciples, who remains anonymous and seems to drop unobtrusively out of the story. This figure of an anonymous disciple has often been thought to be the disciple John elsewhere calls "the disciple Jesus loved."[44] That disciple is never named within the Gospel, and he could not, of course, here on first acquaintance with Jesus yet be described as "the disciple Jesus loved." But there is, it seems to me, a largely unnoticed but clinching argument for identifying this anonymous disciple of ch. 1 with the Beloved Disciple. The Beloved Disciple is portrayed in the Fourth Gospel as the ideal witness to Jesus. It is his witness that the Gospel embodies (21:24). But in that case this disciple must surely fulfill the qualification that this Gospel itself lays down for witnesses to Jesus: "You also are to testify because you have been with me from the beginning" (15:27). In line with this principle this disciple does indeed appear right at the beginning, modestly it might seem in that he is so unobtrusive in the narrative that one might well not notice, let

43. R. Bauckham, "John for Readers of Mark," in R. Bauckham, ed., *The Gospels for All Christians: Rethinking the Gospel Audiences* (Grand Rapids: Eerdmans, 1997) 147-71.

44. The latest discussion is R. Tansmuth, *The Disciple with Many Faces: Martin Hengel's and James H. Charlesworth's Theories Concerning the Beloved Disciple* (University of Helsinki Ph.D. thesis, 2004) 194-97, cf. 215.

alone identify him, but rather immodestly in that he displaces Peter from the position of absolute priority.

There is also a typically subtle way in which the Gospel of John indicates the identity between one of the two disciples who were the first followers of Jesus and the disciple Jesus loved. Of the two disciples when they first "followed" Jesus (1:37) the narrative states: "Jesus turned and saw them following" (1:38). At the end of the Gospel narrative, the Beloved Disciple's last appearance is indicated thus: "Peter turned and saw the disciple whom Jesus loved following" (21:20). In both passages the "following" of Jesus is literal (walking behind Jesus) but in both cases there is the additional, symbolic connotation of following as discipleship. But the parallel does not end with the Beloved Disciple "following" Jesus; it extends to his "remaining." In the case of the first two disciples, their first words to Jesus are "Rabbi, where are you staying *(meneis)?*" (1:38). In response he invites them to "come and see." The narrative continues: "So they came and saw where he was staying *(menei),* and they remained *(emeinan)* with him that day" (1:39). At the end of the Gospel narrative, in reply to Peter's question about the Beloved Disciple, "Lord, what about him?" Jesus says: "If I will that he remain *(menein)* until I come, what is that to you?" (21:22). This saying of Jesus is then repeated in the next verse as the last words of Jesus in the Gospel. (For the argument of this paragraph in more detail, see chapter 15 below.)

There is a kind of rivalry between Peter and the Beloved Disciple in the later chapters of the Gospel, after the Beloved Disciple reappears in 13:23. There is, for example, the scene in which, hearing that Jesus' tomb is empty, the two disciples race to the tomb. The Beloved Disciple wins the race, arriving first, but does not go in. Peter is the first to enter the tomb, but it is the Beloved Disciple who understands the significance of what they see there. He, not Peter, "saw and believed" (John 20:3-8). In my view this rivalry is not a polemical rivalry, designed to denigrate Peter. It could be seen as more of a friendly rivalry, but one with a very serious purpose, which is to portray the Beloved Disciple as especially qualified to be a witness to Jesus.[45] Peter, we learn in ch. 21 (that this is an integral part of the Gospel will be argued below in chapter 14), is to be the chief shepherd of Jesus' sheep and to lay down his life for Jesus, but the Beloved Disciple has a different role, as the ideal witness, the especially perceptive witness. This is the Gospel's claim to be heard at a time when Mark's Gospel was known to embody the witness of Peter the

45. R. Bauckham, "The Beloved Disciple as Ideal Author," *JSNT* 49 (1993) 21-44; reprinted in S. E. Porter and C. A. Evans, eds., *The Johannine Writings* (Biblical Seminar 32; Sheffield: Sheffield Academic, 1995) 46-68. See also chapter 15 below.

leader of the Twelve, the most eminent of all the disciples, respected in all Christian circles. But, the Fourth Gospel implies, Peter has not said the last word about Jesus or the most perceptive word. The Beloved Disciple, relatively little known though he was in the church at large, has his own witness to bear. His association with Jesus should require a hearing for his witness. So he appears, not only rather unobtrusively ahead of Peter at the beginning of the story, but also with Peter at the end, and is the one about whom Jesus speaks his last words in the Gospel. Though he is not in fact, as some mistakenly understood this word of Jesus (21:23), to remain until the parousia, he is, it seems, to survive Peter because his role is that of the witness who remains and bears his witness after Peter. From the unobtrusiveness of the beginning he emerges at the end as "the disciple who is witnessing to these things and has written them" (21:24). (We shall return to the question of his authorship of this Gospel in chapters 14-16 below.)

John's Gospel thus uses the *inclusio* of eyewitness testimony in order to privilege the witness of the Beloved Disciple, which this Gospel embodies. It does so, however, not simply by ignoring the Petrine *inclusio* of Mark's Gospel, but by enclosing a Petrine *inclusio* within its *inclusio* of the Beloved Disciple. In ch. 1, the anonymous disciple, along with Andrew, appears *just before* Peter, whose importance is then stressed by Jesus' bestowal of the name Cephas on him (1:41-42). In ch. 21 Jesus speaks to the Beloved Disciple (21:22-23) just after Jesus' dialogue with Peter, in which he has made Peter the chief shepherd of his sheep and predicted that Peter will lay down his life for Jesus and his sheep (21:15-19). The giving of the name Cephas (assuming that the name alludes to Peter's role after Jesus' departure, as in Matt 16:18-19) and the giving of the role of chief shepherd doubtless correspond, thus reinforcing the significance of the Petrine *inclusio*. The proximity of the two ends of the *inclusio* of the Beloved Disciple to the two ends of the Petrine *inclusio* functions to indicate that this Gospel's distinctive contribution derives not from Peter's testimony but from the Beloved Disciple's witness. But at the same time it acknowledges the importance of Peter's testimony, as it appears in Mark's Gospel, and the extent to which the narrative of the Gospel of John runs parallel to Mark's, while also diverging to a considerable extent. (The role of the inclusio device in the Gospel of John will be further considered in chapter 15 below.)

Luke's *Inclusio* of the Women

A distinctive feature of Luke's story of Jesus is his emphasis on a much wider group of itinerant disciples than the Twelve (Luke 6:17; 8:1-3; 10:1-20; 19:37;

23:49; 24:9, 33; Acts 1:15, 21-23), many of whom traveled with Jesus in Galilee and many of whom were in Jerusalem at the time of the triumphal entry, the crucifixion, and the resurrection appearances. By contrast, Luke's Gospel rarely refers to the Twelve in material not derived from Mark (only 8:1; 24:9, 10, 33). This is rather remarkable in the light of Luke's strong emphasis on the role of the Twelve in the early chapters of Acts. Of these disciples other than the Twelve, only one male disciple, Cleopas (very probably Jesus' uncle Clopas), is named in the Gospel, although, as we have noticed, others appear in Acts: Matthias and Joseph Barsabbas (1:23), perhaps Apollos (18:24-25) and perhaps Mnason (21:16).[46] But most striking, among Luke's references to disciples other than the Twelve, is his unique introduction of three named women, along with many anonymous women disciples, at an early point in the Galilean ministry (Luke 8:2-3). Mark indicates that the women who observed the crucifixion had followed Jesus in Galilee (Mark 15:40), but he does not refer to them at all until this point in the passion narrative. Matthew says no more than that the women, including the mother of the sons of Zebedee (Matt 20:20), a character unique to his Gospel, followed Jesus from Galilee to Jerusalem (Matt 27:55-56).

Thus Luke is unique among the Gospels in referring to the women already in his account of the Galilean ministry, while two of these women disciples appear by name only in Luke's Gospel (8:3: Joanna and Susanna). But there is another significant fact about the place of the women in the Galilean ministry of Jesus according to Luke. In Luke's account of the visit of the women to the empty tomb of Jesus, the two angels they encounter there call on them to "remember how he told you, while he was still in Galilee, that the Son of Man must be handed over to sinners, and be crucified, and on the third day rise again" (24:6-7). These words take for granted that these women had been in the audience of Jesus' private teaching to his disciples in Galilee (cf. 9:18, 43).[47]

However, the full significance of these ways in which Luke has made the

---

46. Acts 21:16 speaks of Mnason of Cyprus, a very early disciple. The word *archaios* could mean that he had been a disciple since the beginning of Jesus' ministry, like the Twelve and others, but it could also mean that he was a founding member of the Jerusalem church (cf. Acts 11:15; 15:7) and not a personal disciple of Jesus at all. That he was a native of Cyprus (most probably he would have come from Cyprus and settled in Jerusalem) makes the former less likely, but by no means impossible.

47. This significance of Luke 24:6 was explored in a pioneering way by C. Ricci, *Mary Magdalene and Many Others* (tr. P. Burns; Minneapolis: Fortress, 1994) 182-87; cf. also M.-L. Rigato, ""Remember" . . . Then They Remembered': Luke 24:6-8," in A.-J. Levine, ed., *A Feminist Companion to Luke* (Sheffield: Sheffield Academic, 2002) 269-80.

women disciples a constituent part of his whole story of Jesus emerges from one further feature. Luke first refers to the women, naming three (Mary Magdalene, Joanna, Susanna) at 8:2-3. He does not, like Matthew, Mark, and John, name them when he refers to their presence at the cross (23:49). Instead, he reserves that information until the end of his story of the women's visit to the empty tomb: "Now it was Mary Magdalene, Joanna, Mary the mother of James, and the other women with them who told this to the apostles" (24:10). Again there are three women named, but Mary the mother of James replaces Susanna. These two passages that name some of the women place them alongside the Twelve (8:1-3 and 24:10) and form a literary *inclusio* bracketing all but the earliest part of Jesus' ministry. In Luke's account the women may not quite match the qualification of those male disciples who had followed Jesus from the time of John the Baptist's ministry and who also witnessed the resurrection, but they come close to doing so. Following Mark, Luke has made sure that Simon Peter is both the first and the last disciple to be individually named in his Gospel (4:38; 24:34), thus acknowledging the incorporation of the Petrine witness of Mark's Gospel into his own work. But within the Petrine *inclusio* he has also placed another *inclusio,* that of the women, only somewhat less inclusive than Peter's, and it is surely significant that near the end of this *inclusio* Luke (24:6) reminds his readers that they have been disciples of Jesus attending to Jesus' teaching throughout his narrative since the opening of the *inclusio* in 8:2-3. The implication is surely that Luke owed some of his special traditions to one (most likely Joanna) or more than one of them.[48]

So three of the four Gospels evidently work quite deliberately with the idea that a Gospel, since it tells the whole story of Jesus, must embody the testimony of witnesses who were participants in the story from beginning to end — from the time of John the Baptist's ministry to the time of the resurrection appearances. These three Gospels all use the literary device of the *inclusio* of eyewitness testimony in order to indicate the main eyewitness source of their story. This does not, of course, exclude the appropriation also of material from other eyewitnesses, and we shall see that these Gospels also do that.

Matthew's Gospel seems not to allude to the principle of eyewitness testimony from beginning to end. In what way this Gospel was associated with Matthew is a mystery, but it does not seem to cast Matthew in the same kind

---

48. I have explored this suggestion more fully in R. Bauckham, *Gospel Women: Studies of the Named Women in the Gospels* (Grand Rapids: Eerdmans, 2002) 186-94. Of very interesting relevance to it is C. Schersten LaHurd, "Re-Viewing Luke 15 with Arab Christian Women," in Levine, ed., *A Feminist Companion to Luke,* 246-68.

of role as that in which Mark's Gospel places Peter or the Fourth Gospel the Beloved Disciple. Matthew is undoubtedly there at the end of the Gospel that is called by his name: he is included in the eleven to whom Jesus appears and speaks his final words (28:16-17). But he is not distinguished from the other ten (as Peter is in Mark 16:7). Moreover, Matthew is not called as a disciple until ch. 9 of the Gospel, when much, including the Sermon on the Mount, has already happened. In general this Gospel, unlike the others, seems not concerned to claim the authority of any specific eyewitnesses. (This point seems coherent with a feature apparent from Table 5: Matthew adds no names [other than that of Jesus' father Joseph and several names of "public" figures] to those occurring already in Mark, while actually dropping several of the names in Mark.)

The *Inclusio* of Eyewitness Testimony in Lucian's *Alexander*

It may be that the literary device I have called the *inclusio* of eyewitness testimony was invented by Mark and borrowed from him by Luke and John. But it also possible that Mark borrowed it from the conventions of popular biographical works of the kind that the Gospels resemble in genre. Unfortunately few of these works, of which there were undoubtedly many in the first and second centuries CE, have survived. Only a biography of a near-contemporary person dependent to a large extent on one major eyewitness could employ the *inclusio* of eyewitness testimony. There are even fewer of these. But there are at least two Greek biographies in which the *inclusio* of eyewitness testimony can be identified. Both were written considerably later than the Gospels, but they resemble the Gospels in being biographies of significant religious figures (though of very different kinds).

The first of these works is the life of Alexander of Abonoteichus by Lucian of Samosata, which he calls *Alexander or the False Prophet (Alexandros ē Pseudomantis)*. Lucian (born between 115 and 125 CE) was a satirist who for much of his life made his living as a traveling orator specializing in satirical dialogues. His life of Alexander is the latest of his many works, written some time after 180, probably about ten years after Alexander's death (before 175). It is a biography of a man Lucian regarded as a villain, written with the purpose of exposing Alexander as a charlatan and a man of many vices. Evidently it was commissioned by a patron, an Epicurean called Celsus, to whom it is dedicated and addressed, but Lucian feels the need to justify expending his literary talents on "a man who does not deserve to have polite people read about him, but rather to have the motley crowd in a vast amphitheatre see him being torn to pieces by foxes or apes" (§2).[49] He cites as a literary precedent Arrian's life of the bandit Tillorobus, by comparison with whom Alexander was "a far more savage brigand" who "filled the whole Roman Empire . . . with his brigandage" (§2). With these intentions it is not surprising that Lucian has nothing good to say of his subject other than his imposing appearance and his misused talents.

Alexander established in his home town of Abonoteichus, on the Black Sea coast of Paphlagonia, a cult and oracle of the snake-god Glycon, who was understood to be the reincarnation of Asclepius. As well as conducting the mysteries and propagandizing for the cult, Alexander himself functioned as Glycon's interpreter (prophet), especially in delivering oracular answers to questions people put to Glycon (as in similar well-established oracles in the Hellenistic world). The reputation of the oracle grew rapidly throughout the Roman world and Alexander became a figure of influence, with devotees even at the imperial court in Rome and among the senatorial aristocracy of Rome. Abonoteichus became a flourishing new religious center. It was exactly the kind of cult that men of a rationalist temper like Lucian thought they could see right through and had a duty to expose as a confidence trick.

As Barry Baldwin remarks, "Lucian liked few things so much as the composition of an invective."[50] But there is much more than that to this anti-biography, as we might call it, of Alexander. It seems likely that to some extent Lucian is parodying the kind of encomiastic biography that would glorify a religious figure like Alexander, telling stories of his origins, his miracles, and his oracular utterances in order to authenticate both him and his cult. There may well have been one or more such popular lives of Alexander himself to which Lucian was deliberately writing a skeptical and parodic alternative.[51] In form, at least, such lives of Alexander might not have looked very different from Mark's Gospel, though Lucian's parody is a more sophisticated production on a higher literary level.

Lucian's attack consists in attributing base motives to Alexander and in exposing all the apparently supernatural features of the cult and the oracle as ingenious trickery. The god Glycon himself, for example, was nothing but a tame snake (brought by Alexander from Pella, a place famous for its tame snakes) with an artificial head and an elaborate device to make it appear to speak. Though questions put to the god were submitted in sealed scrolls and

49. Quotations from Lucian's *Alexander* are all from the translation by A. M. Harmon in the Loeb Classical Library: *Lucian*, vol. 6 (Cambridge: Harvard University Press, 1925) 173-253.

50. B. Baldwin, *Studies in Lucian* (Toronto: Hakkert, 1973) 104.

51. This is suggested by D. L. Tiede, *The Charismatic Figure as Miracle Worker* (SBLDS 1; Missoula: Scholars, 1973) 63-64.

returned with the seal intact, Alexander had ways of breaking the seal and re-storing it as though unopened. In such ways Lucian recounts what a popular encomiastic biography might have related as tales of miracle and magic, but at the same time thoroughly debunks them. He also construes Alexander's motives as vicious, accusing him of the stock crimes of avarice, adultery, sex with boys, and (attempted) murder.

The historical existence of Alexander and the nature of the cult of Glycon at Abonoteichus are independently evidenced and indubitable.[52] The extent to which the details of Lucian's account are accurate has been de-bated,[53] but much of what he says coheres with what is known of the social and religious context of the time and makes good sense.[54] The scurrilous ac-count of Alexander's early life may be largely malicious fiction, and it is hard to believe that Lucian could have known that his rationalistic explanations of all the phenomena of the cult and the oracle were as a matter of fact the case. He presumably hypothesized them for the most part, and some of the tricks were of the kind that other ancient writers also expose. As for Alexander's motives and vices, we can hardly put much trust in a biographer so deter-mined to damn his subject. But these aspects aside, there is no reason why most of Lucian's account of Alexander's career should not be historically reli-able. Wholesale fiction, written well within living memory of the events, would hardly have served his purpose.

Lucian claims to have been an eyewitness of a rather small part of his story, although in his telling of it this part functions as the climax of Alexander's villainy. In a visit to Abonoteichus that Lucian made around the year 165 he was lavishly entertained by Alexander but then, leaving by ship, narrowly escaped an attempt on his life instigated by Alexander. But from what source or sources did Lucian gain the rest of his information about Alexander? For his account to be taken seriously one would expect him to indicate this in some way. He could, of course, have learned a lot from any of the many visitors to the shrine, while some of Alexander's more significant oracles were doubtless well known (such as the one cited in §36, which Lucian says "was to be seen everywhere written over doorways as a charm against the plague"). At one point, Lucian reports a dialogue between the god Glycon and Sacerdos, "a man of Tius," claiming that he had read it in a gilded inscription in Sacerdos's own house (§43).

52. Much of the evidence was already presented by F. Cumont, *Alexandre d'Abonotichos. Un Épisode de l'Histoire du Paganisme au IIe siècle de notre ère* (Brussels: Hayez, 1887).

53. E.g., C. Robinson, *Lucian and His Influence in Europe* (London: Duckworth, 1979) 59-60, thinks the work quite largely fiction.

54. See especially C. P. Jones, *Culture and Society in Lucian* (Cambridge: Harvard University Press, 1986) chapter 12.

But there is one obvious candidate for the source of much of Lucian's account: the Roman aristocrat Rutilianus. Publius Mummius Sisenna Rutilianus is a known historical person who was consul in 146.[55] He was an enthusiastic and highly influential propagandist for Alexander (§§30-31), and, at the age of sixty, he married Alexander's daughter (allegedly Alexander's child by the moon goddess Selene) in obedience to one of Alexander's oracles (§35). Lucian claims to have known Rutilianus personally and to have advised him against the marriage (§54), and there is no reason to doubt him.[56] He wrote his work soon after Rutilianus's death (cf. §35) and it is possible he deliberately waited until Rutilianus was dead, not so that he could falsely claim acquaintance with him (other members of the family would still be able to refute this, were it not true), but so that he could give his frank opinion of Rutilianus, whom he evidently thought a gullible fool driven crazy by superstitious religion (§30-31), and so that he could expose Alexander as a fraud without having to fear the consequences from Rutilianus, who was a very powerful individual.[57]

Lucian claims to have read a letter from Alexander to Rutilianus, in which Alexander compared himself with Pythagoras (§4; entirely plausible in view of other neo-Pythagorean aspects of Alexander's cult), and he quotes three oracular responses on personal matters given to Rutilianus (§33-35). Table 12 below shows how references to Rutilianus by name occur throughout the book. Apart from Alexander himself, there are far more references to Rutilianus than to any other character. Just like the Petrine *inclusio* in the Gospel of Mark, Rutilianus is both the first character in the story, apart from Alexander, to be named and the last to be mentioned by name. The way in which the first mention of his name is made is particularly noteworthy. Rutilianus does not actually figure in the story until Alexander's fame reaches Rome (§30) halfway through the book. But Lucian contrives to make him the first named character, other than Alexander, to be mentioned by citing a letter from Alexander to him before he has begun to tell the story, in connection with his account of Alexander's natural talents (§4). As for Lucian's final reference to Rutilianus, the whole story of Alexander, following a gruesome death (§59), concludes thus:

55. Jones, *Culture*, 141; see also M. Caster, *Études sur Alexandre ou Le Faux Prophète de Lucien* (Paris: Société d'Édition "Les Belles Lettres," 1938) 52-58.

56. Robinson, *Lucian*, 60, does doubt this, but Jones, *Culture*, 145, finds it consistent with other evidence that Lucian had friends among the Roman aristocracy.

57. J. Schwartz, *Biographie de Lucien de Samosate* (Collection Latomus 83; Brussels: Latomus, 1965) 21.

135

It was inevitable, too, that he should have funeral games worthy of his career — that a contest for the shrine should arise. The foremost of his fellow conspirators and imposters referred it to Rutilianus to decide which of them should be given the preference, should succeed to the shrine, and should be crowned with the fillet of priest and prophet. Paetus was one of them, a physician by profession, a greybeard, who conducted himself in a way that befitted neither a physician nor a greybeard. But Rutilianus, the umpire, sent them off unfilleted, keeping the post of prophet for the master after his departure from this life (§60).

Whether or not Lucian was really very close to Rutilianus — close enough to advise him against marrying Alexander's daughter — is not really important, since in any case he has so positioned Rutilianus in his narrative as to imply that Rutilianus was his main eyewitness source. In doing so, he may have been playing with a literary convention, because his depiction of Rutilianus hardly portrays him as likely to be a very trustworthy witness. Having described him as superstitious, Lucian then speaks of Rutilianus's first impressions of Alexander thus:

> When [Rutilianus] heard the tales about the oracle, he very nearly abandoned the office which had been committed to him and took wing to Abonoteichus. Anyhow, he sent one set of messengers after another, and his emissaries, mere illiterate serving-people, were easily deluded, so when they came back, they told not only what they had seen but what they had heard as if they had seen it, and threw in something more for good measure, so as to gain favor with their master. Consequently, they inflamed the poor old man and made him absolutely crazy. Having many powerful friends, he went about not only telling what he had heard from his messengers but adding still more on his own account (§30-31).

It is possible that an encomiastic life of Alexander that Lucian is parodying relied on Rutilianus's testimony as its main eyewitness source and that Lucian is ironically exposing the unreliability of Rutilianus's testimony at the same time as basing his own account on it. He himself is a skeptical historian not taken in by the stories of his credulous informant, whom he cites only to show him up as a fool.

To argue from a parody to aspects of the kind of work that is parodied is clearly somewhat hazardous. However, the resemblance between the way that Rutilianus, Alexander's most eminent follower, appears in Lucian's narrative and the way that Peter, Jesus' most prominent disciple, appears in the Gospel of Mark indicates that there may have been a literary convention — the *inclusio* of eyewitness testimony — that belonged to the genre of the popular life of a charismatic or prophetic figure. Mark would then have borrowed from popular works that are no longer extant the convention that Lucian parodied. If it was a recognized convention then it is the more understandable that Luke and John recognized Mark's use of it and followed Mark in making their own use of it.

The *Inclusio* of Eyewitness Testimony in Porphyry's *Life of Plotinus*

The second example of this literary convention occurs in the earliest extant biography of a philosopher by a pupil of his after Xenophon's *Memorabilia* of Socrates. Porphyry, himself a Neo-Platonist philosopher, wrote a biography of his teacher, Plotinus (204-70 CE), the founder of Neo-Platonism, at the beginning of the fourth century, some thirty years after Plotinus's death.[58] (This is comparable with the lapse of time between the death of Jesus and the Gospel of Mark.) He designed it as an introduction to his edition of Plotinus's works (the full title is *On the Life of Plotinus and the Order of His Books*), and this explains why Porphyry is especially concerned with the origins of Plotinus's writings and the periods of his life in which they were written (see especially §§3-6), as well as with his own role as the disciple who was entrusted with editing the master's works. Richard Valantasis has argued that the work contains an unresolved enigma about the way in which Plotinus functions as a teacher, and that it is designed in this way to point to the books — Plotinus's writings interpreted and edited by Porphyry[59] — as the true spiritual guide that the reader is seeking.[60]

In the latter part of Plotinus's life, when he resided in Rome and wrote all his extant works, he had a school, doubtless modeled on the school of

58. The text is available in P. Henry and H.-R. Schwyzer, eds., *Plotini Opera,* vol. 1 (Museum Lessianum Series Philosophica 33; Paris: Desclée de Brouwer/Brussels: L'Édition Universelle, 1951) 1-46; and English translations in Plotinus, *The Enneads* (tr. S. MacKenna; third ed. revised by R. S. Page; London: Faber, 1962) 1-20, and M. J. Edwards, *Neoplatonic Saints: The Lives of Plotinus and Proclus by Their Students* (Translated Texts for Historians 35; Liverpool: Liverpool University Press, 2001). My quotations are from Edwards's translation.

59. On Porphyry's editing, see D. J. O'Meara, *Plotinus: An Introduction to the Enneads* (Oxford: Clarendon, 1993) 8-10.

60. R. Valantasis, *Spiritual Guides of the Third Century: A Semiotic Study of the Guide-Disciple Relationship in Christianity, Neoplatonism, Hermetism, and Gnosticism* (HDR 27; Minneapolis: Fortress, 1991) chapter 3.

Ammonius Saccas, his own teacher in Alexandria. It was a group of close friends and disciples[61] who were in constant attendance on Plotinus, in his household and at the "conferences" where he expounded his ideas, throughout the time when they were associated with him. Porphyry names fifteen of them, twelve men[62] and three women.[63] The men are Amelius Gentilianus the Etruscan; Paulinus, a doctor from Scythopolis; Eustochius, a doctor from Alexandria; Zoticus, a poet and critic; the Arab Zethus (Zayd), a doctor and politician (Plotinus took summer holidays on Zethus's estate in Campania and died there); Castricius Firmus, a politician; Marcellus, Orontius[64] and Sabinillus, Roman senators; Rogatianus, also a senator, though he dropped his political career to live like a philosopher; Serapion, a rhetorician and financier from Alexandria; and, last to be named, Porphyry himself, the philosopher from Tyre (§7). Of these twelve, only Amelius and Porphyry were "professional" philosophers, devoting their lives to philosophy. The three women disciples are Gemina, who owned the house where Plotinus lived, her daughter, also called Gemina, and Amphiclea, the daughter-in-law of the Neo-Platonic philosopher Iamblichus. All three were "fervently devoted to philosophy" (§ 9). The two lists of disciples are reminiscent of the Gospels, which, as well as listing the Twelve, have a strong tendency to instance three names of women disciples (Matt 26:56; Mark 15:40; 16:1; Luke 8:2-3; 24:10; John 19:25). Whether these parallels with the Gospels are coincidental or deliberate on Porphyry's part we shall consider shortly.

In most cases, Porphyry does not tell us how long these persons were members of Plotinus's school, though he does note that Paulinus, Zoticus, and Zethus died before Plotinus (and so would have been unavailable as eyewitness sources for Porphyry's biography) and that Eustochius had been with Plotinus only toward the end of his life (§7). Porphyry does, however, even before giving the list of disciples that Amelius[65] heads, explain that Amelius spent twenty-four years in Plotinus's company, joining the group of disciples

---

61. On these and all other persons mentioned in the *Life of Plotinus*, see the prosopography by L. Brisson in L. Brisson, M.-O. Goulet-Cazé, R. Goulet, and D. O'Brien, *Porphyre: La Vie de Plotin*, vol. 1 (Paris: Vrin, 1982) 55-114.

62. But if Marcellus and Orontius are understood as the two names of one person, there are only eleven.

63. See the table in L. Brisson, "Notices sur les Noms Propres," in Brisson, Goulet-Cazé, Goulet, and O'Brien, *Porphyre*, 56.

64. Edwards, in his translation (*Neoplatonic Saints*, 15), takes Marcellus and Orontius to be two distinct people; but Brisson, "Notices sur les Noms Propres," in *Porphyre*, 56, 102, treats Orontius (or Orrontius) as the family name of Marcellus.

65. On Amelius, see Brisson, "Notices," 65-69.

only two years after Plotinus first arrived in Rome in 245 CE, when Plotinus was thirty (§3). He must have remained close to Plotinus until 269, the year before Plotinus's death.[66] Porphyry thereby makes it clear that Amelius was well qualified to be the eyewitness whose testimony embraced very nearly all of Plotinus's career as master of his school. There is no indication that any of Plotinus's other disciples came anywhere near rivaling this.

Porphyry certainly regarded Amelius and himself as the two most prominent and distinguished disciples of Plotinus, as indeed they were. His own place last in the list of the twelve male disciples is probably not due to humility,[67] of which he shows none in this work, but for emphasis. It enables him to end the list with the information that he was the one whom Plotinus himself asked to edit his works, a distinction Porphyry thought the most important of all among the disciples of Plotinus. But he does not supplant Amelius's obviously deserved place at the head of the list, where his seniority is underlined by other remarks: that Plotinus gave him his nickname (the punning Amerius), that Amelius himself gave Paulinus his nickname, and that Castricius Firmus not only revered Plotinus but also served Amelius as a loyal retainer (as well as being a close friend to Porphyry; §7). It was Amelius who was most active in defending his master's teaching in writing (§18). Sometimes Porphyry brackets himself with Amelius as "Amelius and I" (§5) or "we" (§§10, 16), indicating their joint status as the disciples closest to the master, as well as most influential with him (§§5, 18). But, for all that, out of the twenty-six years Plotinus spent in Rome (244-70 CE), Porphyry can claim to have spent only five or six years in Plotinus's company (262/3-68/9), arriving when the master was fifty-nine and Amelius had already spent eighteen years in his circle (§§4-5).

The *Life of Plotinus* shows a clear concern with indicating its eyewitness sources and meticulously indicates the periods of Plotinus's life about which they were informed. The work opens with the story of how Amelius managed to get a portrait of Plotinus painted despite Plotinus's refusal (§1). We shall return to this rather surprising opening. But Porphyry then proceeds to narrate Plotinus's last illness and death, in accordance with the Platonic view that the purpose of life is to prepare the soul's escape from the body at death. At the time of Plotinus's death on the estate of his by then deceased disciple Zethus in Campania, only the doctor Eustathius was with him. Porphyry ex-

---

66. Edwards, *Neoplatonic Saints*, 7, n. 47.

67. Unless Porphyry had, of all the twelve, spent the least time in Plotinus's circle. If this were the case, it is understandable that he does not explicitly point this out, though he does state that he was with Plotinus only five or six of the twenty-six years.

plicitly notes that at the time he himself was staying at Lilybaeum in Sicily (he explains this absence in §11), while Amelius was in Apamea in Syria and Castricius in Rome. (Does he mean to indicate that these three, along with Eustochius, were by then the only remaining members of the circle of twelve disciples?) Clearly, if Porphyry's account of Plotinus's last words and death was to be credible, its eyewitness authority needed to be explained. So, no less than three times in this short narrative, Porphyry states that his information came from Eustochius. Only for this narrative, however, was Eustochius a credible informant, since he had joined Plotinus's circle not long before Plotinus died (§7).

Porphyry continues with an account of Plotinus's early life and time with Ammonius in Alexandria, introduced by the information that the account came from Plotinus himself who "told us [presumably the disciples as a group, including Porphyry], as he was wont to do in conversation" (§3).[68] However, when he comes to the later years of Plotinus in Alexandria, Porphyry notes that here his information came from Amelius, taking this opportunity to explain that Amelius joined Plotinus within two years after he had left Alexandria and took up residence in Rome, and that Amelius stayed with him for twenty-four years (§3). This surely serves as a way of indicating that from this point on Amelius is Porphyry's eyewitness source, except for information for which Porphyry himself could vouch. After this one reference to Amelius as his source, Porphyry never again gives an explicit indication that he was, but he did not need to. After this first reference the matter should be evident. Porphyry draws on his own reminiscences of Plotinus (especially §§3, 11, 13, 15, 18), and it is not always possible to distinguish what Porphyry remembered from firsthand acquaintance with Plotinus and what he learned from Amelius. But there is much that is easily attributable to the latter (see especially §§1, 3, 8, 9, 10, 11, 12, 14).[69]

68. Cf. the "we" at the beginning of §23, presumably referring to the disciples as a group, but perhaps to Porphyry and Amelius specifically.

69. P. Cox, *Biography in Late Antiquity* (Berkeley: University of California Press, 1983) 65, suggests that Porphyry's descriptions of the proceedings of Plotinus's school derive partly from Amelius's "collection of notes." She is referring to the "notes *(scholia)* of the seminars" made by Amelius and later written up by him in "some hundred books of notes, which he dedicated to" his adopted son (§3). However, Amelius's notes must have been summaries of the philosophical discussions (and were probably used by Porphyry in editing Plotinus's works) and would hardly have provided the kind of material Porphyry relates in the life of Plotinus. Of discussions in the seminar, only §§13-15 provide any detail; it is possible that §14 is indebted to Amelius's work, but it could be based on Porphyry's own observations, while §13 and §15 turn on Porphyry's own contributions to the discussions. Since §3 clearly refers to oral communication by Amelius to Porphyry it is natural to suppose that most of Porphyry's indebtedness to Amelius in the Life

Porphyry's indebtedness to Amelius is further indicated by his use of the *inclusio* of eyewitness testimony. Amelius appears already in the third sentence of the work, without any introduction. He is both the disciple of Plotinus who is first named in the biography and the one, apart from Porphyry himself, who is last named. Indeed, apart from Plotinus and Porphyry, he is the person named first and last in the work. As can be seen from Table 13, the pattern of his appearances is very similar to that of Peter in the Gospel of Mark[70] and of Rutilianus in Lucian's life of Alexander. (Note also that Amelius heads the list of twelve disciples, just as Peter does in the Synoptic Gospels.) Amelius's name occurs thirty-eight times, more often than that of anyone else except Plotinus, exceeding even the twenty-five occurrences of Porphyry's name.[71] Amelius is not only more prominent within the story than anyone except Plotinus and Porphyry; he also rather emphatically encompasses the whole story, being named no less than eight times after anyone else among contemporaries (except Plotinus and Porphyry) has been named in the last parts of the narration. Like Rutilianus in Lucian's life of Alexander, Amelius makes his final appearance in the narrative after the death of the biography's subject. He is named as the one who asked the oracle of Apollo where the soul of Plotinus had gone (§22). (The oracle that Apollo is said to have given, followed by Porphyry's elaborate interpretation of it [§§22-23], occupies the last section of this *Life of Plotinus* prior to the appendix [§§24-26], in which Porphyry explains the order in which he has arranged the content of Plotinus's *Enneads* in the edition that follows.)

Thus the *inclusio* of eyewitness testimony, indicating that Amelius was the eyewitness source whose testimony extended to virtually all of Plotinus's career, is easily seen to be coherent with what we could in any case gather from the rest of the work about Amelius's importance as an eyewitness source.

Despite the prominence Porphyry gives to Amelius in his work, we can also detect a sense of rivalry. Porphyry seems to have understood himself to be engaged in a contest for the true succession to his master. It appears that Eustochius had already published an edition of Plotinus's works,[72] and it was

---

was of this nature. In §17 Porphyry quotes explicitly and at some length from one of Amelius's treatises defending Plotinus's work, which Amelius addressed to Porphyry.

70. Differences from Mark are that Porphyry often appears as a character in his own narrative and that there are few anonymous characters in Porphyry's work, whereas there are many in Mark.

71. Edwards, *Neoplatonic Saints*, xxxvii, is mistaken in saying that "No pupil's name occurs in the *Plotinus* more often than that of Porphyry."

72. Brisson, "Notices," 81.

surely with this in mind that Porphyry, while praising Eustochius the doctor as having acquired "the character of a true philosopher by his exclusive adherence to the school of Plotinus," also notes that he made Plotinus's acquaintance only toward the end of his life (§7). But Amelius, well recognized as a philosopher and one who had been a disciple of Plotinus for no less than twenty-four years, was the more serious rival. According to Mark Edwards, it was not Porphyry but Amelius "who was generally regarded as the vicegerent of Plotinus."[73] Therefore the prominence Porphyry can hardly avoid giving to Amelius is balanced by two complementary strategies: Porphyry plays up his own importance as disciple of Plotinus and contrives also to denigrate Amelius.

Porphyry's emphasis on his own role in the story appears in the very way he refers to himself. He chooses to write of himself in the first person, but, to ensure that his readers or hearers remain fully aware of his identity, nineteen times he writes "I Porphyry," combining the pronoun *(egō)* with his name. This is an indication of the self-aggrandizement that appears in many more specific ways throughout the work. At one meeting of the seminar, when Porphyry read a poem, Plotinus, Porphyry records, said: "You have proved yourself simultaneously a poet, a philosopher, and a teacher of sacred truth" (§15). Porphyry even claims to have once had the mystical experience of union with the One that he also says Plotinus attained four times in the period he was with him (§23).

It is in relation to Plotinus's writings that Porphyry especially plays up his own role. Although Plotinus had already written twenty-one books before Porphyry met him, he notes that he was among the few who received copies of them (§4).[74] Plotinus wrote a further twenty-four books in the period Porphyry belonged to his circle. These were written records of discussions in the seminars, which Porphyry and Amelius begged him to put in writing (§5). Nine more works were written by Plotinus in the last period of his life after Porphyry had moved to Sicily. The first five of these were sent to Porphyry, the last four not. Porphyry comments that the works written before he knew Plotinus were immature, while those produced in his last years, when Porphyry was away in Sicily, were written when his failing health impaired his genius. Only the twenty-four written in the period when Porphyry was with him "display the maturity of genius" (§6)! This was the period in which, having been entrusted with Plotinus's works for future editing (§7), he urged Plotinus to expound his teachings at greater length in writing (§18). At this point, for-

---

73. Edwards, *Neoplatonic Saints,* xxxvi.

74. For this meaning, see Edwards, *Neoplatonic Saints,* 8 n. 54, which Edwards concludes with the statement: "His [Porphyry's] self-aggrandisement is typical."

getting his earlier admission that Amelius was also urging Plotinus to write (§5), Plotinus instead claims to have inspired Amelius also to write (§18).

The beginning of Porphyry's *Life of Plotinus* reads thus:

> Plotinus, the philosopher who lived in our time, seemed like one who felt ashamed of being in a body. Feeling as he did, he could not endure to talk about his race, his parents or his country of birth. Painters and sculptors were unendurable to him — so much so indeed that, when Amelius begged him to have a portrait done of himself, he said, "Is it not enough to carry the image that nature has put about me?" Did Amelius think that he would agree to leave a more enduring image of the image as though it were some piece worthy of display? So he said no and refused to sit for this purpose; but Amelius had a friend Carterius, the best of the painters living then, whom he got to enter and attend the meetings — it was, in fact, open to anyone to come into the meetings — and accustomed him, by being present more and more, to retain more vivid impressions of what he saw. Then Carterius drew a sketch from the figure that was stored up within his memory, and Amelius helped to make a better likeness of the outline. Carterius had the talent to produce, without the knowledge of Plotinus, a very faithful portrait of him (§1).[75]

This story, while it certainly highlights Amelius, is not exactly to his credit. Edwards calls his role "a foolish and idolatrous attempt to steal the features of his master for a portrait."[76] Porphyry uses the incident to illustrate his opening statement that Plotinus "seemed like one who felt ashamed of being in a body," and for this reason never spoke of his birth or background, the topics with which a biography was expected to begin. But Edwards argues that the story of the portrait also serves to imply that Porphyry's biography will give a truer portrait of Plotinus than the painted one Amelius contrived, against Plotinus's will, to have executed. It subtly anticipates, according to Edwards, Plotinus's contrast between Amelius's accounts of Plotinus's seminar, which were unauthorized, and his own edition of Plotinus's works, which the master commissioned (§§3, 7).[77]

If the story of the portrait implicitly denigrates Amelius at the beginning

75. Translation from Edwards, *Neoplatonic Saints*, 1-2.

76. Edwards, *Neoplatonic Saints*, xxxvi. Cox, *Biography*, 108-11, gives a very different interpretation and speaks of Porphyry's "obvious delight" in the existence of the portrait (108).

77. M. J. Edwards, "A Portrait of Plotinus," *Classical Quarterly* 43 (1993) 480-90, especially 489-90. Unlike Edwards, I do not think that the references to Amelius's copies of Plotinus's writings in §§19-20 are intended as criticism: Porphyry here in fact defends Amelius against the criticism made by Longinus.

of the work, references to Amelius in the latter part of §20 and the earlier part of §21, which are among the last references to Amelius in the book, are the only explicitly negative ones. Here Porphyry quotes and endorses Longinus's criticism of Amelius's own philosophical works, a criticism Porphyry is keen to claim that, in Longinus's view, his own works escaped: "he was perfectly aware that I had in all respects avoided the unphilosophical ramblings of Amelius and was looking to the same goal as Plotinus in my writings" (§21). (After this reference to Amelius there is only one further reference to him, as the one who enquired of the oracle of Apollo about Plotinus after the latter's death [§21].) Here Porphyry claims not only to be the disciple whom Plotinus himself entrusted with editing his writings, but also the true successor to Plotinus in his own philosophical writings. It seems that, while properly acknowledging the importance of Amelius as an eyewitness source of external facts about Plotinus's life, Porphyry at the same time implies that Amelius did not truly understand his master, while Porphyry, who even had the experience of union with the One in common with Plotinus, was the true continuator of Plotinus's philosophy.

This is rather reminiscent of the roles of Peter and the Beloved Disciple in the Gospel of John. Both the Beloved Disciple and Porphyry present themselves as more insightful regarding their respective masters than the generally acknowledged principal disciple and eyewitness, respectively Peter and Amelius. Both present themselves as having been commissioned by the master to represent his legacy after his death, the Beloved Disciple as the witness to Jesus who eventually put his witness into writing, Porphyry as the editor of Plotinus's writings. It is even possible that, just as the Gospel of John incloses the Petrine *inclusio* eyewitness testimony within another such *inclusio*, that of the Beloved Disciple, so Porphyry encompasses the *inclusio* that acknowledges Amelius's testimony with a reference to himself just before and just after the first and last appearances of Amelius in the work. Porphyry's last "I Porphyry" occurs in §23, referring to the fact that he, like Plotinus, experienced union with the One. This is the only occurrence of his name after the last reference to Amelius in §22, and it belongs to Porphyry's interpretation of the oracle of Apollo that Amelius received. Amelius obtained the oracle, but it is Porphyry who truly understood it! However, for an initial reference to Porphyry before the first reference to Amelius we would have to assume that his name as author appeared with the title at the beginning of the work. This may have been the case, but it cannot be taken for granted. The practice of putting a title at the beginning of a scroll was a rather late development.[78]

---

78. J. P. Small, *Wax Tablets of the Mind: Cognitive Studies of Memory and Literacy in Classical Antiquity* (New York: Routledge, 1997) 34.

Mark Edwards has suggested that the *Life of Plotinus* "was intended as a pagan gospel, whose hero, like the Christ of the Fourth Evangelist, is inhabited by a deity."[79] In other words, Porphyry, who wrote fifteen books *Against the Christians,* perhaps around the same time as the *Life of Plotinus,* deliberately portrayed Plotinus as the pagan alternative to the incarnate god of the Christians. His Plotinus is not merely a godlike philosopher but a god sojourning in the flesh among humans like the Johannine Christ.[80] Christianity, to which he strongly objected, was increasingly a serious rival to the kind of religious philosophy that Porphyry, more than Plotinus himself, made of Platonism. Another contemporary work, by Sossianus Hierocles, contrasted the works of Jesus Christ unfavorably with those of Apollonius of Tyana, and drew a response from the Christian theologian and historian Eusebius of Caesarea.[81] Porphyry's fellow disciple Amelius actually spoke with enthusiasm about the prologue to the Gospel of John, evidently giving it a Neo-Platonic interpretation (Eusebius, *Praeparatio Evangelica* 11.19.1; Augustine, *Civitas Dei* 10.29). Porphyry would not have agreed, but he must have known the Gospels quite well, and he was writing at a time when "it had never been more fashionable to treat the lives of intellectual figures as apologetic or controversial weapons."[82]

Thus it is quite possible that the parallels we have pointed out between the *Life of Plotinus* and the Gospels were deliberate on Porphyry's part.[83] Was his use of the *inclusio* of eyewitness testimony also modeled on the Gospels? It is impossible to be sure, but if it was, it is significant for our argument that Porphyry recognized this feature of the Gospels. He is more likely to have done so if he was in any case familiar with this biographical literary device.

79. Edwards, *Neoplatonic Saints,* xxxv, and, in more detail, M. J. Edwards, "Birth, Death, and Divinity in Porphyry's *Life of Plotinus,*" in T. Häag and P. Rousseau, eds., *Greek Biography and Panegyric in Late Antiquity* (Berkeley: University of California Press, 2000) 52-71.

80. Edwards, "Birth," 52-53, here takes issue with Cox, *Biography,* 52, who classifies the *Life of Plotinus* as the sort of biography that portrays a divine philosopher as godlike rather than, as in other cases, as the son of a god.

81. Edwards, *Neoplatonic Saints,* xxxiv.

82. Edwards, *Neoplatonic Saints,* xxxiv. On the other hand, G. Clark, "Philosophic Lives and the Philosophic Life: Porphyry and Iamblichus," in Häag and Rousseau, eds., *Greek Biography,* 42-43, expresses skepticism about the importance of Christianity for Porphyry.

83. Note also the suggestive parallel between the opening sentence of the *Life of Plotinus* — "Plotinus, the philosopher who lived in our time, seemed like one who felt ashamed of being in a body" — and John 1:14: "the Word became flesh and dwelled among us." Both statements substitute for the facts about birth and background with which a biography would commonly begin.

Conclusion

Scholars have often supposed that the Gospel writers cannot have attached much importance to eyewitness testimony since they do not indicate named eyewitness sources of the traditions they use. In previous chapters we have argued that the occurrence of specific personal names in some Gospel stories indicates the eyewitnesses with whom these particular stories were connected in the tradition. We have also argued that the list of the Twelve, carefully preserved and presented in all three Synoptic Gospels, functions as naming the official body of eyewitnesses who had formulated and promulgated the main corpus of Gospel traditions from which much of the content of these Gospels derives.

In the present chapter we have shown that three of the Gospels — those of Mark, Luke, and John — make use of the historiographic principle that the most authoritative eyewitness is one who was present at the events narrated from their beginning to their end and can therefore vouch for the overall shape of the story as well as for specific key events. This principle highlighted the special significance of the Twelve but also of others who were disciples of Jesus for much of the period of his ministry. Accordingly, these three Gospels use the literary device we have called the *inclusio* of eyewitness testimony. This is a convention also deployed in two later Greek biographies, by Lucian and Porphyry, which may lend further weight to the identification of the *inclusio* of eyewitness testimony in three of the Gospels. Though later than the Gospels, these two works may well attest a literary convention that belonged to the tradition of Greco-Roman biographies, of which most examples contemporary with the Gospels have not survived. But however much weight should be given to these parallels outside the Gospels, the data within the Gospels is itself adequate to attest the convention as one that the Gospel writers deliberately deployed. Especially important in establishing the *inclusio* of eyewitness testimony is the way in which Luke and John seem clearly to have recognized Mark's use of the device and to have adapted it to their own narratives and purposes.

Mark's use of the device singles out Peter as the most comprehensive eyewitness source of his Gospel. Luke and John both acknowledge the importance of Peter's testimony by using the device with respect to Peter. In Luke's case, this is his acknowledgement of his use of Mark's Gospel — taken by Luke to embody principally Peter's testimony — as providing the overall structure of his own narrative as well as much specific content. Luke's preface claims firsthand access to people who were eyewitnesses "from the beginning." These can include Peter because Luke takes Mark's Gospel to be substantially Peter's testimony. Probably the women disciples of Jesus were also an important eyewitness source for Luke, indicated by an *inclusio* of the women that is rather less inclusive than the Petrine *inclusio,* but nevertheless very comprehensive (from the Galilean ministry to the empty tomb). John's use of the Petrine *inclusio* is rather more subtle. By creating an *inclusio* of the Beloved Disciple's witness that trumps Peter's by inclosing more, but only a very little more, of John's narrative, John acknowledges the special importance of Peter's testimony, embodied in Mark's Gospel, for his readers' knowledge of Jesus, but also stakes his own Gospel's claim for the, in some respects, superior role of the Beloved Disciple's witness, embodied in John's Gospel.

Thus, contrary to first impressions, with which most Gospels scholars have been content, the Gospels do have their own literary ways of indicating their eyewitness sources. If it be asked why these are not more obvious and explicit in our eyes, we should note that most ancient readers or hearers of these works, unlike scholars of the twentieth and twenty-first centuries, would have expected them to have eyewitness sources, and that those readers or hearers to whom the identity of the eyewitnesses was important would have been alert to the indications the Gospels actually provide.

Table 11: Named Persons in the Gospel of Mark
(excluding Jesus, public figures and OT persons)

	Peter	Sons of Zebedee	Others of the Twelve	Others
1:16	Simon (2)		Andrew	
1:19		James son of Zebedee, John		
1:20				Zebedee
1:29	Simon	James, John	Andrew	
1:30	Simon			
1:36	Simon			
2:14				Levi son of Alphaeus
3:16-19	Simon/Peter	James, son of Zebedee, John brother of James	list of 9	
5:22				Jairus
5:37	Peter	James, John brother of James		
6:3				Mary, James, Joses, Judas, Simon
8:29	Peter			
8:32	Peter			
8:33	Peter			
9:2	Peter	James, John		
9:5	Peter			
9:38		John		
10:28	Peter			
10:35		James, John, sons of Zebedee		
10:41		James, John		
10:46				Bartimaeus son of Timaeus
11:21	Peter			
13:3	Peter	James, John	Andrew	
14:3				Simon the leper
14:10			Judas Iscariot	
14:29	Peter			
14:33	Peter	James, John		

	Peter	Others
14:37	Simon, Peter	
14:43		Judas (Iscariot)
14:54	Peter	
14:66	Peter	
14:67	Peter	
14:70	Peter	
14:72	Peter	
15:21		Simon of Cyrene, father of Alexander and Rufus
15:40		Mary Magdalene
		Mary mother of James the little and Joses
		Salome
15:43		Joseph of Arimathea
15:45		Joseph (of Arimathea)
15:46		Joseph (of Arimathea)
15:47		Mary Magdalene
		Mary mother of Joses
16:1		Mary Magdalene
		Mary mother of James
		Salome
16:7	Peter	

Table 12: Named Persons in Lucian's *Alexander*
(excluding Lucian, his dedicatee Celsus, Alexander, historical and mythological persons, and persons invented by Alexander)

	Rutilianus	others	contemporary persons mentioned but not taking part in the story
4	Rutilianus		
6		Cocconas	
9		Cocconas	
10		Cocconas	
25		Lepidus	
27		Severianus	
			Osroes
30	Rutilianus		
33	Rutilianus		
	Rutilianus		
34	Rutilianus		
35	Rutilianus		
39	Rutilianus	Rutilia	
43		Sacerdos	
		Sacerdos	
		Sacerdos	
		Lepidus	
		Lepidus	
45		Demostratus	
48	Rutilianus		
			emperor Marcus
54	Rutilianus		
	Rutilianus		
55	Rutilianus		
56		Xenophon	
57			king Eupator
			Timocrates
		Avitus	
	Rutilianus		
60	Rutilianus		
		Paetus	
	Rutilianus		

Table 13: Named Persons in Porphyry's *Life of Plotinus*
(excluding Plotinus, historical and mythological persons,
and emperors named only for dating purposes)

	Amelius	Porphyry	others
1	Amelius		
	Amelius		
			Carterius
	Amelius		
			Carterius
2			Eustochius*
			Zethos
			Zethos
			Castricius
			Castricius
			Eustochius*
			Eustochius
			Eustochius*
		I Porphyry	
	Amelius		
			Castricius
			Eustochius
3			Ammonius (Saccas)
			Ammonius (Saccas)
			emperor Gordian (III)
			Ammonius (Saccas)
			emperor Gordian (III)
			Herennius
			Origen
			Ammonius (Saccas)
			Ammonius (Saccas)
			Herennius
			Origen
			Herennius
			Ammonius (Saccas)
	Amelius*		
	Amelius		
			Lysimachus
			Hostilianus Hesychius
4		I Porphyry	
			Antonius
	Amelius		
		I Porphyry	
		I Porphyry	
		Porphyry	

*indicates that at this point Porphyry explicitly indicates that this person was a source of the information he gives.

	Amelius	Porphyry	others
5		Porphyry	
	Amelius		
		I Porphyry	
7	Amelius		
			Paulinus
	Amelius		
			Eustochius
			Zoticus
			Paulinus
			Zethos
			Theodosius
			Ammonius (Saccas)
			Castricius Firmus
	Amelius		
		I Porphyry	
			Marcellus
			Orontius
			Sabinillus
			Rogatianus
			Serapion
		I Porphyry	
9			Gemina (I)
			Gemina (II)
			Amphiclea
			Ariston son of Iamblichus
			Potamon
10			Olympius
			Ammonius
			Olympius
			Olympius
	Amelius		
11			Chione
			Polemon
		I Porphyry	
			Probus
12			emperor Gallienus (III)
			Salonina
13		I Porphyry	
			Thaumasius
		Porphyry	
		Porphyry	
14			Ammonius (Saccas)
			Longinus
			Longinus
			Origen
			Origen

	Amelius	Porphyry	others	contemporary persons mentioned but not taking part in the story
15		Porphyry		
			Diophanes	
		I Porphyry		
			Diophanes Eubulus	
		I Porphyry		
16				Adelphius Aquilinus
	Amelius			
		I Porphyry		
17	Amelius			
			Trypho	
	Amelius			
		I Porphyry		
			Longinus Cleodamus	
		I Porphyry		
			Cleodamus	
	Amelius Amelius			
18		I Porphyry		
	Amelius Amelius Amelius			
		Porphyry		
	Amelius			
		I Porphyry		
	Amelius			
19			Longinus	
	Amelius Amelius			
20	Amelius Amelius			
	Amelius Gentilianus Amelius			
			Longinus	
			Marcellus	
				Euclides Democritus Proclinus
	Gentilianus Amelius			
				Themistocles Phoibion

153

	Amelius	Porphyry	others	contemporary persons mentioned but not taking part in the story
				Annius
				Medius
				Heliodorus
			Ammonius	
			Origen	
				Theodotus
			Eubulus	
			Origen	
			Eubulus	
				Herminus
				Lysimachus
				Athenaeus
				Musonius
				Ammonius (Peripatetic)
				Ptolemaeus
				Ammonius (Peripatetic)
				Euclides
				Democritus
				Proclinus
				Annius
				Medius
				Phoibion
				Heliodorus
	Gentilianus			
	Amelius			
	Amelius			
	Gentilianus			
	(Amelius)			
	Amelius			
	Amelius			
21	Amelius			
	Amelius			
		I Porphyry		
	Amelius			
		I Porphyry		
22	Amelius			
23		I Porphyry		

154

7. The Petrine Perspective in the Gospel of Mark

We have seen that Mark's Gospel has the highest frequency of reference to Peter among the Gospels, and that it uses the *inclusio* of eyewitness testimony to indicate that Peter was its main eyewitness source. Can we go further than this, on the internal evidence of the Gospel itself, in detecting features that relate it closely to Peter? Is there any sense in which the stories are told from a Petrine perspective? Does Peter have an individual significance within the narrative, or is he merely representative of the disciples of Jesus in general? Some older scholarship, inclined to give some credence to the evidence of Papias, who claimed that Mark's Gospel derives from Peter's preaching, sought to identify specifically Petrine characteristics in at least parts of the Gospel.[1] But the tendency of recent scholarship, which has been largely dismissive of Papias's claim, has been to deny that the Gospel shows any sign of being based on traditions mediated by Peter.[2] From most of the scholarly literature it would be easy to get the impression that any connection between the Gospel of Mark and Peter has been conclusively refuted. Since the denial that the Gospel itself shows signs of connection with Peter usually goes hand-in-hand with the view that Papias is untrustworthy in his information about the origins of Mark's Gospel, it is also easy to get the impression that only if one's view of the Gospel is prej-

---

1. E.g. V. Taylor, *The Gospel according to St. Mark* (London: Macmillan, 1952) 82. This is notable in Taylor, a scholar who took full, though not uncritical, account of form criticism.

2. R. E. Brown and J. P. Meier, *Antioch and Rome* (London: Chapman, 1983) 195-96. This sweepingly negative view is representative. P. Perkins, *Peter: Apostle for the Whole Church* (second edition; Edinburgh: Clark, 2000) 53, states bluntly: "Scholars today recognize that Mark is not based upon memories of the apostle Peter."

udiced by Papias is one likely to find Petrine characteristics in the Gospel. We will take a fresh look at Papias on Mark in chapter 9. Here we will offer arguments purely from the internal evidence of Mark's Gospel. From this Gospel's use of a Petrine *inclusio* of eyewitness testimony we already have reason to be open to recognizing further indications of Peter's special connection with this Gospel. The evidence presented in this chapter suggests that such a connection deserves to be given serious consideration again.

The Plural-to-Singular Narrative Device

In a neglected article published in 1925, Cuthbert Turner argued that a characteristic aspect of Mark's narrative composition shows that the story is told from the perspective of a member of the Twelve and that this must be because Mark closely reproduces the way Peter told the story.[3] Major English Gospels scholars of the mid-twentieth century were impressed by the evidence: Thomas Manson accepted the argument but proposed that it be used to distinguish Petrine and non-Petrine sources in Mark,[4] while Vincent Taylor, though partly critical, thought that "it would be fair to claim that these usages suggest that Mark stands nearer to primitive testimony than Matthew or Luke."[5] I am not aware that the evidence adduced by Turner has been subsequently discussed,[6] but it certainly deserves reconsideration.

Turner drew attention to twenty-one passages in Mark in which a plural verb (or more than one plural verb), without an explicit subject,[7] is used to describe the movements of Jesus and his disciples, followed immediately by a singular verb or pronoun referring to Jesus alone. We shall call this nar-

3. C. H. Turner, "Marcan Usage: Notes Critical and Exegetical, on the Second Gospel V. The Movements of Jesus and His Disciples and the Crowd," *JTS* 26 (1925) 225-40; cf. also idem, *Catholic and Apostolic: Collected Papers* (ed. H. N. Bate; Milwaukee: Morehouse, 1931) 183-84. Turner's article is reprinted, along with the rest of his eleven "Notes on Marcan Usage," in J. K. Elliott, *The Language and Style of the Gospel of Mark* (NovTSup 71; Leiden: Brill, 1993). My references are to the original article.

4. T. W. Manson, *Studies in the Gospels and Epistles* (ed. M. Black; Manchester: Manchester University Press, 1962) 40-43.

5. Taylor, *The Gospel according to St. Mark*, 48.

6. S. Byrskog, *Story as History — History as Story* (WUNT 123; Tübingen: Mohr, 2000; reprinted Leiden: Brill, 2002) 289 n. 181, makes brief mention of Manson's argument based on Turner's.

7. Turner rather misleadingly called this an "impersonal plural." He meant that the subject is not expressed. However, a definite personal subject (not merely "people" in general) is implied.

rative pattern "the plural-to-singular narrative device." I have reproduced
Turner's list in Table 14, with two modifications: I have added one instance
that Turner neglected (Mark 9:9) and omitted one for which the textual evidence for the plural verb is extremely weak (11:11). A few examples will illustrate the phenomenon:

> They came to the other side of the sea, to the country of the Gerasenes.
> And when he had stepped out of the boat . . . (5:1-2).

> They came to Bethsaida. Some people brought a blind man to him . . .
> (8:22).

> On the following day, when they came from Bethany, he was hungry
> (11:12).

> They went to a place called Gethsemane; and he said to his disciples . . .
> (14:32).

All but three of the plural verbs in these twenty-one passages are verbs of
movement (the exceptions are in 14:18, 22, 26a).[8] This narrative pattern is thus
overwhelmingly used to refer to the movements of Jesus and the disciples
from place to place. It refers to the itinerant group formed by Jesus and the
closest disciples who traveled with him. Shortly we shall specify the group
more precisely.

This characteristic of Mark's narrative appears much more striking
when we compare the usage of Matthew and Luke in parallel passages (see Table 14). In some cases there is no parallel to the Markan passage at all or the
particular clause containing the plural verb(s) is dropped by Matthew and/or
Luke. In cases where there is a parallel, Matthew retains the plural in nine instances and Luke in only two instances. On six occasions Matthew has a singular verb referring to Jesus alone where Mark has the plural, and Luke similarly has a singular verb on six occasions (not all the same as those in
Matthew). Thus Matthew and Luke have a clear tendency to prefer a singular
verb to Mark's plurals encompassing both Jesus and the disciples. Moreover,
this same tendency is also, very strikingly, reflected in the variant readings of
Mark. In no less than eleven of Mark's twenty-one instances of this narrative
feature, there is a variant reading (more or less well supported) that offers a
singular verb in place of the plural. (In all these cases both Turner and the
printed editions of the Greek New Testament rightly opt for the reading with

8. In fourteen cases the verb is *erchesthai* or a compound of it.

the plural as the more likely original, since it is both the harder reading and consistent with Markan style throughout these passages.[9]) Since the scribes had a tendency to harmonize the texts of the Synoptic Gospels, we might think that these variant readings are the result of their assimilation of the text of Mark to that of Matthew or Luke, but Table 14 shows that this explanation is inadequate, since in five of these cases there is no parallel in Matthew or Luke (Mark 8:22; 9:33; 11:15, 19-21, 27). The scribes must be influenced by the same reasons that led Matthew and Luke to prefer the singular. Further evidence for this, not noted by Turner, can be found in the variant readings of Matthew and Luke. In three cases where Matthew retains Mark's plural and in two where Luke does so, there are variant readings offering the singular. One further piece of the evidence, which Turner neglected to note, is that Luke does have two instances of the plural-to-singular narrative device in passages where there is no Markan parallel. (This brings the total of instances of this device in Luke to four.) Again, in one of these cases there is a variant reading with the singular verb. Interesting as these independent Lukan instances of the feature are, they do not alter the overall picture of the plural-to-singular narrative device as overwhelmingly Markan.

We should note that in some cases the difference between Mark and the other two Synoptics may result simply from the habitual tendency of Matthew and Luke to abbreviate the Markan narratives. But this cannot account for all instances, nor does it explain the phenomenon of the variant readings. Turner's view was that

> the natural and obvious explanation is that we have before us the experience of a disciple and apostle who tells the story from the point of view of an eyewitness and companion, who puts himself in the same group as the Master. . . . Matthew and Luke are Christian historians who stand away from the events, and concentrate their narrative on the central figure.[10]

Turner thought the Markan third-person plurals in these passages were modifications of a first-person plural, used by an eyewitness "to whom the plural came natural as being himself an actor in the events he relates."[11] If "we" is

9. The case where there is serious disagreement among the commentators is Mark 1:29, where the plural makes for a rather incoherent sentence, and some therefore prefer the singular. However, for the same reason, the plural is the harder reading, likely to have been corrected by scribes for the sake of an easier sense. B. M. Metzger, *A Textual Commentary on the Greek New Testament* (Stuttgart: United Bible Societies, 1975) 75, reports this as the majority view on the UBS Committee.

10. Turner, "Marcan Usage," 225.

11. Turner, "Marcan Usage," 226.

substituted for "they" in these passages, they read more naturally, since a distinction between first and third-person is then added to the difference between plural and singular. Turner argued that one passage, awkwardly expressed in Mark's Greek, makes better sense if an underlying "we" is reconstructed. This is 1:29, where the "they" can scarcely include more people than Jesus, Simon, Andrew, James, and John, since these four are so far the only disciples (cf. 1:21):

> In one passage in particular, i 29, "they left the synagogue and came into the house of Simon and Andrew with James and John", the hypothesis that the third person plural of Mark represents a first person plural of Peter makes what as it stands is a curiously awkward phrase into a phrase which is quite easy and coherent. "We left the synagogue and came into our house with our fellow-disciples James and John. My mother-in-law was in bed with fever, and he is told about her. . . ."[12]

Before assessing Turner's argument, we should clarify more precisely whom the "they" of these Markan passages comprises. Sometimes this is quite clear in the Markan context (e.g., Mark 11:11-12), sometimes it has to be inferred. In all cases it is clear that the reference is to Jesus along with some of his disciples. In a few cases, the disciples are named: Peter and Andrew, James and John (1:21, 29), sometimes Peter, James, and John (5:38; 9:9, 14-15), who in this Gospel are represented as the inner circle of the Twelve, those closest to Jesus (cf. also 14:33). In other cases, those following Jesus' arrival in Jerusalem, it is clear that the disciples in question are the Twelve (11:12, 15, 19-21, 27; 14:18, 22, 26-27, 32). In the remaining cases, the issue impinges on the general question of the extent to which Mark's references to Jesus' disciples include disciples other than the Twelve. There are a few cases where Mark refers unequivocally to disciples other than the Twelve (2:14-15; 4:10; 10:32; 15:40-41).[13] I am inclined to the view that Mark implicitly tends to focus exclusively on the Twelve, allowing other disciples to fall out of view.[14] I am also inclined to think that in all the remaining cases of the plural-to-singular narrative device in Mark, the unidentified "they" are probably Jesus and the Twelve rather than a larger group of disciples.

---

12. Turner, "Marcan Usage," 226.

13. The arguments of R. P. Meier, *Jesus and the Twelve: Discipleship and Revelation in Mark* (Grand Rapids: Eerdmans, 1968) chapter 6, to the effect that Mark never refers to disciples other than the Twelve, seem to me to require very implausible interpretations of these texts.

14. Thus to a large extent (limited only by my comment in the previous note) I agree with the general thesis of Meier, *Jesus and the Twelve*.

One of these passages is instructive:

> They were on the road, going up to Jerusalem, and Jesus walking ahead of them; they were amazed, and those who followed were afraid. He took the twelve aside again and began to tell them what was to happen to him (10:32).

Here there has to be a distinction between the "they" who "were amazed" and "those who followed," and the first of these groups must be the same as the disciples implied in the initial "they" who were "on the road." Since Mark never suggests any distinction among followers of Jesus other than the Twelve and others, it is best to take the Twelve to be the subject, along with Jesus, of the first plural verb, and the subject, in contrast with Jesus, of the second plural verb. The rest of the disciples who accompanied Jesus on his journey to Jerusalem are those who "were afraid."[15] Having introduced this group, Mark must specify the Twelve as the group Jesus took aside for private teaching. This passage is also interesting in that begins, as usual in these passages of Mark, by representing Jesus and the Twelve as a single group, and then distinguishes Jesus as walking ahead of the others, visually distinguished from the group. Of course, there is a special reason. Mark is illustrating Jesus' determination, puzzling to his disciples, to go to Jerusalem, the place of most danger to him and them. This distinctive portrayal of Jesus and the Twelve "on the road" highlights by contrast the way in which our Markan feature, comprising both Jesus and the disciples in the same plural verb, represents the group in a companionable rather than hierarchical way. "On the road" Jesus' place as the Master is not evident, though what happens when they arrive somewhere always then serves to single Jesus out as the focus of the narrative.

The plural-to-singular narrative device does not appear in all Markan passages that describe Jesus' movement from place to place. We can divide the other such passages into two broad categories: one in which the disciples (or specified disciples) are mentioned as accompanying Jesus but not included in the generalized way that the plural-to-singular narrative device enables,[16] and another category in which Jesus alone is mentioned as moving.[17] There are about twelve instances of each category, as compared with twenty-one of the plural-to-singular narrative device. In almost all instances of the first cate-

---

15. So C. E. B. Cranfield, *The Gospel according to St Mark* (CGTC; Cambridge: Cambridge University Press, 1959) 335, against more than one different interpretation by other commentators.

16. Mark 2:23; 3:7, 13; 6:1; 7:17; 8:27; 9:2; 11:11, 19; 13:1; 14:17, 33.

17. Mark 1:39; 2:1; 2:13-14; 3:1, 19b; 4:1; 5:21; 6:6b; 7:24, 31; 10:1, 17.

gory (Jesus and disciples explicitly mentioned) it is possible to discern a reason why Mark on this occasion should prefer this style to the plural-to-singular narrative device. (For example, in 3:7, Mark wishes to distinguish the disciples from the crowd, while indicating that both were with Jesus.) This is also the case with a few instances in the second category (Jesus alone) but not with most. These two categories are also those most used in Matthew and Luke when they describe Jesus' movement from place to place.

Thus the plural-to-singular narrative device is the characteristically Markan way of describing Jesus' arrival in a new place, though it is not the only way Mark does so. It is a way of speaking that evidently the other two Synoptic Evangelists and also the scribes who copied the Gospels did not find natural in many cases. In some cases, it seems to be little more than a narrative habit, but in many cases its effect, for readers of Mark, is that they approach a place within, as it were, the group of disciples around Jesus, and then view what happens in the following scene — usually what Jesus does — from the vantage point of the disciples who have arrived there with Jesus. Turner was right to see this narrative feature as adopting the "point of view" of the group of disciples or of someone within the group. If we are to construe this point of view consistently through all these passages, then it should be that of one of the inner group of disciples — Peter, James, and John — since in some cases it is only they and Jesus who are the understood subject of the plural verb. Mark's use of the plural-to-singular narrative device is consistent with the evidence (some of it adduced by Turner) that, by comparison with the more important role of the crowds in Matthew and Luke, Mark is characteristically the Gospel of the disciples or, more precisely, the Gospel of the Twelve. Turner shows, for example, that Mark seems especially concerned to mark out the disciples or the Twelve, distinguished, as a group, from the people in general.[18] That the perspective in the passages we are considering may be understood as from among the inner group of three within the Twelve is also, of course, consistent with the Gospel's references to Peter by name. As we pointed out in chapter 6, Peter is both the first and the last discile to be named in the Gospel, encompassing the whole scope of Jesus' ministry, while Peter is also the most often named disciple in Mark, as well as being named proportionately more often in Mark than in the other Gospels.

It is also relevant to observe that Mark first uses the plural-to-singular narrative device on the first and last occasions Jesus goes anywhere with a group of disciples (1:21; 14:32). Though used sporadically in the intervening narrative rather than at every point, the plural-to-singular narrative device

18. Turner, "Marcan Usage," 227, 234-35.

therefore seems to be used very deliberately by Mark, to make the perspective it gives readers the predominant, though not the only, one through the Gospel's story of Jesus' ministry. This *inclusio* design parallels closely, therefore, the *inclusio* formed by the references to Peter. The first (double) reference to Peter (1:16) is followed very soon by the first use of the plural-to-singular narrative device (1:21), and the next pair of references to Peter coincide with the second occurrence of the plural-to-singular narrative device (1:29-30). The last use of this device is the last time the Twelve are together and with Jesus (14:32), but references to Peter follow thick and fast for a while (14:33, 37, 54, 66, 67, 70, 72). In the story of Peter's denials (14:66-72) the perspective from among the Twelve can be understood as having narrowed to Peter's sole perspective.

Table 15 enables us to see at a glance how there is special emphasis on Peter around the earliest uses of the plural-to-singular narrative device and around the final uses of it. The Petrine *inclusio* is the wider of the two, but its two ends are closely connected with the two ends of the *inclusio* formed by the use of the plural-to-singular narrative device. Uses of the plural-to-singular narrative device and references to Peter also cluster around the mid-point in the narrative (8:22–9:33). There is much to suggest that these two features of Markan composition are closely related. If the perspective provided by the plural-to-singular narrative device is not simply from within the company of Jesus' disciples, but more precisely from within the inner group of Jesus' closest disciples, then its correlation with the references to Peter is readily explicable.

Turner wrote long before the idea of "point of view" (also called "focalization") became widely used in the literary-critical analysis of narrative, and even longer before this narratological usage was applied by Gospels scholars to the study of Mark as narrative.[19] Such scholars rightly point out that the Gospel has an "omniscient" narrator who provides the overriding ideological perspective on the whole story, can tell us information not evident to the characters within the story (e.g., 5:3-5), can access the mind and emotions of any character (e.g., 1:41; 2:6-8; 3:5), and can enable us to see a scene from more than one spatial vantage point (2:2-5). However, within these various possibilities of different kinds of point of view, there is a significant place for what is called, most precisely, internal focalization. Internal focalization

---

19. N. R. Petersen, "'Point of View' in Mark's Narrative," *Semeia* 12 (1978) 97-121; J. Dewey, "Point of View and the Disciples in Mark," *SBL Seminar Papers* (1982) 97-106; S. H. Smith, *A Lion with Wings: A Narrative-Critical Approach to Mark's Gospel* (Sheffield: Sheffield Academic, 1996) chapter 5.

enables readers to view the scene from the vantage point, spatial and (optionally) also psychological, of a character within the story. (External focalization is sharing the view of the narrator who is external to the story.) Internal focalization may be from the perspective of the character portrayed only in an exterior way, in which case the focalization is only spatial and visual or auditory, or in an interior way, in which case the scene can be viewed through the thoughts and feelings of the character.[20] Adequate analysis of narrative requires these categories in addition to the overarching role of the "omniscient" narrator. It is this overarching narrator who describes in words the perspective of a character and who can shift this internal focalization from one character to another.[21] The plural-to-singular narrative device in Mark meets the test for internal focalization (already applied by Turner): that it is possible to rewrite the passage, substituting first-person forms for the third-person references to the focalizing character(s).[22]

Studies of point of view in Mark have missed the plural-to-singular narrative device,[23] characteristic though it is of Mark's Gospel. It is a form of internal focalization, which, as we have argued, enables the readers to view the incident that follows from the perspective of the disciples who have arrived on the scene with Jesus. In a few cases, this perspective soon shifts to another (e.g. 11:15-18), but for the most part it is maintained at least through the pericope that the plural-to-singular narrative device introduces, whereas in many other cases, where this device is not used, the internal focalization shifts once or even a number of times within a single narrative (e.g. 2:2-12; 3:1-6, 20-34; 5:21-43; 6:1-6a, 47-52; 9:14-29). Such shifts of focalization are common in many types of narrative, have their own effectiveness and are not a sign of poor narrative construction.[24] But the fact that Mark does not usually shift the internal focalization in passages introduced by the plural-to-singular nar-

---

20. See S. Rimmon-Kenan, *Narrative Fiction: Contemporary Poetics* (New York: Routledge, 1989) 74-76. M. Bal, *Narratology: Introduction to the Theory of Narrative* (second edition; Toronto: University of Toronto Press, 1997) 142-44, uses "focalization" (which she prefers to G. Genette's term "perspective") only for what Rimmon-Kenan calls "internal focalization." The whole field is rife with terminological differences, which requires that a reader be sure in what sense any particular theorist is using a particular term. There is also a variety of complex typologies of different kinds of "point of view."

21. W. Martin, *Recent Theories of Narrative* (Ithaca: Cornell University Press, 1986) 146.

22. Rimmon-Kenan, *Narrative Fiction*, 75.

23. Dewey, "Point of View," 101, states that the "Markan narrative is almost entirely nonfocalized — presented directly by an omniscient and omnipresent narrator," and then notes a few exceptions, but does not mention this device.

24. Martin, *Recent Theories*, 143-46.

rative device is further proof that he uses this characteristic narrative feature deliberately and with a view to its function for internal focalization.

In most of the passages introduced by the plural-to-singular narrative device, it is only in an exterior way that readers are given the perspective of the disciples. Readers or hearers arrive, as it were, on the scene with the disciples, look over their shoulders, and see and hear the whole scene from that angle. In only a few cases are readers/hearers taken into the disciples' minds in order to share their thoughts and feelings (9:34; 10:32, 34; 14:19). In fact, the inner perspective of the disciples is not very often portrayed in Mark (4:41; 6:49, 51-52; 8:16; 9:6, 10, 32; 10:26, 41). We should recall that in almost all of the passages introduced by the plural-to-singular narrative device the plural verb is one of movement. It is primarily a device for getting readers into spatial position vis-à-vis the scene in which Jesus then acts.

The device is evidently deployed in Mark's narrative strategy in a deliberate and calculated way. It is not, as Turner's argument tends to suggest, a *mere* relic of the way Peter told his stories orally. But in that case, need it be explained with reference to an oral background at all? Is Mark's use of it as a literary device not sufficient explanation of its place in his narrative? Two points are relevant. First, we should recall that, in the Gospels, it is an unusual device, used independently of Mark only twice in Luke, and a device that, in many cases, both the other Synoptic Evangelists and the scribes evidently felt to be inappropriate. It is out of the ordinary and therefore requires an explanation adequate to that fact. Secondly, we should recall how it seems to operate in parallel with the *inclusio* of eyewitness testimony, forming its own *inclusio* around the whole ministry of Jesus, and closely related to the pattern of references to Peter. While the Petrine *inclusio* is Mark's literary means of indicating Peter as the main eyewitness source of the Gospel, the plural-to-singular narrative device appropriately makes the dominant perspective (internal focalization) within the Gospel's narrative the perspective of Peter and those closest to him. It enables readers to share the *eyewitness* perspective on the events that Peter's testimony embodied. Of course, the freedom of the omniscient narrator to shift perspective frequently means that Peter's is by no means the only perspective readers of Mark are given. But there is sufficiently frequent reestablishment of the Petrine perspective for it to be the dominant form of internal focalization, just as there are sufficient references to Peter to keep readers aware of Peter's special relationship to this narrative.

This understanding of the literary function of the plural-to-singular narrative device in Mark makes it, in effect, Mark's way of deliberately reproducing in his narrative the first-person perspective — the "we" perspective — from which Peter naturally told his stories.

The Role of Peter in Mark

Given our conclusion about the function of the plural-to-singular narrative device, we need now to look more closely at the figure of Peter himself in the Gospel of Mark. We have noted the frequency with which his name appears in the Gospel, as well as the way these references seem to relate to the plural-to-singular narrative device, which gives the reader a point of view from within the disciple group, larger or smaller. The two features cluster, we have seen, around the same parts of the Gospel narrative. However, it is also the case that only four pericopes that are introduced by this narrative device are pericopes in which Peter appears as a character (1:29-31; 11:19-25; 14:26-31, 32-42), leaving eight other pericopes in which the narrative device is not used but Peter appears (1:16-20, 35-39; 5:35-37; 8:27-30, 31-33; 9:2-8; 10:23-31; 14:[54], 66-72).[25] Again it may be significant that pericopes in which both features are found occur at the beginning and end of the sequence: 1:29-31 is the second passage introduced by the plural-to-singular narrative device, while 14:32-42 is the last that is introduced in this way. In this way the two features are closely linked at the beginning and the end of the sequence. But what of those pericopes that lack the narrative device but do feature Peter as a character? Does this appearance of Peter as an individual who acts and speaks also give us a Petrine perspective on the events?

Studies of Mark's Gospel usually state that Peter appears, not in his own right, but as representative of the disciple group, whether this be the larger group, the Twelve, or the inner circle of three or four (Peter, James, John, and sometimes Andrew). Timothy Wiarda, in a rather cogent argument against this view,[26] has pointed out that the idea of Peter as "representative" is used in two rather different senses. In one sense Peter, within the narrative world of the Gospel, intentionally acts as a spokesman for the other disciples, whereas, in the other sense, in relation to the reader or hearer of the Gospel, he is representative of the group of the disciples in the sense of exemplifying or sharing the characteristics of the group.[27]

In the latter sense Peter is merely a typical disciple, the one the Evangelist chooses to name. In 14:37-38, when Jesus finds Peter, James, and John sleeping in Gethsemane, he first addresses Peter in particular ("Simon, are you asleep? Could you not keep awake one hour?"), but continues with a plural address to

25. In 16:1-8 Peter is named but does not appear.
26. T. Wiarda, "Peter as Peter in the Gospel of Mark," *NTS* 45 (1999) 19-37. In what follows I am especially indebted to Wiarda's article, though I have framed the issues in a different way and do not agree with all of his argument.
27. T. Wiarda, "Peter," 20-21.

all three ("Keep awake and pray . . ."). Peter is evidently typical of the three.[28] If we ask why, in that case, Peter is singled out, the reason has to do with Jesus' prediction that Peter would deny him (14:30). In view of the fervency of Peter's assertion of loyalty to Jesus (14:31), his falling asleep in Gethsemane, though typical of the disciples, is especially notable in his case, and prepares the way for the narrative in which his disloyalty to Jesus exceeds that of the other disciples, when he denies Jesus (14:54, 66-72).[29] Another instance in which Peter's role is typical of the group seems to be in 11:21, where there is no reason to think Peter is deliberately acting as spokesman for the other disciples, but where what he says could, it seems, have been said by any of them.[30] Hence Jesus' reply is addressed to them all (11:21-25). In 1:36-37, where the subject of the plural verbs is "Simon and those with him" (presumably James, John, and Andrew), Peter is clearly typical of the whole group, but the specific mention of Peter (Simon) by name may suggest that he plays the initiating or leading role.[31]

In 9:5-6, Peter's inept suggestion is explained by the fact that he "did not know what to say, for they were terrified" (9:6). Here Peter shares the fear of all three disciples and presumably a common failure to understand what they see. In that sense Peter is typical, and this is reinforced by the address of the heavenly voice to all three disciples (9:7). But Peter's suggestion is surely his own thinking. He is not a spokesman for the others, voicing their thoughts, but takes an individual initiative. In this case his role goes beyond that of typical disciple, but does not fall into the category of spokesman.[32]

A case in which Peter is often said to be speaking for the group is 8:29.[33] Here Jesus' question ("But who do you say that I am?") is addressed to all the disciples, but it is Peter who answers with the confession that Jesus is the Messiah. It is hard to tell to what extent Peter here voices what all the disciples think. His role may be less spokesman than "opinion leader."[34] After the generalized words of the disciples in v. 28, the attribution of the confession in

28. In Matthew's version Jesus addresses himself to Peter, but what he says is entirely directed, in the second person plural, to the disciples generally (26:40-41). Luke omits all reference to Peter at this point (22:46).

29. Wiarda, "Peter," 31-32; R. E. Brown, *The Death of the Messiah*, vol. 1 (New York: Doubleday, 1994) 194-95.

30. Matthew's version here substitutes a question asked by all the disciples (21:20). There is no parallel in Luke.

31. Cf. Wiarda, "Peter," 27-28.

32. Cf. Wiarda, "Peter," 30, against, e.g., R. T. France, *The Gospel of Mark* (NIGTC; Grand Rapids: Eerdmans, 2002) 354.

33. E.g., France, *The Gospel of Mark*, 329.

34. Wiarda, "Peter," 28, 34. C. A. Evans, *Mark 8:27–16:20* (WBC 34B; Nashville: Nelson, 2001) 45, says merely that Peter plays "a leading role."

v. 29 specifically to Peter needs explanation. The insight may be Peter's own, which, once he has spoken it, Jesus implicitly approves and therefore assumes the other disciples will now share. In any case, Peter's words take their place in a continuing conversation of Jesus with the disciples generally about his messiahship (8:30-31). When Peter then takes Jesus aside, to rebuke him (v. 32), we may think the scene has shifted to a private conversation between Jesus and Peter. However, Jesus' response to Peter is pictured thus: "turning and looking at his disciples, [Jesus] rebuked Peter." The significance must be that Jesus thinks the other disciples also deserving of the rebuke he delivers to Peter. Thus, to some extent, Peter's attitude must be typical of the disciples. Probably only he has the temerity to express it, and he takes Jesus aside so as not to embarrass him before the group. But there is no reason to think that he is speaking on behalf of the others. Again, Peter's role goes beyond, while also including, the typical, but should probably not be characterized as that of spokesman. It is more a case of individuality, as in v. 29.

Something similar is also the case in 14:27-31. Jesus predicts that all of the Twelve will desert him. Peter protests, "Even though all become deserters, I will not" (v. 29), thus making himself a potential exception among the group. Jesus predicts his denials, at which Peter again protests: "Even though I must die with you, I will not deny you." Then the others agree: "all of them said the same" (14:31). There is a delicate interaction here between Peter as typical and as individual. As in 8:29, Wiarda's term, "opinion former,"[35] may be justified. Peter as an individual vows his complete loyalty to Jesus and de-termination to follow this through, even if the others fail to do so. But the others follow his lead.

There is just one case where it is clear that Peter acts as spokesman for the group: in 10:28 he speaks in the first person plural, representing all the disciples. Peter's role, we must conclude with Wiarda, is only very rarely that of spokesman.[36] Wiarda points out that there are many passages in the Gos-pel where a spokesman for the disciples could have been used, but where the disciples in fact speak corporately ("they said"). There is also one case where John plays the role of spokesman (9:38).[37] The role that Peter does often play is that of typical disciple, to some degree at least, a role that is underlined by the fact that Jesus only once addresses him purely as an individual (the pre-diction of his denials: 14:30). Even when Jesus calls Peter to be a disciple, he

35. Wiarda, "Peter," 34.

36. Wiarda, "Peter," 34. Matthew makes a little more use of Peter as a spokesman for the disciples: 15:15; 18:21.

37. Wiarda, "Peter," 26-27.

addresses his brother Andrew too (1:17). In other cases where Jesus addresses Peter specifically, he is also looking over Peter's shoulder, as it were, to include the rest of the group (8:33; 14:37). In addition there are cases where Peter's words to Jesus evoke a response that Jesus addresses generally to all the disciples with no specific address to Peter at all (8:30; 11:22). Peter, we could say, is always aligned with the other disciples, whether as typical or as giving a lead. Even before the story of the denials, Peter has much more individuality in this Gospel than any of the other disciples, but it is an individuality that always emerges within the context of the group.

This is a significant conclusion because it coheres closely with what we discovered was the function of the plural-to-singular narrative device in Mark. That device functions to give the readers a perspective on events *from within* the circle of the disciples, sometimes more precisely from within the inner circle of Peter, James, and John. If we understand this perspective as Peter's, we could call it Peter's "we" perspective (as distinguished from his "I" perspective), stressing that it is Peter's perspective as member of the discipleship group. This is coherent with the fact that, when Peter is named, he is always aligned with the others to a significant extent, and his individuality, when it emerges, does so in the context of that group membership. He is distinguished from the other disciples only at the same time as he is identified with them. He initiates, he leads, he speaks out when others do not, he even professes greater loyalty to Jesus than they have, but he never relates to Jesus as an individual unrelated to the group.

In this way Peter as an individual acts, narratologically, as a further means of focalization for the reader or hearer, continuous with the effect of the plural-to-singular narrative device but more specified. The plural-to-singular narrative device gives readers or hearers a perspective on events from within the group of disciples, larger or smaller. Readers or hearers seem to be traveling with the group of Jesus and his disciples and arriving with them at a scene where they then observe Jesus from the perspective of the disciples. When Peter takes a role as a named individual in a scene, readers or hearers are given more specifically Peter's perspective on events. Now they view not merely from within the group of disciples, but with one disciple who for the time being is distinguished from the others. They see not only Jesus but also the other disciples from Peter's point of view. This happens most effectively in 8:27-33 and 14:27-31 (the two instances in the Gospel where Jesus addresses Peter individually), in 9:5-6 (where Peter's inner motivation is explicitly disclosed), and also, of course, in the story of Peter's denials, the only passage in which readers or hearers go with Peter into a situation physically removed from the other disciples (14:54, 66-72).

So far we have seen that Peter is often typical of the disciples, rarely a spokesman for them, but often emerges as an individual who is both typical and yet more than typical of the disciples. If we focus on this combination of typicality and individuality, we will be able to clarify further the specific narrative role of Peter in the Gospel. The portrayal of the male disciples (especially the Twelve) in Mark's Gospel revolves around two main themes: understanding–non-understanding–misunderstanding and loyalty–apostasy.[38] In both cases, the disciples oscillate between the possibilities, but the negative pole in each case (misunderstanding and apostasy) tends to predominate, resulting in the overall portrayal of them as fallible and failing disciples, whose inability to understand the necessity for Jesus' suffering and death is connected with their failure to remain faithful to him when his passion begins. (There is a contrast here with the women disciples, who alone remain faithful to Jesus when the male disciples have all deserted him, though there is no indication that the women understand Jesus' messianic destiny any better than the men.)

In regard to both of these main themes, Peter is both typical of the disciples in general and also carries the theme, for either good or ill, beyond the extent to which it characterizes the other disciples. This is apparent in the two main narrative sequences which feature Peter.

In the first of these sequences (8:27–9:13) the theme is understanding-misunderstanding. It is Peter who first understands Jesus to be the Messiah (8:29) — a turning point in the Gospel narrative — and also Peter who so far misunderstands what this means that he actually rebukes Jesus, who therefore calls him "Satan" (8:32-33). However precisely one construes the relationship of Peter to the other disciples in these instances, he surpasses them in both understanding and misunderstanding. Then in 9:5-6, while he shares James and John's fear and misunderstanding, it is Peter who actually comes out with an embarrassingly inappropriate suggestion.

The second sequence runs from the Last Supper to Peter's denials of Jesus, and here the theme is loyalty-apostasy. When Jesus predicts that all the disciples will desert him and that Peter will deny him, Peter himself claims that his loyalty to Jesus is greater than that of the others (14:29), who nevertheless join him in determining to die rather than deny Jesus (v. 31). Peter already begins to fail in Gethsemane, though neither more nor less than the others (v. 37-38). However, when the rest of the disciples desert Jesus (v. 50), Peter really does surpass them in loyalty, following Jesus, albeit cautiously at a distance, to the high priest's house (v. 54). But this surpassing loyalty is then

---

38. Smith, *A Lion*, 64.

matched by surpassing disloyalty, for it is only Peter who actually denies having anything to do with Jesus (v. 66-72). Just as his failure to understand Jesus took the extreme form of rebuking him (8:32), so his failure to stand by Jesus in danger takes the extreme form of denying Jesus. (The extreme nature of this apostasy is underlined by the fact that 14:71 probably means that Peter invoked a curse on Jesus.[39]) Thus the story of Peter's denials is not really an exception to the rule that Peter is always to some degree aligned with the other disciples. He is typical of them all in his failure, but surpasses them in the manner of his failure.[40]

We might suppose that neither the Twelve in general nor Peter in particular recover either from their failure to understand Jesus or from their apostasy, but the reference to "his disciples and Peter" in the message of the angel in the tomb (16:7) points to a reunion in which, surely, they will recognize Jesus' true identity and be forgiven their apostasy.[41] All the disciples need this, but none more than Peter. Hence the seemingly redundant specification of Peter alongside "his disciples" (16:7). Peter is the first and the last among the disciples, not only literally in the text of the Gospel (1:16; 16:7), but also in being the foremost in understanding and loyalty while failing the most miserably and blatantly in both. On this account of the main roles Peter plays in the narrative, we can see that they are integral to the two main concerns of the Gospel: the nature of Jesus' identity and mission and the nature of discipleship. (These two are, of course, closely connected with each other.)

If we relate this finding to the way the pattern of reference to Peter forms an *inclusio* of eyewitness testimony (see chapter 6), then we can see how Mark has deployed his main eyewitness source in the interests primarily of these two main concerns of his Gospel. As with the plural-to-singular narrative device, we must recognize that Peter's role in the Gospel is not *merely* a reflection of the way Peter himself told the stories. It is too well integrated into the overall message of the Gospel and into the way in which Mark's masterly composition of his narrative is controlled by his main concerns as an author. But this is no argument against the claim that Peter himself was Mark's major eyewitness source or that the prominence of Peter in the Gospel reflects this. It simply means that Mark is an author in full control of his sources.

39. France, *The Gospel of Mark*, 622; R. E. Brown, *The Death of the Messiah*, vol. 2 (New York: Doubleday, 1994) 604-5.

40. This conclusion is almost the direct opposite of that reached by E. Best, *Mark: The Gospel as Story* (Edinburgh: Clark, 1983) 28: "If the information about Peter's failures came from Peter himself, then Mark has turned our attention away from Peter and towards the other disciples."

41. Best, *Mark*, 47-48.

What is most notably lacking in Mark's portrayal of Peter, when we compare it with the other Gospels, is treatment of Peter's preeminent role in the early Christian community after the resurrection such as we find in Matt 16:13-19; Luke 22:31-32; and John 21:4-19. As well as these passages we should note the difference between Mark and Luke in their account of the call of Peter and the three other fishermen. In Mark Jesus' promise "I will make you fish for people" (1:17), which probably does envisage the disciples' future missionary role after the resurrection, is addressed to both Peter and Andrew and should probably be understood as repeated to James and John (1:20). But in Luke, who links the call with the miraculous catch of fish, a symbol of future missionary success, the narrative is highly focused on Peter (5:4-10) and Jesus' promise is addressed individually to him (5:10). Luke already in this passage portrays Peter as called to a preeminent role in the community's future mission.

The absence of this Petrine theme from Mark[42] is perhaps best understood as due to the very focused purpose of this short Gospel: to demonstrate Jesus' true messianic identity and the kind of discipleship that it entails. The issue of leadership in the community of Jesus' disciples is very minor and appears in Mark only in Jesus' insistence that it be a matter of service in accordance with his own messianic exemplification of service and suffering (9:33-35; 10:35-45). Mark's main treatment of this theme focuses on James and John (10:35-45) rather than Peter and constitutes the most substantial instance of a focus in the Gospel on named male disciples other than Peter (cf. 1:19-20; 2:14-15; 9:38-41). We should probably conclude that this motif was attached to James and John rather than Peter in the traditions Mark knew. The absence in Mark of any allusion to Peter's preeminence in the Christian movement has one significant implication: the reason for Peter's prominence in this Gospel is not connected with the role he would later play in the Christian community and its mission.

What then accounts for Peter's prominence in Mark? We need to account for the large extent to which the point of view that the narrative gives its readers or hearers is either Peter's "we" perspective (the plural-to-singular narrative device) or Peter's "I" perspective (when Peter acts as an individual in the story). Taken together, these features make Mark a Gospel that presents, to a far larger degree than the others, a Petrine perspective on the story of Jesus. The explanation must have two aspects: relating to the source of Mark's traditions and to the way in which Mark has shaped these traditions in the service of his main concerns in his overall composition of the Gospel.

---

42. Though Mark 3:16 states that Jesus gave Simon the name Peter, no explanation of the name is given.

With regard to Mark's sources, the evidence is at the very least consistent with, at most highly supportive of, the hypothesis that Mark's main source was the body of traditions first formulated in Jerusalem by the Twelve, but that he knew this body of traditions in the form in which Peter related them. We can hardly expect to be able to distinguish features peculiar to Peter's version of these traditions, since he was doubtless already prominent in the traditions as the Twelve told them. But we should raise at this point an objection that has often been made to the hypothesis that Peter's preaching stands behind Mark's Gospel: Why then do we not find much more in the way of personal reminiscences of Peter in the Gospel? Does not the way in which Peter, despite being so prominent in the Gospel, is always aligned with the other disciples, never alone with Jesus, and only rarely addressed individually by Jesus tell against the claim that Peter himself was the source of the Petrine material? At least part of the answer to this objection entails asking what kind of personal reminiscences we should expect Mark to have heard from Peter. We should not imagine an aged apostle reminiscing expansively in autobiographical mode, but an apostle fulfilling his commission to preach the Gospel and to teach believers, relating the traditions he has been recounting throughout his life as an apostle in the forms in which he had cast the memories of the Twelve and himself for ease of teaching and communication.

Furthermore, we must not neglect the role of Mark's own composition. Judging from the wide range of Jesus traditions attested in the other canonical Gospels, not to mention noncanonical Gospel traditions, it is clear that Mark has been quite selective in choosing material for his very short Gospel. It is, for example, hardly conceivable that Mark knew no traditions of the sayings of Jesus other than those he includes in his Gospel, which are surprisingly few in the light of his emphasis on Jesus as a teacher. We cannot tell what interesting memories of Peter Mark has left aside in a narrative that is so strongly focused on certain definite concerns.

The Characterization of Peter in Mark

We have defined Peter's role in Mark's narrative, but what of Peter's character? The tendency of scholars to treat Peter merely as representative of the disciples in general has usually been accompanied by a parallel tendency to claim that Peter merely shares the characterization Mark gives the disciples or the Twelve as a character group. Clifton Black, for example, writes that "Peter's blend of attributes, favorable and unfavorable, is not unique to him but, instead, embodies the general virtues and failings of the Twelve."[43] We have seen that Peter is by no means merely typical of the Twelve, but emerges as an individual, albeit an individual member of the group of the disciples. In doing so we have followed Timothy Wiarda. But Wiarda argues not only that Peter has an individual role in the narrative (as do many other individuals, such as Bartimaeus or Pilate); he also argues that Peter is individually characterized.[44]

He rightly argues that recognition of this should not be impeded either by a social-scientific picture of ancient Mediterranean society as group-oriented rather than individualistic or by the literary argument that ancient literature offered only stock characters or types, not characters individually differentiated by specific character traits.[45] On the first point we need only argue that, quite apart from whether the Hellenistic world had in fact a stronger concept of the individual than standard social-scientific descriptions of "Mediterranean persons" allow,[46] in any case the latter merely require that individuals understood themselves and were understood as related to a group, as "dyadic" or, better, "polyadic"[47] and "socially embedded" persons.[48] We have already argued that Peter appears in Mark as an individual who is never

43. C. C. Black, *Mark: Images of an Apostolic Interpreter* (second edition; Minneapolis: Fortress, 2001) 205.

44. Wiarda does not himself make this distinction between role and characterization; he seems to be operating with a notion of individuality in narrative that combines the two.

45. Wiarda, "Peter," 22-25.

46. G. W. Burnett, *Paul and the Salvation of the Individual* (Biblical Interpretation Series 57; Leiden: Brill, 2001) Part 1; F. W. Burnett, "Characterization and Reader Construction of Characters in the Gospels," *Semeia* 63 (1993) 11-12 (evidence from Greek and Roman portraiture). In addition, Louise Lawrence, *An Ethnography of the Gospel of Matthew: A Critical Assessment of the Use of the Honour and Shame Model in New Testament Studies* (WUNT 2/165; Tübingen: Mohr, 2003) chapter 7, provides an important critique, well based on the social scientific literature, of the use of Mediterranean anthropology by Bruce Malina and his school on the matter of individualism and collectivism. She concludes: "Anthropology attests the significance of individualistic traits even in primarily collectivist cultures. Both Graeco-Roman and Jewish voices witness to both individualistic and collectivist traits. . . . [While] the people populating Matthew's world are certainly concerned with collectivist group identity and their relationships with others, this focus does not deny the importance of individualistic self-understanding" (258-59).

47. This term is used by Lawrence, *An Ethnography,* 249, as preferable to "dyadic."

48. B. J. Malina, *The Social World of Jesus and the Gospels* (New York: Routledge, 1996) 37-44. Note also, from a literary perspective, D. McCracken, "Character in the Boundary: Bakhtin's Interdividuality in Biblical Narratives," *Semeia* 63 (1993) 29-42, arguing that "Character conceived in individual terms is inadequate for biblical character, which involves an essential relationship to others, an *inter*dividuality of the sort described by Bakhtin" (29).

unrelated to the group of disciples of Jesus. This certainly involves his sharing some general characteristics that Mark attributes to the disciples in general (loyalty and disloyalty, perceptiveness and obtuseness),[49] but it does not rule out characteristics that especially distinguish him as an individual within the group.[50]

As for the tendency of ancient literature to portray only character types, this can easily be exaggerated. Certainly the ancients lacked our modern sense of idiosyncratic and psychologically complex personalities, a difference that partly correlates with the fact that characters are constructed by their actions more than by psychological introspection.[51] Writing of Greek drama, Christopher Pelling says:

> The playwrights combine in their characters traits which group naturally, and do not furnish any paradoxical or unique combinations; in that sense they are far removed from what we are accustomed to find in modern works. But that in itself does not render these characters "types": Oedipus' energetic intelligence in *Oedipus Tyrannus* groups perfectly naturally with his other traits, as does Ajax's strong adherence to an exaggerated Homeric ethic, or Antigone's singleminded harshness to her sister. These are not reducible to a single "Sophoclean hero," but in each case the new trait combines very readily with the old ones. This is not an idiosyncratic character-mix, then, but one which might readily recur in another human being or dramatic creation; yet in each case we have an individual, grasped and realized as distinct and different, none the less.[52]

It is also important to recognize, in ancient literary accounts of persons, a spectrum from type to individual that can operate within a single text, such that it is possible "even for the typical character to fluctuate between type and individuality."[53] Fred Burnett comments that therefore

---

49. Wiarda, "Peter," 32-33.

50. Nor does it rule out the kind of wholly self-interested behavior Peter displays when he denies Jesus: cf. Malina, *The Social World*, 38: "Behavior that indicates self-concerned individualism is noticed, but it is disdained and variously sanctioned."

51. Cf. R. A. Burridge, *What Are the Gospels?* (SNTSMS 70; Cambridge: Cambridge University Press, 1992) 121; S. Halliwell, "Traditional Greek Conceptions of Character," in C. B. R. Pelling, ed., *Characterization and Individuality in Greek Literature* (Oxford: Clarendon, 1990) 56-59; Burnett, "Characterization," 11, 15-16.

52. C. B. R. Pelling, "Conclusion," in Pelling, ed., *Characterization*, 254-55; cf. also Burnett, "Characterization," 12-13.

53. Burnett, "Characterization," 15. Burnett himself applies this understanding to the character of Peter in Matthew's Gospel (20).

it would seem wise to understand characterization, for any biblical text at least, on a continuum. This would imply for narratives like the Gospels that the focus should be on the degree of characterization rather than on characterization as primarily typical.[54]

This makes it plausible to claim that, in the Gospel of Mark, Peter is not only typical of the disciples to some degree, but also the *most fully* characterized individual in the Gospel, apart from Jesus.[55]

Mark's distinctive characterization of Peter, not surprisingly, does not employ direct character description, but constructs Peter's character by means of his acts and words. Peter is a man of initiative (1:36?) and self-confidence, the one who speaks out when others do not (8:29, 32; 10:28), sometimes with insight (8:29), sometimes altogether too impulsively (8:32; 9:5-6). Even in these latter cases, Peter means well and shows his concern for Jesus even as he misunderstands him. In his enthusiastic and self-confident loyalty to Jesus he thinks himself second to none (14:29-31). He does display more courage in his loyalty to Jesus than the others do (14:50, 54), but loyalty and fear are at odds in his motivation. In his fearful, self-interested denial of Jesus he slips from a relatively mild dissociation from Jesus to the most extreme repudiation (14:68-71). But his loyalty and love for Jesus regain their primacy and express themselves in emotional remorse (14:72).[56] The implication here of a moment of self-recognition, as his illusory self-confidence is destroyed, is also important in showing that Peter is not a *static* character, but one who acquires fresh self-awareness in a life-changing experience.

Some scholars have interpreted Mark's portrayal of Peter, with its strongly negative features, as polemic against Peter,[57] just as his portrayal of

---

54. Burnett, "Characterization," 15; cf. also 18-19.

55. Note also the argument of Lawrence, *An Ethnography*, 246-48, that in Matt 16:13-26 Matthew's Peter is strongly characterized as an individual: "Peter is marked out as a character with individual traits that set him apart from the other disciples." This refers especially to vv. 17-19, which are not paralleled in Mark, but it shows that a scholar well versed in the social scientific literature on individualistic and collectivist cultures can recognize strongly individualizing features in another Gospel's portrayal of Peter. The argument at least opens up the possibility that individual characterization of Peter also occurs in Mark.

56. On the acute translation problem in v. 72, see Brown, *The Death of the Messiah*, vol. 2, 609-10. That Peter wept is not in doubt, but the meaning of the preceding verb *(epibalōn)* here seems impossible to determine with confidence. It must however have functioned to stress Peter's extreme grief.

57. T. V. Smith, *Petrine Controversies in Early Christianity* (WUNT 2/15; Tübingen: Mohr, 1985) 187-90, discusses the views of earlier scholars who have taken this view, concluding: "It is *possible* that the anti-Peter stance should be seen as anti-Peter *polemic*" (190).

the disciples in general (or the Twelve) is similarly understood as polemical.[58] One way in which this can be seen to be mistaken is by observing how Mark takes the trouble to maintain his readers' or hearers' sympathy with Peter. The negative elements in Mark's narratives of Peter are clearly not condoned by the Gospel writer: readers and hearers are expected to disapprove of Peter's behavior on the two occasions when it earns a rebuke from Jesus (8:33; 14:37-38), as well when he disowns and curses Jesus (14:66-72). In themselves this series of incidents could have the effect of alienating readers or hearers from Peter, putting him at an increasing distance from them.[59] However, as Thomas Boomershine argues, this effect is forestalled by the steps Mark takes to maintain or to reestablish their sympathy for Peter. In the case of Peter's misunderstanding of Jesus' messiahship (8:32), very serious though Jesus' response shows it to be (8:33), it follows Peter's perception that Jesus is the Messiah (8:29), which will incline readers or hearers to see him as well-meaning, even though impetuous and foolish. Moreover, very soon after this serious mistake on Peter's part, readers or hearers are once again drawn into sympathy with Peter in the transfiguration narrative. Inept as Peter's suggestion of building booths for Jesus and his heavenly visitors is, Mark immediately explains it: "He did not know what to say, for they were terrified" (9:6). This glimpse into Peter's thoughts and feelings "is clearly an appeal for identification with Peter whose feelings are presented as the way any person would feel in such company."[60]

Similar sympathetic notes of explanation are provided by the author when Peter and the others fail Jesus by falling asleep in Gethsemane. In the first place, Jesus himself says: "the spirit is willing, but the flesh weak" (14:38), implying that they meant well. Secondly, the author comments: "their eyes were very heavy and they did not know what to say to him" (14:40). Boomershine suggests that the first part of this could remind readers or hearers of the customary consumption of a considerable amount of wine at a Passover meal and continues:

---

58. E.g., T. J. Weeden, "The Heresy That Necessitated Mark's Gospel," *ZNW* 59 (1968) 145-58; idem, *Mark: Traditions in Conflict* (Philadelphia: Fortress, 1971); W. Kelber, *Mark's Story of Jesus* (Philadelphia: Fortress, 1979); idem, *The Oral and the Written Gospel: The Hermeneutics of Speaking and Writing in the Synoptic Tradition, Mark, Paul and Q* (Philadelphia: Fortress, 1983). For critique of this view, see E. Best, "The Role of the Disciples in Mark," *NTS* 23 (1976-77) 377-401; R. C. Tannehill, "The Disciples in Mark: The Function of a Narrative Role," *JR* 57 (1957) 386-405; T. E. Boomershine, "Peter's Denial as Polemic or Confession: The Implications of Media Criticism for Biblical Hermeneutics," *Semeia* 39 (1987) 47-68.

59. Cf. Smith, *A Lion*, 67.

60. Boomershine, "Peter's Denial," 57.

The internal description of their inability to find something to say concretizes their shame. What does one say when a beloved friend has been disappointed in his hour of greatest need, even if it couldn't be helped? These narrative comments are inside views explaining their situation and their feelings. The comments do not in any way indicate that the disciples' going to sleep was anything other than wrong. But the narrative function of these comments is to enable the listeners to understand and sympathize with their inability to stay awake. Thus, the episode is an appeal for sympathetic identification and prevents alienation or negative distance.[61]

As for the story of Peter's denials, which might have been the climax of a process of alienation from Peter on the part of readers or hearers, it ends with what Boomershine calls "the most extensive and poignant inside view in his entire narrative."[62] Readers or hearers share Peter's anguished remembering and grief. They also recognize the potentially transforming nature of his self-recognition as a culpable and abject failure.

Thus the full and nuanced characterization of Peter has the effect of encouraging readers or hearers to sympathize and identify with him,[63] further promoting that focalization or seeing from Peter's perspective that we have already seen to be a function of his appearance as an individual distinguished from the other disciples.

A remarkable feature of this characterization of Peter is that it remains constant through all four canonical Gospels. Petrine material in the other Gospels that is not parallel to Mark's displays the same character traits in Peter: impetuosity, self-confidence, outspokenness, and extravagant devotion to Jesus (Matt 14:28-33; Luke 5:8; 22:33; John 6:68-69; 13:6-10; 20:2-10; 21:7, 15-19). Is this to be explained by the impact of the historical Peter preserved in various traditions independently? Or by the influence of Mark's portrayal of Peter on the other Gospel writers? Or by some kind of character stereotype of Peter in the early Christian movement that influenced all the traditions? New Testament scholars do not seem to have addressed this issue, which deserves attention that cannot be given it here.

It has long been debated whether Mark's predominantly negative portrayal of Peter, as the foolishly self-confident disciple who misunderstands Jesus and fails him, could plausibly derive from Peter's own self-depiction.[64] On the

61. Boomershine, "Peter's Denial," 58.
62. Boomershine, "Peter's Denial," 58.
63. Wiarda, "Peter," 36.
64. E.g., Black, *Mark*, 204-5.

one hand, it can be argued that no one in the early church other than Peter himself would have dared or wished to highlight the weakness and failure of the revered apostle with the candor Mark's narrative does.[65] On the other hand, Pheme Perkins claims that "the unfavorable elements attached to Peter in Mark would hardly be found in a Gospel dependent on his testimony,"[66] while Joel Marcus makes the point more specific, claiming that, since Peter was involved in some bitter controversies in the early church, he "could ill have afforded . . . to weaken his position by passing on stories that put himself in a bad light."[67]

Three comments can be made. One is that, despite many attempts by scholars to depict Peter as a controversial figure, the evidence does not support such a view.[68] Gal 2:11-14 depicts a single incident in which Paul thought that Peter acted in an unprincipled way. Elsewhere Paul speaks of Peter only with respect. 1 Cor 1:12 tells us nothing about controversy involving Peter, only that one of the factions that vied for social prestige in the Corinthian church chose to invoke as their patron the most prestigious apostle, as they thought. Peter seems to have been a figure held in respect across all the various currents of the early Christian movement. Secondly, if the story of Peter's denials of Jesus has a historical basis,[69] then it must have been Peter who first told it and authorized it to be told as part of the passion story.[70] Thirdly, that this Markan narrative is a rare case of a story that all four canonical Gospels tell suggests that it could not have been generally understood as merely discrediting or denigrating Peter.

The discussion of whether it is plausible that the story could have been told by Peter himself has focused too much on its purely negative character, its exposing of Peter as a failure, without attending to the transformative charac-

---

65. E.g., W. Schadewaldt, in M. Hengel, *Studies in the Gospel of Mark* (tr. J. Bowden; London: SCM, 1985) 104-6; Brown, *The Death of the Messiah*, vol. 2, 615; C. Blomberg, *Jesus and the Gospels* (Leicester: Inter-Varsity, 1997) 124.

66. Perkins, *Peter*, 53.

67. J. Marcus, *Mark 1–8* (AB 27; New York: Doubleday, 1999) 24.

68. By "controversial figure" I mean a figure whom some opposed while others supported him, and I am referring to evidence from the first century. Smith, *Petrine Controversies*, studies Peter in Christian, including Gnostic, literature up to the third century, and concludes that, where there is controversy, it is usually among pro-Peter groups (212) rather than between pro-Peter and anti-Peter groups. Where he finds a clear anti-Peter stance it is in some Gnostic literature, especially the *Gospels of Mary* and *Thomas*.

69. Brown, *The Death of the Messiah*, vol. 2, 614-21, gives a useful survey of the debate for and against historicity. In favor of historicity, see also J. P. Meier, *A Marginal Jew*, vol. 3: *Companions and Competitors* (New York: Doubleday, 2001) 242-44.

70. The claim of Brown, *The Death of the Messiah*, vol. 2, 615, that "others could have known and reported it," is very implausible.

ter of Peter's experience, as producing a kind of self-recognition that was necessary for Peter's future discipleship. Since all readers or hearers of Mark would know that this failure was followed by restoration, and the Gospel itself appeals to such knowledge in 16:7, Peter's extreme remorse (14:72) would not be understood in an entirely negative way, but as purging Peter of his false self-confidence and making way for a more adequate faith in the crucified and risen Jesus. In this sense, we could agree with Boomershine's description of the story as Peter's "confession" — it is a further step in the transformative journey that began with the confession in 8:29. Only by failing as a disciple could Peter come to understand the necessity for the Messiah to take the way of the cross. Taken in this broader context the story of Peter's denial of Jesus is in some respects comparable with Paul's unhesitating confession of his persecution of the church before his calling to be an apostle of Jesus Christ (Gal 1:13; 1 Cor 15:9; cf. 1 Tim 1:12-14). As part of the larger narrative of Paul's calling, this functioned as testimony to the grace of God (1 Cor 15:9-10). In this sense it is not difficult to imagine Peter telling this story of his own failure, perhaps with a corresponding account of his restoration (cf. John 21:15-19).

Conclusion

Mark's Gospel not only, by its use of the *inclusio* of eyewitness testimony, claims Peter as its main eyewitness source; it also tells the story predominantly (though by no means exclusively) from Peter's perspective. This Petrine perspective is deliberately, carefully, and subtly constructed. Mark's Gospel is no mere transcript of Peter's teaching, nor is the Petrine perspective merely an undesigned survival of the way Peter told his stories. While it does correspond to features of Peter's oral narration, Mark has deliberately designed the Gospel in such a way that it incorporates and conveys this Petrine perspective. Several literary features combine to give readers/hearers Peter's "point of view" (internal focalization), usually spatial and visual or auditory, sometimes also psychological. It is this literary construction of the Petrine perspective that has so far gone almost unnoticed in Markan scholarship. Not only has Mark carefully constructed the Petrine perspective; he has also integrated it into his overall concerns and aims in the Gospel so that it serves Mark's dominant focus on the identity of Jesus and the nature of discipleship. Thus, in deliberately preserving the perspective of his main eyewitness source through much of the Gospel, Mark is no less a real author creating his own Gospel out of the traditions he had from Peter (as well as, probably, some others).

The perspective is that of Peter among the disciples, whether the inner group of three or more generally the Twelve. The perspective is Peter's "we" perspective, the perspective of Peter *qua* member of the group of disciples, rather than an "I" perspective, that of an individual relating to Jesus without reference to the others. (Only in the story of Peter's denials does the "we" perspective narrow to an "I" perspective, and even here Peter does not step outside his narrative role as one of Jesus' disciples.) Therefore there are no "private" reminiscences of Jesus, such as modern readers might expect in a work closely based on Peter's eyewitness testimony. Such expectations are inappropriate because it is Peter's *teaching*, not his autobiographical reminiscence, that lies behind Mark's Gospel. The Gospel reflects the way Peter, as an apostle commissioned to communicate the gospel of salvation, conveyed the body of eyewitness traditions that he and other members of the Twelve had officially formulated and promulgated. Even the story of Peter's denials, though it must have derived from Peter, was probably part of such a body of traditions that was not peculiar to Peter. No doubt Peter adapted, varied, and augmented the common traditions, recounting them from his own perspective, but he did not turn them into autobiography. Purely personal reminiscences of Jesus — even if Peter did relate such reminiscences in private conversation — would have been out of place in the public apostolic teaching of Peter on which Mark's Gospel is based.

In Mark's Gospel Peter is always in some sense aligned with the other disciples. But he does not appear purely as a typical or representative disciple. In his narrative role he is at the same time typical and more than typical of the other disciples. It is within his commonality with the others that he emerges as a distinctive individual, the most fully characterized of all Mark's characters other than Jesus, and it is entirely plausible that this kind of individuality is the kind that was conveyed by Peter's own recounting of the Gospel stories. The sequence of events in which Peter emerges most clearly as an individual who has his own story — his own story *as a disciple of Jesus,* that is — is the one that runs from his protestations of loyalty at the last supper to his distraught condition after denying Jesus. Here Peter exceeds the other disciples both in loyalty and in failure. This personal story does not serve merely to denigrate Peter — whether as hostile criticism from some anti-Petrine faction or as self-denigration by Peter himself — but actually qualifies Peter for his apostolic task. It is a story of personal transformation through failure, self-recognition and restoration (the latter something to which Mark's narrative points, without recounting it), a dramatic example of the encounter with the meaning of the cross that every Markan disciple must undergo. In this respect too it is both credibly the story Peter told about himself and a significant component of the story Mark has told.

Table 14: The Plural-to-Singular Narrative Device in the Synoptic Gospels

Mark	VL (variant reading)	Matthew	Luke
1:21*		No parallel	Sing
1:29-30*	Sing	Sing	Sing
5:1-2	Sing	Sing	Plur (VL Sing)
5:38**	Sing	Sing	Sing
6:53-54		Plur	No parallel
8:22	Sing	No parallel	No parallel
9:9**		Plur**	No parallel
9:14-15**	Sing	Plur** (VL Sing)	Plur** (VL Sing)
9:30		Plur	No parallel
9:33	Sing	No parallel	No parallel
10:32		Sing	No parallel
10:46		Plur (VL Sing)	Sing
11:1	Sing	Plur (VL Sing)	Sing
11:12	Sing	Sing	No parallel
11:15	Sing	No parallel	No parallel
11:19-21	Sing (v. 19)	No parallel	No parallel
11:27	Sing	No parallel	No parallel
14:18		Plur	No parallel
14:22		Plur	No parallel
14:26-27		Plur	No parallel
14:32		Sing	Sing

Luke

9:56-57			
10:38	Sing		

Note: Columns 2, 3 and 4 refer to the verb that is plural in the passages given in column 1.

*In these cases the plural refers to Jesus, Simon, Andrew, James, and John.
**In these cases the plural refers to Jesus, Peter, James, and John.

Table 15: The Plural-to-Singular Narrative Device and References to Peter in the Gospel of Mark

Plural-to-Singular	Peter
	1:16 (twice)
1:21*	
1:29-30*	1:29-30 (twice)
	1:36
	3:16
5:1-2	
	5:37
5:38**	
6:53-54	
8:22	
	8:29
	8:32-33 (twice)
	9:2
	9:5
9:9**	
9:14-15**	
9:30	
9:33	
	10:28
10:32	
10:46	
11:1	
11:12	
11:15	
11:19-21	11:21
11:27	
13:3	
14:18	
14:22	
14:26-27	
	14:29
14:32	
	14:33
	14:37 (twice)
	14:54
	14:66
	14:67
	14:70
	14:72
	16:7

*In these cases the plural refers to Jesus, Simon, Andrew, James, and John.
**In these cases the plural refers to Jesus, Peter, James, and John.

8. Anonymous Persons in Mark's Passion Narrative

Many scholars have postulated that Mark's passion narrative is based on an earlier pre-Markan source[1] that already told a connected story of events leading up to and following Jesus' death. Some such hypothesis is almost essential if much of this material is considered to be in any way traditional and not simply invented by Mark. Whereas much of the rest of Mark's Gospel consists of single units — stories or sayings — that could well have been known simply as independent stories or sayings, many of the events of the passion narrative presuppose their place in a sequence of events forming an overall story. Mark may well have arranged some of this material and created connections between stories, but it is hard to imagine that in doing so he did not have at his disposal some already existing sequence of such events, whether in written or oral form.

On the scope and origin of such a pre-Markan passion narrative scholars differ widely. It would be plausible to think it began with Jesus' entry into Jerusalem (Mark 11:1-11), though some scholars propose that it began even earlier than this and many that it began only later in Mark's narrative. In any case, it is not to be supposed that everything in Mark's passion narrative belonged to this source (I think, for example, that chs. 12-13 likely did not). This is not the place to try to distinguish sources or between source and redaction. Such distinctions are very speculative. Here we shall be content with the plau-

---

1. See the survey in M. L. Soards, "Appendix IX: The Question of a PreMarcan Passion Narrative," in R. E. Brown, *The Death of the Messiah*, vol. 2 (New York: Doubleday, 1994) 1492-1524.

sibility of the view that chs. 11 and 14-16 of Mark are to some degree dependent on a pre-Markan passion narrative, without attempting to be precise about the scope and content of such a source.

One of the more recent contributions to discussion of the pre-Markan passion narrative is Gerd Theissen's essay "A Major Narrative Unit (the Passion Story) and the Jerusalem Community in the Years 40-50 C.E."[2] He argues that various features of Mark's passion narrative reflect the situation of the Jerusalem church in or around the decade 40-50 C.E. Some of these features concern named and unnamed persons in the narrative. We shall focus here on his argument about anonymous persons.

Up to this point in this book I have argued that the presence of anonymous characters is quite normal in the Gospels and that what needs explanation is not why some characters are unnamed but why some others are named. I have also pointed out that named characters other than Jesus and the Twelve are rare in Mark's Gospel prior to the passion narrative, whereas they occur much more frequently in chs. 15 and 16, where their significance is probably that they function as the eyewitness sources of this part of the narrative, from which Peter and the Twelve are absent. Following these arguments, a study of anonymous characters in the passion narrative may seem redundant. However, there are characters, especially in ch. 14 of Mark's Gospel, whose anonymity is not just the anonymity we expect of many Gospel characters, but a little strange. It merits a closer look.

Theissen on Protective Anonymity

We begin with Theissen's argument.[3] Theissen points out, as commentators have often noticed, how difficult it is to tell from Mark's account of the arrest of Jesus in Gethsemane (14:43-52) whether either of two anonymous persons — the man who cut off the ear of the high priest's servant and the young man who fled naked — is a disciple of Jesus or not.[4] It is hardly likely that the former is a member of the arresting party who injures one of his own group by mistake; there would seem to be little point in such an incident being recorded. But "one of those who stood near" is an odd way to speak of one of

2. G. Theissen, *The Gospels in Context* (tr. L. M. Maloney; Minneapolis: Fortress, 1991) chapter 4.

3. Theissen, *The Gospels,* 184-89.

4. There is a full account of the various views in R. E. Brown, *The Death of the Messiah,* vol. 1 (New York: Doubleday, 1994) 266-68. He thinks the man is neither a disciple nor a member of the arresting party but "one of a third group, the bystanders" (266).

the Twelve, who in Mark's narrative have accompanied Jesus from the last supper to Gethsemane. When Mark elsewhere uses a similar phrase — "some of the bystanders" (*tines tōn parestēkotōn,* 15:35) — he refers to the people who stand watching Jesus on the cross (cf. also 14:69-70). In the Gethsemane narrative, are we to envisage people, not disciples of Jesus, who just happened to be there at the time? But why should such a person have taken a sword to the high priest's servant? Although it is hard to see that Mark can be referring to anyone other than one of the Twelve, the reference is peculiarly obscure.

That Mark's reference to this person is odd we can also see from the way Matthew and Luke clarify it. Matthew speaks of "one of those with Jesus" (*heis tōn meta Iēsou,* Matt 26:51), Luke of "one of them" (*heis tis ex autōn,* Luke 22:50), that is, of "those who were around him" (*hoi peri auton,* 22:49). These phrases refer unambiguously to disciples of Jesus.

Matthew and Luke entirely omit the second anonymous person in Mark's account, the young man who flees naked. Does the fact that he "followed" *(synēkolouthei)* mean that he was a disciple, though not one of the Twelve, or simply that he was an inquisitive outsider? Did he continue to follow Jesus when "all" the rest had fled (Mark 14:50) or does Mark mean him to be an illustrative example of the flight of all the disciples, even though Mark has hitherto spoken only of the Twelve as accompanying Jesus to Gethsemane? The account of this young man also raises many other questions, which have been extensively discussed, but we need not address them at this point. What Theissen's argument emphasizes is that, not only is the presence of this anonymous character in the narrative puzzling in itself, but his relationship to Jesus is also left obscure.

When Theissen offers an explanation for the anonymity of the two unnamed persons in Gethsemane, he is explaining not simply why they are unnamed but also why they are not even clearly identified as disciples of Jesus:

> It seems to me that the narrative motive for this anonymity is not hard to guess: both of them [had] run afoul of the "police." The one who draws his sword commits no minor offense when he cuts off someone's ear. Had the blow fallen only slightly awry, he could have wounded the man in the head or throat.[5] This blow with a sword is violence with possibly mortal consequences. The anonymous young man has also offered resistance. In the struggle, his clothes are torn off, so that he has to run away naked. Both these people were in danger in the aftermath. As long as the high

---

5. It seems to me likely that in Mark's narrative the man intends to deliver a mortal blow and misses to the extent that he only cuts off an ear.

priest's slave was alive (and as long as the scar from the sword cut was visible) it would have been inopportune to mention names; it would not even have been wise to identify them as members of the early Christian community. Their anonymity is for their protection, and the obscurity of their positive relationship with Jesus is a strategy of caution. Both the teller and the hearers know more about these two people.[6]

From this Theissen draws a conclusion about the pre-Markan passion narrative:

> If we are correct in our hypothesis of protective anonymity, the location of the Passion tradition would be unmistakable. Only in Jerusalem was there reason to draw a cloak of anonymity over followers of Jesus who had endangered themselves by their actions. The date could also be pinpointed: parts of the Passion account would have to have been composed within the generation of the eyewitnesses and their contemporaries, that is, somewhere between 30 and 60 C.E.[7]

This conclusion is supported by other arguments we cannot reproduce here, but one is worth noticing because it concerns yet another case of anonymity.[8] Although Mark refers by name to Pilate (15:1) and evidently expects his readers to know that Pilate was the Roman governor, he does not give the name of the high priest Caiaphas but refers merely to "the high priest" (14:53). The other Evangelists name him (Matt 26:57; Luke 3:2; John 18:13-14, 24), though Luke does not do so in the passion narrative itself (22:54), and readers of Luke might have difficulty knowing whether Annas or Caiaphas was in charge of the proceedings that condemned Jesus.

Caiaphas was son-in-law to Annas, and several other members of the powerful family of Annas were high priest in the following decades. They held the high priestly office themselves almost continuously down to 42 CE, and the family remained powerful thereafter. It seems to have been primarily this high-priestly family that followed up its action against Jesus by persecuting Jesus' followers, the Jerusalem Christian community, in the succeeding

---

6. Theissen, *The Gospels*, 186-87. With regard to the man with the sword, Theissen is far from the first to make this argument. For example, already, H. B. Swete, *The Gospel According to St Mark* (third edition; London: Macmillan, 1909) 352, wrote: "During the early days of the Church of Jerusalem when the evangelical tradition was being formed, prudential reasons (cf. Jo. xviii.26) may have suggested reticence as to the name of the offender and even the fact of his connexion with the Christian body."

7. Theissen, *The Gospels*, 188-89.

8. Theissen, *The Gospels*, 171-74.

period.[9] Annas's son Ananus II was responsible for the execution of James, Jesus' brother and leader of the Jerusalem church, in 62. The power of the house of Annas and their hostility to Christians would have made it diplomatic for Christian traditions formed in Jerusalem in that period not to refer explicitly to the name of Caiaphas in an account of the death of Jesus. Pilate, on the other hand, was a quite different case. He lost office in 37 CE with a bad reputation and there was no reason he should not be explicitly blamed for the death of Jesus as he commonly was for other abuses of power.[10]

Anonymous Supporters of Jesus

In the rest of this chapter we shall take Theissen's suggestions about protective anonymity further and suggest that there is at least one other important character in Mark's passion narrative who is unnamed for this same reason.

However, before coming to that character, I want to draw attention to the atmosphere of danger and protective secrecy that Mark's passion narrative conjures especially by means of the two rather strange stories in each of which Jesus sends two disciples on a mission: to fetch the colt which Jesus will ride into Jerusalem (Mark 11:1-7) and to prepare the Passover meal (14:12-16). Does Jesus in these stories display miraculous foreknowledge or has he made prior arrangements? The stories are sufficiently similar to require that the answer must be the same in both cases. The second story would scarcely make any sense unless it is presupposed that Jesus has already arranged with the owner of the house in question that he and his disciples will use the guest room for the Passover meal. The first story can appropriately be read in the sense of a king's right to requisition things for his need, but it still needs to be explained that "the bystanders" (another vague phrase like the one in 14:47) allow two perfect strangers to walk off with a colt simply on the strength of the words Jesus tells them to say. These words must be a kind of "password" that Jesus has already arranged in order to identify his disciples as people authorized to borrow the colt. But we should have expected the arrangement to have been made with the owner(s) of the colt. How does it come about that mere "bystanders" know the password? And why does Jesus not tell the disciples to go to the house of a named person (say, Simon son of Dositheus) in order to borrow his colt. The absence of reference to the owner of the colt, whether by name or not, is surely strange.

9. J. C. VanderKam, *From Joshua to Caiaphas: High Priests after the Exile* (Minneapolis: Fortress, 2004) 478.

10. Theissen, *The Gospels*, 173-74.

Once again, we can confirm that the story is strange by observing how Matthew and Luke treat it. Matthew abbreviates drastically, adapting Jesus' words to the disciples and recording no detail of the way they carried them out (Matt 21:3, 6), but Luke, abbreviating Mark's narrative only slightly, substitutes "its owners" (i.e., the owners of the colt) for Mark's "some of the bystanders" (Luke 19:33). This is what we would have expected Mark to have said, and Luke's text only highlights the oddity of Mark's.

Mark's account of Jesus' riding into Jerusalem (11:7-10) is less explicitly messianic than those in the other Gospels. He does not quote Zech 9:9 (as Matthew and John do), and the acclamation by the crowds, while undoubtedly messianic in significance, does not, in Mark's version, explicitly identify Jesus as the messianic king, the son of David, as the versions in the other Gospels do in differing ways. Nevertheless, there can be no doubt that Mark does see this incident as Jesus' public declaration of his messianic role. As such it must be the first of the events that led the temple authorities to see Jesus as a dangerous troublemaker who should be removed and that made it possible for Jesus to be put to death for claiming to be "king of the Jews." The owner of the colt, who had evidently arranged beforehand to let Jesus ride it, could be seen as complicit in a politically subversive act. It may well be that Jesus, in Mark's story, recognizes the danger and makes the arrangements in such a way that the owner need not be directly implicated by loaning the colt. Mark's narrative, with its curious avoidance of reference to the owner, indicates to readers that from this point on Jesus enters a danger zone in which he must employ caution and subterfuge.

The second story is equally strange. The man with the water jar is obviously a prearranged sign (even if the disciples' meeting with him is providential timing foreseen by Jesus) and is unmistakable as such since women usually carried water jars. But why does Jesus employ such an elaborate procedure to enable the disciples to find the house? Evidently, he wants the fact that he and his disciples are to be eating the Passover meal in that particular house to remain secret, as readers of Mark realize because by this time Mark has told them of the plot to arrest Jesus. But why does Jesus not simply tell the two disciples how to find the house of a named person (say, Menahem the priest) and to go there without telling anyone, taking care to keep the location secret? This is more or less what he does say in Matthew's abbreviated account: "Go into the city to a certain man, and say to him, 'The Teacher says . . .'" (Matt 26:18). Here a better translation than "a certain man" (ton deina) would be "So-and-so." Jesus names someone but Matthew does not tell us the name, doubtless because he did not know it. In Matthew, therefore, Jesus behaves as we might have expected. Why the more roundabout and clandestine arrangements in Mark? Probably because Jesus already knows that Judas is going to deliver him to the chief priests, but the other members of the Twelve do not know this. In order to keep the place where they will eat the Passover secret from Judas, Jesus must keep it secret from the Twelve. So the stratagem insures that even the two disciples sent to prepare the room do not know where it is until they get to it. Once again Mark's narrative conjures the atmosphere of danger and the consequent need for secrecy, now heightened since the plot to kill Jesus has been made and Judas has offered to make his arrest possible. Of course, Jesus already expects to be arrested, but he does not wish this to happen until he has shared the Passover meal with his disciples. So the location must be very carefully kept secret.

I do not mean that we should necessarily have expected Mark to name the owner of the colt or the owner of the house if it were not for the prudential considerations that he implicitly attributes to Jesus in these two stories. In accordance with Mark's policy elsewhere, we should expect them to be named only if they were members of the early Christian community and likely to be known by name to some at least of Mark's readers. These two characters must have been closely enough associated with Jesus for it to be likely that they did join the early Christian movement and were members of the Jerusalem church. Even so, we cannot be sure that they were particularly well known by name, and their roles in the story are not such as to make them likely to be eyewitness sources of traditions. So it is no more than a possibility that the narrative protects them — at the time of its formulation in the Jerusalem church — as it does the two anonymous men in Gethsemane, according to Theissen's hypothesis. Nevertheless, the two stories do give us a sense of the danger, not only to Jesus but to those close to him, during his last days in Jerusalem and the secrecy and subterfuge this required. The danger would certainly, for some of those close to Jesus at that time, people who could be regarded as complicit in the events that led to his arrest and condemnation to death, continue for many years afterward if they belonged to the early Christian community in Jerusalem and its environs.

The Woman Who Anointed the Messiah

One such person is the woman who anointed Jesus (Mark 14:3-9). Like the two nameless men in Gethsemane, she is peculiarly unspecified. Not only is her name not given, but there is no indication at all of who she is. Her introduction in v. 3 is remarkably abrupt and unexplanatory: "a woman came." Whether she belongs to the household (a relative of Simon the leper?) or is a guest or has simply come in from the town (like the woman in Luke 7:37) is unexplained, as is her connection with Jesus and her motive. It could be said that all this is due to the Evangelist's focus on Jesus' interpretation of her act, but in fact it is this that makes her *anonymity* quite extraordinary and not at all comparable to the many unremarkable cases of anonymity in Mark's Gospel. What she has done is going to be told in remembrance of her wherever the Gospel is preached in the whole world, and yet she is unnamed. This is more than "somewhat in tension with the point of the saying."[11] Commentators regularly notice the problem while offering no solution.

Ben Witherington offers an explanation in terms of genre: the story is a biographically focused *chreia* (anecdote) in which all the attention is on the biographee, Jesus. Accordingly, it is what the woman "did for Jesus, on whom the personal spotlight shines, not who she is, that is of consequence in such a biography."[12] But this is not entirely convincing because it is not the case that names of characters other than the biographee never appear in biographically focused *chreiai*.[13] More importantly, in this story Jesus does not say simply that the woman's act will be remembered, but that it will be told "in remembrance of her." The remembrance is not going to separate her act from her personal identity.[14]

The solution to this anomaly in Mark's text (reproduced also by Matthew) is Theissen's category of "protective anonymity." At the time when this tradition took shape in this form in the early Jerusalem church, this woman would have been in danger were she identified as having been complicit in Jesus' politically subversive claim to messianic kingship. Her danger was perhaps even greater than that of the man who attacked the servant of the high priest, for it was she who had anointed Jesus as Messiah.

A number of scholars have seen this woman's anointing of Jesus as the anointing entailed by the term Messiah (Anointed One), comparable with the anointing of kings in the Hebrew Bible.[15] The woman is acknowledging or

---

11. C. A. Evans, *Mark 8:27–16:20* (WBC 34B; Nashville: Nelson, 2001) 362.

12. B. Witherington III, *The Gospel of Mark: A Socio-Rhetorical Commentary* (Grand Rapids: Eerdmans, 2001) 366.

13. E.g,. this happens quite often in Lucian's *Demonax*.

14. Cf. R. T. France, *The Gospel of Mark* (NIGTC; Grand Rapids, Eerdmans, 2002) 555: "Presumably it is the act and its symbolism . . . which are to be remembered, rather than the identity of the person who performed it, but the final phrase in that case remains curiously personal."

15. Most recently Evans, *Mark 8:27–16:20*, 359, with references to others who argue for this view; see also E. K. Broadhead, *Prophet, Son, Messiah: Narrative Form and Function in Mark 14–16* (JSNTSup 97; Sheffield: Sheffield Academic, 1994) 37 n. 2. For the anointing of kings in the Old Testament, see 1 Sam 10:1; 16:1, 13; 1 Kgs 1:39; 19:15-16; 2 Kgs 9:3, 6; Ps 89:20.

even designating Jesus as the royal Messiah. Evans is correct in saying that the anointing "would in all probability have been perceived in a messianic sense," but I do not see how he knows that the woman's "action was spontaneous and impromptu and would not have been interpreted in any official sense."[16] There is no reason in the text why she should not have planned it in association with others, who may have thought it best to take Jesus by surprise and so encourage him to undertake the messianic role about which he may have seemed to them very ambivalent. In any case, for our present purposes the woman's own motivation is less important than the fact that, in the charged atmosphere of this time in Jerusalem and with the question whether Jesus was the messianic son of David certainly being widely asked, the woman's action could easily be perceived by others as of messianic significance. Admittedly, it would no doubt be very surprising for the Messiah to be anointed by a woman, but she might have been seen in the role of a prophet, like Samuel, inspired by God to recognize and designate his Anointed One (cf. 1 Sam 16:1-13).[17]

Not all scholars who think the woman's act had messianic significance in its original historical context think that Mark's narrative preserves that significance,[18] and not all scholars who think Mark sees messianic significance in the anointing think this was originally intended or perceived.[19] Reasons for denying that the anointing, either historically or in Mark's story, carries messianic significance are: (1) Anointing the head in the context of a banquet was by no means confined to kings,[20] but was a common custom at feasts. (2) The messianic significance is not explicit in Mark's text.[21] (3) Mark's narrative

16. Evans, *Mark 8:27–16:20*, 360.

17. So E. Schüssler Fiorenza, *In Memory of Her: A Feminist Theological Reconstruction of Christian Origins* (New York: Crossroad, 1985) xiii-xiv; R. A. Horsley, *Hearing the Whole Story: The Politics of Plot in Mark's Gospel* (Louisville: Westminster John Knox, 2001) 217-218. Schüssler Fiorenza's view is repeated with updated references in E. Schüssler Fiorenza, "Re-Visioning Christian Origins: *In Memory of Her* Revisited," in K. J. O'Mahony, ed., *Christian Origins: Worship, Belief and Society* (JSNTSup 241; Sheffield: Sheffield Academic, 2003) 240-42.

18. E.g. J. K. Elliott, "The Anointing of Jesus," *ExpT* 85 (1973-74) 105-107; E. Schüssler Fiorenza, *Jesus: Miriam's Child, Sophia's Prophet* (London: SCM Press, 1994) 95.

19. E.g., C. E. B. Cranfield, *The Gospel According to Saint Mark* (CGTC; second edition; Cambridge: Cambridge University Press, 1963) 415: "It is not likely that the woman thought of herself as anointing the Messiah, but Mark doubtless intended his readers to recognize the messianic significance of her action."

20. K. E. Corley, "The Anointing of Jesus in the Synoptic Tradition: An Argument for Authenticity," *JSHJ* 1 (2003) 66-67; France, *The Gospel*, 552.

21. Presumably this is why many commentators do not even mention the possibility; cf. also E. Y. L. Ng, *Reconstructing Christian Origins? The Feminist Theology of Elisabeth Schüssler Fiorenza: An Evaluation* (Paternoster Biblical and Theological Monographs; Carlisle: Paternoster, 2002) 146-47.

"goes on to interpret the festal gesture in terms of death and burial rather than of messianic commissioning."[22] The first point is correct and therefore means that the messianic significance is not self-evident but dependent on the context, including the wider context in Mark's passion narrative outside this story itself. In Mark's narrative presumably those who object to the waste of the ointment do not perceive the messianic meaning of the anointing. The second point can be answered by referring to Mark's narrative of Jesus' riding the colt into Jerusalem. As we have noticed, the messianic significance is left implicit in Mark's narrative, but it can hardly be doubted that it is there. The story of the anointing is similar. The third point poses a false alternative. What happens in the story is that Jesus recognizes the messianic significance of the anointing but interprets it according to his own understanding of his messianic vocation as entailing suffering and death. Just as readers of Mark know that Jesus' riding into Jerusalem on a colt does not signify messianic triumph of the generally expected kind but constitutes a journey to his death, so the messianic anointing by the woman is redirected by Jesus toward his burial, coherently with the characteristically Markan (though not, of course, only Markan) connection between messiahship and the cross.

What has not been generally recognized is the significance of Mark's placing of this story between his account of the plot by the Jewish authorities to arrest and kill Jesus (14:1-2) and his account of Judas's visit to the chief priests in order to offer to hand Jesus over to them (14:10-11). This is a typically Markan "sandwich" construction, like, for example, the placing of the account of Jesus' demonstration in the temple (11:15-19) between the two parts of the story of the withered fig tree (11:12-14, 20-25). The "sandwich" implies a close connection of meaning between the story that forms the two outer parts and the story that is sandwiched between them. One suggestion about this connection is that "the evangelist creates a vivid contrast between the devotion and faith of the unnamed woman, on the one hand, and the faithlessness and treachery of the named disciple, 'Judas Iscariot, one of the twelve,' on the other."[23] But there is a more obvious connection and one that does justice to the sandwiching of the anointing story between *both* parts of the story of the plot against Jesus. We should surely understand that Judas reports the incident of the anointing to the chief priests, for whom it must constitute significant evidence that Jesus and his disciples are planning an imminent messianic uprising. Perhaps we should also suspect that it was this incident — with its unavoidable confirmation by Jesus that he will undertake

22. France, *The Gospel,* 552.
23. Evans, *Mark 8:27–16:20,* 364.

the messianic role only on his own terms as a vocation to die — that led Judas to defect. Thus the anointing provides both added cause for the chief priests to take swift action against Jesus and also the means to do so in the shape of Judas's offer.

That the anointing is related in this way to the actions of the chief priests and Judas is not, of course, explicit in the story, but this is not a valid objection to it. There is similarly no explicit connection between the story of the withered fig tree and the demonstration in the temple, but most commentators believe that, by means of the Markan "sandwich" construction, the former functions as a comment on Jesus' attitude to and action in the temple. But we should also notice the surely studied reserve in Mark's passion narrative as to what led the Jewish authorities to suppose both that Jesus was so dangerous that action must be taken swiftly and that a charge of claiming messiahship could be made to stick and represented to Pilate as a political challenge to Roman rule. Three events in Mark's narrative provide the priests' motivation: Jesus' entry into Jerusalem, his demonstration in the temple, and his anointing by a woman. But in all three cases the messianic significance is notably subdued in Mark's telling. The author seems wary of making explicit the aspects of these events that made them construable as evidence for the charge on which Jesus was put to death, namely that he was claiming to be the messianic "king of the Jews" and planning an uprising.

The messianic significance of all three events would have been clear to Mark's first readers or hearers, but Mark's apparent strategy of leaving it for them to perceive, rather than highlighting it himself, coheres rather strikingly with the strategy of "protective anonymity" in relation to certain characters in this narrative. What put these persons in danger in Jerusalem in the period of the earliest Christian community would be their complicity in Jesus' allegedly seditious behavior in the days before his arrest. Furthermore, the whole Christian community was potentially at risk for its allegiance to a man who had been executed for such seditious behavior. We can readily understand that, just as the pre-Markan passion narrative protected certain individuals by leaving them anonymous, so it protected the community by not making too obvious the messianic meaning of the events that had constituted the chief priests' evidence for treating Jesus as a dangerously seditious figure. Just as the members of the Jerusalem church who first heard the narrative would know who the anonymous persons were, so they would understand the messianic significance of these events without needing it spelled out for them.

So it seems that the atmosphere of danger and precaution that pervades Mark's narrative in chs. 11 and 14 characterized both the historical events themselves, for Jesus and his disciples, and also the context in which they were first retold, for Jesus' early followers in the early Jerusalem church. The danger the latter were still in was the danger Jesus himself had been in during those days before his arrest. Thus cautious behavior within the narrative corresponds with the cautious way in which it is composed. All this we must suppose was true of the passion narrative as formulated in the Jerusalem church, such that when Mark wrote it was characteristic of the traditional way in which the narrative was still told.

The Anonymous in Mark Are Named in John

We are now in a position to understand why it is that several of the persons who are anonymous in Mark's passion narrative are named in John, thus:

woman who anoints	Mary, sister of Martha (John 12:3)
man who wields sword	Simon Peter (John 18:10)
servant of the high priest	Malchus (John 18:10).

These should not be regarded as instances of some alleged tendency for names to get added in the tradition. As we have seen in chapter 3 there is little evidence of such a tendency before the fourth century. Moreover, such an explanation neglects the specificities of these particular cases in the passion narrative. As we have seen there may be very good reasons for the anonymity of these characters in Mark. We have seen that not only are the woman who anoints and the man who wields the sword nameless in Mark but that there is also a more general obfuscation of their identities, leaving their relationships to Jesus and his disciples very unclear. On the other hand, the naming of the characters in John serves specific purposes. We may take the Gethsemane story first. The identification of the man who wields the sword with Peter could certainly be explained as an aspect of John's character portrayal.[24] This action fits so well the character of the impetuous Peter, devoted to Jesus, ready to lay down his life for Jesus, but seriously misunderstanding Jesus' vocation and intentions, that John has sketched especially in 13:36-38. Identifying the man in Gethsemane as Peter could have been an inspired guess on the Evangelist's part. But it is less easy to understand the naming of Malchus.

It is notable that in all four Gospels this character is called "*the* servant of the high priest" (Matt 26:51; Mark 14:47; Luke 22:50; John 18:10). The high

---

24. As we noticed in chapter 7, John's portrayal of Peter's character is very similar to Mark's.

priest certainly had many more servants or slaves than one, and according to John 18:26 more than one such were members of the arresting party in Gethsemane. Commentators have therefore been hard pressed to explain the definite "the" in this case. Perhaps the meaning is that this servant of the high priest was the officer in charge of the arresting party. He was the most important person in that party, but his name may have been remembered in the early Jerusalem church not simply for that reason but also because the injury to him remained, so to speak, an unsolved crime of which Peter was the as yet undetected perpetrator. Malchus was an influential person in the high priest's entourage with a personal grudge against the disciples of Jesus.

In John's Gospel, uniquely, he is mentioned again in the account of Peter's third denial of Jesus (John 18:26). Against the background of John's account of the events in Gethsemane, we recognize that Peter is afraid of being identified not just as a disciple of Jesus but as the one who assaulted the servant of the high priest. A connection is drawn between John's identification of the man who wielded the sword as Peter and Peter's abject failure in denying Jesus. The connection is historically plausible, though doubtless it could also be seen as narrative ingenuity on the part of the expert storyteller that this Evangelist is. But in the light of our discussion, we certainly cannot maintain that the connection is historically unlikely simply because it is made only in John's Gospel. It could not have been made in the pre-Markan passion narrative (on which not only Mark but, by way of Mark, the other Synoptic Evangelists at this point depend), without also identifying Peter as the man who cut off the high priest's servant's ear. The extent of the fear that motivated Peter's denial could not be explained without blowing his cover. Conversely, by identifying Peter as the man who wielded the sword, John is able to explain more fully why Peter failed so miserably.

Of course, John wrote at a time (after Peter's death) when Peter no longer needed the protection of anonymity in his narrative. Unlike Matthew and Luke, John had independent access to the early Jerusalem traditions in which it was tacitly well known who the man who assaulted the high priest's servant was. As for John's naming of Malchus (in 18:10, though not in 18:26) it probably serves to highlight the danger in which Peter was as a result of his action. The identity of the man he assaulted was widely known.

Given the reasons we have suggested for the anonymity of the woman who anointed Jesus in Mark and given John's independent access to traditions of the early Jerusalem church, there is no difficulty in understanding how it is that the anonymous woman becomes, in John, Mary the sister of Martha and Lazarus. But if we accept that John correctly identifies her, there is a further interesting consequence. There is a character in John's passion narrative who would have needed "protective anonymity" in the pre-Markan passion narrative as much as or even more than the woman who anointed Jesus did: her brother Lazarus. John's Gospel explicitly reports that "the chief priests planned to put Lazarus to death as well" as Jesus (12:10). Lazarus could not have been protected in the early period of the Jerusalem church's life by telling his story but not naming him. His story was too well known locally not to be easily identifiable as his however it was told. For Lazarus "protective anonymity" had to take the form of his total absence from the story as it was publicly told.

The strongest objection to the historicity of John's story of Lazarus — or even to a historical basis of some kind for it — has always been that it does not appear in the Synoptics. Of course, there were stories of Jesus' miracles that were included only in one corpus of Gospel traditions and not in another. For example, there are stories in Luke's special material, such as the raising of the son of the widow of Nain, the closest Gospel parallel to the raising of Lazarus, that are not to be found in Mark. We should not expect the same stories to appear in every such collection of Jesus traditions, and it is not an adequate argument against the historicity of a story that it occurs only in one. Nevertheless, the raising of Lazarus is a special case because of the key importance it has in John's Gospel, not simply on a theological level, but in John's explanation of the course of events that led to Jesus' death. In John's Gospel it is because of the raising of Lazarus and its effect on the people that the Jewish authorities decide that Jesus must die (11:45-53). It is for this reason, according to John, that Jesus is already in mortal danger when he arrives in Bethany a week before his death. If the raising of Lazarus was not only the remarkable event that John portrays but also such a key event in leading to Jesus' death, its absence from Mark — and so, presumably, from the pre-Markan passion narrative — is certainly puzzling. But the difficulty is removed when we recognize that the need for "protective anonymity" in Lazarus's case would require his complete absence from any public telling of the passion narrative in the early Jerusalem church.

One further aspect of the differences between Mark and John in their passion narratives can support the case that John has independent access to the facts of these politically charged events. John dates the anointing of Jesus by Mary at the beginning of the passion week (12:1-8), before the entry into Jerusalem (12:12-19), whereas Mark, as we have seen, sandwiches it between the plotting of the Jewish authorities, which is dated two days before the Passover (Mark 14:1), and Judas's visit to them (14:10-11). Mark's arrangement is surely determined by his desire to link the anointing with this particular context, rather than by a traditional dating of the anointing itself two days before the Passover. As an accurate date for the anointing itself, John's is historically very plausible.[25] Jesus is anointed as the Messiah in Bethany before riding into Jerusalem as the Messiah the next day. Although John, in his account of the anointing, has obscured its messianic significance even more than Mark by having Mary anoint Jesus' feet rather than his head (12:3), he has at the same time preserved its messianic significance by placing it in immediate connection with Jesus' riding into Jerusalem.

Once Again: The Naked Youth

Finally, we may return to the second anonymous character in Mark's account of the arrest of Jesus in Gethsemane. The young man who fled naked is not even mentioned in the other Gospels. But there is one interesting point to notice about him. If the episode is based on a real event and is not just a fictional embellishment of the passion narrative, then the story can only have come from the young man's own telling of it. (The incident is not likely to have been observed by the other disciples, and the account is not likely to have come from members of the arresting party.) It is an example of eyewitness testimony from a person involved in the events. Other such eyewitnesses, especially in the passion narrative, are named in Mark. As we have noticed, this is the main reason why some characters in Mark have names, when many do not. But the young man in this story is the exception that proves the rule. As an eyewitness in need of "protective anonymity" he could not, in the pre-Markan passion narrative, be named, though doubtless those who heard the story knew very well who he was. But then why did Mark (or, for that matter, the early passion narrative) relate the incident at all?

The enigmatic nature of the incident has intrigued scholars and stimulated a large range of more or less speculative interpretations, ranging from the highly symbolic to much more matter-of-fact reconstructions of what lay behind the incident and attempts to identify the young man.[26] To understand the story as constructed purely for allegorical or symbolic reasons would be out of character with the rest of the Markan narrative and furthermore tends to neglect this incident's narrative connection with the preceding account of Jesus' arrest in Gethsemane.[27] It clearly bears some relationship to the fact that all

25. This is recognized by Elliott, "The Anointing," 107.

26. Brown, *The Death of the Messiah*, vol. 1, 294-302, provides a useful overview of the proposed interpretations.

27. Against symbolic interpretations, see also Brown, *The Death of the Messiah*, vol. 1, 302-3.

the others who were with Jesus "deserted him and fled" (14:50) and probably means that this young man was initially an exception to this general dispersion of the disciples. He tried to continue to follow Jesus as the temple police led him away, but he too took flight when an attempt was made to arrest him.

Howard Jackson has usefully assembled parallels from Greek literature to the motif of a person abandoning one's garment and fleeing naked. He points out how easily this could happen:

> Ancient cloaks and mantles of the sort our youth's *sindōn* is likely to have been, . . . were merely . . . simple (i.e. sleeveless) rectangles of cloth, and they were regularly wrapped or draped around the body without any belt or fasteners of any kind to hold them on; even in the best of circumstances, consequently, they were likely to slip off with the normal movements of the body. With any sudden violent action, particularly any involving the arms or legs, the garment was practically assured of being thrown off.[28]

So what happened to the youth was not unusual in ancient life and needs no elaborately symbolic explanation:

> Whether our episode originated with Mark or was inherited from early and what may be historically accurate tradition (the latter much more likely, in my view), the shared experience of daily life was enough to commend Mark's inclusion of the shed garment and naked flight in his account of the youth. Capping the account of the arrest, the motif's vivid picture of abject terror and shameful nudity in cowardly flight admirably reinforces a scene in which the ruling emotion is the desperate impulse to save one's own skin, the mood of "Every man for himself!" By use of the motif Mark ensures that the desertion of Jesus is given a hard-hitting climax with a powerful visual image of universal personal appeal.[29]

So it may be that the purpose of Mark's inclusion of this incident is no more than to reinforce the picture already created by v. 50. But the ordinariness of what happens to the young man could also mean that Mark reports a historical incident for the purpose of drawing attention to the presence of this particular young man in Gethsemane. In modern times the idea that the young man was John Mark himself, understood to be the author of the Gos-

28. H. M. Jackson, "Why the Youth Shed His Cloak and Fled Naked: The Meaning and Purpose of Mark 14:51-52," *JBL* 116 (1997) 280. But note that B. Saunderson, "Gethsemane: The Missing Witness," *Bib* 70 (1989) 230, claims that clips or clasps were used to hold the garment in place.
29. Jackson, "Why the Youth," 285-86.

pel, has proved very appealing. As Theodor Zahn put it, Mark "paints a small picture of himself in the corner of his work."[30] (This is more than a picturesque way of putting it: it makes a comparison with the practice of European painters. John Painter offers a more modern analogy: "like the fleeting appearance of Alfred Hitchcock in his films."[31] Such comparisons are suggestive, but they cannot substitute for evidence of a literary convention in ancient literature. Such evidence does not seem to have been adduced.)

We should at once separate this suggestion — that the young man is the author of the Gospel — from the elaborate scenarios so often associated with it that attempt to conclude from the young man's clothing that he had been in bed and dressed in a great hurry.[32] It was usual to wear two items of clothing — the tunic and the cloak — but it was not indecent or necessarily inadequate to wear only one. Mark points out that in this case the young man was wearing only his cloak (doubtless quite decently wrapped around him) because this was why, when he slipped out of it, he was in the embarrassing and shameful state of nakedness (though possibly wearing a loin cloth).[33] So the young man's dress should not prevent us supposing that he had accompanied Jesus and his disciples from the house where the last supper had taken place, or, alternatively, that he happened to be on the slopes of the Mount of Olives for some other purpose, such as among pilgrims camping there.[34] The former seems more likely, since the young man would surely not have continued to follow Jesus and his captors after everyone else had fled if he had been motivated by nothing more than curiosity. Moreover, the arresting party tried to arrest him too, evidently treating him as someone on Jesus' side. There is no good reason why he should not have been a supporter of Jesus who accompanied the other disciples to Gethsemane. Simply because Mark is usually only interested in the Twelve and mentions other disciples only rarely and incidentally, we need not suppose that only the Twelve were at the last supper.

If the namelessness of this young man is a case of "protective anonymity," as, following Theissen, I have argued, then it seems quite redundant also to suppose that he is John Mark's anonymous presentation of himself. More-

30. Quoted in V. Taylor, *The Gospel according to St. Mark* (London: Macmillan, 1952) 562.

31. J. Painter, *Mark's Gospel: Worlds in Conflict* (NT Readings; New York: Routledge, 1997) 193. Painter himself does not think the young man is Mark.

32. Cf. Brown, *The Death of the Messiah*, vol. 1, 299.

33. The suggestion made by some scholars that he was wearing both a cloak and a tunic and fled wearing only his tunic is unconvincing. Whether or not this condition of wearing only a tunic could be described as being "naked" *(gymnos)*, it would not be shameful in the way this incident surely requires for the matter to be worth mentioning.

34. Saunderson, "Gethsemane," 232, suggests the latter.

over Papias, whom, we have seen, there is more reason to trust than many recent scholars have supposed, claims that Mark neither heard nor was a disciple of Jesus (Eusebius, *Hist. Eccl.* 3.39.15). Another suggested identification of the young man, which would fit very well indeed with our arguments about "protective anonymity," is with Lazarus.[35] That Lazarus was a wanted man would explain both the attempt to arrest the young man and his anonymity in Mark's story. Michael Haren's further suggestion that the young man's linen garment was Lazarus's shroud, worn so that he could be exhibited in Jerusalem as a living proof of the miracle of his resurrection,[36] is an unnecessary speculation (because the young man's garb, as we have seen, does not need any special explanation) that also seems to run counter to the idea that Lazarus was in fear of his life. But the identification of the young man with Lazarus in itself could be right. Perhaps the pre-Markan passion narrative, unable for reasons of protective anonymity to tell the story for which Lazarus was truly famous, acknowledged his importance by allowing him this brief, anonymous appearance in Gethsemane. Unfortunately, in the nature of the case, no degree of certainty seems possible.[37]

Barbara Saunderson has argued that the young man is the eyewitness source, not only of the story of his own flight, but also of the preceding narrative about the events in Gethsemane. No source other than the Twelve or Peter in particular need be required for vv. 43-50 of Mark 14, but Mark's account of Jesus' prayers in Gethsemane (14:32-42) is another matter. Ostensibly, there is a problem: not only does Jesus seem to put himself out of earshot of the disciples or at least of all but the privileged three, but also these three fall asleep and so cannot overhear Jesus' prayers. The problem can be ameliorated by pointing out that it would be a very wooden interpretation of Mark's narrative to suppose that the disciples immediately fell asleep on all three occasions and were not awake enough of the time to gather the general tenor of Jesus' prayers, which is after all surely all that Mark is likely to be reporting. But Barbara Saunderson has suggested that the young man who fled naked is "the missing witness"[38] who could have overheard Jesus while Peter, James,

35. M. J. Haren, "The Naked Young Man: A Historian's Hypothesis on Mark 14,51-52," *Bib* 84 (2003) 525-31.

36. Haren, "The Naked Young Man," 530-31.

37. There is less to be said for the suggestion of J. A. Grassi, *The Secret Identity of the Beloved Disciple* (New York: Paulist, 1992) 111, that the young man is the Beloved Disciple of John's Gospel.

38. Saunderson, "Gethsemane." E. Lohmeyer, *Das Evangelium des Markus* (Göttingen: Vandenhoeck und Ruprecht, 1963) 324, suggested that the young man is included as a witness to the arrest.

and John were soundly asleep nearby. In this book, of course, we have argued that in general the eyewitness sources of particular traditions in the Gospels are indicated by *names,* but in the case of this young man we may have a special case. The need for "protective anonymity" may have overridden the convention of naming the eyewitnesses. Saunderson's suggestion could be correct, but it is impossible to be very confident about it.

9. Papias on Mark and Matthew

In chapter 2 we discussed an excerpt, preserved for us by the church historian Eusebius, from the Prologue to the *Exposition of the Logia*[1] *of the Lord* by Papias of Hierapolis, and we found reason to take quite seriously what Papias said about the connection between Gospel traditions and the eyewitnesses. In that passage Papias was concerned only with oral information, but, it seems, later in his Prologue[2] he also discussed the written Gospels he knew. Eusebius, who, despite his own reservations about Papias's doctrinal reliability, evidently valued at least part of what Papias said about the origins of the Gospels, quotes two passages from Papias, referring specifically to the Gospels of Mark and Matthew. The statements about Mark are attributed by Papias to "the Elder," who is probably John the Elder, that long-lived disciple of Jesus to whom Papias already referred in the passage we discussed in chapter 2. Whether Papias also attributed the comment about Matthew to John the Elder we cannot be sure, but the way Eusebius introduces it suggests that he probably did.[3]

These are the passages with Eusebius's introductions to them:

---

1. Because the meaning of the Greek *logia* here is disputed I have left it untranslated. It probably means something like "accounts of what Jesus said and did." See the discussion below.

2. Eusebius does not say explicitly that these excerpts are from the Prologue, but this would seem to be the natural place for them in Papias's work.

3. R. H. Gundry, *Mark: A Commentary on His Apology for the Cross* (Grand Rapids: Eerdmans, 1993) 1031.

We must now add to his [Papias's] statements quoted above a tradition about Mark, who wrote the Gospel, which has been set forth in these words:

The Elder used to say: Mark, in his capacity as Peter's interpreter [*hermēneutēs*], wrote down accurately as many things as he [Peter?] recalled from memory — though not in an ordered form [*ou mentoi taxei*] — of the things either said or done by the Lord. For he [Mark] neither heard the Lord nor accompanied[4] him, but later, as I said, [he heard and accompanied] Peter, who used to give his teachings in the form of *chreiai*, but had no intention of providing an ordered arrangement [*suntaxin*] of the *logia* of the Lord. Consequently Mark did nothing wrong when he wrote down some individual items just as he [Peter?] related them from memory. For he made it his one concern not to omit anything he had heard or to falsify anything.

This, then, is the account given by Papias about Mark. But about Matthew the following was said:

Therefore Matthew put the *logia* in an ordered arrangement [*sunetaxato*] in the Hebrew language [*hebraidi dialectō*], but each person interpreted them as best he could. (Eusebius, *Hist. Eccl.* 3.39.14-16)

What Papias says here about the Gospel of Mark is the earliest explicit occurrence of the claim that Peter's teaching lies behind this Gospel. It was therefore subjected to close scrutiny and discussion during the first hundred years or more of modern Gospels scholarship. Some scholars up to the present time have continued to treat it very seriously as important evidence about the origins of the Gospel of Mark,[5] but during the twentieth century it came to be widely regarded as historically worthless. Although the attribution of the Gospel to a certain Mark may be accurate, there is no reason, according to this widespread view, to suppose that this was the John Mark of the New Testament (Acts and Epistles), since this Latin name *(Marcus)* was in very common use, in Greek *(Markos)* as well as Latin. We know from Eusebius that Papias cited 1 Peter (*Hist. Eccl.* 3.39.17), almost certainly as evidence of the close association of Peter with the Mark known from the New Testament.

4. The usual translation is "followed," but in contemporary English this is potentially misleading. The meaning of the verb *parakoloutheō* is not so much "come after" as "go closely with."

5. E.g., M. Hengel, *Studies in the Gospel of Mark* (tr. J. Bowden; London: SCM, 1985) 47-53; Gundry, *Mark*, 1026-45; S. Byrskog, *Story as History — History as Story: The Gospel Tradition in the Context of Ancient Oral History* (WUNT 123; Tübingen: Mohr, 2000; reprinted Leiden: Brill, 2002) 272-92; B. Witherington, *The Gospel of Mark: A Socio-Rhetorical Commentary* (Grand Rapids: Eerdmans, 2001) 22-26.

Papias, it is suggested, wishing to give apostolic authority to a Gospel ascribed to an unknown author called Mark, used 1 Pet 5:13 to identify this Mark with Peter's close associate, thus creating the connection he asserts between the Gospel and Peter.[6]

However, there are some good reasons why we should be prepared to look again at Papias's statements about Mark. In the first place, we have argued in chapter 6 that the Gospel of Mark itself, by means of the literary device of the *inclusio* of eyewitness testimony, indicates that Peter was the principal eyewitness source of this Gospel and that the authors of the Gospels of Luke and John both understood Mark to be making this claim. This is probably the most important reason for reconsidering Papias's evidence. However, in addition, we adduced in chapter 7 other evidence internal to the Gospel indicating that it frequently adopts Peter's perspective on events. Moreover, thirdly, we have found that the information Papias gives in Eusebius's earlier extract from his work, considered above in chapter 2, is credible and consistent with other evidence, including that of the Gospels themselves.

Finally, Papias claims to offer, not his own opinion about the origins of the Gospel of Mark, but what "the Elder used to say." If this refers (as is very likely) to John the Elder, whom we know from Papias's earlier account to have been a personal disciple of Jesus, then the time at which he was making this statement about Mark could hardly have been later than 100 CE. If Papias reports accurately what he said, then this is evidence from a relatively early date and from someone who was in quite a good position to know in what way Mark's Gospel was related to the oral teaching of Peter. To be sure, we cannot easily suppose that Papias quotes the words of the Elder *verbatim*. After all, he does not report what the Elder said on a specific occasion, but what the Elder "used to say" on this topic. Some scholars have wished to limit how much of Papias's words about Mark are represented by him as a quotation from the Elder, treating the rest as Papias's own comment on the Elder's words. But it is difficult to divide the material in this way.[7] More likely, Papias offers his own paraphrase of what he remembered the Elder to have said. We cannot tell how far he has attributed to the Elder his own glosses on what the Elder said, but

---

6. E.g., K. Niederwimmer, "Johannes Markus und die Frage nach dem Verfasser des zweiten Evangeliums," *ZNW* 58 (1967) 186; J. Marcus, *Mark 1–8* (AB 27; New York: Doubleday, 1999) 21-24; C. M. Tuckett, "Mark," in J. Barton and J. Muddiman, eds., *The Oxford Bible Commentary* (Oxford: Oxford University Press, 2001) 886; cf. C. C. Black, *Mark: Images of an Apostolic Interpreter* (Minneapolis: Fortress, 2001 [originally published in 1994 by University of South Carolina Press]) 89.

7. J. Kürzinger, *Papias von Hierapolis und die Evangelien des Neuen Testaments* (Regensburg: Pustet, 1983) 45.

we must suppose that, unless he is fabricating, the Elder did say something about the way Mark's Gospel reflected the teaching of Peter. In that case, 1 Pet 5:13 is unlikely to be the basis of the claim that the author of Mark's Gospel was connected with Peter. Papias will have cited this verse rather as corroboration of what the Elder said. To suppose that the statements of the Elder were simply invented by Papias to further support his novel idea that Mark's Gospel derived from Peter's teaching is gratuitous skepticism. Clifton Black asks why, if this idea had been mere speculation by Papias on the basis of 1 Pet 5:13, "would he not have ascribed that tradition to Peter himself, an esteemed apostle and the supposed author of the letter, rather than to a comparatively superfluous middleman like John the presbyter."[8] We should need rather good reasons for doubting that Papias learned of Peter's connection with the Gospel from John the Elder.

Mark as Peter's Interpreter

Precisely what Papias meant by his statements about the origins of Mark's Gospel has been disputed at several points. The first issue we must clarify is what is meant by the claim that Mark was "Peter's interpreter." The Greek noun *hermēneutēs* is related to the verb *hermēneuō,* which Papias uses later in his statement about Matthew's Gospel ("each interpreted them"). Both words can refer to interpretation in the sense of either (1) translation from one language to another, or (2) explanation and exposition. Does Papias (reporting the Elder) mean that Mark acted as Peter's translator or as an expositor who explained what Peter's teaching meant? Although many scholars have opted for the latter possibility, what Papias goes on to say about Mark makes this option unlikely. The whole paragraph seems designed to assert that Mark reproduced in his Gospel exactly what he heard Peter say. This is how Papias excuses what would otherwise be a serious deficiency in Mark's Gospel: its lack of "ordered arrangement." Mark intended to do no more than write down what Peter said just as he recalled it. This emphasis coheres much more naturally with calling Mark Peter's "translator" than with conceding Mark freedom to interpret what Peter said.

Would Peter have needed a translator? Many scholars have thought not, because Peter was surely able to speak Greek. In light of Peter's early life in the dominantly Gentile context of Bethsaida, Markus Bockmuehl speaks of "a very strong likelihood that Peter grew up fully bilingual in a Jewish minority

8. Black, *Mark,* 87-88.

setting."[9] Moreover, Peter could easily have improved his Greek in the course of his evangelistic ministry. But this does not mean that he may not have preferred to teach with the help of a translator who could render his words in a more natural and polished Greek, such as John Mark, who came from a Diaspora Jewish family and was presumably educated in Jerusalem,[10] could plausibly have supplied. Another suggestion is that, if the setting Papias envisages is in Rome, Mark may have translated Peter's words into Latin, but this is less likely, since Greek was widely spoken in Rome and remained the language of the Christian community in Rome throughout the second century. If Mark translated Peter's Aramaic into Greek, this could mean that he habitually did this when Peter was preaching in a Greek-speaking context, but it could mean only that he did so in order to put Peter's words down in writing. The latter could well be what Papias meant to say. Peter might be content with his own rather rough Greek in his oral teaching, but when it came to having his words recorded he preferred to express himself in his native Aramaic and allow Mark to translate into more accurate and readable Greek. It is worth recalling that even the Jewish historian Josephus, who could certainly speak Greek well, used secretaries to assist him with writing good literary Greek (*C. Apion.* 1.50). Mark's Greek has no literary pretensions, but it could well have been sufficiently better than Peter's for his role as translator to have been thought useful in recording Peter's teaching in writing.

If this were Papias's understanding of the situation, it gives a somewhat different impression from what scholars have often seen in his words. In this case we are not to conceive of Mark regularly acting as Peter's interpreter in situations of oral communication and then later, on his own (whether before or after Peter's death), recalling as well as he could what Peter said and writing it

---

9. M. Bockmuehl, "Simon Peter and Bethsaida," in B. Chilton and C. Evans, eds., *The Missions of James, Peter, and Paul* (NovTSup 115; Leiden: Brill, 2004) 82. On the other hand, it is worth noting that Philip, also from Bethsaida, and Peter's brother Andrew, rather than Peter himself, are regarded as the disciples most proficient in Greek in John 12:21-22. Perhaps Peter was not so proficient in Greek.

10. Here I presume the identification of Mark the author of the Gospel with the John Mark of Acts (12:12, 25) and the Mark of the Pauline letters (Col 4:10). As we have noted, this identification has been doubted by recent scholars who reject the possible connection of the Gospel with Peter. Furthermore, Black, *Mark,* doubts whether there is only one Mark portrayed in the New Testament: "the evidence is simply insufficient to establish that these depictions all refer to one and the same figure" (67). Against this, the very fact that Mark was a very common Latin and Greek name suggests that, since early Christian writers could refer to someone called "Mark" without further specification (as in Col 4:10; Phlm 24; 2 Tim 4:11; 1 Pet 5:13) and expect him to be identifiable, there must have been only one Mark who was well known as a leader in the early Christian movement.

down (whether or not with freedom to expound it in his own words). Rather Papias may be envisaging that Peter and Mark sat down together to make a written record of the traditions of Jesus' words and deeds as Peter was in the habit of reciting them.[11] Mark translated and wrote as Peter spoke.[12] (As we shall see, if this is correct, then Papias must mean that there were several or many occasions, on each of which Peter related some of his traditions about Jesus and Mark wrote them down in Greek translation, so that Mark, not Peter, was responsible for the order in which they were compiled to form the Gospel.)

Before pursuing this reading of Papias a little further, we must mention a third possible understanding of his claim that Mark was Peter's *hermēneutēs*. The word, as we have seen, could mean either translator or interpreter in the sense of one who explains and expounds. But Josef Kürzinger has argued that in this case it means no more than intermediary or reporter, designating Mark simply as one who passed on what Peter taught. For this meaning he relies on the use of the verb *hermēneuō* in rhetorical terminology.[13] A major contribution Kürzinger has made to the study of the fragments of Papias is his demonstration that Papias, in the excerpts given by Eusebius, makes use of the vocabulary of ancient literary criticism or study of rhetoric. In chapter 2, we have already followed his suggestions in this regard in translating and understanding the fragment of Papias that we studied there. We shall see that this insight of Kürzinger's proves illuminating also in later parts of Papias's words about Mark. But in this particular instance it is hard to accept Kürzinger's proposal. It would certainly be coherent with the general tenor of what Papias says about Mark — that he reproduced exactly what Peter said. In this respect, Kürzinger's proposal makes as good contextual sense as the meaning "translator." Moreover, it is true that the verb *hermēneuō* was used in discussion of literary composition to mean "convey" or "express," while the adjective *hermēneutikos* and the noun *hermēneia* could be used similarly (see, e.g., Lucian, *Hist. Conscr.* 24, 34, 43). But in such cases the words "refer to the movement within a man by which his thoughts become words,"[14] not to the report-

11. This seems to be how Gundry, *Mark,* 1036, understands Papias.

12. This entails taking the aorist participle *genomenos* as referring to action concurrent with the main verb *egrapsen* rather than prior to it: hence the translation "in his capacity as Peter's interpreter," rather than "having become Peter's interpreter." Both are grammatically possible. See Kürzinger, *Papias,* 47; Gundry, *Mark,* 1035-36.

13. Kürzinger, *Papias,* 45-46. He is followed, e.g., by B. Orchard in B. Orchard and H. Riley, *The Order of the Synoptics: Why Three Synoptic Gospels?* (Macon: Mercer University Press, 1987) 188-89.

14. W. R. Schoedel, *The Apostolic Fathers,* vol. 5: *Polycarp, Martyrdom of Polycarp, Fragments of Papias* (Camden: Nelson, 1967) 107.

ing of one person's words by another. Even more importantly, there seems to be no evidence for the use of the noun *hermēneutēs* to mean someone who transmits the teaching of another. The meaning "translator" is not only common but also seems more natural in this context.

Consistent with the role of Mark as mere translator of Peter is Papias's claim that Mark "made it his one concern not to omit anything he had heard or to falsify anything." This is a version of the common stock formula by which an author claims to have neither omitted nor added anything.[15] The formula was a cliché especially of historiography. It could describe the character of the most reliable eyewitness testimony (e.g., Lucian, *Hist. Conscr.* 47), a historian's fidelity to his sources (e.g., Dionysius of Halicarnassus, *De Veterum Censura* 5) or his care to recount everything important in the course of events and add nothing redundant (e.g., idem, 8). But it is important to note that the formula could also be used of the work of a translator.

For example, Philo, describing the work of the translators of the Greek (Septuagint) version of the Pentateuch, says that they were very conscious that they must "not add or omit or transfer anything, but must keep the original form and shape" (Philo, *De Vita Mosis* 2.34).[16] A Latin writer (writing under the pseudonym of Cornelius Nepos) claims:

> When I was busying myself with many things at Athens, I discovered the history of Dares Phrygius written in his own hand. I loved it greatly and translated it line for line. I thought nothing should be added or omitted lest the history be changed and appear to be my own.[17]

Here is a translator who wants to assure readers that they can rely on his reproduction of his source. Had he exceeded the task of translating, he would have interposed another layer of possible distortion between the events and the readers.

This is exactly Papias's concern: Mark's approach is praiseworthy because he puts readers into direct touch with Peter's oral teaching. By doing more than translate Mark puts readers in touch with a primary source, Peter's eyewitness testimony, instead of constituting a secondary source that dis-

---

15. W. C. van Unnik, "De la règle Μήτε προσθεῖναι μήτε ἀφελεῖν dans l'histoire du canon," *Vigiliae Christianae* 3 (1949) 1-36, collects and discusses many instances of this formula, but neglects the historiographic use.

16. The *Letter of Aristeas* (311) and Josephus (*Ant.* 12.109) use this language with reference rather to the obligation to preserve the text unaltered after it has been made public.

17. This translation from the Latin quoted in S. J. D. Cohen, *Josephus in Galilee and Rome* (Leiden: Brill, 1979) 28, who differs from van Unnik on the meaning of the second sentence (28 n. 15).

tances readers further from the events. That Papias varies the usual formula, stating that Mark neither omitted *nor falsified* anything, is probably not intended to allow the possibility that Mark did add to Peter's oral teaching. Papias evidently liked to vary standard expressions, as in the case of the "living voice" in the fragment we discussed in chapter 2, where Papias gives a unique variation: "a living and abiding voice." But these variations are not just a matter of literary style. In the present case Papias varies the phrase in order to make its point more explicit. A translator who added to his source would be *falsifying* it. Papias is not envisaging additional traditions derived by Mark from a source other than Peter but the possibility that Mark might have falsified the Petrine traditions by exceeding the task of a translator and expanding them with his own additions.

Translators did not always stick to translating. For example, it is rather remarkable, but by no means exceptional,[18] that Josephus claims his history of the Jewish people — the *Antiquities of the Jews* — to be no more and no less than a translation of the Hebrew scriptures (*Ant.* 1.5, 17; 4.196). The following instance of this claim is especially comparable with the passage already quoted from Pseudo-Nepos:

> But let no one reproach me for recording in my work each of these events as I have found them in the ancient books, for at the very beginning of my History I safeguarded myself against those who might find something wanting in my narrative or find fault with it, and said that I was only translating *(metaphrazein)* the books of the Hebrews into the Greek tongue, promising to report their contents without adding anything of my own to the narrative or omitting anything therefrom (*Ant.* 10.218; cf. 1.17; 6.196; 14.1; 20.260-63).[19]

Of course, this is far from strictly true. By comparison with the Hebrew Bible, Josephus frequently both adds and omits entire episodes and makes all manner of detailed changes. In passages such as the one just quoted he is merely parroting historiographic commonplaces that he does not seem to take seriously.[20] Admittedly, he uses verbs (*metaphrazō* here; *methermēneuō* in 1.5)

---

18. Cohen, *Josephus,* 27.

19. On this and related passages see S. Inowlocki, "'Neither Adding Nor Omitting Anything': Josephus' Promise not to Modify the Scriptures in Greek and Latin Context," *JJS* 56 (2005) 48-65.

20. Inowlocki, "Neither Adding," argues that Josephus's claim is justified by an ancient view of translation as faithful transmission of content and adaptation to context, but even this can hardly stretch to describing Josephus's practice as a whole.

that, like Papias's designation of Mark as *hermēneutēs,* allow a "translator" scope for paraphrase. Perhaps Papias would have allowed this also to Mark. But Papias's emphasis, like Josephus's, is entirely on the claim that the "translator" made no substantial changes to his source. Unlike Josephus, he seems to have taken this claim seriously.

The reason he does so emerges when we remember the fragment of Papias we studied in chapter 2. Papias there, commenting on his care in collecting Gospel traditions in oral form, justified it by saying: "I did not think that information from books would profit me as much as information from a living and surviving voice" (Eusebius, *Hist. Eccl.* 3.39.4). We argued that this does not indicate a general preference for oral rather than written sources. Rather it expresses a preference, following good historiographic practice, for reports as close as possible to those of the eyewitnesses themselves. The preference is for "a living and *abiding* voice," that is, oral communication from eyewitnesses who are still alive. Such oral eyewitness testimony, even though Papias received it at second or third hand, was preferable to written sources, since the latter could be falsified or even forged (falsely attributed to an eyewitness).[21] While the eyewitnesses were still alive, so that both they and the intermediary tradents could be interviewed and questioned, this preference made sense, but it would no longer make sense once all the eyewitnesses were dead, as they were by the time Papias wrote his Prologue. So in this Prologue Papias needed to discuss the extent to which written Gospels were adequate substitutes for oral transmission from the eyewitnesses. In Mark's case, although Mark was not an eyewitness himself, he was reproducing Peter's testimony as Peter recited it. Papias portrays Mark as no more than a translator scrupulously accurate in reproducing Peter's oral testimony because in that case his Gospel would be free of the falsifications introduced by "translators," even those who claim to report the testimony of eyewitnesses. Short of a text actually written by an eyewitness, Mark's Gospel, as represented by Papias, would be as good a historical source as one could get in the period after all eyewitnesses had died.

Everything Peter Remembered

I have suggested that Papias called Mark Peter's interpreter, not in the sense that he acted as such when Peter was teaching orally, but in the sense that he

---

21. A. D. Baum, "Papias, der Vorzug der *Viva Vox* und die Evangelienschriften," *NTS* 44 (1998) 146.

translated Peter's words when he and Peter engaged in a process of setting them down in writing. Whether this view is correct depends partly on the meaning of two other clauses in Papias's account. According to the translation given above, Mark "wrote down accurately as many things as *he recalled from memory* [*emnēmoneusen*]," and "wrote down some individual items just as *he related them from memory* [*apemnēmoneusen*]." In the translation above I have also suggested that the subject of both these verbs of remembering — *recalled from memory* and *related from memory* — may be Peter. But this is debatable: many scholars have thought that the person remembering is Mark. Grammatically either reading is possible. The two phrases are quite closely parallel and so we should probably take the subject to be the same in both cases. In the first case, the word order in the sentence facilitates identifying the subject as Peter. But more importantly, if the subject is not Peter, then this sentence fails actually to say what Papias clearly intended: that it was Peter's teaching that Mark wrote down. Moreover, Papias's emphasis in the whole passage, as we have already remarked, is on the fact that Mark recorded exactly what Peter said. This is much better conveyed by saying that Mark wrote what Peter remembered rather than that Mark wrote what he remembered Peter saying.[22] As the last sentence of the passage puts it, what Mark did was to write everything he *had heard*. Throughout the passage the complementary roles of Peter and Mark are that Peter *remembered* and Mark *heard and wrote*. Furthermore, we should note that Papias uses two different verbs of remembering: in the first case *mnēmoneuō* and in the second the much rarer form of the verb with the prefix *apo: apomnēmoneuō*. While it is possible that the two verbs are used interchangeably and that both refer to Mark's remembering as he wrote, the second more properly has the meaning either of "relate from memory" or of "record from memory." It would not make sense to say either that Mark "wrote down some individual items just as *he [Mark] related them from memory*" or that Mark "wrote down some individual items just as *he [Mark] recorded them from memory*,"[23] but it makes very good sense to say that Mark "wrote down some individual items just as *he [Peter] related them from memory*."[24]

In that case, the aorist form of both the verbs of writing *(egrapsen,*

22. On the theme of "remembering" with reference to oral transmission, see J. D. G. Dunn, *Jesus Remembered* (Grand Rapids: Eerdmans, 2003) 278-80; S. Byrskog, "A New Perspective on the Jesus Tradition: Reflections on James D. G. Dunn's *Jesus Remembered*," *JSNT* 26 (2004) 463-67.

23. Kürzinger, *Papias*, 48-49, opts for the meaning "record in writing" for both *mnēmoneuō* and *apomnēmoneuō*.

24. This is argued by Gundry, *Mark*, 1036.

grapsas) and the verbs of remembering *(emnēmoneusen, apemnēmoneusen)* suggests specific occasions on which Peter recalled and related what he remembered while Mark heard, translated, and wrote. These aorists contrast with the imperfect *epoieito* (Peter *"used to give* his teachings in the form of *chreiai"*), referring to Peter's habitual method of teaching. Because this was the way in which Peter was in the habit of giving his teachings about the words and deeds of Jesus, it was naturally also the way in which he recounted them to Mark on those occasions when Mark recorded them in writing.

If it is correct that Papias uses the verb *apomnēmoneuō* in the sense of "to relate from memory" and with Peter as the implied subject, then there is a comment to be made about this choice of terminology. This is the verb from which the noun *apomnēmoneumata,* meaning "memoirs" or "reminiscences," derives. The noun was used in the titles of literary works, most famously Xenophon's "Memoirs"[25] of Socrates. Such books were usually memoirs written by an eyewitness about a famous person, most often a philosopher.[26] Xenophon's introduction to the main part of his work is worth quoting: "I propose to show how Socrates benefited his companions by both his deeds and his words, and, in order to do so, I shall relate as many of them as I remember *(diamnēmoneusō)"* (*Memorabilia* 1.3.1). There is a rather striking parallel (in ideas rather than vocabulary) in Papias's reference to "as many things as he [Peter] recalled from memory . . . of the things either said or done by the Lord." This is doubtless not a direct reminiscence of Xenophon but an instance of the kind of standard clichés that were common in this kind of writing. But it does suggest that in using the verb *apomnēmoneuō* Papias may well have been characterizing Mark's record of what Peter remembered as Peter's *apomnēmoneumata* of Jesus.[27] It would be another instance of Papias's use of technical or semi-technical terms from literary and rhetorical discussion.

However, the most notable coincidence is between Papias's use of *apomnēmoneuō,* with Peter as the subject, and the reference by Justin Martyr (writing around the middle of the second century) to the Gospel of Mark as

---

25. The commonly used Latin title *Memorabilia* was invented only in 1569.

26. A. Momigliano, *The Development of Greek Biography* (Cambridge: Harvard University Press, 1993) 52-54; M. C. Moeser, *The Anecdote in Mark, the Classical World and the Rabbis* (JSNTSup 227; Sheffield: Sheffield Academic, 2002) 64-65; N. Hyldahl, "Hegesipps Hypomnemata," *ST* 14 (1960) 77-83; L. Abramowski, "The 'Memoirs of the Apostles' in Justin," in P. Stuhlmacher, ed., *The Gospel and the Gospels* (Grand Rapids: Eerdmans, 1991) 326-28.

27. R. M. Grant, *The Earliest Lives of Jesus* (New York: Harper, 1961) 18; V. K. Robbins, *Jesus the Teacher: A Socio-Rhetorical Interpretation of Mark* (Minneapolis: Fortress, 1992) 66.

Peter's *apomnēmoneumata* (*Dialogue* 106.3).[28] This is the only occasion on which Justin uses this term to describe one specific Gospel as the memoirs of one specific eyewitness, but he frequently refers to the Gospels in general as the *apomnēmoneumata* of the apostles (*1 Apologia* 66.3; 67.3; and thirteen times in *Dialogue* 107-17). The description is somewhat anomalous, in that *apomnēmoneumata* were usually said to be "of" their subject rather than their author (thus, for example, Xenophon wrote *apomnēmoneumata* of Socrates). But the shift in usage is understandable enough. Justin therefore thought of the Gospels as the "reminiscences" of the apostolic eyewitnesses, and in the case of Mark's Gospel the "reminiscences" of Peter. It is unlikely that he derived this description from the passage of Papias we are studying, where the use of the verb *apomnēmoneuō* is too incidental to have created such a description for the first time.[29] More likely, Papias is evidence that the term *apomnēmoneumata* was already used to describe Mark's Gospel as Peter's "Memoirs" of Jesus in Papias's time. It has been suggested that Justin's description of the Gospels as the *apomnēmoneumata* of the apostles is due to the importance Xenophon's *apomnēmoneumata* of Socrates had for Justin,[30] but although Justin refers to material in this work of Xenophon on one occasion (*2 Apologia* 11.2-3) and certainly esteemed Socrates very highly, he does not actually refer to Xenophon's *apomnēmoneumata* by this term, its title. It may have had some influence on Justin's special preference for this way of describing the Gospels, but already established usage, suggested by Papias's use of *apomnēmoneuō* with Peter as subject, is more likely to have been determinative of Justin's usage.

On one occasion Justin refers to the *apomnēmoneumata* "composed (*syntetachthai*) by his apostles and those who accompanied them" (*Dialogue* 103.8; cf. Papias's implicit statement that Mark "accompanied" Peter). The statement may be echoing the prologue to Luke's Gospel (Luke 1:1, 3). Did Justin think some Gospels (Matthew and John?) were composed by apostles and others by their followers (Mark and Luke?)? Or that Mark's Gospel was composed by an apostle (Peter), like Matthew's?[31] Or that one Gospel was composed both by an apostle (Peter) and his follower (Mark)? Most likely — since Mark's Gospel seems never to have had a distinguishing title other than

28. On the authenticity of the extant text and the evidence that Justin here refers to Mark's Gospel, see G. N. Stanton, *Jesus and Gospel* (Cambridge: Cambridge University Press, 2004) 101; Abramowski, "The 'Memoirs,'" 334-35.

29. C. E. Hill, *The Johannine Corpus in the Early Church* (Oxford: Oxford University Press, 2004) 339-40, argues for Justin's dependence on Papias.

30. Abramowski, "The 'Memoirs,'" 328.

31. Cf. Stanton, *Jesus*, 100-101.

the one that ascribes it to Mark[32] — he shared Papias's view that this Gospel comprised Peter's memoirs but was actually written down by Mark. But if Justin reflected on his use of the verb *syntetachthai* (*syntassō:* literally "put in order"), he did not share Papias's view (which we will discuss below) that Mark's Gospel lacked ordered arrangement *(syntaxis).*

Peter's Anecdotes

In the translation of Papias's statements about Mark at the beginning of this chapter it is said that Peter "used to give his teachings in the form of *chreiai,* but had no intention of providing an ordered arrangement [*syntaxin*] of the *logia* of the Lord." Two points of translation need discussion here. Papias's use of the term *logia* here, as well as in his comment about Matthew and in the title of his own work *(Exposition of the Logia of the Lord),* has been much discussed. But the context in these statements about Mark strongly suggests that it means not "sayings of the Lord"[33] or "prophetic oracles of the Lord"[34] or "prophetic oracles about the Lord" but something like "short reports of what the Lord said and did."[35] This is because "the *logia* of the Lord" must be parallel to the earlier phrase "the things either said or done by the Lord." The content of what Peter did not put in order must be the same as what he recalled from memory and Mark wrote down.

The second point of translation is more important. The phrase translated above as "in the form of *chreiai*" *(pros tas chreias)* used to be commonly translated as "according to needs." Papias was understood to be saying that Peter "adapted his teachings as needed,"[36] or "used to adapt his instructions to the needs [of the hearers]."[37] Read in this way, Papias's words might be thought in surprising agreement with the approach to the study of the Gospels known as form criticism.[38] This maintained that the Gospel traditions

---

32. Hengel, *Studies,* chapter III.

33. This is argued most fully by A. D. Baum, "Papias als Kommentator evangelischer Aussprüche Jesu," *NovT* 38 (1996) 257-76.

34. A. Stewart-Sykes, *From Prophecy to Preaching: A Search for the Origins of the Christian Homily* (*Vigiliae Christianae* Supplements 59; Leiden: Brill, 2001) 206-8.

35. U. H. J. Körtner, *Papias von Hierapolis* (Göttingen: Vandenhoeck und Ruprecht, 1983) 151-67; Kürzinger, *Papias,* 50-51.

36. J. B. Lightfoot, J. R. Harmer, and M. W. Holmes, *The Apostolic Fathers* (Leicester: Apollos, 1990) 316.

37. Hengel, *Studies,* 50.

38. T. F. Glasson, "The Place of the Anecdote," *JTS* 32 (1981) 150.

were transmitted orally in the contexts *(Sitze im Leben)* in the life of the church in which they were put to use and were shaped or even created to meet the needs of such contexts. The form critics themselves, however, were evidently too convinced of the worthlessness of Papias's account of the origins of Mark to notice this point of agreement.

The translation of *pros tas chreias* as "according to needs" has now been largely abandoned in favor of the view that Papias uses *chreia* here as a technical rhetorical term to describe the form in which Peter delivered his teachings about Jesus. The argument was first made by R. O. P. Taylor in 1946. He pointed out that the *chreia* was a rhetorical form defined and described in the ancient handbooks of rhetoric that were guides to elementary education. He quoted the definition given by Aelius Theon: "A Chreia is a concise and pointed account of something said or done, attributed to some particular person" (Theon, *Progymnasmata* 3.2-3). Taylor also observed "that the definition exactly fits the detachable little stories of which so much of Mark consists — which are, indeed, characteristic of the first three Gospels."[39] Taylor's interpretation was taken up by Robert Grant.[40] Then, without reference to Taylor, the same interpretation of Papias's phrase was later championed by Kürzinger,[41] who made it part of his broader argument for the use of rhetorical terminology throughout the fragments of Papias quoted by Eusebius. Since then it has been quite widely accepted.[42]

In the light of Papias's use of rhetorical terms elsewhere, this interpretation of *pros tas chreias* seems very likely correct, especially as we can see that it corresponds sufficiently to the short units of which Mark's narrative is composed for Papias to have regarded Mark as a collection of Peter's *chreiai* about Jesus. Whether he was justified in representing Mark as no more than such a collection of *chreiai* is an issue to which we will need to return later, but at this point it is worth pointing out that the term *chreia* evidently covered quite a wide range of types of content. On the basis of Theon's examples, it is possible to classify *chreiai* as brief narratives containing only actions, as brief narratives containing only sayings, and mixed types containing both actions and

---

39. R. O. P. Taylor, *The Groundwork of the Gospels* (Oxford: Blackwell, 1946) 76.

40. Grant, *The Earliest Lives*, 17-18.

41. Kürzinger, *Papias*, 51-56 (this material was first published in 1977).

42. E.g., Orchard in Orchard and Riley, *The Order*, 188, 190; C. Bryan, *A Preface to Mark* (New York: Oxford University Press, 1993) 126-27; Byrskog, *Story*, 272; Gundry, *Mark*, 1037; Witherington, *The Gospel of Mark*, 22. Kürzinger's view is questioned by W. D. Davies and D. C. Allison, *The Gospel according to Saint Matthew*, vol. 1 (ICC; Edinburgh: Clark, 1988) 16, while M. Black, "The Use of Rhetorical Terminology in Papias on Mark and Matthew," *JSNT* 37 (1989) 34-36, 38, seems undecided.

sayings.[43] The English term "anecdote" seems the best equivalent, for an anecdote is also a brief story about a particular person, focusing on a particular action or saying or both. However, we should note that Theon apparently also regarded as a *chreia* an attributed saying, that is, a brief literary unit that contained, in addition to the saying, only "So-and-so said" or equivalent.[44] Precision of definition[45] is also rather blurred by the use of other terms, such as *apophthegma* and *apomnēmoneuma,* which seem to overlap the usage of *chreia* and may themselves be used interchangeably.[46] An *apomnēmoneuma,* for example, seems to be treated either as a longer unit than a *chreia* or as the more general term of which the *chreia,* distinguished by its brevity, was one type.[47] The *chreia* was essentially brief, but nevertheless the rhetoricians taught pupils both to abbreviate and to expand *chreiai.*[48] Many of Mark's narrative units are probably too long to qualify strictly as *chreiai,* but the term is sufficiently flexible for it to be understandable that Papias, by way of a very broad generalization, could think of Mark's Gospel as composed of *chreiai.*

Would it have been credible to think of Peter relating the deeds and words of Jesus in the form of *chreiai?* Students encountered *chreiai* at every level of Greek edicuation, including the earliest stages, at which *chreiai* were used to teach reading and writing.[49] But since Papias evidently thought that Peter needed Mark to translate his Aramaic into reasonably good Greek, he is unlikely to have thought that Peter had an elementary education in Greek. However, we should remember that the definitions and classifications of the grammarians, such as Theon, were descriptive as well as prescriptive. Essentially they were *describing* the various sorts of anecdotes that people, educated or not, told. In a predominantly oral culture everyone was familiar with various forms of relating short narratives or reporting sayings and would adopt such forms without needing to reflect on the matter at all. In fact, it would be difficult for anyone to tell a short anecdote that did not come within Theon's definition and

43. Moeser, *The Anecdote,* 70-72. For Theon's more elaborate subdivisions of types of *chreia,* see Moeser, *The Anecdote,* 77-78.

44. See the first example given by Moeser, *The Anecdote,* 70.

45. For further definitions of the *chreia* by Theon and other writers, see Moeser, *The Anecdote,* 75-76.

46. Moeser, *The Anecdote,* 64-68.

47. Moeser, *The Anecdote,* 65-66.

48. Moeser, *The Anecdote,* 80; V. K. Robbins, "Chreia and Pronouncement Story in Synoptic Studies," in B. L. Mack and V. K. Robbins, eds., *Patterns of Persuasion in the Gospels* (Sonoma: Polebridge, 1989) 17-18.

49. R. F. Hock, "The *Chreia* in Primary and Secondary Education," in J. M. Asgeirsson and N. van Deusen, eds., *Alexander's Revenge: Hellenistic Culture through the Centuries* (Reykjavik: University of Iceland Press, 2002) 11-35.

qualify as one of his subtypes. Education would simply heighten self-conscious reflection on the forms of anecdote in common use and teach people effective use of anecdotes in persuasion and argumentation.[50]

Greek education taught people how to use such anecdotes in argumentative rhetoric intended to persuade. Theon prescribed eight exercises for students to do with *chreiai,* including memorizing *chreiai,* grammatical exercises, commenting on, confirming and refuting, all with a view to the use of *chreiai* in speeches aimed at persuading people.[51] In order to relate the deeds and sayings of Jesus in the form of short anecdotes Peter certainly did not need to have had such rhetorical training. We simply do not know how Peter would have *used* such anecdotes in his preaching, if Papias is correct in implying that he did. In spite of the assumption of the form critics that Gospel traditions functioned in a homiletic context in which their message was applied, Peter may in fact, for all we know, simply have rehearsed the traditions. Certainly, within the Gospel of Mark, the context of the traditions is a narrative, not a speech. The Gospel doubtless aims to persuade, but only in the way that a narrative can do, quite differently from the way a speech can. In my view it is therefore a mistake to apply the exercises with *chreiai* prescribed by the grammarians to analysis of *chreiai* in the Gospels.[52] There is no reason why Peter could not have given many of the *chreiai* in Mark their basic forms in his oral rehearsing of the words and deeds of Jesus.

Mark's Lack of Order

According to Papias, Peter related his *chreiai* about Jesus individually and haphazardly. He did not compile them in an ordered arrangement *(syntaxis).* Consequently, when Mark translated them and wrote them down, presumably in the course of several sessions with Peter, he transcribed them accurately, but not in order *(taxis).* Since he was no more than a translator, he did not add to his material by investing it with artistic arrangement. Papias thinks

50. Cf. W. Shiner, *Proclaiming the Gospel: First-Century Performance of Mark* (Harrisburg: Trinity, 2003) 6: "The techniques of rhetoric found in the handbooks could be learned even if one never attended a rhetorical school. Indeed, Augustine says it is easier to learn eloquence by reading and hearing eloquent men than by studying rules" (the reference is to Augustine, *De Doctrina Christiana* 4.3.4-5).

51. Moeser, *The Anecdote,* 79-87.

52. *Contra* Mack and Robbins, *Patterns of Persuasion,* who make much of the technique of argumentative elaboration of a *chreia.* My objection is also raised by Witherington, *The Gospel of Mark,* 15.

Mark was entirely justified in this because the value of his work is precisely that it reproduced Peter's teachings just as Peter gave them orally. But Papias evidently also thinks this lack of order would be a very serious deficiency if the Gospel were to be regarded as historiography. Compare what he says of Mark here with what he said about his own work earlier in the Prologue:

> I will not hesitate to put into properly ordered form *(synkatataxai tais hermēneiais)* for you everything I learned carefully in the past from the elders and noted down *(emnēmoneusa)* well, for the truth of which I vouchsafe (Eusebius, *Hist. Eccl.* 3.39.3).

As we noticed in chapter 2, here Papias is describing his own work as following good historiographic practice. Good historiography had two main characteristics: truth and artistic composition, and Papias claims both of them. He first collected the oral reports he received from those who had received them from the eyewitnesses. He carefully noted these down when he received them. Then, in a subsequent stage of work, he compiled them into a properly ordered form. When we compare this passage with Papias's comments on Mark, it is clear that, in Papias's view, Mark had done the first stage of this process exceptionally well: he had faithfully recorded everything Peter related. But this was all he did, with the result that his Gospel is a haphazard collection of *chreiai*. It is not real history, in Papias's view, but more like the notes from which historians composed their work.

As in other cases of Papias's usage that we have noted, *taxis* and *syntaxis* are rhetorical terms. What sort of order might Mark have given to his material, had he worked like a true historian? Mark's Gospel is not unusual among Greek and Roman biographies in being a collection of *chreiai*. There are even some that appear to be as haphazard in their arrangement of *chreiai* as Papias thought Mark to be. Lucian's *Demonax*, a "life" *(bios)* of the Cynic philosopher, has a beginning and an end that form a chronological framework for the rest of the work. (Even Papias must have recognized that Mark also has at least this minimal degree of chronological structure.) Otherwise, however, Lucian seems to offer simply a randomly arranged collection of *chreiai* and some longer anecdotes about Demonax.[53] They are simply placed side by side with no attempt to forge literary links among them. Since this is not Lucian's method in other biographies, those of Peregrinus and Alexander of Abonoteichus, which have a continuous and broadly chronological narrative, it has been plausibly argued that in his *Demonax* Lucian deliberately adopted a rhetorical style appropriate

---

53. For a study of the forms and functions of the *chreiai* in *Demonax*, see Moeser, *The Anecdote*, 89-105.

to his Cynic subject.[54] It is worth noticing another feature of this work which parallels Papias's account of Mark. At the end of this short work, Lucian makes the conventional apology: "These are a very few things out of the many I might have related from memory *(apemnēmoneusa)*" (*Demonax* 67). Papias notices that Mark's Gospel is short. Not only are its contents detached anecdotes, but there are few of them: "Mark wrote down some individual items as Peter related them from memory *(enia grapsas hōs apemnēmoneusen)*."[55] There must be an implicit contrast with other, fuller Gospels, but Papias does not blame Mark for the incompleteness of his compilation, since he "did not omit anything he had heard" from Peter. Once again, what might otherwise seem a deficiency in Mark is justified by the fact that Mark was doing no more than translate and record Peter's teachings in the form of *chreiai*. (Mark's incompleteness would probably not be, in Papias's eyes, a deficiency additional to lack of order, but an aspect of its lack of proper literary order.[56])

It is likely that not even Lucian himself would have classified his *Demonax* as history, not because it lacked truth but because it lacked order *(taxis)*. In his advice on writing history, putting his material into artistically pleasing order is the essential final stage of the historian's task (*Hist. Conscr.* 48, 51). He strongly disapproves of disjointed composition, such as the mere compilation of detached anecdotes in Mark's Gospel or Lucian's own *Demonax* produced:

> [A]ll the body of the history is simply a long narrative. So let it be adorned with the virtues proper to narrative, progressing smoothly, evenly and consistently, free from humps and hollows. Then let its clarity be limpid, achieved, as I have said, both by diction and the interweaving of the matter. For he will make everything distinct and complete, and when he has finished the first topic he will introduce the second, fastened to it and linked with it like a chain, to avoid breaks and a multiplicity of disjointed narratives; no, always the first and second topics must not be merely neighbours but have common matter and overlap (*Hist. Conscr.* 55).[57]

54. B. B. Branham, "Authorizing Humor: Lucian's Demonax and Cynic Rhetoric," *Semeia* 64 (1993) 33-48.

55. On this phrase, see T. Y. Mullins, "Papias on Mark's Gospel," *Vigiliae Christianae* 30 (1976) 189-92. With Papias's use of *enia* here, cf. Lucian, *Demonax* 12 (introducing the collection of *chreiai*): "I should like to cite a few *(enia)* of his well-directed and witty remarks."

56. Schoedel, *Polycarp*, 106, cites Quintilian (*Institutio Oratoria* 7, preface 3) asserting that a rhetorician would "repeat many things, omit many things" if his "order" were inadequate.

57. For *taxis* with reference to historiography, see also Josephus, *Ant.* 1.17; 4.197 *(taxai)*; *War* 1.15; Lucian, *Hist. conscr.* 6, 48; Dionysius of Halicarnassus, *De Veterum Censura* 9; *Epistula ad Pompeium* 3 *(taxai)*.

Evidently here the order envisaged by Lucian is topical rather than chronological. Others thought history was best arranged in a continuous chronological sequence, as Dionysius of Halicarnassus put it in his critical essay on Thucydides: "history should be presented as an uninterrupted sequence of events" (*De Veterum Censura* 9).

Readers did not necessarily have the same expectations of biography *(bioi)* as they did of historiography. The two were distinct genres, but some biographies were much closer to the ideals of historiographic practice than others.[58] They also varied as to whether their principles of arrangement were primarily chronological, primarily topical, or a balance of both.[59] Most have at least the minimal chronological framework (birth and early life at the beginning, death at the end).[60] (Burridge, indeed, opines that Xenophon's *Memorabilia* [*apomnēmoneumata*] is not a true *bios,* because, although the anecdotes about Socrates are carefully grouped by topic, there is not even a chronological framework.[61]) Biographies also differed in the extent to which they offered a mere sequence of anecdotes or wove their material into a seamless narrative: "The more sophisticated the writer, generally the less obvious are the junctures between the particular stories and the units of tradition that make up the work."[62]

As several scholars have rightly pointed out, *taxis* and *syntaxis* in Papias's comments on Mark do not refer to chronological sequence as such, but to the orderly arrangement of material in a literary composition.[63] The opposite of them is not a non-chronological arrangement but the lack of any coherent arrangement of material at all. However, this does not exclude the

---

58. In distinguishing between biography and historiography, too much weight has sometimes been placed on the way Plutarch distinguishes them in *Alexander* 1.2. A. Wardman, *Plutarch's Lives* (London: Elek, 1974), ends his discussion of this passage and its implications: "Thus the form of Plutarchan biography is closer to historiography than his utterance in *Alex.* 1 would, at first, have us believe" (10). He also comments: "The biographer therefore is not so far removed from the historian as his theoretical statement [in *Alexander* 1.2] would make it seem" (154). Cf. also R. A. Burridge, *What Are the Gospels?* (SNTSMS 70; Cambridge: Cambridge University Press, 1992) 63-65.

59. Bryan, *A Preface,* 39-40. Friedrich Leo in 1901 influentially classified ancient biographies as Plutarchian (mainly chronological) and Suetonian (mainly topical), but this classification is too simple to accommodate all biographies; cf. A. Dihle, "The Gospels and Greek Biography," in Stuhlmacher, ed., *The Gospel,* 373-74.

60. Burridge, *What,* 139-41, 169-71.

61. Burridge, *What,* 140.

62. Bryan, *A Preface,* 48; cf. Burridge, *What,* 141-42.

63. F. H. Colson, "Τάξει in Papias (The Gospels and the Rhetorical Schools)," *JTS* 14 (1912) 62-69; Kürzinger, *Papias,* 49.

possibility that Papias (or John the Elder before him) thought that the kind of *taxis* appropriate to such a work as a Gospel should be chronological. Papias's view seems to have been that of someone concerned for best practice in historiography, and, since it is such historiographic practice that he professed to follow in his own composition of a work about the sayings and deeds of Jesus, it is plausible that he expected a *bios* of Jesus to be of the sort that resembled historical writing. It is also plausible that he agreed with Dionysius of Halicarnassus that chronological sequence was the best principle for arranging historical material. Chronological order was the form of arrangement preferred by Papias's distinguished contemporary Plutarch in his long series of *Parallel Lives* and by the Roman historian Tacitus, who wrote his biography of *Agricola* in 98 CE.

That Papias did have chronological order in mind when he stated that Mark's Gospel lacked *taxis* is clear from the way he explained this lack of *taxis*: "For he neither heard the Lord nor accompanied him, but later . . . [he heard and accompanied] Peter." It was because Mark was not himself an eyewitness of the history of Jesus that he was unable to supply the order that Peter had failed to give to his material. There seems no reason why a non-eyewitness should not arrange traditions about Jesus in an appropriate topical order.[64] The kind of order which Mark could have imposed on Peter's *chreiai* only if he had himself been an eyewitness must surely be chronological.[65]

In conclusion, what Papias found lacking in Mark's Gospel was any kind of aesthetic arrangement *(taxis, suntaxis)* of the individual *chreiai* that Mark recorded, along with any attempt to combine them into a continuous narrative (as perhaps *suntaxis* especially implies). The sort of aesthetic arrangement Papias would have expected from an Evangelist who had been an eyewitness would have been chronological sequence. Mark's Gospel did have the considerable value, in Papias's eyes, that it was virtually a transcript of Peter's testimony, and Mark should not be criticized for having confined himself to translating and recording Peter's teachings as accurately and completely as possible. He was right not to attempt an ordering of the material that, not being an eyewitness himself, he could not have achieved satisfactorily.

Whether this was an accurate assessment of Mark's Gospel is a question we shall postpone until we have considered how Papias assessed the other Gospels with which he could compare Mark.

---

64. The way that Kürzinger, *Papias*, 49-50, explains this is unconvincing.
65. A. Wright, "Τάξει in Papias," *JTS* 14 (1913) 298-300; Hengel, *Studies*, 154 n. 67.

Mark, Matthew, and John

Following an interjection by Eusebius himself, his quotations from Papias continue with a statement about Matthew that is much shorter than that about Mark:

> Therefore Matthew put the *logia* in an ordered arrangement [*sunetaxato*] in the Hebrew language [*hebraidi dialectō*], but each person [*hekastos*] interpreted [*hērmēneusen*] them as best he could (Eusebius, *Hist. Eccl.* 3.39.16).

We do not know whether in Papias's report of what the Elder said this sentence followed immediately on the account of Mark's Gospel as Eusebius reproduces it or whether there was intervening material that Eusebius has omitted. The latter seems more probable, because the "therefore" *(oun)* at the beginning of this statement about Matthew seems to presuppose something that has been omitted, unless, with Robert Gundry, we suppose that, according to Papias, it was because Mark's Gospel lacked order that Matthew gave order to his collection of the *logia*.[66] That would make this earliest of all accounts of the origins of the Gospels a witness to Markan priority over Matthew. But it seems more likely that Eusebius has omitted some material, perhaps to the effect that Matthew, unlike Mark, was a personal disciple of Jesus. Eusebius may have thought this obvious and therefore redundant. Alternatively, Eusebius has omitted something of which he did not approve. He had his own ideas about the origins of and differences among the Gospels (see especially *Hist. Eccl.* 3.24.5-16) and is likely to have suppressed material in Papias that was not consistent with them.

Kürzinger has offered a novel interpretation of this sentence of Papias. He takes *hebraidi dialectō* to mean, not "in the Hebrew language," but (taking *dialectos* as a technical rhetorical term) "in the Semitic style of composition"; he takes "each person *(hekastos)*" to be Mark and Matthew; and he takes the verb *hermeneuō* — consistently with his interpretation of *hermeneutēs* with reference to Mark — in the sense of "communicate" or "transmit."[67] The result is the following translation: "Now Matthew put the *logia* into literary form in a Hebrew style. Each of them [i.e., Mark and Matthew] conveyed the *logia* as he was in a position to do."[68] On this interpretation, Papias does not

---

66. R. H. Gundry, *Matthew: A Commentary on His Handbook for a Mixed Church under Persecution* (second edition; Grand Rapids: Eerdmans, 1994), 614.

67. Kürzinger, *Papias*, 9-24.

68. "Matthäus nun hat in hebräischem Stil die Worte (über den Herrn) in literarische Form gebracht. Es stellte sie ein jeder so dar, wie er dazu in der Lage war" (Kürzinger, *Papias*, 103).

refer to a work composed by Matthew in Hebrew or Aramaic and subsequently translated into Greek but to the Greek Gospel of Matthew, composed in Greek but in a style characteristic of Jewish literature. The second half of the sentence refers neither to the translation nor even the interpretation of Matthew's Hebrew composition, but sums up the whole discussion of Mark and Matthew by saying that each conveyed the *logia* in the way each was able: Mark in the form of Peter's teachings, without literary arrangement, and Matthew in a literary arrangement in Semitic style.

However, these suggestions have proved the least convincing of Kürzinger's fresh interpretations of Papias.[69] The occurrence of both *hebraidi dialectō* and *hermēneusen* in the same sentence strongly suggests that Papias is talking about translation from one language to another, not style and transmission.

Both the interpretation of Papias's statements about Mark argued above and the traditional rendering of his statement about Matthew can be supported by observing the parallelism and contrast between what, on these views, Papias says about each of these Gospels:

Mark	*Matthew*
Peter, an eyewitness,	Matthew, an eyewitness,
related *logia (chreiai)* about Jesus	put the *logia* about Jesus
orally	in writing
in Aramaic	in Aramaic/Hebrew
but not in literary order.	in literary order.
Mark, not an eyewitness,	Each person, not an eyewitness,
translated Peter's teachings	translated Matthew's written *logia*
and put them in writing	
accurately and omitting nothing.	as well as they were able.

In each case there are two stages, one the activity of an eyewitness, the other the activity of one or more non-eyewitnesses. In the case of Mark's Gospel, Peter spoke in Aramaic and Mark translated into Greek and recorded in writing. In the case of Matthew's Gospel, Matthew himself wrote in Aramaic or Hebrew (*hebraidi dialectō* could be either) and others translated into Greek. Mark's Gospel is "not in order" because Peter did not relate the material in

69. Cf. Schoedel, *Polycarp,* 110; Black, "The Use," 33-34; Black, *Mark,* 91; Davies and Allison, *Matthew,* 16; D. A. Hagner, *Matthew 1–13* (WBC 33A; Dallas: Word, 1993) xliv-xlv. But Kürzinger is partly followed by Gundry, *Matthew,* 619-20; Byrskog, *Story,* 293. Gundry, *Matthew,* 619, points out that the *men . . . de* structure of the sentence requires that *hekastos* refer to each interpreter of Matthew, not to Mark and Matthew.

order, while Mark, not being an eyewitness, rightly did not attempt to put it "in order." Matthew, on the other hand, was an eyewitness who was able and did put the *logia* in order in his original Gospel, but this order was spoiled by those who translated his work into Greek. Thus Papias is concerned throughout with two aspects of each Gospel: its origin from eyewitness testimony and the question of "order." In both cases he wants to explain why a Gospel with eyewitness origins lacks proper "order."

Apparently Papias thought there had been more than one translation of Matthew's original work into Greek. He probably knew something about the Greek Gospels bearing the name of Matthew and related to our canonical Matthew (the *Gospel of the Nazarenes* and the *Gospel of the Ebionites*[70]), which were used by Jewish Christians in Palestine and Syria. He knew they exhibited major divergences from the Gospel of Matthew used in his home church in Hierapolis and neighboring churches. He referred to these various Greek Matthews, including the one he knew and used, in order to show that none of them could be presumed to preserve accurately the "order" *(suntaxis)* of the original Hebrew or Aramaic Matthew. Quite probably Papias continued, after the sentence quoted by Eusebius, to make it more explicit that the original order given to his work by the eyewitness Matthew had suffered in translation. Unlike Mark's scrupulosity in translating and recording no more or less than Peter said, the translators of Matthew had made major alterations to the apostle's text. (Eusebius would not have approved of such a view and would have censored anything more that Papias said about it.)

Such a view, of course, presupposes that a "translated" work was not necessarily a mere translation. In supposing that the translators of Matthew had heavily edited the text, Papias was not positing anything unusual. A "flexible concept of translation" was common in the ancient world.[71] Translators often felt free to improve the work they were translating by rearranging material and adding material from other sources. We have already noticed Josephus's claim that his *Antiquities of the Jews* was a translation — no more and no less — of the Hebrew Scriptures (*Ant.* 1.5, 17; 4.196; 10.218).[72] In fact, of

---

70. But the *Gospel of the Ebionites* may be of later date than Papias's work; cf. R. Bauckham, "The Origin of the Ebionites," in P. J. Tomson and D. Lambers-Petry, eds., *The Image of the Judaeo-Christians in Ancient Jewish and Christian Literature* (WUNT 158; Tübingen: Mohr, 2003) 162-81.

71. G. Kennedy, "Classical and Christian Source Criticism," in W. O. Walker, ed., *The Relationships among the Gospels: An Interdisciplinary Dialogue* (San Antonio: Trinity University Press, 1978) 144. Inowlocki, "Neither Adding," provides evidence from Porphyry, Aristobolus, Cicero, Plato, and book 16 of the *Corpus Hermeticum*, as well as from Josephus.

72. Cf. Cohen, *Josephus*, 24-33.

course, Josephus extensively rewrites, rearranges, and makes omissions from and very substantial additions to the biblical narratives.[73] Papias could easily have imagined the translators of Matthew proceeding similarly and thereby obscuring the "order" Matthew had originally given to his work. But we must distinguish this understanding of Papias's words from the attempt that has frequently been made to identify the *logia* written in Hebrew or Aramaic by Matthew with the hypothetical Gospel source Q.[74] Since Q consists almost entirely of sayings of Jesus, this identification has usually entailed thinking that by the *logia* of the Lord Papias means sayings of Jesus. However, we have seen that in his discussion of Mark Papias uses the term for short accounts of both what Jesus said and what Jesus did.[75] From the Greek Matthew he knew (presumably our canonical Matthew) Papias could easily see that the building blocks for much of the Gospel were the same kind of short units *(chreiai)* of which Mark was composed, and he is unlikely to have thought that this in itself was due to the translator-editors. It was for disturbing the composition Matthew had initially created out of them that he blamed the translator-editors.

Some scholars have supposed that Papias was comparing Mark's Gospel with Matthew's to the disadvantage of the former.[76] Certainly, Papias might have thought Matthew, in the Greek version he knew, somewhat preferable to Mark in its literary order: it begins with an account of the birth of Jesus, as biographies were generally expected to begin, and much of Jesus' teaching is collected into several lengthy discourses. But if, as we have argued, the kind of literary order Papias missed in Mark was primarily chronological, then Matthew could not have seemed much of an improvement on Mark, since it largely follows the same sequence of brief narratives. If we take seriously the implication that the order originally given to his Gospel by Matthew was spoiled by the translators, then it becomes much more plausible to suppose that Papias is comparing the lack of order in both Mark and Matthew with the presence of order in another Gospel: that of John.[77]

There should be no doubt that Papias knew John's Gospel.[78] We no-

---

73. Cohen, *Josephus*, 35-42.

74. This is still maintained, e.g., by Davies and Allison, *Matthew*, 17.

75. See also Kürzinger, *Papias*, 24-26; B. Reicke, *The Roots of the Synoptic Gospels* (Philadelphia: Fortress, 1986) 157-58.

76. E.g., R. Pesch, *Das Markusevangelium*, vol. 1 (HTKNT, third edition, Freiburg: Herder, 1980) 5-6; Gundry, *Matthew*, 619.

77. J. B. Lightfoot, *Essays on the Work Entitled Supernatural Religion* (London: Macmillan, 1889) 165; Wright, "Τάξει in Papias," 300; Hengel, *Studies*, 48.

78. Among those who deny this is Körtner, *Papias*, 197.

ticed in chapter 2 that Papias's list of seven disciples of Jesus (Eusebius, *Hist. Eccl.* 3.39.4) is a distinctively Johannine list, following the order in which six of them appear in John's Gospel (John 1:40-44; 21:2: Andrew, Peter, Philip, Thomas, James, John).[79] From that Johannine sequence only Nathanael is omitted, because doubtless Papias wished to keep the list to the symbolic number seven and wished to include the non-Johannine disciple Matthew on account of his importance as the author of a Gospel. In addition, we may note that Irenaeus (*Adversus Haereses* 5.36.1-2) ascribes to "the elders" a passage including a quotation from John 14:2, a passage Irenaeus probably derived from Papias.[80] (There is also an Armenian reference to Papias which seems to depend on a comment he made on John 19:39,[81] though the reliability of this evidence may be not entirely secure.) Eusebius doubtless had his own reasons for not quoting what Papias said about John's Gospel, especially if, as I believe, Papias ascribed the Gospel not to John the son of Zebedee but to the disciple of Jesus he calls John the Elder.[82] But Eusebius also had his own ideas about the chronological sequencing in the Gospels and maintained there was no incompatibility among them in this respect (*Hist. Eccl.* 3.24.5-16).[83] His interest in quoting Papias is in the apostolic origin of the Gospels, not in Papias's view on their respective order or lack of order. Papias himself, however, seems to have been interested, not in arguing for the apostolic origin of the Gospels he discusses, but rather in explaining how Gospels which were agreed to be of apostolic origin came to differ so much in their "order."

The only reason Papias could have had for thinking that the Gospels of Matthew and Mark both lacked the kind of order to be expected in a work deriving from an eyewitness is that he knew another Gospel, also of eyewitness origin, whose chronological sequence differed significantly from Mark's and Matthew's and whose "order" Papias preferred. From later patristic discussions of the differences among the Gospels, we know that the differences of order among the Synoptic Gospels did not greatly matter to ancient readers by comparison with the more obvious differences in sequence between John and the Synoptics, especially in the case of the events recounted early in each Gospel (Origen, *Commentary on John* 10.2, 6, 14-15; Epiphanius, *Panarion*

79. M. Hengel, *The Johannine Question* (tr. J. Bowden; London: SCM, 1989) 17-21.
80. J. B. Lightfoot, *Biblical Essays* (London: Macmillan, 1893) 67-68, idem, *Essays*, 194-202.
81. Fragment 24 in Kürzinger, *Papias*, 132-35 = fragment 25 in Lightfoot, Harmer, and Holmes, *The Apostolic Fathers*, 327.
82. See chapter 16 below.
83. R. Bauckham, "Papias and Polycrates on the Origin of the Fourth Gospel," *JTS* 44 (1993) 52-53. This passage of Eusebius is discussed in the appendix to chapter 16 below.

51.4.5-10, 17.11-18.1, 18.6, 21.15-16, 22.1-2, 28.6, 30.14;[84] cf. *Muratorian Canon* lines 16-26; Tertullian, *Adversus Marcionem* 4.2.2). Tatian's *Diatessaron,* which carefully wove the narratives of the four canonical Gospels into a single narrative, was no doubt also motivated more by discrepancies in order among the Gospels than by differences among them in parallel pericopes. Tatian did not consistently prefer the Johannine order, but he tended to accept John's authority where his Gospel made explicit chronological statements.[85]

Papias, of course, claimed that he had put his own collection of the logia of the Lord gathered from oral sources in order (*synkatataxai,* Eusebius, *Hist. Eccl.* 3.39.3).[86] But since in his comment on Mark he makes it clear that only an eyewitness could be a reliable source of the kind of order Papias expected in a Gospel, he could not have thought his own work provided this kind of order unless he derived the order itself from an eyewitness source. Unfortunately, we do not know whether Papias's own work arranged the Gospel traditions he collected in a topical order or within the chronological structure he knew from John's Gospel, but most likely he did follow one of these two possible methods of ordering his material.

The Gospel of John offers a far more precise chronological structure than any of the Synoptic Gospels, never leaving the reader in serious doubt as to the period of Jesus' carefully dated ministry in which a particular event occurred. In addition, it largely lacks the disjointed structure characteristic of the Synoptics and produced by the accumulation of short units loosely, if at all, tied together. John's narratives and discourses are generally longer and they are often more closely connected with each other. It is easy to see that John's Gospel could appear to Papias much closer to good historiography than the Gospels of Mark and Matthew were. Not only does it have a clear chronological sequence; it is also closer to the ideal of continuous seamless narrative to be found in the best historiography (Lucian, *Hist. Conscr.* 55).

In summary, then, we find that Papias was contrasting the lack of order in the Gospels of Mark and Matthew with the order to be found in the Gospel of John.[87] He took for granted that all three Gospels originated from eyewit-

84. In these passages Epiphanius is reporting the criticism of the Gospel of John made by the people he calls Alogoi (= without the Logos) who are said to have rejected all the Johannine literature. The Alogoi have commonly been associated with Gaius of Rome, but the whole question is now in debate; for the latest treatment, see C. E. Hill, *The Johannine Corpus in the Early Church* (Oxford: Oxford University Press, 2004) chapter 4.

85. Grant, *Earliest Lives,* 23-26.

86. For this interpretation of the passage, see Kürzinger, *Papias,* 77-82; and chapter 2 above.

87. In Bauckham, "Papias," 53-56, I argued that the Muratorian Canon is dependent on

ness testimony, but, whereas the Gospel of John was actually written by an eyewitness, the Gospels of Mark and Matthew (in the form available to Papias) were at one stage of transmission removed from the direct report of the eyewitness in question himself. In Mark's case, Peter's oral testimony was translated and recorded by Mark, and this accounts for its lack of order, that is, the lack of literary arrangement, which in the case of a Gospel Papias, concerned as he was with best historiographic practice, expected to be chronological. Mark himself was not to be criticized but rather praised for limiting himself to recording Peter's testimony, no more and no less, and refraining from giving the material an order that, not being an eyewitness himself, he was not capable of supplying. Mark's Gospel, then, in Papias's view was really an incomplete historical work: Mark had accomplished the first stage of the historian's task, that of recording the eyewitness source, but was not able to complete the work by putting the material in order.[88] Given this limitation, Papias valued Mark's Gospel because of its scrupulously accurate record of the *chreiai* as Peter related them. Matthew's Gospel, in the Greek form Papias knew, also, when similarly set against the standard of John's Gospel, lacked order, but the reason for this was different. The original Hebrew or Aramaic work written by the eyewitness Matthew himself must have had the accurate order Matthew would have been able to give it, but Papias thought this order had been disrupted by those who exercised considerable freedom in their rendering of the Gospel in Greek. These evaluations of the Gospels of Mark and Matthew make excellent sense once we realize that Papias valued above all the Gospel of John, which was directly written by an eyewitness and offered a much more precise chronological sequence of events. It was by comparison with John that Papias had to see the Gospels of Mark and Matthew as lacking order, but, not wishing to dismiss these Gospels, Papias set out to explain why they lacked order but were nevertheless of great value because of their closeness to eyewitness testimony.

We can now expand our earlier chart of the parallels and contrasts Papias sees between Mark and Matthew by including also the implicit comparison with John:

Papias when it claims that John the Evangelist was "not only an eyewitness and hearer but also a writer of the miracles of the Lord in order." See also chapter 16 below.

88. Kennedy, "Classical and Christian Source Criticism," 148, argues that Papias was not describing the composition of the Gospel of Mark itself but the preliminary notes that Mark would have taken before composing the Gospel. But it is then difficult to understand why Papias describes this preliminary stage of composition so emphatically, while making no reference to the Gospel as he and his readers knew it. It is more plausible that Papias considered the Gospel itself to be no more than the preliminary stage of gathering notes.

John	Mark	Matthew
John, an eyewitness,	Peter, an eyewitness,	Matthew, an eyewitness,
put the logia about	related *logia (chreiai)* about	put the *logia* about
Jesus	Jesus	Jesus
in writing	orally	in writing
in Greek	in Aramaic	in Aramaic/Hebrew
in literary order.	but not in literary order.	in literary order.
	Mark, not an eyewitness, translated Peter's teachings and put them in writing accurately and omitting nothing.	Each person, not an eyewitness, translated Matthew's written *logia* as well as they were able.

Was Papias engaged in a polemical defense of the Gospels of Mark and Matthew against critics who denigrated them because of their lack of order, or, alternatively, in a polemical defense of the Gospel of John against critics who compared it unfavorably with Mark and Matthew? Either of these interpretations is a possibility, but we do not really need to postulate critics to whom Papias was replying in order to understand what he says. He need only be explaining the differences among the Gospels as he himself observed them. He might reasonably have supposed that these differences would be problematic to serious readers (as indeed they proved, according to our evidence, later in the second century) and intended to set any such misgivings to rest. But critics who had voiced specific criticisms that Papias felt obliged to answer need not be in his view.

What of the fact that Papias claims to be giving the views of the Elder, at least in the case of Mark and probably also in the case of Matthew? We have noticed that he probably intended to offer the gist of the Elder's opinions, not exact quotations. We may therefore easily suppose that some of this discussion, such as the use of rhetorical terminology, is Papias's elaboration of the Elder's views as he had heard them. But it is entirely possible that the basic points were made by the Elder himself who, if correctly identified as John the Elder, a personal disciple of Jesus, can hardly have been teaching to this effect much later than c. 90 CE. Very plausibly it would have been the initial "publication" of the Gospel of John that required some such comment on the most obvious difference between this Gospel and those of Mark and Matthew, which were already known as based very closely on the eyewitness testimony of Peter and Matthew. The Elder, without wishing to deny these eyewitness claims, vindicated the eyewitness claims of the Gospel of John by explaining that it alone presented a chronological sequence that reliably derived from an eyewitness. If, as I believe,[89] John the Elder was actually the author of the Gospel of John, then this would have been his way of explaining the differences between his own Gospel and others. In chapter 15 we will observe the strategy of John's Gospel itself for establishing its author's claim to offer eyewitness testimony additional and in some respects superior to that of the much better known eyewitness Peter, embodied in Mark's Gospel.

Is Mark's Gospel Really "Not in Order"?

Only now that we understand the reasons for what Papias says about Mark are we in a position to ask whether it is consistent with what we can observe for ourselves about the Gospel of Mark. Does Mark's Gospel really consist solely of *chreiai* set down one after another in random order?

It is certainly true that the Gospel is largely composed of discrete narrative units and that often they are linked by no more or little more than "and" *(kai)*. However, it is also obvious that they are not placed randomly together. There are, for example, topical collections (controversy stories in 2:1–3:6 and 11:27–12:40; parables in ch. 4). There is the overall chronological framework of the transition from the ministry of John the Baptist to that of Jesus (1:4-15) and the death and burial of Jesus and the empty tomb. There are elements of plot development in which one thing leads to another: the stories of controversy in 2:1–3:6 issue in the plotting of the Pharisees to destroy Jesus (3:6), or the request of James and John (10:35-40) leads to a conflict and Jesus' teaching about leadership as service (10:41:45). In the passion narrative there are many episodes that, for causal or chronological reasons, necessarily belong in the sequence that Mark presents. There are references back and forth within the narrative, such as the anticipation of Jesus' death as early as 2:20, and the three passion predictions. Mark often uses time and place to structure his narrative and connect the episodes (e.g., time: 1:32, 35; 2:1; 4:35; 6:47; 9:2; 11:12, 20; 14:1, 12, 17; 15:1, 25, 33, 42; 16:1; place: 1:14, 16, 21, 39; 2:1, 13; 3:7; 4:1; 5:1; 6:1, 32, 45, 53; 7:24, 31; 8:10, 22, 27; 9:30, 33; 10:1, 32, 46; 11:1, 12, 15, 27; 13:1; 14:3, 32; 15:22; 16:7). There is the use of *inclusio*, such as the correspondence between the two healings of blind men in 8:22-26 and 10:46-52, framing a section within which there are almost no miracles but a development of the theme of suffering. There is Mark's well-known "sandwich" technique of including one episode within the two parts of another (e.g.,

---

89. Bauckham, "Papias," 24-69. See also chapters 16 and 17 below.

5:21-43; 11:12-25), a form of chiasm or concentric structuring. These are only the more obvious features among many that have led most recent scholars to detect a highly sophisticated arrangement of the material, such that the whole (the complete narrative) is very much more than the sum of its parts (the individual pericopes).[90]

Papias's contention that Mark did no more than record, with scrupulous accuracy, the *chreiai* as Peter related them, is mistaken.[91] However, we should remember that it is from the perspective of his own ideals of historiographic composition that Papias views Mark's Gospel. Two aspects of this perspective are relevant. First, we must attempt to place Mark in the literary spectrum of Greek and Roman biography. Most such works depend on particular sources, written or oral, and units of tradition, like the Markan pericopes. But they differ considerably in the literary sophistication with which they create a narrative whole out of these sources. Christopher Bryan makes this point and goes on to place Mark in the spectrum:

> The more sophisticated the writer, generally the less obvious are the junctures between particular sources and the units of tradition that make up the work. Tacitus's and Plutarch's narratives usually flow as elegant and continuous wholes. In the *Life of Secundus*,[92] by contrast, the four pieces [i.e., the four discrete units that make up this *Life:* a novella, a passion, a diatribe and a dialogue] stand simply side by side, and are easily identified. Yet even a sophisticated writer like Lucian may choose to structure a work very simply; *Demonax* is essentially a collection of anecdotes strung together in no particular order in a biographical framework.
>
> In Mark's use of sources, I place him somewhere between Plutarch and Tacitus on the one hand, and *Demonax* and *Secundus* on the other. . . . [W]hile Mark does not combine his materials into a continuous whole with anything like the grace of a Plutarch or a Tacitus, still he does make

90. For Mark's Gospel as a host of minor narratives composed within an overall narrative superstructure with its own plot, see C. Breytenbach, *The Gospel of Mark as an Episodic Narrative: Reflections on the "Composition" of the Second Gospel = Scriptura*, special issue 4 (1989) 1-26.

91. I therefore differ from B. Orchard, "Mark and the Fusion of Traditions," in F. van Segbroeck, C. M. Tuckett, G. van Belle, and J. Verheyden, eds., *The Four Gospels 1992: Festschrift Frans Neirynck*, vol. 2 (Leuven: Leuven University Press/Peeters, 1992) 779-800, who thinks that the Gospel is a transcript of public lectures given by Peter and taken down verbatim in shorthand.

92. This is the *Life of Secundus the Philosopher* (second half of second century CE); see B. E. Perry, *Secundus the Silent Philosopher* (Philological Monographs 22; New York: American Philological Association, 1964).

considerably more effort in this direction than does the writer of *Secundus*.[93]

We should remember at this point that Papias evidently expects of a life of Jesus the highest standards of contemporary historiography. In literary character, therefore, he is looking for something toward the end of the spectrum represented by Plutarch's *Parallel Lives* rather than that represented by the two very different but essentially unstructured works *The Life of Secundus* and the *Demonax* of Lucian. Reading Mark, he is more likely to have been struck by its resemblance to a work like the latter, with its almost entirely unstructured collection of anecdotes, than by the elements of structure that also characterize Mark's Gospel. Whereas Bryan can say that, considering the whole spectrum of such biographies, "Mark's narrative certainly needs no apology or explanation,"[94] for Papias it did need, precisely, apology and explanation, such as he offers in his account of how Mark recorded only what Peter related as discrete units. He is measuring it against the highest standards of literary historiography, and by these standards it compared badly with the Gospel of John, which, while it lacks the stylistic skills of a Plutarch, is much more chronologically precise and much more obviously a continuous narrative whole than Mark's Gospel is.[95]

Secondly, however, we should note that the ways in which Mark does structure his narrative are mostly characteristic of oral composition. This point has been elucidated especially in a series of articles by Joanna Dewey.[96] She summarizes her arguments as follows, linking them to an interpretation of Papias's words that coheres exactly with our argument about the latter:

> [T]he Gospel of Mark works well as oral literature. It is of an appropriate length for oral performance. A storyteller could learn it from simply

93. Bryan, *A Preface*, 48-49; cf. Burridge, *What*, 172-73, 201.

94. Bryan, *A Preface*, 40.

95. Burridge, *What*, 227: "The Fourth Gospel is more of a continuous whole than the synoptic gospels, despite the occasional break or seam in the narrative."

96. J. Dewey, "Oral Methods of Structuring Narrative in Mark," *Int* 53 (1989) 32-44; eadem, "Mark as Interwoven Tapestry: Forecasts and Echoes for a Listening Audience," *CBQ* 53 (1991) 221-36; eadem, "The Gospel of Mark as Oral/Aural Event: Implications for Interpretation," in E. Struthers Malbon and E. V. McKnight, eds., *The New Literary Criticism and the New Testament* (JSNTSup 109; Sheffield: Sheffield Academic, 1994) 145-63; eadem, "The Survival of Mark's Gospel: A Good Story?" *JBL* 123 (2004) 495-507. Cf. also Bryan, *A Preface*, Part II. Witherington, *Mark*, 15-16, while agreeing that Mark's rhetoric is oral in character, denies that Mark's Gospel was intended for oral performance, apparently on the basis of 13:14, which he takes to refer to the private reader of the Gospel. It is debatable whether this verse refers to the reader of the Gospel or the reader of Daniel. Dewey, "Oral Methods," 35-36, adopts the latter view.

hearing it performed. As I and others have argued elsewhere, its composition consists of oral composition techniques. Briefly, the story consists of happenings that can be easily visualized and thus readily remembered. It consists of short episodes connected paratactically [i.e., by no more or little more than "and," thus placing events side by side rather than subordinating one to another]. The narrative is additive and aggregative [short narratives accumulate rather than creating a climactic linear plot]. Teaching is not gathered into discourses according to topic but rather embedded in short narratives, which is the way oral cultures remember teaching. Indeed, I would suggest that it is the lack of a more literate chronological and topical order that Papias had in mind when he said Mark's story was "not in order." . . . *It followed oral ordering procedures, not proper rhetorical form.*

The plot as well as the style is typical of oral composition. The structure does not build toward a linear climactic plot; the plot to kill Jesus is first introduced in Mark 3:6 but not picked up and developed until Mark 11, and it does not really get under way until Mark 14. Rather than linear plot development, the structure consists of repetitive patterns, series of three parallel episodes, concentric structures, and chiastic structures. Such structures are characteristic of oral literatures, helping the performer, the audience, and new performers and audiences to remember and transmit the material. From what we know of oral literature there is no reason why it could not have been composed and transmitted in oral form.[97]

As Dewey herself points out, none of this enables us to tell whether Mark's Gospel was actually composed orally or was composed in writing using the oral techniques of a skilled oral storyteller. She does think it more probable than not that the Gospel was "refined in writing," thus accounting for some structural elements that are widely separated in the text.[98] But the Gospel could depend closely on an already existing oral narrative, whether or not composed orally by the author of the Gospel, so that the written Gospel is a written "performance" of an oral narrative. Alternatively, it could be that Mark composed the narrative in writing, making use of oral techniques because he was writing for oral performance of his text. In any case, it seems clear that the Gospel was indeed composed for oral performance, and that the oral structuring techniques it employs would have assisted such oral performance and aural reception.[99]

97. Dewey, "The Survival," 499, italics added.
98. Dewey, "Oral Methods," 43-44; eadem, "The Survival," 499-500, n. 19.
99. On oral performance of Mark, see Shiner, *Proclaiming*; and D. F. Smith, *Can We Hear*

For our main concern at this point, which is to explain how Papias was able to judge Mark's Gospel lacking in "order," the important implication is that Papias, with his literary preoccupations, would likely not have recognized oral methods of structuring a narrative as really "order." It would be easy for him to overlook the evidence that Mark did not confine himself to reporting the individual *chreiai* as Peter related them. Mark's ways of shaping the discrete units into a narrative whole were not what Papias was looking for.

We can understand, therefore, how easy it was for Papias to exaggerate Mark's lack of order. But this exaggeration also served his purpose well. Papias was engaged in explaining the differences between John's Gospel and Mark's in a way that favored John's "order" without *denigrating* Mark's Gospel. Had he recognized Mark's structured character, he would have had either to attribute it to Peter, thus acknowledging a serious conflict between two eyewitnesses (Peter and John), or else to blame Mark for providing an order that, not being an eyewitness, he was not qualified to construct with accuracy. Papias's solution to the problem of the differences between John and Mark was one that came easily to him because it cohered very closely with his own view of the historian's task, as we can gather it from the extracts Eusebius has provided. On the one hand, Papias held that the best sources for the historian were oral, not far removed from their eyewitness source, but, on the other hand, he considered the collecting of these sources no more than the historian's first task. Mark was right to limit himself to this task because he had no reliable resources for going beyond it. Thus Mark's Gospel is of great value because it preserves so accurately Peter's testimony, but it lacks order. For order Papias thought one must turn to John's Gospel, which meets his criteria for a finished work of historiography. Since John was himself an eyewitness, he was competent to put the material in proper chronological order, and he has done so in a way that conforms to best historiographic practice by shaping his material into a continuous literary whole, with chronological and geographical precision and with a developing plot that builds to a climax.

If Papias was not merely putting words into John the Elder's mouth but putting the gist of what the Elder used to say into Papias's own words, then the literary-critical aspect of his words may well be attributable to Papias. The Elder may have said that the difference in order between John's and Mark's Gospels was explicable by the fact that, whereas the former was in correct

What They Heard? The Effect of Orality upon a Markan Reading-Event (Ph.D. thesis, University of Durham, 2002).

chronological order, Mark, working only from Peter's preaching, was unable to arrange much of the material in accurate chronological order. As far as it goes, this is plausible enough. But what about Mark's sophisticated use of oral methods of structuring his narrative? We cannot tell how far Mark had already structured his narrative in this way before writing it. At least some of it — the passion narrative — is widely regarded as already structured before Mark wrote it, and our argument in earlier chapters has accepted that as probable. We could well attribute the order of Mark's passion narrative to Peter himself, this narrative being, as we have suggested earlier, Peter's individual version of the official eyewitness testimony formulated by the Twelve. Whether Peter had any hand in other elements of order and structure in the Gospel it is probably impossible to tell. But these uncertainties are no impediment to accepting the Elder's general claim that the oral testimony of Peter lies not at several removes but immediately behind the text of Mark's Gospel. There are, of course, other reasons alleged for not believing this claim, and we shall turn to them shortly, after first briefly noticing other external evidence that corroborates the claim.

Mark as Peter's Gospel

We have already referred to Justin Martyr's description of Mark's Gospel as "the memoirs" *(apomnēmoneumata)* of Peter *(Dialogue* 106.3), and noted the connection with Papias's statement that Mark "wrote down some individual items just as [Peter] related them from memory *(apemnēmoneusen).*" Since Justin regularly referred to the Gospels generally as "the memoirs of the apostles" and since Papias's use of the verb is not especially conspicuous in his account solely of the origin of Mark's Gospel, it is hardly likely that Justin's description of Mark as Peter's memoirs is dependent on Papias. More likely, the Gospel was already sometimes called Peter's memoirs when Papias wrote and his use of the verb *apomnēmoneuō* is an echo of that usage.

Later references to Mark's Gospel as a record of Peter's preaching, such as those by the Muratorian Canon,[100] Irenaeus, Clement of Alexandria, Tertullian, and the so-called Anti-Marcionite Prologue to Mark, are probably

100. Only the last words of the Muratorian Canon's comment on Mark's Gospel survive: "at which nevertheless he was present and has thus set it down *(quibus tamen interfuit et ita posuit)*" must mean that Mark, not being an eyewitness, was not present at the events of Jesus' history, but *was* present at Peter's preaching and recorded it.

dependent on Papias and do not provide independent testimony to a tradition more widespread than Papias's own writing. But there are two intriguing instances which *may* provide such independent testimony. We cannot be sure, but they seem worth discussing because they are hardly ever even mentioned in this connection.

One is Saying 13 of the *Gospel of Thomas:*

> Jesus said to his disciples, "Make comparisons; tell me whom I am like."
>
> Simon Peter said to him, "You are like a righteous angel."
>
> Matthew said to him, "You are like a wise philosopher."
>
> Thomas said to him, "Master, my mouth is completely unable to say whom you are like."
>
> Jesus said to him, "I am not your master, for you have drunk, you have become drunk from the bubbling spring which I have dug."
>
> And he took him aside and spoke three words to him.
>
> And when Thomas returned to his companions, they asked him, "What did Jesus say to you?"
>
> Thomas said to them, "If I speak one of his words which he said to me, you will take up stones and throw them at me. And fire will come from the stones and consume you."[101]

The passage clearly compares Peter's and Matthew's characterizations of Jesus with Thomas's appreciation of the ineffable nature of Jesus, and regards the former as lacking insight and misleading. But why are Peter and Matthew selected for this role? It would be easy enough to explain the appearance of Peter from the fact that he was the apostolic figure of unrivalled prominence and authority among the "orthodox" Christians from whom this Gospel wishes to distinguish itself. But why Matthew? Matthew would be one of the most obscure of the Twelve had not a Gospel been attributed to him. The saying in the *Gospel of Thomas* must presuppose the existence of Matthew's Gospel and its attribution to Matthew. By citing Matthew's view of Jesus it is deliberately denigrating the Gospel of Matthew and upholding the superiority of the *Gospel of Thomas* with its sayings derived from Thomas. This is confirmed by the fact that Matthew's description of Jesus as "like a wise philosopher" is quite appropriate as a reference to Matthew's Gospel. In no other Gospel is Jesus' ethical teaching as prominent as it is in Matthew's. In the ancient world ethics was the domain of philosophers, and an ethical teacher like

101. This translation is from W. D. Stroker, *Extracanonical Sayings of Jesus* (SBL Resources for Biblical Study 18; Atlanta: Scholars, 1989) 26-27. I have corrected the typographical error "thrown" to "throw."

the Jesus of Matthew could well be described as "a wise philosopher." The *Gospel of Thomas* itself is only minimally concerned with ethics.

If Matthew in this passage represents Matthew's Gospel, then it becomes highly likely that Peter represents Mark's Gospel. Peter's statement that Jesus is "like a righteous angel" is presumably a deliberate substitute for Peter's confession in Mark (8:29: "You are the Messiah"), made because the *Gospel of Thomas* has no interest in the Hebrew Bible or the Jewish messianic expectation. The term "a righteous angel" may simply reflect the evidently supernatural character of Mark's Jesus. Alternatively it could be a misunderstanding of the biblical quotation with which Mark's Gospel begins: "See, I am sending my messenger *(angelos)* ahead of you" (Mark 1:2). The author of Saying 13 of *Thomas* would have read this mistakenly as a reference to Jesus rather than to John the Baptist.

That most scholars have not seen these probable references to the Gospels of Mark and Matthew in Saying 13 of *Thomas*[102] may in part be due to the conviction of many scholars that the *Gospel of Thomas* is independent of the canonical Gospels. We need not enter that discussion here but only point out that, whatever the sources of the sayings of Jesus in *Thomas* might be in most cases, this particular saying looks very much as though it were composed for the written collection to justify it over against the "orthodox" Gospels of Mark and Matthew. It demonstrates no more than that the final redactor was aware of these Gospels. Unfortunately, scholars remain deeply divided over the date of the *Gospel of Thomas* in the form we have it (as also over the dates of hypothetical earlier versions), and the date of the composition of this saying therefore remains difficult to determine. Many scholars date the *Gospel* as early as or earlier than Papias, and in that case this saying would provide evidence of the close association of the Gospel of Mark with Peter independently of Papias. But the present state of scholarship on the *Gospel of Thomas* leaves this possibility highly debatable.

The second reference to Mark's Gospel as a record of Peter's preaching that may be independent of Papias is rather indirect. According to Clement of Alexandria (*Stromateis* 7.106.4), writing c. 200 CE, the Egyptian Gnostic teacher Basilides claimed that he had been taught by a certain Glaucias, "the interpreter *(hermēnea)* of Peter." This parallel to Papias's description of Mark as "the interpreter *(hermēneutēs)* of Peter" can hardly be accidental. Though

---

102. They were seen by A. F. Walls, "The References to Apostles in the Gospel of Thomas," *NTS* 7 (1960-61) 269. T. V. Smith, *Petrine Controversies in Early Christianity* (WUNT 2/15; Tübingen: Mohr, 1985) 115-16, and T. A. Wayment, "Christian Teachers in Matthew and Thomas: The Possibility of Becoming a 'Master,'" *JECS* 12 (2004) 289-311, both think that, by referring to Matthew and Peter, the *Gospel of Thomas* intends reference to the figure of Peter in Matthew's Gospel, especially to Matt 16:16-19.

the words translated "interpreter" in each case are different *(hermēneus, hermēneutēs)*, they are closely related and synonymous.

Since Clement knew and quoted Basilides' own works, we can be confident that the claim to have been a disciple of Glaucias goes back to Basilides himself. As for Basilides' dates, Clement states vaguely that he was active in the reigns of Hadrian and Antoninus Pius (117-61 CE), but Clement's apparent concern to show that he could not have been taught by a disciple of Peter may mean that his broad indication of dates errs on the late side. Eusebius's *Chronikon* gives the precise date of 132-33 CE for Basilides, but we do not know to what specific event this date refers.[103] It seems likely that Basilides was claiming to have been the disciple of Peter's interpreter Glaucias around the time when Papias was writing or perhaps somewhat later.

Scholars who have argued that Papias's statements about the Gospels were motivated by anti-Gnostic apologetic[104] have sometimes seen in his description of Mark as Peter's interpreter a polemical response to Basilides' authorization of his teaching by reference to Glaucias the interpreter of Peter. But there is little to be said for the idea that Papias was concerned with anti-Gnostic apologetic, and the idea has generally been abandoned.[105] It is much more likely that Basilides' claim was imitative of the description of Mark as Peter's interpreter. He meant to authorize his own claim to esoteric tradition transmitted orally from Peter by paralleling the claim that Mark's Gospel conveyed Peter's teaching. He may have known this latter claim either directly from reading Papias[106] or indirectly from Papias's influence, but the chronology makes it rather more plausible that he knew it as a tradition about Mark's Gospel independently of Papias. Also in favor of this view is the special association of both Mark and his Gospel with Alexandria, where Basilides had his philosophical school. This association was known to Clement of Alexandria (Eusebius, *Hist. Eccl.* 2.16.1[107]). It is very plausible that Mark was known as "Peter's interpreter," with reference to the authorship of his Gospel, in Egypt from an early date. Therefore, as with the testimony of the *Gospel of Thomas*, we cannot be sure that this is evidence for the association of Peter with Mark's Gospel independent of Papias, but in this case the indications that it is are quite strong.

103. A. Harnack, *Die Chronologie der altchristlichen Litteratur bis Eusebius,* vol. 1 (Leipzig: Hinrichs, 1897) 290-91.

104. E.g., Niederwimmer, "Johannes Markus," 186; W. Bauer, *Orthodoxy and Heresy in Earliest Christianity,* ed. R. A. Kraft and G. Krodel (Philadelphia: Fortress, 1971) 184-89.

105. Cf. Schoedel, *Polycarp,* 100-101, 112; Byrskog, *Story,* 273.

106. This is the view of M. Hengel, *The Four Gospels and the One Gospel of Jesus Christ* (tr. J. Bowden; London: SCM, 2000) 58.

107. Also, if authentic, the *Letter to Theodore,* published by Morton Smith.

A Petrine Gospel?

Kurt Niederwimmer, in an influential article,[108] offered three arguments against the historical credibility of what Papias said about Mark's Gospel. The first is that the Gospel's vague and even erroneous indications of Galilean geography are incompatible with an author of Jewish Palestinian origin, as the John Mark of the New Testament was.[109] The second is that the Gospel's references to Jewish rites (Mark 7:1-5) display ignorance of Jewish customs and suggest that the author must have been a Gentile.[110] These two arguments are against identifying the author of the Gospel as John Mark of Jerusalem (and could in principle be compatible with the view that an otherwise unknown Mark acted as Peter's interpreter). The third argument is against the claim that Peter was the source of the Gospel's contents. Niederwimmer finds this incompatible with the findings of form criticism and redaction criticism, which have shown that the traditions in the Gospel are the product of a long and complex tradition history.[111]

The first and second of these arguments have been very adequately answered by others[112] (including Joel Marcus, who does not regard Papias's statement about Mark as historically credible), and the refutations need not be repeated here. But we may note some evidence that points in the opposite direction. The author of Mark seems to have been bilingual, competent in both Greek and Aramaic, a characteristic that suggests a Palestinian, and most plausibly a Jerusalem Jew. Martin Hengel points to the many Aramaic terms that have been preserved in the Gospel: "I do not know any other work in Greek which has so many Aramaic or Hebrew words and formulae in so narrow a space."[113] More recently Maurice Casey has argued that substantial parts, at least, of this Gospel were translated from Aramaic.[114]

Niederwimmer's third argument opens up the whole issue of the nature of the Gospel traditions, their transmission in the earliest churches and their relationship to the eyewitnesses, which we shall discuss in the following chapters.

108. Niederwimmer, "Johannes Markus."

109. Niederwimmer, "Johannes Markus," 178-83.

110. Niederwimmer, "Johannes Markus," 183-85.

111. Niederwimmer, "Johannes Markus," 185.

112. Geography: Hengel, *Studies*, 46, 148 n. 51; idem, *Between Jesus and Paul* (tr. J. Bowden; London: SCM, 1983) 193 n. 19; Marcus, *Mark 1–8*, 21. Jewish rites: Hengel, *Studies*, 148-49 n. 52; Marcus, *Mark 1–8*, 19-20.

113. Hengel, *Studies*, 46.

114. M. Casey, *Aramaic Sources of Mark's Gospel* (SNTSMS 102; Cambridge: Cambridge University Press, 1998).

10. Models of Oral Tradition

The argument of this book — that the texts of our Gospels are close to the eyewitness reports of the words and deeds of Jesus — runs counter to almost all recent New Testament scholarship. As we have indicated from time to time, the prevalent view is that a long period of oral transmission in the churches intervened between whatever the eyewitnesses said and the Jesus traditions as they reached the Evangelists. No doubt the eyewitnesses started the process of oral tradition, but it passed through many retellings, reformulations, and expansions before the Evangelists themselves did their own editorial work on it.

Scholars differ widely as to how conservative or creative the tradition was, and so on the extent to which the contents of the Gospels reliably preserve what Jesus actually said and did. It would be misleading to suggest that this view of the transmission of Jesus traditions in the early church necessarily leads to historical skepticism about the reliability of the Gospels' accounts of Jesus. Many scholars suppose that the communities that handed on the traditions were careful to preserve them, not without adaptation and interpretation, but broadly with faithfulness to the form in which they received them. As we shall see later in this chapter, oral transmission is quite capable of preserving traditions faithfully, even across much longer periods than that between Jesus and the writing of the Gospels, and we shall see reason to support those scholars who see the early Christian transmission of Jesus traditions as a relatively conservative process. Other scholars, however, working with the dictum that the Jesus traditions are in the first place evidence about the Christian communities that transmitted them, conclude that they tell us much more about those communities than about Jesus. The traditions were not only adapted, but in many cases created for the use to which the Christian churches put them, in preaching or teaching. The transmission process was a highly creative one. The Gospels are unreliable sources for the history of Jesus not merely because of the fallibility of human memories but more decisively because the Christian communities had no real interest in preserving traditions about the past but formulated Jesus traditions for the quite different purpose of witnessing to the present, living Lord Jesus.

The main purpose of this chapter and the next is to consider the implications of putting the eyewitnesses back into the picture, not merely as the original sources of gospel traditions, but as people who remained accessible sources and authoritative guarantors of their own testimony throughout the period between Jesus and the writing of the Gospels. For this purpose we cannot avoid the key issues involved in discussion of the nature of the transmission of Jesus traditions in the early church. The role we attribute to the eyewitnesses will be fully credible only if we can set it within this wider context and engage constructively with the range of scholarly discussion of the wider issues. To keep the discussion within reasonable bounds, we must take care to focus on the issue of the eyewitnesses, but in order to support our view of the eyewitnesses and to show what a decisive difference putting them back in the picture makes, we must also range more widely. However, we shall restrict discussion to the Synoptic Gospels, since it is generally agreed that the Gospel of John is a special case (however this specialness is understood). Issues about the transmission of traditions are different in this case. We reserve the Gospel of John for full discussion in chapters 14-16.

In this chapter we will discuss the three main models of oral tradition that have been used to understand the process of the transmission of Gospel tradition in the early church. They are associated with the names of Rudolf Bultmann, Birger Gerhardsson, and Kenneth Bailey.

Form Criticism

The dominant scholarly picture of the transmission of Jesus traditions in the early church has its origins, some eighty-five years ago, in the methodology for Gospels studies that is generally known in English as form criticism — not quite a translation of the German term *Formgeschichte* ("form history").[1]

---

1. For useful accounts of form criticism, see B. S. Easton, *The Gospel before the Gospels* (London: Allen and Unwin, 1928) chapter 2; S. H. Travis, "Form Criticism," in I. H. Marshall, ed., *New Testament Interpretation* (Grand Rapids: Eerdmans, 1977) 153-64; V. K. Robbins, "Form

It is a curious fact that nearly all the contentions of the early form critics have by now been convincingly refuted, but the general picture of the process of oral transmission that the form critics pioneered still governs the way most New Testament scholars think.

The form criticism of the Gospels was pioneered and developed by three German scholars in enormously influential works: Karl Ludwig Schmidt's *Der Rahmen der Geschichte Jesu* ("The Framework of the Story of Jesus," 1919),[2] Martin Dibelius's *From Tradition to Gospel* (1919),[3] and Rudolf Bultmann's *The History of the Synoptic Tradition* (1921).[4] Schmidt is generally included among the pioneers because his argument was foundational for the whole approach. He drew attention to the way in which Mark's Gospel is composed of short units — stories about Jesus or sayings of Jesus — and argued that the overall framework that links these together is largely secondary, a creation of the Evangelist. The units (pericopes) preexisted the Gospel as distinct traditions transmitted orally until Mark first put them in writing and supplied the "string" on which they are now threaded like pearls. The framework is therefore mostly artificial and the order of pericopes in Mark determined by topical and other non-historical considerations. But the result that was the starting point for form criticism was the recognition that Mark, like the other Synoptic Gospels, breaks down into short units that could have existed separately in the oral tradition. Mark's Gospel is to be seen as a kind of oral literature that incorporates the oral traditions much as they already existed. This insight opened the way, for the first time, to serious study of the oral phase of transmission of the gospel traditions. This is what the form critics undertook to pursue.

Criticism: New Testament," *ABD* 2.841-843. See also R. Bultmann, "The New Approach to the Synoptic Problem," in idem, *Existence and Faith* (tr. S. M. Ogden; London: Hodder and Stoughton, 1961) 35-56 (this essay first appeared in German in 1926). For the antecedents of form criticism and the influence of the Old Testament scholar Hermann Gunkel on the New Testament form critics, see M. J. Buss, *Biblical Form Criticism in Its Context* (JSOTSup 274; Sheffield: Sheffield Academic, 1999) chapter 12.

2. K. L. Schmidt, *Der Rahmen der Geschichte Jesu* (Berlin: Trowizsch, 1919). This has never been translated into English. The fullest account of it in English is in D. R. Hall, *The Gospel Framework: Fiction or Fact?* (Carlisle: Paternoster, 1998), which is also a strong critique. Schmidt's subsequent book has now been translated: *The Place of the Gospels in the General History of Literature* (tr. B. R. McCane; Columbia: University of South Carolina Press, 2002).

3. M. Dibelius, *From Tradition to Gospel* (tr. B. L. Woolf; London: Nicholson and Watson, 1934). The German original, *Die Formgeschichte des Evangelium*, was first published in 1919, but the English translation is of the enlarged second edition (Tübingen, 1933).

4. R. Bultmann, *The History of the Synoptic Tradition* (tr. J. Marsh; Oxford: Blackwell, 1963; second edition 1968). The German original, *Die Geschichte der synoptischen Tradition,* was first published in 1921 (Göttingen: Vandenhoeck und Ruprecht), but the English translation includes the supplement added to the second German edition (1958).

That the individual units of the Synoptic Gospels are close to the oral forms in which they previously existed and that in oral transmission they were not necessarily linked together as they are in the Gospels remain, in my opinion, the most significant insights of form criticism and have not been refuted. We have already seen how this characteristic of Mark was already, in essence, recognized by Papias. To be sure, even the form critics admitted exceptions. Mark's passion narrative, if it preexisted Mark's telling of it at all, must have existed as a connected narrative of some kind (and many scholars take the view we have endorsed in chapter 8: that it goes back to the Jerusalem church in, at the latest, the 40s). There are also parts of Mark's Gospel — such as a string of short sayings of Jesus, a collection of parables, a collection of controversy stories — which could well have existed as small collections of Gospel traditions already before Mark.[5] It is also easy to dispute Schmidt's view that Mark's chronological and geographical framework is completely unhistorical and his own creation. The very broad outline of the story could well have been adopted by Mark from the type of "kerygmatic summary" that is to be found in the speeches of Peter and Paul in Acts and that, in my opinion, existed in early Christian tradition as a distinct form from the gospel traditions themselves, that is, from the individual stories and sayings.[6] If this book's argument for a close relationship between Mark's Gospel and Peter's oral testimony is accepted, one could even argue that Mark, when editing the individual traditions he had received from Peter, deployed a general knowledge of the course of Jesus' ministry that he owed to Peter. But there would still be much that is artificial — that is, that does not reproduce the chronological sequence of the life of Jesus — in Mark's actual arrangement of the material.[7] That for the most part he was arranging units that probably not even Peter could have put in exact chronological order is clear. He was evidently guided to a large extent by the good storyteller's need to lay out the material in a way that facilitates the readers'/hearers' appreciation of it. That most of the individual pericopes in all three Synoptic Gospels retain broadly the shape in which they existed in oral transmission is a sound insight.

5. W. R. Telford, "The Pre-Markan Tradition in Recent Research (1980-1990)," in *The Four Gospels 1992* (F. Neirynck FS; Leuven: Leuven University Press/Peeters, 1992) vol. 2, 693-723, provides a comprehensive survey (for the specified period) of scholarly views on this topic.

6. R. Bauckham, "Kerygmatic Summaries in the Speeches of Acts," in B. Witherington, ed., *History, Literature and Society in the Book of Acts* (Cambridge: Cambridge University Press, 1996) 185-217; cf. also G. N. Stanton, *Jesus of Nazareth in New Testament Preaching* (SNTSMS 27; Cambridge: Cambridge University Press, 1974).

7. This seems to me the most that the significant critique of Schmidt by Hall, *The Gospel Framework,* has demonstrated. Cf. also V. Taylor, *The Formation of the Gospel Tradition* (second ed.; London: Macmillan, 1935) 38-41.

But this is only the starting point for form criticism. It enabled the form critics to classify the Gospels as folk literature, close to their oral origins, and to focus on the "form" *(Gattung)* of each unit. They produced a typology of different forms, which were supposed to be determined by compositional character, though content also played a significant part in the classification. The details of the classification need not detain us here, but by way of illustration we list the five forms identified by Dibelius in the narrative units of the Gospels. They were: the paradigm (for which Bultmann preferred the term apophthegm, and Vincent Taylor originated the label that became customary in English-speaking scholarship: pronouncement story), the tale, the legend, the passion story, and the myth. The tradition took these shapes within the early Christian communities, where each form was determined by a specific *Sitz im Leben* ("setting in life") of the church and each had a distinctive function. The *Sitz im Leben* is a typical situation, such as preaching, worship, catechesis, or apologetic. The form critics claimed to discover how each Gospel pericope had functioned in its oral form in the life of the community.

It is in this sense that the gospel traditions are said to inform us primarily about the life of the early church rather than about the historical life of Jesus. It was a short step to assuming that the traditions were not only adapted to their functions in the church but in many cases actually created for those functions. However, it should be said that the more moderate scholars, especially English-speaking scholars,[8] who adopted German form criticism critically, often argued that understanding the way a tradition functioned in the life of the church by no means entailed that it originated in that context and could not also go back to a *Sitz im Leben Jesu*. But the possibility that gospel traditions could plausibly be understood as creations of the community was what gave rise to the whole discussion of criteria for authenticity of sayings of Jesus. Such criteria for authenticity (that is, for having originated as words of Jesus) by which to sift the sayings of Jesus in the Gospels derived from the form critical movement's claim to be able to place the traditions in the life of the church and thereby to explain the origin of inauthentic sayings.

Bultmann in particular developed form criticism as a tool for tracing the origin and tradition history of gospel traditions. This was possible, in his view, because of a number of factors. One was that most of the pericopes as we have them in the Gospels are not pure examples of their form: they dis-

---

8. See, e.g., Easton, *The Gospel,* chapter 3; Taylor, *The Formation;* R. H. Lightfoot, *The Gospel Message of St. Mark* (Oxford: Clarendon, 1950) 102: "The tendency to modify the narrative for particular purposes is undoubtedly present in the gospels, and was recognized long before form criticism was heard of; but there is no reason to think that it is present to a disconcerting degree, or to call in question the reliability of the record as a whole."

play elaborations of the pure forms or do not fit unequivocally into any one form but must be classified as mixed types. Bultmann assumed that each tradition must originally have existed in the pure form and that the deviations from pure form are traces of the history the tradition has gone through between its origin and its incorporation in a Gospel text. In addition, Bultmann attempted to establish laws of the tradition that would have generally affected all the forms. He did so especially by observing the changes that Markan pericopes undergo when taken over by Matthew or Luke and assuming that the laws of this literary relationship were a mere continuation of those operative in the preceding oral transmission. But laws of tradition were also to be found through the study of folktales, popular anecdotes, and folksongs, which Bultmann thought to be the same kind of oral literature as the Gospels. Such study would enable us to distinguish traditions of earlier and later origin, and even to reconstruct a form of a tradition earlier than any that has been preserved.

Although the form critics used examples from Hellenistic and rabbinic literature to help identify the specific forms that the Gospel traditions take, the analogy with folk literature as studied by the folklorists of the day was decisive for much of their understanding of the Gospel tradition. For the form critics it was axiomatic that folk literature was anonymous and to be attributed to the community, not to individuals, certainly not named individuals. Bultmann also assumed that in such a context traditions were freely created and modified according to the needs of the community. Such communities were not interested in the past and had no reason to attempt to preserve historical accounts for their historical value.

This contention not only rested on the supposed folkloric analogy, but had also a theological dimension. The Jesus who mattered for the early communities, especially the "Hellenistic" (as opposed to Palestinian) communities, was Jesus the risen and exalted Lord, who was in direct relationship with the community. This contemporary Jesus addressed the community through the Christian prophets, whose words were often incorporated in the Gospel traditions and came to be attributed in the Gospels to the pre-Easter Jesus. The communities had no historical consciousness such that would have required them to care about the distinction between the pre- and post-Easter Jesus. This virtually axiomatic lack of interest in the genuinely past life and teaching of Jesus on the part of the early Christian communities is central to Bultmann's skepticism about the historical value of the traditions generally. For the same reason the communities presumably attached no importance to the eyewitnesses and would not have had recourse to them even if they had been accessible. Any role they had would have been confined to the Palestinian origins of the Christian movement and absent from the Hellenistic communities in which the gospel traditions as we have them took shape.

Criticisms of Form Criticism

Virtually every element in this construction has been questioned and rejected by some or even most scholars. Many of these criticisms are rooted in the much better and fuller information that is now available about the way oral traditions operate in predominantly oral societies.

(1) Bultmann's assumption that traditions originated in pure form is highly questionable: there is no reason why they should not have existed from the beginning in modified or mixed forms.[9] The fact that so few of the Gospel pericopes actually conform to the ideal types postulated by the form critics indicates that a more nuanced approach to form is requisite.

(2) There is no strict correlation between a form and a *Sitz im Leben*. The same traditions often perform several different functions in different contexts, while a variety of forms can be utilized in the same context.[10]

(3) More generally, the assumption of "homeostasis" (the term used by anthropologist Jack Goody), that is, a perfect correspondence between traditions and their use to the society that transmits them, was exaggerated by the form critics. Jan Vansina writes of oral traditions generally that "there is congruence but there is no total congruence of content with the concerns of the present. . . . The presence of archaisms in various traditions gives homeostasis the lie."[11] In other words, historical information can be preserved even when it corresponds to no clear function in the community. Vansina's further comment on this issue is very significant for our later discussion of the extent to which early Christians were interested in the past: "Homeostasis theories cannot explain why history is valued more in some societies than in others."[12] More specific cultural features come into play.

---

9. Travis, "Form Criticism," 158-59; R. Blank, *Analyse und Kritik der formgeschichtlichen Arbeiten von Martin Dibelius und Rudolf Bultmann* (Basel: Reinhardt, 1981) 201.

10. G. N. Stanton, "Form Criticism Revisited," in M. Hooker and C. Hickling, eds., *What about the New Testament?* (C. Evans FS; London: SCM, 1975) 23; idem, *Jesus of Nazareth*, 181; R. Riesner, *Jesus als Lehrer* (WUNT 2/7; Tübingen: Mohr, 1981) 12-13. The point is made about oral traditions generally by J. Vansina, *Oral Tradition as History* (Madison: University of Wisconsin Press, 1985) 101: traditions "often serve multiple purposes and uses."

11. Vansina, *Oral Tradition*, 121; cf. S. Byrskog, "A New Perspective on the Jesus Tradition: Reflections on James D. G. Dunn's *Jesus Remembered*," *JSNT* 26 (2004) 468-69.

12. Vansina, *Oral Tradition*, 122.

(4) E. P. Sanders's work is generally regarded as having shown that there are no laws of tradition operating consistently throughout the gospel traditions. From his study of the manuscript traditions and the apocryphal Gospels (i.e., in the postcanonical tradition, where there is relatively hard evidence) he concluded that "On all counts the tradition developed in opposite directions,"[13] though in the case of some of the criteria that have been used to distinguish early and late there is a more or less pronounced tendency for the tradition to develop in one direction rather than the opposite.[14] (Sanders followed Bultmann's assumption that oral and literary developments are closely comparable.)

These four points of criticism effectively demolish the whole edifice of tradition history erected on the basis of form criticism. Form criticism, it turns out, can really only deal with matters of form and cannot function to determine the origins or relative ages of traditions.[15] Since these points are widely admitted, the inability of form criticism to tell us how the gospel traditions were transmitted between the eyewitnesses and Gospel texts should be generally agreed. But there is more:

(5) The assumption of comparability with folklore — freely altered and created in transmission — can be questioned at several points. The time span between Jesus and the Gospels is much shorter than the periods of time spanned by the traditions studied by folklorists. Moreover the nature of the traditions is very different.[16] If the analogy with oral traditions in traditional societies is to carry any weight, there must be much more careful distinction between different types of traditions and the different ways in which they are treated.

(6) Folklorists themselves have abandoned the "romantic" idea of the folk as collectively the creator of folk traditions in favor of recognizing the roles of authoritative individuals in interaction with the community.[17]

(7) The form critics worked with a preconceived notion of the development of early Christianity, for example Bultmann's emphasis on the sharp

---

13. E. P. Sanders, *The Tendencies of the Synoptic Tradition* (SNTSMS 9; Cambridge: Cambridge University Press, 1969) 272.

14. Sanders, *The Tendencies*, 275; cf. Riesner, *Jesus*, 14-17.

15. Cf. Easton, *The Gospel*, 81: "Form criticism may prepare the way for historical criticism, but form criticism is not historical criticism."

16. E. E. Ellis, "The Synoptic Gospels and History," in B. Chilton and C. A. Evans, eds., *Authenticating the Activities of Jesus* (NT Tools and Studies 28, 2; Leiden: Brill, 1999) 54-55; idem, "New Directions in Form Criticism," in idem, *Prophecy and Hermeneutic in Early Christianity* (WUNT 18; Tübingen: Mohr, 1978) 244.

17. Blank, *Analyse*, 200-201.

distinction between Palestinian and Hellenistic communities.[18] Tradition history was not derived simply from the study of the gospel traditions but was constructed according to the expected pattern.

(8) That the gospel traditions were transmitted purely orally for several decades was assumed by the form critics rather than demonstrated. The world of the early Christian communities was not a purely oral one, but a predominantly oral society in which written texts had a place that was closely related to orality.[19] The possibility that there was some form of written traditions before the Gospels as such were written will be explored briefly in the next chapter (11).

(9) Vernon Robbins,[20] James Dunn,[21] and Werner Kelber[22] have all charged the form critics, especially Bultmann, with using a literary model for understanding the process of oral transmission. Dunn writes:

> This becomes most evident in [Bultmann's] conceptualization of the whole tradition about Jesus as "composed of a series of layers."[23] The imagined process is one where each layer is laid or builds upon another. Bultmann made such play with it because, apart from anything else, he was confident that he could strip off later (Hellenistic) layers to expose the earlier (Palestinian) layers. The image itself, however, is drawn from the literary processes of editing, where each successive edition (layer) is an edited version . . . of the previous edition (layer). But is such a conceptualization really appropriate to a process of oral retellings of traditional material?[24]

Dunn's answer is no. We should think of each *performance* of an oral tradition as differing from others, but not in such a way that each builds on the earlier. With oral tradition there is no linear development, layer on layer. We shall return to Dunn's model of oral transmission as varied performances later, but for the moment we should note the consequence: the kind of tradition history that Bultmann thought could be reconstructed did not exist. As

18. N. T. Wright, *The New Testament and the People of God* (London: SPCK, 1992) 420-21.

19. Ellis, "The Synoptic Gospels," 53; Travis, "Form Criticism," 159.

20. Robbins, "Form Criticism," 842.

21. J. D. G. Dunn, "Altering the Default Setting: Re-Envisaging the Early Transmission of the Jesus Tradition," *NTS* 49 (2003) 144-45; idem, *Jesus Remembered* (Grand Rapids: Eerdmans, 2003) 194-95, 248-49.

22. W. H. Kelber, "The Case of the Gospels: Memory's Desire and the Limits of Historical Criticism," *Oral Tradition* 17 (2002) 64.

23. R. Bultmann, *Jesus and the Word* (New York: Scribner, 1935) 12-13.

24. Dunn, *Jesus Remembered*, 194-95.

Dunn says, "The unknown factors and variations so characteristic of oral tradition put the tradition-history — or better, performance-history — beyond reach."[25]

Even a few of these criticisms would be sufficient to undermine the whole form-critical enterprise. There is no reason to believe that the oral transmission of Jesus traditions in the early church was at all as Bultmann envisaged it.[26] It is remarkable that this is not more widely acknowledged explicitly, though, once one is aware of it, it is not difficult to see that many contemporary Gospels scholars acknowledge it implicitly by ignoring form criticism in its classical form. But what form criticism has bequeathed as a long enduring legacy is the largely unexamined *impression* that many scholars — and probably even more students — still entertain: the impression of a long period of creative development of the traditions before they attained written form in the Gospels. The retention of such an impression is not defensible unless it is justified afresh, for the arguments of the form critics no longer hold water.

The Scandinavian Alternative

In 1961 the Swedish scholar Birger Gerhardsson published his book *Memory and Manuscript*,[27] in which he developed the insights of his teacher Harald Riesenfeld and proposed a radical alternative to form criticism's understanding of the oral transmission of Jesus tradition. He provided a major study of oral transmission in rabbinic Judaism and argued that early Christianity must have adopted the same methods and practices. Thus, unlike the form critics, he provided a particular model of oral tradition as practiced in a specific historical context and presented it as the nearest available parallel to the Jesus tradition. The disciples of rabbis were expected to memorize their masters' teaching, and importance was attached to preserving the exact words. Mnemonic techniques and other controls were used to minimize deviation from the version learned. The emphasis on Jesus' teaching of his disciples

---

25. Dunn, "Altering," 172.

26. Robbins, "Form Criticism," 843, who is a relatively sympathetic critic, lists five enduring strengths of form criticism, but none of them support the actual model of oral transmission used by the form critics or the ways in which they actually traced tradition histories.

27. B. Gerhardsson, *Memory and Manuscript: Oral Transmission and Written Transmission in Rabbinic Judaism and Early Christianity* (Lund: Gleerup, 1961). Gerhardsson's more important later writings on the same topic are collected in English translation in idem, *The Reliability of the Gospel Tradition* (Peabody: Hendrickson, 2001).

throughout the Gospels indicates that he would have expected them to memorize his teaching. In the early Jerusalem church the Twelve would have functioned as a kind of rabbinate formulating, controlling, and passing on the Jesus tradition. Thus the tradition would have been preserved much more carefully and faithfully than the form critics envisaged.

Gerhardsson did allow for some development and changes in the tradition, such as can be seen in rabbinic literature, but such deliberate expansions of the tradition and interpretative changes were made by the authorized controllers of the tradition, and were therefore relatively restricted, by contrast with the free creativity of the community postulated by Bultmann. Gerhardsson emphasized the named apostles as the individuals who originated (after Jesus) the tradition and controlled it, by contrast with the anonymous and collective origin of traditions presumed by the form critics. Finally, it is also important to recognize that, whereas the form critics usually supposed that the traditions were transmitted and developed in the course of their actual use in the community for various functions, Gerhardsson distinguished the transmission of the traditions from their use. Quite apart from their use, the traditions were handed down in a channel of transmission that was independent of other practices and functions. This is an important point to which we shall return.

It was unfortunate that Gerhardsson published his work at a time when New Testament scholars were becoming very aware of the pitfalls of using rabbinic traditions as evidence for Judaism prior to 70 CE. Continuity between pre-70 Pharisaism and the rabbis of the Mishnah could not be taken for granted anymore. Moreover, first-century Palestinian Judaism was no longer thought to be dominated by the Pharisees but pictured as a much more diverse phenomenon. Consequently, Gerhardsson was easily accused of anachronism in taking the practices of rabbinic tradition as a model for understanding early Christianity.[28] This was not entirely fair, since, although Gerhardsson probably did assume too much continuity between Pharisaism and rabbinic Judaism and too readily supposed that it was the Pharisaic traditioning that would have been the most obvious model for early Christians to follow, the value of his analogy is not necessarily linked to these assumptions. Rabbinic Judaism could be an illuminating parallel despite being later than the New Testament period. Furthermore, the actual methods of

28. E.g., S. Talmon, "Oral Tradition and Written Transmission, or the Heard and the Seen Word in Judaism of the Second Temple Periods," in H. Wansbrough, ed., *Jesus and the Oral Gospel Tradition* (JSNTSup 64; Sheffield: Sheffield University Press, 1991) 132-33; P. Davids, "The Gospels and Jewish Tradition: Twenty Years after Gerhardsson," in R. T. France and D. Wenham, eds., *Gospel Perspectives*, vol. 1 (Sheffield: JSOT, 1980) 76-81.

oral transmission used by the rabbis were not peculiar to them, but were in fact the common educational methods, even at elementary level, of the ancient world. Rainer Riesner's work has particularly made this apparent.[29]

Besides this charge of anachronism, the reasons most scholars were not convinced by Gerhardsson's work were mainly two: (1) this model of memorization and the transmission of exact words is too rigid to explain the actual extent of variation in the Jesus traditions as we can observe them in the Gospels;[30] and (2) there is insufficient evidence to support Gerhardsson's view that the apostolic college in Jerusalem functioned to control the tradition in such an extensive way as he supposes.[31] In other words, transmission was less rigid and controlled. It should be said that Gerhardsson's position on both these points is easily exaggerated, and one suspects that some scholars have been tempted to represent the form critics and Gerhardsson as opposite extremes, the former postulating an entirely informal, uncontrolled process in which all kinds of creative developments could be imagined, the latter a rigidly controlled process in which tradition was transmitted virtually verbatim. With regard to the first point, Gerhardsson recognized that changes occurred even in rabbinic halakhah[32] and did allow for a degree of change and development in the gospel traditions.[33] On the second point, his attitude to the dominant role of the Twelve softened in later work, where he allows that there were also other streams of gospel traditions, so that "[n]one of the evangelists worked with traditions taken only from one source."[34]

One further criticism may be mentioned. It is that, like the form critics, Gerhardsson assumes that before the Gospels the Jesus tradition was purely oral and made no use of writing.[35] He may, in this respect, have been misled by the later rabbis' principle of exclusively oral transmission of "oral Torah"[36] (expressed in b. Gittin 60a: "Words orally transmitted you may not write"). This principle probably originated only in the Amoraic period (i.e., from the third century)[37] and should not be projected back onto the first century.

29. Riesner, *Jesus als Lehrer,* chapter 3.
30. Dunn, *Jesus Remembered,* 198; Ellis, "The Synoptic Gospels," 56.
31. Davids, "The Gospels," 87-88.
32. Gerhardsson, *The Reliability,* 54.
33. Gerhardsson, *The Reliability,* 51-57, 71, 79-81; idem, "The Secret of the Transmission of the Unwritten Jesus Tradition," *NTS* 51 (2005) 15-16.
34. Gerhardsson, *The Reliability,* 50.
35. Davids, "The Gospels," 79; Talmon, "Oral Tradition," 146-48.
36. Cf. Gerhardsson, *Memory,* 201-2.
37. M. S. Jaffee, *Torah in the Mouth: Writing and Oral Tradition in Palestinian Judaism 200 BCE–400 CE* (Oxford: Oxford University Press, 2001) chapter 7. Jaffee argues that it was influ-

There is no evidence that the Pharisees abstained from writing their "traditions of the fathers."[38] There is even less reason to suppose that an insistence on oral transmission alone characterized other Jewish groups at the time of Jesus, such as the (highly literary) Qumran community.[39] However, again it is not true that Gerhardsson entirely neglected the role of written materials: he postulated that, just as private notebooks were in fact used by the rabbis and their pupils, so writing, as an aid to memory, could have been used in early Christian circles prior to the Gospels. Small collections of sayings of Jesus or stories about Jesus in notebooks could have prepared the way for fuller collections like Mark's.[40]

A Middle Way?

In 1991 Kenneth Bailey, a New Testament scholar who has worked for more than thirty years in the Middle East, published an important article on oral tradition and the Gospels[41] which, because it appeared in a journal not often consulted by New Testament scholars, has taken some time to receive the attention it deserves. But now both N. T. Wright[42] and James Dunn[43] have adopted the form of oral tradition Bailey proposes as a model for the way in which the Jesus traditions would have been transmitted in the early church.

Bailey draws on his extensive experience of Middle Eastern village life and his close observation of the way oral tradition operated in such contexts in the recent past. He also organizes his observations into a typology of three types of oral transmission, which he specifies as *informal uncontrolled* tradition, *informal controlled* tradition, and *formal controlled* tradition. The first is the way he describes the model of tradition with which form criticism worked. Bultmann, he says,

---

enced by the wider view in Greco-Roman culture that knowledge from books is less valuable than knowledge gained from the embodiment of books in the form of a living teacher.

38. Jaffee, *Torah*, chapter 3.

39. On Qumran see Jaffee, *Torah*, chapter 2.

40. Gerhardsson, *Memory*, 202; idem, "Illuminating the Kingdom: Narrative Meshalim in the Synoptic Gospels," in Wansbrough, ed., *Jesus*, 307.

41. K. E. Bailey, "Informal Controlled Oral Tradition and the Synoptic Gospels," *Asia Journal of Theology* 5 (1991) 34-51; reprinted in *Themelios* 20 (1995) 4-11. My references are to the latter publication. Cf. also idem, "Middle Eastern Oral Tradition and the Synoptic Gospels," *ExpT* 106 (1995) 363-67.

42. N. T. Wright, *Jesus and the Victory of God* (London: SPCK, 1996) 133-37.

43. Dunn, *Jesus Remembered*, 205-10.

does not deny that there *is* a tradition stemming from Jesus, but asserts that it has, for the most part, faded out. The community, he feels, was not interested in preserving or controlling the tradition. Furthermore, the tradition is always open to new community creations that are rapidly attributed to the community's founder. It is *informal* in the sense that there is no identifiable teacher nor student and no structure within which material is passed from one person to another. All is fluid and plastic, open to new additions and new shapes.[44]

In this model the transmission is uncontrolled — that is, there are no limits placed on the degree to which the tradition can change and develop — and informal — that is, there is no structure of identified individuals responsible for preserving and transmitting the tradition.

Interestingly, Bailey comments that this kind of tradition does exist in the contemporary Middle East:

> The *informal uncontrolled* oral tradition can be labeled "rumour transmission." Tragedies and atrocity stories naturally slip into this category and when tragedy or civil strife occur, rumour transmission quickly takes over. From 1975 to 1984 the present writer was *awash* with such oral transmission in Beirut, Lebanon. A story of three people killed in a bread line in front of a bakery by a random shell quickly became a story of 300 people massacred in cold blood when the account was retold by angry compatriots of the victims.[45]

This kind of transmission is what modern western people often envisage when they assume that oral tradition must be highly unreliable. But we should note that it occurs in circumstances where some people are strongly motivated to distort the tradition and where there are no social mechanisms to control the transmission. The key to appreciating how oral tradition can operate with much less scope for change is to understand the kinds of control that predominantly oral societies have at their disposal for preserving traditions they wish to retain faithfully over long periods.

Bailey classifies Gerhardsson's account of rabbinic tradition and, by analogy, the Jesus tradition in early Christianity as *formal controlled* tradition:

> It is *formal* in the sense that there is a clearly identified teacher, a clearly identified student, and a clearly identified block of traditional material that is being passed on from one to the other. It is *controlled* in the sense

44. Bailey, "Informal," 5.
45. Bailey, "Informal," 5.

that the material is memorized (and/or written), identified as "tradition" and thus preserved intact.[46]

Again, this kind of tradition does exist in the contemporary Middle East. It "is most publicly visible in the memorization of the entire Qur'an by Muslim sheiks and in the memorization of various extensive liturgies in Eastern Orthodoxy."[47] Memorization of the whole Qur'an and works of Islamic learning[48] is perhaps not entirely parallel to Gerhardsson's account. In such a tradition, the written text of the Qur'an may not be "considered an independent mode of expression," but it does surely have an indispensable place in this scholarly culture in relation to orality. It is the complete text of the Qur'an, a written document, that is memorized, without any verbal deviation at all being tolerated. It is doubtful whether such completely verbatim memory of a text as large as the Qur'an could be preserved were there no written text available. While it is the oral memory that matters in daily use, the written text does exist as a control on the memory. This goes beyond the rabbinic analogy and amounts to a tradition that is textually controlled as well as controlled by the teaching situation of individual masters and teachers.

However, what Bailey says about the importance of orality in a teaching and learning process of this kind is important, and of wider application to other situations, such as early Christianity: "the passing on of memorized tradition provided opportunity for explanation and discussion as to its meaning, while the cold lifeless book did not."[49]

Of these two forms of tradition, those adopted by the form critics and the Scandinavians respectively, Bailey states that they

> are both still very much alive in the Middle East. The first results from natural human failings; the second is a carefully nurtured methodology of great antiquity that is still practised and held in high regard by both Christians and Muslims.[50]

Bailey does not exclude the possibility that the second, in particular, may be helpful as a partial analogy for the transmission of Jesus traditions,[51] but he

46. Bailey, "Informal," 5.
47. Bailey, "Informal," 5.
48. Bailey, "Informal," 5-6.
49. Bailey, "Informal," 6. Bailey here refers to the famous passage in Plato, *Phaedrus* 274C-275A.
50. Bailey, "Informal," 6.
51. Cf. Bailey, "Informal," 10: "We are not suggesting absolute categories. The pedagogy of the rabbinic schools may well lie behind some of the material."

offers as more generally helpful for understanding the latter a form of oral tradition in contemporary (or recent) Middle East village life that he categorizes as *informal controlled* oral tradition. Here he justifiably claims to offer "new data,"[52] though it is true, of course, that his evidence is "anecdotal"[53] rather than collected systematically with the methods of anthropological research.

His basic discussion of the process is this:

> The traditional setting is the gathering of villagers in the evening for the telling of stories and the recitation of poetry. These gatherings have a name: they are called *haflat samar*. *Samar* in Arabic is a cognate of the Hebrew *shamar*, meaning to preserve. The community is *preserving* its store of tradition. By *informal* we mean that there is no set teacher and no specifically identified student. As stories, poems and other traditional materials are told and recited through the evening, anyone can theoretically participate. In fact, the older men, the more gifted men, and the socially more prominent men tend to do the reciting. The reciters will shift depending on who is seated in the circle. . . . I have often been seated in such circles when some piece of traditional oral literature is quoted. I might not happen to know the story and so proceed to ask what it is all about. Someone then says, "Elder so-and-so knows the story." The ranking social/intellectual figure then proceeds to tell the story with pride. By contrast, in the recitation of *formal controlled* oral tradition there is a specifically identified teacher and a specifically identified student.[54]

While in the *haflat samar* there is no official storyteller and many participate in the rehearsal of tradition, there are limits on who can do so. A reliable person for this role must have grown up in the village and known the village's traditions all his life.[55]

In this model it is the *community* that exercises control to ensure that the traditions are preserved faithfully. Depending on the type of tradition, more or less flexibility is allowed in such preservation. Bailey classifies the types of material transmitted as proverbs, story riddles, poetry, parable or story, and historical accounts (of the important figures in the community's history). It is very important to note that he specifies the degree of flexibility permitted in each case. In the case of proverbs and poems, verbatim reproduction is mandatory. A mistake of even a single word by the person reciting

---

52. Bailey, "Informal," 6.
53. Dunn, *Jesus Remembered,* 206, 209.
54. Bailey, "Informal," 6.
55. Bailey, "Informal," 6.

will be emphatically corrected by the listeners in general, and if the reciter hesitates he will be assisted by the group, drawing on their "collective memory." By contrast, *some* flexibility is allowed in the case of parables and historical accounts of people and events "important to the identity of the community."[56] Here there are both flexibility and control. In the example Bailey provides there is a story with three main scenes and a proverb as a punch line at the end of the story. An adequate recitation of this story would require the following items:

> The proverb that appeared in the story (the punch-line) had to be repeated verbatim. The three basic scenes could not be changed, but the order of the last two could be reversed without triggering the community rejection mechanism. The basic flow of the story and its conclusion had to remain the same. The names could not be changed. The summary punch-line was inviolable. However, the teller could vary the pitch of one character's emotional reaction to the other, and the dialogue within the flow of the story could at any point reflect the individual teller's style and interests. That is, the story-teller had a certain freedom to tell the story in his own way as long as the central thrust of the story was not changed.[57]

What is important here is not merely the balance of continuity and flexibility, but that specific aspects of the tradition are considered inviolable, while other specific aspects can be varied to a degree. This means that the story cannot change into another. Its basic features are fixed. Here are obvious analogies with the way the stories in the Gospels vary to some degree in the different versions but preserve key features and structures, including, frequently, a punch line that occurs with nearly verbatim equivalence in the several versions of the story.

None of the five categories of material Bailey has listed can be treated with unrestricted flexibility, that is, without control. This is allowed only for such material as "the casual news of the day." Control is absent when the material is "*irrelevant to the identity of the community* and is not judged *wise* or *valuable*." Such material "does not enter the tradition and is soon forgotten or reshaped beyond recognition." It is difficult to imagine that the traditions of the words and deeds of Jesus could have been treated in this way in the early Christian communities.

One implication of this model that is not explicitly developed by Bailey is seen by Dunn as confirmation of his most decisive criticism of form criti-

56. Bailey, "Informal," 7.
57. Bailey, "Informal," 7.

cism, namely that the form critics worked with a literary model of oral transmission in which one "layer" is laid on a previous one:

> the paradigm of literary editing is confirmed as wholly inappropriate: in oral tradition one telling of a story is in no sense an editing of a previous telling; rather, each telling starts with the same subject and theme, but retellings are different: each telling is a performance of the tradition itself, not of the first, or third, or twenty-third "edition" of the tradition. Our expectation, accordingly, should be of the oral transmission of Jesus tradition as a sequence of retellings, each starting from the same storehouse of communally remembered events and teaching, and each weaving the common stock together in different patterns for different contexts.[58]

Problems with the Threefold Typology

James Dunn, like N. T. Wright, has adopted Bailey's model as the most appropriate one for understanding the gospel tradition in the early church. His main reason seems to be that, by providing a middle way between Bultmann and Gerhardsson, the model accounts best for the actual phenomena of stability and variability that we find in the Gospels.[59] Neither a totally uncontrolled nor a totally rigid process of transmission explains the evidence of the Gospel traditions as we have them. Dunn does a good job of showing, through study of a range of examples from the Gospels, that parallel texts in the Gospels are best understood as varying performances of tradition, varying within the kind of limits that Bailey describes operating in modern Middle Eastern villages.[60]

However, there is a serious problem in Dunn's adoption of Bailey's model of *informal controlled* tradition as the middle way between Bultmann and Gerhardsson. Dunn seems to assume that the balance between flexibility and stability in the kind of tradition that Bailey describes is a function of the *informality* of this traditioning process, that is, the fact that it is the community that exercises control rather than official storytellers or the like. But we should note that there are two quite different issues to be distinguished here. One is: who does the controlling, the community or specified individuals? This question addresses the difference between "informal" and "formal" in Bailey's usage. The second question is: how is the control exercised? In other

58. Dunn, *Jesus Remembered*, 209.
59. Dunn, "Altering," 155-56.
60. Dunn, *Jesus Remembered*, 210-49.

words, in what respects and how far is flexibility permitted in the rehearsal of the traditions? There is no reason why Bailey's account of the balance of stability and flexibility should not be applicable to a *formal* controlled tradition as well as to an *informal* controlled tradition. In this respect, the threefold typology has probably had a somewhat misleading effect on scholars who favor Bailey's *informal* controlled tradition as the best analogy for the Gospel tradition. Because the most frequently voiced criticism of Gerhardsson is that the rabbinic analogy does not account for the extent of variability we can actually observe in the Gospel traditions, this alleged inflexibility in transmission has been associated with the model of a *formal* controlled tradition as though it were entailed by this model. In fact, the model as such does not entail such inflexibility, for the threefold typology is based on differentiating according to two factors only: controlled or uncontrolled, formal or informal. The balance of stability and flexibility is really a third factor. The balance Bailey describes as characteristic of the processes he has observed could in fact characterize a formal controlled example of oral tradition just as well as an informal controlled example. But the threefold typology has misled readers into supposing that the former is not an option.

The threefold typology is not nuanced enough to enable a sufficiently precise account of how the transmission of Jesus tradition in the early church worked. We need to ask the following questions:

(1) Was the tradition *controlled* in any way? (1a) For what *reasons* would control over the tradition have been thought necessary?
(2) If the tradition was controlled, what were the *mechanisms of control?*
(3) Were *different kinds or aspects of traditions* treated differently with regard to the degree of flexibility permitted? (3a) What was the *relative balance of stability and flexibility* in the treatment of these different kinds or aspects of traditions?
(4) How are the Gospels related to the oral tradition?

Clearly if the answer to (1) is no, the other questions need not be answered. This would be the case if the form critics were right. We have already found sufficient reason to agree with Bailey, Dunn, and many other recent scholars in discounting the form-critical model. But we should note that we have not yet explored question (1a), which is an important subsidiary question. The form critics did not think the early communities had any reason to wish to preserve the tradition carefully, for they lacked a sense of history and were not interested in the past life and words of Jesus as genuinely past and to be distinguished from the presence of the exalted Christ. If the form critics were wrong, we need to establish that the early Christians had reasons for re-garding the stability of the tradition as important. We know that oral societies can, if they choose, operate mechanisms of control that ensure conservative transmission of tradition. We need, in the early Christian case, to establish why they should have chosen to do so.

Whatever the merits of Bailey's model, we cannot regard it as having answered question (2). Bailey shows that informal control by a whole com-munity can operate very efficiently in such a way as to preserve tradition with relative stability. But this is not the only sort of control exercised by predomi-nantly oral societies, many of which have particular individuals charged with the responsibility of guarding the tradition. The importance of the eyewit-nesses in the early Christian movement, which our argument in this book has highlighted, suggests that they may have had an important role in the control of the traditions of the words and deeds of Jesus. The question of mecha-nisms of control is therefore a key one for our specific concerns in this book.

With regard to questions (3) and (3a) Bailey's model does provide a plausible analogy to the Gospel traditions. Within the scope of this book, we cannot engage in detailed discussion of the traditions as we have them in the Gospels. Dunn's work is important in this respect, though he would certainly agree that he has really been able only to make a start on the kind of fresh look at the Synoptic traditions that is needed if the phenomenon of stability and variability in various forms of oral tradition is to be fully exploited in Gospels studies. Extracanonical sources also need to be brought into this dis-cussion so that the full range of evidence can be studied in this way.

There is one point that is of great importance for our own concerns and which seems to me to follow from Dunn's treatment of oral tradition, though he himself does not explicitly make it. As we have seen, against the form-critical conception of oral tradition operating like successive editions of a lit-erary text, Dunn insists that each performance of a tradition is a performance of the tradition as such, not a further development of the last such perfor-mance. There are no layers of tradition, only various performances, differing within the limits allowed.[61] It would seem to follow from this that there is no good reason to suppose that the range of variation of particular traditions was even greater than the range we find in the Gospels themselves. There are no laws of tradition that can take us back to more original forms of a tradi-tion and show how the version of it we find in the Gospels developed from something very different. Traditions in performance just had the relative sta-

---

61. Dunn, *Jesus Remembered*, 248-49; cf. also idem, "Altering," 153-54, where Dunn also rightly criticizes the Jesus Seminar for making the same mistake as the form critics at this point.

bility and variability that the Gospel versions — where we have more than one version — display. When we have only one version, we may reasonably suppose that this tradition in performance had the degree of stability and variability we find in instances where the Gospels provide more than one version, but not that there was ever a significantly greater degree of variation.

Question (4) brings us back to the contention of this book that the testimony of the eyewitnesses lies not distantly, but closely behind the texts of our Gospels. We will be able to return to this question after discussing questions (1), (1a), and (2) in the next chapter, where our whole endeavor will be to put the eyewitnesses back into the picture both of the oral tradition and of the origins of the written Gospels.

Bailey and Dunn on the Eyewitnesses

The account we have given of Bailey's model may seem to discount the role of the eyewitnesses no less thoroughly than the form critics did. But this impression would not be entirely fair. Recall that, in his description of the *haflat samar,* Bailey stresses that there are no official storytellers, that any member of the community can be a reciter of the traditions of the village, but that to qualify as a reciter in the *haflat samar* one must have grown up hearing the stories. He cites an example of a man in his sixties who did not qualify because he had lived in the village only thirty-seven years.[62] Bailey also states that it is the elders — the older, more gifted, more socially prominent men — who tend to do the reciting. In this description of the *haflat samar,* Bailey is not concerned to distinguish between traditions about events within living memory and traditions from an earlier period, and so the role of eyewitnesses seems not to arise. However, when he turns to drawing some conclusions, all too briefly, for the study of the Synoptic Gospels, he apparently argues that, in the early Christian communities, those who were qualified to recite the tradition in the public gathering of the community were specifically the eyewitnesses.

Bailey relies on the reference in Luke's preface to "those who were eyewitnesses and ministers of the word" (1:2) to argue that the qualified reciters of the Jesus traditions had to have been eyewitnesses. The passage that follows contains a misleading sentence and so must be quoted here at length and explained:

62. Bailey, "Informal," 6.

It is my suggestion that up until the upheaval of the Jewish-Roman war *informal controlled* oral tradition was able to function in the villages of Palestine. Those who accepted the new rabbi as the expected Messiah would record and transmit data concerning him as the source of their identity. Then in AD 70 many of the settled villages of Palestine were destroyed and many of the people dispersed. Thus the Jewish-Roman war would have disrupted the sociological village structures in which the *informal controlled* oral tradition functioned. However, anyone twenty years and older in that year would have been an authentic reciter of that tradition. It appears that the earliest church may have refined the methodology already functioning naturally among them. Not everyone who lived in the community in the village and heard the stories of Jesus was authorized to recite the tradition. The witness was required to have been an eyewitness of the historical Jesus to qualify as a *huperetes tou logou* [minister of the word] (cf. Lk. 1:2). Thus, at least through to the end of the first century, the authenticity of that tradition was assured to the community through specially designated authoritative witnesses.[63]

As this stands, the fifth sentence ("However, anyone twenty years old . . .") is in flat contradiction to what follows. This sentence refers to anyone aged twenty or more in the year 70. But people so young could not possibly be the eyewitnesses of the historical Jesus who are later said to have been the only ones qualified to recite the tradition. (Moreover, Bailey later states quite clearly that Paul was not qualified to be "a reciter of the *informal* controlled oral tradition.") We must presume that something has gone wrong in this passage, probably as a result of abbreviation. The fifth sentence must be meant to refer to those who were twenty or older in the year of Jesus' crucifixion, not in the year 70.[64] In other words, Bailey supposes that in gatherings of the local Christian communities in pre-70 Palestine the only people who would recite the tradition would have been eyewitnesses. He apparently supposes that there would be many such, so that the scene would resemble the *haflat samar* he describes, where the elders tend to do the reciting.

This does provide a plausible setting for one aspect of the eyewitness testimony as we have discussed it in previous chapters. We proposed that

63. Bailey, "Informal," 10.

64. Dunn, *Jesus Remembered*, 209, is misled by this statement, and Wright, *Jesus*, 135, seems also to have misunderstood the distinction Bailey makes between eyewitnesses and others. According to Bailey, *informal controlled* oral tradition operated only with eyewitnesses as the qualified reciters. Where this was not the case, as in Paul's Corinth, *formal controlled* tradition evidently takes over.

those Gospel stories in which specific persons (otherwise insignificant in the Gospel story) are named were first told by the persons named. These would not be eyewitnesses to more than a small part of the Gospel tradition, but in the setting proposed by Bailey we can imagine Jairus telling the story of his daughter's resuscitation, Bartimaeus telling the story of his own healing, and so on. But Bailey does not distinguish these "minor" eyewitnesses, of whom there were certainly very many (including the five hundred to whom 1 Cor 15:6 refers), from those who were eyewitnesses "from the beginning," those disciples of Jesus who could bear comprehensive witness to the whole course of Jesus' ministry and beyond. Moreover, his picture of Christian groups in the villages of Palestine takes no account of the special authority of the mother church in Jerusalem, which was special no doubt in part because of the leadership of Peter and the Twelve, eyewitnesses "from the beginning." Such eyewitnesses would surely have played a more important role as authoritative guarantors of the tradition than Bailey's model seems to allow.

Bailey seems to be proposing that, when the Jewish-Roman war put an end to the sociological basis for the *informal controlled* tradition in Palestinian villages, the tradition became more controlled. It was then that the major eyewitnesses came into their own as "specially designated authoritative witnesses." This seems a rather late stage (the youngest would now be about fifty) for them to assume a novel role, and it seems more plausible that they had exercised a controlling function in relation to the tradition from the start. The difficulties Bailey's argument encounters when it tries to do justice to the role of the eyewitnesses suggest that the model he proposes of a tradition controlled only by the community as a whole is after all not entirely appropriate.

Dunn also has difficulty fitting the eyewitnesses into the model he adopts from Bailey. He stresses that the control was exercised by the *community,* and, so far as one can tell, he assumes, unlike Bailey, that all members of the community — or at any rate, not just the eyewitnesses — could recite the tradition. Of the eyewitnesses he writes:

> In focusing particular attention on the communal character of the early traditioning process we should not discount the more traditional emphasis on the individual figure of authority respected for his or her own association with Jesus during the days of his mission.[65]

In a response to Dunn's book, Samuel Byrskog commented on this sentence:

---

65. Dunn, *Jesus Remembered,* 243; cf. his account of "Apostolic Custodians" (180-81).

It remains unclear how their [the eyewitnesses'] "continuing role" becomes manifest in Dunn's picture of how the group identifies itself by the corporate remembering of tradition.[66]

To this Dunn replied at some length.[67] To a large extent he still endorses the form-critical picture of an oral tradition for which the eyewitnesses were only a starting point. The memories of the original disciples reached the Gospel writers mainly because they had fed these into the oral tradition at an early stage. The original disciples could not have maintained a presence in every Christian community. But

> I see no difficulty, then, in merging the insights of oral tradition as community tradition and recognition of the importance of individual eyewitnesses in providing, contributing and in at least some measure helping to control the interpretation given to that tradition.[68]

This is progress. We shall attempt to expand on it in the next two chapters.

---

66. Byrskog, "A New Perspective," 467.

67. J. D. G. Dunn, "On History, Memory and Eyewitnesses: In Response to Bengt Holmberg and Samuel Byrskog," *JSNT* 26 (2004) 482-85.

68. Dunn, "On History," 484.

11. Transmitting the Jesus Traditions

In this chapter and the next we shall outline the character of the transmission process of the Jesus traditions as a formal controlled tradition in which the eyewitnesses played an important part.

Pauline Evidence for Formal Transmission

We have unequivocal evidence, in Paul's letters, that the early Christian movement did practice the formal transmission of tradition. By "formal" here I mean that there were specific practices employed to ensure that tradition was faithfully handed on from a qualified traditioner to others.[1] The evidence is found in Paul's use of the technical terms for handing on a tradition (*paradidōmi*, 1 Cor 11:2, 23, corresponding to Hebrew *māsar*) and receiving a tradition (*paralambanō*, 1 Cor 15:1, 3; Gal 1:9; Col 2:6; 1 Thess 2:13; 4:1; 2 Thess 3:6, corresponding to Hebrew *qibbēl*).[2] These Greek words were used for formal transmission of tradition in the Hellenistic schools and so would have been familiar in this sense to Paul's Gentile readers. They also appeared in Jewish Greek usage (Josephus, *Ant.* 13.297; *C. Ap.* 1.60; Mark 7:4, 13; Acts 6:14), corresponding to what we find in Hebrew in later rabbinic literature (e.g.,

---

1. M. Dibelius, *From Tradition to Gospel* (tr. B. L. Woolf; London: Nicholson and Watson, 1934) 15-16, comes close to acknowledging this.

2. For this terminology, see M. S. Jaffee, *Torah in the Mouth: Writing and Oral Tradition in Palestinian Judaism 200 BCE–400 CE* (Oxford: Oxford University Press, 2001) 73-75, 80.

m. 'Avot 1.1). Paul also speaks of faithfully retaining or observing a tradition (*katechō*, 1 Cor 11:2; 15:2; *krateō*, 2 Thess 2:15, which is used of Jewish tradition in Mark 7:3, 4, 8, corresponding to the Hebrew *'āḥaz*) and uses, of course, the term "tradition" itself (*paradosis*, 1 Cor 11:2; 2 Thess 2:15; 3:6, used of Jewish tradition in Matt 15:2; Mark 7:5; Gal 1:14; Josephus, *Ant.* 13.297).

Paul uses this terminology to refer to a variety of kinds of tradition that he communicated to his churches when he established them. These certainly include "kerygmatic summaries" of the gospel story and message (for which the best evidence is 1 Cor 15:1-8), ethical instruction, instructions for the ordering of the community and its worship, and also Jesus traditions (for which the best evidence is 1 Cor 11:23-25).[3] It is obvious that Paul took over the technical terminology for tradition from the usage with which he would have been familiar as a Pharisaic teacher. But it is therefore important to note that there is sufficient evidence of this terminology in early Christian literature outside the Pauline letters to show that it was not peculiar to Paul or solely derived from Paul's usage (Jude 3; Luke 1:2; Acts 16:4; *Didache* 4:13; *Barnabas* 19:11). The terminology is of considerable importance, for to "hand on" a tradition is not just to tell it or speak it and to "receive" a tradition is not just to hear it. Rather, handing on a tradition "means that *one hands over something to somebody so that the latter possesses it*," while receiving a tradition "means that *one receives something so that one possesses it*."[4] While this need not entail verbatim memorization, it does entail some process of teaching and learning so that what is communicated will be retained. Moreover, it is clear that the traditions Paul envisages require an authorized tradent to teach them, such as he considered himself to be. In one case where Paul speaks of traditions, he makes clear that his authority for transmitting at least some of them to his churches was not his apostolic status as such, but the fact that he himself had received them from competent authorities (1 Cor 15:3). He thus places himself in a chain of transmission.[5]

From whom did Paul receive traditions? In 1 Cor 15:3, where Paul claims

---

3. For these categories see, e.g., B. Gerhardsson, *Memory and Manuscript: Oral Transmission and Written Transmission in Rabbinic Judaism and Early Christianity* (Lund: Gleerup, 1961) 288-306; P. T. O'Brien, *Colossians, Philemon* (WBC 44; Waco: Word, 1982) 105-6; J. D. G. Dunn, *The Epistles to the Colossians and to Philemon* (NIGTC; Grand Rapids: Eerdmans, 1996) 139-141; idem, *The Theology of Paul the Apostle* (Grand Rapids: Eerdmans, 1998) 185-95.

4. B. Gerhardsson, "Illuminating the Kingdom: Narrative Meshalim in the Synoptic Gospels," in H. Wansbrough, ed., *Jesus and the Oral Gospel Tradition* (JSNTSup 64; Sheffield: Sheffield University Press, 1991) 306.

5. This is also implied by the *kai* in 1 Cor 15:1, 3, meaning "you *in turn* received," "I *in turn* received."

to have received the tradition (including the list of resurrection appearances) that he rehearses in vv. 3-7,[6] some scholars have held that the source of this tradition must have been the "Hellenistic" church in Damascus rather than the Jerusalem apostles.[7] This view is designed to maintain the idea of a separation between "Hellenistic Jewish" Christianity, to which Paul is supposed to have belonged, and the Palestinian Jewish Christianity of the Jerusalem church. But such a separation is hardly compatible with the role Paul gives to the Jerusalem apostles precisely here in 1 Cor 15:5, 7. Moreover, when Paul claims his own apostleship despite its anomalous character (vv. 9-11), he asserts the unanimity between himself and the other apostles on the key matters he has just rehearsed (v. 11). This unanimity existed *because* he had received the tradition in question from the Jerusalem apostles.[8]

It is very notable that in Galatians, even in the context of Paul's strong concern to maintain the independence of his apostleship from Jerusalem, he admits that three years after his call to be an apostle he did visit Jerusalem and spent two weeks with Peter (Gal 1:18).[9] Two weeks of conversation with Peter (for he states that he saw none of the other apostles except James: v. 19[10]) is a lot of conversation. As C. H. Dodd memorably put it, "we may presume they did not spend all the time talking about the weather."[11] We should rather presume that Paul was becoming thoroughly informed of the Jesus traditions as formulated by the Twelve, learning them from the leader of the Twelve, Peter. This is not inconsistent with Paul's insistence that he did not receive the gospel he preached from humans but through the revelation of Jesus Christ at the time of his call to be an apostle (vv. 11-12). It was on the strength of this revelation of the gospel message that he already proclaimed the gospel, with full apostolic authority, in the period before he visited Peter in Jerusalem (vv.

---

6. We need not enter the debate as to how much of these verses constitute the original tradition Paul received. There is no good reason for denying that it comprises the whole of vv. 3-7, though with an annotation ("most of whom are still alive, though some have died") probably added by Paul in v. 6 and the appearance to Paul himself added in v. 8.

7. E.g., J. Héring, *The First Epistle of Saint Paul to the Corinthians* (tr. A. W. Heathcote and P. J. Alcock; London: Epworth, 1962) 158. According to A. Eriksson, *Traditions as Rhetorical Proof* (CB[NT] 29; Stockholm: Almqvist and Wiksell, 1998) 91, "The resulting consensus is that the tradition was derived from Jerusalem, and received its present shape among the Greek-speaking, Jewish, Christians." But the Greek version could easily be Paul's own.

8. Cf. M. Hengel and A. M. Schwemer, *Paul between Damascus and Antioch* (tr. J. Bowden; London: SCM, 1997) 147.

9. I find the account of this visit in Gerhardsson, *Memory*, 297-98, broadly convincing.

10. Note that James is also the only individual besides Peter who is named in 1 Cor 15:3-7.

11. C. H. Dodd, *The Apostolic Preaching and Its Developments* (second edition; London: Hodder and Stoughton, 1944) 16.

15-17). What he lacked, however, was detail about the words and deeds of Jesus, and he may have come to see the need for this during his period of mission in Nabatea (Arabia: v. 17).[12] As James Dunn puts it, "we must allow that his early encounters with those in the new movement before him had a fairly substantive level of 'information content,' to supplement or correct the picture he had gained as a persecutor."[13] Allusions to Jesus traditions in Paul's writings are in fact much more numerous than an older stereotype of Paul allowed.[14]

On the other occasion when Paul explicitly states that he "received" a tradition, he is also explicit about the source: "I received from the Lord what I also handed on to you" (1 Cor 11:23). The tradition is about the words of Jesus at the last supper (vv. 23-25), which he cites as ground for what he goes on to say about the body and blood of the Lord with reference to the Corinthian celebration of the Lord's Supper (11:26-32). Paul certainly does not mean that he received this tradition by immediate revelation from the exalted Lord. He must have known it as a unit of Jesus tradition, perhaps already part of a passion narrative; it is the only such unit that Paul ever quotes explicitly and at length. He cites it in a form that is close to the Lukan version (Luke 22:19-20)[15] and that diverges generally in the same way as Luke's from the version in Mark and Matthew (Mark 14:22-24; Matt 26:26-28). Paul's version is verbally so close to Luke's that, since literary dependence in either direction is very unlikely, Paul must be dependent either on a written text or, more likely, an oral text that has been quite closely memorized.[16] Either or both of the two versions — the Pauline-Lukan version and the Markan-Matthean version — may have been influenced by the Christian practice of the Eucharist,[17] but it

12. For the view that Paul went to Nabatea to begin his apostolic mission to the Gentiles, see Hengel and Schwemer, *Paul between Damascus,* chapter 4; R. Bauckham, "What If Paul Had Travelled East Rather Than West?" *Biblical Interpretation* 8 (2000) 171-84.

13. J. D. G. Dunn, *The Epistle to the Galatians* (BNTC; London: Black, 1993) 74; cf. also N. Taylor, *Paul, Antioch and Jerusalem* (JSNTSup 66; Sheffield: Sheffield Academic, 1992) 80.

14. See D. Wenham, *Paul: Follower of Jesus or Founder of Christianity?* (Grand Rapids: Eerdmans 1995); Dunn, *The Theology,* 189-95.

15. For the text-critical problem and defense of the longer text of Luke here, see J. A. Fitzmyer, *The Gospel according to Luke X–XXIV* (AB 28A; New York: Doubleday, 1985) 1387-91.

16. The argument of M. Casey, *Aramaic Sources of Mark's Gospel* (SNTSMS 102; Cambridge: Cambridge University Press, 1998) 248-49, that Paul himself has extensively rewritten the account to suit his purpose in the context requires him to imply either that Luke is dependent on this Pauline letter or that Luke 22:19b-20 does not belong to the original text of the Gospel. Casey's argument also requires that the version Paul gives in his letter is very different from the version he had previously given the Corinthians, making 1 Cor 11:23a quite misleading.

17. This is less likely than is often supposed. It is rarely realized that Mark and Matthew

is not likely that they were actually liturgical texts recited at the Eucharist.[18] Paul cites the Jesus tradition, not a liturgical text, and so he provides perhaps our earliest evidence of narratives about Jesus transmitted in a way that involved, while not wholly verbatim reproduction, certainly a considerable degree of precise memorization.

Paul's claim to have received this tradition "from the Lord" should be compared with his allusions to specific sayings of "the Lord" in 1 Cor 7:10-16 and 9:14. The former text, 7:10-16, is particularly illuminating in the way it distinguishes sharply and clearly between what Paul knew as Jesus' words in a traditional saying of Jesus (vv. 10-11) and his own instruction (vv. 12-16), which he sees as providing for a situation not envisaged in Jesus' own teaching. Paul's own instruction is not given as mere opinion, but as carrying his apostolic authority. Yet it is clearly distinguished from the words of Jesus, a fact that tells importantly against the view of the form critics that new sayings of Jesus were readily created and attributed to him in the churches. Just as Paul cites sayings of Jesus in 7:10-11 and 9:14, so his introduction to the tradition about the Lord's Supper in 11:23 ("I received from the Lord") focuses on the source of the sayings of Jesus, which are the point of the narrative, and claims that they truly derive from Jesus. He therefore envisages a chain of transmission that *begins from Jesus himself* and passes through intermediaries to Paul himself, who has already passed it on to the Corinthians when he first established their church. The intermediaries are surely, again, the Jerusalem apostles, and this part of the passion traditions will have been part of what Paul learned (in the strong sense of learning a tradition such that he could later recite it) from Peter during that significant fortnight in Jerusalem. Given Paul's concern and conviction that his gospel traditions come from the Lord Jesus himself, it is inconceivable that Paul would have relied on less direct means of access to the traditions. Though Paul may not want to draw attention to the fact, since his relationship with the Jerusalem apostles was a touchy subject for him, in this respect he was indeed dependent on those apostles. While he may have insisted that his authority to recite and transmit the Jesus traditions belonged to him as an apostle directly appointed by the Lord, the authenticity of the traditions he transmitted in fact depended on

---

do not record these words at the supper for the sake of narrating the institution of the Eucharist, but in order to provide a sacrificial interpretation of the death of Jesus that they go on to narrate. Thus the words requiring repetition of the acts in remembrance of Jesus could have been omitted as not serving Mark's and Matthew's purpose.

18. A. B. McGowan, "'Is There a Liturgical Text in This Gospel?' The Institution Narratives and Their Early Interpretive Communities," *JBL* 118 (1999) 73-87; A. C. Thiselton, *The First Epistle to the Corinthians* (NIGTC; Grand Rapids: Eerdmans, 2000) 868.

their derivation from the Jerusalem apostles. We might note that his claim, as an apostle, to have the same right as the Jerusalem apostles to material support from his converts (1 Cor 9:3-6) is based on a number of reasons, but the final and clinching argument is a saying of the earthly Jesus (9:14).

We have considered *from whom* Paul received his traditions, but *to whom* did he transmit them? Whenever Paul makes this clear, it is to his addressees as a whole, the Christian community to which he writes, that he says he has handed on the traditions. This is the case, for example, in the two specific cases we have considered (1 Cor 11:23; 15:1-3). Paul never speaks of having transmitted the traditions to specific persons within the communities, people who might act as authoritative guardians and teachers of the traditions. The retaining and maintaining of the traditions is always represented as the responsibility of all Paul's readers (1 Cor 11:2; 15:2; 2 Thess 2:15). So we might suppose that, whatever was the case up to the point at which the traditions were received by Paul's newly established churches, from then on we must envisage a process of control by the community as a whole. We could invoke here Bailey's model of the Middle Eastern village, discussed in the last chapter, although Bailey himself applies this model only to Jewish Christian communities within Palestine.[19] According to this model, there are deliberate processes of learning and faithfully preserving tradition, but they are exercised generally by the community, not as the responsibility of specially authorized individuals.

However, we know that there were persons expressly designated as teachers in the Pauline churches (Rom 12:7; 1 Cor 12:28-29; Gal 6:6; Eph 4:11), as in other parts of the early Christian movement (Acts 13:1; Heb 5:12; Jas 3:1; *Didache* 15:1-2). James Dunn, in spite of his adoption of Bailey's model, stresses their role as, so to speak, local storehouses of the traditions.[20] Did Paul's transmission of tradition ignore the special role of designated teachers within the community?

A parallel in what Josephus says about the Pharisees is illuminating:

> I want to explain here that the Pharisees passed on *(paredosan)* to the people *(tǭ dēmǭ)* certain ordinances from a succession of fathers *(ek paterōn diadochēs)*, which are not written down in the laws of Moses. For this reason the party of the Sadducees dismisses these ordinances, averring that one need only recognize the written ordinances, whereas those

19. K. E. Bailey, "Informal Controlled Oral Tradition and the Synoptic Gospels," *Themelios* 20 (1995) 10.

20. J. D. G. Dunn, *Jesus Remembered* (Grand Rapids: Eerdmans, 2003) 176-77; idem, "On History, Memory and Eyewitnesses: In Response to Bengt Holmberg and Samuel Byrskog," *JSNT* 26 (2004) 482.

from the tradition of the fathers *(ek paradoseōs tōn paterōn)* need not be observed *(Ant.* 13.297).[21]

In the light of Josephus's general usage, Steve Mason argues that he has borrowed the phrase "from a succession of fathers" from the Pharisees' own usage.[22] The term "succession" *(diadochē)* was commonly used with reference to the Hellenistic schools of philosophy: "Plato, Aristotle, Epicurus and Zeno all passed the direction of their schools on to 'successors,' who viewed their task as the preservation and exposition of the master's original philosophy."[23] It is clear that "the fathers" from whom the Pharisees received their traditions were not the people in general, but a chain of individual teachers. We should imagine something like the chain of succession later defined in Pirqe 'Avot: "Moses received the Law from Sinai and committed it to Joshua, and Joshua to the elders, and the elders to the Prophets; and the Prophets committed it to the men of the Great Synagogue," after which follows a list of individual sages (Simeon the Just, Antigonus of Soko, et al.) who transmitted it from the men of the Great Synagogue down to Hillel and Shammai (m. 'Avot 1:2-12).

The important point for our purposes is that Josephus uses the language of "passing on" tradition both for the transmission from one teacher to another and also for the transmission from the Pharisees *to the people.* The fact that the Pharisees taught the traditions to the people in general is entirely consistent with the fact that Pharisaic teachers received the traditions from earlier teachers and taught them to pupils who in turn became part of the chain of transmission. Similarly, the fact that, in one sense, Paul transmitted traditions to each Christian community as a whole and expected the whole community to recall them when he alludes to them is quite consistent with the probability that he also transmitted the traditions to a few designated persons in each community, people with the skills and gifts necessary for preserving the traditions and for being a resource for the traditions that belonged to the community as a whole. Thus, even within the Pauline communities, we should reckon with the role of specially authorized guarantors of the traditions, and thus a more formal process of preservation and transmission of the traditions than Bailey's model envisages. The rather important result is that designated persons in each Pauline community knew the Jesus traditions through a chain of only two links between themselves and Jesus himself, namely Paul and the Jerusalem apostles.

21. Translation from S. Mason, *Flavius Josephus on the Pharisees* (Leiden: Brill, 1991) 217.

22. Mason, *Flavius Josephus,* 239.

23. Mason, *Flavius Josephus,* 234.

Thus Paul provides ample evidence of the formal transmission of traditions within the early Christian movement, and good evidence more precisely for *the formal transmission of traditions of the words and deeds of Jesus.* Paul himself learned such traditions from Peter by a formal process of learning, and he probably transmitted them by a similar process of formal learning, not merely to the communities he founded as a whole, but also, with special attention, to persons designated as teachers within each community. Finally, we should remember that Paul did not work alone in his missionary work but with colleagues, some of whom had been prominent members of the Jerusalem church: Barnabas, Mark, and Silvanus (= Silas in Acts).[24] They would have had considerably more opportunity to become thoroughly familiar with the Jesus traditions of the Jerusalem church, and it may be that they took part of the responsibility for transmitting the Jesus traditions to the churches in whose founding they participated with Paul. (They did not participate in this way at Corinth.) Barnabas in particular may have helped to enrich Paul's own knowledge of these traditions.

Remembering the Past of Jesus

Before proceeding to discuss further the means of control that early Christians exercised over the Jesus tradition, it will be useful to consider at this stage for what reasons they would have wished to preserve faithfully traditions about the sayings of Jesus spoken during his ministry and about events of Jesus' history in the past. There is no doubt that oral societies generally and in particular the societies in which the early Christian movement developed had means of preserving traditions from more than minor changes in the course of transmission. Whether a particular oral society actually takes the trouble to preserve particular traditions from major alteration depends on its attitude to those traditions.

It is important to recall a feature of Bailey's observation of oral tradition in Middle Eastern villages: that different types of tradition are treated in different ways. This is generally true of oral societies.[25] Jan Vansina, in his authoritative account of oral tradition, observes that there are no general rules.

24. The evidence of Acts about these figures is sufficiently confirmed by Paul's own letters for there to be no serious doubt of its reliability.

25. Cf. the comment on rabbinic literature by P. S. Alexander, "Orality in Pharisaic-Rabbinic Judaism at the Turn of the Eras," in Wansbrough, ed., *Jesus and the Oral Gospel Tradition,* 182: "The degree of variation will differ according to the type of material: halakhic traditions are noticeably more carefully preserved than *aggadot.*"

Whether or to what extent a society intends to preserve a tradition faithfully must be investigated with regard to each type of tradition in each given society, as must the means employed for faithful preservation and the success achieved when faithful preservation is attempted.[26] This is an immensely important principle to grasp since it rules out many of the claims that have been made about the Jesus traditions of the early church on the grounds that such-and-such is the way oral tradition supposedly operates.

Equally important is Vansina's observation that oral societies often distinguish between tales and historical accounts. Tales "are considered to be fiction."[27]

> Every performance is a premiere and appreciated as such by the audience. The public likes to hear known tales in new garb. This is similar to the attitude of the public towards production of an opera, where the performance should be original in setting, style of singing, acting, costume, and other details, but not alter either score or wording. The public of a tale expects partly novel wording and novel expression. Over time tales alter much more than accounts and in a different way. . . . Among tales occur historical tales. They differ from accounts in that they are told for entertainment and are subject to the dynamics of fiction. Names and settings can be changed at will.[28]

Such "historical tales" are treated as fictional and are not equivalent to what Vansina calls historical "accounts," which are regarded as truthful accounts of the past and treated accordingly. This does not mean that they do not change, but that they change differently and largely as a result of incorporation into a community's larger corpus of such traditions: "In general, they tend to become shorter and be single anecdotes. . . . The whole corpus of group accounts is constantly and slowly reshaped or streamlined."[29] Accounts treated as historical change less and more slowly than tales:

> Variability is often much less pronounced. There is substantial commonality in plot, setting, personages, and even succession of episodes. . . . The time span of a tradition is important in this respect. If it is small, then we can come close to the message told by contemporaries after eyewitness

26. J. Vansina, *Oral Tradition as History* (Madison: University of Wisconsin Press, 1985) 42.

27. Vansina, *Oral Tradition*, 25.

28. Vansina, *Oral Tradition*, 26.

29. Vansina, *Oral Tradition*, 20-21.

accounts have been conflated with rumor. More often we come close to the message as it stabilized in the generation after that.[30]

Here we must remember (as we observed in chapter 2) that Vansina defines oral tradition as tradition transmitted beyond the span of living memory. When eyewitnesses are still available, we are dealing, in his terminology, with oral history rather than oral tradition. In the passage we have just quoted he is speaking of what happens when eyewitness memories have been absorbed into the community's corpus of tradition and begin to change slowly because of that incorporation. We must return later to the question of the difference this issue of the eyewitnesses makes. We need note here only that even when Vansina speaks of the comparatively small change that historical accounts undergo in oral tradition, the time span he envisages is longer than that between the events of Jesus' history and the Gospels. Nevertheless, what is important for our present purposes is that oral societies treat historical tales and historical accounts differently and in such a way that the latter are preserved more faithfully. In the latter case there is an intention to preserve faithfully, which is lacking in the former.[31]

This distinction between tales and accounts refutes all claims that Gospels scholars, from the form critics onward, have made to the effect that early Christians, in the transmission of Jesus traditions, would not have made any distinction between the past time of the history of Jesus and their own present *because oral societies and their traditions do not make such distinctions.*[32] This is untrue. Moreover Vansina dissents from the view of anthropologist Jack Goody that complete "homeostasis" exists between a society and its traditions, such that the traditions change in complete correspondence to society and cannot correspond to a past reality.[33] Vansina agrees that there is congruence between a society and its traditions, but "no total congruence of content with the concerns of the present." This is proved by the fact that archaism — features of historical accounts that have been simply preserved and

---

30. Vansina, *Oral Tradition*, 53-54; cf. 161.

31. Cf. Alexander, "Orality," 182, on rabbinic literature: "What preserved a text — whether written or oral — against substantial change was not the medium of its transmission, but a prior attitude towards its nature and authority which dictated that it should not be changed." Alexander is arguing that it is not necessarily the case that oral traditions change more than written texts.

32. E.g., W. Kelber, *The Oral and the Written Gospel* (second edition; Bloomington: Indiana University Press, 1997) 199-209.

33. See also S. Byrskog, *Story as History, History as Story* (WUNT 123; Tübingen: Mohr, 2000; reprinted Leiden: Brill, 2002) 131-33.

not adjusted to conform to present circumstances — survives in historical traditions.[34] Indeed, a failing of homeostasis theories is precisely that they

> cannot explain why history is valued more in some societies than others. . . . Beyond homeostasis fundamental cultural options, differing worldviews must be taken into account and they are not wholly conditioned by the present social organization.[35]

The question, then, is not whether oral societies as such distinguish history from the present and preserve historical traditions in such a way as to preserve them from radical adaptation to the social context, but whether as a matter of fact the early Christian communities did so. Whether the Jesus traditions themselves show evidence of this is crucial, but it is also important to establish the early Christian movement's attitude to the past, specifically the history of Jesus, and why this past history mattered to them.

It was not, of course, a matter of purely antiquarian interest in the past for its own sake, an attitude that is rare even in modern societies (though by no means completely unknown among scholars even in pre-modern societies, including Greco-Roman antiquity). The question is whether a particular society has any use for historical accounts that it regards as genuinely about the past:[36]

> Traditions about events are only kept because the events were thought to be important or significant. A selection process is already underway, starting in fact with the eyewitnesses or contemporary reports.[37]

But this is as far as generalization can take us. Beyond that it is a matter of the cultural particularities of a society, and this is especially the case when we are dealing, as in the case of the early Christian movement, with communities formed in the context of a culturally sophisticated society, one that already

34. Vansina, *Oral Tradition*, 120-21.
35. Vansina, *Oral Tradition*, 122.
36. Vansina, *Oral Tradition*, 114-16, gives a highly illuminating example, comparing the oral traditions of Burundi and Rwanda. Despite being neighboring societies with much in common, the former lacks historical accounts whereas the latter has rich historical traditions that are of widespread interest. This is explained by the "difference in socio-political systems," particularly in the fact that in Rwanda government needed historical legitimation. The result is considerable difference in attitudes to and interest in the past between the two societies. Cf. also Vansina, *Oral Tradition*, 91-92, for traditions that intend to transmit history, though not with the merely antiquarian aim of transmitting nothing but history for its own sake.
37. Vansina, *Oral Tradition*; 118, cf. 91-92 on the uses of historical accounts.

has a written body of authoritative Scripture and a rich heritage of traditions from the past as well as a tradition of serious historiography.[38] It is when past history matters in a particular cultural context that historical accounts are preserved with a real intention and effort to insure an important degree of stability and continuity.

That early Christians in fact had a genuine sense of the past as past and were concerned to preserve memories of the past history of Jesus has often been demonstrated.[39] Two particularly important books should be mentioned. The first, published as early as 1974, is Graham Stanton's *Jesus of Nazareth in New Testament Preaching*.[40] In my view, Stanton too readily accepted many of the contentions of form criticism — especially the view that missionary preaching was the primary *Sitz im Leben* of the gospel traditions — which now appear much more questionable. But with this qualification it is all the more significant that he was able to demonstrate that what we know of the early church's preaching of the gospel itself shows considerable evidence that the past history of Jesus mattered and that reference to it was an integral part of the church's preaching itself: "The early communities have retained traditions about Jesus which provide such a rich and full portrait of him that we must conclude that the church began to look back to the past . . . at an early stage in its development."[41]

While Stanton's work concerned the church's preaching, the second book dealt with the Gospels. It is Eugene Lemcio's *The Past of Jesus in the Gospels*.[42] He succeeds in amply demonstrating that the Gospel writers distinguished the time of Jesus' past history from their own present. The Gospel writers' careful effort to make this distinction

> transcended merely putting verbs in past tenses and dividing the account into pre- and post-resurrection periods. Rather, they took care that the

38. Cf. S. Byrskog, "A New Perspective on the Jesus Tradition: Reflections on James D. G. Dunn's *Jesus Remembered*," *JSNT* 26 (2004) 469-70: "One must take seriously that in the first century oral conventions were deeply influenced by the written word, which created an element of abstract thinking and reflection about the past."

39. E.g., C. F. D. Moule, "Jesus in New Testament Kerygma," in idem, *Essays in New Testament Interpretation* (Cambridge: Cambridge University Press, 1982) 37-49 (this essay was first published in 1970); J. Roloff, *Das Kerygma und die irdische Jesus* (Göttingen: Vandenhoeck und Ruprecht, 1970).

40. G. N. Stanton, *Jesus of Nazareth in New Testament Preaching* (SNTSMS 27; Cambridge: Cambridge University Press, 1974).

41. Stanton, *Jesus of Nazareth*, 170-71.

42. E. E. Lemcio, *The Past of Jesus in the Gospels* (SNTSMS 68; Cambridge: Cambridge University Press, 1991).

terminology appropriate to the Christian era does not appear beforehand. Vocabulary characteristic prior to Easter faith falls by the wayside
afterwards. Words common to both bear a different nuance in each. Idiom suits the time. And these are not routine or incidental expressions.
They reveal what Jesus the protagonist and the Evangelists as narrators
believe about the gospel, the Christ, the messianic task, the nature of salvation, etc. . . . Kerygmatic expressions of "faith" found outside of the
gospels were not projected back onto the narrative.[43]

A simple illustration is the fact that the ways in which the pre-Easter Jesus refers to himself in the Gospel narratives do not correspond to the ways in which
early Christians referred to him. He calls himself "Son of Man" (used only in
sayings of Jesus in the New Testament, with the single exception of Acts 7:56),
almost never "Messiah" (even in the Gospel of John) or "Son of God" (in the
Synoptics, but the usage is rare even in John). Not only do the sayings of Jesus
in the Gospels display a characteristic vocabulary and idiom not found in early
Christian usage, but the way the Evangelists speak of such matters as faith, discipleship, and salvation in the pre-Easter period differs from the way they
themselves portray these matters in the post-Easter context.

Lemcio's work coheres strongly with the general, though quite recent,
acceptance in Gospels scholarship that, generically, the Gospels are biography
— or, more precisely, they are biographies *(bioi)* in the sense of ancient
Greco-Roman biography.[44] Different as this genre is from modern biographies, it nevertheless entails a real sense of the past as past and an intention to
distinguish the past from the present. No ancient reader who identified the
Gospels as *bioi* could have expected their narrative form to be merely a way of
speaking of the risen, exalted Christ in his present relationship to his people.
They would expect the narratives to recount the real past and not to confuse
this with the present.

However, might one not suppose that this "biographical" sense of history as really past was applied to the Jesus traditions by the Gospel writers,
who, by incorporating the traditions into a biographical narrative frame,
adopted them into a form of historical consciousness that was foreign to the
traditions themselves, particularly in their oral form? For example, Helmut
Koester states that the incorporation of a tradition into a biographical context
"may fundamentally change [its] form and function . . . because it is now
transferred from its situation in the life of the community into the context of

43. Lemcio, *The Past of Jesus,* 1-2.
44. See especially R. A. Burridge, *What Are the Gospels? A Comparison with Graeco-
Roman Biography* (SNTSMS 70; Cambridge: Cambridge University Press, 1992).

the life of Jesus."[45] This kind of argument could preserve the form-critical view of the oral tradition while accepting the view, which the form critics so strongly rejected, that the Gospels themselves are biographies. But it must be said that much of Lemcio's evidence, while it is marshaled to prove his thesis about the Gospels as such, must also apply to the traditions as they existed orally before the Gospels. Certainly something happened when the traditions were appropriated by the writers of the Gospels, but it could not have been so discontinuous with the attitude of the oral traditions themselves. The nature of the traditions — as soon as we consider them outside the perspective the form critics brought to them — shows that they made reference to the real past history of Jesus. The fact that this is stated in the excellent textbook *The Historical Jesus,* by Gerd Theissen and Annette Merz,[46] shows how far the mainstream of Gospels scholarship has moved since the heyday of form criticism.

The early Christian movement was interested in the genuinely past history of Jesus because they regarded it as *religiously relevant.* But why should this have been the case? Dunn offers a sociological explanation: The early Christians, distinguished from other groups by terms referring to Jesus ("Nazarenes" and "Christians"), "would almost certainly have required a foundation story (or stories) to explain, to themselves as well as to others, why they had formed distinct social groups."[47] It was for purposes of self-identity that Christians transmitted Jesus traditions and wrote Gospels. While this explanation has the advantage of cross-cultural comparison,[48] it is lacking in the cultural specificity necessary for an adequate explanation. Early Christians were less concerned with self-identity than with salvation, though the two are in their case closely related. Jesus was more than the founder of their movement; he was the source of salvation. Moreover, this salvation was understood within the thoroughly Jewish context of Christian origins. It was fulfillment of the promises made by the God of Israel to his people Israel in the past. It was a new chapter — the decisive, eschatological chapter — in God's history with his people and the world. The events of Jesus' history were charged with all the history-making significance of the activity of Israel's God. Thus, at the deepest level, it was for profoundly theological reasons — their understanding of God and salvation — that early Christians were concerned with faithful memory of the really past story of Jesus. The present in

45. H. Koester, "Written Gospels or Oral Tradition?" *JBL* 113 (1994) 296.

46. G. Theissen and A. Merz, *The Historical Jesus* (tr. J. Bowden; London: SCM, 1998) 102-4.

47. Dunn, *Jesus Remembered,* 175.

48. Cf. B. A. Misztal, *Theories of Social Remembering* (Philadelphia: Open University, 2003) 132-39.

which they lived in relationship with the risen and exalted Christ was the effect of this past history, presupposing its pastness and not at all dissolving it.

An "Isolated" Tradition

The most essential and, at the same time, the simplest way in which the early Christian movement strove to preserve the traditions about Jesus faithfully, without major alteration, was by transmitting the traditions for their own sake and in their own right, not as part of something else. The assumption of the form critics (for which they produced no evidence) was that the church's evangelistic preaching and its communal instruction of believers were the contexts in which the Jesus traditions were passed on. They provided the *Sitze im Leben* for which the forms of the tradition were intended. This meant that the tradition was entirely pliable to the uses to which it was put in the church's kerygmatic and parenetic practices, that is, its proclamation of the gospel and its instruction of believers in the Christian way. The constant development and expansion of the tradition were due to the fact that it was transmitted by means of its *use*. (Dibelius, it is true, supposed that the sayings of Jesus were handed down *both* as collections *and* in parenetic use, but that the latter was the principal means.) It was Gerhardsson, following his teacher Harald Riesenfeld,[49] who argued, to the contrary, that the Jesus tradition was transmitted *independently of its use,* as what he called an "isolated" tradition.[50] The primary *Sitz im Leben* of the tradition was this transmission process itself.

For evidence that the Jesus tradition was in this sense "isolated," we need look no farther than the Pauline passages we discussed earlier in this chapter. The mere fact that Paul speaks of a formal process of handing on (Jesus) tradition (1 Cor 11:23) requires us to suppose that it had an existence in its own right and was transmitted as such. The clear distinction Paul maintains between the saying of Jesus about divorce that he cites and the further instructions he himself adds (1 Cor 7:10-16) shows how the tradition of the sayings of Jesus was kept distinct from their use in parenetic instruction. Other-

---

49. H. Riesenfeld, "The Gospel Tradition and Its Beginnings," in idem, *The Gospel Tradition* (Oxford: Blackwell, 1970) 1-29.

50. B. Gerhardsson, *Memory and Manuscript: Oral Transmission and Written Transmission in Rabbinic Judaism and Early Christianity* (Lund: Gleerup, 1961) 335; idem, *The Reliability of the Gospel Tradition* (Peabody: Hendrickson, 2001) 22-23, 41-65. The terminology ("die Isolierung der Jesustradition") was evidently first used by G. Kittel in 1926 (cited in Gerhardsson, *The Reliability,* 64).

wise, how easy it would have been for Paul to present his own teaching in this case as an implication of what Jesus had already said, absorbing the former into the tradition of the latter. Moreover, even more significantly, early Christian instruction (as we have it in various New Testament letters and in the Apostolic Fathers) rarely cites the sayings or deeds of Jesus as such. Allusions are made, more or less frequently; instruction is given that is clearly indebted in its spirit and thrust to the sayings of Jesus; but actual citations are very rare. There is no way in which parenesis of this kind could have preserved the sayings of Jesus *at all*. Very often, when explicit citations are made, it is clear that readers are being reminded of what they already know (e.g., 1 Cor 11:23; Acts 20:35; 1 *Clement* 13:1; 46:7-8) — not from the parenesis, but from the tradition of the sayings of Jesus as such.

This does not mean that the Jesus traditions as we know them from the Gospels in no way reflect the context of the early Christian movement to which they were found relevant. But adaptations to this later context (i.e., later than the ministry of Jesus) are moderate. They do not effect radical reshapings of the tradition. Frequently, the traditions in fact betray no hint of the way in which the early Christians interpreted them with reference to their own needs and situations.

The Gospels themselves would be hard to explain unless the oral Jesus traditions before them were transmitted for their own sake, "isolated" from other types of Christian tradition. For the Gospels themselves are "isolated": they alone of early Christian literary productions transmit the traditions about Jesus and they transmit exclusively traditions about Jesus. No other teachers (with the special exception of John the Baptist) play any role. The disciples do not supplement Jesus' teaching with contributions — adding or interpreting — in their own name.[51] This is, of course, appropriate to their genre as *bioi* (ancient biographies) of Jesus, but *bioi* of Jesus would hardly have been possible or the need for them felt had the oral Jesus traditions not already had an existence independent of other forms of early Christian tradition.[52]

---

51. Gerhardsson, *The Reliability*, 63.

52. This observation is relevant to an interesting comparative question: why did rabbinic Judaism, unlike early Christianity, produce no biographies of its rabbis? See J. Neusner, *Why No Gospels in Talmudic Judaism?* (Brown Judaic Studies 135; Atlanta: Scholars, 1988).

Controlling the Tradition: Memorization

Memorization was universal in education in the ancient world.[53] Learning meant, to a significant degree, memorizing. This could mean memorizing books[54] or selections from them (cf. 2 Macc 2:25), or memorizing oral material.[55] Although Dominic Crossan has argued that a sharp distinction should be made between these two,[56] such a distinction is inappropriate in a society that, though predominantly oral, did make use of written texts.[57] There is no doubt, for example, that the later rabbis memorized both the text of Scripture and oral traditions, while, in the latter case, as we shall note further in the next section, they sometimes at least used notebooks as aids to memory. Where books existed not so much to be read as to be heard and their contents to be held in the memory and transmitted orally as well as in writing, we should not draw too sharp a distinction between the memorizing of written and of oral material.

It is much more important to recognize that different kinds of material might require different *degrees* of memorization:

> [O]ne has to differentiate. Rhetors could memorize verbatim their own speeches (Eunapios, *Vit. Soph.* 2.8), pupils learnt by heart large parts of classical literature to have examples for imitation (Quintilian, *Inst. Orat.* 2.7.2-4), but a school tradition could also be handed down with considerable variation by altering and expanding it (Seneca, *Epist.* 33.4).[58]

In basic Hellenistic education *chreiai* about famous men and the sayings of great teachers were memorized, but pupils were also taught ways of varying the *chreiai* — abbreviating, expanding, and so forth.[59] The intention was that

53. B. Gerhardsson, *Memory and Manuscript: Oral Transmission and Written Transmission in Rabbinic Judaism and Early Christianity* (Lund: Gleerup, 1961) 123-26; R. Riesner, *Jesus als Lehrer* (WUNT 2/7; Tübingen: Mohr, 1981) 440-43.

54. As we noted in the last chapter, K. E. Bailey observes how this kind of practice of memorization is still alive in the Middle East: "Informal Controlled Oral Tradition and the Synoptic Gospels," 5; cf. also W. Shiner, *Proclaiming the Gospel: First-Century Performance of Mark* (Harrisburg: Trinity, 2003) 104, 106.

55. Shiner, *Proclaiming*, 106-7.

56. J. D. Crossan, *The Birth of Christianity* (San Francisco: HarperCollins, 1998) chapter 3.

57. Cf. Quintilian's advice on memorizing written texts, quoted and discussed in J. P. Small, *Wax Tablets of the Mind: Cognitive Studies of Memory and Literacy in Classical Antiquity* (New York: Routledge, 1997) 117-22.

58. R. Riesner, "Jesus as Preacher and Teacher," in Wansbrough, ed., *Jesus and the Oral Gospel Tradition*, 203.

59. M. C. Moeser, *The Anecdote in Mark, the Classical World and the Rabbis* (JSNTSup 227; Sheffield: Sheffield Academic, 2002) 79-87.

this would be useful in making speeches or in clever conversation. Word-for-word reproduction was the aim of memorizing some kinds of material, but less precise memorization was appropriate for other kinds of material. In the retelling of a story the plot is more important than the words, though there might be key statements that would need more or less precise reproduction. In a Jewish context Scripture would certainly be memorized verbatim, but other written narratives, like the *Biblical Antiquities* of Pseudo-Philo, might well be memorized for oral performance in a synagogue, with the degree of performative variation normally expected in such cases.[60]

Thus memorization would not always entail completely verbatim learning by rote, but some degree of memorization was indispensable to any deliberate attempt to learn and transmit tradition faithfully. It was the necessary alternative to trusting the unreliable vagaries of undisciplined memory. It is sometimes supposed that in predominantly oral societies the faculty of memory is better developed than in our own.[61] It would be better to say that, in societies where reliance on memory is essential in large areas of life in which it no longer matters much to us, people took the trouble to remember and used techniques of memorizing. Memory was not just a faculty, but a vital skill with techniques to be learned.[62] In a revealing passage in the *Apocalypse of Baruch,* God says: "Listen, Baruch, to this word and write down in the memory of your heart all that you shall learn" (2 *Baruch* 50:1). Here the memory is pictured as a book in which the owner writes memories down (so also Prov 3:3; 7:3).[63] In other words, committing to memory is a deliberate and skilled act, comparable to recording words in a notebook. Later Baruch would transfer these remembered words from the notebook of his memory to the literal writing of a book. Similarly, Irenaeus says, of the traditions he heard from Polycarp, that he "made notes of them, not on paper but in my heart" (*apud* Eusebius, *Hist. Eccl.* 5.20.7).

The longest Pauline example of rehearsing Jesus tradition — to which, because of its demonstrably early date, we have already referred more than once — is here again instructive. The close verbal parallelism between 1 Cor 11:23-25 and Luke 22:19-20 cannot plausibly be explained by a literary relationship between the texts, since Luke's Gospel cannot have been available to

60. Cf. H. G. Snyder, *Teachers and Texts in the Ancient World* (New York: Routledge, 2000) 174-77.

61. Against this, see Small, *Wax Tablets,* 4.

62. On "mnemotechnics," see Byrskog, *Story as History,* 163-64; Small, *Wax Tablets,* chapters 7-9.

63. Similarly, memory was often conceived as a wax tablet in the mind: Byrskog, *Story as History,* 162.

Paul and Luke shows no acquaintance with Paul's letters. Only strictly memorized oral tradition (memorized in Greek) can explain the high degree of verbal resemblance. We should note that, although Paul seems to expect his hearers to know the memorized oral text, it is entirely possible that he expects only a general familiarity on the part of the community as a whole, while the exact form, with a high degree of memorized wording,[64] would be preserved by teachers specifically commissioned to be guardians of the tradition.

In a predominantly oral society, not only do people deliberately remember but also teachers formulate their teachings so as to make them easily memorable. It has frequently been observed that Jesus' teaching in its typically Synoptic forms has many features that facilitate remembering. The aphorisms are typically terse and incisive, the narrative parables have a clear and relatively simple plot outline. Even in Greek translation, the only form in which we have them, the sayings of Jesus are recognizably poetic, especially employing parallelism, and many have posited Aramaic originals rich in alliteration, assonance, rhythm, rhyme, and wordplay.[65] These teaching formulations were certainly not created by Jesus ad hoc, in the course of his teaching, but were carefully crafted, designed as concise encapsulations of his teaching that his hearers could take away, remember, ponder, and live by. We cannot suppose that Jesus' oral teaching consisted entirely of such sayings as these. Jesus must have preached much more discursively, but offered these aphorisms and parables as brief but thought-provoking summations of his teaching for his hearers to jot down in their mental notebooks for frequent future recall. (Obviously, therefore, it was these memorable summations that survived, and when the writers of the Synoptic Gospels wished to *represent* the discursive teaching of Jesus they mostly had to use collections of these sayings.)

This kind of encapsulation of teaching in carefully crafted aphorisms to be remembered was the teaching style of the Jewish wisdom teacher. As Rainer Riesner puts it, "Even the form of the sayings of Jesus included in itself an imperative to remember them."[66] Jesus' hearers would readily recognize this and would apply to memorable sayings the deliberate practices of committing to memory that they would know were expected. To suppose that memorable sayings merely happened to stick in the memory, like politicians' "sound-bites" in the undisciplined memories that characterize the oral di-

---

64. To say that the tradition here is "in wholly fixed verbal form," as T. Holtz, "Paul and the Oral Gospel Tradition," in Wansbrough, ed., *Jesus and the Oral Gospel Tradition*, 383, does, is only slightly exaggerated.

65. Riesner, *Jesus als Lehrer*, 392-404.

66. Riesner, "Jesus as Preacher and Teacher," 202.

mension of our own culture, would be to mistake the cultural context of Jesus and the tradition of his sayings.

However, Werner Kelber, recognizing the mnemonic characteristics of the sayings of Jesus, attempts a sharp distinction between mnemonics and memorization:

> That many dominical sayings are mnemonically shaped so as to acousti-cally effect an oral and, we should add, visual appreciation among hearers is self-evident. But we distance ourselves from the assumption that mne-monics *eo ipso* entail memorization. That information is couched in mnemonically usable patterns is a commonplace of ancient and medieval rhetorical conventions. Customarily, mnemonics operate in the interest of assisting memory and of facilitating remembering in the oral process-ing of knowledge and information. They allow for, indeed thrive on, hermeneutical inventiveness and compositional freedom in performance. Memorization, by contrast, enforces the inculcation of words through ceaseless repetition, and displays little interest in accommodation to so-cial contexts and live audiences.[67]

Kelber is concerned to make room for the creative appropriation of the tradi-tion by those who continued it. But we should notice, first, that this is appli-cable to teachers who performed the Jesus tradition, not to those who simply appropriated it for meditative application in their own lives. These latter would not be at all interested in accommodating it to social contexts and live audiences. They simply wanted to remember it for its practical value. Second, creative adaptation of the tradition presupposes some degree of memoriza-tion of it. Third, the distinction drawn by Kelber between mnemonics and memorization seems to be a confusion of categories. Mnemonics (in the sense in which Kelber is here using the term) is the way the teacher makes the teaching memorable; memorization is the way the audience appropriates the teaching. Kelber offers no other description of the way an audience remem-bers if it is not by memorization. In all oral cultures, and in particular in first-century Mediterranean culture, repetition in order to remember is normal. Fourthly, the extent to which memorization would be verbally exact or rather focused on structure or plot would vary according to the type of material be-ing memorized.

Verbally exact memorization is not foreign to oral tradition generally, but is one specific form of memorization, employed for specific, appropriate

---

67. W. H. Kelber, "The Case of the Gospels: Memory's Desire and the Limits of Historical Criticism," *Oral Tradition* 17 (2002) 60.

types of material. Thus Vansina writes of the "slogans" of the Kuba clan of Rwanda, of which many recorded performances can be compared:

> Comparative analysis of versions yields in this case very short set speech patterns, which have been learned by heart. Such patterns are very stable in many cases, encompass the message of the tradition, and are the parts that were once composed by a single individual.[68]

In the case of Jesus' teaching, we should expect that the short and pithy aphorisms would be memorized word-for-word: it is hard to imagine in what other way they could be remembered. But narrative parables might be memorized rather as a narrative structure, with just key phrases learned exactly. So far we have discussed sayings of Jesus, but the principle that the form of memorization would vary according to the type of material being remembered is most clearly illustrated in the well-known difference between the tradition of the sayings of Jesus and that of the stories about Jesus. Our extant examples of differing versions show that exact wording is much more likely to be preserved in the case of sayings of Jesus than in that of narratives about Jesus. In other words, performative variation was evidently freer in the latter than in the former.

From the argument so far it should be clear that Jesus must have expected his sayings to be deliberately learned by hearers who took his teaching seriously, especially his disciples. That nothing is said in the Gospels about his requiring his sayings to be memorized or teaching by repetition is no argument to the contrary.[69] Something that would be so self-evident in the cultural context of the texts did not need mentioning. (However, Rainer Riesner has shown that Luke 9:44a probably refers to memorization.[70]) Still, it is a further question whether Jesus expected his disciples to transmit his teaching to others. The evidence for an affirmative answer to this question lies in the strong tradition within the Gospels that Jesus sent out his disciples to spread his message during his ministry (Matt 9:36–10:15; Mark 6:7-13; Luke 9:1-6; 10:1-16),[71] supported especially by the saying that equates their mission as his messengers with that of himself as their sender: "He who receives you receives me . . ." (Matt 10:40, with variant versions in Mark 9:37; Luke 10:16; John

68. Vansina, *Oral Tradition as History,* 51. Cf. also R. Finnegan, quoted in Riesner, "Jesus as Preacher and Teacher," 207-8.

69. *Pace* M. Hengel, *The Charismatic Leader and His Followers* (tr. J. C. G. Greig; Edinburgh: Clark, 1981) 80; Dunn, *Jesus Remembered,* 198.

70. Riesner, *Jesus als Lehrer,* 444-45.

71. Riesner, *Jesus als Lehrer,* 453-75, provides a detailed treatment of this subject.

13:20). The Evangelists characterize the message of the disciples of Jesus very briefly, but in the same terms in which they summarize Jesus' own proclamation (Matt 10:7; Mark 6:12; Luke 9:2; 10:9). For this same message the disciples must have employed the same sayings in which Jesus himself had crystallized his teaching.[72]

In that sense a formal transmission of Jesus' teaching by authorized tradents, his disciples, began already during Jesus' ministry. The same probably cannot be said, however, of the stories about Jesus' activity. These too would certainly have been told during Jesus' ministry. In some cases, as we suggested in chapter 3, these stories will have been first told by the persons whose names are still attached to them in the Gospels. Bartimaeus will have been telling his story to anyone who would listen doubtless from the start. Jesus' disciples were surely already telling the stories of Jesus' healings and exorcisms at least to other disciples during his ministry. But this would have been a matter of informal transmission. Only when formulated and transmitted by the eyewitnesses and especially, though not exclusively, by the Twelve after the resurrection of Jesus would the narrative traditions about Jesus have become more formal, in the sense of tradition authorized by an acknowledged competent tradent and formally delivered to others. Perhaps, in the case of narrative traditions, more informal transmission also continued.

As we noted in the last chapter, a principal objection to Gerhardsson's account of the tradition as controlled by scrupulous practices of memorization has been that it fails to account for the actual variation in the versions of the Jesus traditions that we have in our extant sources.[73] It is clearly an essential requirement of any account of the way the traditions were transmitted that it explain this actual variation in the written texts. However, we should recall at this point that the model of the tradition offered by the form critics has been shown to be mistaken, and that, as a result, there is no reason to postulate that the oral traditions once varied to a much greater extent than they do in the extant versions in the Gospels. There is no need to postulate extensive development of the traditions prior to the versions we have in the Gospels. We may reasonably suppose that the extent of variation we can observe in the extant records (the canonical Gospels along with the early extracanonical material) is

72. For the argument of this paragraph, see the pioneering and influential article by H. Schürmann, "Die vorösterlichen Anfänge der Logientradition. Versuch eines formgeschichtlichen Zugangs zum Leben Jesu," in H. Ristow and K. Matthiae, eds., *Der historische Jesus und der kerygmatische Christus* (Berlin: Evangelische, 1962) 342-70.

73. Dunn, *Jesus Remembered*, 198; and cf. Gerhardsson's response to Dunn on this point: B. Gerhardsson, "The Secret of the Transmission of the Unwritten Jesus Tradition," *NTS* 51 (2005) 15-16.

the same — no greater or less — as the extent to which the traditions varied in oral performance.

With this presupposition, we can explain the variability of the traditions by reference to five main factors (in addition, of course, to failures of memory and mere mistakes, which must occur in any such process): (1) We must allow for the probability that Jesus himself used varying versions of his own sayings on different occasions, and that sometimes the traditions have preserved these. (2) Some verbal differences will result from translation variants (in translation from Aramaic to Greek). (3) Many differences, especially in narrative, will be due to the variability normal in oral performance and to the degree considered appropriate for the type of material being transmitted.[74] This kind of variation probably accounts for many differences in the triple tradition (the material common to Matthew, Mark, and Luke). Matthew and Luke varied their Markan written source in the same kinds of ways they would have done had they been performing oral tradition.[75]

(4) Many differences, especially in the sayings material, must be deliberate interpretative alterations or additions, by which a tradent sought to explain or to adapt the teaching when the post-Easter situation seemed to require this. Such changes, it should be noted, are entirely compatible with word-for-word memorization of, for example, aphorisms of Jesus, since the changes would be made quite deliberately to a known form of exact words. Such changes are also quite compatible with a formal process of transmission, since it would be authorized tradents who, from their own familiarity with the tradition, would be competent to make such changes. The Gospel writers, too, would have made such changes, and these are what are commonly treated as redactional changes of the more significant sort, as distinct from merely stylistic and incidental variations. (5) Finally, there are changes the Gospel writers have made in order to integrate the traditions into the connected narrative of their Gospels. (This may be to some extent a continuation of what had been done in the making of earlier small collections of sayings or narratives.)

In order to clarify further the difference between factors (3) and (4), we should recognize that the idea of performative variation depends on a distinction between key elements, which remain stable in all performances, and other elements, which are treated as flexible. In many cases, the key elements

74. Note the important statement of G. Theissen, *The Miracle Stories of the Early Christian Tradition* (tr. F. McDonagh; Edinburgh: Clark, 1981) 195: "The relationship between variability and continuity must be determined for each genre [used in the Gospel traditions] specifically."

75. This is shown by means of specific examples in Dunn, *Jesus Remembered*, 210-24; idem, "Altering the Default Setting: Re-Envisaging the Early Transmission of the Jesus Tradition," *NTS* 49 (2003) 156-63.

would be remembered verbatim, while others would not. Factor (3) represents the ordinary variability of the more flexible parts of the tradition, while factor (4) explains the changes that occur *in the key elements* of the traditions and the substantial additions to the traditions. These arguments, of course, require extensive testing against the phenomena of the Jesus traditions as we have them, which unfortunately cannot be pursued here.

In short, memorization was a mechanism of control that preserved the Jesus traditions as faithfully as the early Christian movement required. It was exercised to the extent that stable reproduction was deemed important and in regard to those aspects of the traditions for which stable reproduction was thought appropriate. While memorization accounts (in part) for the stability of the tradition, several other factors account for its variability. Factors making for stability and factors making for variability should not be considered in tension with each other. Each balanced the other to produce the combination of fixity and flexibility that was considered appropriate to each of the various types of Jesus tradition.

Controlling the Tradition: Writing?

Whether Jesus traditions, before the writing of the Gospels, were transmitted not only orally but also in written form in notebooks, is a question Graham Stanton has recently said should certainly be reopened.[76] E. Earle Ellis has for some time maintained that the writing of Jesus traditions and the circulation of such written records among Jesus' disciples could well have begun already during Jesus' ministry,[77] while Alan Millard has recently argued this case on the basis of the widespread presence of writing in Jewish Palestine at the time of Jesus.[78]

Any discussion of this issue must recognize that in the predominantly oral culture of the ancient world, including the early Christian movement, writing and orality were not alternatives but complementary.[79] For the most

76. G. N. Stanton, *Jesus and Gospel* (Cambridge: Cambridge University Press, 2004) 186.

77. E. E. Ellis, "New Directions in Form Criticism," in idem, *Prophecy and Hermeneutic in Early Christianity* (WUNT 18; Tübingen: Mohr, 1978) 242-47; idem, "The Synoptic Gospels and History," in B. Chilton and C. A. Evans, eds., *Authenticating the Activities of Jesus* (NT Tools and Studies 28, 2; Leiden: Brill, 1999) 53-54; cf. also Riesner, *Jesus als Lehrer*, 491-98.

78. A. Millard, *Reading and Writing in the Time of Jesus* (Sheffield: Sheffield Academic, 2000), especially chapters 7-8.

79. H. Y. Gamble, *Books and Readers in the Early Church* (New Haven: Yale University Press, 1995) 28-32.

part writing existed to supplement and to support oral forms of remembering and teaching.[80] But as a supplement to orality, more for the sake of reminding than of remembering, it had a place even among the later rabbis, those who insisted on the necessarily oral character of the Oral Torah, as Gerhardsson already explained.[81] Martin Jaffee has recently argued for a thorough "interpenetration" of oral and written composition in the rabbinic traditions behind the Mishnah.[82] But what we know the rabbis used were not so much books as private notebooks.[83] They were notes of material known in oral transmission and were not in any sense intended to replace the oral traditions but rather to serve as aids to memory precisely in learning and recalling the oral traditions.

Such notebooks were in quite widespread use in the ancient world (2 Tim 4:13 refers to parchment notebooks Paul carried on his travels).[84] It seems more probable than not that early Christians used them. It is true that the extent of literacy in Jewish Palestine is debated and may have been very small,[85] but we should also notice that the followers of Jesus, both during his ministry and in the early Jerusalem church, were drawn from all classes of people. There would undoubtedly be some who could write and more who could read.[86] These would be not only members of the educated elite but also professional scribes and copyists. The old suggestion that, among the Twelve, it would be Matthew the tax collector who would most likely, owing to his profession, be able to write[87] might after all be a sound guess and a clue to the perplexing question of the role he might have played somewhere among the

80. Cf. Byrskog, *Story as History*, 116: "Writing was not avoided as such, but functioned mainly as a memorandum of what the person already should remember from oral communication."

81. Gerhardsson, *Memory*, 157-63; idem, *The Reliability of the Gospel Tradition* (Peabody: Hendrickson, 2001) 12-13.

82. Jaffee, *Torah in the Mouth*, chapter 6.

83. Gerhardsson, *Memory*, 160-61.

84. On the sorts of notebook (wax tablets, ink leaf tablets, and parchment and papyrus booklets) and their use, see L. A. Alexander, "Ancient Book Production and the Circulation of the Gospels," in R. Bauckham, ed., *The Gospels for All Christians: Rethinking the Gospel Audiences* (Grand Rapids: Eerdmans, 1998) 73-75, 82-84; Stanton, *Jesus*, 173-78, 187-88. For many examples of note-taking in antiquity, see C. S. Keener, *The Gospel of John: A Commentary*, vol. 1 (Peabody: Hendrickson, 2003) 55-56.

85. Against Millard, *Reading*, who argues for widespread literacy, C. Hezser, *Jewish Literacy in Roman Palestine* (TSAJ 81; Tübingen: Mohr, 2001) believes it was well below 10%, perhaps only 3%.

86. Riesner, *Jesus*, 497-98.

87. For the possibility that a tax collector would be literate, see Hezser, *Jewish Literacy*, 499-500.

sources of the Gospel of Matthew.[88] We can be fairly confident that some quite sophisticated scribal activity, in the form of intensive work on expounding the biblical prophecies with reference to Jesus and his followers, akin to the learned commentaries produced by the Qumran community, went on at a very early date, presumably in the Jerusalem church, whence its influence can be seen throughout the New Testament writings.[89] The first Christians were not all illiterate peasant laborers and craftsmen, as the form critics supposed, but evidently included people who studied the Scriptures with current exegetical skills and could write works with the literary quality of the letter of James.[90] Leaders who were not themselves literate could employ the services of other believers who were. Moreover, as Martin Hengel has proposed, it would surely have been in Jerusalem, where Greek-speaking Jews from the Diaspora became prominent in the Christian community, that Jesus traditions were first translated into Greek.[91]

In such a context it does seem unlikely that no one would have even noted down Jesus traditions in notebooks for the private use of Christian teachers. Such notebooks would not be a wholly new factor in the process of transmission through memorization that we described in the last section. They would simply have reinforced the capacity of oral transmission itself to preserve the traditions faithfully. They should not be imagined as proto-Gospels, though they may account for some of the so-called Q passages where Matthew and Luke are in almost entirely verbatim agreement.[92] In general, their closeness to orality must make it virtually impossible for us to distinguish them from oral sources.

Whether or not writing already served as a control on the transmission of the tradition before the writing of the extant Gospels, there is no doubt that with the composition of these Gospels writing came into its own as means of ensuring the faithful preservation of the Jesus traditions. We shall return to this point in the next chapter.

---

88. E. J. Goodspeed, *Matthew, Apostle and Evangelist* (Philadelphia: Winston, 1959).

89. R. Bauckham, *Jude and the Relatives of Jesus in the Early Church* (Edinburgh: Clark, 1990) 233-34.

90. For the authenticity of the letter of James, who may have secured the assistance of a native Greek speaker in composing it, see R. Bauckham, *James: Wisdom of James, Disciple of Jesus the Sage* (New York: Routledge, 1999).

91. M. Hengel, *Between Jesus and Paul* (tr. J. Bowden; London: SCM, 1983) 26.

92. Stanton, *Jesus*, 188.

12. Anonymous Tradition or Eyewitness Testimony?

Communities or Individuals?

Of crucial importance for our whole argument in this book is the role of individual authors and tradents of Jesus traditions. We have suggested that the traditions were originated and formulated by named eyewitnesses, in whose name they were transmitted and who remained the living and active guarantors of the traditions. In local Christian communities which did not include eyewitnesses among their members, there would probably be recognized teachers who functioned as authorized tradents of the traditions they had received from the eyewitnesses either directly or through very few (authorized) intermediaries.

This picture is very different from the model presented both by the form critics, for whom the tradition was throughout attributed to the community as a collective, and from Bailey's model as it is adopted and developed by James Dunn. Dunn does indeed attribute to the eyewitnesses an important role in the formation of the Jesus traditions, but he stresses the way in which the traditions were already a matter of "shared memory" among the disciples during Jesus' ministry. Tradition-forming, he declares, "is a *communal* process, not least because the tradition is often constitutive of the community as community."[1] At this point Dunn's view is wholly in continuity with the form-critical emphasis on the *Sitz im Leben* of the tradition as a sociological category. It is the community that forms and structures the Jesus traditions

1. J. D. G. Dunn, *Jesus Remembered* (Grand Rapids: Eerdmans, 2003) 240-41.

with a view to their communal functions. Tradition, he asserts, "has to be distinguished from individual memory, though it could be described as corporate memory giving identity to the group which thus remembers."[2]

Here we must also identify the influence of the Durkheimian sociological notion of "collective memory" (developed above all by Maurice Halbwachs),[3] which has had considerable influence in social science, cultural theory, and oral history. Some theorists in this tradition have dissolved the notion of individual memory in that of collective, social, or cultural memory, while others have worked with a close relationship between the two.[4] Apparently Dunn envisages something more like the latter when, having stressed the shared memories of the early discipleship groups, he writes:

> Nor should we forget the continuing role of eyewitness tradents, of those recognized from the first as apostles or otherwise authoritative bearers of the Jesus tradition. . . . Such indications as there are from the pre-Pauline and early Pauline period suggest already fairly extensive outreach by such figures . . . and a general concern to ensure that a foundation of authoritative tradition was well laid in each case. In focusing particular attention on the communal character of the early traditioning process we should not discount the more traditional emphasis on the individual figure of authority respected for his or her own association with Jesus during the days of his mission.[5]

However, this attempt to reinstate authoritative individuals to some degree evidently makes no difference to the way in which Dunn envisages the relationship of the oral traditions to the written Gospels:

> [I]t is almost self-evident that the Synoptists proceeded by gathering and ordering Jesus tradition which had already been in circulation, that is, had already been well enough known to various churches, for at least some years if not decades. Where else did the Evangelists find the tradition? Stored up, unused, in an old box at the back of some teacher's

2. Dunn, *Jesus Remembered*, 173 n. 1.

3. This is also pointed out by S. Byrskog, "A New Perspective on the Jesus Tradition: Reflections on James D. G. Dunn's *Jesus Remembered*," *JSNT* 26 (2004) 464. Major parts of Halbwachs's most significant work, *Les cadres sociaux de la mémoire* (1925), are available in English translation with an introduction by L. A. Coser, in M. Halbwachs, *On Collective Memory* (Chicago: University of Chicago Press, 1992).

4. For a brief overview, see A. Green, "Individual Remembering and 'Collective Memory': Theoretical Presuppositions and Contemporary Debates," *Oral History* 32 (2004) 35-43.

5. Dunn, *Jesus Remembered*, 242-43.

house? Stored up, unrehearsed, in the failing memory of an old apostle? Hardly![6]

It is surely strange — and indicative of the continuing hold of the form-critical picture of things over the mind of a scholar quite willing to criticize the form critics in other ways — that at this point Dunn can envisage a direct relationship between the eyewitnesses and the Gospels only by conjuring the absurd picture of an apostle whose memories had been "unrehearsed" until a Gospel writer tapped them in order to write a Gospel. Dunn knows very well that, for example, the Papias tradition about the relationship of Peter's preaching to Mark's Gospel envisaged nothing of this kind, but claimed that the Gospel was related, via the sole intermediation of Mark, to the oral teaching of Peter as he gave it throughout his career as probably the most active of all the eyewitnesses who devoted themselves to church-planting and ministry.

What is clear is that Dunn cannot take seriously a role for the eyewitnesses once their testimony had been absorbed into the oral tradition — the collective memory — of the various Christian communities.[7] The alternative to the dominant view that Dunn shares is not the quite implausible hypothesis he rightly ridicules. It is that the traditions as transmitted in the churches explicitly acknowledged their sources in the eyewitnesses and the authority of the eyewitnesses for their reliability. Of course, the Synoptic Gospel writers would have known the oral traditions that were doubtless frequently rehearsed in whatever Christian communities (by no means necessarily only one for each author) they were familiar with, but they would most likely also have heard eyewitnesses themselves rehearse their own traditions on many occasions, in these same communities or elsewhere. They would know that the traditions as transmitted by authorized tradents in communities which had no eyewitnesses as members themselves referred back to the eyewitnesses as their authority. Gospel writers would certainly not be content to record the traditions as transmitted in such a church. They would want to get closer to the source if possible. This would especially be the case if, as is certainly true in Luke's case, they envisaged their work as historiographic and knew anything of the methods and standards enjoined by ancient historians.

To further substantiate this statement of *a priori* probability, we need

6. Dunn, *Jesus Remembered,* 250.

7. This is again clear in his response to Byrskog's criticism that he obscures the role of individuals: Dunn, "On History, Memory and Eyewitnesses: In Response to Bengt Holmberg and Samuel Byrskog," *JSNT* 26 (2004) 482-83.

first to clarify the main point at which this book's proposal parts company with the *informal controlled* model of tradition that Dunn has adopted from Bailey and proposes instead a *particular* kind of *formal controlled* model. We have argued that the transmission of the Jesus tradition was *controlled* by memorization and perhaps also by writing, though the latter would probably not make a substantial difference to the control ensured in any case by memorization. But how was the control exercised? This is where we dissent from the *informality* of Bailey's model, where it is the whole community that insures that the tradition is as faithfully preserved as is desired by the community. Memorization (in some degree and in some respects, as we have explained) can and, indeed, must, if anything much is to be preserved at all, operate as a control, but on Bailey's model it is the community as a whole that is responsible for insuring that it does operate as well as is desired. By contrast, according to Bailey's typology, a *formal controlled* model introduces an institutional (or at least semi-institutional) element into the process of control: "there is a clearly identified teacher, a clearly identified student, and a clearly identified block of traditional material that is passed on from one to the other."[8] We have already confirmed that there was indeed, in the early Christian movement, an "isolated" tradition of the words and history of Jesus, passed on simply as such, in a formal process of transmission. The "clearly identified" teachers would be, in the first place, eyewitnesses, and their "clearly identified" students would be community teachers authorized as tradents because they had learned the tradition from the eyewitnesses. They passed on the tradition *as the eyewitnesses' testimony,* to which in many cases the names of the individual eyewitnesses remained attached.

We will return later to the issue of "collective memory." For the time being we wish to show that, whatever truth there may be in speaking of a collective memory in the early Christian movement, it did not prevent early Christians from treating Jesus traditions as the testimony of specific eyewitnesses. At this point we may usefully return to our starting place in chapter 2 of this book: what Papias said about the eyewitnesses:

> I shall not hesitate also to put into properly ordered form for you (sing.) everything I learned carefully in the past from the elders and noted down well, for the truth of which I vouch. For unlike most people I did not enjoy those who have a great deal to say, but those who teach the truth. Nor did I enjoy those who recall someone else's commandments, but those

8. K. E. Bailey, "Informal Controlled Oral Tradition and the Synoptic Gospels," *Themelios* 20 (1995) 5.

who remember the commandments given by the Lord to the faith and proceeding from the truth itself. And if by chance anyone who had been in attendance on the elders should come my way, I inquired about the words of the elders — [that is,] what [according to the elders] Andrew or Peter said *(eipen)*, or Philip, or Thomas or James, or John or Matthew or any other of the Lord's disciples, and whatever Aristion and the elder John, the Lord's disciples, were saying *(legousin)*. For I did not think that information from books would profit me as much as information from a living and surviving voice (Eusebius, *Hist. Eccl.* 3.39.3-4).[9]

We may note that Papias shows no interest at all in anonymous community traditions but only in traditions formulated and transmitted by individuals: the disciples of the elders (i.e., individuals who had listened to the elders teaching and then happened to pass through Hierapolis), the elders (individual teachers in the churches of the province of Asia, doubtless known by name to Papias), and the disciples of Jesus (members of the Twelve and at least a few others). No doubt he was supplementing the Jesus traditions that had been transmitted to his own Christian community in Hierapolis, but, in view of his attitude to such traditions as we can gather it from this and other fragments, he is unlikely to have been interested in anonymous collective tradition even in the community to which he belonged. He probably knew the established local Jesus traditions as the testimony of named eyewitnesses. We recall that Philip the evangelist and his prophet daughters settled in Hierapolis, and the latter were evidently personally known to Papias, who recorded stories they had told him. Whatever had been true of the Jesus traditions in Papias's church at an earlier stage of its history, once Philip and his daughters arrived there this church would have acquired a whole body of traditions from persons who had known many of the eyewitnesses well. There is no reason, then, why the traditions Papias knew from local transmission should have been any less closely connected with named eyewitnesses than those he collected from his visitors. Finally, we should recall also that, though he wrote at a later date, the time *about which* Papias was writing in this fragment must have been around the time that Matthew, Luke, and John were writing their Gospels. His concern for traditions transmitted from named eyewitnesses cannot therefore be seen as an apologetic concern from a period

---

9. Apart from the first sentence and the translation of *parēkolouthēkōs tis* as "anyone who had been in attendance on," this translation is from J. B. Lightfoot, J. R. Harmer, and M. W. Holmes, *The Apostolic Fathers* (Leicester: Apollos, 1990) 314, with the words in square brackets added. For discussion of issues of translation in this passage, see chapter 2 above.

later than the Gospels. It is more likely to correspond to the way the Gospel writers themselves thought of Jesus traditions.

Papias's notion of tradition transmitted from named eyewitnesses through other individual teachers is common to patristic writers thereafter. A passage from Irenaeus's *Letter to Florinus* (part of which was quoted in chapter 2 above) is of special interest because, like Papias, Irenaeus here offers personal testimony. Writing in the 190s, he is reproaching Florinus, a Valentinian teacher, for his views:

> These opinions, Florinus, to say no more, are not of sound judgment; these opinions are not in harmony with the Church, and involve those who adopt them in the greatest impiety; these opinions not even the heretics outside the Church ever dared to espouse openly; these opinions the elders before us, who also were disciples of the apostles, did not hand down to you. For when I was still a boy I saw you in lower Asia in the company of Polycarp, faring brilliantly in the imperial court and trying to secure his favour. For I distinctly recall the events of that time better than those of recent years (for what we learn in childhood keeps pace with the growing mind and becomes part of it), so that I can tell the very place where the blessed Polycarp used to sit as he discoursed, his goings out and his comings in, the character of his life, his bodily appearance, the discourses he would address to the multitude, how he would tell of his conversations with John and with the others who had seen the Lord, how he would relate their words from memory; and what the things were which he had heard from them concerning the Lord, his mighty works and his teaching, Polycarp, as having received them from the eyewitnesses (*autoptōn*) of the life of the Logos, would declare altogether in accordance with the scriptures. To these things I used to listen diligently even then, by the mercy of God which was upon me, noting them down not on papyrus but in my heart (*apud* Eusebius, *Hist. Eccl.* 5.20.4-7).[10]

Some scholars have been dubious about how far Irenaeus's vivid memories of his boyhood may be trusted. But he is right about the clarity of early memories in later life (though this was probably something of a topos, since Seneca the Elder made a similar claim [*Controversiae* preface 3-4]). The scenes that Irenaeus describes would indeed have been memorable. Since he is appealing to Florinus's own memories of himself sitting at the feet of Polycarp, he can hardly have been consciously exaggerating. More important, however, is

---

10. Translation from R. M. Grant, *Second-Century Christianity* (London: SPCK, 1946) 115-16.

Irenaeus's explicit account of what a chain of tradition from the eyewitnesses would have been like. Again, there is reference to the community only as recipients of tradition, not itself transmitting tradition. In this respect there is close resemblance with Josephus's account of the traditions of the Pharisees (*Ant.* 13.297), which was quoted in chapter 11 above. There too the traditions are delivered to the people in public teaching, but the perpetuation of the traditions takes place through a chain of individuals, authorized tradents.

One conclusion should be quite clear: the model we are proposing for the transmission of Jesus traditions cannot be said to reflect modern western individualism.[11] Papias and Irenaeus were not modern individualists! Whether they were right or wrong about the transmission of Jesus traditions, they were using a conventional ancient model to describe it, the same that Josephus applied to the Pharisees. Indeed, the idea of transmission of tradition from a teacher through individual named disciples was commonplace in the second century. Not only does Irenaeus use it in other forms as well as the one quoted;[12] his Gnostic opponents also claimed their own lines of named individuals through whom the esoteric teaching of the apostles had reached them. James was supposed to have passed on what was revealed to him by Jesus to Addai, who wrote it down and transmitted it to others (2 *Apocalypse of James* 36:15-25). Basilides was said to have received his teaching from Glaucias, a personal disciple of Peter, while Valentinus claimed to have received his tradition from Theudas, a disciple of Paul (Clement of Alexandria, *Stromateis* 7.106.4). On the orthodox side, Clement of Alexandria believed that the risen Jesus "gave the tradition of knowledge to James the Just and John and Peter, these gave it to the other Apostles and the other Apostles to the seventy, of whom Barnabas also was one" (*apud* Eusebius, *Hist. Eccl.* 2.1.4).

Of course, in these instances there are strong apologetic concerns involved. The issue is that of a reliable tradition of sound doctrine, passed down from Jesus through named intermediaries, who could be held to guarantee a true tradition more convincingly than any claim to collective tradition could have done. The apologetic concern is wholly explicit in the passage we quoted from Irenaeus's *Letter to Florinus*. However, it is indubitable that this model of the transmission of teaching was available independently of its apologetic use by catholic Christians and Gnostics. As we noted, when discussing Josephus's account of Pharisaic tradition, the model was widely used in the

11. Cf. the remarks of Dunn, *Jesus Remembered*, 240.

12. See the very useful diagrams in B. Mutschler, "Was weiss Irenäus vom Johannes-evangelium? Der historische Kontext des Johannesevangeliums aus der Perspektive seiner Rezeption bei Irenäus von Lyon," in J. Frey and U. Schnelle, eds., *Kontexte des Johannesevangelums* (WUNT 175; Tübingen: Mohr, 2004) 708, 711, as well as Table 17 below (after chapter 17).

Hellenistic philosophical schools, and also features in the list of a succession of Pharisaic traditioners in Pirqe 'Avot. The latter may have some apologetic overtone, but this does not seem to be the dominant concern.[13] Finally, despite several scholars' attempts to read Papias as driven by apologetic concerns, in fact nothing in the fragments of his writings that we have gives any indication of doctrinal conflict or polemic. The idea of a chain of teachers/disciples was a well-established way of representing the passing down of a tradition through a formal process of delivery and reception by authorized tradents. If the Christian movement in the New Testament period were concerned with such a formal process, as we know from the Pauline evidence above all that it was, then we should expect the Jesus traditions to have been attached to named individuals among the disciples of Jesus and to have been transmitted by teachers who preserved these named sources.

Nowhere in early Christian literature do we find traditions attributed to the community as their source or transmitter, only as the recipient. Against the general form-critical image of the early Christian movement as an anonymous collectivity, we must stress that the New Testament writings are full of prominent named individuals. As Martin Hengel puts it, "Individual figures kept standing out in the earliest community, despite its collective constitution. They — and not the anonymous collective — exercised a decisive influence on theological developments."[14] Compared with the prominence of named individuals in the New Testament itself, form criticism represented a rather strange depersonalization of early Christianity that still exercises an unconscious influence on New Testament scholars.[15]

Of particular interest is the number of individual members of the Jerusalem church who appear in our sources, since we should expect a large number of the eyewitnesses to have been members of this church. Of those who appear in Acts, the following are known to have been eyewitnesses: Peter (chs. 1–15), James (12:2) and John (3:1–4:31; 8:14-25) the sons of Zebedee, and the rest of the original Twelve (1:13), Matthias (1:23-26), James the Lord's brother (12:17; 15:13-21; 21:18-25) and the other brothers (1:14: not named),[16] Barnabas (4:36-37; 9:27; 11:22-26, 30; 12:25–15:39), Joseph Barsabbas (1:23), Mary the

---

13. A. Tropper, "Tractate *Avot* and Early Christian Succession Lists," in A. H. Becker and A. Y. Reed, eds., *The Ways That Never Parted: Jews and Christians in Late Antiquity and the Early Middle Ages* (Tübingen: Mohr, 2003) 159-88.

14. M. Hengel, *Between Jesus and Paul* (tr. J. Bowden; London: SCM, 1983) 149 n. 124.

15. Cf. B. Gerhardsson, *The Reliability of the Gospel Tradition* (Peabody: Hendrickson, 2001) 74.

16. Luke never names the other brothers, but according to Mark (6:3) and Matthew (13:55) they were Joses/Joseph, Simon, and Judas (Jude).

mother of Jesus (1:14),[17] Mnason (21:16),[18] and Silas (15:22–18:5; = Silvanus in Paul).[19] Other members of the Jerusalem church mentioned in Acts and not known to have been eyewitnesses, though they may have been, are Agabus (11:28; 21:10-11), Ananias and Sapphira (5:1-10), John Mark (12:12, 25; 13:5, 13; 15:37-39), Judas Barsabbas (15:22-34), Mary the mother of John Mark (12:12), Stephen (6:5–8:1), Philip the evangelist (6:5-6; 8:4-40; 21:8-9) and the rest of the Seven (6:5), Philip's daughters (21:9), and Rhoda (12:13-15). Readers inclined to doubt the evidence of Acts should also note the members of the Jerusalem church whom Paul finds occasion to mention. Those who were eyewitnesses are Peter (1 Cor 1:12; 3:22; 9:5; 15:5; Gal 1:18; 2:9, 11-14), John the son of Zebedee (Gal 2:9), the rest of the Twelve (1 Cor 15:5), James the Lord's brother (1 Cor 15:7; Gal 1:19; 2:9, 12) and the other brothers (1 Cor 9:5), Barnabas (1 Cor 9:6; Gal 2:1, 13; Col 4:10), Andronicus and Junia (Rom 16:7),[20] and Silvanus (2 Cor 1:19; 1 Thess 1:1; 2 Thess 1:1). Mark, also mentioned (Col 4:10; Phlm 24), is not known to have been an eyewitness.

It is a weakness of Bailey's and Dunn's models that they focus on the early transmission of Jesus traditions in Palestinian Jewish villages, ignoring the Jerusalem church. Doubtless there were groups of followers of Jesus in the villages as early as during Jesus' ministry. But after the resurrection it was the Jerusalem church, under the leadership of the Twelve and later of James the Lord's brother, that became the mother church of the whole Christian movement. Given Jerusalem's place at both the literal and the symbolic center of the Jewish world, this was a natural development, as well as conforming to the eschatological self-understanding of the Christian community as the place from which the word of the Lord would go out to the ends of the earth and to

17. Note also the general reference to other women in Acts 1:14, very likely including the three women named in Luke 24:10 (Mary Magdalene, Joanna, and Mary the mother of James).

18. The description of Mnason as *archaiǭ mathētę̄* (Acts 21:16) probably means "an original disciple," that is, one of the founding members of the Jerusalem church, who must therefore also have been a personal disciple of Jesus.

19. The reason for supposing Barnabas and Silas/Silvanus to have been eyewitnesses is that Paul evidently considered them apostles (Barnabas: 1 Cor 9:6; Silvanus: 1 Thess 1:1 with 2:7). Paul's use of "apostles" entails that they were commissioned by the risen Christ in a resurrection appearance (cf. 1 Cor 9:1; 15:7). This in turn makes it likely that they had been disciples of Jesus during his ministry, but we cannot know this for certain.

20. That Paul calls these two "apostles" must mean that they had been present at a resurrection appearance of Jesus and therefore most likely were members of the Jerusalem church, which also likely follows from the fact that Paul says they were Christians before he was; see R. Bauckham, *Gospel Women: Studies of the Named Women in the Gospels* (Grand Rapids: Eerdmans, 2002) 165-86, where I also conjecture that Junia may have been the Latin name of Jesus' disciple Joanna (Luke 8:3; 24:10).

which the redeemed of Israel and the nations would come (see especially Isa 2:2-3). The authority of this church over the whole movement was widely recognized,[21] as we can see in a particularly striking way from the fact that even Paul, who was probably, among the Christian leaders of the first generation, the most independent of Jerusalem, nevertheless in his own way recognized the centrality of Jerusalem (Gal 2:1-10; Rom 15:19). His collection for the community there was his way of acknowledging it (cf. Rom 15:25-27).[22] Though Luke's depiction of the early history of the Christian movement in the first half of Acts is doubtless somewhat schematized, the role he attributes to Jerusalem, as the center that oversaw the growing movement elsewhere and to which this movement looked for definitive leadership, should not be dismissed as merely a theological tendency of Luke's, as some scholars, habitually skeptical of Acts, have thought. It coheres well with what we should expect in the context of first-century Judaism, and other evidence confirms it.

When we recognize this central significance of the Jerusalem church for the Christian movement throughout Palestine and the Diaspora, it becomes obvious that it must have had a key place in the formulation and transmission of Jesus traditions,[23] especially as, in the early years, most of those Christian leaders who had been disciples of Jesus were based there, along with other eyewitnesses who may not have been in the leadership of the movement but whose eyewitness testimony to the words of Jesus and the events of his story was valued. In this context the special role of the Twelve as a body of official witnesses, as Luke depicts it in Acts and as we have seen to be the implication of the lists of the Twelve in the Gospels (see chapters 5-6 above), is readily intelligible. We should probably envisage a carefully compiled and formulated collection of Jesus traditions, incorporating other important eyewitness testimony as well as that of the Twelve themselves, but authorized by the Twelve as the official body of witnesses. In this context, it is also easy to account for the particular role of Peter, the leader of the Twelve, as an expo-

21. See R. Bauckham, "James and the Jerusalem Church," in R. Bauckham, ed., *The Book of Acts in Its Palestinian Setting* (The Book of Acts in Its First Century Setting 4; Grand Rapids: Eerdmans, 1995) 417-27.

22. A rarely noticed indication of the importance Paul attributed to Jerusalem is 1 Cor 14:36 (if this passage is genuinely Pauline), where Paul sarcastically asks the Corinthians, "Was it from you that the word of God went forth?" echoing Isa 2:3: "For out of Zion shall go forth instruction and the word of YHWH from Jerusalem." In accordance with prophecy Jerusalem was the geographical source of the gospel.

23. This point is made by T. M. Derico, *On the Selection of Oral-Traditional Data: Methodological Prolegomena for the Construction of a New Model of Early Christian Tradition* (M. Phil. dissertation, University of St. Andrews, 2001) 55-56.

nent of this official tradition (chapters 6-7), and therefore the apostle to whom Paul went to learn (Gal 1:18-19). There is no reason to think that this tradition was the only channel of eyewitness testimony about Jesus either in Jerusalem itself or in the wider Christian movement. But it must have had special prestige.

Anonymous Gospels?

The assumption that Jesus traditions circulated anonymously in the early church and that therefore the Gospels in which they were gathered and recorded were also originally anonymous was very widespread in twentieth-century Gospels scholarship. It was propagated by the form critics as a corollary of their use of the model of folklore, which is passed down anonymously by communities. The Gospels, they thought, were folk literature, similarly anonymous. This use of the model of folklore has been discredited, as we saw in chapter 10, partly because there is a great difference between folk traditions passed down over centuries and the short span of time — less than a lifetime — that elapsed before Gospels were written. But it is remarkable how tenacious has been the idea that not only the traditions but the Gospels themselves were originally anonymous. There are three main reasons for rejecting this view of both the traditions and the Gospels:

(1) In three cases — Luke, John, and Matthew — the evidence of the Gospel itself shows that it was not intended to be anonymous. All four Gospels are anonymous in the formal sense that the author's name does not appear in the text of the work itself, only in the title (which we will discuss below). But this does not mean that they were intentionally anonymous. Many ancient works were anonymous in the same formal sense, and the name may not even appear in the surviving title of the work. For example, this is true of Lucian's *Life of Demonax (Dēmōnactos bios),* which as a *bios* (ancient biography) is generically comparable with the Gospels. Yet Lucian speaks throughout in the first person and obviously expects his readers to know who he is. Such works would often have been circulated in the first instance among friends or acquaintances of the author who would know who the author was from the oral context in which the work was first read. Knowledge of authorship would be passed on when copies were made for other readers, and the name would be noted, with a brief title, on the outside of the scroll or on a label affixed to the scroll. In denying that the Gospels were originally anonymous, our intention is to deny that they were first presented as works without authors.

The clearest case is Luke because of the dedication of the work to Theophilus (1:3), probably a patron.[24] It is inconceivable that a work with a named dedicatee should have been anonymous.[25] The author's name may have featured in an original title, but in any case would have been known to the dedicatee and other first readers because the author would have presented the book to the dedicatee. Of course, this in itself does not guarantee that the author was named Luke; the attribution to Luke could be later and erroneous. But we are not, at this point, concerned with establishing the real authorship of each Gospel, only with refuting the idea that the Gospels were presented and received as anonymous works whose contents would have been taken as coming from the community rather than from known authors.

In the case of John's Gospel, 21:23 is important in showing that the Beloved Disciple — ostensibly, at least, the author (21:24)[26] — was an identifiable figure, someone about whom a rumor could circulate, at least in some circles. Although he remains anonymous within the Gospel, its first readers must have known his name.

The case of Matthew is more complex. It requires the connection of two facts about the Gospel. One is that the figure of Matthew, who in the other Gospels appears only as a name in the lists of the Twelve in Mark and Luke, acquires a higher profile in the Gospel of Matthew. In this Gospel, he is dubbed "the tax collector" in the list of the Twelve (10:3), while in the story about the call of a tax collector, whom Mark and Luke call Levi, the tax collector is named Matthew (9:9). This definite, albeit quite small, emphasis on the character Matthew within the Gospel cannot be unconnected with the other relevant fact: that the title of the Gospel associates it with Matthew ("according to Matthew") in a way that, while it may not necessarily indicate authorship as such, certainly treats the apostle Matthew as in some way this Gospel's source. We shall consider the titles of the Gospels shortly, but here we need take the title of Matthew simply as evidence from some early stage of the Gospel's trans-

24. Cf. L. Alexander, *The Preface to Luke's Gospel: Literary Convention and Social Context in Luke 1.1-4 and Acts 1.1* (SNTSMS 78; Cambridge: Cambridge University Press, 1993) 190-91.

25. The point is generally overlooked by commentators, probably because they rarely treat the title of the work as part of the text on which they comment. But note F. Bovon, *Luke 1* (Hermeneia; Minneapolis: Fortress, 2002) 18: "The absence of the author's name in the prologue remains a riddle to me, despite the church's tradition of anonymity and the possibility that the name was mentioned in the title of the work." By "the church's tradition of anonymity" he apparently means the form critics' view that the gospel traditions were transmitted anonymously.

26. For an argument that 21:23 and 24 both belong to the original text of the Gospel, see chapter 14 below.

mission. It is hardly likely that the Gospel came to be associated with Matthew on the basis of the references to him in 9:9 and 10:3. These references are surely not prominent enough to have made readers think Matthew must be the author. Much more likely, the author was responsible both for these references to Matthew and for the attribution of the work to Matthew, which would therefore have been original, presumably included in a title. Since it is not likely that the apostle Matthew wrote the Gospel as we have it (see my argument at the end of chapter 5), the attribution could either be a pseudepigraphal claim to Matthean authorship or could reflect a role that the apostle Matthew actually played in the genesis of the Gospel, while not being its final author. In either case, the Gospel was not presented originally as the anonymous product of the community. (The use of a pseudonym is not equivalent to anonymity. Pseudepigraphal works were produced in literary traditions in which works were expected to have author's names attached to them.)

(2) Secondly, we consider the evidence of the traditional titles of the Gospels. Throughout the early manuscript tradition, from c. 200 onward, the only titles for all four canonical Gospels are in the form "Gospel according to . . ." *(euangelion kata . . .)*, with the exception of manuscripts Vaticanus and Sinaiticus which have the short form "According to. . . ." Martin Hengel has argued persuasively, not only that the longer form was the earlier form, but also that the meaning is not "the Gospel writing written according to the tradition that derives from Mark," but "*the* Gospel (i.e., the one and only gospel message) according to Mark's account." The usual genitive for the author's name has been avoided in favor of the very unusual "according to . . ." *(kata . . .)* formula, in order to "express the fact that here the gospel was narrated in the particular version of the evangelist in question."[27] Each of these titles therefore presupposes the existence of other Gospel writings (not necessarily all three of the other canonical ones), from which the Gospel in question needed to be distinguished.[28] A Christian community that knew only one Gospel writing would not have needed to entitle it in this way. Even a Gospel writer who knew other Gospels to be circulating around the churches

27. M. Hengel, *Studies in the Gospel of Mark* (tr. J. Bowden; London: SCM, 1985) 65. G. N. Stanton, *Jesus of Nazareth in New Testament Preaching* (SNTSMS 27; Cambridge: Cambridge University Press, 1974) 78, agrees.

28. The extant Coptic manuscript of the *Gospel of Thomas* has this form of title as a *subscriptio* at the end of the work: "The Gospel according to Thomas." But this is probably a scribal imitation of the established titles of the four Gospels. The original title of the work forms the beginning of the text: "These are the secret sayings which the living Jesus spoke and which Didymus Judas Thomas wrote down." So H. Koester, *Ancient Christian Gospels* (London: SCM, 1990) 20-21.

could have himself given this form of title to his work. (In the first century CE, most authors gave their books titles, but the practice was not universal.[29])

Whether or not any of these titles originate from the authors themselves, the need for titles that distinguished one Gospel from another would arise as soon as any Christian community had copies of more than one in its library and was reading more than one in its worship meetings. For the former purpose, it would have been necessary to identify books externally, when, for example, they were placed side-by-side on a shelf. For this purpose a short title with the author's name would be written either on the outside of the scroll or on a papyrus or parchment tag that hung down when the scroll was placed horizontally on a shelf.[30] In the case of codices, "labels appeared on all possible surfaces: edges, covers, and spines."[31] In this sense also, therefore, Gospels would not have been anonymous when they first circulated around the churches. A church receiving its first copy of one such would have received with it information, at least in oral form, about its authorship and then used its author's name when labeling the book and when reading from it in worship.

Hengel argues that, given that the Gospels must have acquired titles at a very early stage, the titles that survive in the earliest manuscript tradition (c. 200 onward) are these "original" titles.[32] In favor of this is the fact that no evidence exists that these Gospels were ever known by other names. The unusual form of the titles and the universal use of them as soon as we have any evidence suggest that they originated at an early stage. Once the Gospels were widely known it would be much more difficult for a standard form of title for all four Gospels to have come into universal use. Helmut Koester, who thinks Marcion was the first person to use the word "Gospel" for a book, rejects Hengel's argument that the full form "Gospel according to . . ." could have been used to entitle the Gospels already early in the second century, though he does not necessarily deny that the ascriptions to authors may be early.[33] However, Graham Stanton supports Hengel's argument on the basis of other early instances of the term "Gospel" *(euangelion)* used for a written Gospel.[34]

29. Hengel, *Studies,* 74; J. P. Small, *Wax Tablets of the Mind: Cognitive Studies of Memory and Literacy in Classical Antiquity* (New York: Routledge, 1997) 33-35.

30. H. Y. Gamble, *Books and Readers in the Early Church* (New Haven: Yale University Press, 1995) 48.

31. Small, *Wax Tablets,* 50.

32. Hengel, *Studies,* 64-84; cf. also idem, *The Four Gospels and the One Gospel of Jesus Christ* (tr. J. Bowden; London: SCM, 2000) 116-27.

33. H. Koester, "From the Kerygma-Gospel to Written Gospels," *NTS* 35 (1989) 375-76 and n. 6; idem, *Ancient Christian Gospels,* 33-34.

34. Stanton, *Jesus,* 79-80.

Whether or not the actual form of title, "Gospel according to . . ." was already used when the Gospels first circulated around the churches, it is very likely that the ascription of the Gospels to Matthew, Mark, Luke, and John dates from this very early stage, since this is the only way that one of the Gospels could have been distinguished from another. Our evidence offers no alternative way in which this could have been done. Again the universality of these ascriptions of authorship and the fact that they seem never to have been disputed indicate that they became established usage as soon as the Gospels were circulating.

(3) These two lines of argument establish that as soon as the Gospels circulated around the churches they had author's names attached to them, even though such names were not part of the text of the Gospels. Our further question about anonymity concerns the contents of the Gospels: do the Gospel-writers present the traditions they preserve as derived from named eyewitnesses or as anonymous community tradition to which no specific names could be attached?[35] Here we need only to resume the evidence we discussed in chapters 3-8: (i) Where the names of relatively minor characters are given in the Gospels, the reason is usually that the tradition to which the name is attached derived from that person. (ii) In all three Synoptic Gospels, the explanation of the care with which the list of the Twelve has been preserved and recorded is that they were known to be the official body of eyewitnesses who had formulated a body of traditions on which the three Synoptic Gospels depend. (iii) Three of the Gospels — Mark, Luke, and John — deploy a literary device, the *inclusio* of eyewitness testimony, to indicate the most extensive eyewitness source(s) of their Gospels. Mark's use of the device points to Peter (indicating that Mark's traditions are those of the Twelve in the form that Peter told and supplemented). Luke also acknowledges Peter as the most extensive eyewitness source of his narrative, but by making also a secondary use of the device he indicates that the group of women disciples of Jesus were also an important eyewitness source of his Gospel. John's Gospel plays on Mark's use of this device in order to stake its claim for the Beloved Disciple as an eyewitness as important as — even, in a sense, more important than — Peter. (We shall discuss in chapter 14 other ways in which the Gospel of John claims the Beloved Disciple as not only its principal eyewitness source but also its author.)

These arguments show not simply that, as a matter of fact, the tradi-

---

35. Historians in antiquity did not name their eyewitness sources as a matter of course, but in specific cases they did: S. Byrskog, *Story as History — History as Story* (WUNT 123; Tübingen: Mohr, 2000; reprinted Leiden: Brill, 2002) 149-53.

tions in the Gospels have eyewitness sources but, very importantly, that the Gospels themselves indicate their own eyewitness sources. Once we recognize these ways in which the Gospels indicate their sources, we can see that they pass on traditions not in the name of the anonymous collective but in the name of the specific eyewitnesses who were responsible for these traditions.

Controlling the Tradition: Eyewitnesses and Gospels

In the last chapter we discussed memorization as a means of controlling the tradition, in the sense of preserving it faithfully with a minimum of change. But whose memories were being preserved? In the process of transmission, was the testimony of the eyewitnesses absorbed into an anonymous body of Jesus traditions in each community, a body of traditions which the community ascribed to its own collective memory rather than to named eyewitnesses sources? Our argument so far implies that this would not have taken place. If the Gospel writers knew the traditions they recorded as the testimony of the Twelve, of other groups of named disciples, and of various individual named disciples, then it is natural to suppose that this is how they were known as oral traditions in the churches. As we saw in chapter 2, this also seems to have been the situation that Papias knew in the latter part of the first century, when the Gospels were being written. Throughout the process from the founding of a Christian community down to the stage, probably in the early second century, when written Gospels superseded oral traditions in the same community's knowledge of Jesus traditions, the community would have known the Jesus traditions, whether oral or written, as traditions attributed to their eyewitness sources.

As we have learned in previous chapters, communities that are predominantly oral have ways of preserving traditions faithfully when the character and use of these traditions make this desirable. Such communities have ways of checking oral performances for accuracy. Jan Vansina writes:

> Where . . . the performers intend to stick as closely as possible to the message related and to avoid lapses of memory or distortion, the pace of change can almost be stopped. In some cases controls over the faithfulness of the performance were set up and sanctions or rewards meted out to the performers. . . . In Polynesia ritual sanctions were brought to bear in the case of failure to be word-perfect. When bystanders perceived a mistake the ceremony was abandoned. In New Zealand it was believed that a single mistake in performance was enough to strike the performer

dead. Similar sanctions were found in Hawaii. . . . Such . . . beliefs had visible effects. Thus in Hawaii a hymn of 618 lines was recorded which was identical with a version collected on the neighboring island of Oahu. . . . Sometimes controllers were appointed to check important performances. In Rwanda the controllers of *ubwiiru* esoteric liturgical texts were the other performers entitled to recite it.[36]

In the early Christian movement we may suppose that the authorized tradents of the tradition performed this role of controllers, but among them the eyewitnesses would surely have been the most important. We must remind ourselves, as we have quite often had occasion to do, that Vansina and other writers about oral tradition are describing processes of transmission over several generations, whereas in the case of the early church up to the writing of the Gospels we are considering the preservation of the testimony of the eyewitnesses *during their own lifetimes.* They are the obvious people to have controlled this in the interests of faithful preservation.

In favor of this role of the eyewitnesses, we should note that the early Christian movement, though geographically widely spread, was a network of close communication, in which individual communities were in frequent touch with others and in which many individual leaders traveled frequently and widely. I have provided detailed evidence of this elsewhere.[37] First or secondhand contact with eyewitnesses would not have been unusual. (The community addressed in Hebrews had evidently received the gospel traditions directly from eyewitnesses: see 2:3-4.) Many Jewish Christians from many places would doubtless have continued the custom of visiting Jerusalem for the festivals and so would have had the opportunity to hear the traditions of the Twelve from members of the Twelve themselves while there were still some resident in Jerusalem. Individual eyewitnesses of importance, such as Peter or Thomas, would have had their own disciples, who (like Mark in Peter's case) were familiar enough with their teacher's rehearsal of Jesus traditions to be able to check, as well as to pass on, the traditions transmitted in that eyewitness's name as they themselves traveled around. This is the situation envisaged in the fragment of Papias's Prologue from which we began our investigations in chapter 2.

36. J. Vansina, *Oral Tradition as History* (Madison: University of Wisconsin Press, 1985) 41-42.

37. R. Bauckham, "For Whom Were Gospels Written?" in idem, ed., *The Gospels for All Christians* (Grand Rapids: Eerdmans, 1998) 30-44; cf. also M. B. Thompson, "The Holy Internet: Communication between Churches in the First Christian Generation," in the same volume, 49-70.

This is an appropriate point at which to consider Paul's references to eyewitnesses in the "kerygmatic summary" (summary of the gospel history) of 1 Cor 15:3-8. It is the earliest example we have of a genre of which there are many later examples: a summary of the gospel history in a series of short clauses. The evidence suggests that this was a flexible genre; that is, a recital of such a summary could draw on a fund of items not all of which were always included and could even add additional items.[38] In 1 Corinthians, Paul's purpose in the context accounts for the fact that the summary starts with the death of Jesus and focuses on the resurrection appearances, which are catalogued at length. Paul himself has added the reference to himself in v. 8 as well as the second half of v. 6. But the attempt to determine precisely the parameters of the tradition Paul cites and the degree to which he has modified it is inappropriate to the nature of the genre. For our present purpose it is quite sufficient that Paul relates this as a tradition he himself received — surely from the Jerusalem church — and handed on to the Corinthian Christians when he founded their church:

> For I handed on to you as of first importance what I in turn
>   had received:
> that Christ died for our sins in accordance with the scriptures,
> and that he was buried,
> and that he was raised on the third day in accordance
>   with the scriptures,
> and that he appeared to Cephas,
> then to the twelve.
> Then he appeared to more than five hundred brothers and sisters
>   at one time,
> most of whom are still alive, though some have died.
> Then he appeared to James,
> then to all the apostles.
> Last of all, as to one untimely born, he appeared also to me
> (1 Cor 15:3-8 NRSV).

The list of the resurrection appearances has clearly been formulated to summarize the witness of the eyewitnesses. It corresponds in more detail to those parts of the kerygmatic summaries in the speeches of Acts, where Peter speaks of the members of the Twelve as witnesses to Jesus' resurrection (Acts

38. R. Bauckham, "Kerygmatic Summaries in the Speeches of Acts," in B. Witherington, ed., *History, Literature, and Society in the Book of Acts* (Cambridge: Cambridge University Press, 1996) 185-217 (211-12 on 1 Cor 15:3-7).

2:32; 3:15; 10:40-41) and Luke's Paul also speaks, not of himself but of those who have been personal disciples of Jesus, as the witnesses to the resurrection (13:31). There can be no doubt that in his own recital of a kerygmatic summary in 1 Corinthians 15 Paul is citing the *eyewitness testimony* of those who were recipients of resurrection appearances, including the most prominent in the Jerusalem church: Peter (Cephas), the Twelve, and James the brother of Jesus. This is the only occasion on which Paul ever refers to the Twelve as such. In Paul's understanding of apostleship — as referring to all who had been commissioned by the risen Jesus to proclaim the Gospel[39] — "all the apostles" were a wider category than the Twelve. Paul takes it for granted that most of these people were still alive when he was writing, but makes the point explicit in his remarkable reference to the (otherwise unknown) appearance to more than five hundred believers: "most of whom are still alive, though some have died [literally 'fallen asleep']."[40] The explicitness of this detail — which looks like one that Paul has added to the traditional form — shows that he intends it to be a kind of authentication: if anyone wishes to check this tradition, a very large number of the eyewitnesses are still alive and can be seen and heard.[41] Paul thus takes for granted the *continuing accessibility and role* of the eyewitnesses, even extending to a very large number of minor eyewitnesses as well as to such prominent persons as the Twelve and James.

One reason Gospels were written was to maintain this accessibility and function of the eyewitnesses beyond their lifetimes.[42] Many quite recent writers have argued against the view that the written Gospels immediately replaced the oral tradition of the sayings and stories of Jesus. This view has re-

39. J. D. G. Dunn, *Jesus and the Spirit* (London: SCM, 1975) 273.

40. Against the theory that this refers to the same event as that described in Acts 2 (Pentecost), see Dunn, *Jesus*, 144-46.

41. A. C. Thiselton, *The First Epistle to the Corinthians* (NIGTC; Grand Rapids: Eerdmans, 2000) 1205. By contrast, A. Eriksson, *Traditions as Rhetorical Proof: Pauline Argumentation in 1 Corinthians* (CB[NT] 29; Stockholm: Almqvist and Wiksell, 1998) 253-54, who maintains that the passage has nothing to do with offering evidence for the reality of Jesus' resurrection, takes Paul's addition in v. 6 to indicate that the problem about resurrection at Corinth was that some believers had died, thus contradicting the view that believers had already entered the new age with Jesus and were not to die. But there is no evidence in the rest of the chapter that this was the problem the Corinthians had with resurrection. It is much more plausible — and in accord with recent understanding of the kinds of problems that had arisen in the Corinthian church — that some of the Corinthians found bodily resurrection incredible on the basis of the ordinary Greco-Roman hope of purely spiritual survival of death.

42. In "For Whom Were Gospels Written?" I stressed that the Gospels were *written* to communicate across distance, that is, to be circulated around the Christian communities, but I neglected this further important function: to give permanence to eyewitness testimony beyond the lifetime of the eyewitnesses.

308

lied rather heavily on the evidence of Papias's preference for oral sources, mistakenly taking this to be true of the time when Papias was writing, in the early second century, rather than of the time when eyewitnesses were still alive (as we have explained in chapter 2). To this extent the question of the survival of oral tradition beyond the time when written Gospels were widely known may need some reappraisal, but it remains probable that oral traditions did not immediately die out. Rather, the Gospels took their place within a still predominantly oral context, and will have operated in relation to orality, as written texts do in predominantly oral societies, rather than as a complete alternative to it.[43] In other words, the Gospels stepped into the role of the eyewitnesses, which they had vacated through death. They interacted with the oral tradition, influencing it, doubtless becoming partially oralized in the form of new oral traditions, but also functioning as the guarantor of the traditions, as the eyewitnesses had in their lifetimes, and as controls on the tradition, making it possible to check its faithfulness to the testimony of the eyewitnesses as now recorded in writing.

The form critics saw the Gospels as folk literature more or less continuous with the oral traditions as formed and transmitted anonymously by the communities. Our argument is rather that the continuity of the Gospels is with the testimony of the eyewitnesses, not via a long period of community transmission but through, in many cases, immediate access to the eyewitnesses or, in other cases, probably no more than one intermediary. However, we cannot ignore the extent to which redaction criticism and literary criticism qualified the form critics' view of the Gospels by stressing how far the Gospel writers themselves shaped the traditions they received in both theological and literary ways. Redaction criticism was often carried to excess, and can now be seen to have made too much of minor verbal and narrative differences among the Synoptics that may be better seen as the kind of performative variations normal in oral tradition, not necessarily embodying highly nuanced ideological divergences. But it remains the case that the Gospel writers should be seen as sophisticated authors who ordered and shaped their traditions into narrative wholes with distinctive understandings of Jesus and Christian faith. It is unlikely that the traditions as formulated and recounted by the eyewitnesses were able to do this to more than a fairly small extent

43. On the complementarity of orality and written texts in early Judaism, see S. Talmon, "Oral Tradition and Written Transmission, or the Heard and the Seen Word in Judaism of the Second Temple Period," in H. Wansbrough, ed., *Jesus and the Oral Gospel Tradition* (JSNTSup 64; Sheffield: Sheffield Academic, 1991) 121-58. For such complementarity in the Greco-Roman world generally, see P. J. Achtemeier, "*Omne Verbum Sonat:* The New Testament and the Oral Environment of Late Western Antiquity," *JBL* 109 (1990) 3-27.

(with the exception of the eyewitness who wrote the Fourth Gospel, as we shall see in chapters 14-17). It was left to the Gospel writers to integrate their testimonies into biographies *(bioi)* of Jesus.

To allow both for the Gospels' faithful preservation of the eyewitnesses' testimony as they themselves recounted it and also for the creative work of the Gospel writers as true authors, we have an adequate model in the kind of ancient historiography, resembling modern oral history, that Samuel Byrskog has described:

> The ancient historians exercised autopsy directly and/or indirectly, by be-ing present themselves and/or by seeking out and interrogating other eye-witnesses. . . . They acted very much like oral historians, aiming to hear the living voices of those who were present. They also permitted the ac-counts of the eyewitnesses to become a vital part of their own written sto-ries. The accounts of the eyewitnesses, whether they were the accounts of the historians themselves or of other persons, were heard and recorded in view of their retrospective character.[44]

In their close relationship to eyewitness testimony the Gospels conform to the best practice of ancient historiography. For ancient historians this rela-tionship required that good history be contemporary history, written in the lifetimes of the eyewitnesses. So the Gospels were written over the period, from the death of Peter to that of the Beloved Disciple, when the eyewitnesses were ceasing to be available.

Individual and Collective Memories

For the form critics it was the community that "remembered" Gospel tradi-tions. It is interesting to note that they were writing around the time at which the French sociologist Maurice Halbwachs was inventing the notion of "col-lective memory."[45] Highly congruent though this concept is with the model of oral tradition employed by the form critics, they do not seem to have been influenced by it or, indeed, to have given concepts of memory any serious at-tention.[46]

44. Byrskog, *Story as History*, 64.
45. M. Halbwachs, *Les cadres sociaux de la mémoire* (Paris: Alcan, 1925).
46. Cf. W. H. Kelber, "The Case of the Gospels: Memory's Desire and the Limits of His-torical Criticism," *Oral Tradition* 17 (2002) 65: Bultmann's works "display no sustained reflec-tion on memory. The concept is without mention in his scholarly work. This vacuum seems to

Halbwachs's work, which stressed the social formation of individual memory to the point of making all memory collective, has exercised a considerable influence in anthropology, sociology, cultural history, and oral history.[47] As a result these disciplines have tended to emphasize collective memory at the expense of individual memory, whereas psychological study of memory, as we shall see in the next chapter, has focused overwhelmingly on individual memory with little attention to the social dimensions of memory. In both cases, however, there have been recent efforts to redress the balance.[48] Thus James Fentress, an anthropologist, and Chris Wickham, a medieval historian, state at the outset of the book they co-wrote on collective memory that

> an important problem facing anyone who wants to follow Halbwachs in this field is how to elaborate a conception of memory which, while doing full justice to the collective side of one's conscious life, does not render the individual a sort of automaton, passively obeying the collective will.[49]

Barbara Misztal, similarly critical of the strong tendency to social determinism in Halbwachs's work, also seeks a way beyond either social determinism or the excessive individualism that disregards the social dimension. She proposes an "intersubjective" approach in which remembering, while constructed from cultural forms and constrained by social context, is an individual mental act. Individuals engage in an active process of remembering, but

---

be related to his inadequate understanding of both orality and gospel textuality. . . . His focus was entirely on determining the original form of a saying or story and its setting in the life of the community, and not on the rhetorical, performative, memorial aspects of speech."

47. For examples of the treatment of collective memory in these disciplines, see P. Connerton, *How Societies Remember* (Cambridge: Cambridge University Press, 1989); P. Burke, "History as Social Memory," in idem, *Varieties of Cultural History* (Cambridge: Polity, 1997) 43-59; E. Tonkin, *Narrating Our Past: The Social Construction of Oral History* (Cambridge: Cambridge University Press, 1992); and D. Mendels, *Memory in Jewish, Pagan and Christian Societies of the Graeco-Roman World* (LSTS 48; London: Clark [Continuum] 2004).

48. For examples in psychological studies, see, e.g., J. Bruner and C. Fleisher Feldman, "Group Narrative as a Context of Autobiography," and W. Hirst and D. Manier, "Remembering as Communication: A Family Recounts Its Past," both in D. C. Rubin, ed., *Remembering Our Past: Studies in Autobiographical Memory* (Cambridge: Cambridge University Press, 1996).

49. J. Fentress and C. Wickham, *Social Memory* (Oxford: Blackwell, 1992) ix. A frequent criticism of Halbwachs, as of his teacher Durkheim, has been that the emphasis on community, consensus, and cohesion in society ignores the reality and importance of dissent, and therefore of the coexistence of various collective memories in conflict: e.g., Burke, "History as Social Memory," 55-56; B. A. Misztal, *Theories of Social Remembering* (Philadelphia: Open University, 2003) chapter 3; Green, "Individual Remembering," 40-43. This is important for the study of early Christianity as a movement with a different social memory from that of the societies in which it developed.

always as individuals related to the world, interacting with collective traditions and expectations.[50] Memory is "intersubjectively constituted," and, "while it is the individual who remembers, remembering is more than just a personal act."[51]

For our purposes it is important to make some distinctions that are not often made in such discussions. One is between personal or recollective memory, in which the person remembering has the experience of "reliving" the recollected experience, and, on the other hand, memory for information. It is possible to remember information even about one's own past without personal recollection of it. Someone may know (from a diary, for example, or from other people) that she attended a particular friend's wedding forty years ago, but may have no recollection of it. This is memory for information, and differs from recollection, with its sense of reliving one's own experience. The latter kind of memory, recollection, can only be had by the person who experienced the event recalled (although there are, of course, cases of false memory, in which people have the experience of recollecting experiences they did not have). When passed on to others, this kind of memory necessarily ceases to be personal recollection and becomes information about what happened to the person who experienced it.

Much of what is called "collective memory," "social memory," or "cultural memory" is shared memory of information about the past. This is what is entailed, for example, when a large social group "commemorates" a notable event in its past, although, while the event is still within living memory, individuals with personal memories of the event may participate in the commemoration and may enrich the collective memory with their personal testimonies. Thus individual memory, shared with others, is the prime source of collective memory and can feed into the latter at any stage while the individuals in question are still alive and actively remembering their own past. As a result, partly, of this connection between individual and social memory, most discussions of collective memory, if they consider individual recollection at all, subsume it into collective memory.[52] Thus Misztal, for example, when she stresses that it is the individual who remembers, does not mean that the individual has his or her own recollections or, at least, she is not interested in distinguishing this from knowledge the individual may have about the collective past, from whatever source. Generally she is speaking about memory of a past

50. Misztal, *Theories*, especially chapter 4.

51. Misztal, *Theories*, 6.

52. It is also unfortunate that, despite the clear phenomenological difference between personal recollection and memory for information, there seems to be no generally accepted and unambiguous way of distinguishing between them in terminology.

of which no one who shares the memory has personal recollection. In effect, memory here means the same as tradition.[53] Taking up again the distinction Jan Vansina makes between oral history and oral tradition (see chapter 2), we could say that personal recollections are the main focus of oral history, while oral tradition deals in the collective memories of a group passed down across generations. Individual recollection has a time limit — the death of the person remembering — but collective memory does not.

We can make further progress if we distinguish three categories: (1) the social dimension of individual recollection, (2) the shared recollections of a group, and (3) collective memory. In order to avoid too individualistic a concept of individual memory, the first of these three categories is important, but it should not be confused with the others. It is as members of the groups to which they belong that individuals remember even their personal recollections, and scholars who apply the categories of Mediterranean anthropology to the ancient world would say that this was more the case in the ancient world than it is in the context of modern western individualism. Even with reference to modern culture, however, Misztal is right to state that "individual remembering takes place in the social context — it is prompted by social cues, employed for social purposes, ruled and ordered by socially structured norms and patterns, and therefore contains much that is social."[54]

We will develop this a little more in the next chapter. Here it is important to note that the social dimension of personal recollection does not at all contradict the individual's sense of ownership of a recollection of what he or she experienced. In the recounting of such a recollection — normally in the first person singular — the social dimension need not be expressed at all. Nor is it by any means confined to memory. Individuals are dependent on the shared resources of their culture in all their thinking and have to reckon with cultural expectations in all their communication with others.

The social dimension of individual remembering therefore does not require us to dissolve the distinctiveness of personal recollection. Nor does it authorize us to subsume it into some more collective form of memory. There is, however, (2) a form of memory in which a group of people who have shared the same experiences share their recollections of those experiences. Every family has its own group memories of this kind. A fund of memories common to the group develops out of some degree of merging of individual recollections. But individuals continue to have individual memories, their

53. Cf. the treatment of "Tradition as Information Remembered," chapter 6 in Vansina, *Oral Tradition*.
54. Misztal, *Theories*, 5.

own perspectives on events experienced by the group as well as recollections of events not recalled by the rest of the group.[55]

This is the kind of group memory to which James Dunn refers when he very plausibly conjectures that already during the ministry of Jesus his disciples must have been sharing their memories of the events.[56] We can imagine more than one group of disciples doing this. Such informal sharing of memories would have preceded the more official formulation of a body of traditions by the Twelve at some point in the early history of the Jerusalem church. This would have had its source in the shared memories of the Twelve, but it probably would also have included the testimony of others, such as the women disciples who recounted the events of the death and burial of Jesus and discovery of the empty tomb, events not witnessed by any of the Twelve. This would be a step from shared memories to the collecting of memories, not all of them recollections of the Twelve themselves. It would therefore also be a step in the direction of the third category, collective memory. Neither the sharing of memories by the disciples nor the collecting and formalizing of memories by the Twelve would have prevented the continuing recounting also of individual recollections by individual disciples.

(3) I use the term "collective memory" to refer to the traditions of a group about events not personally recollected by any of the group's members. The period when the eyewitnesses of Jesus were alive and accessible would have formed a transition from individual and shared memories to such purely collective memory. Groups of Christians who were not eyewitnesses were appropriating as their community tradition the testimonies of the eyewitnesses, which came to them either as the testimony of individuals or as the shared memories of a group, notably the Twelve.[57] We have seen reason to suppose that, as this happened, the traditions continued to be ascribed to the eyewitnesses who had formulated these traditions from their own recollections. The communities did not simply take them over as anonymous traditions which could now be ascribed only to the community, but continued to know them as owned by the eyewitnesses who originated them. The term "collective memory" should not be allowed to obscure this.

55. Cf. Misztal, *Theories*, 11. Hirst and Manier, "Remembering as Communication," 273, report that "collective memories accepted by all participants [in the group] are more richly recollected than are memories constructed by individuals outside the group."

56. Dunn, *Jesus Remembered*, 239-41.

57. Those who view conflict as an all-pervasive and determining feature of the early Christian movement will want to stress that such groups of disciples, the Gospel writers, and the first gospel audiences were in competitive relationships, each advancing rival claims to the collective memory. I am less inclined to stress conflict in this context.

In the Gospels the individual and shared memories of the eyewitnesses were given written form still, as we have seen, with indications of their named eyewitness sources incorporated into their narratives. These written traditions came to form the church's collective memory of Jesus thereafter. The fact that it was the four canonical Gospels that, after a period of lively controversy about which Gospels were reliable, became the permanent sources of the church's collective memory of Jesus meant that this collective memory always retained some sense of its origins in the personal recollections of the eyewitnesses to the events. The church itself did not "remember" Jesus in the same sense as, for example, Peter did, but in a secondary sense that could not be real were it not rooted in the recollective memories of Peter and others.

The distinctions we have made should warn us against too unreflectively applying to the Jesus traditions in the New Testament period what sociologists and historians say about collective memory. The latter has come to mean, in many cases, more or less all the ways in which societies know about their collective pasts,[58] regardless of whether personal recollection has any role at all in these ways of knowing the past. The emphasis is very much on how societies construct their collective pasts in ways that are meaningful and useful in the present. The uses to which scholars in fields such as cultural history put the concept of collective memory do not usually make it relevant or of interest to consider the personal recollections of individuals as the sources of collective memories. Where there is some consideration of these, there is a strong tendency to use the social dimension of individual memory as a way of eliding the difference between it and collective memory.[59] This, we have argued, is illegitimate. There is a real and important difference between the way in which individuals' personal recollections are influenced by their social context and, on the other hand, the kind of collective memory that is common to a social group and consists of memory for information about the group's collective past. The recollections of individuals may help to form collective memory, but they are not the same as collective memory. In particular circumstances such as that of earliest Christianity, the recollections of individuals may be of decisive importance *as* the personal recollections of individuals. The facts that such individuals are group-related and their memories belong to a social con-

58. E.g., as media of the transmission of social memory, Burke, "History as Social Memory," 47-49, lists oral traditions, memoirs and other written records, visual images, commemorative acts, and places where memories are located. Connerton, *How Societies Remember,* focuses on "commemorative ceremonies" and "bodily practices."

59. This tendency, with its influence on oral history, is analyzed by A. Green, "Individual Remembering," who argues that the pendulum has swung too far toward collective memory and away from individual memory.

text do not diminish their significance as individuals, or the significance of their personal recollections of experiences unique to them, recollections valued by the group precisely for this reason.

There is another area in which discussion of collective memory connects with a strong concern in our account of the transmission of Jesus traditions. One inheritance from Durkheim and Halbwachs, besides the tendency to absorb individual memory into collective memory, has been the closely related tendency to absorb memory into its present usefulness to the group. Again there is a striking convergence here with form criticism and its legacy in Gospels study throughout the twentieth century.[60] Misztal labels this tendency the "presentist" approach to collective memory, characterized by the contention that "the past is moulded to suit present dominant ideology."[61] It places memory wholly in the service of group identity and highlights the invention of the past in the form of new traditions and rituals designed to create or maintain group identity. When attention is given to who controls or imposes such invented memories, social memory comes to be understood as ideology serving the interests of the powerful. In Misztal's judgment, memory here becomes "a prisoner of political reductionalism and functionalism."[62] The identification of social memory solely with dominant ideology is avoided by the approach she calls the "popular memory" approach to collective memory. This approach, inspired by Michel Foucault's notions of popular memory and counter-memory, observes that memories may be socially constituted "from below" ("bottom up") as well as "from above." Critical of even Foucault's undervaluation of the power of popular memories to resist control by the dominant power and ideology, the Popular Memory Group of oral historians is devoted to the study of alternative memories.[63]

Finally, Misztal discusses the "dynamics of memory" approach, which is important for its resistance to the tendency to absorb memory into its present

60. Kelber, "The Case of the Gospels," 55-86, a discussion that is well informed by studies of memory in the tradition of Halbwachs, highlights the category of memory rather than that of tradition, and is critical of form criticism's focus on the original form of traditions, but insists that "remembering" in the Jesus tradition and the Gospels was overwhelmingly controlled by present needs and aspirations. This absorption of the past into the present gives Kelber's approach an important continuity with form criticism.

61. Misztal, *Theories*, 56. Note especially E. Hobsbawm and T. Ranger, eds., *The Invention of Tradition* (Cambridge: Cambridge University Press, 1985).

62. Misztal, *Theories*, 61.

63. Misztal, *Theories*, 61-63. P. F. Esler, *Conflict and Identity in Romans: The Social Setting of Paul's Letter* (Minneapolis: Fortress, 2003) 174-75, introduces the notion of collective memory into Pauline studies, but, by contrast to Halbwachs and others, is concerned with the way rival groups contend for the possession and interpretation of collective memory.

uses.[64] Here social memory is seen as an ongoing process of negotiation with the past, showing that there are "limits to the power of actors in the present to remake the past according to their own interests." The past is not purely a contemporary construct, but is "highly resistant to efforts to make it over." Recounting the past is a continuous attempt to understand the relationship of past and present. This relationship is constantly changing, and therefore social memory is always developing and fluctuating, but the process is not simply one of inventing the past, but of the constant interaction of the past with social memory.[65] This approach to collective memory among historians is precisely parallel to Vansina's critique of anthropologist Jack Goody's principle of complete homeostasis (congruence) between oral traditions and their use in oral societies. We noticed this as one reason for doubting the approach of form criticism to gospel traditions (chapter 10). Vansina insists that "there is congruence but there is no total congruence of content [in oral tradition] with the concerns of the present," and observes that "the presence of archaisms in various traditions gives homeostasis the lie."[66] In other words, social memory or oral tradition has to be constantly negotiating the relationship of the present to the past. In this negotiation the past has a voice that has to be heard. It cannot be freely invented.

One of the roles of the eyewitnesses in earliest Christianity was to articulate this voice in a social context in which the group was strongly committed to hearing the past's own voice, not for the past's own sake, but in order to understand the relationship of the group's present to the decisive events that constituted, for this group, not only the basis of its identity, but also God's acts for the salvation of the world. Of course, the negotiation of present meaning with memory of the past was already taking place in the traditions as formulated by the eyewitnesses themselves, but to a limited degree, owing to the "isolated" nature of the gospel tradition (see chapter 11). To a large extent, the eyewitnesses represented a kind of resistance of memory to complete absorption into its present uses. Collective memory or tradition as it developed recognized and accepted this resistance as integral to its self-understanding. Whereas the complete taking over of Jesus traditions by the community, the attribution of the traditions to the community, would have facilitated the kind of invention of traditions postulated by the form critics, the need to authenticate tradition by reference to the eyewitnesses favored the

64. As notable examples Misztal cites M. Schudson, *Watergate in American Memory* (New York: Basic Books, 1992); and B. Schwartz, *Abraham Lincoln and the Forge of National Identity* (Chicago: University of Chicago Press, 2000).

65. Misztal, *Theories*, 67-73.

66. Vansina, *Oral Tradition*, 121; cf. also Byrskog, "A New Perspective," 468-69.

tradition's faithfulness to its origins. Individual recollective memory did not lose its own identity through absorption into collective memory, but maintained that identity even when it was transmitted by the collective memory. The incorporation of the testimony of the eyewitnesses into the Gospels insured the permanence of that identity. Christianity's continual fresh discovery of the relevance of the story of Jesus to new circumstances has always taken the form of negotiating past and present. All such negotiation has had to account for itself with reference to the Jesus represented in the four Gospels, the Jesus of eyewitness testimony.

13. Eyewitness Memory

We all know from experience that memory is fallible. We seem to forget far more than we remember. Memories get distorted. Different people remember the same things quite differently. Memory plays tricks on us, so that even when we feel certain our memories are correct they turn out to be false. People can remember things that never happened at all. On the other hand, we also know from experience that for most everyday purposes memory is reliable enough. Human society could not be sustained otherwise. And we know, if we reflect on it, that memories can survive with a considerable degree of accuracy over a long period. How are we to gauge the reliability or otherwise of the gospel traditions? How far would they have been accurately preserved even within the memories of the eyewitnesses themselves? Even if our argument so far in this book is valid to the effect that the Gospels put us in much closer touch than has often been thought recently with the traditions as the eyewitnesses themselves framed and transmitted them, can we have any confidence in these eyewitness memories?

Psychologists have been studying recollective memory for well over a century. There is a large body of data and interpretation available that is highly relevant to these questions about the reliability of eyewitness memories. New Testament scholars have rarely made any use of these resources,[1]

1. Exceptions are J. D. Crossan, *The Birth of Christianity* (San Francisco: HarperCollins, 1998) 59-68; R. K. McIver and M. Carroll, "Experiments to Develop Criteria for Determining the Existence of Written Sources, and Their Potential Implications for the Synoptic Problem," *JBL* 121 (2002) 667-87; A. D. Baum, "Der mündliche Faktor: Teilanalogien zu *Minor Agreements* aus

and this chapter represents a first attempt to access the relevant data and theory and relate them to the gospel traditions in a systematic way.

In preparation for this psychological approach to the memories of the eyewitnesses of Jesus, we will present two anecdotal instances that illustrate both how unreliable and how remarkably reliable eyewitness testimony in ordinary life (i.e., outside the legal context of evidence in court) can be. They will set up the possibilities and the problem.

When Rossini Met Beethoven

Jan Vansina offers the following as a warning of how unreliable eyewitness testimony can be:

> The famous story of the reminiscences of Rossini about his early meeting with Beethoven may serve as a warning to the unwary. When first told, a few years after Beethoven's death, Rossini said that he went to Beethoven's house, had great difficulty in being admitted, and in the end did not speak to the master whose command of Italian (Rossini's language) was insufficient. This last bit we may doubt — at least from this source. Towards the end of Rossini's life the story had become quite a tale. It involved the tortured master, in the throes of creation, receiving Rossini, advising him to continue his great work, and above all praising *Il Barbiere di Siviglia* as the greatest comic work ever written.[2]

This example illustrates how an eyewitness may himself reshape an autobiographical memory radically during the course of retelling the story over many years. The motive in this case is obvious. Rossini emerges as a thoroughly untrustworthy witness. But did he believe his own story in its later form? Quite possibly.

---

der Oral Poetry-Forschung und der experimentellen Gedächtnis-Psychologie," *Biblica* 85 (2004) 264-72. By contrast, cognitive psychology has been put to quite extensive use by classical scholars: J. P. Small, *Wax Tablets of the Mind: Cognitive Studies of Memory and Literacy in Classical Antiquity* (New York: Routledge, 1997); G. S. Shrimpton, *History and Memory in Ancient Greece* (McGill-Queen's Studies in the History of Ideas 23; Montreal and Kingston: McGill-Queen's University Press, 1997) 52-60; E. Minchin, *Homer and the Resources of Memory: Some Applications of Cognitive Theory to the* Iliad *and the* Odyssey (Oxford: Oxford University Press, 2001).

2. J. Vansina, *Oral Tradition as History* (Madison: University of Wisconsin Press, 1985) 9-10.

The Case of the Rotting Fisherman

On the other hand, accurate recall of events after many years is also possible. In the following rather remarkable instance an eighty-three-year-old man remembered accurate details of an event that happened more than seventy years previously. The example is particularly interesting because it is difficult to find cases of very long-term memories for which the evidence is available to test their accuracy.

In June, 1901 a local newspaper in Norfolk, England, carried the following report:

> **STRANGE TRAGEDY AT WINTERTON**
> **Body Found in the Sandhills**
>
> Late on Tuesday, a gruesome find was made on the sandhills at Winterton, a large fishing village eight miles north of Yarmouth. It appears that a fisherman with his dog, accompanied by a Yarmouth gentleman, was walking along the cliff, when they came across the body of a man hanging from a post driven high up in the sandhills and partially covered with sand. The body was hanging by a piece of stout cord, which had been neatly fastened to the post, evidently driven into the sands by the deceased's own hand. The features were quite unrecognizable, and covered with fungus. From the clothing the body was believed to be that of a fisherman named Gislam, who had been missing from home for about five weeks, and who was supposed either to have been drowned or to have gone to sea. So it was subsequently identified. The spot is a very wild and lonely one, and very rarely visited by Winterton people, and the body would probably not have been discovered had it not been that the dog in question called the attention of his master to it.

The inquest was held the next day and was reported in the paper thus:

> The first witness called was the deceased's brother-in-law, Albert Robert George, also a fisherman, living at Winterton. Deceased, he said, was thirty-six years of age. He was at times very strange in his manner, and witness could not say whether on those occasions he was wholly responsible for his actions. He last saw him alive on the 8th of May near his own home. Deceased then put his arms around his little three-year-old son Stanley, said "Good-bye" and walked away. Witness supposed he was going to sea. He did not know that anything had occurred to upset him. The deceased's widow, Susannah Boulton Gislam, concurred with the evidence given by the previous witness, her brother. Her late husband's life,

she said, was insured in the Prudential. There was no quarrel between him and her before he left home on May 8th, which was the last occasion when she saw him alive; but he had been upset by being served with a County Court summons. She did not think that he fully knew what he was doing at times, though she had never heard him threaten to commit suicide, or even mention such a thing.

The jury gave a verdict of "suicide while temporarily insane."

Then it so happened, in 1973, that a man being interviewed volunteered an account of this event to illustrate a point about village practices in the past:

Respondent: Well — long story, 1910 this was. This woman wanted her husband to get away to sea or be earning some money — they'd none. Well, you could understand the woman's a' being — getting on to him about getting of a . . . At the same time, if he couldn't he couldn't. He went on the beach one day, and he was last seen — at an angle — and he went — as people saw him, to the south. But he was artful. When he knew people were all down . . . down home after their dinners, he turned and went north. They . . . ransacked the hills . . . they went to Yarmouth to see if he went on a boat. And nobody found him. No one. And they gave it up. Well, his poor wife didn't hardly get — well she didn't go out of doors. . . . The result was — a man one evening — this happened in May, and six weeks following, so that'd be in June — perhaps the fore-part of July, I won't say exactly, a man was . . . well, like they used to go walking along the water's edge. . . . He had a dog with him, perhaps he'd got — come out to give this dog a good run. And this dog would not leave this place. That got up on the hills. And he kept barking and yapping, barking and yapping, good way from Winterton, toward the north. And he thought to himself, whatever on the earth's that. He called him several time. The result was he had to go see — and there was this here man, tied to a post, about that high. And he — well, he was picked by the birds. Awful. Weren't fit to look at. Of course he got the dog away. . . . Well he had to come home to Winterton and got the coast guard and report it. And of course that was — soon a — well, hullaballoo. There was some people were against her, so much as if they dressed up an effigy, lit it up — didn't do it 'til it got dark at night, ten or eleven o'clock, and went round against where they lived. I don't know what they sung now, I was only ten. I forget . . . But that poor old girl — well she didn't go mad but she had to go to the hospital, so she died there.

Interviewer: People felt she'd driven, nagged him into it?

Respondent: Yes. Yes.

Interviewer: You said it happened in 1910 and you just said you were ten years old?

Respondent: Well, I was ten years old.

Interviewer: You were born?

Respondent: 1890.

Interviewer: If you were ten that would be 1900.

Respondent: Well, didn't I tell you 1900?

Interviewer: I think you said 1910.

Respondent: Ah well, 1900 might be. Just into the nineteenth-twentieth century. That was June, that . . . May when he done it and — I can't tell you the exact date — but he was buried — in Winterton churchyard.[3]

In personal recollections, dating is the element least likely to be accurate, and so it is very noteworthy that, not only did the witness place the events in the correct months of the year, but also provided a correct absolute date in terms of his age at the time, even though he mistook the year until questioned about it. Everything in the witness's statement is consistent with the newspaper reports, and the considerable added detail is entirely plausible, though it is not possible to tell whether some of it (such as, "And he thought to himself, whatever on the earth's that") is the kind of minor elaboration natural in storytelling. Particularly interesting is the way the witness's statement and the newspaper report of the trial offer different perspectives that could well dovetail together in fact. At the trial we find the dead man's wife and her brother evidently very anxious to avoid any possible implication that she might have driven her husband to his death. In the witness's memories we find that such an allegation was indeed abroad among some of her neighbors and that it did not lack some basis in the couple's situation and relationship.

That this witness remembered this event so well, even though he was not personally involved and only ten at the time, can be attributed to the very unusual, indeed macabre nature of the event that made it naturally very memorable, perhaps especially to a ten-year-old boy. But we should also presume that the memory had been rehearsed quite often, both by the witness himself and probably also by others in his presence. Frequent rehearsal, as we shall see, is an important element in the preservation of memories.

3. Cited in A. Baddeley, *Your Memory: A User's Guide* (London: Prion, 1982) 136-40.

Recollective Memory

The kind of memory with which we are concerned in this chapter is what we shall call, following William Brewer, recollective memory.[4] In the literature it goes under a variety of names, including "episodic memory," "personal memory" and "autobiographical memory." But Brewer treats "autobiographical memory" as a broader term and helpfully distinguishes four kinds of autobiographical memory. There is (1) recollective memory, which is personal memory (with mental images) of a specific event in one's life; there is (2) generic personal memory, which is a personal memory (with mental imagery) of repeated occurrences or circumstances but not of any specific instance; there is (3) autobiographical fact, which is knowing about an event in one's past without mental imagery or the phenomenon of "reliving" the experience; and finally there is (4) the self-schema, which is the general conception of oneself that one has acquired through many experiences.[5]

Most episodic narratives in the Gospels, if they are based on eyewitness testimony, would come into the first category. There is some generalized material that may be placed in the second category. But sayings of Jesus, other than those that are integral parts of a narrative, do not belong among these categories. As we have argued in the previous chapter, they would have been memorized to some degree and reproduced like other information that has been committed to memory and recalled. Presumably even the eyewitnesses would not usually have recalled a specific occasion and place at which Jesus pronounced the saying, or, even if they did, that memory would be incidental to the procedure of recalling and transmitting the saying. In this chapter we are concerned with the psychology of such recollective memories as eyewitnesses would have and which would have been the source of episodic narratives in the Gospels.

Brewer provides a carefully considered description of the characteristics of recollective memory:

> Recollective memory is memory for a specific episode from an individual's past. It typically appears to be a "reliving" of the individual's phe-

4. W. F. Brewer, "What Is Recollective Memory?" in D. C. Rubin, ed., *Remembering Our Past: Studies in Autobiographical Memory* (Cambridge: Cambridge University Press, 1996) 19-66. Earlier he had used the term "personal memory": W. F. Brewer, "What Is Autobiographical Memory?" in D. C. Rubin, ed., *Autobiographical Memory* (Cambridge: Cambridge University Press, 1986) 25-49. For other terms that have been used, see idem, "What Is Recollective Memory?" 21, 32.

5. Brewer, "What Is Autobiographical Memory?" 25-32.

nomenal experience during that earlier moment. Thus, these memories typically contain information about place, actions, persons, objects, thoughts and affect. They do not contain any direct representation of time. The information in this form of memory is expressed as a mental image. Compared to visual perception, recollective memory images are dim, unclear, sketchy and unsteady. The point of view of recollective memory images can be from the original perspective or from an observer's point of view. The image may contain irrelevant detail. Recollective memories also appear to include propositional (nonimage) information. They are accompanied by a belief that the remembered episode was personally experienced by the individual in that individual's past. Recent recollective memories tend to be fairly veridical unless they are influenced by strong schema-based processes. Recollective memories give rise to high confidence in the accuracy of their content and that confidence can frequently predict objective memory accuracy.[6]

Copies or (Re)constructions?

An important theoretical issue in the study of memory — by philosophers as well as psychologists — is whether a particular recollective memory is a copy of the original experience or a reconstruction of the original experience. This is a matter of divergent *theories,* for which the available experimental data are important evidence but still open to interpretation. Reconstructive theories have in recent years become dominant in the psychological literature.[7] However, the appeal that is sometimes made to the experiments and conclusions of Sir Frederick Bartlett in his classic study *Remembering* (1932),[8] as having made the case for the reconstructive nature of recollective memories,[9] is quite unjustified, since Bartlett tested memory for texts, stories, and pictures, not for personally experienced events. On the other hand, the phenomenon of false memories, in which a person can recall an experience he or she has not in fact had and with the same kind of certainty that accompanies true memo-

6. Brewer, "What Is Recollective Memory?" 60-61. This builds on his early description in "What Is Autobiographical Memory?" 34-35.

7. References in Brewer, "What Is Recollective Memory?" 40.

8. F. C. Bartlett, *Remembering: A Study in Experimental and Social Psychology* (Cambridge: Cambridge University Press, 1932).

9. C. R. Barclay, "Schematization of Autobiographical Memory," in Rubin, ed., *Autobiographical Memory,* 82: "most autobiographical memories are *reconstructions* of past episodic events (Bartlett, 1932)."

ries, is evidence suggesting at least that a copy theory of memory by itself is not adequate.

David Lieberman writes that, according to the copy theory, "Memory . . . resembles a video recorder: We first accurately record whatever we experience and then, when we need the record, we reproduce it exactly."[10] We should note immediately that this is a misleading image of what happens when we mentally record an event. Perception of an event is already selective and interpretative. Reconstructive theories of memory propose that the process of retrieval is also a constructive process, not merely a replay of the original experience. To some extent, the issue concerns how memories are stored. Reconstructive theories propose that a recollective memory is not stored as such in the memory's knowledge base. Rather, the retrieval of a memory involves the creative bringing together of different elements of autobiographical knowledge: "memory is a constitutive process involving a complex retrieval system sampling an extensive knowledge base."[11] On this view, "memories are temporary or transitory mental representations that only exist in the context of some specific processing episode."[12] To support this view there is experimental evidence that when a person recalls the same experience on different occasions there are both stability and variability in the details.[13]

It is important to note, with David Rubin, that a constructive theory of recollective memories "does not mean that they are either accurate or inaccurate, but that they are not encoded, stored and retrieved as wholes but rather are created at retrieval using components."[14] When memories are accurate, as undoubtedly they very often are, such a theory explains how it is that they are accurate. But, in the nature of the case, even accurate memories are selective and interpretative. According to much psychological theory, the memory works with "schemata" ("frames" or "scripts" are other terms with similar meaning), patterns that enable the mind to organize data in a usable way.[15] These may include general concepts of what is usually the case and what usually happens, narrative patterns that organize perceptions into stories, and the "self-schema" that includes one's overall sense of one's identity and char-

10. D. A. Lieberman, *Learning and Memory: An Integrative Approach* (Belmont: Wadsworth, 2004) 442.

11. M. A. Conway, "Autobiographical Knowledge and Autobiographical Memories," in Rubin, ed., *Remembering Our Past*, 86.

12. Conway, "Autobiographical Knowledge," 76.

13. Conway, "Autobiographical Knowledge," 80-81.

14. D. C. Rubin, "Introduction," in idem, ed., *Remembering Our Past*, 4.

15. Barclay, "Schematization," 82-83. On the use of the notion of schemata in historical study, see P. Burke, *Varieties of Cultural History* (Cambridge: Polity, 1997) 39-41, 95-97, 176-78.

acter.[16] (Psychologists often write about these matters in seemingly very individualistic terms, and we may note in passing that the "self-schema" need not represent one's self in isolation but can portray it in its necessary relationships to others.) Because schemata and especially self-schemata may change over time, the organizing principles used by the mind may produce variation in the way a memory is recalled. Moreover, the purpose for which the memory is recalled and communicated (for remembering is always communication) may strongly affect the construction of the memory.

Memories are not freely constructed. There are clearly constraints in the remembering process that account for the relative accuracy and the broad element of stability in memories recalled on different occasions. But a reconstructive theory explains how significant inaccuracies can arise. If a person cannot recall sufficient accurate detail to reproduce an experience, the mind may fill in the gaps from its other stores of knowledge. The experience of one woman recalling her early memories is a nice illustration. She writes that one day she was reliving a memory of the Russian revolution of 1905, when she was five years old:

> I was looking out of the window, with my eyes on two women running past, just underneath, each frightened in her own way. They had neither hats nor kerchiefs and their hair was bobbed. "The Revolutionaries," Mother said, close behind me: I turned my head to her. To my amazement I realized that the room I was looking at was the sitting-room of the house to which we moved when I was thirteen!

She goes on to explain that this later house was quite similar to the one in which they lived in 1905.[17] Her memory had misled her by supplying for this episodic memory information from a generic personal memory (i.e., of a house she had lived in) that was close to, but not the correct generic memory. Craig Barclay, who quotes this example, comments:

> Perhaps many autobiographical memories acquire schematic properties in this way. That is, through similarities in certain perceptual or conceptual features the past is reconstructed such that the person adds or takes

16. Barclay, "Schematization," 87, quotes the definition given by H. Markus: "Self-schemata are cognitive generalizations about the self, derived from past experience, that organize and guide the processing of self-referenced information contained in an individual's social experiences."

17. Quoted in Barclay, "Schematization," 85, from E. Salaman, *A Collection of Moments: A Study of Involuntary Memories* (London: Longman, 1970) 32.

away information to make a story coherent and believable to themselves and others at some particular time.[18]

Another way in which the reconstructive process can be misled so that distorted memories occur is through misinformation acquired by persons about an event they remember. Such misinformation can be unconsciously adopted into their memory and become part of it.[19] In extreme cases persons told about an event that allegedly happened to them can come to believe they actually remember it, even though the event never happened. An experimental case concerns a fourteen-year-old boy named Chris. His older brother was persuaded

> to ask Chris if he could remember an incident that happened when Chris was 5 years old and became lost in a shopping mall. At first, Chris couldn't remember it — quite rightly, as it never happened — but his brother prompted him with details, and gradually Chris began to remember. After about 2 weeks, Chris reported having a clear and vivid memory of the incident.[20]

Entirely false memories of this kind, not deliberately set up in this way, seem very often to be memories of childhood,[21] such as this example from Mark Twain:

> I used to remember my brother Henry walking into a fire outdoors when he was a week old. It is remarkable in me to remember a thing like that, and it is still more remarkable that I should cling to the delusion for thirty years that I did remember it — of course, it never happened; he would not have been able to walk at that age.[22]

Perhaps a child's memory is particularly susceptible, either to its own imagination, as presumably in this case, or to visualizing events talked about by others.

As for adults, Barclay reports an experiment in which people were provided, at several points over a period of two and a half years, with their own original records of everyday events they had experienced along with "foils," which were records of everyday experiences of someone else who shared the same kind of daily experiences. Analysis of the quite complex data showed

18. Barclay, "Schematization," 86.
19. Lieberman, *Learning*, 445.
20. Lieberman, *Learning*, 446.
21. References in Brewer, "What Is Autobiographical Memory?" 43-44.
22. Quoted in Barclay, "Schematization," 82.

that, when people mistakenly identified foils as their own experience, they tended to identify with such events as were most similar to their genuine experiences.[23] While this suggests that memory reconstruction works in part with a concept of what is likely to have happened to a person in the past, it also suggests that memories for unusual events are least likely to be false memories. Memorable events stick with us; it is with the ordinary and the everyday that our memories may sometimes deceive us.

Brewer argues for a partially reconstructive view of recollective memory, including an element of copying. On the whole, he judges that the evidence for reconstruction, though not very considerable (and some of the claimed evidence he argues is not valid), is greater than the evidence for copying, but the phenomenon of irrelevant details, often found in recollective memory, seems hard to account for on a purely reconstructive view. His hypothesis is that "recent (days to weeks) personal memories are, in fact, reasonably accurate copies of the individual's original phenomenal experience." But reconstruction may occur subsequently: "with time, or under strong schema-based processes, the original experience can be reconstructed to produce a new nonveridical memory that retains most of the phenomenal characteristics of other personal memories (e.g. strong visual imagery, strong belief value)."[24]

Brewer reports an experiment that shows the accuracy of short-term recall (as well as throwing some doubts on the value of the experiment reported by Barclay):

> [S]ubjects carried a random alarm device for several weeks. When the alarm went off they wrote down the events that were occurring (e.g. actions, thoughts) and other descriptive information (e.g. location, time). At several periods over the next few months they were given a cued-recall test (using different probes such as actions, location, time) for the events they had recorded previously. A qualitative analysis of these recalls showed that they made many errors (roughly 50%). However, almost all of these errors were retrieval errors (the subjects appeared to be recalling the wrong event to the probe). In only 1.5% of the cases did the subjects make true reconstructive errors in which they appeared to be recalling

23. Barclay, "Schematization," 91-95. My account of the experiment and the conclusions to be drawn from it are very simplified. However, it is not clear to me from Barclay's account whether people in this experiment who identified a foil as a memory of their own actually had the experience of "reliving" the event, i.e., a properly recollective memory, or simply made a judgment that they likely experienced the event reported. For doubts about the value of the data from this experiment, see also Brewer, "What Is Recollective Memory?" 40-41.

24. Brewer, "What Is Autobiographical Memory?" 41-44.

the original event but recalled information that was in conflict with what they had originally recorded about the event. I argued that this relatively low rate of reconstructive memory errors for ordinary events was in fair agreement with my earlier partially reconstructive view.[25]

Brewer also claims that the data on so-called "flashbulb" memories (vivid and detailed memories of the occasion when people first heard of some dramatic event, such as the assassination of John F. Kennedy) can be understood as consistent with his partially reconstructive view, rather than the more thoroughgoing reconstructive view that others have based on such data.[26]

It seems safe to conclude that recollective memory has a reconstructive element, but the extent to which a copy element is also important, especially in short-term recall, is still very debatable. But reconstruction does not in itself entail inaccuracy. The memory is capable of very accurate, though inevitably selective, reconstruction. (This makes the term "reconstruction" preferable to "construction." For example, the use of generic personal memory to fill gaps in episodic memory may be fully justified.) Reconstruction, however, can lead to inaccuracy (even occasionally to completely false memories). Interpretative elements in the reconstruction of memories (as also in the original perception) are always at work, seeking an account that is meaningful in the context of recall, but again such interpretation, while going beyond mere reproduction, by no means necessarily distorts memory. We may think of a reconstructed memory, perhaps, as more like a painting than a photograph.[27]

Further conclusions about the accuracy of recollective memories cannot be drawn from this general discussion of copy and reconstructive theories. It requires discussion of types and characteristics of recollective memories. Are there aspects of particular recollective memories or of the ways in which they are recalled that indicate greater probability of accuracy in these than in other cases?

The Reliability of Recollective Memory

We can now draw on more specific conclusions that can be drawn from the study of recollective memory by psychologists. What sort of events are remembered best? What sort of memories are more likely to be reliable? The following factors seem to be important:

25. Brewer, "What Is Recollective Memory?" 41.
26. Brewer, "What Is Recollective Memory?" 41-42.
27. The image is suggested by Brewer, "What Is Recollective Memory?" 29.

(1) *Unique or unusual event.* An event that we generally consider "memorable" is likely to be unique or unusual. The common notion that such events are more likely to be remembered[28] is confirmed by studies that "consistently find that low-frequency events show better memory" than high-frequency (i.e., repeated) events.[29] A hypothesis that may relate to these findings is that "repetition of events leads to the development of generic personal memories at the expense of the individual personal memories that are repeated."[30] Closely connected with this criterion is the finding that the *unexpectedness* of an event also makes it more memorable.[31]

(2) *Salient or consequential event.* Also in mind when we commonly speak of a "memorable" event is that it is one that is important for us. This too is confirmed by studies.[32] What we more easily forget is the trivial and the insignificant (which, of course, may be significant for other people, but not for ourselves).

(3) *An event in which a person is emotionally involved.* Although there are studies that seem to show that events that provoked high emotion (positive or negative) are better remembered, this finding is less secure. Such events also tend to be unusual or important events, so that it is less clear whether emotion is an independent factor.[33] The evidence on the effect of emotion on memory is in fact quite complex, as the conclusions to two recent studies will illustrate:

> We conclude that emotional events in real-life situations are retained well, both with respect to the emotional event itself and the central, critical detail information of the emotion-eliciting event, that is the information that elicits the emotional reaction. It also seems that certain critical detail information of emotion-arousing events and some circumstantial

28. Cf. G. Cohen, *Memory in the Real World* (Hillsdale: Erlbaum, 1989) 118: "In the ordinary language of everyday, we often speak of an experience as 'unforgettable,' and, in fact, we probably do have quite accurate intuitions about what kinds of events someone ought to be able to remember."

29. Brewer, "What Is Recollective Memory?" 50, 57.

30. Brewer, "What Is Autobiographical Memory?" 45; cf. idem, "What Is Recollective Memory?" 51.

31. Brewer, "What Is Autobiographical Memory?" 44.

32. Brewer, "What Is Recollective Memory?" 50; A. Baddeley, *Human Memory: Theory and Practice* (revised edition; Hove: Psychology, 1997) 218-219. This is also well recognized by oral historians: see S. Byrskog, *Story as History — History as Story* (WUNT 123; Tübingen: Mohr, 2000; reprinted Leiden: Brill, 2002) 28 ("A person involved remembers better than a disinterested observer" [summarizing Paul Thompson]), 165-66.

33. Brewer, "What Is Recollective Memory?" 50.

information is less susceptible to forgetting compared with neutral detail information over time. However, memory for information associated with unpleasant emotional events, that is, information preceding and succeeding such events, or peripheral, noncentral information within an emotional scenario, seems to be less accurately retained. . . . Whereas memory for central emotional event information is relatively accurate, memory for emotions seems to be quite inaccurate (e.g. the intensity and frequency with which we experience emotions).[34]

In general, emotion seems to have a positive effect on memory, increasing memory vividness, accuracy, completeness, and longevity. But emotion's effects are not uniformly positive. Many emotional events contain a prominent visual stimulus, and, if so, emotion seems to promote a focus on this stimulus in a fashion that impairs memory for the event's periphery. Emotion assigned to an event after the fact may also spur memory reconstruction based on too little information, and this may foster reconstructive error. And, finally, extremely intense emotion may work against memory, perhaps by interrupting the biological processes needed for memory consolidation.[35]

(4) *Vivid imagery.* Recollective memories are usually characterized by visual imagery. Brewer reports an experiment that showed that "most recollective memory gave rise to reports of visual imagery. Accurate recollections tended to show stronger imagery than inaccurate recollections."[36]

(5) *Irrelevant detail.* As we have noted already, Brewer has argued that recollective memories frequently include irrelevant details, and this is an argument for a copy component in recollective memory. Such details have been especially associated with flashbulb memories; in fact, they are not peculiar to flashbulb memories but are found also in other recollective memories.[37] However, he states that "[i]t is difficult to find data that directly address the

34. S.-A. Christianson and M. A. Safer, "Emotional Events and Emotions in Autobiographical Memories," in Rubin, ed., *Remembering Our Past,* 238.

35. D. Reisberg and F. Heuer, "Memory for Emotional Events," in D. Reisberg and P. Hertel, eds., *Memory and Emotion* (Oxford: Oxford University Press, 2004) 35. See also B. A. Misztal, *Theories of Social Remembering* (Philadelphia: Open University, 2003) 80-81.

36. Brewer, "What Is Recollective Memory?" 35-36, cf. 43. On vivid memories, see also M. A. Conway and D. A. Bekerian, "Characteristics of Vivid Memories," in M. M. Gruneberg, P. E. Morris, and R. N. Sykes, eds., *Practical Aspects of Memory,* vol. 1: *Memory in Everyday Life* (Chichester: Wiley, 1988) 519-24.

37. Brewer, "What Is Recollective Memory?" 37.

hypothesis that occurrence of irrelevant detail in recollective memory is related to memory accuracy."[38]

(6) *Point of view.* Recollective memories take two forms with respect to point of view. One is "field memories," in which the memory images present the original scene from the point of view from which it was originally experienced. The other is "observer memories," in which the memory images present the original scene as an external observer might experience it. There are data suggesting that "field memories" are more likely in the case of recent memories than in that of older memories.[39] But it seems also to be true that people can switch the point of view of a memory from field to observer and vice versa.[40] There seems no reason to think that "field memories" are more accurate than "observer memories."

(7) *Dating.* There is much evidence that recollective memories "exclude absolute time information from most events." While a typical recollection will include information on location, actions, persons, emotions, and thoughts and may include information about the time of day, dates are very uncommon. If people wish to date these memories, they usually do so by inference from other information that the memory does contain.[41]

(8) *Gist and details.* Some writers, particularly those who emphasize the likelihood of inaccuracy in long-term recollective memory, argue that the "gist" of the memory is likely to be accurate, even when the details are not. Barclay maintains that recollective memories are "true in the sense of maintaining the integrity and gist of past life events."[42] Baddeley, who observes that studies show "a very high level of recall of autobiographical events, and a low level of distortion, given adequate cueing,"[43] also says:

> [M]uch of our autobiographical recollection of the past is reasonably free of error, provided that we stick to remembering the broad outline of events. Errors begin to occur once we try to force ourselves to come up with detailed information from an inadequate base. This gives full rein to

38. Brewer, "What Is Recollective Memory?" 44.

39. Brewer, "What Is Recollective Memory?" 37; Conway, "Autobiographical Knowledge," 89.

40. Brewer, "What Is Recollective Memory?" 45; Conway, "Autobiographical Knowledge," 89.

41. Brewer, "What Is Recollective Memory?" 52; cf. also Cohen, *Memory*, 126-28.

42. Barclay, "Schematization," 82. See also idem, "Truth and Accuracy in Autobiographical Memory," in Gruneberg, Morris, and Sykes, eds., *Memory in Everyday Life*, 289-93, where he develops the idea that autobiographical memories are inaccurate but "true" in the sense of conveying "the essence of one's self" (290).

43. Baddeley, *Human Memory*, 221.

various sources of distortion, including that of prior expectations, disruption by misleading questions, and by social factors such as the desire to please the questioner, and to present ourselves in a good light.[44]

The "gist" of a memory is commonly the sequence or structure that makes the event meaningful to the person who initially perceives and then recalls. Forming such a gist is an act of interpretation, but this need not involve inaccuracy.

(9) *Frequent rehearsal.* Frequent recall is an important factor in both retaining the memory and retaining it accurately.[45] This may involve constructing the memory in a standard narrative form that is then remembered as a piece of information rather than as a recollective ("relived") memory.[46]

The following account of the results of two studies illustrates how some of these factors determining memorability come together to promote and preserve memory of specific events:

> Rubin and Kozin (1984)[47] asked a group of students to describe three of their clearest memories, and to rate them for national importance, personal importance, surprise, vividness, emotionality, and how often they had discussed the event. The most commonly reported events concerned injuries or accidents, sports, and encounters with the opposite sex. Memories which were more vivid also received higher ratings for importance, surprise, and emotionality. Cohen and Faulkner[48] also reported that memory vividness correlated significantly with emotion, importance, and the amount of rehearsal. In their study, the relative power of these factors shifted with the age of the person who was remembering. For younger people, characteristics of the event itself, such as emotionality and importance, were the best predictors of memory vividness, but for elderly people the amount of rehearsal was the most powerful factor. The vividness of their remote memories was preserved because the events were often thought about and talked about. The events that were most often remembered were: births, marriages and deaths (22.2%); holidays

44. Baddeley, *Human Memory,* 222.

45. Baddeley, *Human Memory,* 213.

46. Conway, "Autobiographical Knowledge," 89-90. Bartlett, *Remembering,* 93, already observed that "[w]ith frequent reproduction the form and items of remembered detail very quickly become stereotyped and thereafter suffer little change," though he was speaking of reproductions of a story, not of autobiographical memory.

47. D. C. Rubin and M. Kozin, "Vivid Memories," *Cognition* 16 (1984) 81-95.

48. G. Cohen and D. Faulkner, "Lifespan Changes in Autobiographical Memories," in Gruneberg, Morris, and Sykes, eds., *Memory in Everyday Life,* 277-82.

(11.8%); trivia (8.2%); illness/injury (8%); education (8%); family (7.5%); war (6.1%); love affairs (5.1%); recreations/sports (4.9%). Events in which the subjects were actors were remembered better than events in which they were only bystanders, and unique occasions and first times were remembered more often than generic events or last times.[49]

These studies illustrate the way several of the factors discussed above — events that are unique, salient, surprising, vivid, often rehearsed — tend to occur in combination, making it difficult to gauge their relative importance.

Schematization, Narrativization, and Meaning

In this section we shall look more closely at the interpretative structuring that characterizes all recollective memory (as well as, in other ways, all types of memory). We are already structuring events, selecting and ordering, seeking coherence and meaning, when we experience and perceive the events, but even more so when we recall and recount them. In order to understand how we do this, psychologists posit knowledge structures, already existing in the memory, which function to order and interpret new data, as we perceive and recall them. Bartlett, in this as in other respects a pioneer of modern psychology, used the term "schema" to refer to a mental model, formed by the mind as a kind of distillation of information gained in frequent everyday experience. In his famous study of how a particular story ("The War of the Ghosts") was reproduced after various intervals by a number of individuals, he observed the largely unwitting "rationalization" of the story that occurred over the course of several reproductions. The features and details that seemed incoherent or puzzling to the individual tended to be omitted or adapted, and explanatory connections and additions were made.[50] Bartlett's explanation of this was that the individual was making the material meaningful by normalizing it according to the mental models, which Bartlett called schemata, already present in his memory.[51] Related terms that have been used in subsequent studies refer to particular types of schemata: scripts are the schemata for events and stories, frames[52] for knowledge about objects and places.[53]

49. Cohen, *Memory*, 124-25.

50. Bartlett, *Remembering*, 84-89.

51. Bartlett, *Remembering*, 201.

52. Misztal, *Theories of Social Remembering*, 82-83, uses this term in dependence on E. Goffman.

53. On schema theory in general, see Cohen, *Memory*, 71-72, 207-9, where she also dis-

When it comes to memories of events, we must take special account of story schemata, which are derived not so much from our direct experience of events as from hearing and reading stories and unconsciously learning the kinds of narrative structures that are commonly employed to tell a meaningful story, whether real or fictional.[54] Some such narrative structures are common across cultures, others more culture-specific. In perception and recall we are constantly narrativizing experience — by selection, connection, and explanation of items — and must employ such narrative structures as are available to us as established schemata in our memories. This is the only way to make sense of events in the way that stories do. It is part of the quest for meaning (what Bartlett called the "effort after meaning") that is inherent in remembering. But two misunderstandings need to be corrected.

One is the idea that this process is a procrustean forcing of all experience into narrowly preconceived patterns. Narrative patterns are infinitely subtle and adaptable. Moreover, interesting narratives are often those that feature unique or surprising events that disrupt the schema-based expectations of their hearers (and so, in the first place, of their tellers too). But such surprises are possible because the narrative nevertheless still follows some well-known narrative conventions. We can only contemplate the strange in the context of the more ordinary and familiar, against which it is strange precisely through standing out. At the limit of such disruptions of schemata there is also to be found the quite incoherent memory, which persists because of the puzzlement it induces, its refusal to fit into a person's meaning-making. Such incoherence provokes attempts at meaning for as long as it is remembered, testifying both to the human need to remember through making sense and at the same time to the opposite: the priority of what is remembered over the sense that can be made of it.

The second, closely related misunderstanding is that the mind's use of narrative schemata to order events in remembering and recalling necessarily distorts reality, as though we are constantly imposing structures alien to the material we structure. Do schemata impede our access to what happens? On the contrary, they enable it. As Bruner and Feldman put it, "[N]arrative patterning does not 'get in the way' of accurate autobiographical reporting or interpreting, but rather provides a framework for both telling and understanding."[55] Of course, misleading simplifications and distortions occur often

---

cusses how schema theory attempts to deal with the irrelevant detail often found in recollective memories.

54. Misztal, *Theories of Social Remembering*, 10.

55. J. Bruner and C. Fleisher Feldman, "Group Narrative as a Context of Autobiography," in Rubin, ed., *Remembering Our Past*, 291.

enough, but we are well enough familiar with ways of challenging and correcting these. We know there can be no finally definitive account of any event, but we also know that there are better and worse accounts, accounts that are more or less faithful to what they seek to report. The theory of schemata is no warrant for a general distrust of memory or for dissolving memory in postmodern epistemological skepticism. Furthermore, when the schemata go beyond the empirically verifiable in their quest for meaning in events, this does not mean that they must distort or reject the empirical.

Implicitly we have already brought the social context of individual memory into play. We are not concerned here with the notion of collective memory (discussed in the last chapter), but only with the necessarily social context of an individual's remembering.[56] "We cannot divorce the act of remembering from the act of communicating," write Hirst and Manier. "Recollections arise not from the depths of a storehouse in the head, but from a desire to communicate with others about the personal past."[57] But it would be better to substitute "both . . . and" for that "not . . . but." It is the desire or the need to communicate that draws at least the makings of our recollections out of the storehouse of memory. Or rather, this is very often the case. We do sometimes remember quite spontaneously, for no purpose, and sometimes we remember purely for our own purposes (to while away an empty hour, for example), but mostly we remember in order to tell other people. Often the telling to other people is the remembering. We need to put our memories into socially available scripts if we are to succeed in communicating them to others.

The social shaping of our memories occurs at all stages. When we perceive and store experiences we are already shaping them with structures of meaning that belong to us because they belong to our social context. Even when we remember privately, we are formulating our memories into a story we tell ourselves, and the structures of narrative and meaning we deploy are not, even in the highly individualistic culture of the contemporary West, wholly private ones. What we tell ourselves privately participates in the discourses to which we belong socially. The more we tell our memories, privately and socially, the more the scripts, the expectations, and the goals of our social contexts serve to interpret them. Much psychological study of memory, with its emphasis on self-schemata, tends to neglect this, but a more socially orientated approach, recognizing the extent to which individ-

56. Cf. Misztal, *Theories of Social Remembering*, 5-6.

57. W. Hirst and D. Manier, "Remembering as Communication: A Family Recounts Its Past," in Rubin, ed., *Remembering Our Past*, 271.

ual identity is inseparable from group identity, has become apparent in some studies.[58]

Fact and Meaning, Past and Present

Two further aspects of the formulations of memories as meaningful stories need to be noticed. Remembering occurs at the place we could characterize both as the conjunction of information and meaning and as the interaction of past and present. For the first of these, what John Robinson calls the first-person perspective of remembering is crucial:

> [I]n autobiographical memory research we need to examine memory from both third-person and first-person perspectives. . . . For some aspects of experience agreement (between experimenter and subject, or among participants) or conformity with some documentary information may be given priority. For the interpretive aspects of experience the first-person perspective has priority.[59]

The rather individualistic approach of Robinson's work, while it rightly recognizes the different ways in which individuals may experience and remember the same event, neglects the possibility of shared meaning among persons who experience and remember together.[60] He reads the "first-person perspective" as an "I" perspective, without attending to the possibility of a "we" perspective. In cases of group experience and remembering, we may have to reckon with an interplay of "I" and "we" perspectives. But the distinction between first-person perspectives and third-person perspectives is valid and significant.

We could also call these two categories participant perspectives and observer perspectives, and we may recall that the first kind of eyewitness testimony is what the historians of the ancient world especially valued because it provided access to the "insider" significance of the event, which a detached observer could not supply. We have also noticed how this participant perspective is embodied in the "gist" of an event that is remembered even when

58. For example, Bruner and Fleisher Feldman, "Group Narrative," and Hirst and Manier, "Remembering as Communication."

59. J. A. Robinson, "Perspective, Meaning and Remembering," in Rubin, ed., *Remembering Our Past*, 214.

60. He does recognize the influence of social context on the way the individual remembers and retells: "Perspective," 202-3.

details are inaccurate. Psychologists such as Robinson who wish to validate the importance of first-person (subjective) perspectives provide some insight into the inadequacy of a simplistic modern distinction between objective fact and subjective experience:

> The focus on perspectives places personal meaning at the center of in-quiry. Accuracy and completeness have been the conventional standards for assessing memory. In the world of cognitive research, the criteria for accuracy and completeness are usually defined from a third-person point of view. The investigator knows what really happened and can specify ex-actly how any person's account deviates from some canonical reality. But these discrepancies are neither absolute nor unambiguous. . . . A third-person or observer perspective provides indispensable information, and societies may decide that for certain purposes it should be privileged, but it needs to be joined to a thorough analysis of first-person perspec-tives. . . . Accepting the need to include the personal in our science does not leave us stranded in relativism. We can objectively characterize first-person perspectives as consistent or inconsistent with (1) those of other participants and observers, (2) each person's established ways of experi-encing, and (3) their previous reports of events.[61]

Robinson's work focuses on why it is that meaning in personal memo-ries changes or remains stable over time. "Remembering," he observes, "is al-ways embedded in a developmental history."[62] He analyzes meaning as in-volving the following four factors making for change or stability:

> *The multiplicity of potential meanings:* Some events are inherently am-biguous (with respect, for example, to a person's motivation and in-tentions), such that even "third-person" observers at the time must infer and interpret and may well do so differently.
>
> *Deferred meaning:* "Meaning is not always fully explicated when events occur." Later information or insight may explicate previously puz-zling events or show that initial interpretation, though justified, was limited and should be expanded with additional meaning.
>
> *Changing meaning:* "The meaning of any experience can change over time. New information or an altered perspective can prompt us to reinterpret specific experiences or entire segments of our personal history."

61. Robinson, "Perspective," 200.
62. Robinson, "Perspective," 203.

> *Negotiating meaning:* As we have already noticed, the social context of remembering can significantly shape the way remembered events are understood.[63]

In his discussion of these categories Robinson veers between two poles. On the one hand, he recognizes that in the rememberer's search for meaning the rememberer is seeking an interpretation that best accounts for the objective character of what he or she has experienced. The quest for meaning does not take leave of the objectivity of the remembered past. On the other hand, Robinson insists that varying interpretations can be seen as equally authentic, to be categorized not as true or false but as authentically reflecting differences and changes in personal perspective, and so to be judged by the criterion of authenticity rather than accuracy. We need to hold on to both poles of this divergence. On the phenomenological level of how people understand what they are doing in interpretative remembering, they are concerned with adequacy to the event as well as with adequacy to their current beliefs, values, and goals. This is why learning more about a key event can cause a radical revaluation of it. Meanings remain stable, take on additional dimensions or change by the discarding of previous understanding and its replacement with new insight. The adequacy of interpretation to the event itself may increase or decrease according to the way in which perspectival factors operate. This is why people can differ or argue about the significance of events by discussing the event itself rather than or as well as their interpretative categories.

If information and meaning come together in remembering, so do past and present. Indeed, this is the defining characteristic of memory. It straddles past and present in such a way that the past influences the present at the same time as the present affects the way in which the past is recalled. As with information and meaning, both poles of this dialectic need to be kept in view. Those who recall the past really do intend to recall the past, not to create it to suit present needs and purposes. At the same time memories are recalled in order to be put to use in the present. As Bartlett put it in his *Encyclopaedia Britannica* article on memory,

> The critical questions [remain] as they have been ever since remembering began to be investigated: how to understand and reconcile the conflicting demands for the accurate and literal reinstatement of events and experiences at the time when they "go into storage," and the equally urgent requirement that when they come "out of storage," it should be in forms

63. Robinson, "Perspective," 200-203.

sufficiently flexible to meet the challenges of a constantly changing world.[64]

It is interesting to note how close Bartlett comes here to the philosopher Paul Ricoeur, who speaks of "the task of showing how the epistemic, *veridical* dimension of memory is united with the *practical* dimension tied to the idea of the *exercise* of memory."[65] From the perspective of a phenomenology of memory, Ricoeur, very conscious of the way in which the present affects the way the past is recalled, nevertheless insists that memory intends to speak of the past and is engaged in a search for truth. This is what differentiates memory from imagination:

> in spite of the traps that imagination lays for memory, it can be affirmed that a specific search for truth is implied in the intending of the past "thing," of *what* was formerly seen, heard, experienced, learned. This search for truth determines memory as a cognitive issue.[66]

Remembering Jesus

We have sketched some of the arguments and findings of psychology that have relevance for our interest in the eyewitness memories behind the Gospels. In turning to the gospel narratives, we shall begin by taking up our list of nine factors that are important in relation to the reliability of memories.

(1) *Unique or unusual event.* It is easy to see that most of the gospel narratives recount events that we would ordinarily regard as "memorable" because of their often unique, often unusual, often surprising characteristics. Nothing is ordinary or trivial. There are some kinds of events that, although unusual from a general point of view, evidently recurred often in Jesus' ministry: healings and exorcisms. Most of the stories of these have their own very distinctive features that would have made them memorable as single events even for disciples who witnessed many such healings and exorcisms. Such disciples would also have had generic personal memories of these kinds of events, and these could have influenced their memories of specific cases. In one or two cases a narrative is so short on differentiating features that it may be a case of a

64. F. C. Bartlett, quoted in J. A. Robinson, "Autobiographical Memory: A Historical Prologue," in Rubin, ed., *Autobiographical Memory*, 23.

65. P. Ricoeur, *Memory, History, Forgetting* (tr. K. Blamey and D. Pellauer; Chicago: University of Chicago Press, 2004) 55.

66. Ricoeur, *Memory*, 55.

story constructed almost entirely from generic memory (Mark 1:23-28; Matt 9:27-31). For the most part these narratives have specific features that are central, not merely peripheral, making them memorable as specific events.

(2) *Salient or consequential event.* Similarly, it is easy to see that most of the gospel narratives would be memorable to the eyewitnesses for this reason too: they would have been of huge personal (and group) significance, among the most memorable events of their lives, in many cases perhaps *the* most memorable events of their lives. They were the landmark events that stood out among all their memories.

(3) *An event in which a person is emotionally involved.* The gospel eyewitnesses, as we have often stressed in this book, were not detached observers but participants, close to the action even when not among the actors, deeply affected by the events. The eyewitnesses' emotions at the time are only rarely mentioned (e.g., Mark 9:6; 14:72 — in both these cases Peter's), and so the question of the accuracy of the memory of the emotion itself hardly arises. The proposal that emotion promotes a strong visual memory of central features of the event at the expense of peripheral detail is reasonably compatible with the gospel narratives, in which peripheral detail is in any case scarce.

(4) *Vivid imagery.* Most gospel narratives have little in the way of vivid visual imagery. Where it is found, this is particularly characteristic of Mark, and it is significant that in Matthean and Lukan parallels to this material the vivid imagery is usually not present (e.g., Mark 2:4;[67] 4:37-38; 6:39-40; 7:33-34; 9:20; 10:32, 50; 11:4). The reason is that Matthew and Luke tell these stories much more concisely than Mark does (Matthew generally more so than Luke). Vivid detail is among the features that have to be dropped to make space for all the non-Markan material that both Matthew and Luke include in their Gospels. This is a simple matter of space, since both were attempting a much more comprehensive collection of Jesus traditions than Mark's, but needed to keep within the limit of the ordinary size of a papyrus scroll if their books were not to be prohibitively expensive to copy and use. At the same time their short narratives were presumably still within the range of possible variation in oral performances. This raises the question whether oral performances of these stories might often have been longer, with more vivid detail, than even Mark's written performances of them.[68] John's narratives are lon-

67. In this case, Matthew omits the whole incident of letting the man down through the roof, but Luke (5:19) has replaced Mark's Palestinian detail (the clay roof of a house in Capernaum) with a presumably more familiar tiled roof.

68. The discussion of "smaller story units" within the narratives of the Hebrew Bible, by A. F. Campbell, "The Storyteller's Role: Reported Story and Biblical Text," *CBQ* 64 (2002) 427-41, is very suggestive for study of the Gospels.

ger than typical Synoptic pericopes, but vivid detail is less common than in Mark (e.g., 9:6; 11:44; 13:5; 18:18; 20:6-7, 12). Typically Johannine narratives, skillfully told though they are, focus more on conversation than on visual detail. Of course, the vivid detail in Mark can scarcely be used as evidence of Mark's closeness to eyewitness testimony, since a good storyteller (whether Mark or his oral source) can create vivid detail, and details not essential to a story are likely to be performative variations.[69]

(5) *Irrelevant detail.* There is little irrelevant detail in the gospel narratives. Most details are significant for narrative or theological reasons. It is true that Gospels scholars have a deep-rooted desire to explain all detail as significant, and so it may be that on occasions where their explanations are disputed or implausible we should more willingly accept that some details are irrelevant survivals of eyewitness memory. Sometimes, such as in regard to the "other boats" in Mark 4:36, scholars resort to considering the detail to be a remnant of an earlier form of the story in which it did have significance.[70] But if Mark could retain a detail that was not significant for his own narrative purpose, he could just as easily have retained it from eyewitness memory as from a version of the story in which it was significant. But the general absence of such details is not evidence against eyewitness provenance. It rather indicates that these stories have already been honed for ease of remembering. The eyewitnesses themselves would surely have pruned irrelevant detail from their own stories when they formulated them in manageable units of tradition that could be passed on to others.

(6) *Point of view.* As we have noted, people remembering events can readily switch point of view in the way they tell the story. We should not expect a consistently participant point of view in gospel stories that the eyewitnesses have formulated for communication and handing on and that the Gospel writers have naturally adapted to their overall narrative composition. In fact, point of view shifts frequently in the gospel narratives. In chapter 7 we observed a special phenomenon in the Gospel of Mark that does seem to be the Gospel writer's way of preserving the participant perspective of the disciples, more precisely of Peter within the group of the disciples. But we should stress at this point that the lack of such a phenomenon in other cases is no ev-

69. Cf. R. T. France, *The Gospel of Mark* (NIGTC; Grand Rapids: Eerdmans, 2002) 17-18.
70. R. A. Guelich, *Mark 1–8:26* (WBC 34A; Dallas: Word, 1989) 265 (citing G. Schille). But V. Taylor, *The Gospel according to St. Mark* (London: Macmillan, 1952) 274, writes: "This detail, so unnecessary to the story, is probably a genuine reminiscence," and France, *The Gospel of Mark,* 223, agrees: "It is hard . . . to see any other reason for their inclusion beyond the circumstantial reminiscence on the part of whoever told the story (Peter?) that as a matter of fact their boat was not alone on the lake that evening."

idence that eyewitness testimony does not lie behind gospel narratives. Eyewitnesses themselves may tell their stories from an observer point of view even though they participated in the events.

(7) *Dating.* Recollective memories rarely include datings (as distinct from temporal indications such as the time of day that may be integral to the recollection) since dates are not usually intrinsic to events as experienced. In the Synoptic Gospels, whereas the narratives are quite often localized, the Evangelists evidently did not know at what point in Jesus' ministry most of their narratives occurred, with the exception of those necessarily attached to its beginning or end. Significantly, the greater chronological precision in John's Gospel hinges on the relationship of events to the Jewish festivals. While this issue deserves further study, it is relatively easy to see that the chronological data in the Gospels fit the phenomena of recollective memory, in which memories would include indications of dating (whether absolute or relative to other remembered events) only for specific reasons.

(8) *Gist and details.* A distinction between "gist" and details may be somewhat misleading. Some details are the way in which the gist of the memory is perceived and recalled. It would be better to distinguish between details essential to the gist of the story and inessential details. For example, in the narrative of the feeding of the five thousand (Matt 14:13-21; Mark 6:32-44; Luke 9:10-17; John 6:1-15), it seems clear that some numerical details (five loaves, two fish, five thousand men) are treated as essential to the story. All four versions emphasize them. The story is unlikely ever to have been told in more general terms, referring merely to a little food and a lot of people. Such details as the *five* loaves, the *two* fish, and the *five* thousand men are memorable and would have been essential to the story as it was formulated and transmitted by the eyewitnesses and therefore also as it was transmitted subsequently by others, including the Gospel writers. In this particular case they are what make the story of the feeding of the five thousand *a different story* from that of the feeding of the *four* thousand from *seven* loaves and a few fish (Matt 15:32-39; Mark 8:1-10) and suggest that we should not regard these two stories as variants of a single story but as stories which, from their first tellings, were distinguished by different details.[71]

A good example of the consistency of the gist along with variation in inessential detail is the story of Peter's three denials of Jesus as told in all four Gospels (Matt 26:58, 69-75; Mark 14:54, 66-72; Luke 22:54-62; John 18:15-18, 25-27). The consistent points across all four versions are that Peter sat with others around the fire in the courtyard of the high priest's residence, that three

71. France, *The Gospel of Mark*, 306-7.

times he was asked whether he was one of Jesus' disciples, the first time by a maid, and that after his third denial the cock crowed. All other details, including the identity of the second and third questioners and the actual words of their questions and Peter's answers, vary. Since it is probable that Mark's account was known to the other three Evangelists, whether or not their variations from Mark are due entirely to redaction or also to independent versions of the story, it seems likely that they regarded the degree of variation in detail that they exhibit as justified in different performances of the tradition. The "gist" of the story that they all preserve conveys the common significance of the story in all their versions. It is this that would have been consistent in Peter's own telling of the story on various occasions. It is what he would certainly have remembered and would have taken the trouble to remember accurately. Whether he himself varied other details or whether this was done only by others who subsequently performed the oral tradition he transmitted to them is of no great importance. Some of the additional details may be accurate reminiscences of Peter, but were not treated as essential to the story.

In such examples we can see that the gist of an eyewitness memory, preserved in all tellings even if other details are not accurately preserved, and the gist of an oral tradition, preserved in all performances even when other details are varied, can readily coincide. This is a most important conclusion for the study of gospel traditions. It is a conclusion that recognizes the realistic extent to which memory can be relied upon, in the case both of the memory of the eyewitness and of the memory of the performer of oral tradition. The transition from the one to the other need not entail a significant decrease in reliability, though of course this is possible.

(9) *Frequent rehearsal.* This aspect is crucial for any assessment of the likely reliability of the eyewitness testimony of the Gospels. In the first place, we can be sure that the eyewitnesses of events in the history of Jesus would have first told their stories very soon after the event. After a healing or exorcism, for example, the recipient of the miracle would be telling the story to friends and neighbors (as the Gospels themselves indicate) — after all, this is how Jesus became well-known throughout Palestine as a miracle worker — but Jesus' disciples who had been present would also be telling the story to other disciples. They would certainly have gone on doing so. The nature of such reporting indicates that an eyewitness's story would acquire a fairly fixed form quite soon. Some key words of Jesus might be remembered precisely, and the story line or structure would be stabilized. It would have been in such stereotyped forms that the stories of the eyewitnesses would also have become, through a natural process of sharing memories within groups of disciples, part of a store of shared memories among those closest to Jesus. As a

345

general rule, frequent rehearsal would have the effect of preserving an eyewitness's story very much as he or she first remembered and reported it. Of course, we cannot exclude the universal human tendency to "improve" or embellish a good story, but we can exclude the frailties and distortions of memory to a large extent.

The eyewitnesses who remembered the events of the history of Jesus were remembering inherently very memorable events, unusual events that would have impressed themselves on the memory, events of key significance for those who remembered them, landmark or life-changing events for them in many cases, and their memories would have been reinforced and stabilized by frequent rehearsal, beginning soon after the event. They did not need to remember — and the Gospels rarely record — merely peripheral aspects of the scene or the event, the aspects of recollective memory that are least reliable. Such details may often have been subject to performative variation in the eyewitnesses' tellings of their stories, but the central features of the memory, those that constituted its meaning for those who witnessed and attested it, are likely to have been preserved reliably. We may conclude that the memories of eyewitnesses of the history of Jesus score highly by the criteria for likely reliability that have been established by the psychological study of recollective memory.

Schematization, Narrativization, and Meaning

We have seen that all recollective memory employs schemata of various kinds, among which, in memories of events, story schemata or scripts are naturally of key significance. Already in the process of perceiving events and recording the data in memory, however exactly this happens, such story scripts are being deployed. They assist the selective and meaning-making process that is essential to experiencing and remembering events. Story scripts are no doubt especially operative in the processes of retrieving and telling memories. They are part of the "reconstructive" process that is by no means necessarily a distorting or fabrication of the events, but the way in which meaningful recollective representations of events are possible. We have also noticed that a social dimension to the operation of story scripts and other schemata is present at all stages. Those that are not simply necessary structures of all human thought have been socially acquired. Even in private recollection we tell stories structured by socially derived schemata. But, in addition, most recollection is at the same time communication. Memories must be told in forms corresponding to socially available schemata if those who tell their memories are to be successful in communicating with others. We have noted also that this formation of memories according to already existing schemata should not be construed too rigidly. Story scripts are infinitely flexible. Because the point of telling a memory is often precisely its very particular, even very surprising or unique, content, story scripts function to frame such particularity in a way that effectively communicates it. Moreover, particular stories often work by transgressing the expectations set up by a well-recognized schema. Schemata may be adapted so that new story scripts become available in a social context in which they have become necessary or desirable, whether through the need to recount some kind of event not adequately served by existing scripts or through the interpretative needs of the search for meaning in events. The formation of fresh schemata in this way may well begin with the eyewitnesses who struggle, in recalling and communicating memories, to do justice to their experiences.

All this was neglected by the form critics, who, in their intensive focus on the forms in which the gospel narratives (and sayings) are cast, took it for granted that such forms must have evolved in the process of the Christian communities' development of the material for community use. This is the point at which we need to engage the critique leveled by Dennis Nineham, in the name of form criticism, against the possibility of any significant involvement of the eyewitnesses in the formation of the Gospel traditions other than at the very beginning. In a series of three articles published in 1958 and 1960,[72] Nineham argued that, whereas the case for the involvement of the eyewitnesses, as made, for example, by Vincent Taylor, was an a priori argument from what one would expect to have happened, the case against such involvement was an a posteriori argument from the evidence of the Gospels themselves.[73] The form critics had demonstrated that the forms in which the Gospel traditions are cast were the result of a long process of development in community use. It is likely that these articles of Nineham were very influential, in British scholarship at least, in insuring the disappearance of the eyewitnesses from Gospels scholarship.

This is how Nineham stated his case at the outset:

72. D. E. Nineham, "Eye-Witness Testimony and the Gospel Tradition, I," *JTS* 9 (1958) 13-25; "Eye-Witness Testimony and the Gospel Tradition, II," *JTS* 9 (1958) 243-52; "Eye-Witness Testimony and the Gospel Tradition, III," *JTS* 11 (1960) 253-64. These articles doubtless had an important part in Nineham's work that produced his commentary on Mark, in which he adopted a thoroughgoing form-critical approach: *The Gospel of St. Mark* (revised edition: London: Black, 1968; first published by Penguin, 1963).

73. Nineham, "Eye-Witness Testimony and the Gospel Tradition, I," 14-16.

According to the form-critics, eye-witnesses played little direct part in the *development* of the Gospel tradition, however much they may have had to do with its original formulation. The point is too well known to need elaboration, but it may be pointed out that this opinion is no accidental or peripheral feature of the form-critical position. For it is of the essence of the form-critical approach that it starts from the internal evidence of the gospels in their finished form; and the characteristics of the finished gospels to which it points as the key features for their proper understanding are precisely those which are incompatible with any theory of much direct eye-witness influence after the initial stage. The formal, stereotyped character of the separate sections, suggestive of long community use, the absence of particular, individual details such as would be irrelevant to community edification, the conventional character of the connecting summaries, all these point to a development which was controlled by the impersonal needs and forces of the community and not immediately by the personal recollections of the individual eye-witness. Indeed it would not be too much to say that it is the absence of the characteristics we should expect in eye-witness testimony — knowledge of the particular, inclusion of the merely memorable, as opposed to the edifying, exact biographical and topographical precision and the like — which forms the very foundation of the form-critical edifice. And so it is a basic article of belief [!] of the form-critic that the Gospel tradition owed the form in which it reached our evangelists almost entirely to community use and its demands, and hardly at all to direct intervention or modification on the part of the eye-witnesses.[74]

Because Nineham's competent account of the form-critical case puts so much weight on the claim that it is an a posteriori case, proceeding from the internal evidence of the Gospels themselves, it is important to point out that the case argued in this book is also based on internal evidence provided by features of the Gospels themselves (chapters 2-7). This evidence accounts for much of the novelty in the argument of this book, according to which the Gospels themselves indicate their closeness to the testimony of the eyewitnesses.

Much of Nineham's account of the proven conclusions of form criticism has already been addressed and refuted in chapters 10-12. That the forms of the pericopes in the Synoptic Gospels are the product of a long process of development in the communities and that the forms were governed, even created, by the requirements of community use in preaching and teaching and so forth are highly questionable contentions. They have, in fact, been abandoned

74. Nineham, "Eye-Witness Testimony and the Gospel Tradition, I," 13.

in much Gospels scholarship, which no longer assumes that the forms can each be identified with specific community functions or that the development of each tradition can be traced according to laws of tradition and in accordance with the assumption that each tradition existed originally in pure form, rather than in the modified or mixed fashion that it has in the Gospels. We are left with this question: how did the traditions acquire the literary forms that can be distinguished in analysis of the Gospel pericopes? We should note that the forms are by no means as tidily distinguished and classified as the form critics proposed, but it remains the case that the form or structure of, for example, a miracle story can be analyzed and features common to such stories in the Gospels can be isolated and listed.[75]

In a 1981 article, "The Place of the Anecdote: A Note on Form Criticism,"[76] T. Francis Glasson provided a perceptive critique of the form-critical contention that, because stories in the Gospels can be classified as in various different forms, it follows that they are the product of a long process of oral development in which details not relevant to the use to which the community put the story have fallen away and the structure of the story streamlined to conform to a stereotyped form. Apart from some reference to the use of *chreiai* (anecdotes) in ancient biographies, Glasson's argument was largely from contemporary practice and experience, and this may account for the relatively little influence it seems to have had. But Glasson was really arguing (citing in support the Old Testament form-critical work of Old Testament scholars Hermann Gunkel and Klaus Koch) that all human utterances employ stereotyped forms that can be classified:

> [I]f it is true that we cannot speak or write without falling into some utterance which can be classified and identified as a particular Form, how fallacious it is to argue that, because the Gospel material can be classified into various Forms, this is an infallible sign of community transmission.[77]

Focusing on the "anecdote" (for which Glasson employed a very broad definition) as the form which so many gospel narratives take, Glasson argued that the "reduction" of such stories to essential features, without irrelevant details, is entirely to be expected, without the need to postulate lengthy oral

---

75. An excellent contribution to defining and analyzing Gospel miracle stories is G. Theissen, *The Miracle Stories of the Early Christian Tradition* (tr. F. McDonagh; Edinburgh: Clark, 1983).

76. T. F. Glasson, "The Place of the Anecdote: A Note on Form Criticism," *JTS* 32 (181) 142-50.

77. Glasson, "The Place of the Anecdote," 147.

development. Using the example of the apophthegm or pronouncement story, where the main interest lies in a striking saying of Jesus, Glasson points out that this "reduction" happens all the time in the telling of such stories today:

> Quite often the original "ear-witness" of today himself trims the story to its bare essentials; and at other times (a most important matter) the one who first writes it down, keeping an eye on his space, trims it. In neither case is there any question of the influence of community transmission or a long period of oral repetition.[78]

He offers an example:

> I have in my possession a letter from the famous conductor Sir Adrian Boult, which contains an anecdote from his own experience, a pronouncement story as we might call it. It begins: "I was once rehearsing and a chap in the wood-wind, who was known to enjoy his drinks a great deal, had a cough. . . ." It is unnecessary to give the story in full here. It consists of only four sentences and it will be noticed that no date is given, no indication of place, the man is not named, the piece of music is not specified, even the instrument the man was playing is not mentioned — not because these details have slowly dropped off in the course of decades of oral transmission, but because they are immaterial to the main point. . . . Yet Sir Adrian is reporting an incident at which he was present and in which he took part.[79]

Glasson's argument from common experience is important, because scholars rather easily lose touch with common experience when dealing in technicalities such as the classification of Gospel pericopes according to forms. But we can give it greater substance by appeal to the psychological studies of recollective memory we have studied. The structuring of stories according to "forms" occurs even before the eyewitness first tells his or her story. Such forms will be further honed in the eyewitness's telling of the memory over the course of the first few such rehearsals. This is a *rapid* process in the rehearsal of the story by the *individual* eyewitness (in a social context). In order to account for the forms, there is absolutely no need to postulate a long process of "impersonal" (Nineham's term) community tradition. In the eyewitness's own early rehearsals of the story a distinction would al-

78. Glasson, "The Place of the Anecdote," 145.
79. Glasson, "The Place of the Anecdote," 145.

ready have been made between, on the one hand, the features essential to the story and its point, and, on the other hand, inessential details that would be merely optional features serving the storytelling attractiveness of the story. A grasp of the gist of the story, essential to the meaning the eyewitness had found in the event, would be necessary for all communication of the story, whether by the eyewitness or as repeated by others.

The form critics never really addressed the question of where the forms came from, sometimes giving the impression that they were created in the course of community development of the traditions, but also citing parallels either from classical antiquity or from international folklore. The psychological notion of schemata should enable research into the extent to which gospel narratives use cross-cultural story scripts that recur wherever people tell stories, being more or less inherent in the nature of telling a story, or conform to more culturally specific story scripts. Studies of the forms that stories take in the work of known ancient authors recounting their own experiences are also needed to substantiate the point that the relatively stereotyped forms of the Gospel traditions could be those given them by their earliest, eyewitness tellers. The death of the form-critical paradigm, which has been slowly exhausting itself for several decades, should liberate Gospels scholars to pursue a whole field of research into narrative forms on the lines we have suggested.

Fact and Meaning, Past and Present

In the section with this title earlier in this chapter, we argued that recollective memories have two poles: the objectivity of the event and the rememberer's insight into its meaning. Without some perception of meaning (such as the way in which occurrences were causally related) there is unlikely to be a coherent memory that can be narrated, but at the same time, given that, experientially, to remember is to recall *the past*, events are not endlessly malleable to suit any interpretation. Depending on the use to which the memory is being put, people who recollect may be more or less concerned with accurate representation of what happened, but to some degree all recollection entails reference to the real past. Interpretation is therefore the search for meaning adequate to the event as well as conforming to the values and expectations of the person remembering and the audience. Interpretation of memories can change for various reasons — and the memory itself can thus be said to change — but this process of change should not be envisaged, as it is rather too often in Gospels studies, as one in which "objective facts", such as there are, are merely given at the beginning of the process, which then evolves by a process of interpretation away from these facts. The continuing process of interpretation, which may go on, in the eyewitness's thinking and telling, long after the event was first recollected, is, in part, a search for an interpretation adequate to the event as remembered. Information and interpretation interrelate for as long as the latter changes.

It is a familiar claim that the Gospel narratives are written in the light of their endings, that the Jesus whose story they tell is the risen and exalted Lord of the community. This is not in question, but just how this process of interpreting the past in the light of more recent events or experience took place already in the oral traditions, as told by the eyewitnesses, and in the composition of the Gospels requires far more detailed discussion than can be offered here. But the four factors we noted that John Robinson postulated as making for change or stability in recollective memories are relevant to that discussion. Perhaps especially important is the category of deferred meaning, according to which both later information or later reflection and insight may — without abolishing the meaning already recognized — expand that meaning. Events that are initially, to some extent, puzzling may come to make much more sense in this way.

One important factor in the first Christians' realization of such deferred meaning in the events they had themselves, in many cases, experienced, was certainly the study of the Scriptures in the light of the realization, via the resurrection and exaltation of Jesus, of who he was within the purpose of God already outlined and promised by the prophets. John's Gospel makes this quite explicit:

Jesus found a young donkey and sat on it; as it is written:

Do not be afraid, daughter of Zion.
Look, your king is coming, sitting on a donkey's colt! [Zech 9:9]

His disciples did not understand these things at first; but when Jesus was glorified, then they remembered that these things had been written of him and had been done to him (John 12:14-16; cf. also 2:22; 7:37-39; 20:9).

As well as such reference to the scriptural insights brought to bear on their memories by the disciples only after Jesus' resurrection, there are other explicit indications in the Gospel that the meaning of events in Jesus' ministry were and could be understood adequately only from this retrospective perspective. When Jesus washes the disciples' feet, he says, "You do not know now what I am doing, but later you will understand" (13:7; 16:25). It is ironic that these explicit examples of "deferred meaning" occur in the Gospel that is so commonly thought to have transfigured the earthly Jesus already with the glory of his exaltation.

It is no accident that the Johannine motif of misunderstanding especially focuses on the death of Jesus on a cross (e.g., 2:19-20; 8:21-28; 12:27-33; 13:26-30). The originally incomprehensible character of this end to Jesus' life is reflected also in the passion predictions and the graphic portrayal of the disciples' negative reactions to them in the Synoptics (Mark 8:31-33; 9:9-10, 31-32). The memories of the passion and death of Jesus must have been the most obstinately meaningless and at the same time the most unforgettable of the traditions, even in the light of the resurrection. It took scriptural interpretation, which is now woven into the passion narratives, to make these memories even tolerable, but also unexpectedly full of inexhaustible meaning.

In some respects it is remarkable how little subsequent interpretation many Synoptic narratives have received. Their context in the whole gospel story as each Gospel writer tells it provides them with more meaning than the individual pericope, abstracted from this context, would have. With reference to the stories of Jesus' healings and exorcisms, Gerd Theissen points out how the stories almost entirely lack eschatological interpretation as signs of the arrival of the kingdom of God. Theissen thinks that this was the meaning Jesus himself gave his miracles of exorcism and healing, but it is found, not in the miracle stories themselves, only in the sayings tradition (Matt 11:2-6, 20-24; 12:29; Mark 3:24-27; Luke 10:18). Theissen explains this by claiming that the miracle stories have undergone a "popular adaptation" in which the distinctive character of Jesus' miracles has been smoothed out. This in turn he explains by postulating that the miracle stories were formulated and handed down by ordinary people outside the circle of Jesus' followers.[80] It is doubtful whether this explanation is sufficient to justify the claim about "popular adaptation." That stories of Jesus' miracles would have circulated independently of the circles (plural!) of his disciples can hardly be doubted. But that all the miracle stories entered the stock of gospel traditions among the earliest Christians from such a source is unlikely. The disciples themselves are also bound to have told these stories from the beginning, and it is not plausible that their accounts are wholly unrepresented among the miracle stories of the Gospels. If there were two kinds of miracle stories, some with and some without the eschatological interpretation, Theissen's argument would be much more plausible. That the absence of such interpretation is universal in the traditions is much more easily explained by supposing that miracle stories as

80. Theissen, *Miracle Stories,* 276-86; G. Theissen and A. Merz, *The Historical Jesus* (tr. J. Bowden; London: SCM, 1998) 301-2.

such never contained within themselves the kind of interpretation Jesus himself gave to his healings and exorcisms. They were confined to telling the story in a fairly simple and memorable form, with no more interpretation than, in some cases, an emphasis on the need for the recipient's faith and/or a recognition of Jesus' unique authority to do such things.[81] But, if they were from early on told normally within the context of other Jesus traditions, they would not need to embody their own interpretation; the interpretation could be given by their context, as it is in the Gospels as we have them. We should not, as the form critics sometimes did, imagine that each Gospel story was designed to be used alone in preaching and to convey "the gospel in a nutshell."[82] There is no good reason why this should be the case.

The important conclusion for our present purposes is that the stories of Jesus' healings and exorcisms have been little affected by the way Jesus himself interpreted these events in his teaching or by the way that similar interpretation of them was current in early Christian circles. The stories themselves preserve the more simply meaningful character of the first reports and are given more meaning by the context of other Gospel traditions that were told alongside them.

In considering the conjunction of information and meaning in the Gospel narratives we have also dealt with the conjunction of past and future. In understanding recollective memories, we need to retain the dialectic of past and future that is always at work in such memories. Memory as such makes reference to the real past, and it is impossible to imagine a self-conscious activity of memory that would not embody an intentional reference to the past. We have already, in the previous chapter, adduced evidence for the importance of the history of Jesus as genuinely past events for the early Christians. In the memories of the eyewitnesses the past and present were surely in constant interaction. But the present should not be conceived here primarily as the *community use* to which the traditions were put. As we have argued in chapters 10-12, the traditions were preserved independently of their use, and each tradition may have been put to a variety of uses in Christian preaching and teaching. Nineham's conviction, along with the form critics in general, that the shape of the stories in the Gospels must have been given them through community use over a long period is not well founded in the evidence. Far more important than the use of the traditions in shaping them must have been the fresh light in which everything in Jesus' ministry

81. Cf. Theissen, *Miracle Stories*, 276-7.

82. Cf. S. H. Travis, "Form Criticism," in I. H. Marshall, ed., *New Testament Interpretation* (Grand Rapids: Eerdmans, 1977) 162.

had to be seen after the cross, the resurrection, and the growing understanding of these events. However, even this seems to have affected only to a small extent the way many of the stories were told. As Theissen and Merz put it,

> The "Easter gulf" has not transformed the traditions into an undifferentiated ahistorical whole. Pre-Easter recollections stubbornly persist. . . . Back-projections from the period after Easter are particularly concentrated on the person of Jesus and on giving meaning to his death. So they can be limited to particular points and be relativized by the demonstration of pre-Easter "relics" even in these spheres.[83]

This continuity of tradition before and after the resurrection was made possible by the eyewitnesses, who themselves saw their stories in a new light after the resurrection, but whose memories already had a degree of stability that severely limited the degree to which they were changed by further interpretative insight. We return to a point made earlier: that the stereotypical form of each tradition would already have been relatively fixed in the eyewitness's memory after only a short period of frequent rehearsal. The relatively small extent to which the stories have been affected by post-resurrection interpretation has to be explained by the probability that it was the stories in the fairly fixed form already given them by the eyewitnesses during Jesus' ministry that survived the revolution in understanding consequent on the cross and the resurrection. The eyewitnesses were still around. They remained the authoritative source of their traditions. And the impact of the past itself, along with a conviction that the past history of Jesus mattered as past event, gave stability to their memories long after the crucial theological developments that took place in the earliest Christian circles.

A Note on Eyewitness Testimony in Court

Psychologists studying recollective memory have, for obvious reasons, given much attention to the use of eyewitness testimony in legal processes.[84] Juries

83. Theissen and Merz, *The Historical Jesus*, 100.

84. E.g., D. F. Ross, J. D. Read, and M. P. Toglia, eds., *Adult Eyewitness Testimony: Current Trends and Developments* (Cambridge: Cambridge University Press, 1994); W. A. Wagenaar, "Autobiographical Memory in Court," in Rubin, ed., *Remembering Our Past*, 180-96; P. B. Ainsworth, *Psychology, Law and Eyewitness Testimony* (Chichester: Wiley, 1998). There is a trenchant critique of psychological work on eyewitness testimony by a philosopher: C. A. J. Coady, *Testimony: A Philosophical Study* (Oxford: Clarendon, 1992) chapter 15, though it should be noted that he refers to no studies subsequent to 1984. For critique see also the brief but penetrating remarks of Ricoeur, *Memory*, 162.

tend to attach great importance to eyewitness testimonies and to assume that they are accurate. Psychologists have been concerned to point out that this cannot be assumed, that there are various ways in which eyewitness testimony can be mistaken, and to recommend ways in which interviewing procedures, identification parades, and the assessment of eyewitness testimony can be improved.

An important problem for the use of eyewitness testimony in court is that, as we have noticed, recollection is usually accurate as far as the central features of an event are concerned but often unreliable in remembering peripheral details. But it is often precisely the latter that a court needs: exact words of a statement made long ago, exact times of day, voice recognition of a person met only once, faces of people merely glimpsed fleetingly. Witnesses may have been wholly uninvolved bystanders who had no reason to notice or remember the details required. The effect of fear on victims may be to narrow their attention to the focus of fear, which is vividly remembered, while at the same time excluding peripheral matters from observation and recall. Interviewing techniques, especially leading questions, may serve to feed information to witnesses who come to think they remember it.

But these aspects of testimony in court that have led psychologists to question its accuracy in significant respects bear scarcely at all on the kind of eyewitness testimony with which we are concerned in the Gospels. The witnesses in these cases were not mere uninvolved bystanders, but participants in the events. What their testimonies needed to convey were not peripheral details but the central gist of the events they recalled. They were not required to recall faces (so important in modern legal trials), nor were they pressed to remember what did not come easily to mind.

It is worth quoting again Alan Baddeley's assessment:

> [M]uch of our autobiographical recollection of the past is reasonably free of error, provided that we stick to remembering the broad outline of events. Errors begin to occur once we try to force ourselves to come up with detailed information from an inadequate base. This gives full rein to various sources of distortion, including that of prior expectations, disruption by misleading questions, and by social factors such as the desire to please the questioner, and to present ourselves in a good light.[85]

The eyewitnesses behind the Gospel accounts surely told what was prominent in their memories and did not need to attempt the laborious processes of retrieval and reconstruction that make for false memories.

85. Baddeley, *Human Memory*, 222.

Finally, since some psychological studies of memory give the impression that it is radically unreliable, the way that Gillian Cohen sums up her survey of the whole subject is also worth quoting:

> Research has tended to emphasize the errors that occur in everyday memory functions. The picture that emerges is of an error-prone system. This emphasis is partly an artefact of research methodology. In experiments it is usually more informative to set task difficulty at a level where people make errors so that the nature of the errors and the conditions that provoke them can be identified. . . . People do make plenty of naturally occurring errors in ordinary life situations, but, arguably, the methodology has produced a somewhat distorted view of memory efficiency. In daily life, memory successes are the norm and memory failures are the exception. People also exhibit remarkable feats of remembering faces and voices from the remote past, and foreign-language vocabulary and childhood experiences over a lifetime. As well as such examples of retention over very long periods, people can retain large amounts of information over shorter periods, as when they prepare for examinations, and sometimes, as in the case of expert knowledge, they acquire a large amount of information and retain it for an indefinitely long time. Considering how grossly it is overloaded, memory in the real world proves remarkably efficient and resilient.[86]

86. G. Cohen, *Memory*, 222. I am grateful to Malcolm Jeeves for his careful reading of this chapter and his expert comments.

14. The Gospel of John as Eyewitness Testimony

The Beloved Disciple "Wrote These Things"

One of the Gospels claims not only to be based on eyewitness accounts but to have been actually written by an eyewitness. These are the concluding verses of the Gospel of John:

> This is the disciple who is testifying to these things and has written them, and we know that his testimony is true. But there are also many other things that Jesus did; if every one of them were written down, I suppose that the world itself could not contain the books that would be written (21:24-25, NRSV).

The disciple in question is the disciple who appears as an anonymous figure at key points in the Gospel's narrative, usually described as "the disciple Jesus loved." Taken at face value, this conclusion to the Gospel seems to claim that this disciple wrote it. This was the traditional understanding of the words until the modern period. But most modern scholars have been reluctant to accept this claim. One rather popular way of evading it has been the suggestion that v. 24 does not really claim that the Beloved Disciple was the author of the Gospel. The language used need not mean actual authorship but may point to a rather less direct relationship between the Beloved Disciple and the Gospel.

This argument depends on the notion that the Greek verb *graphein* ("write") may be used here in a "causative" sense, meaning "to cause to write."

358

Then the disciple is not said to have written "these things," but to have "caused them to be written." The only evidence that has ever been presented for this sense of the verb was given by J. H. Bernard in his commentary of 1928.[1] All other commentators who adopt this idea appear to depend solely on Bernard's evidence, directly or indirectly. He cited only biblical evidence, essentially in two categories.[2] The first, appealing to the usage of the Gospel of John itself, refers to 19:19 (cf. 21-22), according to which (translating the Greek literally) "Pilate wrote an inscription and put it on the cross." It is reasonable to suppose, as Bernard does, that this "means Pilate was responsible for the wording of the *titulus,* but hardly that he wrote himself on the wooden board." The second category of Bernard's evidence relates to the Pauline letters. Paul seems usually to have dictated his letters to a scribe (Rom 16:22; cf. Gal 6:11; 1 Pet 5:12), and yet can say "I am writing" (Rom 15:15; 1 Cor 4:14; 5:9; 9:15; 14:37).[3]

What this evidence proves is that *graphein* can refer to authorship by dictation to a scribe. Many ancient authors did not themselves wield the pen when they composed their writings, for writing was a craft better left to those who had been trained to do it well. However, we should be clear that in this slightly extended sense of *graphein* the author dictates the words. While Pilate probably did not write the inscription on the cross with his own hands, John's narrative makes it completely unambiguous that he dictated the precise words used (cf. 19:21-22). Of course, it is also true that an ancient writer, like modern writers, might receive assistance with his work but not consider himself any less its author. A scribe taking dictation of works such as Paul's letters might exercise discretion in minor grammatical or stylistic matters, just as a modern secretary taking dictation or a publisher's copy-editor preparing an author's text for publication might do. We know that the Jewish historian Josephus, for example, employed secretaries to improve his Greek style. But in such cases the author reads, approves, and takes responsibility for the final text. It is not that the author has merely caused the work to be written, but that he or she has been assisted in writing his or her own work. This kind of assistance does not require a special "causative" sense of "to write."

Many scholars, from Bernard himself onward, have taken the evidence that *graphein* could refer to writing by dictation as a warrant for interpreting

---

1. J. H. Bernard, *A Critical and Exegetical Commentary on the Gospel according to St. John,* vol. 2, ed. A. H. McNeile (ICC; Edinburgh; Clark, 1928) 713.

2. He also refers to Judges 8:14 LXX, where the A text more appropriately reads *apegrapsato.*

3. Bernard himself does not give the references to 1 Corinthians, and it is not impossible that Paul wrote 1 Corinthians with his own hand.

John 21:24 as attributing to the Beloved Disciple a relationship to the Gospel considerably less direct than Pilate's to the inscription on the cross or Paul's to his letters. Bernard's own position is moderate: "the Beloved Disciple *caused these things to be written.* They were put into shape by the writer who took them down, and afterwards published them, not as his own, but as 'the Gospel according to John.'"[4] It is not very clear what this "putting into shape" is supposed to have involved, but other scholars have stretched it a long way. Writing in the hugely influential *Theological Dictionary of the New Testament,* Gottlob Schrenk first cited the Pauline evidence that *graphein* can refer to dictation and then continued:

> In the light of this incontrovertible fact it may be asked whether the *ho grapsas tauta* ["who has written these things"] of Jn. 21:24 might not simply mean that the beloved disciple and his recollections stand behind this Gospel and are the occasion of its writing. This is a very possible view so long as we do not weaken unduly the second aspect. Indeed, it would be difficult to press the formula to imply other than an assertion of spiritual responsibility for what is contained in the book.[5]

The progression of thought in these three sentences is breathtaking. Somehow Schrenk finds it possible to move from the "incontrovertible fact" that *graphein* can refer to dictation to claiming "it would be difficult to press the formula" to mean more than that the Beloved Disciple had "spiritual responsibility for what is contained in the book." Not a single example is given of the use of *graphein* to assert no more than "spiritual responsibility" for the content of a book. No evidence at all is added to the Pauline evidence that *graphein* can refer to authorship by dictation.

What is even more remarkable is the way in which this staggeringly faulty piece of argument has been uncritically followed by scholar after scholar. One of the great Johannine scholars of the later twentieth century, Raymond Brown, in his commentary on the Gospel, first cites Montgomery Hitchcock, who, in an article of 1930 that has been largely ignored, completely refuted Bernard's case, though he went too far in denying that *graphein* can even refer to authorship by dictation.[6] Brown then cites Bernard himself as suggesting what he calls a "moderate causative sense" for *graphein* in John

4. Bernard, *A Critical and Exegetical Commentary,* 713.

5. G. Schrenk in G. Kittel, ed., *Theological Dictionary of the New Testament,* vol. 1 (tr. G. W. Bromiley; Grand Rapids: Eerdmans, 1964) 743. The German original was published in 1933.

6. F. R. M. Hitchcock, "The Use of γράφειν," *JTS* 31 (1930) 271-75.

21:24. Finally, Brown states that "others think that 'wrote' can include author-ship in a much more remote sense," and cites Schrenk's three sentences as we have quoted them above. He then simply notes that he follows Schrenk's in-terpretation,[7] later putting it in his own words: "has written them" in John 21:24 "means no more than the claim that the beloved Disciple is the one who has borne the witness echoed in the written Gospel."[8] Brown offers not a shred of argument or evidence for preferring Schrenk's view to Hitchcock's or Bernard's.

It must be stressed that no one has yet produced any evidence that *graphein* can be used to refer to a relationship between "author" and text more remote than that of the dictation of a text to a scribe. No one seems even to have looked for such evidence. Yet the notion that John 21:24 asserts no more than that the Beloved Disciple's witness lies somewhere at the source of the tradition that later, in other very creative hands, produced the Gospel, has become common.[9] Scholar after scholar has evidently found it sufficient that previous Johannine scholars have found this view credible despite the lack of linguistic evidence. This must be because they have found it so hugely improbable that the Beloved Disciple could himself be the author of the Gos-pel that they have grasped like a dying man at the straw of possibility that 21:24 does not say that he was. But whatever reasons a scholar might have to doubt that the Beloved Disciple wrote the Gospel, these cannot serve, in the absence of linguistic evidence, to determine *the meaning of the words* "has written them" in John 21:24. Only evidence of linguistic usage can do that.

Kevin Vanhoozer, who approaches this issue as an expert in hermeneu-tics, is worth hearing at this point. Having cited the views of scholars such as Schrenk and Brown, he asks:

> Does it make sense to say that it is the Beloved Disciple "who has written" or even "had these things written" if he is only a source? And even if he were the prime or only source, can we really say, with Schrenk, that the

---

7. R. E. Brown, *The Gospel according to John XIII–XXI* (AB 29A; New York: Doubleday, 1966) 1122.

8. Brown, *The Gospel according to John XIII–XXI*, 1127. In R. E. Brown, *An Introduction to the Gospel of John* (ed. F. J. Moloney; New York: Doubleday, 2003) 194, he states that he considers the "causative" interpretation of *ho grapsas* "possible." It "would imply that the B[eloved] D[isciple] and his recollections stand behind the Gospel and enabled its writing."

9. E.g., G. R. Beasley-Murray, *John* (WBC 36; Waco: Word, 1987) 415; J. H. Charlesworth, *The Beloved Disciple* (Valley Forge: Trinity, 1995) 24-26, 46; F. J. Moloney, *The Gospel of John* (Sacra Pagina 4; Collegeville: Liturgical, 1998) 561; D. M. Smith, *John* (Abingdon NT Commen-taries; Nashville: Abingdon, 1999) 399-400; A. T. Lincoln, *Truth on Trial* (Peabody: Hendrickson, 2000) 153.

Beloved Disciple is "spiritually responsible" for the contents of the Gospel? Is this not a bit like saying that Paganini was "responsible" for Rachmaninov's variations and modifications of his theme? Surely the mind and spirit behind "Rhapsody on a Theme of Paganini" is distinctly Rachmaninov's. Paganini did not author or compose the "Rhapsody," nor could he have.

Historical critics, in their zeal to solve one riddle about authorship, have created a new one: how can a distant source be responsible for a text over which he had no final control? . . . The Fourth Gospel . . . is a finely tuned work, dependent on subtleties of structure, irony and so forth to achieve its effect. It is difficult to see how the substance of the witness could be preserved if the beloved Disciple were not also responsible for its form. But if he is responsible for its form and substance, would he then not be the sole author?[10]

So far we have assumed, with the scholars to whom we have referred, that the "these things" of John 21:24 — to which the Beloved Disciple testifies and which he has written — are the contents of the Gospel. A few scholars have dissented from this view and supposed the reference to be either to ch. 21 alone or to a written source that the author of the Gospel used in composing the Gospel. These views would allow us to give the words "has written them" in 21:24 their natural sense without supposing that they claim the Beloved Disciple as author of the Gospel. But they are very improbable. Most scholars agree that vv. 24 and 25 belong together, and when they are read together it is impossible to read them as referring only to chapter 21. They are plainly a conclusion to the whole Gospel and "these things" must be the deeds of Jesus recounted throughout the Gospel. It also seems inadequate to take the sense in which the Beloved Disciple wrote them to be only that he wrote a source used by the author. Later we shall show that 20:30-31 and 21:24-25 form together a carefully composed two-stage conclusion to the Gospel. This requires that "written" has the same sense in both 20:30-31 and 21:24. In both cases it refers to the writing of "this book," not of a source.

John 21:24 means that the Beloved Disciple composed the Gospel, whether or not he wielded the pen. He could have received assistance of various kinds in the process of composition or his work could have been edited by someone else, but the statement requires that he was substantially responsible both for the content and for the words of the book. A scholar who has reason to find this claim incredible may, of course, take it to be factually in-

10. K. J. Vanhoozer, "The Hermeneutics of I-Witness Testimony," in idem, *First Theology* (Downers Grove: InterVarsity, 2002) 261-62.

correct. In that case, there are basically two alternative explanations of how this misleading claim came to be made in these closing verses of the Gospel. One is that 21:24-25 was added at a late stage in the process of the Gospel's composition by a redactor who mistakenly thought the Beloved Disciple was the author.[11] Alternatively, the real author of the Gospel has fictitiously attributed his work to the Beloved Disciple. In that case the Gospel is pseudepigraphal, whether the pseudepigraphy is understood as a fraudulent claim or as an acceptable literary device.

The possibility that the Gospel could be pseudepigraphal will be raised again and discussed in the next chapter. Here we must take up at once the possibility that 21:24-25 is a late addition to the Gospel and that therefore its evidence as to the authorship of the Gospel may well be quite unreliable. This issue is inseparable from the question of the original ending of the Gospel. A very large majority of modern scholars[12] have supposed that the Gospel originally ended at the end of chapter 20, since 20:30-31 reads, to these scholars, like a conclusion that appropriately brings the Gospel narrative to a close. It follows that chapter 21 is a kind of appendix added later, and, while 21:24-25 could have been an original part of this appendix, a tendency to think of the Gospel growing by redactional accretions has made many scholars think it likely that these verses are later than the rest of chapter 21. Some think that v. 24 was added on its own and v. 25 only subsequently. Against all such theories that deconstruct the final parts of the Gospel into a series of successive additions, I will argue that the Gospel was originally designed to end just as it does in the version we have and never existed without the claim about its authorship that 21:24 makes.

11. So B. Lindars, *The Gospel of John* (New Century Bible; London: Marshall, Morgan and Scott, 1972) 641; idem, *John* (NT Guides; Sheffield: Sheffield Academic, 1990) 22-23.

12. Exceptions include Bishop Cassian (Serge Besobrasoff), "John xxi," *NTS* 3 (1956-57) 132-36; H. Thyen, "Entwicklungen innerhalb der johanneischen Theologie und Kirche im Spiegel von Joh 21 und der Lieblingsjüngertexte des Evangeliums," in M. de Jonge, ed., *L'Évangile de Jean. Sources, rédaction, théologie* (BETL 44; Gembloux: Duculot/Leuven: Leuven University Press, 1977) 259-99; P. S. Minear, "The Original Functions of John 21," *JBL* 102 (1983) 85-98; D. A. Carson, *The Gospel according to John* (Grand Rapids: Eerdmans, 1991) 665-68; W. S. Vorster, "The Growth and Making of John 21," in F. van Segbroeck, C. M. Tuckett, G. van Belle, and J. Verheyden, eds., *The Four Gospels 1992*, vol. 3 (F. Neirynck Festschrift; Leuven: Leuven University Press/Peeters, 1992) 2207-21; T. L. Brodie, *The Gospel according to John: A Literary and Theological Commentary* (Oxford: Oxford University Press, 1993) 572-82; R. Bauckham, "The 153 Fish and the Unity of the Fourth Gospel," *Neotestamentica* 36 (2002) 77-88; C. S. Keener, *The Gospel of John: A Commentary*, vol. 2 (Peabody: Hendrickson, 2003) 1213, 1219-22; A. J. Köstenberger, *John* (Grand Rapids: Baker, 2004) 583-86. Others are listed in B. R. Gaventa, "The Archive of Excess: John 21 and the Problem of Narrative Closure," in R. A. Culpepper and C. C. Black, eds., *Exploring the Gospel of John* (D. M. Smith FS; Louisville: Westminster John Knox, 1996) 249-50 n. 8.

The End of the Gospel

The structure of the concluding parts of the Gospel is quite coherent: there is a narrative epilogue (21:1-23) framed by a conclusion divided into two carefully designed stages (20:30-31 and 21:24-25). One reason the conclusion comes in two stages is that they serve to fence off the narrative in ch. 21 from the main narrative of the Gospel, thus indicating its status as an epilogue. An epilogue, it should be noticed, is not the same as a subsequently added appendix. While being deliberately set apart from the main narrative, an epilogue may be fully part of the design of a work. In the case of this Gospel, the Epilogue balances the Prologue at the beginning of the Gospel (1:1-18). The Prologue sketches the prehistory to the Gospel's story, while the Epilogue foresees its posthistory. Just as the Prologue goes back in time to creation, so the Epilogue previews the future mission of the disciples, symbolized by the miraculous catch of fish, and focuses especially on the different roles that Peter and the Beloved Disciple are to play in it. The time projected by the Epilogue runs to the parousia (future coming) of Jesus. Its last words, in v. 23, are Jesus' words "until I come,"[13] corresponding at the other end of time to the first words of the prologue: "In the beginning" (1:1).

The correspondence between Prologue and Epilogue is confirmed by an element of numerical composition (of which this is one of many in the Gospel[14]). The prologue consists of 496 syllables, appropriately since 496 is both a triangular number[15] and a perfect number[16] and is also the numerical value of the Greek word *monogenēs* (meaning "only son" and used in 1:14, 18).[17] Odd though these considerations may seem to us, people in the New Testament period were fascinated by certain special sorts of numbers, including triangular and perfect numbers,[18] and were used to the idea that words had numerical values, which were easily calculated because all the letters of the Greek alphabet were also used as numerals. But the importance of the

---

13. Some manuscripts add "what is that to you?" *(ti pros se)*, as in v. 22, but this is probably not the original reading. Scribes would have added these words, drawing on v. 22, in order to complete the otherwise incomplete sentence at the end of v. 23.

14. I shall demonstrate this in work currently in progress.

15. It is the triangle of 31, i.e., the sum of all integers from 1 to 31.

16. I.e., it is equal to the sum of its divisors. 496 is third in the series of perfect numbers, following 6 and 28.

17. M. J. J. Menken, *Numerical Literary Techniques in John: The Fourth Evangelist's Use of Numbers of Words and Syllables* (NovTSup 55; Leiden: Brill, 1985) 21.

18. Menken, *Numerical Literary Techniques,* 27-29; R. Bauckham, *The Climax of Prophecy: Studies on the Book of Revelation* (Edinburgh: Clark, 1993) 390-93.

number 496 for our immediate purpose is that it links the Prologue and the Epilogue together. For, while the Prologue has 496 syllables, the Epilogue (a considerably longer passage) has 496 *words*. That the correspondence should be between the number of syllables in the Prologue and the number of words in the Epilogue is quite appropriate, because the Prologue is a poetic composition, in which one might expect the number of syllables to be important, whereas the Epilogue is a narrative. Further evidence of numerical composition can be found in the fact that the two stages of the conclusion to the Gospel (20:30-31 and 21:24-25), framing the epilogue, each consists of 43 words.[19] This provides an initial indication that they should be read together and in parallel.

We must compare in detail these two stages of the Gospel's conclusion. These are the texts:

> Now Jesus did many other signs in the presence of the disciples, which are not written in this book. But these are written so that you may believe that Jesus is the Messiah, the Son of God, and that through believing you may have life in his name (20:30-31, NRSV altered).

> This is the disciple who is testifying to these things and has written them, and we know that his testimony is true. But there are also many other things that Jesus did; if every one of them were written down, I suppose that the world itself could not contain the books that would be written (21:24-25, NRSV).

These two stages of the conclusion are parallel but not repetitive. At every point where they are parallel, the second stage of the conclusion takes the matter on a stage further from the first. For example, both parts of the conclusion speak of what is and is not written in this book. The first stage speaks of "many other *signs* that Jesus did" that are not included in the book, in addition to those signs that are narrated.[20] The second stage of the conclusion speaks more generally of "many other *things* that Jesus did" besides those that are included in the book, and develops the hyperbolic notion that the world itself could not contain the books that would be needed to record everything Jesus did (a standard historiographic topos[21]). This could less convincingly

19. This is pointed out by C. Savasta, "Gv 20,30-32 e 21,24-25: Una Doppia Finale?" *BeO* 43 (2001) 130. There are 43 words in 20:30-31 if the reading that omits "his" *(autou)* is preferred in 20:30.

20. For the meaning of "signs" in this verse, see the thorough study of G. Van Belle, "The Meaning of σημεῖα in Jn 20,30-31," *ETL* 74 (1998) 300-325.

21. For many examples, see Keener, *The Gospel of John*, vol. 2, 1241-42.

be said of the "signs." So the progression in the parallel statements is from signs in particular to deeds in general. In this Gospel's specific use of the term "signs," Jesus did many things that were not signs. For example, the miracle in ch. 21 is not a "sign," since it does not serve to reveal Jesus' glory and thus to enable belief in him, as the "signs" do (2:11; 20:31), but rather to symbolize the coming mission of the church. So the first stage of the conclusion accurately and appropriately indicates the end of the Gospel's narrative specifically of "signs" and with it the completion of the Gospel's main aim of enabling christological faith, while the second stage equally accurately and appropriately marks the end of the whole Gospel.

If we now turn to what the two stages of the conclusion say about the witness on which the Gospel is based, we will see that there is a carefully designed two-stage disclosure of the Beloved Disciple's role in the production of the Gospel. The first stage speaks generally of Jesus' disciples, the second stage of one disciple, the one Jesus loved. While the first stage of the conclusion does not use the term "witness," it implies it in speaking of signs Jesus did "in the presence of the disciples." The reader will naturally suppose that it is from the witness of these disciples that the Gospel's narratives of the signs are derived and may well recall 15:27, addressed to the disciples: "you also are to testify because you have been with me from the beginning." The second stage of the conclusion explicitly introduces the term "testify" and also specifies the Beloved Disciple in particular as the witness. The reason for the narrowing of focus from the witness of the disciples in general to, in the second stage, that of the Beloved Disciple in particular becomes apparent when we consider the next element of parallelism between the two stages. Both stages speak of the writing of the Gospel's narrative, but the first stage avoids revealing its author by using, twice, the passive voice: "are written." The second stage reveals that it was by the Beloved Disciple that they were written: "This is the disciple who is testifying to these things and has written them" (21:24). Why does the Gospel in this way withhold revealing its author until the very end? We shall return to this question in the next chapter.

Another way in which the two stages of the conclusion parallel each other is that both stages have a link with the Gospel's Prologue, helping to form an *inclusio* between the beginning and the end of the Gospel. The links are different in the two cases but also closely connected. In the first stage of the conclusion, the statement of purpose, "*so that you may believe* that Jesus is the Messiah, the Son of God," recalls the statement in the Prologue about John the Baptist, who "came for a witness to testify to the light, *so that all may believe* through him" (1:7). The second stage of the conclusion also recalls John the Baptist, since its use of "witness" language for the Beloved Disciple is paralleled in the Prologue by the "witness" language used of John in v. 15 as well as in vv. 7-8. The conclusion enables readers finally to see how it is that John the Baptist's witness could be "so that *all* may believe through him." Incorporated in the Beloved Disciple's testimony and written, it continues to witness to all who read the Gospel, just as the Beloved Disciple himself does. So the Beloved Disciple's present-tense testifying (*is* testifying) in 21:24 is matched by John the Baptist's present-tense testifying (he *testifies*) in 1:15.

Next we must consider the way in which each of the two stages of the conclusion relates to its context. In the case of the first stage this involves both what precedes and what follows. What precedes is the story of Jesus' appearance to Thomas, climaxing in his christological confession, the only fully adequate one on the lips of a character in the Gospel. Jesus then says: "Have you believed because you have seen me? Blessed are those who have not seen and yet have come to believe" (20:29). The first stage of the conclusion builds on this by explaining how it is that those who have not seen, such as readers of the Gospel, are to come to believe. This will be possible because the testimony of those who have seen, the disciples who were present when the signs occurred, has been written "in this book," which therefore mediates between those who did see and those who do not, making it possible for the latter to believe on the strength of the testimony of the disciples. Appropriately, the Epilogue (21:1-23) then follows, previewing symbolically the church's mission, which is how the witness of the disciples will enable many to believe and to have life.

The Epilogue compares and contrasts the roles of Peter and the Beloved Disciple, first in the event of the miraculous catch of fish, then in Jesus' conversation with Peter. The Beloved Disciple, with his "It is the Lord!" (21:7), appears in the role of witness, identifying Jesus, while Peter, hauling in the net (21:11), takes the more active role in mission. In his conversation with Jesus, we then learn that Peter will have the active role of the shepherd who tends the flock and will die for it (21:15-19). The contrasting destiny of the Beloved Disciple, on the other hand, is conveyed more cryptically in Jesus' saying, "If I will that he remain until I come . . ." (21:22, 23). This saying is not quoted and discussed solely for the rather banal purpose of correcting the way it had been over-literally misunderstood (21:23). The Beloved Disciple's own Gospel does not end with the anticlimactic revelation that, contrary to expectations, he is going to die. Rather this saying of Jesus is given a characteristically Johannine level of hidden meaning, and this becomes clear in the second stage of the conclusion, which immediately follows (21:24-25). While the Beloved Disciple may not personally survive to the parousia, he will continue to fulfill the purpose Jesus has given him until the parousia because, as the conclusion says, that role is to witness and, moreover, he has written his witness and so his witness remains.[22] Thus the Gospel withholds the revelation that the Beloved Disciple wrote the Gospel until this can be shown to be the hidden meaning of a cryptic saying of Jesus. This particular disciple's writing of a Gospel is finally authorized by the explanation that he did so in fulfillment of the role that Jesus himself assigned him.

At the second stage of the conclusion, if not at the first, readers will recall the only previous verse in the Gospel that spoke of *one specific witness* to an event in the Gospel story: "He who saw this has testified so that you also may believe. His testimony is true and he knows that he tells the truth" (19:35). This statement anticipates both stages of the conclusion: "so that you also may believe" anticipates the first stage, both verbally and conceptually, while what is said about this person's testimony and its truth corresponds closely to the second stage. We should notice, however, what is carefully withheld here, to be revealed only in the Gospel's conclusion. The witness is not said to have written his testimony, nor is it clear who the witness is. Readers divide between those who think this must be the Beloved Disciple, because the latter appeared at the cross, with no other male disciples, several verses previously (19:26-27), and those who think this cannot be the Beloved Disciple, because if it were we should expect that to be made clearer.[23] The identity of this figure with the Beloved Disciple is left designedly ambiguous.[24] It becomes unmistakable only when readers reach 21:24, with its clear echo of the language of 19:35. Only then are we supposed to learn that the witness behind the Gospel is specifically that of the Beloved Disciple and that he wrote it.

If this argument is persuasive, then we cannot think that the identification of the Beloved Disciple as the author of the Gospel is a later, secondary accretion to the Gospel. The Gospel, with its Epilogue and its two-stage conclusion, has been designed to reveal only at the end the role of the Beloved Disciple in its making. This revelation enables readers then to see retrospectively that the role of the Beloved Disciple within the narrative, both plainly and obscurely present, is such as to qualify him especially well for the role of witness to Jesus and author of the Gospel. How this is so and why it is that the

22. Similarly D. Tovey, *Narrative Art and Act in the Fourth Gospel* (JSNTSup 151; Sheffield: Sheffield Academic, 1997) 93, though he misses the point that this is a characteristically Johannine interpretation of a cryptic saying.

23. E.g., M. Casey, *Is John's Gospel True?* (London: Routledge, 1996) 159.

24. Cf. J. L. Staley, *The Print's First Kiss: A Rhetorical Investigation of the Implied Reader in the Fourth Gospel* (SBLDS 82; Atlanta: Scholars, 1988) 40: "The narrative trick for the Fourth Gospel then is that the implied author is able to withhold the narrator's identity and his role in the story from the implied reader until the final two sentences of the book."

Gospel so carefully withholds the information that the Beloved Disciple is its author we shall consider in the next chapter.

Who Are the "We" of 21:24?

There is a remaining puzzle in the passage that reveals the Beloved Disciple's authorship: "This is the disciple who is testifying to these things and has written them, and we know that his testimony is true" (21:24). Who are the "we" who "know" that the Beloved Disciple's "testimony is true"? There are four main possibilities. First, the "we" could include the readers along with the author (the Beloved Disciple), meaning that we all know that his witness is true. But this is unlikely, since first-time readers or hearers of the Gospel are scarcely in a position to know this. Second, the most common view is that "we" are a circle of teachers or elders who have added their testimony to the Gospel, identifying its author and recommending it.[25] But this would seem scarcely possible if, as I have argued, these final verses of the Gospel (21:24-25) belong integrally to the original author's design of the Gospel. Moreover, it is difficult to see what value these people's corroboration of the Beloved Disciple's testimony could have since they do not identify themselves, leaving readers with no way of telling what authority they have to make this statement.[26]

Third, the "we" could be a circle of leaders or eyewitnesses within which the Beloved Disciple includes himself.[27] The alternation of third person reference to the Beloved Disciple and this first person plural ("we know") need not be a problem. The narrative has previously spoken of this disciple in the third person and this was a standard practice for authors portraying themselves as a character in their narrative. But in this verse the author needs to make the transition from third person reference to himself, as in the preceding narrative, to the first person speech addressed to the readers that is necessary now that he, so to speak, steps out of the narrative and reveals himself to be the author.

While the third view is quite possible, especially when this verse is considered alone, there is a further and final possibility that is arguably prefera-

---

25. E.g., Brown, *The Gospel according to John XIII–XXI*, 1122-25; M. Hengel, *The Johannine Question* (tr. J. Bowden; London: SCM, 1989) 84.

26. J. Chapman, "'We Know That His Testimony Is True,'" *JTS* 31 (1930) 381.

27. E.g., Smith, *John*, 400; E. C. Hoskyns, *The Fourth Gospel*, ed. F. N. Davey (London: Faber and Faber, 1947) 559-60; Tovey, *Narrative Art*, 95; Keener, *The Gospel of John*, vol. 2, 1240-41. This interpretation probably lies behind the account of the writing of the Gospel of John in the Muratorian Canon (see chapter 16 below).

ble. This is that the "we" is not a genuine plural but stands for "I."[28] It might be objected that then we should expect "we" rather than "I" in v. 25 too, but in fact ancient writers of Greek seem to have slipped easily from first person plural to first person singular or vice versa when speaking of themselves. An example (one of many that could be cited) that is especially interesting because it occurs in the conclusion to a treatise is in the essay of Dionysius of Halicarnassus on *Demosthenes* (§58), where the concluding three sentences are:

> I would have given you examples of what I have said but for the risk of becoming a bore, especially as it is you that I am addressing. That is all we have to say about the style of Demosthenes, my dear Ammaeus. If god preserves us, we shall present you in a subsequent treatise with an even longer and more remarkable account than this of his genius in the treatment of subject-matter.[29]

Stephen Usher, the translator in the Loeb edition, translates the Greek first-person plurals in the last two sentences here as English first-person singulars, doubtless because he found the transition from singular to plural too awkward in English. This underlines that we should be cautious about judging the significance of such a transition by the standards of English usage. In the next section we shall notice another example of this particular Greek usage within the Johannine literature itself.

The argument for regarding the first person plural in 21:24 as a substitute for "I" depends on observing the similarity between this statement ("we know that his testimony is true") and several other passages in the Johannine literature that, when looked at together, seem all to be examples of a Johannine idiomatic usage that we can call "the 'we' of authoritative testimony." We must now examine the other examples of this usage.

The "We" of Authoritative Testimony

We shall discover in this section that John 21:24 employs a particular Johannine idiom that occurs elsewhere in the Johannine writings (i.e., the Gospel and the three letters of John) in John 3:11; 1 John 1:1-5; 4:14; and 3 John

---

28. E.g., Carson, *The Gospel according to John,* 684. According to Chapman, "We Know," 379, 385, this was the view of the Greek Fathers.

29. Translation adapted from Dionysius of Halicarnassus, *The Critical Essays,* vol. 1 (tr. S. Usher; Cambridge: Harvard University Press, 1974) 455.

9-10, 12. Whether the same author was responsible for the Gospel of John and all three Johannine letters is debated, but for our present purposes we need not resolve this issue. It is in any case generally recognized that these Johannine writings share characteristic linguistic usages, whether these belong to the "idiolect" of one author or to the "sociolect" of a school of Johannine writers. Parallels in the Johannine letters are therefore relevant to establishing the meaning of related passages in the Gospel of John.

The idiom in question we shall call "the 'we' of authoritative testimony." A use of the first person plural (pronouns and verbs) as a substitute for "I" was identified in some of these passages by Adolf von Harnack in an important but largely forgotten study of 1923,[30] and Howard Jackson has recently drawn attention to Harnack's work, developing it in his own way.[31] These writers speak of a "we" of "authority" or of "augmented empowerment,"[32] but the credit for identifying testimony as a common element in all the Johannine uses of this idiom should go to a neglected article by John Chapman, published in 1930.[33] It is this common element that justifies my use of the term "'we' of authoritative testimony." I have learned from all three of these earlier studies while not agreeing entirely with any of them. In what follows we must examine the texts in question in some detail in order to establish adequately that they share a common idiom, the "we" of authoritative testimony.

It will be useful to begin by identifying the three basic ways in which "we" (first person plural pronouns and/or first person plural verbs) can be used in ancient Greek (as in many other languages):

(1) the *associative*[34] "we" is used when an author includes him/herself and his/her reader(s) in a "we," such that "we" means "I and you";

(2) the *dissociative* "we" is used when an author distinguishes between a group to which he/she belongs and his/her reader(s), such that "we" means "I and my associates";

---

30. A. von Harnack, "Das 'Wir' in den Johanneischen Schriften," *SPAW,* Philosophisch-historischen Klasse (1923) 96-113. Harnack is followed by Hengel, *The Johannine Question,* 28-29, 164-65 n. 22.

31. H. M. Jackson, "Ancient Self-Referential Conventions and Their Implications for the Authorship and Integrity of the Gospel of John," *JTS* 50 (1999) 1-34.

32. Jackson, "Ancient Self-Referential Conventions," 12.

33. Chapman, "We Know," 379-87.

34. I have borrowed the terminology "associative" and "dissociative" from Jackson, "Ancient Self-Referential Conventions," 12. R. E. Brown, *The Epistles of John* (AB 30; New York: Doubleday, 1982) 499, uses the terms "nondistinctive" and "distinctive" in the same sense.

(3) "we" is used as a *substitute for "I,"* when the intention is not to refer to any other persons along with the speaker but to give added force to the self-reference. This is sometimes called a plural of majesty or a plural of authority. It may be used by an author, much like the authorial "we" in English, presumably to add a sense of augmented authority. It may also be used by a speaker who is in some sense superior to those he/she addresses.[35] This resembles the royal "we" in English, but was more widely used in ancient Greek than this particular English usage, which is more or less confined to the monarch (although Margaret Thatcher famously adopted it for herself). Again, the plural intensifies the authority expressed. It is worth noting again at this point that, in this Greek usage of "we" as a substitute for "I," alternation between "we" and "I" is common. James Moulton writes of "examples from late Greek literature and from papyrus letters, which prove beyond all possible doubt that *I* and *we* chased each other throughout these documents without rhyme or reason."[36]

3 John 9-12 We begin our investigation of the "we" of authoritative testimony with 3 John 9-10, 12. V. 8 has clear instances of an associative "we," the author ("the elder") including himself and his addressee Gaius in a larger group of all true Christians. But this meaning is impossible for the four first person plurals in vv. 9, 10, and 12. Some scholars take these to be dissociative "we"s, in which the writer associates himself with others (not including Gaius), probably with a group of Christian leaders.[37] The difficulty with this view is that the "us" of vv. 9 and 10 would seem to be different from "the brothers" of v. 10, apparently traveling missionaries associated with the elder, while the "we" of v. 12 must be different from the "all" of that verse, who are

35. Thus, in a striking instance in Josephus, *Ant.* 2.68-69, where Joseph addresses Pharaoh's disgraced butler, he is probably anticipating his rise to a position superior to the butler. Hengel, *The Johannine Question*, 30, also refers to the "authoritative 'we' for a leader of a religious group" in 4QMMT. However, E. Qimron and J. Strugnell, *Qumran Cave 4.V: Miqṣat Maʿaśe Ha-Torah* (DJD 10; Oxford: Clarendon, 1994) 114, write: "There is no reason to postulate an auctorial 'we,' with the first person singular meaning, in this document. Such a usage is unattested in early Hebrew, although frequent in Greek literature and epistolography. These pronouncements of law are therefore to be taken as uttered in the name of the community which practised them."

36. J. H. Moulton, *A Grammar of New Testament Greek*, vol. 1 (third edition; Edinburgh: Clark, 1908) 86, citing K. Dick, *Der schriftstellerische Plural bei Paulus* (1900).

37. E.g., Brown, *The Epistles*, 717, 724; B. F. Westcott, *The Epistles of St John* (London: Macmillan, 1883) 229-30; I. H. Marshall, *The Epistles of John* (NICNT; Grand Rapids: Eerdmans, 1978) 88 n. 2, 93 n. 8.

presumably all Christians in the communities to which the elder and Gaius belong (cf. also "the friends" of v. 15). It seems unnecessarily complex to hypothesize yet another group as the referent of the "we" of these verses. Once we recognize that the alternation between "we" and "I" in vv. 9 and 10 is not unexpected in cases of the Greek use of "we" as a substitute for "I," it is easiest to take the "we" in all three verses (9, 10, 12) as a substitute for "I."

This does not mean that the "we" is a merely arbitrary variation on "I." It is plausible that in vv. 9 and 10 the use of the first person plural functions to stress the writer's authority in a context where it is being challenged.[38] The phrase "does not acknowledge our authority" in the NRSV of v. 9 is an interpretative translation of the Greek, which would be more literally rendered "does not receive us." The verb (*epidechesthai*, "receive, accept, welcome") is the verb translated "welcome" in v. 10 of the NRSV. The verb does not in itself imply acknowledgement of authority, but naturally has this nuance in appropriate contexts (e.g., 1 Macc 10:1). Even in v. 10, where the brothers are presumably the authoritative envoys of the elder, there is probably something of this nuance implied in the reference to receiving or welcoming them.

The second half of v. 12, "We also testify for him, and you know that our testimony is true," can then easily be understood to continue the use of a "we" of authority. Even apart from this feature, the statement is extraordinarily emphatic. The word "true" picks up "the truth itself"[39] in the preceding statement, claiming, as entirely evident to Gaius, the participation of the elder's testimony in the truth itself. This example of a Johannine authoritative "we" is of particular interest to our present enquiry because it is the authority of *testimony* that is asserted. Of course, this passage by itself could not establish a particular Johannine idiom relating to authoritative testimony. For that purpose it will need to be brought into relationship with the other examples we shall cite. But it is worth noting at once how very close indeed the formulation of this statement in 3 John 12 is to John 21:24: "This is the disciple who is testifying to these things, and has written them, and we know that his testimony is true."[40]

1 John 1:1-5   1 John makes considerable use of the associative "we" (1:6-

38. Chapman, "We Know," 384; Jackson, "Ancient Self-Referential Conventions," 13.

39. This personified "truth" has been interpreted as God, Jesus (cf. John 14:6), or the Spirit (cf. 1 John 5:6), but it would seem odd to put a divine Witness between the witness of "all" and that of the elder, and so it is probably better to understand the phrase less specifically: "if the truth could speak, it too would testify that Demetrius's life was in accord with its own standards" (Marshall, *The Epistles*, 93).

40. For similar statements not employing the "we" of authoritative testimony, see John 5:32; 19:35.

10; 2:1, 3, 5, 18, 19, 25, 28; 3:1, 2, 14, 16, 18, 19-24; 4:7, 9-13, 16, 17, 21; 5:2-4, 9, 11, 14, 15, 18-20), but this cannot be the sense of the "we" in this prologue to 1 John, since the "we" in 1:1-5 is clearly distinguished from "you," the addressees (1:1, 2, 3, 5). Many commentators have understood the "we" in these verses as a dissociative "we" in which the writer speaks on behalf of a larger group. Those who think that the writer himself was an eyewitness of the history of Jesus have no difficulty identifying the group as eyewitnesses in general or the apostles,[41] while those who do not believe the author could have been an eyewitness himself try to understand him to be speaking on behalf of a group of "authoritative bearers of the tradition"[42] who have known the eyewitnesses and continued their testimony.[43] But, while reading a dissociative "we" may seem quite plausible in vv. 1-3, it encounters a serious obstacle in v. 4: "We are writing these things."[44] This could make sense if others were actually associated with the author in his writing of the letter, as Paul's colleagues are with Paul in many of his letters, but this is not what is usually claimed for the dissociative "we" in this passage. Moreover, in all other cases (no less than twelve times) where the author of 1 John speaks of writing his letter, he speaks in the first person singular: "I am writing" (2:1, 7-8, 12-14, 21, 26; 5:13). For the "we" of 1:1-5 to be dissociative, v. 4 has to mean "I am writing on behalf of the others." This is what most commentators who take this view seem to think, usually without comment on the difficulty of such an interpretation. But, if this were the meaning, then the sense of the "we" would change significantly between vv. 1-3 and v. 4. In vv. 1-3 there would be a straightforward, ordinary use of the dissociative "we": what is said is as true of the others as it is of the author. But in v. 4, what is said is not really true of the others at all. Rudolf Schnackenburg is thus obliged to admit that in v. 4 the author "incorrectly retains the plural."[45]

The usual objection to taking the "we" of this passage to be a substitute for "I" is that elsewhere the writer speaks of himself in the first person singular.[46] This is true of the twelve occasions already mentioned where he speaks

41. E.g., Westcott, *The Epistles*, 3; A. E. Brooke, *A Critical and Exegetical Commentary on the Johannine Epistles* (ICC; Edinburgh: Clark, 1912) 2-3; Marshall, *The Epistles*, 106-7.

42. J. Painter, *1, 2, and 3 John* (Sacra Pagina 18; Collegeville: Liturgical, 2002) 128; cf. Brown, *The Epistles*, 160: "The tradition-bearers and interpreters who stand in a special relationship to the Beloved Disciple in their attempt to preserve his witness."

43. E.g., J. Lieu, *The Theology of the Johannine Epistles* (Cambridge: Cambridge University Press, 1991) 23-24; R. Schnackenburg, *The Johannine Epistles* (tr. R. and I. Fuller; New York: Crossroad, 1992) 55; Painter, *1, 2, and 3 John*, 128-31, 135.

44. Note that the "we" (*hēmeis* placed after the verb) here is emphatic.

45. Schnackenburg, *The Johannine Epistles*, 51.

46. E.g., Brown, *The Epistles*, 158.

of himself as writing the letter (2:1, 7-8, 12-14, 21, 26; 5:13). But this is a valid objection only if no reason can be given for the presence of a different usage in 1:1-5. Such a reason is readily available once we recognize the phenomenon of a "we" of authoritative testimony in these and other Johannine passages. This passage is full of the language of testimony: not only the word "testify" itself (v. 2), but also the recurrent verbs of hearing and seeing. None of the later passages in which the author writes of himself in the first person concern testimony. The prologue to the letter is quite evidently designed to state emphatically the author's authority to address his readers on the basis of his having heard and seen the reality of which he speaks. The augmented authority that the use of the first person plural gives to his claims makes the use of the first person plural in this solemnly formulated introduction to his work easily intelligible.

The transition from this authoritative "we" of vv. 1-5 to the associative "we" of vv. 6-10 is not problematic. Whereas in v. 5 the distinction between "we" and "you" is explicit, the fact that no such distinction is being made in the following verses is very soon clear. Such a transition occurs frequently and naturally in English use of the authorial "we," where a writer may well say, for example, "we have seen that . . ." (meaning: "I and you, my readers, have seen that . . .") and continue immediately with, for example, "we shall now demonstrate that . . ." (where "we" = "I").

1 John 4:11-16 In my view the "we" of 4:14 should be understood as a "we" of authoritative testimony.[47] To some extent interpretation of this "we" depends on interpretation of the "we" of 1:1-5. Some of those scholars who see a dissociative "we" there find it also in 4:14, on the grounds of the similarity of the claim ("we have seen and do testify").[48] One would expect that Harnack[49] and Jackson,[50] who find an authoritative "we" (a subsitute for "I") in 1:1-5, would do the same in 4:14, but in fact they join the majority of scholars in regarding the "we" of 4:14 as an associative "we," in which the author includes his readers in the claim that "we have seen and do testify that the Father has sent his Son as the Savior of the world."[51]

47. So also Chapman, "We Know," 384.

48. E.g., Brooke, *A Critical and Exegetical Commentary*, 121-22 (he thinks the dissociative "we" also continues into v. 16); Schnackenburg, *The Johannine Epistles*, 219; Painter, *1, 2, and 3 John*, 274-75.

49. Harnack, "Das 'Wir,'" 101-2.

50. Jackson, "Ancient Self-Referential Conventions," 14-15. Both Harnack and Jackson make the methodological mistake of determining the meaning of 4:14 before considering 1:1-5. Readers, on the other hand, will read 4:14 in the light of 1:1-5.

51. So also, e.g., Marshall, *The Epistles*, 106, 220; Brown, *The Epistles*, 522-23.

There are two main reasons adduced by scholars who find an associative "we" here in 4:14 rather than either a dissociative "we" or the "we" as a substitute for "I." One is that this verse is surrounded by other "we"s, of which the "we" of v. 13 is indubitably associative, and the "we" of v. 16 is very likely associative. Harnack and Jackson point out that the "we" of v. 14 is the tenth of a series of twelve "we"s in vv. 11-16, the first nine of which are universally held to be associative.[52] This argument from the context is obviously a strong one and to dissent from it requires a strong indication in v. 14 itself that the "we" here is different from the "we" of the preceding verses. But, once we have recognized the "we" of authoritative testimony in 1:1-5, such an indication is in fact very clear. Alone among the "we"s of 4:11-16, that of v. 14 uses the language of testimony: "we have seen and do testify." As Schnackenburg points out, this is virtually a quotation from 1:2 ("we have seen it and do testify to it").[53] (The words for "see" are different in the two cases. Johannine usage seems to vary the two verbs *horan* and *theasthai* indiscriminately, and the latter is used in 1:1 as well as in 4:14. But both are in the perfect tense, and there are no "it"s in the Greek of 1:2.) We also find the same phrase in passages in the Gospel of John where it refers to the unique testimony of someone who has "seen" what others have not: "I [John the Baptist] myself have seen and have testified that this is the Son of God" (1:34); "the one who has seen [the blood and the water flow from Jesus' side] has testified" (19:35); "we [Jesus] testify to what we have seen" (3:11); "he [Jesus] testifies to what he has seen and heard" (3:32). In one of these cases (3:11), the "we" of authoritative testimony is used, as we shall argue later, and it is worth noting that the authority of the testimony is strengthened in other ways in two of the other parallels: by the emphatic "I myself" *(kagō)* in 1:34, and by the following assertion ("his testimony is true, and he knows that he tells the truth") in 19:35. Thus the language of 1 John 4:14 strongly indicates that the "we" here is distinguished from the "we" of previous verses. We have noted above — with reference to English use of the authorial "we" — that there is no real difficulty in alternation between the associative "we" and the "we" that substitutes for "I." The same alternation occurs between 1:5 and 1:6.

The second main reason alleged for choosing an associative "we" in 4:14 rather than either a dissociative "we" or the "we" as a substitute for "I" is that what is said is not distinctive of a group or individual but is true of all Christians (or, some commentators would prefer to say, of "Johannine" Christians belonging to the author's group). It is pointed out that the testimony is to

52. Harnack, "Das 'Wir,'" 101; Jackson, "Ancient Self-Referential Conventions," 14.
53. Schnackenburg, *The Johannine Epistles,* 219.

something ("the Father has sent his Son as the Savior of the world") that cannot have been "seen" by physical sight.[54] We will have to return to the issue of what is meant when Johannine eyewitnesses testify to what they have "seen." But, in the first place, it should surely be clear (though not admitted by all scholars) that the language of 1:1-3 is designed to include, even to emphasize apprehension by the physical senses: "what we have heard, what we have seen with our eyes, what we have looked at and touched with our hands. . . ." What was seen may go beyond what could have been empirically observed by anyone present, but it is hard to see how the author could have referred more clearly to apprehension by the physical senses. Since 4:14 echoes 1:1-3, this connotation of physical sight must carry over into 4:14. Secondly, it may be, as Schnackenburg argues,[55] that, since 4:14 is an abbreviated version of 1:1-3, the real object of "we have seen" in 4:14 is not the clause that is the object of "do testify" ("that the Father has sent his Son as the Savior of the world"), but the object implied in 1:1-3: the physical presence of the incarnate Son. Thirdly, in any case the parallels from the Gospel of John noted above show that, while the meaning of "see" may fluctuate (a vision in the case of John the Baptist, at least physical sight of an empirically observable event in 19:35), when used with "testify" the reference is always to the unique experience of an eyewitness who testifies to others what he alone has seen. The testimony is given to others, so that they may believe, by one who has been privileged to "see." While all true Christians "*confess* that Jesus is the Son of God" (4:15), only the one who has "seen" can "*testify*" (4:14). If "testify" (with a christological object) were here the activity of all Christians and equivalent to "confess," this use of the verb would be unique in the Johannine writings.

Thus, while the testimony in 4:14 ("that the Father has sent his Son as the Savior of the world") is the result of believing recognition of what God was doing in the events of Jesus' presence on earth, it is what could only be given by one who was present at those events, both seeing the empirically observable and perceiving the divine activity. In the context of 1 John, with its emphatic opening declaration of the author's privileged claim to have seen and so to be able to testify, 4:14 is very easily recognized as another instance of this Johannine "we" of authoritative testimony.

John 3:10-13 The first person plurals in Jesus' words in John 3:11 have puzzled commentators, especially since the statements in the first person plural are themselves introduced by a statement in the first person singular, al-

---

54. E.g., Brown, *The Epistles,* 522; J. L. Houlden, *A Commentary on the Johannine Epistles* (BNTC; London: Black, 1973) 115.

55. Schnackenburg, *The Johannine Epistles,* 219.

beit a standard formula ("Very truly, I tell you"), while v. 12 reverts immediately to the first person singular. We should also notice that Nicodemus has addressed Jesus using the first person plural in v. 2 ("Rabbi, we know that you are a teacher come from God"), presumably speaking on behalf of the aristocratic Pharisees of whom he is one, though some think he has come to Jesus accompanied by a group of disciples.[56] It is presumably in response to this plural used by Nicodemus that Jesus switches from second person singular to second person plural address in the course of v. 11. But unlike the first person plural used by Jesus in v. 11, the second person plural continues through v. 12, where there are four more instances.

Interpretations which take the "we" of v. 11 to be a real plural vary between those who take it to include with Jesus persons that Jesus could, in the presumed historical context, have considered to be already witnesses — God, the prophets, John the Baptist, Jesus' disciples[57] — and on the other hand those who think of a situation after the ministry of Jesus. In the latter case, the plural implies either that Jesus anticipates the witness of his disciples continuing his own witness in the future[58] or that Jesus is here merely a mouthpiece for the church or the Johannine community.[59] The view has become quite popular that v. 11 reflects the debate, at the time of the writing of the Gospel, between two communities: Johannine Christians and the synagogue.[60] Against all such interpretations, the natural meaning of the verse in context is that Jesus refers to what he uniquely, as the only one who has descended from heaven (3:13), has seen in heaven (cf. 5:19-20). This is strongly supported by 3:31-32, where the same claim is made simply of Jesus in the third person singular: "The one who comes from heaven is above all. He testifies to what he has seen and heard. . . ." If the claim refers to the testimony that only Jesus can make on the basis of what he has seen in heaven, then not even his disciples in the future can say "*we* testify to what *we* have seen," only that Jesus testified to what *he* had seen.

56. F. P. Cotterell, "The Nicodemus Conversation: A Fresh Appraisal," *ExpT* 96 (1984-85) 238.

57. E.g., E. C. Hoskyns, *The Fourth Gospel*, ed. F. N. Davey (London: Faber, 1947) 215-16.

58. R. Schnackenburg, *The Gospel according to St John*, vol. 1 (tr. K. Smyth; London: Burns and Oates, 1968) 276.

59. E.g., G. H. C. Macgregor, *The Gospel of John* (London: Hodder and Stoughton, 1928) 75-76; B. Witherington III, *John's Wisdom* (Louisville: Westminster John Knox, 1995) 98.

60. E.g., C. K. Barrett, *The Gospel according to St. John* (second edition; London: SPCK, 1978) 211; F. J. Maloney, *Belief in the Word* (Minneapolis: Fortress, 1993) 115-16; Lincoln, *Truth*, 66-71; J. F. McGrath, *John's Apologetic Christology* (SNTSMS 111; Cambridge: Cambridge University Press, 2001) 212; cf. Tovey, *Narrative Art*, 163.

We should also note the significance of the fact that the saying in 3:11 is introduced by the formula "Very truly, I say to you," which is more literally translated: "Amen, amen, I say to you." This formula, which occurs twenty-five times in John, is this Gospel's unique equivalent to the Synoptic Gospels' "Amen, I say to you." The doubling of the "Amen" strengthens the sense of solemn asseveration. Andrew Lincoln identifies it as a "swearing formula" that relates to the theme of Jesus' unique witness within the larger metaphorical complex of judicial trial in the Gospel of John. It underlines the character of Jesus' testimony as uniquely self-authenticating.[61] The attribution to the church or the Johannine community of a saying introduced by this formula would seriously contravene the significance of the formula as declaring Jesus' unique authority.

On the view that in 3:11 we hear the voice of the Johannine community, it is also difficult to understand why the first person plural appears only here. Why does it not continue into the next verse, where it would appropriately match the second person plural that indicates (on this view) the synagogue community that the Johannine community is addressing? The same problem of explaining why the second person plurals continue through v. 12, while the first person singular reappears in v. 12, is a serious obstacle for the explanation that in v. 11 "Jesus is sardonically aping the plural that Nicodemus affected when he first approached Jesus."[62]

Recognizing here the "we" of authoritative testimony does justice to the uniqueness of Jesus' testimony that the context indicates and also explains why the first person plural is limited to these words in v. 11. The "we" is used precisely because here Jesus speaks of his testimony. There is only one other place in the words of Jesus in this Gospel where Jesus could be understood to use the first person plural as a substitute for "I" (9:4), but in this case the plural is easily understood as an associative "we" in which Jesus includes his disciples with himself. Conversely, there are several occasions in the Gospel where Jesus uses the word "testify" in the first person singular (5:31; 7:7; 8:14, 18; 18:37), but in none of these cases is there a solemn declaration of his testimony, such as we have in 3:11. Thus the Johannine Jesus uses "we" as a substitute for "I" only on the one occasion when the "we" of authoritative testimony is required by Johannine style.

John 21:24-25   In the light of the previous examples, it is now unmistakable that 21:24 uses the "we" of authoritative testimony. The same person,

61. Lincoln, *Truth*, 30-31.

62. Carson, *The Gospel according to John*, 198-199; also R. E. Brown, *The Gospel according to John I–XII* (AB 29; New York: Doubleday, 1966) 132.

the writer, speaks of himself first as "the disciple who is testifying to these things." This third person reference is necessary to make the transition from the narrative (up to 21:23) in which he had appeared as a character in the third person. Then, now revealed as the author and directly addressing his readers, he switches to the first person. He uses the first person plural ("we know") because this is Johannine idiom when solemnly claiming the authority of testimony. Finally, he uses the first person singular ("I suppose") as the natural way to address his readers when it is no longer a matter of solemn testimony. Awkward as these shifts may seem to us, they are readily intelligible once we recognize the idiomatic "we" of authoritative testimony.

It is interesting to compare 21:24 with the only other explicit reference to the Beloved Disciple's witness in the Gospel. The two statements "we know that his testimony is true" (21:24) and "he knows that he tells the truth" (19:35) are exactly equivalent, one phrased in the first person, the other in the third person. The emphatic "he" *(ekeinos)* in 19:35 functions to provide "augmented empowerment" for the testimonial claim,[63] just as the first person plural does in 21:24. 19:35 also illustrates that, at least for some of the most important elements in the Beloved Disciple's testimony, there is no one other than himself who can vouch for the truth of his witness. In both 19:35 and 21:24 all he can do is to solemnly aver that his testimony is true. Other people cannot corroborate this; they can only believe it.

John 1:14-16   John 1:14 is the sixth and final case in the Johannine writings in which we may be justified in recognizing the "we" of authoritative testimony. I have left it to last because it is less clear than the other five examples. Unlike the others, this one does not use the words "testify" or "witness," although the verb "to testify" is used, with John the Baptist as subject, in the following verse (1:15). However, as we have already observed, a claim to see is regularly linked with a claim to testify, both in cases of the "we" of authoritative testimony (1 John 1:1-2; 4:14; John 3:11) and in other cases (John 1:32, 34; 3:32; 19:35). Even without the use of the words "testify" or "witness," the phrase "we have seen his glory" would seem to be rather clearly the language of testimony.

However, we must take account of the fact that 1:14 and 16 contain two other first person plurals. (Thus in the whole Gospel, there are just four instances in which the author, as distinct from one of his characters, uses the first person plural: 1:14 [twice], 16; 21:24.) Who are the "us" in "the Word became flesh and lived among us"? Who are the "we" in "From his fullness we

---

63. Cf. also 5:37: "the one who sent me, the Father, has himself *(ekeinos)* testified on my behalf."

have all received"? Many commentators consider all three first person plurals in these verses to be associative "we"s that include the author with all his readers or all Christians. This is certainly correct in the case of the "we" of v. 16, but that "we" seems to be deliberately distinguished from the "we" of v. 14 in that the former is no mere "we" but "we all." There is a distinction here between eyewitness testimony ("we have seen his glory") and the experience of all Christians, who are not all eyewitnesses but who have all received grace from the fullness of grace in Jesus Christ.

More problematic is the relationship between "among us" and "we have seen" in v. 14. If these have the same reference, then both must refer to the disciples of Jesus, and "we have seen" would have to be a genuine plural — a dissociative "we" meaning "I and the other eyewitnesses"[64] — rather than the "we" of authoritative testimony. Alternatively, "among us" could refer to humanity in general: Jesus, the Word incarnate, lived a human life among human beings. Then the "we" of "we have seen his glory" could be equivalent to "I," the "we" of authoritative testimony. I am inclined to think that this is ultimately the true meaning, not only because of the general evidence for a Johannine idiom of this kind, but also because this "we" of authoritative witness in the prologue to the Gospel would then match and form an *inclusio* with the "we" of authoritative testimony in 21:24. Yet the first-time reader/hearer of 1:14 would not be able to discern this. Even if such a reader were familiar with the idiomatic "we" of authoritative testimony, the lack of the term "witness" in this verse might leave some ambiguity as to whether this is an instance of it. Such a reader would not be able to tell whether this initial claim to eyewitness testimony in the Gospel points to a single witness who wrote the Gospel or a group of disciples on whose behalf one of them has written, forming some kind of corporate testimonial authorship. This ambiguity would cohere with the way, even at the first stage of the conclusion to the Gospel (20:30-31), all that is implied is the witness of Jesus' disciples in general. Only at the second stage of the conclusion, as we have seen, is one particular disciple in the narrative revealed to be the primary witness and the actual author. Then, like other passages of the Gospel, including 19:35, 1:14 could be reread in the light of the revelation of the Gospel's authorship. Then it could be seen that 1:14 need not suggest a plurality of witness so much as the authoritative "we" of the Beloved Disciple's own claim. Once again I must add that I am leaving until the next chapter why the identity of the author as primary witness and author is withheld from readers until the very end of the Gospel.

64. So, e.g., Keener, *The Gospel of John: A Commentary,* vol. 1, 411.

A Prophetic Precedent for the "We" of Authoritative Testimony

There is one more passage in the Gospel that can be illuminated by recognition of the "we" of authoritative testimony. The case we have made for recognizing that idiom in 21:24 and 1:14 needs no further support and does not depend at all on the argument in the present section. Yet, if this argument is persuasive, it will provide further corroborative evidence of the author's deliberate awareness of this Johannine idiom.

John 12:38 quotes the Septuagint Greek version of Isa 53:1 as part of John's conclusion to the public ministry of Jesus, in which he stresses that the general response has been unbelief. He sees this unbelief as fulfillment of prophecies by Isaiah, both Isa 53:1 and Isa 6:10, which John goes on to quote in vv. 39-40. The quotation of Isa 53:1 is highly suitable for the purpose of summing up Jesus' public ministry prior to the beginning of his passion, for this verse occurs early in the famous Isaianic account of the Suffering Servant of God (Isa 52:13–53:12), a passage that John, like many other early Christian writers, undoubtedly understood as prophetic of the passion and death of Jesus.[65]

Yet how exactly does he interpret Isaiah 53:1? In particular, who are the speakers in this verse according to John's reading of it? Commentators have often and correctly pointed out that the two lines of the quotation correspond very aptly to the two aspects of Jesus' public ministry: the first to Jesus' words ("our message" or "what we have heard") and the second to Jesus' works or signs (effected by "the arm of the Lord").[66] But most commentators refrain from identifying the speaker(s) in the quotation. They cannot be preachers of the Christian gospel, as they are in Paul's quotation of this verse (Rom 10:16),[67] since in the context it must be *Jesus'* message that has not been believed by those who heard his words and saw his signs in the gospel narrative up to this point. So Beasley-Murray, for one, suggests, though only tentatively, the correct explanation, that in its context in John this Isaianic prophecy is to be read as though the speaker were Jesus. Jesus can describe his words as "what we have heard" or "our report" because, according to this Gospel, Je-

65. Cf. R. Bauckham, *God Crucified: Monotheism and Christology in the New Testament* (Grand Rapids: Eerdmans, 1998) 63-68.

66. Bernard, *A Critical and Exegetical Commentary*, 450; Brown, *The Gospel according to John I–XII*, 485; C. K. Barrett, *The Gospel according to St. John* (second edition; London: SPCK, 1978) 431; Carson, *The Gospel*, 448; B. G. Schuchard, *Scripture within Scripture: The Interrelationship of Form and Function in the Explicit Old Testament Citations in the Gospel of John* (SBLDS 133; Atlanta: Scholars, 1992) 88-89.

67. A. T. Hanson, *The Prophetic Gospel* (Edinburgh: Clark, 1991) 166.

sus' words were what he had heard from the Father (3:34; 7:16; 8:26; 12:49).[68] But these words were also, as again the Gospel makes very clear, Jesus' testimony (3:11, 32; 5:31; 7:7; 8:14, 18; 18:37). So it is entirely appropriate that, as in 3:11, he should employ here, in the words of Isa 53:1, the "we" of authoritative testimony. This is also appropriate in the Isaianic context of the quotation, if this verse is taken to be the words of the Suffering Servant himself complaining that his message from God has been rejected. For the Servant is also God's witness (Isa 43:10; 55:4). John would have been well aware of this, because, as we will see in the next chapter, the important theme of witness and related metaphors in his Gospel is dependent on deutero-Isaiah's depiction of the cosmic trial of the truth in which both the Servant and Israel are to testify as God's witnesses. It is even possible that it was precisely because John found the "we" of authoritative testimony on the lips of the Suffering Servant in Isa 53:1 that he attributed this idiom to Jesus, speaking of his testimony, in his Gospel (3:11).

68. G. R. Beasley-Murray, *John* (WBC 36; Waco: Word, 1987) 216.

15. The Witness of
   the Beloved Disciple

What Sort of Witness?

In the last chapter we demonstrated that, according to John 21:24, the Beloved Disciple was both the primary witness on whose testimony the Gospel is based and also himself the author of the Gospel. We must now take a closer and harder look at the concept of "witness" as it is used in this connection in the Gospel of John.

In this book we took our initial bearings from Samuel Byrskog's work, in which he compared the role of oral history in ancient historiography with the role of eyewitnesses in relation to the Gospel traditions. This means that we have been interested in the *eyewitnesses,* people who had been in direct contact with Jesus and the events of his history. We have tried to show that the texts of the Gospels are closer to the reports of these eyewitnesses than has usually been allowed in the Gospels scholarship of the last few decades. We have borne in mind Byrskog's observation that the historians of the ancient world preferred the evidence of involved participants rather than merely dispassionate observers, because the former were in a position to understand and to interpret the significance of what they had seen. We noted that therefore, according to Byrskog, the eyewitnesses were "as much interpreters as observers."[1] In the case of the Gospels, too, the eyewitness informants who transmitted the traditions and remained active guarantors of the tradition as long as they were alive

---

1. S. Byrskog, *Story as History — History as Story* (WUNT 123; Tübingen: Mohr, 2000; reprinted Leiden: Brill, 2002) 149.

would not only have remembered and recounted facts but naturally also have interpreted in the process of experiencing and remembering. Nevertheless, our search for the eyewitnesses and their roles in the making of the Gospels has assumed that these people — most of whom had been disciples or adherents of Jesus during his ministry — really had experienced directly the events of which they told and, in narrativizing and interpreting their memories, were functioning as the kind of reliable informants that ancient historians valued.

In this context it seems rather obvious that we should understand the Beloved Disciple's "witness" in this historiographic sense. Moreover, when we remember that the historians considered the very best basis for history to be the historian's own direct experience of the events of which he wrote, then the Fourth Gospel's claim that the Beloved Disciple was not only the primary witness to its history but also its author fits easily into this historiographic frame of reference. In this Gospel, it seems, we have what Byrskog calls "direct autopsy." The Beloved Disciple's claim parallels, for example, that of Josephus for his history of the *Jewish War:* "My qualification as a historian of the war was that I had been an actor in many, and an eyewitness *(autoptēs)* of most, of the events; in short, nothing whatever was said or done of which I was ignorant" (*C. Ap.* 1.55). (Of course, this does not guarantee that Josephus's account is always accurate, let alone objective. He had axes to grind, especially his need to justify his actions and put himself in the best possible light.)

However, is this really the proper frame of reference for understanding the "witness" of the Beloved Disciple in the Fourth Gospel? It will be useful, before going any further, to clarify a possible linguistic confusion that arises from the English use of the words "witness," "testify," and "testimony." These words in the New Testament normally translate the *martureō* word-group in Greek. The word-group has a primarily legal meaning and, when used outside a literal courtroom context, constitutes a legal metaphor. This is also true of the English words "witness" and "testify," though in some uses they have strayed rather far from their legal origins. The confusion arises when we turn to the word "eyewitness." The technical Greek word for an eyewitness or someone who experiences something firsthand is *autoptēs,* used in the passage just quoted from Josephus and also in the preface to Luke's Gospel. This word is not a legal metaphor, but in English we have only a legal metaphor — "eyewitness" — to translate it. This can obscure the fact that in ancient Greek historiographic usage the idea of eyewitness reporting, what Byrskog calls autopsy, is only rarely expressed in legal metaphors.[2] Even *autoptēs* is not often

2. One example is Josephus, *Vita* 360: "You [Justus of Tiberias] had it written twenty years ago, and might have obtained the evidence *(marturian)* of eyewitnesses to your accuracy."

used, but the idea is often conveyed by very ordinary language for seeing or being present and reporting. Thus there is, in Greek, what might be called "literal" eyewitnessing, not expressed in a legal metaphor, although properly speaking in English there is not. The important point is that New Testament use of the *martureō* word-group does not itself come from historiographic usage, though as we shall see this does not prevent its being used with historiographic significance.

So the Gospel of John's talk of the Beloved Disciple's "witness" (John 19:35; 21:24: *martureō, marturia*) does not *linguistically* evoke the historiographic notion of eyewitness reporting, as the English word "eyewitness" might deceive us into thinking. Nevertheless, we might well maintain that the nature of the Beloved Disciple's witness and the role it plays in the Gospel bring it *functionally* very close to historiographic autopsy. This is the point at which we must take up a very important challenge to such a claim. It is made in a significant recent work on the Gospel of John, Andrew Lincoln's *Truth on Trial: The Lawsuit Motif in the Fourth Gospel,*[3] along with his subsequently published article, "The Beloved Disciple as Eyewitness and the Fourth Gospel as Witness."[4] The article draws extensively on the book, but it helpfully focuses Lincoln's response to the specific issue of the Beloved Disciple's testimony.

Lincoln persuasively shows how the motif of a cosmic trial of the truth, derived especially from Isaiah 40–55, forms a broad metaphorical framework for this Gospel's interpretation of the story of Jesus. (In itself this is not a new contribution, but Lincoln develops this understanding of the Gospel more thoroughly than previous scholars who stressed the lawsuit motif in the Gospel.) Within this overall framework of a cosmic lawsuit the Beloved Disciple's witness is only one of several categories of witness and forms part of the whole metaphorical complex. Its function must be understood within this framework as part of the ongoing story of the trial of the truth as the Gospel tells it. In that framework witness is a legal metaphor and the Beloved Disciple's witness cannot be equated with "literal" eyewitness. While not denying a minimal element of literal eyewitnessing in the Beloved Disciple's testimony, Lincoln considers it a literary device in the service of the theological agenda of witness, not a serious claim to historiographic status.

---

3. A. T. Lincoln, *Truth on Trial: The Lawsuit Motif in the Fourth Gospel* (Peabody: Hendrickson, 2000).

4. A. T. Lincoln, "The Beloved Disciple as Eyewitness and the Fourth Gospel as Witness," *JSNT* 85 (2002) 3-26.

The Beloved Disciple among the Witnesses in God's Lawsuit

There can be no doubt that Lincoln is right to stress the metaphorical complex of the lawsuit as a theme that runs through the Gospel and accounts for
the prominence of the idea of witness in the Gospel. The Beloved Disciple's
witness must be connected with this broader motif. Lincoln is also right to see
the prophecies of deutero-Isaiah as the most important source of this motif,
though it is, of course, also important that the Gospel's story of a cosmic lawsuit includes the literal events of judicial proceedings against Jesus by the Jewish authorities, acting in the name of the "law" of Moses, and by Pilate. In
deutero-Isaiah YHWH brings a case against the gods of the nations and their
supporters in order to determine the identity of the true God. He calls on the
worshipers of the other gods to demonstrate their reality and supremacy,
while he himself calls as witnesses his people Israel and the figure of the Servant of YHWH. It is this lawsuit that the Gospel of John sees taking place in
the history of Jesus, as the one true God demonstrates his deity in controversy
with the claims of the world. He does so by calling Jesus as chief witness and
by vindicating him, not only as true witness but also as incarnate representative of God's own true deity. The witnessing role of the Servant in Isaiah is
played by Jesus in the Gospel, while the accompanying role of the witnesses,
God's people Israel, in Isaiah is taken by Jesus' followers in the Gospel. Even
though the decisive verdict against the world is given in the cross, the trial
continues as the followers of Jesus continue to bear witness against the world.

This means that, as Lincoln correctly and helpfully expounds the way
the trial motif functions in the Gospel, there are two phases of the trial and
thus also of witness. In the first phase, which comprises the Gospel's own narrative scope, there are seven witnesses. (In view of other series of sevens in the
Gospel, the number is surely not accidental. Seven witnesses add up to complete, indeed superabundant witness, exceeding the Mosaic law's minimal requirement of two witnesses for adequate witness.) The seven witnesses, in order of appearance, are John the Baptist (1:7, etc.), Jesus himself (3:11, etc.), the
Samaritan woman (4:39), God the Father (5:32), Jesus' works or signs (5:36),
the Scriptures (5:39), and the crowd who testify about Jesus' raising of Lazarus
(12:17). In the second phase of the trial, the phase that lies in the future from
the perspective of the narrative, there are only two witnesses: the Paraclete
(15:26) and the disciples (15:27), of whom the Beloved Disciple is one (19:35;
21:24). This is how the Beloved Disciple's witness fits into the Gospel's much
wider metaphorical motif of the cosmic trial.

The temporal succession of the two phases of the trial is clear. The
seven witnesses bore their witness in the period of the history of Jesus, while

the disciples, with the Paraclete, bear their witness in the period of the Paraclete. But the relationship is more than one of temporal succession. The testimony of the Paraclete and the disciples both continues and explicitly refers back to the witness of Jesus. It has the history of Jesus for its content. The special role of the Beloved Disciple's witness is in part that it puts the witness of the disciples into written form, as the Gospel, and thereby it enables the seven witnesses to continue to testify. There is a nice *inclusio* between the references to the witness of the Baptist in the Prologue and the witness of the Beloved Disciple in the conclusion. Of both it is said that they testify — in the present tense (1:15; 21:24). For the Beloved Disciple this is true because his testimony, now written, continues to testify, remaining indeed until the parousia, while of John the Baptist it is true because the Beloved Disciple has reported John's testimony as part of his own written testimony. The *inclusio* also indicates what is in any case obvious: that the same is true of all the seven witnesses. The Beloved Disciple's written witness encompasses them all and enables them still to testify. To be sure, the Gospel also interprets the seven witnesses: what John the Baptist says, in the Gospel, is doubtless not a mere report of what even the Beloved Disciple heard him say at the time. But the Beloved Disciple's written witness can only interpret the seven witnesses if at the same time it does in some sense report them. Otherwise the temporal succession of the two phases of the trial immediately collapses and the seven witnesses become no more than forms of expression of the Beloved Disciple's own witness. The Gospel's own careful array of witnesses thus sets some limits to the degree of creativity the Beloved Disciple, as author, can be understood to have exercised if his own witness is not to contradict and to refute itself.

From this elucidation of the trial motif itself, therefore, we can see that the place of the witness of the disciples in general and of the Beloved Disciple's witness in particular within the broad metaphorical framework of the lawsuit itself requires a real element of reporting of the past within that witness. We do not have to step outside the framework of meaning provided by the Gospel's lawsuit metaphor in order to say that, when it comes to the Beloved Disciple's witness, the meaning of the metaphor of witness includes a significant element of reporting. At this point, with reference to the Beloved Disciple's witness, there seems no reason why the Gospel's understanding of witness should not take up and in a significant way coincide with the historiographic notion of eyewitness reporting. If that makes the Beloved Disciple's witness in that respect exceptional within the Gospel's broader use of witness terminology, this exceptionality results from the logic of the overall metaphorical structure, not from some alien intrusion into that structure.

A Comparison with Luke-Acts

It begins to look plausible that, in the case of the Beloved Disciple's witness, the Fourth Gospel's usage is intentionally both metaphorical-theological (part of the cosmic trial motif) and historiographic. This can be supported, in the first place, by means of a comparison of the motif of witness in Luke-Acts. In its use of this motif in this respect Luke-Acts is remarkably parallel to that of the Fourth Gospel, though this is rarely noticed:

(a) The only statement in John's Gospel explicitly about the witness of Jesus' disciples in general is: "You also [i.e., in addition to the Paraclete] are to testify *(martureite)* because you have been with me from the beginning" (15:27). This is the only occurrence of the word "witness" applied to the disciples (other than the Beloved Disciple) in John. So it is the more noteworthy that it is so closely linked to a requirement of eyewitness presence at all the events of the history of Jesus. Johannine scholars rarely pay much attention to this or to the very close parallel with Luke's idea of the qualifications required for the role of witnesses to Jesus. (We already discussed this parallel, in much more detail, in chapter 6). In Acts, Peter's speech about the replacement of Judas states that the person who takes the vacant place among the Twelve must have "accompanied us during all the time that the Lord Jesus went in and out among us, beginning from the baptism of John until the day that he was taken up from us — one of these must become a witness *(martura)* with us of his resurrection" (Acts 1:21-22). In the Preface to Luke's Gospel the same idea is differently expressed when he claims as the source of his traditions "those who from the beginning were eyewitnesses *(autoptai)* and servants of the word" (Luke 1:2). These are probably a wider group than just the Twelve, but include the Twelve and are similarly qualified. The phrase that John and Luke have in common — "from the beginning" *(ap' archēs)* — is typically Johannine (cf. John 6:64; 8:25, 44; 1 John 2:7, 13; 3:8, 11; 2 John 5), but in Luke's Preface it has a historiographic background, referring to the appropriate point at which a historical narrative should begin.

(b) If we take John 15:27 seriously, it is clear that for this Gospel the role of witness to Jesus in the period of the Paraclete is strictly limited to a specific group defined by their relationship to Jesus in the time of his ministry. John never suggests that "witness" is something else that later Christian believers also do. Similarly Luke confines the vocabulary of witness almost entirely to those who have been personal disciples of Jesus, with the single major exception[5] of Paul, who is a witness on the basis of his own special experience

---

5. Note also Acts 22:20, where Paul, addressing Jesus, speaks of "the blood of your witness

of the exalted Christ. For both John and Luke witness is something that requires firsthand contact with the events of Jesus' history.[6]

(c) We have noted that the *martyreō* word group, used by both Luke and John, does not belong to the standard terminology of historiography. Therefore Luke does not use it in the preface to his Gospel, where he seems to have deliberately avoided theological vocabulary,[7] calling the witnesses *autoptai* instead. Luke, like John, appears to have drawn his witness terminology from deutero-Isaiah, as the phrase "to the end of the earth" in Acts 1:8 suggests (cf. Isa 49:6). By identifying the disciples as witnesses with the witnesses to God in the Isaianic prophecies Luke places them within the theologically interpretative framework of eschatological events that those chapters of Isaiah provided not only for Luke and John, but also for most of the New Testament writers. Thus it is clear that Luke has deliberately correlated the historiographic notion of eyewitness report with the Isaianic theological notion of God's witnesses. Though John certainly makes more of the lawsuit metaphor from Isaiah than Luke does, the close parallels between their respective understandings of the disciples as witnesses suggest that John also exploits the coincidence between historiographic and theological ideas of witness.[8]

The *Inclusio* of Eyewitness Testimony

At this point we should also remind ourselves of the literary device that we studied in chapter 6, in connection with the idea, common to Luke and John, of witness "from the beginning." There we argued that the Gospels of Mark, Luke, and John all make use of a technique, the *inclusio* of eyewitness testimony, which indicates that disciple of Jesus on whose witness the Gospel in question is primarily based by making him the disciple who is mentioned both first and last in the Gospel's account of Jesus' ministry. We noticed that,

---

Stephen." This usage may be influenced by the reference to Paul's witness in v. 18, but it may also have the literal judicial context of Stephen's witness and death in view.

6. A. J. Köstenberger, *The Missions of Jesus and the Disciples according to the Fourth Gospel* (Grand Rapids: Eerdmans, 1998) 150-51, contests this view for John, but can do so only by an argument from analogy, not from actual Johannine usage.

7. Cf. L. Alexander, *The Preface to Luke's Gospel* (SNTSMS 78; Cambridge: Cambridge University Press, 1993) 124: "Luke goes out of his way to avoid specifically Christian language in the preface."

8. Another interesting parallel in these two authors' understandings of witness is that in both John (15:26-27) and Luke-Acts (Luke 24:46-49; Acts 1:8) the Spirit is related to the disciples' witness.

in John's case, it is the Beloved Disciple who occupies this position, displacing Peter from the position of primary eyewitness he enjoys in Mark, appearing in the narrative a little before Peter and also becoming the object of narrative attention at the very end of the Gospel, just after Peter. If this argument is valid, then the Gospel clearly portrays the Beloved Disciple's witness as the kind of eyewitness testimony that belongs to historiography.

We can reinforce the point here by looking in a little more detail at the way the portrayals of the anonymous disciple in 1:35-40 and the Beloved Disciple in chapter 21 are subtly parallel. The former cannot, in the context of chapter 1, yet be identified as the Beloved Disciple, but he becomes so identifiable retrospectively, both in view of the statement in 15:27 that witnesses to Jesus must have been with him "from the beginning" and also in view of the literary parallelism we shall now examine.

The parallel begins at 1:35 and 21:2. In 1:35 we are introduced to two anonymous disciples (initially of John the Baptist, subsequently of Jesus), while in 21:2 the fishing party is said to consist of five named disciples and two anonymous others. In this way, as Derek Tovey puts it, the author

> creates a "space" for an elusive, unnamed disciple. In both cases the space is created initially by mentioning two unnamed disciples, then partly filled with a particular disciple. But there is a subtle difference. In the first case, the place of one of the unnamed characters is taken by Andrew (1.40), hence by a named and unmistakably identifiable and identified character. He is Simon Peter's brother and features a number of times in the gospel (also at 6.8 and 12.22). However, in ch. 21, one space remains open (as is the case at 1.35-42) while the other is filled by none other than the beloved disciple who, the reader discovers at 21.7, is a member of the party. By this time in the narrative he is a wholly substantial and personalized character, but still unnamed.[9]

This pattern of similarity and difference explains the otherwise rather odd fact that there are *two* anonymous disciples in the fishing party. (Is the one who remains unidentified Andrew, who thus, by comparison with their appearance in 1:35-42, changes places with the Beloved Disciple?)

Of the two anonymous disciples in 1:35 it is said that, having heard John the Baptist's identification of Jesus as the Lamb of God, they "followed" Jesus (1:37). Then "Jesus turned and saw them following" (1:38). This statement is strikingly paralleled towards the end of ch. 21, where the attention is drawn to

---

9. D. Tovey, *Narrative Art and Act in the Fourth Gospel* (JSNTSup 151; Sheffield: Sheffield Academic, 1997) 124.

the Beloved Disciple thus: "Peter turned and saw the disciple whom Jesus loved following" (21:20). (The Greek words for "turned" and "saw" are different in the two cases, but this is not an argument against the significance of the parallel, still less for the view that ch. 21 comes from a different author. Rather the difference is typical of the way this Gospel frequently varies its vocabulary even when repeating the same assertions.[10]) In both passages the "following" of Jesus is literal (walking behind Jesus) but there is also the symbolic connotation of following as discipleship.

The parallel does not end with the Beloved Disciple's "following" of Jesus; it extends to his "remaining." In the case of the first two disciples, their first words to Jesus are "Rabbi, where are you staying *(meneis)?*" (1:38). In response he invites them to "Come and see!" The narrative continues: "So they came and saw where he was staying *(menei),* and they remained *(emeinan)* with him that day" (1:39). (In English a consistent translation of the Greek verb *menein* is not possible here, but it is the same verb that is translated both "stay" and "remain.") At the end of the Gospel narrative, in reply to Peter's question about the Beloved Disciple, "Lord, what about him?" Jesus says: "If I will that he remain *(menein)* until I come, what is that to you?" (21:22). This saying of Jesus is then repeated to form the last words of Jesus in the Gospel, "If it is my will that he remain *(menein)* until I come" (21:23).[11]

The connection here between the two cases of "remaining" may seem somewhat artificial, but when we learn (in 21:24) that the Beloved Disciple is the principal eyewitness behind the Gospel's narrative, the connection becomes much more significant. The day that the Beloved Disciple spent with Jesus at the beginning of Jesus' ministry, before Peter even set eyes on Jesus (1:40-42), indicates that he had the opportunity to get to know Jesus right at the beginning. It strengthens his qualification to be the special witness whose testimony forms this Gospel. The reference at the end of the Gospel to his remaining refers to his activity of bearing witness to Jesus after the Gospel story of Jesus has reached its conclusion. Whereas Peter's destiny is to give his life for Jesus and his people (21:18-19), the Beloved Disciple's destiny is to continue to bear witness to Jesus. Thus the Beloved Disciple's qualifications to bear witness to Jesus began before Peter became a disciple and his activity of bearing witness will continue into the future even after Peter has completed

10. See E. D. Freed, "Variations in the Language and Thought of John," *ZNW* 55 (1964) 167-97.

11. Many manuscripts complete the sentence, adding "what is that to you?" as in v. 22, but the shorter reading is probably to be preferred. Scribes would have hesitated to leave the sentence incomplete in v. 23 and so supplied the rest from v. 22, but the author could well have wished the last words of Jesus in the Gospel to be "until I come."

his discipleship. In a sense it will continue even until the parousia, because it is embodied in the Gospel. In this sense it stretches from Jesus' first "coming" at the time of John the Baptist's testimony (1:29, 30) to Jesus' second "coming" in the future (21:22, 23). In this way the Gospel of John makes typically inventive use of the *inclusio* of eyewitness testimony.

In view of this quite elaborate use of the *inclusio* of eyewitness testimony, we must conclude that the Gospel presents the Beloved Disciple as the disciple whose eyewitness reports are the most important source of the Gospel's historical narrative.

The Beloved Disciple as Ideal Witness and Author

We must now consider in more detail the role the Beloved Disciple plays within the narrative of the Gospel. He appears only on relatively few occasions: 1:35-40; 13:23-26; 19:25-27, 35; 20:2-10; 21:2, 7, 20-24, and perhaps also 18:15-16. All of these passages refer to him, of course, in third-person language. This is in accordance with the best and regular historiographic practice. When ancient historians referred to themselves within their narratives as participating in or observing the events they recount, they commonly referred to themselves in the third person by name, as Thucydides, Xenophon, Polybius, Julius Caesar, or Josephus.[12] Howard Jackson explains this practice as a "self-distancing and self-objectification" that "bestowed an air of disinterested objectivity and impartiality on a narrative."[13] I doubt this explanation. It seems more likely that the convention is a rather obvious way of maintaining the distinction between the author as an actor alongside others in the narrative and the author as the writer who is narrating the account, or, in Meir Sternberg's terminology, between "himself as 'he' in the capacity as agent" and himself as "'I' in the capacity as restricted narrator."[14] An author who appears in his or her own narrative is related to the narrative in these two very different ways. For an author to refer to himself or herself in the first person when recounting his or her role in the events narrated would have the effect of drawing readers'

---

12. For some examples, see C. S. Keener, *The Gospel of John: A Commentary*, vol. 2 (Peabody: Hendrickson, 2003) 918 n. 210.

13. H. M. Jackson, "Ancient Self-Referential Conventions and Their Implications for the Authorship and Integrity of the Gospel of John," *JTS* 50 (1999) 27, 25, and generally 24-30.

14. Quoted in J. L. Staley, *The Print's First Kiss: A Rhetorical Investigation of the Implied Reader in the Fourth Gospel* (SBLDS 82; Atlanta: Scholars, 1988) 40, from M. Sternberg, *Expositional Modes and Temporal Ordering in Fiction* (Baltimore: Johns Hopkins University Press, 1978) 279. Sternberg uses Xenophon as a primary example of this.

attention to the author as the narrator who is telling the story and addressing the readers. Except for special purposes, this is a distraction. The use of the third person keeps the author *as author* hidden behind the narrative as he or she is in the rest of the narrative. As Tovey puts it: "It might be that a first-century writer had no other way to distinguish [the] reporting self from the self who lived then, except by placing a nominal and pronominal distance between the two 'selfs.'"[15] Whether or not any other way of doing this was available to the author of John's Gospel, the use of third-person reference was both an obvious way and well-established historiographic practice.

As well as the difference between the author as an actor in the past events that are narrated and the author as the writer who is now narrating them, it is also, of course, essential to ancient historiography that the two are connected. In what Byrskog calls "direct autopsy," the part the author played in the events is what qualifies him to write reliably about them. We may once again recall Josephus's claim: "My qualification as a historian of the war was that I had been an actor in many, and an eyewitness of most, of the events" (*C. Ap.* 1.55). If a similar claim for the Beloved Disciple is the meaning of John 21:24, then we should expect the role he plays within the narrative to be such as to qualify him for the task of primary witness and author of the Gospel. This, we shall see, turns out to explain most satisfactorily why it is that the Beloved Disciple appears in the narrative on precisely those relatively few occasions when he does.

A popular notion about the Beloved Disciple has been that he is portrayed in the Gospel as the ideal disciple.[16] (Some scholars have taken this notion as far as denying that he is a historical character at all,[17] though this view

---

15. Tovey, *Narrative Art,* 145.

16. E.g., R. A. Culpepper, *Anatomy of the Fourth Gospel* (Philadelphia: Fortress, 1983) 121 ("the ideal disciple, the paradigm of discipleship"); K. Quast, *Peter and the Beloved Disciple* (JSNTSup 32; Sheffield: Sheffield Academic, 1989) 160 ("a symbolic and representative figure with which the readers are drawn to identify themselves"); R. F. Collins, *These Things Have Been Written* (Louvain Theological and Pastoral Monographs 2; Grand Rapids: Eerdmans, 1990) 42-45 ("he is *the* representative figure of the Johannine tradition," "the disciple of Jesus *par excellence*," "the epitome of discipleship"); M. Davies, *Rhetoric and Reference in the Fourth Gospel* (JSNTSup 69; Sheffield: Sheffield Academic, 1992) 341 ("a dramatized representative of the ideal disciple, an example for the reader"), 344 ("not only the ideal disciple, but the ideal Gentile disciple"); C. M. Conway, *Men and Women in the Fourth Gospel* (SBLDS 167; Atlanta: SBL, 1999) 178 ("Most critics now view the character . . . as a representative of the ideal disciple"). Against viewing the Beloved Disciple as an ideal disciple, see now K. S. O'Brien, "Written That You May Believe: John 20 and Narrative Rhetoric," *CBQ* 67 (2005) 296-301.

17. For a survey of such views, see J. H. Charlesworth, *The Beloved Disciple* (Valley Forge: Trinity, 1995) 134-38; and see also M. Casey, *Is John's Gospel True?* (London: Routledge, 1996) 159-64.

seems to entail taking 21:23 as a later misunderstanding of the Beloved Disciple as a particular, known individual.) If this means that the Beloved Disciple represents, as a model for others, the ideal of discipleship, it is certainly misleading. He may perhaps sometimes function in this way, just as do other disciples (such as Nathanael and Mary Magdalene) in this Gospel, but such a function cannot satisfactorily account for most of what is said about him. Even if we confine ourselves to the passages in which the Beloved Disciple is referred to as such, the only undisputed references to him, we find an emphasis on an exclusive privilege which is precisely not representative. In 13:23-26, he has the place of special intimacy next to Jesus at the supper, which it is not possible for more than one disciple to occupy, and he is therefore uniquely placed to inquire and to be enlightened as to Jesus' meaning and purpose. In 20:1-10 his understanding faith in the resurrection is enabled by his observing the empty tomb and the grave clothes: it relates to the role of eyewitness which he here shares with Peter but not with later disciples. The passage most easily susceptible to an interpretation of the Beloved Disciple as ideal disciple is 19:26-27, where he is certainly portrayed as the only one of Jesus' male disciples who is faithful enough to be with him at the cross. The scene may represent symbolically the new relationships established by Jesus' death and resurrection (cf. 20:17), but even here the representativeness of the Beloved Disciple cannot replace his unique and particular privilege. The point is not simply that any faithful disciple becomes the son of Jesus' mother, though to an extent this may be true. The Beloved Disciple uniquely takes the mother of Jesus into his own home.

In interpretations of the Beloved Disciple as the ideal disciple he is usually contrasted with the figure of Peter, understood as a less than ideal disciple. The Beloved Disciple's relationship to Peter, whose portrayal in the Gospel is much more complex and detailed than that of the Beloved Disciple, is certainly important for understanding the role of the latter. It must be significant that in almost all cases where the Beloved Disciple is portrayed in relation to Peter, the Beloved Disciple in some sense takes precedence (1:35-42; 13:23-26; 20:1-10; 21:7; also 18:15-16, if the anonymous disciple in this case is the Beloved Disciple), while in 19:26-27 and 19:35 Peter's absence similarly gives the Beloved Disciple a kind of superiority to Peter.

There is a sense in which, up to and including 21:7, the Beloved Disciple is represented as superior to Peter. But the sense in which this is true becomes apparent only when we see that Peter and the Beloved Disciple represent two different kinds of discipleship: active service and perceptive witness. The story of these two disciples, as it is told especially from ch. 13 to ch. 21, shows how each became qualified for these two different kinds of discipleship. Peter is portrayed as the disciple who is eager to follow and to serve Jesus (13:6-9, 36-37; 18:10-11, 15). He will not let Jesus serve him, until he realizes that he cannot be a disciple otherwise, and then his eagerness exceeds Jesus' intention (13:6-9). He is ready to follow Jesus into mortal danger and to lay down his own life to save Jesus from death (13:37). But just as he does not understand that Jesus must wash his feet, so he does not understand that Jesus the good shepherd must lay down his life for him (cf. 13:37 with 10:11, 15; this lack of understanding appears similarly in 18:10-11). Only after Jesus' death (13:36: "afterward"; cf. 13:7) will he be able to follow Jesus to death (13:36). So Peter's love for Jesus, though eager and extravagant, is expressed in ignorant self-confidence that ends in failure when he denies Jesus (13:38; 18:15-27). It is after the resurrection (when Peter's characteristic of active eagerness reappears: 20:3-6; 21:7-8) that Jesus not merely restores Peter to discipleship but enables Peter to become for the first time a disciple who understands what discipleship means for him and can at last truly follow Jesus to death. To Peter's threefold denial of Jesus corresponds the threefold pledge of love which Jesus now draws from him (21:15-17; note the charcoal fire which links 21:9 with 18:18). To this new Peter, who now loves Jesus as the good shepherd who has given his life for his sheep, can now be given the commission to follow Jesus (21:19, 22; cf. 13:36) as the chief under-shepherd of Jesus' sheep, who is to care for the sheep and, following Jesus, give his own life for them (21:18-19; cf. 12:33; 18:32). In this role Peter's eagerness for service is redeemed, but his self-will is replaced (21:18) by true discipleship.

Thus the point of the Gospel's portrayal of Peter — which can really be appreciated only when ch. 21 is understood as integral to the Gospel — is not to denigrate Peter but to show him as the disciple who through failure and grace is enabled by Jesus to become the chief pastor of the church. The Gospel does acknowledge a minor role for Peter as witness to the events of the Gospel story (20:6-7), and presumably the fact that the Beloved Disciple displaces, but only just displaces, Peter in the *inclusio* of eyewitness testimony also acknowledges this role. But the Gospel gives Peter primarily the role of shepherd. This is not at all the role of the Beloved Disciple, who therefore becomes at the end irrelevant to Peter's own call to discipleship (21:20-22).

The Beloved Disciple is given a superiority to Peter only in respects which qualify him for his own role of perceptive witness to Jesus. This understanding of his role also explains the way in which the Beloved Disciple is portrayed much more adequately than the idea that he is the ideal disciple can. This portrayal can be analyzed as having four elements. In the first place, there is the Beloved Disciple's special intimacy with Jesus, which is stressed already in 1:35-40. He cannot yet, on first acquaintance with Jesus, be called by

the description that stresses precisely this intimacy: "the disciple Jesus loved."
But what is important about the little that is already said of this disciple in
1:35-40 is that it stresses the opportunity he and Andrew had to get to know
Jesus, a point which is not made about the disciples who are recruited subsequently. Although the Beloved Disciple then disappears from the narrative
until ch. 13, the point has been made that he was able to get to know Jesus before any other disciple except Andrew. When he reappears in 13:23-26 it is his
intimacy with Jesus that is stressed, so that he alone is in a position to ask Jesus a delicate question and to hear and observe the way Jesus answers it. His
especially close relationship with Jesus again emerges in 19:26-27, where Jesus
entrusts his mother to him. Sjef van Tilborg argues that these passages portray Jesus and the Beloved Disciple in accordance with the ancient "institution" ("more or less an institutional reality") "of a teacher who loves in a special way one favorite among his disciples" and "who attributes to this disciple
a special role with regard to his succession in the future."[18] This last aspect is
of importance in pointing us to the fact that the Beloved Disciple's special intimacy with Jesus is not just a privilege but an indication that Jesus expected a
special role for him in the future.

The second element in the Gospel's portrayal of the Beloved Disciple as
qualified to be a perceptive witness to Jesus is that he is present at key points
in the story of Jesus. Again, his initial appearance at 1:35 is more significant
than is usually noticed. It makes the Beloved Disciple a witness of John's testimony to Jesus, as well as to the beginning of Jesus' ministry, and it is certainly
not accidental that the Beloved Disciple on his first appearance in the Gospel
hears John the Baptist's testimony to Jesus as the sacrificial lamb of God (1:35;
cf. v. 29). When the Beloved Disciple's own witness is explicitly highlighted at
19:35, it is his eyewitness testimony to the fulfillment of precisely these words
of John the Baptist: he sees the flow of blood and water, along with the fact
that no bone is broken, that show Jesus to be the true Passover lamb (19:31-
37). The fact that the Beloved Disciple is present at the cross makes him superior to Peter not simply as a disciple, but precisely as that disciple — the only
male disciple — who witnesses the key salvific event of the whole Gospel
story, the hour of Jesus' exaltation, toward which the whole story from John
the Baptist's testimony onward has pointed.

If the disciple of 18:15-16 is the Beloved Disciple, this passage also portrays him as present at a key event, Jesus' trial before Annas, along with Peter's
denials. If his entry only into the courtyard of the building makes him more

18. S. van Tilborg, *Imaginative Love in John* (BIS 2; Leiden: Brill, 1993) 246, and cf. in detail his chapter 2.

obviously a witness to Peter's denials than to the trial, nevertheless his relationship to the high priest may well be intended to indicate access to information (cf. also the implications of 18:10, 26). Since it is the disciple's relationship to the high priest rather than to Jesus that matters for his role as witness in this context, this may account for the fact that he is not introduced here as the disciple Jesus loved.

The Beloved Disciple's subsequent appearances are also at key points in the narrative: with Peter he sees the empty tomb (20:3-10), and with six other disciples he meets the risen Christ in the last resurrection appearance narrated in the Gospel, which is interpreted in ch. 21 as previewing the disciples' subsequent mission to the world.

Thirdly, the occasions on which the Beloved Disciple appears in the narrative are marked by observational detail. As Tovey puts it, "at every point where the beloved disciple appears . . . the narrative includes items of close detail which suggest 'on the spot,' eyewitness report."[19] Lincoln objects to this claim: "Vivid details are part and parcel of an omniscient narrator's perspective in good storytelling and in this narrative are also found at points where the Beloved Disciple does not appear."[20] Of course, the presence of such narrative detail cannot prove that the Gospel really does embody eyewitness reporting, but that is not what is being claimed here. The point is rather that the Gospel portrays the Beloved Disciple as one qualified to give eyewitness reports of the occasions on which he was present. Although there is observational detail in other passages of the Gospel, what is notable is how consistently the appearances of the Beloved Disciple are accompanied by such detail.

Thus, in 1:39, there is the "seemingly unmotivated detail"[21] of the specific time: "about the tenth hour," that is, four o'clock in the afternoon. In 13:26, the Beloved Disciple, from his position next to Jesus at the table, observes Jesus dip a piece of bread and give it to Judas. In 18:18 (relevant if the "other disciple" of vv. 15-16 is the Beloved Disciple) there is considerably more vivid detail about the fire than in the Markan parallel (14:54). According to 19:33-35, the Beloved Disciple observed that Jesus' legs were not broken and

19. Tovey, *Narrative Art,* 140.

20. Lincoln, "The Beloved Disciple," 5.

21. C. L. Blomberg, *The Historical Reliability of John's Gospel* (Downers Grove: InterVarsity, 2001) 81. But R. Schnackenburg, *The Gospel according to St. John,* vol. 1 (tr. K. Smyth; London: Burns and Oates, 1968) 309, is probably correct in explaining the significance of this detail thus: "It serves to indicate the length and fruitfulness of the conversation, which went on all the evening. . . . It also suggests the importance of the hour for the disciples — the hour in which they enter into fellowship with Jesus."

that the thrust of the sword into his side produced flows of blood and water. In the empty tomb, Peter "saw the linen wrappings lying there, and the cloth that had been on Jesus' head, not lying with the linen wrappings but rolled up in a place by itself" (20:6-7), and the Beloved Disciple shares this observation (20:8). Finally, ch. 21 has the detail about Jesus' preparing breakfast (21:9) and the exact number of the huge catch of fish (21:11). Such evidence should not be misused. On the one hand, in many cases the detail is, of course, *significant* detail, with a clear role in the narrative, while, on the other hand, vivid detail is the stock-in-trade of a skilled storyteller, such as the author of this Gospel most certainly was. All the same, these details do help to give readers the impression that the Gospel portrays the Beloved Disciple as an observant witness of what happened.

Fourthly, the Beloved Disciple is portrayed as a *perceptive* witness, with spiritual insight into the meaning of the events of the Gospel story. However, despite his special intimacy with Jesus, it is not at all clear that this quality emerges before the resurrection. In 13:25-30 the Beloved Disciple witnesses, more fully than the other disciples, the way in which Jesus designates the betrayer and thus shows his awareness and willing acceptance of the fate that he must undergo as a divine destiny. The Beloved Disciple is given the material for a key insight into the meaning of the events that lead to Jesus' death, but it is not said that he himself at the time *understands* any better than the rest of the disciples (13:28). His breakthrough to understanding seems to come in 20:8-9.[22] The narrative of the two disciples at the tomb skillfully correlates the two. The Beloved Disciple arrives first, but Peter goes in first. Peter has the priority as a witness to the evidence, but the Beloved Disciple has the superiority in perceiving its significance. This point is usually misunderstood by those who see the Beloved Disciple as the ideal disciple. He is not here portrayed as the model for later Christians who believe in the resurrection without seeing (20:29), since it is expressly said that "he saw and believed" (20:8). The point is that, like Peter, he provides the eyewitness testimony that later Christians need in order to believe without seeing, but, unlike Peter, he already perceives the significance of what they both see. The same priority in spiritual recognition of the truth of Jesus is attributed to the Beloved Disciple in 21:7.

These four features of the portrayal of the Beloved Disciple qualify him to be the ideal witness to Jesus, his story, and its meaning. These qualities are

---

22. A useful discussion is B. Byrne, "The Faith of the Beloved Disciple and the Community in John 20," *JSNT* 23 (1985) 83-97, reprinted in S. E. Porter and C. A. Evans, eds., *The Johannine Writings* (Biblical Seminar 32; Sheffield: Sheffield Academic, 1995) 31-45.

displayed to a large extent by way of contrast with Peter, but the point is not a *general* superiority to Peter. The Beloved Disciple is better qualified to be the author of a Gospel, but he is not better qualified to be the chief under-shepherd of Jesus' sheep, which is Peter's mode of discipleship. It is worth no-ticing that whereas in Peter's case, the Gospel emphasizes his love for Jesus, in the Beloved Disciple's case it emphasizes Jesus' love for him. The former em-phasis is appropriate for the active role of discipleship as participation in Je-sus' activity of serving and sacrificing: it corresponds to Jesus' love for his dis-ciples. The latter emphasis is appropriate for the more receptive role of discipleship as witness and corresponds to Jesus' enjoyment of his Father's love (cf. the correspondence between 13:23 and 1:18). The different, comple-mentary roles of the two disciples shows that it is not rivalry between differ-ent branches of early Christianity that is at stake in their relationship. The Gospel acknowledges Peter's leading role in the whole church, while claiming for the Beloved Disciple a role of witnessing to the truth of Jesus which is equally significant for the whole church.

Finally, on the relation between Peter and the Beloved Disciple, we should note that the point of their portrayal, in comparison and contrast with each other, is neither the way each relates to the other nor the way each relates to others within the narrative. Peter is not shown as "shepherd" to other disciples within the narrative, nor does the Beloved Disciple act as a witness to others within the narrative. Except at 21:7, his relation to Peter is not that of mediator to Peter of his superior insight into the truth of Jesus. Rather he is represented as the disciple who was so related to Jesus and the events of Jesus' story that he can bear witness *to the readers/hearers of the Gos-pel*. The point of the double story of the two disciples is to show how each, through his own, different way of following Jesus, relates to the church after the resurrection. Just as Peter's role in the story enables him to become the chief under-shepherd of Jesus' sheep, not within the narrative but later, so the Beloved Disciple's role in the story enables him to witness to others, not within the narrative but later. Although both can serve from time to time in the narrative as representative disciples, models for all Christians, the over-whelming emphasis is on the special roles which their personal discipleship of Jesus enables them to play in the church. In the Beloved Disciple's case, this is his witness as author of the Gospel.

The argument is still repeated that the Beloved Disciple would not have been so presumptuous as to call *himself* "the disciple Jesus loved,"[23] as he must have done were he the author of the Gospel. The argument probably

23. E.g., Culpepper, *Anatomy*, 45.

presupposes too modern a concept of appropriate modesty. But it is also important to realize that by this epithet is not meant only that Jesus singled him out from the other disciples, all of whom he loved, as the Gospel makes very clear (13:1), and made him the recipient of special affection and intimacy. The epithet points not only to a privilege but also to a responsibility and a vocation. Out of his privileged intimacy the Beloved Disciple was to witness. The Gospel was evidently written out of this belief in this disciple's special calling to witness to Jesus and the events in which he had been a privileged participant. He would not have seen such a calling as something to be modest about. Just as Paul had no qualms about claiming his calling to proclaim Christ to all the Gentiles (e.g., Rom 1:1-5; Gal 1:15-16), so the author of the Gospel of John had no inhibitions about describing himself as Jesus' favorite disciple, since this was, after all, his qualification and his authority for writing the Gospel.

As another indication that, in the broader social context, the sort of claim the Beloved Disciple makes for himself (if he is the author of the Gospel) would not have been thought inappropriately presumptuous, we may recall our reading of Porphyry's *Life of Plotinus* in chapter 6. We observed that the relationship of Porphyry and Amelius as disciples of Plotinus is reminiscent of the Beloved Disciple and Peter. Porphyry's immodesty, even self-aggrandizement, is in the interests of his claim of succession to Plotinus, to be the disciple to whom Plotinus entrusted the editing of his works and thereby his legacy after his death. Whether or not Porphyry's work was actually influenced by the Gospel of John, the notion of a favorite disciple who was designated successor of his master (a teacher or philosopher), the one entrusted with keeping his teaching alive, was widespread in the ancient world.[24] It was hardly possible to claim such a role as successor without also claiming the position of favorite disciple in some sense.

The phrase "the disciple whom Jesus loved" must be regarded as an epithet, not a real title. Had it been a title, commonly used by others to refer reverentially to this disciple, it would have had a fixed linguistic form, whereas in fact the Greek verb used in the phrase is usually *agapan* (13:23; 19:26; 21:7, 20) but once *philein* (20:2). Moreover, it is much too cumbersome to have been used as a title. This is why in English discussion the disciple is commonly called "the Beloved Disciple," which contracts the actual phrase the Gospel uses into something concise enough to be easily used as a title. The Gospel could have used the Greek equivalent of this English title *(ho mathētēs ho agapētos)*, but it does not. Howard Jackson is surely correct in concluding that

---

24. Van Tilborg, *Imaginative Love in John*, chapter 2; Keener, *The Gospel of John*, vol. 2, 917.

it was not a title used by others but precisely a self-designation adopted by the author of the Gospel specifically for the purpose of referring to himself in his own narrative.[25]

The Beloved Disciple and the Other Disciples

As we have noticed, the Beloved Disciple explicitly appears in his Gospel on relatively few, though very significant occasions. How far are readers to assume that he was also present at other events where he is not mentioned? The occasions where his presence is explicit certainly cannot be the sum total of his presence with Jesus during Jesus' ministry. Just as, on his first appearance in 1:35, he cannot yet be called "the disciple Jesus loved," so he could hardly be called this in 13:23 if this were the first time he had been in company with Jesus since that momentous first day. The epithet presupposes some longer experience of discipleship on his part. Nevertheless, the Gospel leaves us guessing whether any of the events of chs. 2-12 were directly witnessed by the Beloved Disciple and narrated from his own eyewitness memory. Evidently this is not important, for if it were the Gospel surely would make it clear.

The Gospel's use of the *inclusio* of eyewitness testimony implies that the Beloved Disciple's witness in some way encompasses the whole of his narrative, and this is also suggested by the claim in 21:24 that he "is testifying to these things," where "these things" must be the whole content of the Gospel. But neither of these considerations requires that the Beloved Disciple was personally present at all the events he narrates, since it is also clear from the Gospel that he belonged to the circle of disciples of Jesus and would have had direct and easy access to the eyewitness testimony of those who had been present at events he himself did not witness. While not claiming direct autopsy for his whole narrative, he was closely enough related to all the events to "testify" to them all. Again the implication is similar to Josephus's claim: "My qualification as a historian of the war was that I had been an actor in many, and an eyewitness of most of the events; in short, nothing whatever was said or done of which I was ignorant" (*C. Ap.* 1.55). That he was "an eyewitness of most" is something of an exaggeration, but in any case he has no hesitation in claiming adequate and reliable knowledge even of those few events which he does not claim to have witnessed directly.

At this point it becomes significant, as we observed in chapter 5, that

25. Jackson, "Ancient Self-Referential Conventions," 31.

John's Gospel differs from the Synoptics in having no list of the Twelve. It refers to the Twelve (6:67-71), but gives no clear indication which disciples belonged to this body other than Peter (6:68), Judas Iscariot (6:71), and Thomas (20:24). The function of the lists of the Twelve in the Synoptics, we argued in chapter 5, is to cite their authority as the official sources and guarantors of the main body of Gospel traditions these Gospels contain. Evidently John's Gospel, unlike the Synoptics, does not wish to claim to be based on the official witness of the Twelve.

This coheres with the probability that the Beloved Disciple himself was not one of the Twelve. But we should also notice that the named disciples of Jesus who do appear in the Gospel of John are not, with the exception of Peter, those prominent in the Synoptic Gospels. The sons of Zebedee barely make an appearance (21:2), while those male and itinerant disciples who are prominent are Andrew (appearing independently of his brother, as he does not in the Synoptics) (1:40-42, 44; 6:8-9; 12:22), Philip (1:43-46; 6:5-7; 12:21-22; 14:8-9), Thomas (11:16; 14:5; 20:24-29; 21:2), and Nathanael (who, like the Beloved Disciple himself [see pp. 412-14 below], was not one of the Twelve: 1:45-51; 21:2). Also prominent, of course, are Nicodemus, and the Bethany family, Lazarus, Martha, and Mary. These names may well indicate the circles in which the Beloved Disciple especially moved and his sources for traditions for which he could not depend on his own direct autopsy. That some of them are members of the Twelve does not contradict the observation that this Gospel is not dependent on the core collection of gospel traditions that went under the authority of the Twelve, for that official and corporate witness of the Twelve did not prevent individual members of the Twelve from also being tradents and guarantors of traditions they transmitted as individuals. We observed in chapter 2 that this is an implication of Papias's report that he sought for traditions attributed to individual named disciples, including members of the Twelve. That the Gospel of John draws both on the Beloved Disciple's own direct autopsy and also on traditions he had directly from individual disciples whose specific traditions did not enter the Synoptic traditions of the words and deeds of Jesus can explain in part the distinctiveness of this Gospel's narrative when compared with the Synoptics.

The Meaning of Eyewitness "Seeing"

In the last chapter we found John 1:14 ("we have seen his glory") to be an example of the "we" of authoritative testimony. Many commentators, however, take the "we" to be not eyewitnesses of the events of Jesus' life, death, and resurrection but all Christians or all Johannine Christians. At stake here is not only the identification of the "we," which we discussed in chapter 14, but also the meaning of "seeing" in both this and a number of other passages. Those who deny that "we" in "we have seen his glory" (1:14) are the eyewitnesses correctly point out that to "see his glory" cannot refer merely to the sight of Jesus with the physical eyes that all who came in contact with Jesus had.[26] However, this does not mean that it has no relationship to such empirical contact with Jesus. The preceding context of this statement reads: "The Word became flesh and lived among us. . . ." Whether the "us" in this case are humanity in general or the eyewitnesses in particular, there is undoubted reference here to the physical presence of the Word in the midst of physical humanity. In this context, to "see his glory" must surely be to recognize his divine glory *in this physical presence.* The succeeding context is also relevant, for v. 16 uses another first person plural: "From his fullness we have all *(hēmeis pantēs)* received, grace in place of grace." As we observed in chapter 14, this does not show the "we" of v. 14 to be all Christians, but rather the opposite. The emphatic "we all" introduces a different subject. Only the eyewitnesses saw his glory, but *all* Christians have received grace from his fullness. This understanding of 1:14 means that the basis of the Gospel in eyewitness testimony is already indicated in the Prologue, but in such a way that empirical observation and theological perception are inextricable. It is the testimony of those — or of one — who saw the glory of God in the flesh of Jesus Christ, something that *neither* Jesus' unbelieving contemporaries *nor* later Christian believers did.

An important part of Andrew Lincoln's case for minimizing the significance of what he calls literal or ordinary eyewitness is that "in the discourse of the Fourth Gospel, seeing and testifying are the equivalent of believing and confessing."[27] In other words, seeing and testifying are quite independent of empirical contact with Jesus in the flesh, but refer to the kind of interpretation of the story of Jesus that any believer, knowing the story, could in principle do. Thus Lincoln is able to treat the Beloved Disciple's presence as a literal eyewitness in the story as no more than a literary device[28] that is not important for the nature of the Gospel's witness to Jesus. It seems to be his view that nothing that is distinctive to this Gospel's narrative need be historical (even if it might so happen that some things are) for the Gospel's testimony to be true, because the Gospel's distinctive contribution, its testi-

---

26. E.g., Lincoln, "The Beloved Disciple," 8.

27. Lincoln, "The Beloved Disciple," 25; cf. the argument on pp. 7-9.

28. Lincoln, "The Beloved Disciple," 18-19.

mony, is purely interpretative, the seeing and testifying that are the same as believing and confessing.[29]

That "in the discourse of the Fourth Gospel, seeing and testifying are the equivalent of believing and confessing" is a claim that must be strongly contested. We have already noticed that this Gospel's use of "witness" terminology is confined, in the period of the Paraclete, to the testimony of those who have been personal disciples of Jesus. The Gospel virtually defines witness as entailing this historical qualification: "You also are to testify because you have been with me from the beginning" (15:27). The meaning of "seeing" is a more difficult matter, because it does not seem that the Gospel's rather prolific use of the various verbs of seeing, apparently used interchangeably, can be pinned down to a fully consistent pattern of theological meaning. There may be a few cases where "seeing" is very close to meaning "believing," though even in 12:44-46 the two are probably not quite synonymous.[30] But "seeing" can certainly also be distinguished from "believing," as, for example, in 6:36 ("you have seen me and yet do not believe") and 20:29 ("Blessed are those who have not seen and yet have come to believe"). We have already seen, in chapter 14 above, how this latter saying of Jesus is pivotal for the Gospel's own statement of its purpose. It is the testimony of those who did see and believed that enables those who have not seen also to believe, and it is the Gospel that mediates the testimony of those who have seen to those who have not, so that the latter may also believe.

The issue is not only that of a distinction between empirical sight and spiritual perception. There is also a temporal issue. Not only does seeing the glory of God in the flesh of Jesus entail both empirical sight and spiritual perception. It is also temporally limited to the period in which Jesus lived in the flesh on earth. "We have seen his glory" — in the light of the Gospel's later references to Jesus' glory — refers primarily to the signs (Jesus' miracles) and to the cross, because in these events Jesus' glory was revealed. The seeing occurred when the revelation occurred. Of the first of the signs we are told: "Jesus did this, the beginning of the signs, in Cana of Galilee, and revealed his glory; and his disciples believed in him" (2:11). The glory was revealed — and therefore seen — then and there, in a named place where something happened. Martha saw the glory of God when Lazarus walked out of the tomb (11:40). Even if "seeing" is sometimes used differently, it is this kind of seeing

29. Cf. Lincoln, "The Beloved Disciple," 26: "The truth claims of the Fourth Gospel's narrative are not to its circumstantial accuracy ensured by eyewitness testimony but to the explanation of God's purposes for human existence implied by its narrative discourse."

30. Cf. Lincoln, "The Beloved Disciple," 8.

that belongs with testimony. Some of Lincoln's examples for showing that the seeing that goes with testifying is not empirical sight make this very point.[31] For example, John the Baptist "testified, saying, 'I saw the Spirit descending from heaven like a dove . . .'" (1:32, cf. v. 34). It may be a moot point how non-empirical John's contemporaries would have considered a visionary experience like this, but in any case it refers to an event of revelation that happened then and there. John testifies in the present to what he saw when the revelation was given to him, and the revelation was given, of course, in connection with Jesus in the flesh. It was on the man that John could see with his eyes on whom he saw in vision the Spirit descend and remain. This link between empirical and temporal aspects of seeing and testifying highlights once again how we cannot eliminate the empirical without collapsing the two temporal phases of the Gospel's lawsuit into one.

When John uses the language of "seeing" in a way that correlates with testimony it has empirical and temporal aspects that bring it to that extent close to the language of "seeing" in historiography. For while the legal metaphor of witness does not belong to the standard terminology of historiography, the language of "seeing" does. The historians' preference for eyewitness reports or (better still) their own eyewitness observation was justified by the well-known saying of Heraclitus,[32] quoted by Thucydides (1.73.2) and Polybius (12.7.1) in the form "Eyes are surer witnesses than ears" (here there is an occurrence of "witness" language) and by Herodotus (1.8) and Lucian (*Hist. Conscr.* 29) in the form "Ears are less reliable than eyes." A historian denounced by Lucian began his account: "Ears are less reliable than eyes. I write then what I have seen, not what I have heard." Lucian denounces him not for the principle but for not living up to it (*Hist. Conscr.* 29). It was a cardinal principle of historiography. The contrast between the two senses in Heraclitus's saying is really a contrast between firsthand experience (in which other senses, including hearing, may complement sight, but sight is essential) and merely hearing other people's reports.[33] It is this direct experience to which the Fourth Gospel also refers when it claims "We have seen his glory" (1:14) and "He who saw this has testified" (19:35) or "I have seen the Lord" (Mary Magdalene's claim in 20:18). That the empirical aspect is by no means the whole of what is meant by these claims does not invalidate all kinship with the primacy of sight in historiography. Once again it seems that John's understanding of testimony (in the case of the disciples) unites historiographic and theological aspects inseparably.

31. Lincoln, "The Beloved Disciple," 8-9.
32. Byrskog, *Story as History,* 49-53.
33. Cf. Byrskog, *Story as History,* 93-99.

Why Is the Beloved Disciple's Role as Principal Witness and Author Not Revealed until the End of the Gospel?

We must now return to this question, which we have several times postponed answering. We may usefully begin by tracing the way in which a first-time sequential reading of the Gospel raises the issue of the book's eyewitness basis. Already in the Prologue the author speaks as one of the eyewitnesses (1:14), and so readers know from the beginning that this narrative comes with a strong eyewitness claim, but they cannot tell to which of the disciples in the narrative this claim is attached. They are not necessarily expecting statements in the first person within the narrative, because it was standard historiographic practice for an author who takes part in his own narrative to refer to himself in the third person as one of the characters within the narrative and only to speak in the first person in prefatory or similar non-narrative matter. The Fourth Gospel follows this practice. First-time readers may scarcely notice the anonymous disciple in ch. 1. They may wonder about the identity of "the disciple Jesus loved" when he appears from ch. 13 onward. They learn in 15:27 that the witnesses are disciples who have been with Jesus from the beginning and will assume that the author belongs to this category. They notice the one explicit claim to eyewitness testimony in 19:35, but cannot be sure who the witness is (though he seems to be still alive at the time of writing) or whether his witness is to more than this one occurrence. We have seen how the carefully staged conclusion (20:30-31; 21:24-25) brings them finally to the revelation that the Beloved Disciple is the principal witness and author. Then retrospectively, if they choose, they can trace the indications in the narrative that show him to be qualified for this role.

The Gospel very carefully prepares for the revelation that the Beloved Disciple is its author but equally carefully withholds it until the very end of the Gospel. Why is this? It seems that the Beloved Disciple was not a well-known disciple. He was not completely unknown; otherwise the rumor that he would not die (21:23) could not have existed, but he was not well-known, especially not as a character in Gospel traditions. He was not one of the Twelve, whose names, at least, are carefully preserved in all three Synoptics but not, significantly, in John. He was not one of those prominent few among the Twelve who appear by name in the narratives of the other Gospels. As a character in the Gospel traditions his readers or hearers are not likely to have heard of him — certainly not from Mark's Gospel, which he probably assumes they know, and probably not from whatever other Gospel traditions they may have known. His claim to be qualified to write a Gospel from his own eyewitness testimony is therefore not easy to advance, especially if, as we have seen good reason to think, he and his readers regarded Mark's Gospel as substantially the testimony of Peter himself. The Beloved Disciple's anonymous and unobtrusive appearance in ch. 1 is like saying: "I know you haven't heard of me. I'm not in the Gospel narrative you know, but actually I was there at the beginning, even before Peter." The anonymity of the Beloved Disciple, when he appears as "the disciple whom Jesus loved," is a similar paradoxical combination of modesty and temerity. It acknowledges that he is not a disciple whom most of his readers or hearers will know by name, but at the same time the epithet that substitutes for a name claims a special closeness to Jesus. The claim is not overdone: he appears only a few times but they are points of critical significance in the narrative. Readers gradually learn to see this mysterious person, not only as close to Jesus, but also as especially perceptive. He is privileged to see, empirically, what other disciples do not, but he also, at the empty tomb and again at Jesus' appearance in ch. 21, sees the significance of what happens, at least sooner than others. By the time he is finally revealed as principal witness and author readers or hearers have learned enough about him to credit the claim. But even so the finally and extraordinarily audacious claim to surpass Peter as a witness can be made only with the backing of the cryptic final saying of Jesus in the Gospel, as mysterious as the disciple it concerns.

Authentic or Pseudepigraphal?

Another question we have postponed until now is whether the Gospel's claim to have the Beloved Disciple for its author is authentic or not.[34] Did this disciple really write the Gospel, or did someone else write the Gospel as though it were by the Beloved Disciple, perhaps even completely inventing the figure of the Beloved Disciple as a cover for his or her own authorship?[35] The question is by no means easy to answer. All our arguments so far go to show that the Gospel *portrays* the Beloved Disciple as its principal witness and author, making a historiographic claim about his eyewitness evidence as well as a theological claim about his perceptive understanding. It is another matter whether

34. A scholar who considers the Gospel pseudonymous on the basis of 1:14, but apparently not that it claims the Beloved Disciple for its author, is J. Ashton, *Understanding the Fourth Gospel* (Oxford: Clarendon, 1991) 437-39.

35. T. Thatcher, "The Legend of the Beloved Disciple," in R. T. Fortna and T. Thatcher, eds., *Jesus in Johannine Tradition* (Louisville: Westminster John Knox, 2001) 91-99, uses the anthropological category of "legendary storyteller" to explain how the narrative of the Fourth Gospel came to be attributed to the Beloved Disciple.

this portrayal is historical fact or fiction. In ancient historiography false claims to autopsy, designed to legitimate a historian's work, were undoubtedly made. In the eyes of some, such claims helped to discredit all historians as liars, but they were denounced by more scrupulous historians and by critics, such as Lucian, who wished to defend the authenticity of good history by dissociating it from the fictionalizing tendencies of those historians who placed rhetorical practices of persuasion above concern for historical truth.[36] Where should the Gospel of John be placed in a context in which, according to Samuel Byrskog, "[r]eferences to autopsy now belonged to the cross-section of history and story, reality and history"?[37]

Judgments may have to depend in part on whether the content of the Gospel's narrative is considered historically plausible within the historiographic conventions of the time. However, there is one rather strong argument in favor of the authenticity of the Gospel's claim to authorship that we can only now appreciate at this final stage of our argument. If, as we have argued in the last section, the Gospel presumes the Beloved Disciple to be an obscure figure, unknown in other Gospel traditions, not in a position to advance his claim to be a significant witness to the events of the Gospel story easily, needing to establish his place in the readers' consciousness artfully and gradually, building the credibility on which he can count only at the very end of the Gospel where he reveals his authorship of the work, why should a pseudepigraphal author in search of a suitable pseudonym choose such a character? Why not write, as the authors of other pseudepigraphal Gospels did, in the name of a well-known disciple — Philip or Andrew or Thomas? Why make the task of establishing the credibility of this Gospel narrative so hard for himself or herself? Moreover, why not claim for the Gospel a more explicit and convincing authorization from Jesus than the ingenious but obscure interpretation of a saying of Jesus that ostensibly means nothing of the kind (21:22-24)? For a disciple who could make his audacious claim to testimony more significant than Peter's only by some such means, the combination of modesty and audacity in the Gospel's portrayal of the Beloved Disciple is a brilliant strategy. But it is hard to believe that a pseudepigraphal writer would have invented a character who required such a brilliant strategy to establish his claim to witness.

36. Byrskog, *Story as History,* 119-223.
37. Byrskog, *Story as History,* 214.

The Eyewitness as Historian

There is at least one sense in which the Gospel of John resembles Greco-Roman historiography more closely than the Synoptic Gospels do. All scholars, whatever their views of the redactional work of the Synoptic Evangelists and of the historical reliability of the Gospel of John, agree that the latter presents a much more thoroughly and extensively interpreted version of the story of Jesus. Though the writers of the Synoptic Gospels incorporate and fashion their sources into an integrated whole, a biography *(bios)* of Jesus, they remain close to the ways in which the eyewitnesses told their stories and transmitted the sayings of Jesus. They are collections of such stories and sayings, selected, combined, arranged, and adapted, but with only a relatively small degree of freely created interpretative comment and addition. They have preserved the formal character of their sources to a much greater extent than most Greco-Roman historians did. The latter generally assimilated their sources into seamless, comprehensive narratives strongly expressive of their own developed interpretations of the history they related.[38] This is why, for example, the Gospel of Mark seemed to Papias more like a historian's notes than a finished work of historiography, what Mark took down from the eyewitnesses (in this case Peter) but had not worked up into a developed narrative of his own. Papias, as we have seen, approved of this in Mark's case, since Mark was not an eyewitness and so was not qualified to supply what a fully developed history of Jesus would require (see chapter 9 above).

Papias was thinking especially, though not exclusively, of chronological order, and we have suggested that he preferred John's Gospel, whose greater chronological precision derived, in his view, from the eyewitness who wrote this Gospel. But we can also apply the contrast between Mark (or the Synoptics in general) and John more widely. The greater selectivity of events recorded, the more continuous narrative with its more strongly delineated plot, the lengthy discourses and debates — all these distinctive features of the Gospel of John, as compared with the Synoptics, are what make possible the much fuller development of the author's own interpretation of Jesus and his story, just as comparable features of the works of the Greco-Roman historians enable the expression of their own understanding of the history, making their works much more than mere reports of what the eyewitnesses said. But in the case of the Gospel of John these characteristics are linked with its claim to be entirely the testimony of an author who was himself an eyewitness. In this case, the whole historiographic process of eyewitness observation and participation, in-

38. Cf. Byrskog, *Story as History,* 254-65.

terrogation of other eyewitnesses, arrangement and narrativization in the formation of an integrated and rhetorically persuasive work — all this was the work of an eyewitness, whose interpretation was, of course, in play at every level of the process, but in what one might think of as a cumulative manner, such that the finished Gospel has a high degree of highly reflective interpretation. The eyewitness claim justifies this degree of interpretation for a context in which the direct reports of the eyewitnesses were the most highly valued forms of testimony to Jesus. In the case of the other Gospels it was important that the form of the eyewitness testimonies was preserved in the Gospels. The more reflectively interpretative Gospel of John does not, by contrast, assimilate the eyewitness reports beyond recognition into its own elaboration of the story, but is, as it stands, the way one eyewitness understood what he and others had seen. The author's eyewitness status authorizes the interpretation. Thus, whereas scholars have often supposed that this Gospel could not have been written by an eyewitness because of its high degree of interpretation of the events and the words of Jesus, by contrast with the Synoptics, in fact the high degree of interpretation is appropriate precisely because this is the only one of the canonical Gospels that claims eyewitness authorship.

Conclusion

In all four Gospels we have the history of Jesus only in the form of testimony, the testimony of involved participants who responded in faith to the disclosure of God in these events. In testimony fact and interpretation are inextricable; in this testimony empirical sight and spiritual perception are inseparable. If this history was in fact the disclosure of God, then to have the report of some uncommitted observer would not take us nearer the historical truth but further from it. The concurrence of historiographic and theological concepts of witness in John's Gospel is wholly appropriate to the historical uniqueness of the subject matter, which as historical requires historiographic rendering but in its disclosure of God also demands that the witness to it speak of God. In this Gospel we have the idiosyncratic testimony of a disciple whose relationship to the events, to Jesus, was distinctive and different. It is a view from outside the circles from which other Gospel traditions largely derive, and it is the perspective of a man who was deeply but distinctively formed by his own experience of the events. In its origins and in its reflective maturation this testimony is idiosyncratic, and its truth is not distinguishable from its idiosyncrasy. As with all testimony, even that of the law court, there is a point beyond which corroboration cannot go, and only the witness can vouch for the truth of his own witness.

16. Papias on John

The Identity of the Beloved Disciple

In the previous two chapters we have argued that the Gospel of John portrays and claims as its author the disciple it calls "the disciple Jesus loved," and that this claim to authorship is plausibly authentic. This argument has also entailed supposing that the Beloved Disciple was not one of the Twelve, but a lesser known disciple, not known from the Gospel traditions generally, a disciple who had to establish his claim to a role of privileged witness to Jesus in the minds of readers or hearers who may well know nothing about him.

That the Beloved Disciple was not one of the Twelve, but rather a disciple generally resident in Jerusalem, who did not, like the Twelve and many others, travel with Jesus in his itinerant ministry, has been argued, from the evidence of the Gospel, by many scholars.[1] It differs, of course, from the tra-

---

1. E.g., F. C. Burkitt, *The Gospel History and Its Transmission* (Edinburgh: Clark, 1911) 247-50; A. E. Garvie, *The Beloved Disciple* (London: Hodder and Stoughton, 1922) 202-4; J. N. Sanders, *The Fourth Gospel in the Early Church* (Cambridge: Cambridge University Press, 1943) 43-45; P. Parker, "John the son of Zebedee and the Fourth Gospel," *JBL* 81 (1962) 35-43; O. Cullmann, *The Johannine Circle* (tr. J. Bowden; London: SCM, 1976) 63-85; R. E. Brown, *The Community of the Beloved Disciple* (London: Chapman, 1979) 31-34 (a change of view from that in Brown's commentary: *The Gospel According to John I–XII* [AB 29A; New York: Doubleday, 1966] xcii-xcviii); R. Schnackenburg, *The Gospel according to St John*, vol. 3 (tr. K. Smyth; New York: Crossroad, 1982) 375-88 (also a change from his earlier position: *The Gospel according to St John*, vol. 1 [tr. K. Smyth; London: Burns and Oates, 1968] chapter 5); D. E. H. Whiteley, "Was John Written by a Sadducee?" in W. Haase, ed., *Aufstieg und Niedergang der Römischen Welt*

ditional view that the Beloved Disciple was John the son of Zebedee, a prominent member of the Twelve, a view that is still maintained by a considerable
number of recent scholars.[2]

This is not the place for a full discussion of the arguments for and
against the identification of the Beloved Disciple as one of the Twelve[3] or,
more specifically, as John the son of Zebedee. However, one argument is especially important for our interests in this book. It relates to the sources of traditions in the various Gospels. We have argued that the official tradition of
the Twelve as an authoritative body of eyewitnesses lies especially behind
Mark's Gospel, which reflects this body of tradition in the form in which Peter in particular used to tell it. In this tradition of the Twelve, an inner circle
of three (Peter, James, and John) or four (with the addition of Andrew) members of the Twelve is especially prominent. In Matthew and Luke this inner
group does not appear outside passages parallel to Mark, and, while Peter is
prominent, the sons of Zebedee never appear in non-Markan traditions in

---

II.25.3 (Berlin: de Gruyter, 1985) 2481-2505; G. R. Beasley-Murray, *John* (WBC 36; Waco: Word,
1987) lxx-lxxv; M. Hengel, *The Johannine Question* (tr. J. Bowden; London: SCM, 1989) 76-80;
idem, *Die johanneische Frage* (WUNT 67; Tübingen: Mohr, 1993) 210-19; J. W. Pryor, *John: Evangelist of the Covenant People* (London: Darton, Longman and Todd, 1992) 3; J. A. Grassi, *The Secret Identity of the Beloved Disciple* (New York: Paulist, 1992); R. A. Culpepper, *John the Son of
Zebedee: The Life of a Legend* (Columbia: University of South Carolina Press, 1994) 84-85;
B. Witherington, *John's Wisdom* (Louisville: Westminster John Knox, 1995) 14-15. This position
is also taken by those who identify the Beloved Disciple with Lazarus: see the survey of these
scholars in J. H. Charlesworth, *The Beloved Disciple: Whose Witness Validates the Gospel of John?*
(Valley Forge: Trinity, 1995) 185-92.

2. E.g., J. A. T. Robinson, *The Priority of John* (ed. J. F. Coakley; London: SCM, 1985) 93-
122; D. A. Carson, *The Gospel according to John* (Grand Rapids: Eerdmans, 1991) 68-81; H. N.
Ridderbos, *The Gospel of John: A Theological Commentary* (tr. J. Vriend; Grand Rapids: Eerdmans, 1997) 672-83 (he thinks John the son of Zebedee deliberately concealed his own identity
in the Gospel); A. J. Köstenberger, *Encountering John* (Grand Rapids: Baker, 1999) 22-25; C. L.
Blomberg, *The Historical Reliability of John's Gospel* (Downers Grove: InterVarsity, 2001) 22-41;
C. S. Keener, *The Gospel of John*, vol. 1 (Peabody: Hendrickson, 2003) 82-104; C. G. Kruse, *John*
(Tyndale New Testament Commentaries; Grand Rapids: Eerdmans, 2003) 24-30. Among older
works, the classic case was made by B. F. Westcott, *The Gospel according to St. John* (London:
Murray, 1889) v-xxxiv; see also E. Abbot, A. P. Peabody, and J. B. Lightfoot, *The Fourth Gospel:
Evidences External and Internal of Its Johannine Authorship* (London: Hodder and Stoughton,
1892); W. Sanday, *The Criticism of the Fourth Gospel* (Oxford: Clarendon, 1905); H. P. V. Nunn,
The Son of Zebedee and the Fourth Gospel (London: SPCK, 1927).

3. The Beloved Disciple has occasionally been identified with a member of the Twelve
other than John the son of Zebedee. Charlesworth, *The Beloved Disciple,* defends at length the
view that the Beloved Disciple is Thomas. Andrew, Philip, Judas the brother of Jesus (regarded
as also a member of the Twelve) and even Judas Iscariot have also been proposed: see
Charlesworth, *The Beloved Disciple,* 179-81, 196-97, 170-79.

Matthew and appear only once in non-Markan traditions in Luke (9:54-55). But Matthew and Luke, like Mark, acknowledge their Gospels' indebtedness to the tradition of the Twelve (whether entirely or only partly known to them from Mark's Gospel) by including lists of the Twelve in their Gospels.

In the Gospel of John, however, there is no list of the Twelve, and the role of the Twelve in the narrative (6:67-71; 20:24) is very minor by comparison with the Synoptics. John has some parallels to Markan traditions, but even in these the inner circle of the Twelve — Peter, James, John, and sometimes Andrew — never appears as a group. Instead, the members of the Twelve who appear by name in the Gospel of John are, with the exception of the ubiquitously prominent Peter, disciples not mentioned in the Synoptics outside the lists of the Twelve: Thomas (11:16; 14:5; 20:24-29; 21:2), Philip (1:43-46; 6:5-7; 12:21-22; 14:8-9) and Judas (not Iscariot, 14:22). Andrew, who appears in the Synoptics with his brother Peter and the sons of Zebedee, appears in John's Gospel only once in association with Peter (1:40-42), more commonly in association with Philip, who came from the same place (6:5-9; 12:21-22; cf. 1:44). The sons of Zebedee are mentioned (only in this way, without their personal names) in 21:2, where they take part in a fishing expedition on the sea of Galilee, along with Peter (their fellow fisherman according to the Synoptics). Such a context is where we might expect to find the sons of Zebedee in a Gospel that is generally not concerned with them. In addition to highlighting members of the Twelve other than those prominent in the Synoptics, John's Gospel also gives significant roles to named disciples, not members of the Twelve, who do not appear at all in the Synoptics (Nathanael, Nicodemus, Lazarus, Mary the wife of Clopas) or who appear only once in one of the Synoptics (Mary and Martha of Bethany, who also appear in Luke 10:38-42).

All this suggests that the distinctive narratives of the Gospel of John derive not simply from the Beloved Disciple himself, but from a particular circle of disciples of Jesus in which the Beloved Disciple moved. The circle includes a few of the Twelve, especially Philip and Thomas, but not the inner circle so prominent in Mark. Other disciples who were not members of the Twelve were just as prominent in this circle. It is notable that four of these lived in Jerusalem or its vicinity (Nicodemus, Lazarus, Martha, and Mary), a fact that supports the supposition that the Beloved Disciple himself was a Jerusalem resident. Attempts to identify the Beloved Disciple with one of this circle who is named in the Gospel (Lazarus,[4] Thomas,[5] or

4. See Charlesworth, *The Beloved Disciple*, 185-92.
5. Charlesworth, *The Beloved Disciple*, chapters 4-10. Charlesworth's argument is fully discussed, along with Martin Hengel's identification of the Beloved Disciple with John the El-

Nathanael[6]) fail because they require us to think that the Gospel sometimes refers to the Beloved Disciple as an anonymous figure and sometimes names him. Whatever the function of anonymity in the Gospel's portrayal of the Beloved Disciple, it would be defeated if it were not consistently employed. But the same consideration speaks against the identification of the Beloved Disciple with John the son of Zebedee.[7] The latter does appear in the reference to "the sons of Zebedee" in 21:2, where the list of disciples explicitly includes two anonymous disciples. When readers or hearers discover that the Beloved Disciple is one of this group (21:7), the natural assumption, in view of his anonymity throughout the Gospel up to this point, is that he is one of the two anonymous persons in 21:2. The fact that John the son of Zebedee appears as one of "the sons of Zebedee" in 21:2 actually excludes the possibility that he is the Beloved Disciple.

Many of those scholars who consider that the Beloved Disciple is not John the son of Zebedee are content — or think we are obliged — to leave him anonymous, not identifiable as any historical person otherwise known to us. For the validity of our argument in the last two chapters, this would be sufficient. However, there are two reasons why it will be worthwhile to pursue the question of the identity of the Beloved Disciple further. One is that in chapter 12 we accepted and endorsed Martin Hengel's argument that the Gospels must have been ascribed to Matthew, Mark, Luke, and John as soon as they were circulating in churches that knew more than one Gospel. Thus the ascription of this Gospel to a disciple called John must have been very early. If we also take into account that the identity of the Beloved Disciple was certainly known to some of the Gospel's first hearers or readers, those who had heard the rumor that he would survive to the parousia (21:23), then it becomes very likely that, when the Gospel first circulated beyond the Christian community in which it was written, it was accompanied by at least oral information as to its author and that the ascription of the Gospel to John is correct. We must note, however, that the title of the Gospel conveys no further information about this John, whose name is one of the commonest male

---

der, by R. Tasmuth, *The Disciple with Many Faces: Martin Hengel's and James H. Charlesworth's Theories Concerning the Beloved Disciple* (dissertation, University of Helsinki, 2004). For criticism of Charlesworth's argument, see also Blomberg, *The Historical Reliability*, 36-37.

6. Most recently by D. Catchpole, "The Beloved Disciple and Nathanael," in C. Rowland and C. Fletcher-Louis, eds., *Understanding, Studying, Reading: Essays in Honour of John Ashton* (JSNTSup 153; Sheffield: Sheffield Academic, 1998) 69-92. For previous examples of this identification, see Charlesworth, *The Beloved Disciple*, 181-85.

7. Similarly, it excludes identifying the Beloved Disciple with either Thomas or Nathanael, both of whom are named in 21:2.

names of Palestinian Jews, in fact the fifth commonest (see Table 6). Five percent of Palestinian Jewish men were called John. That the author of John's Gospel was a John other than John the son of Zebedee is not at all unlikely.[8]

The second reason for pursuing this issue here is that in previous chapters we have found that what Papias said about the Gospels should be taken more seriously than recent scholarship has usually allowed. Unfortunately we lack direct evidence of what Papias said about the authorship of the Gospel of John, but we may have indications of it in second-century writers who had read Papias. Most scholars have claimed that the second-century evidence about the authorship of this Gospel is unanimous in considering John the son of Zebedee its author, but we shall see that there are grounds for doubting this. This chapter will argue that the author was the disciple of Jesus whom Papias calls John the Elder,[9] and that some second-century writers who refer to the matter were aware that this man was not John the son of Zebedee. In the course of time, however, the two came to be identified. The earlier evidence has been misunderstood through being read in the light of the later.

8. Keener, *The Gospel of John*, vol. 1, 97, admits that the name John was common among Palestinian Jews, but thinks that "intrinsic probability does not tend to favor a disciple of the Apostle John named John." I am not sure this argument is very cogent, but in any case I am not claiming that the author of the Gospel or John the Elder was a disciple of John the son of Zebedee.

9. At one time it was a not uncommon scholarly view, especially in English-speaking scholarship, that the author of the Gospel of John was John the Elder, but most of the scholars who held this view did not think that the Beloved Disciple was the author of the Gospel, and most combined the view that John the Elder (supposed to have been a disciple of John the son of Zebedee) wrote the Gospel with the traditional view that the Beloved Disciple was John the son of Zebedee. This was the view, e.g., of B. H. Streeter, *The Four Gospels* (London: Macmillan, 1924) 430-81; idem, *The Primitive Church* (London: Macmillan, 1929) 87-97; A. Harnack, *Die Chronologie der altchristlichen Litteratur bis Eusebius,* vol. 1 (Leipzig: Hinrichs, 1897) 659-80. For other examples, see Sanday, *The Criticism,* 18-19. On the other hand, the threefold identification of the Beloved Disciple, the author of the Gospel, and John the Elder for which we are arguing in this chapter has been only occasionally argued: H. K. H. Delff, *Die Geschichte des Rabbi Jesus von Nazareth* (Leipzig: Friedrich, 1889); idem, *Das vierte Evangelium. Ein authenticher Bericht über Jesus von Nazareth* (Husum: Delff, 1890) (though Delff distinguished the Beloved Disciple's work from extensive later interpolations); C. F. Burney, *The Aramaic Origin of the Fourth Gospel* (Oxford: Clarendon, 1922) 133-49; J. Colson, *L'Énigme du Disciple que Jésus Aimait* (Théologie Historique 10; Paris: Beauchesne, 1969); Hengel, *The Johannine Question;* idem, *Die johanneische Frage* (though Hengel argues for a degree of merging of John the Elder and John the son of Zebedee in the figure of the Beloved Disciple); M.-L. Rigato, "L'apostolo ed evangelista Giovanni,' 'sacerdoto' levitico," *Rivista Biblica* 38 (1990) 451-83. Hengel's argument is discussed in detail by Tasmuth, *The Disciple,* and much more briefly by Culpepper, *John,* 304-7.

One More Time — Papias on the Eyewitnesses

We begin by returning, now for the last time, to the passage from Papias's Prologue with which our whole investigation in this book began. Remarkably it has still more light to shed:

> I shall not hesitate also to put into properly ordered form for you (sing.) everything I learned carefully in the past from the elders and noted down well, for the truth of which I vouch. For unlike most people I did not enjoy those who have a great deal to say, but those who teach the truth. Nor did I enjoy those who recall someone else's commandments, but those who remember the commandments given by the Lord to the faith and proceeding from the truth itself. And if by chance anyone who had been in attendance on the elders should come my way, I inquired about the words of the elders — [that is,] what [according to the elders] Andrew or Peter said *(eipen)*, or Philip, or Thomas, or James, or John, or Matthew, or any other of the Lord's disciples, and whatever Aristion and the elder John, the Lord's disciples, were saying *(legousin)*. For I did not think that information from books would profit me as much as information from a living and surviving voice (Eusebius, *Hist. Eccl.* 3.39.3-4).[10]

We recall that Papias probably wrote this passage some considerable time after the time of which it speaks. When he wrote the passage he certainly knew the Gospel of John, and this passage itself gives evidence of that in its initial list of seven of the Lord's disciples: Andrew, Peter, Philip, Thomas, James, John, and Matthew. The first six names occur in the order in which these characters first appear in the Gospel of John (1:40, 41, 43; 11:16; 21:2). This striking correspondence is unlikely to be coincidental. The only member of the Twelve (apart from Judas Iscariot) who is named in the Gospel of John but does not appear in this list is the obscure "Judas (not Iscariot)," mentioned once (14:22). Papias has added Matthew, a disciple who does not appear in John's Gospel, to the list,[11] because, when he was writing, Matthew's

10. Apart from the first sentence and the translation of *parēkolouthēkōs tis* as "anyone who had been in attendance on", this translation is from J. B. Lightfoot, J. R. Harmer, and M. W. Holmes, *The Apostolic Fathers* (Leicester: Apollos, 1990) 314, with the words in square brackets added.

11. The idea that Papias has substituted Matthew for John's Nathanael, perhaps even identified the two on the basis of the similarity in the meanings of their names (cf. Hengel, *The Johannine Question*, 19-20), is excluded by the fact that in that case Nathanael (who appears in John 1:45-51) should appear between Philip and Thomas in Papias's list. Evidently Papias wished his list of seven to include only members of the Twelve and therefore excluded Nathanael.

Gospel was well known and the apostle Matthew therefore an obvious source of oral traditions about Jesus.

If Papias's list of six Johannine disciples comes from the Gospel of John and follows the order of their appearance in that Gospel — which seems probable — there is a very significant consequence. It is that Papias did not think the Beloved Disciple was John the son of Zebedee, who appears last in Papias's list of six before Matthew, following his brother James (the normal order of the two names in the Synoptic Gospels), because "the sons of Zebedee" are the last disciples to be introduced in the Gospel of John (21:2). The Beloved Disciple, of course, occurs much sooner in the Gospel. If Papias recognized the Beloved Disciple in the anonymous disciple of 1:35-39, he would have placed him first in the list (or second, after Andrew), but even if he did not recognize this disciple as the Beloved Disciple, he would certainly not have missed the latter's appearance in 13:23 (the first time he is called "the disciple Jesus loved"). In that case, the Beloved Disciple would have to appear in his list between Thomas and James. It seems that Papias has not included the Beloved Disciple in this list and did not identify him as the son of Zebedee.

There is another possible explanation of the order of Papias's list of seven disciples, which also recognizes its dependence on the Gospel of John. This supposes that, rather than listing the disciples in the order of their appearance in the Gospel, Papias simply combined the "list" of disciples in John 1 with that of John 21:2,[12] in both cases omitting Nathanael:

Papias	John 1:35-51	John 21:2
	anonymous disciple	
Andrew	Andrew	
Peter	Peter	Peter
Philip	Philip	
	Nathanael	
Thomas		Thomas
		Nathanael
James		sons of Zebedee
John		
		2 anonymous disciples
Matthew		

This explanation differs substantially from the previous suggestion only in supposing that Papias took Thomas from the list in John 21:2, rather than

12. Hengel, *The Johannine Question*, 17-19; followed by Culpepper, *John*, 111-12.

from his earlier appearance(s) in the Gospel. It would be more convincing if John 1 really contained a list rather than a narrative in which the various disciples appear one by one. If this second explanation is preferred, there is no necessary consequence for the identity of the Beloved Disciple. However, an intriguing possibility is that Papias identified the two anonymous disciples in John 21:2 as Aristion and John the Elder.[13] But the question of his identification of the Beloved Disciple would still be left open: among the group of disciples in John 21:2, he could have taken the Beloved Disciple to be one of the two anonymous disciples or one of the sons of Zebedee.

In chapter 2 we noticed the key distinction Papias makes between the seven disciples (seven for complete witness) and the two others who are subsequently named (two for adequate witness). He asked visiting disciples of the elders what the seven *had said,* but what Aristion and John the Elder *were saying.* The seven were all dead by the time of which Papias writes,[14] but Aristion and John the Elder were still alive. He was separated from the former by time, but from the latter only by space. Some scholars have been reluctant to admit that Papias regards Aristion and John the Elder as "disciples of the Lord" in the same sense as the seven were, that is, as personal disciples of Jesus, eyewitnesses of his history.[15] But this reluctance stems from a failure to recognize that Papias is not describing the time at which he was writing.[16] At that time (especially if it was as late as 130 CE, as many scholars have thought) there could scarcely have been personal disciples of Jesus still alive. But Papias is speaking of an earlier period of his life. The clear implication of the passage that at least two of Jesus' disciples were then still alive is what enables us to

13. Hengel, *The Johannine Question,* 19.

14. Philip of Side (writing in the fifth century) claimed that Papias in his second book said that John the brother of James (i.e., the son of Zebedee) was put to death by the Jews. This is fragment 16 in J. Kürzinger, *Papias von Hierapolis und die Evangelien des Neuen Testaments* (Regensburg: Pustet, 1983) 128-29 = fragment 5 in Lightfoot, Harmer, and Holmes, *The Apostolic Fathers,* 326. (The same information is given by George the Sinner, perhaps in dependence on Philip of Side: fragment 17 in Kürzinger = fragment 6 in Lightfoot, Harmer, and Holmes.) This claim has been frequently discussed by scholars writing on Papias and the authorship of the Gospel of John. Opinions are so divided as to its authenticity that I have decided not to discuss it in this chapter. Recent supporters of its authenticity include Charlesworth, *The Beloved Disciple,* 240-41; Hengel, *The Johannine Question,* 21. Corroborating evidence is discussed by Culpepper, *John,* 171-74. In my view, John the son of Zebedee in any case had nothing to do with Ephesus.

15. E.g., J. E. Carpenter, *The Johannine Writings* (London: Constable, 1927) 215-16; Schnackenburg, *The Gospel according to St. John,* vol. 1, 89-90; Culpepper, *John,* 111.

16. Brown, *The Gospel according to John I–XII,* xci, is unusual in fully recognizing this point.

know that the period he describes was late in the first century. It was a time when most of Jesus' disciples were dead but at least two, Aristion and John the Elder, were still alive.

John the Elder — the Long-Lived Disciple of Jesus

Could John the Elder have been the Beloved Disciple and the author of the Gospel of John? For a start we might note two interesting facts. The Gospel reports a rumor that the Beloved Disciple will survive until the parousia (21:22-23) and points out that the rumor is mistaken and based on a misunderstanding of something Jesus said. The rumor makes much sense if we postulate that this disciple survived most of the other disciples of Jesus. The expectation of the early Christians that the parousia would occur in the lifetime of the generation of Jesus' contemporaries became, as it were, focused on this particular disciple, after most of the others had died. His exceptional longevity was attributed to the Lord's wish that this disciple should survive until his coming in glory. The period in which this idea would have been circulated is precisely the period of which Papias speaks, when the more famous disciples of Jesus had died but Aristion and John the Elder were still alive. Moreover, we should note the view that appears first in Irenaeus and was then common among the fathers: that John's Gospel was the last of the four Gospels to be written and that its author lived longer than most of his fellow disciples (Irenaeus says he lived into the reign of Trajan, which began in 98 CE, *Adv. Haer.* 3.1.1; 3.3.4).[17] Irenaeus, who knew Papias's book well, may have learned from Papias that John's was the last of the four Gospels to be written. If this John was John the Elder, then again we have a perfect temporal fit with what Papias says in our passage. At the time of which Papias writes, John the son of Zebedee was dead, but John the Elder survived. He would presumably have been writing his Gospel around that time.

We have argued (in chapter 9) that, when he wrote his Prologue, Papias probably thought Mark's Gospel was written during Peter's lifetime. He evidently also thought that Matthew's Gospel was originally written by the apostle Matthew in Hebrew or Aramaic. Thus, at least from the standpoint of his views about the Gospels when he wrote his Prologue, the time he is describing, a time when Peter and Matthew were already dead, was a

---

17. On the plausibility of such longevity, see Hengel, *The Johannine Question*, 133; Keener, *The Gospel of John*, vol. 1, 102-3.

time at which those two Gospels had been written. Peter and Matthew were dead, but John the Elder, author of John's Gospel survived, his Gospel not yet complete. (We know nothing of what Papias thought about Luke's Gospel.)

The other interesting fact that may connect John the Elder with the Gospel of John is his title "the elder," which Papias evidently uses here to distinguish him from John the son of Zebedee. What is the significance of this title? We must first note that in the quoted passage Papias also speaks of "the elders" from whom he expects to be able to receive reports of what such disciples of Jesus as Andrew and Philip had said. The best interpretation of this usage seems to be that the elders were the senior Christian teachers in the cities of Asia at the time of which Papias writes. Irenaeus, who knew Papias's work well, several times quotes traditions attributed to "the elders" (*Adv. Haer.* 2.22.5; 4.28.1; 5.5.1; 5.30.1; 5.36.1, 2; 6.33.3), which many scholars think must come from Papias.[18] Irenaeus understood this term to refer to the generation of Asiatic Christian leaders who had not themselves been disciples of Jesus but had known those who were.[19] It could be that John the Elder and Aristion, who had been personal disciples of Jesus, were nevertheless also counted in this category of "elders" because they survived most of the other disciples of Jesus and so were colleagues of the Asiatic "elders." Papias would then be using this title for John the Elder in order to distinguish him from John the son of Zebedee. Both were disciples of Jesus but only the former counted as one of the "elders."[20]

However, we must also take account of the fact that in another fragment quoted by Eusebius (discussed above in chapter 9) Papias refers simply to "the Elder," almost certainly meaning John the Elder (Eusebius, *Hist. Eccl.* 3.39.15). This suggests we should take the title more seriously as meaning something very distinctive in John the Elder's case. Of all the Asiatic elders it seems that he alone could be designated simply as "the Elder" without ambiguity. This usage of Papias corresponds rather strikingly with the usage of the second and third Johannine letters, whose author designates himself simply as "the Elder" (2 John 1; 3 John 1). This is a remarkable usage, because it is hard to find a parallel to the use, in the prescript of a letter where the author and recipient(s) are specified, of a title of this kind without a personal name. One would expect either just a personal name or a personal name with an

18. E.g., C. E. Hill, *The Johannine Corpus in the Early Church* (Oxford: Oxford University Press, 2004) 385.

19. J. Chapman, *John the Presbyter and the Fourth Gospel* (Oxford: Clarendon, 1911) 13-16.

20. I took this view in R. Bauckham, "Papias and Polycrates on the Origin of the Fourth Gospel," *JTS* 44 (1993) 60.

identifying title, as in all the other New Testament letters.[21] The very unusual usage by both Papias and the author of 2 and 3 John makes a plausible case for identifying the latter with John the Elder.[22]

The meaning of the title as a self-designation of the author of 2 and 3 John is debated.[23] Explanations that make him one out of several or many elders do not do justice to his anonymity, which requires the term "the Elder" to refer unequivocally to one person only. In the Mishnah, this title *(ha-zāqēn)*, is given to three rabbis: Hillel (m. ʿArakhin 2:4; m. Shebuoth 10:3), Shammai (m. ʿOrlah 2:5; m. Sukkoth 2:8) and Gamaliel I (m. ʿOrlah 2:12, etc.). In this last case, the title undoubtedly serves to distinguish Gamaliel from his grandson, Gamaliel II, but this distinguishing function cannot apply in the cases of Hillel[24] and Shammai. It is possible that they acquired the title in their old age when they were regarded as venerable teachers. But there is no evidence that either could be called just "the Elder." This usage remains unique to Papias and the Johannine letters. Since we know that in Papias the Elder's personal name was John and that the letters bear the name John in their traditional titles, it is likely that we are dealing with a special usage in the case of one and the same individual.

It seems plausible that John the Elder was so called not primarily in order to distinguish him from other Johns[25] (though the title does also serve this function in Papias *apud* Eusebius, *Hist. Eccl.* 3.39.4), but because of his longevity. It was a title of honor given to him in his venerable old age, and he himself adopted it as a self-designation.[26] His own use of it in the Johannine letters coheres with his habit of referring to Christians for whom he has pas-

---

21. R. E. Brown, *The Epistles of John* (AB 30; London: Chapman, 1983) 647.

22. Hengel, *The Johannine Question,* 28-30.

23. Brown, *The Epistles,* 647-51, explains and discusses five proposals.

24. He did not need to be distinguished from his very obscure great-grandson (Tosephta Moʿed Qatan 2:15). Rabbi Hillel II lived in the fourth century CE.

25. Hengel, *The Johannine Question,* 28, thinks: "Probably John the elder was given this name in advanced age to distinguish him from the son of Zebedee, who by that time was probably already dead." But surely after the latter's death, there would not normally be any need to make the distinction. The distinction would only be necessary in special contexts, such as the account by Papias *apud* Eusebius, *Hist. Eccl.* 3.39.4. Hengel's view may be influenced by the fact that he wishes to retain the idea of some kind of link between John the son of Zebedee and John the Elder (*The Johannine Question,* 130-32). I see no need to postulate such a link.

26. Cf. Sanday, *The Criticism,* 252: "I suppose that the Apostle thought of himself most of all as memory — the last and strongest link with those wonderful years. It was this especially that gave him his sense at once of dignity and responsibility. When his disciples spoke of ὁ πρεσβύτερος, I imagine that they meant, as we might say, "the Venerable"; they looked up to him with a feeling of awe tempered with affection."

toral responsibility as his "little children" (*tekna, teknia, paidia:* 1 John 2:1, 18, 28; 3:7, 18; 4:4; 5:21; 3 John 4).[27]

If, as I believe, the same author was responsible for the Gospel of John and all three Johannine letters, then our argument leads to the conclusion that John the Elder was the Beloved Disciple and the author of the Gospel of John.[28]

Papias on the Gospel of John

We have seen that when Papias wished to list some of the members of the Twelve, he turned not, as would seem the obvious choice, to the list of the Twelve in Mark's or Matthew's Gospel (both of which he knew), but to John's Gospel, listing six of his seven disciples in the order in which they appear in that Gospel. He could have distinguished (in most cases) members of the Twelve from other disciples in John's Gospel only by employing knowledge of the Synoptic list of the Twelve, but even so he chose to give a Johannine listing. It is evident that Papias valued the Gospel of John highly, more highly than other Gospels he knew.

However, no explicit comments by Papias on the Gospel of John have survived. (Charles Hill has recently claimed that in *Hist. Eccl.* 3.24.5-13 Eusebius has reported what Papias said about the Gospel of John without naming Papias.[29] Attractive as this claim is, I doubt if it can be sustained, and the issue is discussed in an appendix to this chapter.) But in chapter 9 we argued that Papias's comments on Mark and Matthew, as reported by Eusebius (*Hist. Eccl.* 3.39.14-16), are best explained on the supposition that he was comparing both with the Gospel of John. Papias thought that the Gospels of Mark and Matthew both lacked the kind of order to be expected in a work deriving from an eyewitness because he knew another Gospel, also of eyewitness origin, whose chronological sequence differed significantly from Mark's and Matthew's and whose "order" *(taxis)* Papias preferred. This was John's Gospel, which he could well have thought conformed better to best historiographic practice than Mark and Matthew (and Luke, if he knew Luke) did. It was by comparison with John that Papias could not but see Mark and Mat-

---

27. But this usage need not imply that the speaker is older than those he addresses: cf. John 13:33.

28. Note the argument in chapter 14 above that both the author of the Gospel and the author of 1 John claim to have been eyewitnesses of the history of Jesus.

29. C. E. Hill, "What Papias Said about John (and Luke): A 'New' Papian Fragment," *JTS* 49 (1998) 582-629; idem, *The Johannine Corpus*, 385-94.

thew as lacking order, and it was for this reason that, not wishing to dismiss these last two Gospels, he attempted to explain why they lacked order but were nevertheless of great value because of their closeness to eyewitness testimony. Presupposed is his very high evaluation of John's Gospel.

This conclusion about the way Papias compared the Gospels permits us a final observation about the order in which he lists the seven disciples in the passage from his Prologue. As we have noticed, this is Johannine in its *sequence*. The first three names (Andrew, Peter, Philip) are listed in the *order* in which they first became disciples of Jesus according to the first chapter of John's Gospel. If, as we have suggested, the other names (other than the non-Johannine Matthew) follow in order of their appearance in John's Gospel (Thomas, James, John), then Papias's deliberate adoption of Johannine *order (taxis)* is further evidenced. In Mark and Matthew, of course, these disciples first appear in a quite different order. In Mark it is: Peter, Andrew, James, John, Philip, Matthew, and Thomas. We know that the differences readers tended to notice in the Gospels were those between John and the Synoptics, especially in the order of the events recounted early in each Gospel[30] (including the calling of the first disciples). Papias's adherence to a Johannine order in this passage therefore testifies to his deliberate preference for John in this respect.

Papias must have said something about the origin of John's Gospel, comparable with his statements about the Gospels of Mark and Matthew. Why did Eusebius not report it? There may be two reasons. One is that, as we have suggested, Papias ascribed this Gospel to John the Elder. Eusebius himself emphatically draws attention to Papias's distinction between two Johns, the son of Zebedee and the Elder, because he wishes to suggest that the latter was the author of the Book of Revelation (*Hist. Eccl.* 3.39.5-7). Eusebius did not regard Revelation as apostolic or canonical. Since he so emphatically distinguished the two Johns in Papias, Eusebius could not have missed or disguised the fact that according to Papias the author of John's Gospel was not the son of Zebedee. This was a judgment with which Eusebius would have vehemently differed.

Secondly, Eusebius would not have liked Papias's own solution to the problem of differences of order between the Gospels: that John's is correct and the others unreliable in this respect. His own understanding of the way the sequences of events in the four Gospels relate (expounded in *Hist. Eccl.* 3.24.5-16) is that the three Synoptic authors record the ministry of Jesus only after the imprisonment of John the Baptist. John wrote precisely in order to

30. Bauckham, "Papias and Polycrates," 50-51.

fill in the gaps they had left: he records the ministry before the imprison-ment of John the Baptist. This apparently settles the matter. Eusebius evi-dently sees no need to admit that the order in any Gospel ever needs to be preferred to the order in another. It is significant that, despite his interest in recording what early authors said about the Gospels (*Hist. Eccl.* 3.3.3; 3.24.16) and despite the fact that the chronological differences among the Gospels were certainly discussed in some of his sources, he never quotes or refers to such discussions.[31]

Papias's comment on Mark is in fact the only admission of a lack of order in any of the Gospels that Eusebius has allowed into his work. It has slipped through his net because what Papias said about Mark's accuracy in recording Peter's teaching was too valuable to omit. But Eusebius has ob-scured the importance of the question of order in Papias's quoted com-ments on Mark and Matthew by drastically censoring the context from which he selects these quotations. We can well imagine that he would not quote a statement about John's Gospel that was inextricable from Papias's assertion of its superiority in *taxis* to Matthew and Mark, just as he would not include any suggestion that that Gospel's author was not John the son of Zebedee.

Evidence in the Muratorian Canon for Papias on John

If Papias wrote something about the origin of the Gospel of John that Eusebius did not record, we might expect it to have left some trace in other writers who knew Papias's work. In search of such a trace, it will prove profit-able for us to examine the Muratorian Canon, a text whose relationship to Papias has sometimes been noticed[32] but insufficiently studied.

The so-called Muratorian Canon is the earliest known example of a New Testament canon list, though it seems to record the views of an individ-ual on which books should be treated as authoritative Scripture, suitable for reading in worship, and is not an official church document. It survives in a bad Latin translation of its original Greek. It has usually been dated in the late second century, and although this dating has been challenged in favor of a

31. Details in Bauckham, "Papias and Polycrates," 52-53.
32. J. B. Lightfoot, *Biblical Essays* (London: Macmillan, 1893) 100; idem, *Essays on the Work Entitled* Supernatural Religion (London: Macmillan, 1889) 205-7; F.-M. Braun, *Jean le Théologien et son Évangile dans l'Église Ancienne* (Paris: Gabalda, 1959) 355; A. Ehrhardt, "The Gospels in the Muratorian Canon," in idem, *The Framework of the New Testament Stories* (Man-chester: Manchester University Press, 1964) 12-13.

fourth-century date by Albert Sundberg[33] and Geoffrey Hahneman,[34] the resulting discussions[35] may be judged to have vindicated the earlier date.

The Muratorian Canon must have contained comments on the Gospels of Matthew, Mark, Luke, and John, in that order, but the extant text preserves only the last six words of the comment on Mark, followed by comments on Luke and John:

> at which he was present, and thus he wrote them down.
>
> The third book of the gospel is according to Luke. Luke the physician, when Paul had taken him with him after the ascension of Christ, as one skilled in writing, wrote from report in his own name, though he did not himself see the Lord in the flesh and on that account, as he was able to ascertain [events], so [he set them down]. So he began his story from the birth of John.
>
> The fourth of the gospels is of John, one of the disciples. To his fellow-disciples and bishops, who were encouraging him, he said: "Fast with me today for three days, and whatever will be revealed to each of us, let us tell to one another." The same night it was revealed to Andrew, one of the apostles, that all should certify what John wrote in his own name.
>
> Therefore, while various elements may be taught in the several books of gospels, it makes no difference to the faith of believers, for by the one chief Spirit all things have been declared in all: concerning the nativity, the passion, the resurrection, the life with his disciples, and his double advent, first in lowliness and contempt (which has taken place), second in glorious royal power (which is to be).
>
> Why, then, is it remarkable that John so constantly brings forth single points even in his epistles, saying of himself, "What we have seen with our eyes and heard with our ears and our hands have handled, these we write

33. A. C. Sundberg, "Canon Muratori: A Fourth-Century List," *HTR* 66 (1973) 1-41.

34. G. M. Hahneman, *The Muratorian Fragment and the Development of the Canon* (Oxford: Oxford University Press, 1992); idem, "The Muratorian Fragment and the Origins of the New Testament Canon," in L. M. McDonald and J. A. Sanders, eds., *The Canon Debate* (Peabody: Hendrickson, 2002) 405-15.

35. E. Ferguson, "Canon Muratori: Date and Provenance," *Studia Patristica* 17 (1982) 677-83; idem, "Review of Geoffrey Mark Hahneman, *The Muratorian Fragment and the Development of the Canon*," *JTS* 44 (1993) 696; F. F. Bruce, "Some Thoughts on the Beginning of the New Testament Canon," *BJRL* 65 (1983) 56-57; B. M. Metzger, *The Canon of the New Testament: Its Origins, Development, and Significance* (Oxford: Clarendon, 1987) 193-94; P. Henne, "La datation du *Canon de Muratori*," *RB* 100 (1993) 54-75; W. Horbury, "The Wisdom of Solomon in the Muratorian Fragment," *JTS* 45 (1994) 149-59; C. E. Hill, "The Debate over the Muratorian Fragment and the Development of the Canon," *WTJ* 57 (1995) 437-52; idem, *The Johannine Corpus*, 129-34.

to you" [cf. 1 John 1:1, 4]? Thus he professes himself not only an eyewitness and hearer but also a writer of all the miracles of our Lord in order.[36]

The words with which the fragment begins are most easily understood as dependent on what Papias said about Mark *(apud* Eusebius, *Hist. Eccl.* 3.39.15). They cannot mean that Mark was present at the events he recorded, not only because no early tradition suggests this, but also because the subsequent statement about Luke, that "he did not himself see the Lord in the flesh" *(dominum tamen nec ipse vidit in carne)* should probably be translated "he also did not see. . . ." In other words, Luke, like Mark, was not an eyewitness of the ministry of Jesus.[37] Therefore the comment on Mark was probably to the effect that (as Papias said) he had not been a disciple of Jesus but had heard Peter's preaching and set down in writing what he heard from Peter. If the surviving words mean that Mark set down what Peter said just as he heard it, this reflects Papias's own account, not the accounts of Irenaeus *(Adv. Haer.* 3.1.1) and Clement of Alexandria *(apud* Eusebius, *Hist. Eccl.* 6.14.6), which were dependent on Papias. The whole Muratorian Canon is in fact notable for the lack of any sign of Irenaeus's influence.

The last sentence of the quoted section of the Muratorian Canon should also be compared with Papias on Mark. That John was not only an eye- and earwitness but also wrote "all the miracles of the Lord in order" *(per ordinem)* corresponds to Papias's assertion that *Mark* "neither heard the Lord nor accompanied him and did not write in order *(taxei)*" what Jesus said and did. Because John, unlike Mark, was an eyewitness he was able to write "in order." Moreover, the order that the Muratorian Canon validates in this way is that of the Lord's miracles, referring to the most obvious way in which the Gospel of John appears to insist on chronological order: in specifying the first two "signs" as the first and second of a sequence (2:11; 4:54). Though we do not know what the Muratorian Canon said about Matthew, this concluding statement clearly makes John superior to Mark and Luke when it comes to order.

Such a statement is the kind of claim we have already concluded that Papias probably made about the Gospel of John (see chapter 9). The suspicion that the Muratorian Canon is borrowing from Papias here is confirmed by the quotation from 1 John which is used to substantiate the claim that John wrote as an eyewitness and therefore "in order."[38] This can be related to

---

36. Translation (slightly adapted) from R. M. Grant, *Second-Century Christianity: A Collection of Fragments* (London: SPCK, 1946) 118.

37. Lightfoot, *Essays on the Work,* 206; Ehrhardt, "The Gospels," 13.

38. In his discussion of this part of the Muratorian Canon, Ehrhardt ("The Gospels," 26-36) is led astray by connecting the quotation from 1 John with 1 Cor 2:9 and regarding the latter

Eusebius's statement that Papias cited testimonies from 1 John and 1 Peter (*Hist. Eccl.* 3.39.17).[39] The testimony from 1 Peter was probably a quotation of 1 Pet 5:13, adduced in support of what Papias said about the connection between Mark and Peter.[40] A quotation from 1 John 1:1-4, adduced in support of what he said about the Gospel of John, would be an appropriate parallel.

Thus it is likely that the last paragraph in our quoted section of the Muratorian Canon is closely dependent on Papias. The preceding paragraph reflects the author's own apologetic concern about the differences among the Gospels.[41] It is not out of place in the middle of the comments on John because it was no doubt the differences between John and the Synoptics that the author had especially in mind. He makes the observation immediately after the story he has told about the origin of John's Gospel because the story tells how John's fellow disciples certified John's own account. He takes this to mean that John's Gospel cannot really be in disagreement with others. But it is notable that his own concern (which he shares with Tertullian, *Adversus Marcionem* 4.2) seems to be to stress that on essential points of the story of Jesus (including presumably the sequence of events) the four Gospels agree. This is rather different from the point his subsequent statement about John's Gospel seems to make: that as far as order is concerned, John is superior. This confirms that this latter point comes from his source, Papias.

If the Muratorian Canon's quotation from 1 John and the conclusions drawn from it about the Gospel of John very probably follow Papias quite closely, its story about the origin of the Gospel is more problematic. We must allow for the possibility that this story is a considerably embroidered version of what Papias said. Papias's account of the origin of Mark's Gospel was elaborated by Clement of Alexandria and then further by Eusebius (*Hist. Eccl.* 2.15.1-2), even while the latter claimed only to be repeating Papias's and Clement's account. The elaborations in these cases served the apologetic purpose of enhancing the apostolic authority of the Gospel. The same could be true of the Muratorian Canon's story of the origin of the Gospel of John.

We should notice, in the first place, that there is good reason for supposing that this story bears some relation to Papias and treats not John the

---

as a Pauline slogan. The quotation in 1 Cor 2:9 was much too widely used to have been considered a Pauline slogan: see M. E. Stone and J. Strugnell, *The Books of Elijah: Parts 1-2* (Missoula: Scholars, 1979) 42-73.

39. This suggestion was already made by Lightfoot, *Essays on the Work,* 206.

40. Bauckham, "Papias and Polycrates," 46-47.

41. Ehrhardt, "The Gospels," 26, is mistaken in seeing the influence of Papias on this passage.

son of Zebedee, but Papias's John the Elder, as the author of the Gospel.[42] This is shown by the terminology. John himself is "one of the disciples" *(ex descipulis)*. He is encouraged to write by his "fellow-disciples and bishops" *(condescipulis et episcopis)*, one of whom is Andrew, "one of the apostles" *(ex apostolis)*. The contrast between John, one of the disciples, and Andrew, one of the apostles, is striking. We recall that, in the passage from Papias's Prologue that Eusebius quotes *(Hist. Eccl.* 3.39.4), Papias uses the term "disciples of the Lord" for all who were personal disciples of Jesus, whether members of the Twelve (such as the seven he lists) or others (such as Aristion or John the Elder). He uses it for members of the Twelve in preference to "apostle" no doubt because it is the fact that they were personal disciples of Jesus that matters to him. The term "apostle" as such did not necessarily convey this meaning since, especially in Asia and even for Papias,[43] Paul was "the apostle." So in the passage from his Prologue Papias uses no term that distinguishes members of the Twelve from other disciples. The author of the Muratorian Canon makes this distinction by calling John "one of the disciples" and Andrew "one of the apostles." He did not need to call Andrew this in order to distinguish him from some other Andrew, but evidently did so in order to distinguish a member of the Twelve from John, who was not a member of the Twelve. That the author of the Muratorian Canon is deliberately working with the categories of disciples Papias distinguishes in his Prologue is further suggested by the fact that the apostle he singles out is Andrew. Papias's list of seven disciples is unique in putting Andrew at its head.

Thus the author of the Muratorian Canon evidently means that John, who was a disciple but not a member of the Twelve, met with his fellow disciples, whom the author supposes to have been also bishops. They would include both members of the Twelve and other disciples, and it was to Andrew, the foremost member of the Twelve who was present, that the revelation came. The greatest obstacle to supposing that this account as such derives from Papias is that it presupposes that when the Gospel of John was written not only Andrew but also a number of other disciples of Jesus were still alive. Papias clearly implies in his Prologue that at the time when he was collecting

---

42. That Streeter, *The Four Gospels*, 439-40, was able to quote the Muratorian Canon without noticing its support for his own view that the author of the Gospel of John was John the Elder is remarkable, and illustrates how far study of the external evidence for the authorship of this Gospel has been dominated by an uncritical assumption that second-century references to "John" as the author of the Gospel must be to the son of Zebedee.

43. Papias refers to Paul simply as "the apostle" in fragment 23 in Kürzinger, *Papias von Hierapolis und die Evangelien* 128-29 = fragment 24 in Lightfoot, Harmer, and Holmes, *The Apostolic Fathers*, 326.

oral traditions not only Andrew but also all other disciples of the Lord whose teaching could have been accessible to him, with the exception of Aristion and John the Elder, were dead. It is unlikely that Papias dated the writing of the Gospel of John much earlier than this, since Irenaeus (*Adv. Haer.* 3.1.1) and Clement of Alexandria (*apud* Eusebius, *Hist. Eccl.* 6.14.7), both of whom knew Papias's work, both thought John's was the last Gospel to be written.

In order to distinguish just what the Muratorian Canon owes to Papias, it will be useful to notice that, whereas its story of the origin of the Gospel of John does not, as a whole, occur in any other extant source, two elements of the story are found elsewhere. These are the two aspects of the part that the other disciples play: they encourage *(cohortantibus)* John to write and they certify *(recogniscentibus)* what John writes as true. The second aspect is likely, as has long been recognized,[44] to be an interpretation of John 21:24 ("we know that his testimony is true"). (We have argued in chapter 14 that this reading of John 21:24 is incorrect, but that does not mean that ancient readers of John could not have misunderstood it in this way, just as many modern readers have.)

This second aspect can also be found in Irenaeus, whose evidence is important because he knew Papias's work well. In *Adv. Haer.* 2.22, Irenaeus wishes, for reasons that need not detain us here, to argue that Jesus was more than 40 years old when he died. He writes:

> For everyone will admit that the age of thirty is that of someone still young and this period of youth extends to the fortieth year.[45] It is only from the fortieth and fiftieth year that a person begins to decline towards old age. This is the age that our Lord possessed while he was still teaching, as the Gospel testifies and all the elders who associated with *(sumbeblēkotes)* John the disciple of the Lord testify *(marturousin)*, [saying that] John transmitted [to them the same tradition]. For he remained with them until the time of Trajan. Some of them saw not only John but also other apostles, and heard the same things from them, and testify to the truth of this report *(testantur de huiusmodi relatione)* (*Adv. Haer.* 2.22.5).[46]

Irenaeus goes on to expound John 8:57 ("You are not yet fifty years old") as implying that Jesus had passed forty, since otherwise the Jews would have

44. B. W. Bacon, *The Gospel of the Hellenists* (New York: Holt, 1933) 36-37.

45. The Latin text of this sentence is corrupt: see the note in A. Rousseau and L. Doutreleau, *Irenée de Lyon. Contre les Hérésies, Livre II*, vol. 1 (SC 293; Paris: Cerf, 1982) 288.

46. My translation from the Latin and the partially preserved Greek (*apud* Eusebius, *Hist. Eccl.* 3.23.3).

said, "You are not yet forty years old." Clearly it is to this text that he refers in the passage just quoted ("as the Gospel testifies"). His further reference to the elders has commonly been taken to mean that he knew a tradition which *also* affirmed that Jesus lived beyond forty years.[47] It is true that Irenaeus several times quotes traditions of "the elders" and sometimes, if not always,[48] derives them from Papias. But in this case the more probable explanation is surely that Irenaeus is referring to John 21:24 ("we know that his testimony is true"). He takes the "we" of that verse to be the elders who knew John in Asia and with those words testified to the truth of all he had written in the Gospel. Thus they testified to the truth of John 8:57 along with every other part of this Gospel's account. They were able to certify the truth of all that John had written, both by testifying that it was John the disciple of the Lord who had transmitted these traditions and, because some of them had in the past also known other apostles, by being able to testify that John's record agreed with what they had heard from other apostles.

So far as it goes, this report that the elders certified the truth of John's Gospel coincides with the story in the Muratorian Canon. What they have in common may well go back to Papias. But there are two important differences. First, Irenaeus, by placing John the disciple of the Lord alongside "the other apostles" seems to include John among the apostles in a way that he does also very occasionally elsewhere. In the next chapter we shall return to Irenaeus's identification of John. But his language thus differs from that of the Muratorian Canon, in which John and Andrew are contrasted as "one of the disciples " and "one of the apostles." The latter must preserve Papias's attribution of the Gospel to John the Elder. Secondly, those who certify the Gospel are, in Irenaeus, the elders who knew John, but in the Muratorian Canon they are John's "fellow-disciples and bishops." An explanation of this difference will confirm that both writers are indebted to Papias.

For Irenaeus, as for Papias himself, the elders were the generation of Christian teachers in the province of Asia who had known the apostles but outlived them. This is how we have interpreted our much discussed fragment from Papias's Prologue in which he speaks both of "elders" and of "disciples of the Lord." But some modern scholars have read the text in such a way as to identify the "elders" with the list of "disciples" that Papias gives: Andrew, Pe-

---

47. Lightfoot, *Biblical Essays,* 56-58; idem, *Essays on the Work,* 245-47; J. Chapman, "Papias on the Age of Our Lord," *JTS* 9 (1908) 53-61 (who thinks Irenaeus misunderstood a statement of Papias); J. J. Gunther, "Early Identifications of the Author of the Johannine Writings," *JEH* 31 (1980) 408.

48. See Chapman, *John the Presbyter,* 16, for the view that he always derives them from Papias.

ter, and the rest.[49] In fact, Eusebius also seems to have read Papias in that way (*Hist. Eccl.* 3.39.7). If we suppose that this was also how the author of the Muratorian Canon read Papias, we can see why his identification of those who certified the Gospel of John differed from that of Irenaeus. Papias, we may suppose, said that John's Gospel was certified by the elders. The author of the Muratorian Canon, misguided by his interpretation of the words of Papias that we know in the fragment of the Prologue, assumed that these elders were the other disciples of the Lord whom Papias then names: Andrew, Peter, and the rest. He therefore calls them the "fellow-disciples" of John (the Elder). Asking himself why they were called elders — and perhaps remembering 1 Pet 5:1-2, where Peter calls himself an elder among other elders — he assumes that they were called elders because they were bishops.[50] So he calls them John's "fellow-disciples and bishops," and, when he wishes to name one of them, he naturally selects the first name in Papias's list of these supposed elders: Andrew. Irenaeus, on the other hand, correctly understood Papias. The elders who vouched for the truth of John's Gospel could do so, not because they themselves had been disciples of the Lord, but because some of them had known other disciples of the Lord besides John himself.

The other aspect of the role of John's fellow disciples according to the Muratorian Canon is that they urged him to write. This has a kind of parallel in Clement of Alexandria, another writer who seems to have known Papias's work. Clement says that John was urged to write by his associates *(gnōrimōn)* (*apud* Eusebius, *Hist. Eccl.* 6.14.7).[51] Perhaps this comes from Papias. On the other hand, we should note that in his account of the origin of Mark's Gospel Clement (*apud* Eusebius, *Hist. Eccl.* 6.14.6) added to what he knew from Papias the information that those who heard Peter's preaching exhorted Mark to write a record of what Peter had said.[52] So it may be that this was a conventional topos to explain why an author put pen to paper and that the resemblance at this point between Clement and the Muratorian Canon is coincidental.

49. E.g., B. Orchard in B. Orchard and H. Riley, *The Order of the Synoptics: Why Three Synoptic Gospels?* (Macon: Mercer University Press, 1987) 176; C. R. Matthews, *Philip: Apostle and Evangelist* (NovTSup 105; Leiden: Brill, 2002) 21-22.

50. This interpretation of the elders who urged John to write his Gospel as bishops is also found in later writers dependent on Irenaeus (Victorinus of Pettau, *Commentary on the Apocalypse* 11:1; Jerome, *De viris illustribus* 9; and the Monarchian Prologue to John); see Bauckham, "Papias and Polycrates," 63-65.

51. The translation that Ehrhardt, "The Gospels," 20, gives has: "urged on by the 'Elders.'" This must be a mistake, but it is a serious one because it makes Clement's words look closer to the elders of Papias and Irenaeus than they really are. John's disciples no doubt are the elders, but Clement does not call them this.

52. The point is further elaborated by Eusebius himself: *Hist. Eccl.* 2.15.1.

We may conclude that what Papias said about the origin of John's Gospel was that John the Elder, the disciple of the Lord, wrote it. He may have said that John was urged to do so by the elders, the leading Christian teachers in the province of Asia, who had known other disciples of Jesus. Papias also, very likely, said that these elders vouched for the truth of the Gospel (referring to John 21:24). He then quoted part of 1 John 1:1-4 in order to show that its author, John the Elder, was both himself an eyewitness of the events of the Gospel history and himself wrote them in his Gospel. Therefore he alone, among the Gospel writers Papias discussed, wrote the *logia* of the Lord in order.

Appendix: Papias as Eusebius's Source in *Hist. Eccl.* 3.24.5-13?

Charles Hill has argued that Papias's views on John's Gospel (as well as a reference to Luke's) are preserved by Eusebius in *Hist. Eccl.* 3.24.5-13.[53] Eusebius's use of a source in this passage is indicated by the words "a record holds" (*katechei logos*, 3.24.5), "the record is certainly true" (*kai alēthēs ge ho logos*, 3.24.8), and the vaguer "they say" (*phasi*, 3.24.7 *bis*, 11). It is clear that at least 3.24.6-7 comes from a single source, and it is likely that 3.24.11 is from the same source. Hill has made a good case for his proposal that Papias was the source. It is not possible here to interact with all the details of Hill's argument. Instead I shall offer several qualifications of it:

(1) Hill does not delimit the source closely enough. In fact, "The record is certainly true" at the beginning of 3.24.8 signals the end of the first passage drawn from the source. The rest of 3.24.8, as well as 3.24.9-10, is Eusebius's own explanatory comment. The source is picked up again in 3.24.11 ("they say") but then probably goes no farther than the end of 3.24.11. Eusebius then adds further comment of his own in 3.24.12-13. These comments may pick up some of the vocabulary of the source, but they are not to be relied on for communicating what the source itself said.

(2) However, there is a further problem about identifying what the source actually said. Even in the passages we have delimited as reporting the source, it is clear that Eusebius is not quoting but paraphrasing. Eusebius can be quite free in his paraphrasing. A nice example is what he reports that Clement of Alexandria (in a no longer extant work) said about the origin of the Gospel of Mark. He does so twice:

---

53. Hill, "What Papias Said." He summarizes his argument very briefly in *The Johannine Corpus*, 386-88.

And again in the same books [the *Hypotyposeis*] Clement has inserted a tradition from the primitive elders, as follows: He said that. . . . When Peter had publicly preached the word at Rome, and by the Spirit had proclaimed the Gospel, that those present, who were many, exhorted Mark, as one who had followed him for a long time and remembered what had been spoken, to make a record of what was said; and that he did this, and distributed the Gospel among those who asked him. And that when the matter came to Peter's knowledge he neither strongly forbade it nor urged it forward (*Hist. Eccl.* 6.14.6-7).

But a great light of religion shone on the minds of the hearers of Peter, so that they were not satisfied with a single hearing or with the unwritten teaching of the divine proclamation, but with every kind of exhortation besought Mark, whose Gospel is extant, seeing that he was Peter's follower, to leave them a written statement of the teaching given them verbally, nor did they cease until they had persuaded him, and so became the cause of the Scripture called the Gospel according to Mark. And they say *(phasi)* that the apostle, knowing by revelation of the Spirit to him what had been done, was pleased at their zeal, and ratified the scripture for study in the churches. Clement quotes the story in the sixth book of the *Hypotyposeis* . . . (*Hist. Eccl.* 2.15.1-2).[54]

Even the first of these passages is not a quotation but a report in indirect speech, but comparison with the second shows how free in rewriting and elaborating a source Eusebius could be when he was paraphrasing. There could therefore be a good deal of Eusebius's interpretative inferences even within his report of the source in *Hist. Eccl.* 3.24.6-8, 11.

(3) Hill argues that Eusebius is quoting a written source rather than an oral tradition. It is certainly unlikely that Eusebius would be directly reliant on an oral source in a matter of this kind. But, while the phrase "a record holds" (*katechei logos*, 3.24.5), which is quite common in Eusebius, can certainly refer to a written source,[55] it is not so clear that "they say" (*phasi*, 3.24.7 [*bis*], 11) can do so.[56] The likely explanation is that Eusebius's written source

54. Translations are by K. Lake in the Loeb Classical Library.

55. H. J. Lawlor, *Eusebiana: Essays on the Ecclesiastical History of Eusebius Pamphili, ca. 264-349 A.D. Bishop of Caesarea* (Oxford: Oxford University Press, 1917, reprinted Amsterdam: Philo, 1973) 21-23.

56. Cf. P. Sellew, "Eusebius and the Gospels," in H. W. Attridge and G. Hata, eds., *Eusebius, Christianity, and Judaism* (Studia Post-Biblica 42; Leiden: Brill, 1992) 117: "Greek historians often use the verb φασί when following a source, either written or oral. . . . Eusebius' typical use of the verb φασί seems to be to report traditions for which he had no clear written authority."

was itself reporting oral tradition. This may well be the explanation of the few other occasions on which Eusebius uses "they say" *(phasi)* when he is reporting a written source.[57] It is surely the case in the first of his two reports of Clement of Alexandria on the origins of Mark's Gospel as we have cited them above. There Eusebius tells us that Clement was relaying "a tradition from the primitive elders" (6.14.5), which fully explains the "they say" *(phasi)* in the second report (2.15.2). If the author of the source in 3.24.6-8, 11, is Papias, then Papias could be citing what he had heard that the elders had said or what he had heard that John the Elder had said.

(4) However, there are difficulties about identifying the source as Papias. One is what is said here about Matthew, as compared with what Papias certainly says about Matthew in the explicit quotation from him in *Hist. Eccl.* 3.39.16 ("Matthew put the *logia* in an ordered arrangement in the Hebrew language, but each interpreted them as best he could").[58] The only point of agreement is that Matthew wrote in Hebrew. The point being made is quite different. In 3.39.16 Papias is concerned with the issue of order in the Gospels, while 3.24.6 is explaining how it was that Matthew was obliged to write his Gospel. The two statements cannot be combined into a single account from the same context in Papias, as Hill seems to think when he cites with approval Hugh Lawlor's suggestion "that this information on Matthew from 3.24.5-6 has come more or less intact from the Papian account of which Eusebius gives only the last lines in 3.39.16."[59] On the contrary, if what is said about Matthew and John in the source Eusebius leaves anonymous in fact comes from Papias, then it must have occurred in a quite different context in Papias's work from that in which the explicit quotation of Papias on Matthew occurred. This is not an insuperable difficulty for ascribing the anonymous source to Papias, but it deprives the case of some of its attractiveness.

(5) Hill points out that Eusebius's source in this passage shares with what we know Papias said about Mark (3.39.15) a concern with the question of "order" in the Gospels, and that, if we make the inferences about what Papias must have said about John that we have made in this chapter, then the two passages also a share a recognition of the differences in order between John and the other Gospels.[60] It is very surprising that he seems not to notice that, while a recognition of the problem is a common factor, the solution to the problem in each case is quite different. Papias freely admits that Mark's

57. Cf. Hill, "What Papias Said," 591 n. 25.
58. For justification of this translation and discussion of the passage, see chapter 9 above.
59. Hill, "What Papias Said," 590, referring to Lawlor, *Eusebiana,* 22.
60. Hill, "What Papias Said," 597-602.

Gospel is not "in order" and excuses Mark for this. The solution to the difference in order between the Gospels that Papias must be inferred to have offered is that John's Gospel does follow a correct chronological order, while the other Gospels (at least Mark and Matthew) do not. In *Hist. Eccl.* 3.24.5-13 the solution is quite different. The four Gospels are reconciled without an admission that any of them is not "in order." John is said to have confined himself to filling in the gap left by the Synoptics at the beginning of their accounts of Jesus' ministry. They narrated only what happened after John the Baptist was put in prison, whereas John narrated what occurred before John the Baptist was put in prison. Eusebius is evidently wholly content with this solution to the whole issue of differences in order between the Gospels. As such it rather obviously fails (does John's account of the feeding of the five thousand narrate a quite different event from that in the Synoptics, an event that occurred even before the Synoptics' accounts of Jesus' ministry begin?), but it is reasonably plausible with respect to the early part of John's narrative (as can be seen from the various references in the four Gospels to the imprisonment of John the Baptist, which Eusebius quotes). It does, therefore, address the problem of differences among the Gospels in the way that that problem seems to have been felt most acutely by ancient readers: with respect to the different ways in which the Gospels begin.[61]

If the source used by Eusebius in *Hist. Eccl.* 3.24.5-13 actually said about the respective order of the Gospels what Eusebius claims it said, then this is not, as Hill asserts, "strong evidence" that the source was Papias.[62] On the contrary, it is strong evidence against that conclusion, for it is quite inconsistent with what Papias says about Mark in the undisputed fragment (3.39.15) as well as with what can probably be inferred as to his view of John's Gospel. It is possible that the source itself said much less than Eusebius made it say. It might have consisted only of 3.24.6-7 and may have said that John thought, not that the events at the beginning of the ministry were *all* that was lacking from the other Gospels (as Eusebius's text of 3.24.7 does), but merely that *one* inadequacy of the other Gospels was their failure to narrate the events at the very beginning of the ministry. This could have been said by Papias. But it is clear that in order to save the attribution to Papias we have to speculate about what the source itself said and how Eusebius has altered it. Attributing the

---

61. Bauckham, "Papias and Polycrates," 50-51; Hill, "What Papias Said," 598-601. The discrepancies between John and the Synoptics that Epiphanius says the "Alogi" cited relate especially to the way the accounts of Jesus' ministry begin (Epiphanius, *Panarion* 51.4.5-10; 51.17.11–18.1; 51.18.6; 51.21.15-16, quoted by Hill, *The Johannine Corpus*, 176). For our present purposes it does not matter whether Epiphanius's ascription of these arguments to the "Alogi" is correct.

62. Hill, "What Papias Said," 601.

source to Papias with such a large qualification makes the passage of little real value for reconstructing Papias's work.

(6) However, even if we could accept the whole of Hill's argument for ascribing this passage to Papias, Hill's conclusion as to what Papias thought about the authorship of the Gospel of John — that he ascribed it to John the son of Zebedee[63] — is not valid. Eusebius himself, of course, believed that the author of John's Gospel was John the son of Zebedee, not the man Papias calls John the Elder. Whatever the source said about this, Eusebius would have adapted it to conform to his own view of the Gospel's authorship, just as he interprets Papias's fragment about the eyewitnesses in this way (*Hist. Eccl.* 3.39.5-6). Eusebius regularly omits or explains away anything in his sources that disagreed with his own views of the authorship of New Testament books. As Philip Sellew comments, "Eusebius will resist with nearly complete success any temptation to include historical information about scripture from writers that he considers somehow religiously suspect."[64] For Eusebius, Papias was most certainly a suspect authority.

In fact, in this case, Eusebius's report of the source contains almost nothing that identifies the John of which it speaks as John the son of Zebedee rather than John the disciple of the Lord whom Papias calls John the Elder. Only once (3.24.11) is John called "the apostle," a term Papias does not use at all in the extant fragments. Of course, Eusebius's placement of the passage within his wider account of John the apostle, the son of Zebedee, requires that it be read as referring to that John. But it is worth considering why Eusebius chose to paraphrase rather than to quote. If the source were Papias, it may well be that only by paraphrasing could Eusebius remove the evidence that Papias was speaking of John the Elder, not the son of Zebedee. On Eusebius's use of "they say" (*phasi,* as in 3.24.7 [*bis*], 11), Sellew writes:

> Eusebius normally cites a tradition with the verb φασί [they say] when repeating oral legends. On occasion, however, Eusebius will resort to this vague authority of φασί when he is not so much unable as unwilling, for reasons of theological scruples, to quote a written authority.[65]

Whatever Eusebius's source in *Hist. Eccl.* 3.24.5-13, we cannot tell what it said about the identity of the John who wrote the Gospel.

63. Hill, "What Papias Said," 613-14.
64. Sellew, "Eusebius and the Gospels," 112.
65. Sellew, "Eusebius and the Gospels," 117-18.

17. Polycrates and Irenaeus on John

Polycrates on John

Apart from what we can reconstruct of Papias's treatment of John's Gospel, the most valuable patristic witness to the identity of its author is Polycrates, who was bishop of Ephesus late in the second century. The association of the John who wrote the Gospel with the city of Ephesus is widely attested from the late second century on. It is found in Irenaeus (*Adv. Haer.* 3.1.1; 3.3.4), the apocryphal *Acts of John,* and Clement of Alexandria (*apud* Eusebius, *Hist. Eccl.* 3.23.6).[1] It may well have been stated already by Papias, but we cannot demonstrate that. However, the best evidence for it is surely Polycrates, himself bishop of Ephesus, who was born no later than 130 CE[2] into a family of prominent Christian leaders long resident in the province of Asia and who must have known local tradition in the church of Ephesus well.

Of his writings we have only an extract, quoted by Eusebius, from a letter he wrote, c. 190-195, to Bishop Victor of Rome. The letter belongs to the Quartodeciman controversy, a long-running debate between the church of Rome and the churches of the province of Asia over the date of Easter. The latter, treating Easter as the Christian Passover, observed the festival on the fourteenth day of the Jewish month Nisan, whatever day of the week that was,

---

1. Cf. also Apollonius of Ephesus (*apud* Eusebius, *Hist. Eccl.* 5.18.14). Although from Eusebius's report it seems that it was John the author of the Apocalypse whom he associated with Ephesus, he probably, like other authors of his time, identified this John with the author of the Gospel.

2. In his letter, quoted below, written c. 190-195, he declares his age to be sixty-five.

and not (as elsewhere) on the following Sunday. The controversy became especially fierce in the time of Bishop Victor, who tried to suppress the Quartodeciman observance. Polycrates' letter therefore sought to defend the local Asian practice as supported by the highest authority in local tradition:

> As for us, then, we keep the day without tampering with it, neither adding, nor subtracting. For indeed in Asia great luminaries have fallen asleep, such as shall rise again on the day of the Lord's appearing, when he comes with glory from heaven to seek out all his saints: to wit, Philip, one of the twelve apostles, who has fallen asleep in Hierapolis, [as have] also his two daughters who grew old in virginity, and his other daughter who lived in the Holy Spirit and rests at Ephesus; and, moreover, [there is] John also, he who leaned back on the Lord's breast, who was a priest, wearing the high-priestly frontlet *(to petalon),*[3] both witness *(martys)*[4] and teacher. He has fallen asleep at Ephesus. Moreover, Polycarp, too, at Smyrna, both bishop and martyr *(martys);* and Thraseas, both bishop and martyr *(martys),* of Eumenia, who has fallen asleep at Smyrna. And why need I mention Sagaris, both bishop and martyr *(martys),* who has fallen asleep at Laodicea? or the blessed Papyrius, or Melito the eunuch who in all things lived in the Holy Spirit, who lies at Sardis, awaiting the visitation from heaven when he shall rise from the dead? These all observed the fourteenth day for the Pascha according to the Gospel, in no way deviating therefrom, but following the rule of faith. And moreover I also, Polycrates, the least of you all, [do] according to the tradition of my kinsmen, on some of whom also I attended as a disciple *(parēkolouthēsa).*[5] Seven of my kinsmen were bishops, and I am the eighth. And my kinsmen always kept the day when the people [that is, Jews] put away the leaven. Therefore I for my part, brethren, who number sixty-five years in the Lord and have conversed with the brethren from all parts of the world and traversed the entire range of holy Scripture, am not affrighted by threats (Eusebius, *Hist. Eccl.* 5.24.2-7).[6]

3. Lawlor and Oulton (see note 6 below) here translate *petalon* as "the sacerdotal plate," but this is inadequate in the light of the evidence presented below that the word refers only to part of the *high priest's* headdress, either his golden crown or its golden frontlet inscribed with the sacred name of God.

4. Lawlor and Oulton here translate *martys* as "martyr," as they do in the subsequent three occurrences of the same word (referring to Polycarp, Thraseas, and Sagaris). The word was used by this time in the special sense of one who bore witness by dying but also retained its older sense of simply "witness."

5. This conveys the sense of *parēkolouthēsa* better than Lawlor's and Oulton's "some of whom also I have followed closely."

6. Translation from H. J. Lawlor and J. E. L. Oulton, *Eusebius Bishop of Caesarea: The Ec-*

Discussions of this passage have usually failed to appreciate its careful artistry. Polycrates adduces *seven* great luminaries of Asia who practiced the Quartodeciman observance. As the number of completeness, seven indicates the sufficiency of their evidence. When Polycrates subsequently refers to his seven relatives, who were bishops and to some of whom he had been a disciple, he is not adducing a second, unnecessary set of witnesses, but claiming the seven great luminaries themselves as his relatives. In the interests of modesty, he does not claim them as his relatives until he has first named them all and then introduced himself, "the least of you all,"[7] as a supernumerary eighth, whose witness is therefore strictly superfluous. In this way he is able to add his own testimony to that of his illustrious relatives in a suitably modest way. Clearly he regards all the seven luminaries as bishops, but uses the word in the list only of those to whom he can attach the phrase "bishop and martyr" (Polycarp, Thraseas, Sagaris).

Polycrates' claim to some kind of family relationship with all seven luminaries is by no means implausible. It is surely significant that, whereas the two daughters of Philip who died at Hierapolis are said to have grown old as virgins, this is not said of the third daughter, who died at Ephesus and who we should assume was therefore an ancestor of Polycrates. It may well be that Polycrates' catalogue of his illustrious episcopal relatives was not compiled especially for this occasion but was one he had proudly rehearsed before. The deliberate limitation of the list to his own relatives as well as to the number seven explains the omission of other Asian notables who could presumably have been cited in support of the Quartodeciman observance, such as Aristion, Papias, or Claudius Apollinarius of Hierapolis.[8]

Polycrates' reference to Philip is of interest before we turn to John. The Philip in question is certainly Philip the evangelist, whose four daughters prophesied, according to Acts 21:8-9. When Polycrates says of one of the daughters that she "lived in the Holy Spirit" he means that she was a prophet. At least two of Philip's daughters had been known to Papias (Eusebius, *Hist. Eccl.* 3.39.9).[9] The

---

clesiastical History and the Martyrs of Palestine, vol. 1 (London: SPCK, 1927) 169, altered at a few points (see the preceding notes).

7. All Greek manuscripts have "you" *(hymōn)*, but it is tempting to follow the Syriac version of Eusebius in omitting it.

8. C. E. Hill, *The Johannine Corpus in the Early Church* (Oxford: Oxford University Press, 2004) 297, is therefore mistaken to infer that Apollinarius disagreed with the Quartodeciman supporters.

9. For a survey of discussion as to whether this Philip known to Papias is the member of the Twelve or the member of the Seven, see C. R. Matthews, *Philip: Apostle and Evangelist* (NovTSup 105; Leiden: Brill, 2002) 31-33.

fact that Polycrates' statement about them differs significantly from Acts, where there are four daughters, all prophets, shows that he is certainly dependent on local tradition about them.[10] But by calling Philip "one of the twelve apostles" Polycrates would seem to have confused the two Philips, the member of the Twelve and the member of the Seven (Acts 6:5; 8:5-40; 21:8-9).[11] It would probably be more accurate to say that he deliberately identified these two figures (as they seem to us) as the same person. Early Christian exegetes of New Testament writings, following the similar practice in Jewish exegesis of the Hebrew scriptures,[12] frequently assumed that characters bearing the same name were the same person.[13] The identification of the two Philips by Polycrates, no doubt following an exegetical tradition of the church in Ephesus, is very similar to the way Mary Magdalene and Mary of Bethany were treated as the same person by most Christian writers later than the New Testament. Thus, in his reference to Philip, Polycrates relates a tradition that draws both on local memory of the evangelist

10. M. Hengel, *Die johanneische Frage* (WUNT 67; Tübingen: Mohr, 1993) 35. By contrast the Montanist writer Proclus (*apud* Eusebius, *Hist. Eccl.* 3.31.4), while knowing the tradition that associated Philip and his daughters with Hierapolis (he claims they were all buried there), refers to four daughters, all prophets. For the possibility that Polycrates implies the existence of a fourth daughter who presumably stayed in Palestine, see Matthews, *Philip,* 24 n. 33.

11. This has been the verdict of most scholars (e.g., M. Hengel, *The Johannine Question* [tr. J. Bowden; London: SCM, 1989] 7; R. A. Culpepper, *John the Son of Zebedee: The Life of a Legend* [Columbia: University of South Carolina Press, 1994] 128). But Matthews, *Philip,* argues that there was in fact only one Philip — the evangelist, who was secondarily added to the list of the Twelve. He supposes that Luke, finding the name Philip in both the list of the Twelve and the list of the Seven, mistakenly supposed they must be distinct persons. I am not convinced, partly owing to the view of the list of the Twelve that I have argued in chapter 5. Matthews (16-18) rightly points out that the name Philip was not common among Palestinian Jews (seven instances if our two Philips count as two), and argues that "it is quite unlikely that two of the earliest prominent Christian figures from Palestine would have shared the name Philip" (18). But there are special circumstances to note. Philip, one of the Twelve, was from Bethsaida (John 1:44), and so was doubtless named after Philip the tetrarch, who ruled that area and who raised the status of Bethsaida to that of city. (On this Philip, see N. Kokkinos, *The Herodian Dynasty* [Sheffield: Sheffield Academic, 1998] 236-40. He refers to a citizen of Panias named after Philip the tetrarch [240].) The Philip who was one of the Seven, on the other hand, was a Greek-speaking Jewish resident of Jerusalem, who was probably born in the Diaspora. The plausibility of his name cannot be judged by reference to the Palestinian Jewish onomasticon.

12. Examples in R. Bauckham, *Gospel Women: Studies of the Named Women in the Gospels* (Grand Rapids: Eerdmans, 2002) 40.

13. When J. J. Gunther, "Early Identifications of the Author of the Johannine Writings," *JEH* 31 (1980) 417, says, "A learned ecclesiastic would be able to recognize that Philip the Evangelist was not one of the Twelve," he mistakes the character of learned exegesis in this period. Eusebius, a very learned ecclesiastic, fully accepts the identification of the two Philips (*Hist. Eccl.* 3.31.2-5).

and his daughters at Hierapolis and Ephesus and also on an exegetical identification of this Philip with the Philip who was one of the Twelve. We shall see that his reference to John displays the same combination of local historical tradition and local exegetical tradition.

Polycrates has this to say of John: "he who leaned back on the Lord's breast, who was a priest, wearing the high-priestly frontlet *(to petalon)*,[14] both witness *(martus)*[15] and teacher. He has fallen asleep at Ephesus." Of the elements of this description, much the most puzzling and debated is the reference to John as a priest who wore the *petalon*. This will therefore be left to last in our discussion. The clause "who leaned back on the Lord's breast" is drawn virtually verbatim from John's Gospel (13:25; 21:20). The allusion is most likely to 21:20, because there the Beloved Disciple is introduced for the last time in the Gospel before being identified as its author in 21:24. The phrase indicates the special intimacy with Jesus that qualified the Beloved Disciple to be the author of the Gospel. Polycrates uses the phrase not only to identify John as the writer of John's Gospel but also to suggest the special value of that Gospel. That Irenaeus uses precisely the same words (*Adv. Haer.* 3.1.1 [= Eusebius, *Hist. Eccl.* 5.8.4]: "he who leaned back on the Lord's breast") to indicate John as the author of the Gospel probably reflects a traditional Asian way of referring to the author of the Gospel[16] rather than Polycrates' dependence on Irenaeus. The sixty-five-year-old bishop of Ephesus did not need to learn from the bishop of Lyons how to refer to Ephesus's own Gospel writer, who was also the most illustrious of his own relatives.[17]

Reference to John as the author of the Gospel probably continues with the word *martus*. It is not the statement that John "has fallen asleep" that prevents *martus* here from referring to death as a martyr,[18] for Polycrates uses

14. See note 3 above.

15. See note 4 above.

16. Hengel, *The Johannine Question*, 7.

17. The treatment of the Johannine question by J. N. Sanders, *The Fourth Gospel in the Early Church* (Cambridge: Cambridge University Press, 1943) is seriously marred by the way he dismisses Polycrates' evidence without discussion as merely dependent on Irenaeus and lacking any independent value (7). He requires us to think that no one in Asia thought of considering John of Ephesus the author of the Gospel of John until Polycrates read Irenaeus and that the aged bishop *of Ephesus* then accepted this entirely novel idea purely on Irenaeus's authority. Local church tradition counted for more than that in the late second century. Unfortunately, Sanders's approach has influenced too many more recent and more cursory discussions of the external evidence for the authorship of John. For the superiority of Polycrates' evidence to that of Irenaeus, see J. Colson, *L'Énigme du Disciple que Jésus Aimait* (Théologie Historique 10; Paris: Beauchesne, 1969) 35.

18. As Gunther, "Early Identifications," 420, and others think.

the same verb of Thraseas and Sagaris, who, like Polycarp, are designated martyrs. But whereas Thraseas, Sagaris, and Polycarp are all called "bishop and martyr" *(episkopos kai martus)*, with *martus* appropriately placed second in the pair of words, John is called "priest . . . and *martus* and teacher," where *martus*, if it referred to his death, would be oddly sandwiched between "priest" *(hiereus)* and "teacher" *(didaskolos)*. It has often been taken to allude to Rev 1:2,9, identifying the author of John's Gospel with the author of the Apocalypse, and referring to his sufferings as a witness on the island of Patmos.[19] But it is more likely to allude to his authorship of the Gospel, which in John 21:24 (cf. 19:35) is treated as equivalent to the Beloved Disciple's witness.[20] The pair of terms "witness and teacher" may well designate John as respectively the author of the Gospel and the author of the Johannine letters.[21]

Polycrates' stress on John's authorship of the Gospel is probably connected with the importance of the authority of John's Gospel for defense of the Quartodeciman observance. Claudius Apollinarius, bishop of Hierapolis (perhaps Papias's immediate successor), writing some years earlier,[22] strongly associates the Quartodeciman observance with the Johannine chronology of the passion and refers to opponents of it who appealed to the Matthean chronology *(apud Chronicon Paschale preface)*.[23] He evidently thought that the Gospels do not disagree, but that the proper way to harmonize them was to take the Johannine chronology as authoritative for correctly interpreting the Matthean.[24] That Polycrates shared this view is suggested by the way he refers to the fourteenth of Nisan as "the day when the people put away the leaven." This means that for him the date was identified not as the day on which the Jews ate the Passover meal (since, according to the Jewish reckoning of the day from sunset to sunset, this took place at the beginning of the fifteenth of Nisan), but as the day of the preparation for the Passover (cf. John 19:14), when leaven had

19. E.g., F.-M. Braun, *Jean le Théologien et son Évangile dans l'Église Ancienne* (Paris: Gabalda, 1959) 339. The identification of the author of the Apocalypse is an even more difficult question than the identification of the author of the Gospel of John. I have deliberately left it aside in this chapter.

20. J. H. Bernard, *A Critical and Exegetical Commentary on the Gospel according to St. John*, vol. 2, ed. A. H. McNeile (ICC; Edinburgh: Clark, 1928) li.

21. That John is called "the teacher" *(ho didaskolos)* in *Acts of John* 37 is probably coincidental.

22. Hill, *The Johannine Corpus*, 296-98, dates his work on the Passover to the 160s, which is possible but not, I think, as certain as he maintains.

23. The fragments of Apollinarius's works are conveniently collected in translation in R. M. Grant, *Second-Century Christianity: A Collection of Fragments* (London: SPCK, 1946) 78-79.

24. R. M. Grant, *The Earliest Lives of Jesus* (New York: Harper, 1961) 30.

to be removed from houses before sunset. In that case, the significance of observing the fourteenth of Nisan can only be, for Polycrates, that, according to the Johannine chronology, it was the day Jesus was crucified. Thus his reference to observing the fourteenth day "according to the Gospel" must be to John's Gospel as authoritative on this point. It is in faithful succession to Papias's preference for the Johannine chronology over the lack of "order" in other Gospels.

Polycrates' final statement about John — that he died in Ephesus — is an obvious claim to local tradition.[25] It means that the tomb of this author of the Gospel was known in Ephesus.[26] It corresponds to Irenaeus's statement, doubtless also based on local Asian tradition, that John wrote the Gospel while living at Ephesus (*Adv. Haer.* 3.1.1). Martin Hengel comments on Polycrates: "The tombs of Philip in Hierapolis and John in Ephesus were the counterparts to the famous *tropaia* [tomb monuments] of the two princes of the apostles in Rome with which the Roman presbyter Gaius [also around the end of the second century] confronts the leading Montanist Proclus."[27]

On the basis of the information so far discussed, it has sometimes been argued that Polycrates was clearly not thinking of John the son of Zebedee.[28] The two main arguments used are suggestive, but not fully conclusive. It is pointed out that whereas Polycrates explicitly calls Philip one of the twelve apostles, this is not said of John. But it could be replied that, if it were generally believed that the John who wrote the Gospel was one of the twelve apostles, Polycrates could take this for granted, while using a description ("he who leaned back on the Lord's breast") that gave him even greater authority: not just one of the Twelve, but that member of the Twelve who was most intimate with the Lord. However, this reply, of course, begs the question whether it *was* generally accepted that the John who wrote the Gospel was one of the Twelve.

It is also pointed out that Philip, first in the list, is given precedence over John, but the order could merely reflect the belief that Philip had died before John, who according to Irenaeus survived until the reign of Trajan.[29] It is pos-

25. That there were local traditions about John at Ephesus is also attested by Apollonius of Ephesus, writing probably a few years later than Polycrates: Eusebius, *Hist. Eccl.* 5.18.14 (for the date, see Hill, *The Johannine Corpus*, 138).

26. On the tomb(s) of John at Ephesus, see Culpepper, *John*, 147-50.

27. Hengel, *The Johannine Question*, 7. He refers to Eusebius, *Hist. Eccl.* 2.25.7.

28. E.g., H. K. H. Delff, *Die Geschichte des Rabbi Jesus von Nazareth* (Leipzig: Friedrich, 1889) 69-72; idem, *Das vierte Evangelium. Ein authentischer Bericht über Jesus von Nazareth* (Husum: Delff, 1890) 2-11; C. F. Burney, *The Aramaic Origin of the Fourth Gospel* (Oxford: Clarendon, 1922) 134; Colson, *L'Énigme*, 35-42; Gunther, "Early Identifications," 420-21; cf. Hengel, *Johannine Question*, 7.

29. Hill, *The Johannine Corpus*, 119.

sible, though we cannot be sure, that the rest of the list continues in chronological order of death. A decisive argument for the view that Polycrates refers to a John other than the son of Zebedee will emerge only when we establish the correct interpretation of the remaining item in his description of him: his priesthood.

John as a Jewish High Priest?

According to Polycrates, John was "a priest, wearing the high-priestly frontlet *(to petalon)*." We must give some attention to the word *petalon*, which I have translated here as "the high-priestly frontlet." The Jewish high priest in the Jerusalem Temple wore an elaborate headdress, which is carefully described by Josephus *(Ant.* 3.172-78).[30] His description is the most detailed we have, and all other descriptions and allusions to the high priest's headdress are quite consistent with it. Over the ordinary linen turban worn by all the priests, the high priest wore another turban embroidered in blue. This was encircled by a golden crown, which had three tiers and was surmounted by a golden "calyx" *(kalyx)* resembling the crown of petals on a flower. The part of the crown that covered the forehead was a band *(telamōn)* of gold, on which were inscribed the four letters of the sacred name of God (YHWH).[31]

Josephus does not use the word *petalon* (which means a leaf of metal), but other Jews and early Christians, writing about the high-priestly headdress do, evidently as a translation of the Hebrew word *ṣîṣ* (literally "flower"). There seem to have been two traditions of interpretation of the meaning of this Hebrew word when it appears in the Pentateuch with reference to the headdress of the high priest. Josephus seems to have taken it to refer to the whole of the golden crown, which had the shape of a flower. This is also how the translators of the Septuagint Greek version of Exodus and Leviticus understood it, using *petalon* (LXX Exod 28:30 [v. 36 in the Hebrew]; 36:38 [39:30 in the Hebrew]; Lev 8:9), and the same tradition of translation was followed by Philo *(De Vita Mosis* 2.114, cf. 116, 132) and probably by Clement of Alexandria *(Excerpta ex Theodoto* 27.1; cf. *Stromateis* 5.6.38.6). On the other hand, in the Hebrew text of

---

30. He gives a briefer description in *War* 5.235.

31. Josephus's statement that what was engraved on the front of the crown was the Tetragrammaton *(Ant.* 3.178; *War* 5.235) is supported by Philo, *De Vita Mosis* 114-15, 132; *Letter of Aristeas* 98; and Clement of Alexandria, *Stromateis* 5.6.38.6. On the other hand Exod 28:36 and 39:30 appear to give the inscription as "Holy to YHWH." J. E. Hodd, "A Note on Two Points in Aaron's Headdress," *JTS* 26 (1925) 74-75, argues that the texts in Exodus should be interpreted in line with the later evidence.

Ben Sira the ṣîṣ was understood to be, not the crown, but the metal frontal on which the sacred letters were engraved (45:12; cf. 40:4). Greek writers who followed this tradition of interpretation of the high priest's ṣîṣ used *petalon* to translate it, just as writers following the other tradition did. Hence in *Letter of Aristeas* 98 and in *Testament of Levi* 8:2 the high priest's *petalon* is the golden plate on the high priest's forehead inscribed with the Hebrew letters YHWH.[32] This is probably a more natural use of the Greek word.

It is impossible to tell whether, when Polycrates refers to the *petalon* worn by John, he is referring to the whole of the high priest's golden crown or only to that part of it that formed a band across the forehead and on which the Tetragrammaton was engraved. What is important is that in either case the reference is to a distinctively high-priestly, indeed *the* distinctively high-priestly item of headdress. Of the various golden garments distinctive to the high priest, the golden crown bearing on its front the sacred letters is always treated as the most important. In the *Letter of Aristeas* (96-99) it appears as the climax of the description of the awe-inspiring garments of the high priest Eleazar, and it similarly climaxes Ben Sira's description of the vestments of Aaron (Sir 45:8-12). Ben Sira claims that the crown with its engraved frontlet was a spectacular sight (45:12). Josephus similarly ends his descriptions of the high-priestly vestments with the crown and its sacred inscription (*War* 5.231-35; *Ant.* 3.159-78). It was the unique privilege of the high priest to bear the divine name, graven in gold, on his forehead. Josephus also indicates that, whereas there could be any number of sets of the other high-priestly vestments (Solomon, he says, made thousands), "the crown on which Moses had inscribed God's name was unique and has remained to this day" (*Ant.* 8.93).[33] There was only one *petalon*, believed to be the original one made for Aaron.

To wear the *petalon*, then, was to officiate as high priest. According to a rabbinic tradition in b. Qiddushin 66a, when king Yannai (Alexander Jannaeus[34]) wished to provoke the Pharisees, who objected to his claiming the high priesthood, by making that claim clear to them, he wore the ṣîṣ. Thus when Polycrates claims that John "was a priest wearing the *petalon*," his words state, as precisely and unambiguously as it was possible to do, that John offici-

32. For the argument of this paragraph in more detail, see Bauckham, "Papias and Polycrates on the Origin of the Fourth Gospel," *JTS* 44 (1993) 34-36.

33. Presumably Josephus thought it was taken, with other temple treasures, to Rome after the fall of Jerusalem (cf. *War* 6.387-91).

34. Because of the parallel to this story in Josephus, *Ant.* 290-93, where the king is John Hyrcanus, many scholars think the tradition has confused John Hyrcanus with Alexander Jannaeus. See J. C. VanderKam, *From Joshua to Caiaphas: High Priests after the Exile* (Minneapolis: Fortress, 2004) 298-301.

ated as high priest in the Jerusalem Temple. They cannot even make him one of the chief priests *(archiereis)* in the wider sense of the term as used in the New Testament and Josephus, whether this means members of the high-priestly families or holders of a number of high offices in the Temple. In fact there is no Greek term for "high priest" that unambiguously distinguishes *the* chief priest from the chief priests (the distinction between high priest and chief priests is made only in English translations). But "a priest wearing the *petalon*" is quite unambiguous. Polycrates' words mean that John officiated precisely as high priest, in succession to Aaron, in the Jerusalem temple, and are an accurately Jewish way of saying this. We may compare Polycrates' description of the fourteenth of Nisan as the day "when the people [the Jews] remove the leaven." This cannot simply be derived from Exod 12:15, but reflects both the contemporary Jewish practice (of removing leaven from houses before the beginning of the first day of unleavened bread) and the technical language for it (cf. m. Pesaḥim 1-2). The use of the simple "the people" *(ho laos)* to mean the Jews is Diaspora Jewish usage, known from inscriptions in Asia Minor.[35] Living close to the large Jewish community of Ephesus and in a church with a strongly Jewish Christian background, it is not surprising that Polycrates can speak of things Jewish in an authentically Jewish way. His doing so may even reflect pride in his own at least partly Jewish ancestry if, as we have suggested, he claimed descent from one of the daughters of Philip.

In any case, there is no evidence that Christian writers of this period ever imagined that the *petalon* was ever worn by anyone other than the Jewish high priest himself when officiating in the Temple.[36] Polycrates' claim that John wore the *petalon* has sometimes been understood as metaphorical.[37]

---

35. E. Schürer, *The History of the Jewish People in the Age of Jesus Christ (175 B.C.–A.D. 135)*, revised edition ed. G. Vermes, F. Millar, and M. Goodman, vol. 3/1 (Edinburgh: Clark, 1986) 89-90; W. Ameling, ed., *Inscriptiones Judaicae Orientis*, vol. 2, *Kleinasien* (TSAJ 99; Tübingen: Mohr, 2004) 138-39, 193.

36. Three other passages in early Christian literature that have sometimes been interpreted otherwise are *Protevangelium of James* 5:1 and two passages in Epiphanius about James the Lord's brother (*Panarion* 29.4; 78.13-14). I have discussed these in detail in Bauckham, "Papias and Polycrates," 37-40, and shown that these are not exceptions to the rule that the *petalon* is always an item of headdress worn only by the high priest. Epiphanius, interpreting Hegesippus's claim that James alone was permitted to enter the Temple sanctuary, took him to mean that James was permitted to officiate on the Day of Atonement, entering the holy of holies as only the high priest could. This tradition about James is probably quite independent of Polycrates' statement about John, but they share the same, evidently stereotyped, way of referring to the exercise of the high priest's office in the Temple: wearing the *petalon*.

37. E.g., Braun, *Jean le Théologien*, 339-40; F. F. Bruce, "St. John at Ephesus," *BJRL* 60 (1978) 343.

The idea that the high priesthood is a metaphor for John's position of authority in the church can claim support from two allegedly parallel usages. First, in *Didache* 13:3 Christians are instructed to give the firstfruits of their produce to the prophets. "for they are your high priests" *(archiereis humōn)*. Secondly, Hippolytus *(Refutatio* 1 proemium 6) claims that the successors of the apostles participate with them in the same grace of high priesthood *(archierateias)*. This may actually be based on a misunderstanding of Polycrates' words about John,[38] but in any case neither the *Didache* nor Hippolytus really parallels Polycrates here. The general idea of high priesthood might occasionally be used metaphorically (or perhaps we should say typologically) of Christian prophets or bishops, whose position in some respects resembled that of Jewish high priests. But in such a usage it would be odd to use the precise expression "wear the *petalon*." Polycrates' words are a straightforward statement that John officiated as high priest in the Temple. Their context offers no indication that they are meant other than literally, while their place in the sequence of statements about John naturally associates them with his early life in Jerusalem, where he had been a disciple of Jesus and could have been a high priest.

The other form of interpretation that has been offered by previous scholars takes seriously the apparently intended literal meaning of Polycrates' words and explains them as a historical reminiscence of the Beloved Disciple or the author of John's Gospel, who, it is suggested, belonged to a priestly family in Jerusalem and perhaps officiated in the Temple in some capacity. The difficulty in interpretations along these lines is that the historical basis they postulate for Polycrates' words is historically plausible only when it is something much less than Polycrates states: that John was high priest. J. H. Bernard's speculation that the *petalon* might sometimes have been worn by ordinary Jewish priests in the late Second Temple period[39] is contradicted by all the evidence. Internal evidence from the Gospel of John (including 18:15) alleged to show that the author — or the source of the author's tradition — belonged to Jerusalem priestly circles may have some force,[40] but does not re-

38. R. Eisler, *The Enigma of the Fourth Gospel* (London: Methuen, 1938) 55, quotes an apparently unpublished fragment of a lost work of Hippolytus that refers to John as "Ephesian high priest" *(archiereus Ephesios)*. Whether genuine or not, this is certainly dependent on Polycrates. If genuine, it would explain Hippolytus, *Refutatio* 1 proemium 6.

39. Bernard, *A Critical and Exegetical Commentary*, vol. 2, 596; cf. Colson, *L'Énigme*, 37, who defies all the evidence in asserting "il n'est pas prouvé que l'usage, au temps de Jésus, n'était pas plus étendu." Of course, the negative cannot be proved, but there is no reason at all to suppose that it was.

40. E.g., Burney, *The Aramaic Origin*, 133-34; Colson, *L'Énigme*, 18-27, 94-97; Hengel, *The*

ally explain why Polycrates should have reached the much more remarkable conclusion that John actually held office as high priest.

The boldest historical speculation is that of Robert Eisler.[41] Following Delff,[42] he identifies John, the author of the Gospel, with the John who appears as a member of the high priestly family in Acts 4:6. Going further than Delff,[43] he claims that this John actually was the high priest, by identifying him with Theophilus the son of Annas (Josephus, *Ant.* 18.123), who was high priest from 37 to 41 CE.[44] He suggests that Theophilus was used as the Greek name roughly equivalent in meaning to Hebrew Yohanan or Yehohanan (John). This is quite possible, but the identification of the John of whom Polycrates speaks with the high priest Theophilus is achieved only by a series of unverifiable guesses and requires us to believe that only Polycrates has preserved any reference to the fact that the high priest Theophilus was a disciple of Jesus.

More recently, Rigato, apparently without knowledge of Eisler's work, has taken Polycrates' statement fully seriously, identified John the author of the Gospel with the John of Acts 4:6,[45] and supposed that this John must at some time have officiated as high priest.[46] Since Josephus (our main source for knowledge of the high priests of the late Second Temple period) does not refer to a high priest named John, Rigato allows three possibilities:[47] (1) that Josephus's record of the high priests is incomplete and does not happen to refer to John (perhaps the name of John, as a Christian, was subject to a kind of *damnatio memoriae*, expunged from the record), (2) that John was another name of one of those mentioned by Josephus, or (3) that on one Day of Atonement John substituted for the high priest, according to the practice of substituting another member of the family if the high priest was ill or ritually impure.[48] Certainly these are possibilities, but it still remains surprising that only Polycrates should have preserved any reference to the remarkable fact that a disciple of Jesus, author of the Gospel of John, was or substituted for

---

Johannine Question, 109-11, 125-26; M.-L. Rigato, "L'apostolo ed evangelista Giovanni,' 'sacerdoto' levitico," *Rivista Biblica* 38 (1990) 469-81.

41. Eisler, *The Enigma,* 36-45.

42. Delff, *Geschichte,* 95.

43. Delff, *Das vierte Evangelium,* 9-10, supposed that this John stood in for the high priest on one occasion. This possibility is also suggested by Rigato, "L'apostolo,'" 464 n. 33 (see below).

44. See VanderKam, *From Joshua,* 440-43.

45. Rigato, "L'apostolo,'" 465-66.

46. Rigato, "L'apostolo,'" 463-65.

47. Rigato, "L'apostolo,'" 464-65 n. 33.

48. VanderKam, *From Joshua,* 409-11.

the high priest. It is worth noting that we know of one occasion when the reigning high priest was unable to officiate on the Day of Atonement owing to ritual impurity. This was the high priest Matthias (5-4 BCE), and the incident, along with the name of the relative who substituted for him (Joseph son of Elim), was not only recorded by Josephus (*Ant.* 17.165-67) but well remembered, as a precedent, in rabbinic tradition (Tosephta Yoma 1:4; b. Yoma 12b; y. Yoma 1:1, 38d). James VanderKam comments: "It is understandable that an event so public as the temporary replacement of a high priest on the Day of Atonement would be remembered in the tradition."[49]

We need to take a closer look at Acts 4:6. The occasion is a meeting of the high priest's council at which the apostles Peter and John are accused of stirring up the people by preaching the resurrection of Jesus. "The high priest's family," we should probably infer, is that of the powerful ex-high priest Annas (high priest 6-15 CE), father-in-law of the reigning high priest Caiaphas and father of no less than five other high priests in the period 16-62 CE. John and Alexander, neither of whom is mentioned by Josephus, presumably also belong to this family. In place of "John" (*Iōannēs*), which is the reading of the majority of manuscripts, there is a variant reading "Jonathan" (*Iōnathas*), which would refer to the son of Annas who was briefly high priest after Caiaphas, according to Josephus (*Ant.* 18.95) and who played quite a prominent role in Josephus's narrative of later events.[50] Since the name John is very frequent in the New Testament while the name Jonathan occurs nowhere else in the New Testament, some have supposed that "Jonathan" was the original reading for which scribes substituted the more familiar name "John."[51] But a more common judgment has been that the well-known historical figure Jonathan has been substituted for the otherwise unknown John by knowledgeable scribes.[52] In fact, it may now be possible to identify this John, since the discovery in Jerusalem of the ossuary of Yehohanah (Joanna) daughter of Yehohanan (John), the son of the high priest Theophilus, who was a son of Annas.[53]

The improbable and speculative nature of Eisler's proposal has distracted attention from the way in which Acts 4:6 really can explain Polycrates'

49. VanderKam, *From Joshua*, 411.

50. VanderKam, *From Joshua*, 436-40.

51. E.g., J. Jeremias, *Jerusalem in the Time of Jesus* (tr. F. H. and C. H. Cave; London: SCM, 1969) 197 n. 161; VanderKam, *From Joshua*, 438 n. 114.

52. B. M. Metzger, *A Textual Commentary on the Greek New Testament* (Stuttgart: United Bible Societies, 1975) 317-18.

53. D. Barag and D. Flusser, "The Ossuary of Yehoḥanah Granddaughter of the High Priest Theophilus," *IEJ* 36 (1986) 39-44.

words about John. The simplest explanation is that Polycrates (or the Ephesian church tradition he followed) identified John the Beloved Disciple, who had died at Ephesus, with the John of Acts 4:6 (whether or not "John" was the original reading, it is so common in the manuscripts that it is easy to suppose it to be the reading known in Ephesus and to Polycrates). But Polycrates made this identification, not because he had any historical information to this effect, but simply as a matter of scriptural exegesis.[54] The tradition that John the Beloved Disciple was a high priest is neither metaphorical nor historical, but *exegetical.*

As we have already noted in connection with Polycrates' identification of the two Philips, it was common practice for early Christian exegetes of the New Testament writings to identify characters who bore the same name. Other examples are the identification, in the second-century *Acts of Paul* (written in Polycrates' time), of the Judas who was Paul's host in Damascus (Acts 9:11) with Judas the Lord's brother (Mark 6:3),[55] or the identification that the *Protevangelium of James* (23-24) makes between Zechariah the father of John the Baptist and the Zechariah who was murdered in the Temple (Matt 23:35). We may also recall how prominent figures of the early post-apostolic church — comparable with John the Elder of Ephesus — were assumed to be the same person as persons of the same name who appear in New Testament writings: Clement of Rome was identified as the Clement of Phil 4:3 (Eusebius, *Hist. Eccl.* 3.4.9), Linus of Rome was identified as the Linus of 2 Tim 4:21 (Irenaeus, *Adv. Haer.* 3.3.3; Eusebius, *Hist. Eccl.* 3.4.8), Hermas the prophet, author of the *Shepherd,* was identified as the Hermas of Rom 16:14 (Origen, ad loc.). These last two instances may have some historical plausibility, but these identifications were doubtless made in the same way as the others — as an *exegetical* procedure.

It is quite likely that the identification of the Beloved Disciple with the John of Acts 4:6 was facilitated by John 18:15, which, if it is understood to refer to the Beloved Disciple, depicts him as intimately acquainted with the high priest. In Acts 4:6 John is listed third after Annas and Caiaphas. Someone who knew that in the late Second Temple period the Jewish high priests mostly held office for short periods only, or who was misled by John 18:13 into thinking the office was filled annually, would easily suppose that such a prominent member of the high-priestly family as the John of Acts 4:6 appears to be must have him-

54. That Polycrates was well acquainted with the early chapters of Acts is shown by his quotation of Acts 5:9 later in his letter.

55. Coptic text of a section of the *Acts of Paul,* translated in E. Hennecke, W. Schneemelcher, and R. McL. Wilson, eds., *New Testament Apocrypha,* vol. 2 (revised edition; Louisville: Westminster/John Knox, 1992) 264.

self held the office of high priest at some time. The motive for identifying John the Beloved Disciple with this John will have been — in addition to the general exegetical practice already mentioned — the natural desire of the Ephesian church to find their own John, author of the Gospel they prized, mentioned somewhere else in the writings of the emerging New Testament canon. But the identification also served well Polycrates' particular purpose in his letter to Victor of Rome: the justification of the Quartodeciman observance in line with the Johannine chronology of the passion. An eyewitness of the passion who actually himself served as high priest could be expected to remember correctly its precise chronological relationship to the Jewish festival.

It is quite likely that Polycrates, who in his letter prides himself on his considerable knowledge of the Scriptures, himself made this identification of his own illustrious relative with the John of Acts 4:6. But whether Polycrates made this identification or inherited it, it is of considerable importance. For it is now clear that *when the Ephesian church looked for its own John, the Beloved Disciple, in New Testament writings other than the Gospel of John, they did not identify him with John the son of Zebedee. The identification of him with the John of Acts 4:6 makes it impossible to identify him with John the son of Zebedee,*[56] who appears in the same narrative as one of the two disciples who are there interrogated by Annas, Caiaphas, John, and Alexander. The Ephesian church's own tradition about their own John evidently made them sure that he could not be John the son of Zebedee and obliged them, even at the end of the second century, to resist this identification, which was already proving irresistible in some other places and seems to have become universal in the next century.

Irenaeus on John

We have argued that in the second-century Christian traditions of the province of Asia, and especially in Ephesus, the John who wrote the Gospel of John and was the one that Gospel calls "the disciple Jesus loved" was not identified with John the son of Zebedee. He was, rather, known as a disciple of Jesus who did not belong to the circle of the Twelve and who, in the later part of his life, lived in Ephesus, was well known in the churches of that area,

---

56. I stress this point because critics of my view as set out in my "Papias and Polycrates" seem not to have taken account of it, apparently supposing that Polycrates could have identified the author of the Gospel of John both with the John of Acts 4:6 and with John the son of Zebedee. This is inconceivable in an expert exegete, as Polycrates was.

and was an especially long-lived disciple of Jesus, who outlived most of his contemporaries. He had been buried in Ephesus, where his tomb was known, and Polycrates bishop of Ephesus toward the end of the century claimed a blood relationship with him. In the sources we have so far considered, John the son of Zebedee is connected neither with the Gospel nor with Ephesus. These associations would come about only through a secondary identification of John of Ephesus, Papias's John the Elder, with the John who belonged to the Twelve. Knowledge of the distinction between the two Johns was not confined to Asia but appears also in the Muratorian Canon, and therefore probably in Rome or Italy, where most scholars have located that document. Indebtedness to the work of Papias seems to be the explanation in this case.

At the beginning of book 3 of his magnum opus, *Against the Heresies* (c. 180), Irenaeus of Lyons provides a brief statement about the apostolic origins of each of the four Gospels that he considers genuinely apostolic. We consider it at this point, in advance of our more general consideration of Irenaeus's views of John, because it has been claimed that this statement was not composed by Irenaeus himself, but was taken by him from the archives of the church of Rome:[57]

> So Matthew published a written Gospel among the Hebrews in their own language, while Peter and Paul were preaching at Rome and founding the church. After their departure, Mark, the disciple and interpreter *(hermēneutēs)* of Peter, did also hand down to us in writing what had been preached by Peter. Luke also, the companion of Paul, recorded in a book the Gospel preached by him [Paul]. Then John, the disciple of the Lord, the one who leaned back on the Lord's breast, himself published a Gospel while he resided in Ephesus (Irenaeus, *Adv. Haer.* 3.1.1; Greek text in Eusebius, *Hist. Eccl.* 5.8.2-4).[58]

It seems to me less than clear that Irenaeus did not compose this passage himself. The notices about Matthew and Mark are evidently dependent on Papias, whose work Irenaeus knew (5.33.4). Irenaeus himself elsewhere calls Luke the "companion" *(sectator, akolouthos)* of the apostles (1.23.1; 3.10.1; cf.

57. B. Mutschler, "Was weiss Irenäus vom Johannesevangelium? Der historische Kontext der Johannesevangeliums aus der Perspektive seiner Rezeption bei Irenäus von Lyon," in J. Frey and U. Schnelle, eds., *Kontexte des Johannesevangeliums. Das vierte Evangelium in religions- und traditionsgeschichtlicher Perspektive* (WUNT 175; Tübingen: Mohr, 2004) 705-6, following C.-J. Thornton, *Der Zeuge des Zeugen. Lukas als Historiker der Paulusreisen* (WUNT 56; Tübingen: Mohr, 1991) 8-67, who dates this Roman source between 120 and 135 (62).

58. For the texts of the *Adversus Haereses* I depend on the volumes edited by A. Rousseau in the Sources Chrétiennes series: vols. 100, 153, 211, 264, and 294.

3.14.1). It does look as though the notice about Matthew is framed from the perspective of the church of Rome, but this could reflect Irenaeus's own association with Rome, the mother church as far as his own church of Lyons was concerned. Of the two descriptions of John, "the disciple of the Lord" is Irenaeus's own regular way of referring to him,[59] though it was also used in Rome (see below). It is true that Irenaeus nowhere else calls John "the one who leaned back on the Lord's breast," but this exact description was, as we have seen, used by Polycrates (Eusebius, *Hist. Eccl.* 5.24.3), bishop of Ephesus while Irenaeus was bishop of Lyons. Though the description is modeled closely on John 13:25, this does not account for the exact verbal correspondence in its two late-second-century occurrences in Polycrates and Irenaeus.[60] It must have been a standard description of John, used to denote that special intimacy with Jesus that gave his Gospel special value. Most likely it was standard usage in the church of Ephesus. From there it could have been taken up in Rome, prior to its use by Polycrates and Irenaeus, but it is simpler to suppose that Irenaeus knew it as the usage of the Ephesian church. Thus it is hazardous to put any weight on the claim that Irenaeus drew these four notices about the Gospels from a single source. He could well have composed them himself from his knowledge of Papias and other sources.

However, Irenaeus's importance for our argument is by no means confined to this particular passage. He refers many times to John the author of the Gospel, and it is relevant to ask whether these references reflect the Asian tradition of a John who wrote the Gospel but was not the son of Zebedee. Since Irenaeus himself came from the province of Asia, probably from Smyrna, we may reasonably expect him to transmit the local knowledge about John of Ephesus. As a young man he sat at the feet of the aged bishop Polycarp of Smyrna, from whom he heard Polycarp's many reminiscences of those of the apostolic generation he had known and the traditions about Jesus they transmitted. He later moved to Lyons in southern France, where, in

59. Mutschler, "Was weiss Irenäus," 705, 707, argues that the form of this phrase that has the genitive ("of the Lord") in the predicative position (as here in 3.1.1) always derives from a source, whereas Irenaeus himself uses the form with the genitive in the attributive position. But the argument is not convincing. The attributive form occurs in ten cases, the predicative form occurs eight times (1.8.5 [bis]; 3.1.1; 3.11.1, 3; 4.30.4; 5.33.3; *Letter to Victor*), and there is one case (2.22.5) where the Greek text has the predicative form but the Latin the attributive, indicating that we cannot entirely rely on the literalness of the Latin translation in a case like this. Of the eight cases of the predicative form, only four are in passages Mutschler attributes to Irenaeus's sources (3.1.1; 3.3.4; 5.33.3; *Letter to Victor*).

60. In *Adv. Haer.* 4.20.11, on the other hand, Irenaeus quotes the exact words of John 21:20 and does not use them to identify John.

177 or 178 CE, he succeeded Photinus, the bishop of Lyons who had died a martyr. Here he found himself in controversy with the Valentinian Gnostics, especially their eminent teacher Ptolemy, and composed his magnum opus *Against the Heresies* in five books around 180 CE, in which he refuted the Gnostics exhaustively and created a classic statement of the emerging orthodoxy. Some time later he wrote a small handbook of Christian apologetics, *The Demonstration of the Apostolic Preaching* (preserved only in an Armenian version). We also have parts of two of his letters, one to Florinus, the Valentinian teacher whom he had known in his youth in Smyrna when both were pupils of Polycarp, and the other (c. 195 CE) to bishop Victor I of Rome in connection with the Quartodeciman controversy (between Rome and the churches of Asia) about the date of Easter.

What does Irenaeus know about John, the author of the Gospel? He considers him the author of all the Johannine literature: Gospel, letters,[61] and Apocalypse. He is the Beloved Disciple (though Irenaeus does not use that term), who reclined on the Lord's breast at the Last Supper. He wrote the Gospel while residing in Ephesus, and he lived there until his death, during the reign of Trajan (which began in 98 CE). Irenaeus often calls him "John, the disciple of the Lord" (see Table 16). He relates one story about John in Ephesus: how, when John saw that the heretic Cerinthus was in the public baths, he fled the building, lest it collapse (*Adv. Haer.* 3.3.4). He quotes what John had claimed was teaching of Jesus about the miraculous fruitfulness of the earth during the messianic age (5.33.4). But his main interest in John is in his Gospel, which is the more authoritative by virtue of its author's closeness to Jesus. A majority of Irenaeus's references to John are to him as the author of the Gospel. Whereas Irenaeus often cites the Synoptic Gospels without mentioning their authors by name, in the case of quotations from the Gospel of John he frequently names its author, often adding his honorific epithet: "the disciple of the Lord."

From what sources (other than the Gospel of John itself) did Irenaeus draw his information about John? Table 17 puts into diagrammatic form the scattered information Irenaeus provides about his sources. There seem to be three direct sources, among which bishop Polycarp of Smyrna clearly takes pride of place from Irenaeus's point of view.[62] Although the following passage has been quoted already in chapter 12, we need to recall it here. Irenaeus is reproaching the Valentinian teacher Florinus for his heretical teaching:

---

61. Irenaeus shows knowledge of only two of these: 1 and 2 John.

62. On Polycarp's importance more generally as a source for Irenaeus, see Hill, *The Johannine Corpus*, 351-57.

These opinions, Florinus, to say no more, are not of sound judgment; these opinions are not in harmony with the Church, and involve those who adopt them in the greatest impiety; these opinions not even the heretics outside the Church ever dared to espouse openly; these opinions the elders before us, who also were disciples of the apostles, did not hand down to you. For when I was still a boy I saw you in lower Asia in the company of Polycarp, faring brilliantly in the imperial court and trying to secure his favour. For I distinctly recall the events of that time better than those of recent years (for what we learn in childhood keeps pace with the growing mind and becomes part of it), so that I can tell the very place where the blessed Polycarp used to sit as he discoursed, his goings out and his comings in, the character of his life, his bodily appearance, the discourses he would address to the multitude, how he would tell of his conversations with John and with the others who had seen the Lord, how he would relate their words from memory; and what the things were which he had heard from them concerning the Lord, his mighty works and his teaching, Polycarp, as having received them from the eyewitnesses (*autoptōn*) of the life of the Logos, would declare altogether in accordance with the scriptures. To these things I used to listen diligently even then, by the mercy of God which was upon me, noting them down not on papyrus but in my heart (*apud* Eusebius, *Hist. Eccl.* 5.20.4-7).[63]

Irenaeus does not, in fact, relay many memories of Polycarp's reminiscences of John. The story of John and Cerinthus in the baths is attributed by Irenaeus to "hearers of Polycarp" (*Adv. Haer.* 3.3.4), and this has been understood to mean that Irenaeus did not himself hear it from Polycarp but only at secondhand from those who did.[64] This is possible, but it is more likely that he includes himself among these "hearers of Polycarp" and means only to indicate that this story was well known among those who had listened to the aged bishop of Smyrna, himself included.[65] It is certainly the sort of memorable — and presumably humorous — tale that would have stuck in his memory since he heard it as a boy. In his letter to Bishop Victor of Rome, Irenaeus recalls Polycarp's visit to Rome in the days of Anicetus (155-166 CE), when Polycarp claimed that the Quartodeciman observance of Easter had been his practice when he observed it with John the Lord's disciple. However, it is not clear that Irenaeus recalls what he himself was present at; the event was doubtless widely known in the churches. For our purposes the really impor-

63. Translation from Grant, *Second-Century Christianity*, 115-16.
64. Mutschler, "Was weiss Irenäus," 709.
65. This seems also to be the view of Hill, *The Johannine Corpus*, 354.

tant information that Irenaeus recalled Polycarp conveying is general information: that Polycarp as a young man had associated with a disciple of Jesus called John, as well as others who had seen Jesus (Aristion would doubtless have been one of these). Irenaeus is hardly likely to have been mistaken about this. Plausibly also Irenaeus knew this John to be the author of the Gospel from Polycarp as well as from other sources.

Irenaeus valued his memories of Polycarp because they put him in touch with Jesus by way of only two intermediaries: Polycarp and John. This was possible only because both were very long lived: John survived, according to Irenaeus, into the reign of Trajan (which began in 98), while Polycarp was eighty-six when he was martyred in Smyrna somewhere in the period 156 to 167 CE. The other oral source of Irenaeus's information about John was doubtless the local traditions of the church of Ephesus, which he would have known when he lived in Smyrna. Finally, Irenaeus had a written source: the works of Papias, which he explicitly cites just once (5.33.4) and from which he would certainly have known what we have inferred that Papias must have said about the Gospel of John and its authorship. Irenaeus calls Papias "a hearer of John and companion of Polycarp" (5.33.4). As we observed in chapter 2, he was probably mistaken about Papias having heard John, but the mistake is geographical rather than chronological. Papias's knowledge of John came through intermediaries who visited Hierapolis. Papias was a contemporary of Polycarp, perhaps slightly older, though he doubtless did not live long enough for Irenaeus to have known him.

Irenaeus also refers generally to the elders, the circle of revered teachers in the province of Asia, contemporaries of Polycarp and Papias, who had been disciples of John and the other apostles or disciples of Jesus who had visited or settled in the area.[66] It is not clear from what sources, oral or written, Irenaeus knew their teachings, but in the case of the few items of information about John that he attributes to them it is likely that Papias was his source. This seems clear in the case of John's report of the teaching of Jesus about the messianic age, which he begins citing from the elders (*Adv. Haer.* 5.33.3) and continues citing from Papias (5.33.4).[67]

What Irenaeus tells us about John of Ephesus is what was known in the churches of the province of Asia where Irenaeus resided. From more than one local source of such knowledge, including Polycarp, who had known John per-

---

66. It is not clear whether "those who had seen John" (5.30.1) are these elders or a wider circle.

67. In chapter 16 we argued that in 2.22.5 Irenaeus's reference to the elders is no more than his own interpretation of John 21:24.

sonally, he knew that this John was the Beloved Disciple, lived in Ephesus, wrote the Gospel there, and survived until around the end of the first century. Most of this is also independently confirmed by Polycrates of Ephesus, writing at about the same time as Irenaeus. We would need very good grounds for doubting the basic accuracy of this account of the authorship of the Gospel of John. The argument we have been pursuing is that this John, disciple of Jesus and author of the Gospel, was not John the son of Zebedee, member of the Twelve, and that this was known in Ephesus as late as Polycrates' letter to Victor of Rome. Was it also Irenaeus's view? It has commonly been assumed and sometimes argued[68] that Irenaeus identified the author of the Gospel with John the son of Zebedee, but this has also been vigorously contested.[69] What is revealing in itself is how difficult it is to find conclusive evidence one way or the other.

Was the Author of John's Gospel John the Son of Zebedee?

We should make it clear that none of Irenaeus's references to John that we have been considering indicate that he was John the son of Zebedee. These references tell us nothing about this John's life prior to his residence in Ephesus beyond identifying him as the Beloved Disciple in the Gospel of John. Irenaeus does also make five unequivocal references to John the son of Zebedee, all alluding to his role in the Synoptic Gospels and Acts. The two references to his role in the Gospels all put him in company with Peter and James, making up the inner circle of three within the wider circle of the Twelve, at the Transfiguration in particular (*Adv. Haer.* 2.24.4)[70] and generally

68. E.g., J. Chapman, *John the Presbyter and the Fourth Gospel* (Oxford: Clarendon, 1911) 42-43. Mutschler, "Was weiss Irenäus," thinks the two Johns (of Ephesus and son of Zebedee) were merged already in the notice about the Gospel in the Roman church archive (to which he attributes Irenaeus's information in 3.1.1) and in Polycrates, as well as in Irenaeus. But this is purely because he assumes that an identification of John of Ephesus with the Beloved Disciple and author of the Gospel must presuppose that this disciple was John the son of Zebedee (703). He apparently does not realize that Papias portrays John the Elder (who he supposes edited the Gospel) as a personal disciple of Jesus.

69. E.g., Burney, *The Aramaic Origin*, 138-42; Gunther, "Early Identifications," 418-19; cf. Colson, *L'Énigme*, 32-34 (Colson thinks Irenaeus confused the two Johns in his memory).

70. The immediately following reference to the people present at the raising of Jairus's daughter is problematic, since Peter and James are mentioned but John omitted. It is not satisfactory simply (with manuscript S) to add John, because the text requires there to be five persons including Jesus (Jesus, Peter, James, the father, and the mother). Perhaps the original text did not count Jesus as the fifth person. See A. Rousseau and L. Doutreleau, *Irénee de Lyons. Contre les Hérésies, Livre II*, vol. 1 (SC 293; Paris: Éditions du Cerf, 1982) 292.

at all the events of Jesus' ministry (3.12.15). The other three references are to John with Peter in the narratives of Acts 3 (3.12.3 [bis]) and Acts 4 (3.12.5). There is nothing in these passages to suggest that this John is the same person as John of Ephesus, the Beloved Disciple and author of the Gospel. Nor is there any emphasis on John's role, such as we might expect if Irenaeus saw in these passages his favorite and most authoritative Gospel writer and the one with whom he was himself in touch at one remove, via his revered teacher Polycarp. John the son of Zebedee appears merely as the last of the group of three (Peter, James, and John) and as the companion of Peter in narratives that give Peter the active role. The same can be said of Irenaeus's single reference to "the sons of Zebedee" (1.21.2), though in this case he is merely citing what his Gnostic opponents said. We should add that none of these references to John the son of Zebedee apply to him Irenaeus's characteristic identifying epithet for the author of the Gospel of John: "the disciple of the Lord."

Irenaeus uses this epithet in nineteen of his fifty-three references to John by name (see Table 16), while on two further occasions he calls him just "the disciple of the Lord" in contexts where it is clear that his reference is to John (3.11.1, 3). (He also once, in a context of discussion of John's Gospel, refers to Jesus as "the teacher of John" [1.9.2].) Irenaeus never uses the singular phrase "the disciple of the Lord" to refer to anyone except John.[71] He often speaks of the disciples of Jesus (usually the Twelve) in the setting of Jesus' ministry, but calls them apostles after the resurrection. He once uses the term to refer to members of the Jerusalem church other than the apostles, paraphrasing Acts 4:23 (Peter and John "went to their own people") as: "they returned to the rest of their fellow-apostles and disciples of the Lord, that is, to the church" (3.12.5).[72]

Clearly the epithet "disciple of the Lord" is meant not so much to put John in a group as to distinguish him uniquely. It conveys his special closeness to Jesus, both historically during Jesus' ministry and theologically in his Gospel.[73] Probably, like the modern term "Beloved Disciple," it is an abbreviated allusion to the Gospel's more cumbersome phrase: "the disciple Jesus loved."[74] Irenaeus's regular use of it must surely derive from his sources, espe-

---

71. Mutschler, "Was weiss Irenäus," 698.

72. The three terms, "church," "apostles," and "disciples of the Lord," are taken up rhetorically later in the same passage, confirming that the last refers to members of the Jerusalem church other than the apostles. Only on one other occasion does Irenaeus seem to distinguish "apostles" and "disciples" of Jesus, and this is a report that the Carpocratians say that Jesus spoke in mystery to his disciples and apostles privately (1.25.5).

73. Mutschler, "Was weiss Irenäus," 699.

74. When Tertullian writes of "John, the Lord's most beloved disciple (*dilectissimum*

cially from Polycarp.[75] It is not Papias's usage in the fragments of his work that we have. Papias uses the plural "disciples of the Lord" for all of Jesus' disciples (members of the Twelve and others such as Aristion), including John, and we have seen that the Muratorian Canon seems to follow this usage in calling John "one of the disciples" (whereas Andrew is "one of the apostles"). As a distinguishing epithet for the John who was still alive in Papias's time, Papias used "the Elder." It is not difficult to imagine why this usage (unattested outside Papias) should not have continued after John's death. The term does not distinguish John from those Irenaeus calls "the elders," the Christian leaders who had known John and were not themselves disciples of Jesus,[76] or even from the ordinary "presbyters" of every church. Instead, "the disciple of the Lord" placed John in the company of personal disciples of Jesus and also suggested the unique relationship of the author of John's Gospel to Jesus. For members of the church of Ephesus and of churches in the province of Asia generally, *the* disciple of the Lord was their own John, the one who reclined on the Lord's breast and wrote his Gospel in Ephesus. The usage was evidently not entirely confined to Asia, since we find it (referring to the author of John's Gospel) in the Valentinian teacher Ptolemy (*apud* Irenaeus, *Adv. Haer.* 1.8.5),[77] who seems to have been the leader of the Valentinian school in Italy around the middle of the second century or a little later.[78] But it seems likely that "John the disciple of the Lord" originated and was predominantly used in Asia.

The other New Testament author whose personal connections with the churches of the province of Asia gave him special prestige in those churches

---

Domino), who used to lean on his breast" (*Praescriptio* 22.5), he seems to be paraphrasing Irenaeus, *Adv. Haer.* 3.1.1: "John, the disciple of the Lord, the one who leaned back on the Lord's breast."

75. In particular, the use in 3.3.4; 5.33.4; and *Letter to Victor* may be intended to indicate that Polycarp and the elders used this term.

76. In *Letter to Florinus* Irenaeus also uses the term for Polycarp, who was one of this group.

77. In another work, his *Letter to Flora,* Ptolemy speaks of the author of John's Gospel as "the apostle" (*apud* Epiphanius, *Panarion* 33.3.6).

78. B. Layton, *The Gnostic Scriptures* (London: SCM, 1987) 277-78. See also the apocryphal letter of John cited by Pseudo-Cyprian, *De Montibus Sina et Sion* 13 ("his [Christ's] disciple John"); *Apocryphon of John* 1:4 ("John, [his, i.e., the Savior's] disciple"); and Heracleon, *apud* Origen, *Commentary on John* 6:3 ("the disciple"). An interesting later survival of this usage is in the apocryphal *Epistle of Titus,* which refers to "John the disciple of the Lord" in introducing a quotation from the apocryphal *Acts of John.* (The *Acts of John* itself does not refer to John in this way.) See Hennecke, Schneemelcher, and Wilson, eds., *New Testament Apocrypha,* vol. 2, 65, 159; E. Junod and J.-D. Kaestli, *Acta Iohannes,* vol. 1 (CCSA 1; Turnhout: Brepols, 1983) 140-41.

in the second century was, of course, Paul. Irenaeus's references to him are very numerous (see Table 16): often just as "Paul" but occasionally "Paul the apostle" (19 times, the same number as the occurrences of "John the disciple of the Lord") and often just as "the apostle," both in contexts where it is clear from previous references that the reference is to Paul but also quite frequently where this is not the case. Paul is the only figure who can be called just "the apostle" without ambiguity. Other uses of "the apostle" as a distinguishing or honorific epithet with a name are confined in Irenaeus to Peter, who is "Peter the apostle" three times, and Matthew, who is "Matthew the apostle" just once. These usages all highlight the special significance of John's unique epithet "the disciple of the Lord."

If we look for any possible clues that Irenaeus identified John "the disciple of the Lord" with John the son of Zebedee, one of the Twelve, the only evidence that is even possibly relevant is Irenaeus's references to John the author of the Gospel as "the apostle" or as one of a group called "the apostles." The evidence is as follows:

> *Adv Haer.* 1.9.2, 3: "the apostle" (used of John)
>
> 3.21.3: four "apostles" (Peter, John, Matthew, Paul) wrote
>
> 3.5.1: those "apostles who put the Gospel in writing" (implicitly including John)
>
> 3.11.9: "the Gospels of the apostles" (three times, contrasted with heretical Gospels and probably referring to Matthew and John and perhaps also Mark and Luke as written by disciples of the apostles)
>
> 2.22.5: the elders "in Asia who associated with John, the disciple of the Lord. . . . Some of them saw not only John, but also other apostles"
>
> *Letter to Victor:* Polycarp observed Easter "with John, the disciple of our Lord and the rest of the apostles with whom he associated"
>
> *Adv. Haer.* 3.3.4, in Irenaeus's conclusion to Polycarp's story of John and Cerinthus in the bathhouse: "Such was the horror which the apostles and their disciples had . . ." (John is thus an instance of "the apostles" and Polycarp an instance of "their disciples")
>
> 3.3.4: "the church in Ephesus, founded by Paul and having John residing among them down to the time of Trajan, is a true witness of the tradition of the apostles"

The two examples of "the apostle" (1.9.2, 3) occur in a context in which it is clear that John the author of the Gospel of John is meant. Irenaeus is debating the interpretation of the Gospel's Prologue with Ptolemy the Valentinian, and it is likely that this usage ("the apostle" for John), found only here among

461

Irenaeus's many references to John, is borrowed from Ptolemy.[79] In Ptolemy's *Letter to Flora* (though this is not the work to which Irenaeus is responding here) Ptolemy refers to the author of the Johannine Prologue as "the apostle" (*apud* Epiphanius, *Panarion* 33.3.6), apparently with no contextual indication that John is meant. But Irenaeus would not have borrowed the term had he thought it actually inapplicable to John. The other passages quoted above show that Irenaeus does include John in a general category of "apostles," even though he never (outside 1.9.2, 3) uses the word in the singular of John in particular.

However, "the apostles" for Irenaeus are not just the Twelve, as his frequent references to Paul as "the apostle" make absolutely clear, and Paul is not the only apostle outside the Twelve: Barnabas is also for Irenaeus an apostle (3.12.14), as he was for Paul (1 Cor 9:1-6). The Seventy whom Jesus sent out in addition to the Twelve are also apostles: Irenaeus follows Luke in speaking of the twelve apostles and "seventy others" (Luke 10:1), but the logic of his argument with his Gnostic opponents in this context (2.21.1) leaves no possible doubt that he considered the Seventy to be apostles like the Twelve.

Perhaps most illuminating is a passage in which Irenaeus calls even John the Baptist an apostle. The reason why Jesus called the Baptist "more than a prophet" (Matt 11:9; Luke 7:26) is this:

> For all other prophets announced the coming of the Light of the Father [cf. John 1:6-7], and desired to be worthy of seeing him whom they preached; but John both announced [his coming] beforehand, just like the other [prophets], and actually saw him when he came, and pointed him out, and persuaded many to believe in him, so that he himself held the office of both prophet and apostle (3.11.4).

If John the Baptist was an apostle by virtue of testifying to Jesus and persuading many to believe in him, then John's namesake the author of the Gospel of John must certainly also be an apostle, regardless of whether he was one of the Twelve.

There is therefore no reason to think that either Irenaeus's Asiatic sources or Irenaeus himself thought the author of the Gospel of John to be one of the Twelve. Only those who presuppose, without argument, that a John who was a personal disciple of Jesus *must* have been John the son of Zebedee are obliged to read Irenaeus in this way. If we come to Irenaeus in-

79. Note, however, that C. Markschies, "New Research on Ptolemaeus Gnosticus," *ZAC* 4 (2000) 225-54, argues that the *Letter to Flora* is the only genuine work of Ptolemy that we have and that the Valentinian work which Irenaeus quotes in *Adv. Haer.* 1.8.5 was not by Ptolemy.

stead with the knowledge that the John who resided in Ephesus and was known as the author of the Gospel in local tradition was not John the son of Zebedee, then nothing that Irenaeus says either about John "the disciple of the Lord" or about John the son of Zebedee even suggests that they might be the same person.[80]

Identification of the Author of John's Gospel with John the Son of Zebedee

There are only two Christian works of the second century that clearly identify the John who wrote the Gospel with John the son of Zebedee. These are the two apocryphal works, the *Acts of John* and the *Epistle of the Apostles*.

The *Acts of John* tells of the activities of John "the apostle" in the area of Asia Minor around Ephesus and Smyrna and clearly identifies this John as the son of Zebedee, one of the Twelve (especially §§88-91). The main part of this work (i.e., other than §§94-102, 109) has usually been dated to the second century. Recent studies suggest the second quarter of the century,[81] c. 150,[82] the second half of the second century,[83] or the first half of the third century.[84] As for its place of composition, recent scholars have argued for Egypt,[85] Asia Minor,[86] and Syria.[87] There has been much discussion about the extent of the

80. Note also the two different ways in which Irenaeus refers to the John known by Polycarp when addressing, respectively, Florinus and Victor. Florinus, as the letter to him reminds him, had himself heard Polycarp's teaching and reminiscences, and so would have no doubt about which John is in mind when he hears of Polycarp's association with "John and those who had seen the Lord." To Victor of Rome, on the other hand, Irenaeus specifies "John the disciple of our Lord."

81. P. J. Lalleman, *The Acts of John: A Two-Stage Initiation into Johannine Gnosticism* (Studies on the Apocryphal Acts of the Apostles 4; Leuven: Peeters, 1998) 268-70.

82. C. E. Hill, *The Johannine Corpus in the Early Church* (Oxford: Oxford University Press, 2004) 259.

83. E. Junod and J.-D. Kaestli, *Acta Iohannes*, vol. 2 (CCSA 2; Turnhout: Brepols, 1983) 694-700.

84. K. Schäferdiek in Hennecke, Schneemelcher, and Wilson, eds., *New Testament Apocrypha*, vol. 2, 167.

85. Junod and Kaestli, *Acta Iohannes*, vol. 2, 689-94; J. Bremmer, "Women in the Apocryphal Acts of John," in J. N. Bremmer, ed., *The Apocryphal Acts of John* (Kampen: Kok, 1995) 55-56.

86. Lalleman, *The Acts of John*, 256-66. He provides a detailed critique of arguments for Egypt and Syria as well as his own arguments for Asia Minor.

87. Schäferdiek in Hennecke, Schneemelcher, and Wilson, eds., *New Testament Apocrypha*, vol. 2, 166.

author's knowledge of Ephesus, where a major part of the action is set, but it is notable that Pieter Lalleman, who argues very strongly for the work's origin in Asia Minor and for some accurate knowledge of Ephesus by the author, thinks it "unlikely that he is personally familiar with the city"[88] and that the work must come from elsewhere in Asia Minor. In my judgment the case for Egypt remains the strongest.

The *Epistle of the Apostles (Epistula Apostolorum)* represents itself as a letter written by the Twelve after the ascension of Jesus to the churches throughout the world. The evidence that it regards the author of John's Gospel as one of the Twelve is that it places John first in its rather anomalous list of the Twelve at the opening of the letter (§2) and that, among the work's Gospel sources, the Gospel of John is certainly preeminent,[89] the latter presumably being the reason for the former. It is noteworthy also that the list has Thomas, a prominent disciple only in John's Gospel, second and, somewhat unusually, includes Nathanael, a uniquely Johannine disciple.[90] There is no indication of John's association with Ephesus or of the specifically Asiatic traditions about John of Ephesus, unless the fact that Cerinthus (along with Simon Magus) is one of the two enemies of Christ said to have gone throughout the world and against whom the Twelve are writing (§§1, 7), is to be connected with Polycarp's story of John and Cerinthus in Ephesus (Irenaeus, *Adv. Haer.* 3.3.4) or with Irenaeus's statements that the Gospel of John was aimed against the teaching of Cerinthus (*Adv. Haer.* 3.11.1). But the reference to Simon and Cerinthus in the *Epistle of the Apostles* may only indicate that these were the two false teachers the author knew to have been active in the period of the apostles.

Although most recent scholars have argued for Egypt as the place of composition of the *Epistle of the Apostles*,[91] Charles Hill has revived and considerably strengthened the earlier argument of Carl Schmidt[92] in favor of Asia

88. Lalleman, *The Acts of John*, 270.

89. Details in Hill, *The Johannine Corpus*, 367-69.

90. Cf. C. E. Hill, "The Identity of John's Nathanael," *JSNT* (1997) 50-52. The list of the Twelve that occurs, with small variation, in the Syriac *Didascalia Apostolorum* (12) and the *Apostolic Church Order* similarly puts John first and includes Nathanael. In second place it puts not Thomas but Matthew, surely because John and Matthew are seen as the two members of the Twelve who wrote Gospels.

91. C. E. Hill, "The *Epistula Apostolorum*: An Asian Tract from the Time of Polycarp," *JECS* 7 (1999) 6-14, presents and discusses the arguments for Egypt offered by A. A. T. Ehrhardt, M. Hornschuh, and C. D. G. Müller.

92. C. Schmidt and I. Wajnberg, *Gespräche Jesu mit seinen Jünger nach der Auferstehung. Ein katholisch-apostolisches Sendschreiben des 2. Jahrhunderts* (TU 43; Leipzig: Hinrichs, 1919) 361-402.

Minor.[93] Although his argument can scarcely be regarded as conclusive, it is the most persuasive to date. As for the time of composition, Hill argues that it was either just before 120 CE or during the 140s (much of his argument depends on accepting Asia Minor as the place of writing). The latter date is more consistent with the evidence of §17, which predicts the parousia after a hundred and twenty years.[94] These are most naturally counted from the fictional time of the prediction during a conversation between the risen Jesus and his disciples.

In the light of the recent discussions of the dates and places of these two works, I am no longer confident of my earlier argument that they indicate that the identification of the author of the Gospel of John with John the son of Zebedee probably originated in Egypt in the second half of the second century.[95] It is quite possible that the identification was made independently at more than one time and place. It was easily made by anyone not familiar with the local tradition in and around Ephesus that distinguished the two Johns. Moreover, since there was nothing obviously incompatible between what was positively known about John "the disciple of the Lord" in Ephesus and what was known of John the son of Zebedee from the Synoptic Gospels and Acts, even someone familiar with the Ephesian traditions could ignore the distinction. It is perhaps more remarkable that the distinction was still observed at the end of the second century by Polycrates and Irenaeus than that others abandoned it. We should remember (from the discussion of Polycrates' letter earlier in this chapter) that Polycrates identified two Philips: the Philip who was one of the Seven, who lived and died in Hierapolis with two of his daughters, and the Philip who was one of the Twelve. That is, he identified the local Philip with the Philip who belonged to the Twelve. We also explained that this kind of identification of scriptural characters bearing the same name was a standard exegetical practice in early Judaism and Christianity. It is why Polycrates himself identified John of Ephesus with the high-priestly John of Acts 4:6. It is hardly surprising that others not inhibited, as Polycrates was, by the Ephesian tradition's merely negative knowledge that their John was not one of the Twelve made the more obvious identification of the author of the Gospel, known (at least

93. Hill, "The *Epistula Apostolorum*," 9-39. His arguments for Smyrna in particular are weaker.

94. The Ethiopic version has 150 years, but most scholars have agreed that the Coptic version is more likely original at this point. A scribe would have extended the period when the 120 years had passed.

95. R. Bauckham, "Papias and Polycrates on the Origin of the Fourth Gospel," *JTS* 44 (1993) 65-66.

to the author of the *Acts of John*) to be associated with Ephesus, with John the son of Zebedee.

Among other Christian writers of the second century,[96] the most potentially interesting for their views on the authorship of John's Gospel are Justin Martyr, who spent some time early in his adult life in Ephesus (*Dialogue* 1.1), and Clement of Alexandria, who probably knew Papias's work.[97] Unfortunately neither of them provides the clarity we would wish. Justin, despite the doubts that some scholars have had about this, very likely did know and make use of John's Gospel,[98] and, as we noticed in chapter 9, he referred to the Gospels as "the memoirs *(apomnēmoneumata)* of the apostles" (*1 Apologia* 66.3; 67.3; and thirteen times in *Dialogue* 107-17). In chapter 9 we discussed his more specific reference to the Gospels as the memoirs "composed by the apostles and those who accompanied them" (*2 Apologia* 11.2-3), most likely meaning that Matthew's and John's Gospels were composed by apostles, while those of Mark and Luke were composed by disciples of the apostles.[99] Justin also says explicitly that the Book of Revelation was written by "John, one of the apostles of Christ" (*Dialogue* 81.4). He probably shared the view of many in the second century that the same John was the author of the Gospel and the Apocalypse. But who, in Justin's usage, were "apostles of Christ"? Although on occasion he refers to the Twelve as the apostles who took the Gospel from Jerusalem throughout the world (*1 Apologia* 39.3; *Dialogue* 42.1), his other references to apostles (*1 Apologia* 42.4; 50.12; 53.3; *Dialogue* 110.2; 114.4; 119.6) provide evidence neither that he limited the term to the Twelve nor that he used it more broadly. We cannot tell whether Justin thought John, the author of the Gospel, was a member of the Twelve.

Clement of Alexandria tells a story he calls "a true tradition about John the apostle preserved in memory." The story locates John in Ephesus after the death of Domitian, when, Clement says, John moved from Patmos to Ephesus (*Quis dives salvetur* 42 = Eusebius, *Hist. Eccl.* 3.23.6). Thus Clement identifies the John in an oral tradition about John of Ephesus with the author of the Book of Revelation and calls him "John the apostle." He very likely took this John to be also the author of the Gospel. But did Clement think he was John the son of Zebedee? Again we cannot be sure. After all, Clement can refer even

---

96. Other second-century writers who call the author of John's Gospel an apostle are the Valentinian teachers Ptolemy (*Letter to Flora, apud* Epiphanius, *Panarion* 33.3.6) and Theodotus (*apud* Clement of Alexandria, *Excerpta ex Theodoto* 7.3; 35.1; 41.3).

97. His account of the origin of Mark's Gospel (*apud* Eusebius, *Hist. Eccl.* 6.14.6) seems indebted to Papias.

98. Hill, *The Johannine Corpus*, 316-37.

99. Cf. Hill, *The Johannine Corpus*, 338-42.

to Clement of Rome as "the apostle Clement" (*Stromateis* 4.17.105.1), even though he could hardly have thought Clement was even a personal disciple of Jesus. Probably he calls Clement of Rome an apostle because he is citing Clement's letter as authoritative Scripture, alongside Paul (called "the apostle"), John (the author of 1 John), Hebrews (ascribed to Paul), the book of Wisdom, and various Old Testament passages (4.16-18). For the same reason he quotes the *Epistle of Barnabas* and ascribes it to "Barnabas the apostle" (2.6.31.2; 2.7.35.5), though in this case he has Paul's precedent for calling Barnabas an apostle (1 Cor 9:1-6). The Scriptures were at this time coming to be described as "the prophets" (Old Testament) and "the apostles" (New Testament),[100] and so any Christian writing deemed authoritative Scripture was in some sense apostolic and its author might be, at least loosely, called an apostle. But by the same token it would be easy for Clement of Alexandria to think of John of Ephesus, author of the Gospel, as "John the apostle" without identifying him with John the son of Zebedee.

The use of the term "apostle" for writers of Scripture can be connected both with the emerging definition of a "canon" of Christian writings considered appropriate for reading in Christian worship alongside the Old Testament Scriptures, and also with the closely related notion of apostolic tradition passed down in the apostolic sees and polemically defended against the claims of Gnostic groups to their own esoteric tradition handed down secretly from the apostles. We can see these concerns at work on those few occasions on which Irenaeus calls the author of the Gospel of John "apostle" or places him in a group called "the apostles." In several such cases Irenaeus includes this John among those apostles who wrote down the apostolic teaching (*Adv. Haer.* 3.5.1; 3.21.3) or more specifically insists on the authority of John's Gospel (2.22.5), while in others he is concerned with the apostolic succession, either securing Polycarp's authority as the link in the chain after the apostles by virtue of his association with John (3.3.4; *Letter to Victor*) or claiming that the church of Ephesus is a reliable witness to apostolic tradition because of its foundation by Paul and its lengthy association with John (*Adv. Haer.* 3.3.4; cf. 2.22.5). It is by contrast with the Gnostic Gospels that Irenaeus refers to "the Gospels of the Apostles" (3.11.9), including John among them. In all such cases the term "apostle" indicates reliable authority, authorized by Christ himself and generally recognized in the churches.

These factors account for the increasing use of the term "apostle" for

---

100. The Muratorian canon uses these terms, and Justin (1 *Apologia* 67.3) says that at Christian worship meetings "the memoirs of the apostles or the writings of the prophets are read."

John of Ephesus. But for those who lacked Irenaeus's access to local Ephesian tradition, the idea of a Gospel author for whom the term "the Lord's disciple" was more appropriate than "apostle" must have been highly anomalous. Mark and Luke qualified as authors of apostolic Gospels because they were disciples of apostles, but John's apostolic authority was not in this sense derivative. It was his own as a personal disciple of Jesus. Once he was regularly termed "apostle" he very easily became indistinguishable from John the son of Zebedee.

Table 16: Named Apostles in Irenaeus
(in *Adv. Haer., Demonstration of the Apostolic Preaching,*
Letter to Florinus and *Letter to Victor*)

	Number of occurrences[102]
John of Ephesus, author of the Johannine literature[101]	
John the disciple of the Lord	19
John	34
the disciple of the Lord	3
the apostle	2
"he who saw the Apocalypse"	1
John the son of Zebedee (indubitable instances)	
Peter, James, and John (in the Gospels)	2[103]
Peter and John (in Acts)	3
Paul	
Paul the apostle	19
Paul	96
the apostle	79[104]
Peter	
Peter the apostle	3
Peter	46
Simon/Simon called Peter	2
Judas Iscariot	
Judas	20
Judas "the twelfth of the apostles"	1
Judas "one of his disciples"	1
Matthew	
Matthew the apostle	1
Matthew	14

101. In most cases the Gospel of John is in view, but there are two references to 1 John (3.16.5, 8), one to 2 John (1.16.3) and six to Revelation (1.26.3; 4.12.2; 4.17.6; 4.18.6; 4.20.11; 4.21.3).

102. These calculations are my own, though I have consulted B. Reynders, *Lexique Comparé du Texte Grec et des Versions Latine, Arménienne et Syriaque de l'"Adversus Haereses" de Saint Irénée*, 2 vols. (CSCO 141-42, Subsidia 5-6; Louvain: Imprimerie Orientaliste, 1954), as well as the indices to the Sources Chrétiennes editions of the *Adversus Haereses*.

103. There is also one reference to "the sons of Zebedee" (1.21.2).

104. I have included in this figure one reference to "he who had received the apostolate to the Gentiles" (4.24.2), one reference to "his [i.e., Jesus'] apostle" (5.2.2) and one to "the blessed apostle" (4.40.4).

Barnabas	7
Philip[105]	
Philip (one of the Twelve)	2
Philip (one of the Seven)	3
James the son of Zebedee	
James	3[106]
Matthias	3
James the Lord's brother	
James	3
Thomas	1
Nathanael	1

105. It is not possible to tell whether Irenaeus distinguished the two Philips or regarded them as one person.

106. There is also one reference to "the sons of Zebedee" (1.21.2).

Table 17: Sources of Irenaeus's Knowledge
of John the Disciple of the Lord[107]

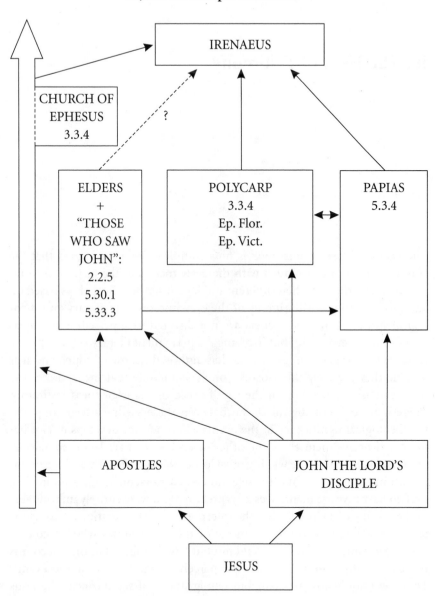

107. This table is based on those in Mutschler, "Was weiss Irenäus vom Johannesevange-lium?" 708, 711, 715, but with modifications.

18. The Jesus of Testimony

The historical task of this book is now complete. We have argued that the Gospels put us in close touch with the eyewitnesses of the history of Jesus. The Gospel writers, in their different ways, present their Gospels as based on and incorporating the testimony of the eyewitnesses. The literary and theological strategies of these writers are not directed to superseding the testimony of the eyewitnesses but to giving it a permanent literary vehicle. In one case, we have argued, an eyewitness has authored his own Gospel, and it is notable that precisely this Gospel, John's, is the one that incorporates the most extensive reflection on the significance of the eyewitness testimony. There is no epistemological chasm between the eyewitness testimony and the theological significance of the events as this author develops it. Not being eyewitnesses themselves, the other Gospel writers are less theologically ambitious. Of course, the writing of a Gospel was significantly an interpretative act in a variety of ways (the selection and arrangement of testimony in a unified narrative are themselves interpretative and were entirely unavoidable in the writing of a Gospel). But the interpretative act of writing a Gospel intended continuity with the testimony of the eyewitnesses who, of course, had already interpreted, who could not but have combined in their accounts the empirically observable with the perceived significance of the events. They were not just reminiscing but telling stories of significance. The Jesus the Gospels portray is Jesus as these eyewitnesses portrayed him, the Jesus of testimony.

In this concluding chapter we must look more closely at this category of testimony, its epistemological status, its role in historiography and its significance as a theological category. Testimony, we will argue, is both the historically appropriate category for understanding what kind of history the Gospels are and the theologically appropriate category for understanding what kind of access Christian readers of the Gospels thereby have to Jesus and his history. It is the category that enables us to surmount the dichotomy between the so-called historical Jesus and the so-called Christ of faith. It enables us to see that the Gospels are not some kind of obstacle to knowledge of the real Jesus and his history but precisely the kind of means of access to the real Jesus and his history that, as historians and as believers, we need.

What Is Testimony and Can We Rely on It?

Kevin Vanhoozer offers this definition of testimony: "Testimony is a speech act in which the witness's very act of stating *p* is offered as evidence 'that *p*,' it being assumed that the witness has the relevant competence or credentials to state truly 'that *p*.'"[1] Let us note immediately three more restricted uses of the term. One is the testimony of witnesses in a law court. Another is testimony from the past by which we know about what happened in the past: the testimony of historical evidence with which the historian is professionally concerned. Finally, there is a very special case which Vanhoozer also defines: "a genre that attempts to convey the fact and meaning of singular events of absolute significance."[2] Each of these can easily be seen to be a special case of the general definition with which we began. It may well be that we are inclined to associate the word "testimony" with one or more of these special cases rather than with the more general phenomenon. All three of the special cases are relevant to our own concern in this book and this chapter: the Gospels as testimony to the history of Jesus. Each of the three has its own characteristics and raises issues distinctive to the Gospels as testimony. But it will prove very useful to attend first to the general definition and the very common phenome-

1. K. J. Vanhoozer, "The Hermeneutics of I-Witness Testimony: John 21:20-24 and the Death of the Author," in idem, *First Theology: God, Scripture and Hermeneutics* (Downers Grove: InterVarsity, 2002) 269. The definition is adapted from the somewhat more elaborate one in C. A. J. Coady, *Testimony* (Oxford: Clarendon, 1992) 42. Vanhoozer puts it even more concisely in idem, *Is There a Meaning in This Text?* (Grand Rapids: Zondervan, 1998) 291: "Testimony is an illocutory act whereby a witness's say-so is itself evidence for the truth of what is said."

2. Vanhoozer, "The Hermeneutics," 269. In this definition Vanhoozer is following P. Ricoeur, "The Hermeneutics of Testimony," in idem, *Essays on Biblical Interpretation* (ed. L. S. Mudge; London: SPCK, 1981) 119-20.

non to which it applies. In doing so we shall be heavily indebted to the land-mark philosophical study of testimony by C. A. J. Coady.

For many people the word "testimony" suggests most immediately the evidence of a witness in a court of law, and we have seen that the Gospel of John makes much use of this kind of witness as a metaphor.[3] But, as Coady points out,

> It does not follow . . . that such legal situations are the only ones in which testimony can exist; it seems rather that the legal framework adapts and solemnizes an everyday phenomenon to which it may not be common to apply such a technical-sounding word. It is indeed uncommon to say, "His testimony was such-and-such," in non-formal contexts; instead we frequently speak simply of "His report . . ." or "His version . . ." or simply, "He says. . . ." When I accept some report and in reply to questioning I stand firm on, "His word is good enough for me," or "Well, it's in *The Times*," then it would seem perverse to hold that simply because there is no legal context this cannot be a case of someone's accepting testimony.[4]

Coady therefore speaks of "formal testimony," meaning legal or quasi-legal testimony, but also of "natural testimony," the much wider usage. Natural testimony occurs in any situation in which

> we have a speaker engaged in the speech act of testifying to the truth of some proposition which is either in dispute or in some way in need of de-termination and his attestation is evidence towards settling the matter.[5]

In the legal context there may be special rules of evidence, varying from one legal system to another, but the same general notion of testimony is operative over a very wide range of everyday situations. We accept testimony whenever we take someone else's word for it, whether this be in ordinary conversational interchange, in our reliance on experts in any field, or as experts ourselves in some field of knowledge or research.[6] We do this hundreds, probably thou-sands, of times a day in trivial ways and in crucially important ways. We rely all the time on "facts" for which we only have other people's testimony. As David Hume put it,

---

3. For the use of this metaphor throughout the New Testament, see A. A. Trites, *The New Testament Concept of Witness* (SNTSMS 31; Cambridge: Cambridge University Press, 1977).

4. Coady, *Testimony*, 26.

5. Coady, *Testimony*, 38.

6. Even in mathematics: Coady, *Testimony*, 12.

[T]here is no species of reasoning more common, more useful, and even necessary to human life, than that which is derived from the testimony of men [*sic*] and the reports of eye-witnesses and spectators.[7]

The fundamental point is that testimony requires trust: "When we believe testimony we believe what is said because we trust the witness."[8] But how can such trust be justified? How does knowledge on the basis of testimony relate to other kinds of knowledge? What is its epistemological status? Do we really know what we accept on the word of another in the same way that we know what we learn from perception or memory or inference? Coady says that the "basic thrust [of his book's argument] is that our trust in the word of others is fundamental to the very idea of serious cognitive activity."[9] His achievement is to have shown that testimony is as basic a form of knowledge as perception, memory, and inference. It has "the same kind of epistemic status as our other primary sources of information, such as perception."[10]

---

7. Quoted in Coady, *Testimony*, 7.

8. Coady, *Testimony*, 46.

9. Coady, *Testimony*, vii.

10. Coady, *Testimony*, 175. Coady's view is followed also by C. S. Evans, *The Historical Christ and the Jesus of Faith* (Oxford: Clarendon, 1996) 334-35. The only critique of Coady's argument that I know is R. Foley, *Intellectual Trust in Oneself and Others* (Cambridge: Cambridge University Press, 2001) chapter 4. He agrees with Coady in rejecting what he calls "epistemic egotism" and "epistemic egoism," but evidently thinks that Coady does not take sufficient account of "the possibility of rational iconoclasm, that is, for the possibility of individuals rejecting the most cherished opinions of their contemporaries or the most deeply held assumptions of their traditions and yet still being rational" (99). He argues that the reason we regularly accept the testimony of others without questioning it is that to do otherwise would be inconsistent with our reasons for trusting our own knowledge. But when others offer testimony that is in conflict with our own knowledge this justifies us in finding reasons for contesting their testimony. In this case there would be a sense in which our trust in the intellectual reliability of others follows from our intellectual self-trust and is therefore not a properly basic form of knowledge with the same status as our own perception and memory. But how are we supposed to know whether this issue of consistency is actually operative in our attitudes to testimony? I think Coady's account gives sufficient justification for intellectual autonomy of the kind Foley values. On Coady's account one need only say that I am justified in doubting another's testimony if it disagrees with views of my own that I consider well grounded. This would be like doubting someone's testimony because I know him or her to be unreliable. Foley ends his treatment by agreeing quite closely with Coady's account of the relationship of intellectual autonomy and intellectual dependence on others: "As intellectual beings, we are both social and autonomous. The latter is in tension with the former but also dependent on it. We become intellectually independent despite the influence of others, but also because of it, if all goes well. Our intellectual training, which we largely receive from others, develops and hones abilities that allow us to evaluate and at times even radically criticize the views, procedure, and standards of

Such a view of testimony, however, swims with difficulty against the stream of modern philosophical epistemology, and Coady finds a significant precedent only in the so-called "common sense" philosophy of the eighteenth-century Scottish philosopher Thomas Reid.[11] Reid classified the exchange of testimony as one of what he called the "social operations of mind." These also include such activities as giving and receiving commands, promising, and asking and answering questions, all of which presuppose interpersonal exchange. He contrasts them with the "solitary operations of mind," and insists that they are not reducible to the latter, as though the solitary operations were basic and the social operations reliable only if we somehow check them by means of the solitary operations.[12] Thus testimony, according to Reid, exposes the social character of knowledge. To trust the testimony of others is simply fundamental to the kind of creatures we are. It does not need to be justified on the basis of other ("solitary") means of knowledge, for it is as basic as they are.

Thomas Reid's approach to testimony is now broadly shared by "many of the most influential contemporary epistemologists,"[13] but this is a recent development. The most important reason it has not been accepted by more philosophers in the modern period — and this is also the reason for the widespread neglect of testimony even as a topic of philosophical study — is the individualism bequeathed to philosophy by the Enlightenment, more specifically an individualistic epistemology inclined to minimize the individual's intellectual reliance on other people.[14] The starting point has been the individual's own perception (What is the nature of *my* knowledge? How do *I* come to know?), which has been accorded epistemological priority over common knowledge (What is the nature of *our* knowledge? How do *we* come to know?).[15] The desire to justify knowledge only as the individual's autonomous knowledge makes testimony problematic. In response to this problem, a tradition of thinking from Hume onward has sought to justify reliance on testimony in terms of allegedly more fundamental forms of knowledge that do not require reliance on others. This requires that one rely on testimony

those around us, the very views, procedures and standards that have intellectually shaped us." This is true, but it remains the case that such criticism, however radical, can never affect more than a very small proportion of the information and opinion we receive from others.

11. Coady, *Testimony*, 23, 54-62.

12. Coady, *Testimony*, 54-55; cf. also Vanhoozer, *Is There a Meaning*, 290.

13. Foley, *Intellectual Trust*, 96. On p. 97 he refers to several.

14. Coady, *Testimony*, chapter 1, suggests that the mathematical theory of probability is a second reason.

15. Coady, *Testimony*, 148-50.

only because one has somehow been able to check the credibility of the witness or to observe that the kind of testimony in question usually turns out to be trustworthy.[16] Coady refutes all such attempts to reduce testimony to other means of knowledge. It is simply not true that each of us has done anything approaching sufficient observation for ourselves of the correlation between testimony and observable facts to justify our reliance on testimony.[17] Further attempts to avoid the conclusion that testimony is a basic form of knowledge probably turn out to rely covertly on trusting others. Coady shows that in fact the very use of a public language in which a testimony is available presupposes the reliability of many of the reports made in that language ("an extensive commitment to believing the reports of others [is] a precondition to understanding their speech at all").[18] Hence "what is suspect is the very idea of an entirely individualistic justification for the phenomenon of communal epistemological trust."[19]

If testimony is as basic a means of knowledge as perception, memory, and inference, then we must understand our epistemic situation in less exclusively individualistic terms and more in communal or inter-subjective terms. But this does not mean renouncing any kind of cognitive autonomy, as though the individual could never think for herself. It means, rather, that epistemic trust in others is the basic matrix within which the individual can acquire and exercise what Coady calls "a robust degree of cognitive autonomy":

> Just as the autonomous agent need not utterly renounce his dependence upon others, even at the deepest levels of his existence, so the autonomous thinker need not entirely renounce some degree of fundamental reliance upon the word of others but rather should deploy it to achieve a genuinely critical stance and a viable independence of outlook. One needs intellectual autonomy to achieve a feasible degree of control over the beliefs one acquires and to ensure that one's thinking is appropriately responsive to one's actual cognitive history and present intellectual environment. None the less, the independent thinker is not someone who works everything out for herself, even in principle, but one who exercises a controlling intelligence over the input she receives from the normal sources of information whether their basis be individual or communal.[20]

16. Coady, *Testimony,* 22-23.
17. Coady, *Testimony,* 79-83.
18. Coady, *Testimony,* 176.
19. Coady, *Testimony,* 152.
20. Coady, *Testimony,* 99-100.

Therefore believing testimony, as we do very frequently indeed, entails a fundamental attitude of trust, but not necessarily uncritical trust:

> When we believe testimony we believe what is said because we trust the witness. This attitude of trust is very fundamental, but it is not blind. As [Thomas] Reid noted, the child begins with an attitude of complete trust in what it is told, and develops more critical attitudes as it matures. None the less, even for adults, the critical attitude is itself founded upon a general stance of trust, just as the adult awareness of the way memory plays us false rests upon a broader confidence in recollective powers.
>
> Contrary to what we are inclined, unreflectively, to suppose, the attitudes of critical appraisal and of trust are not diametrically opposed, though in particular cases, one cannot, in the same breath, both trust what a witness says, and subject it to critical evaluation. What happens characteristically in the reception of testimony is that the audience operates a sort of learning mechanism which has certain critical capacities built into it. . . . We may have "no reason to doubt" another's communication even where there is no question of our being gullible; we may simply recognize that the standard warning signs of deceit, confusion, or mistake are not present. This recognition incorporates our knowledge of the witness's competence, of the circumstances surrounding his utterance, of the consistency of the parts of his testimony, and its relation to what others have said, on the matter. . . . It is important to appreciate the complex relation between trust and critical appraisal.[21]

Testimony, then, of its very nature invites trust. We have no reason to think that as a means of knowledge it is less reliable than perception, memory, and inference. We have no reason to suppose that the perceptions of others, given us in testimony, are less worthy of belief than our own. Comprehensive distrust of everything others tell us defies the communal and inter-subjective reality of the human epistemic situation. A fundamental attitude of trust is not gullibility but a necessary epistemic virtue. Trust is fundamental, while critical evaluation is important but feasible only as a secondary activity, presupposing a more basic attitude of trust. The situation is in principle no different than in the case of our individual perceptions, memories, and inferences, which we have no choice but to trust fundamentally, while also being aware that they can mislead us and require critical evaluation in suspicious cases. It is only the excessive individualism of the modern western ideology that tempts us to the view that testimony should regularly and generally incur our suspicion, while

21. Coady, *Testimony*, 46-47.

our own perceptions, memories, and inferences should not. There may be some difference in that, in many though by no means all cases, there appears to be a wider range and number of possible factors making for distortion and falsification of testimony. This justifies, for example, rigorous cross-examination and assessment of witnesses in a court of law and the modern historian's use of methodologically refined critical tools for assessing the testimonies that come to us from the past, but it does not reverse the necessary priority of trust over critical assessment. As Paul Ricoeur puts it, any human community requires the "prudential rule": "First, trust the word of others, then doubt if there are good reasons for doing so."[22]

Testimony and History

In this book, I have followed Samuel Byrskog in arguing that the Gospels, though in some ways a very distinctive form of historiography, share broadly in the attitude to eyewitness testimony that was common among historians in the Greco-Roman period. These historians valued above all reports of first-hand experience of the events they recounted. Best of all was for the historian to have been himself a participant in the events (direct autopsy). Failing that (and no historian was present at all the events he needed to recount, not least because usually some would be simultaneous), they sought informants who could speak from firsthand knowledge and whom they could interview (indirect autopsy). This, at least, was historiographic best practice, represented and theorized by such generally admired historians as Thucydides and Polybius. The preference for direct or indirect autopsy is an obviously reasonable general rule for acquiring the testimony likely to be most reliable. Not only did it mean that the risks of transmission through a chain of informants were avoided; it also meant that the historians were able to cross-examine their witnesses in a way somewhat similar to legal practice in court. They could draw out the kind of information they most needed and they could form some judgments as to the likely reliability of an informant. Of course, it is not always the case that firsthand testimony is more reliable than other forms of testimony, and even the best historians did not rely exclusively on it. But they sought to rely primarily on it, and this entailed the view that contemporary history — history still within living memory — was the only kind of history that should, properly speaking, be attempted. This did not mean, of

---

22. P. Ricoeur, *Memory, History, Forgetting* (tr. K. Blamey and D. Pellauer; Chicago: University of Chicago Press, 2004) 165.

course, that the historians thought only contemporary history could be *known*. They trusted, to a large extent, historians of the past who had written of the events within living memory in their day. But, generally speaking, they did not think they themselves had any means of doing better than past historians had done in writing of the events of the past.

We should not suppose that the historians relied *uncritically* on testimony. Polybius, for example, described the historian's task as: "to believe those worthy of belief and to be a good critic of the reports that reach him" (12.4.5).[23] The best historians assessed their informants and weighed conflicting testimony, sometimes reporting two different accounts while judging one to be more credible. It could doubtless be claimed that their critical appraisal of testimony lacked the methodological rigor to which modern historians aspire. But it is important to remember their self-limitation to events within living memory. The critical tools of modern historians have been developed largely with a view to investigating the history of earlier, often much earlier, times than those in which the historian lives. Their access to firsthand testimony also gave the Greco-Roman historians the considerable advantage of being able to interrogate their witnesses. By remaining, as it were, within their competence, the best of Greco-Roman historians achieved results that we should not be too ready to suppose a historian equipped with modern historical methods could easily have surpassed.

However, for our present concern it is important to ask whether the role of testimony in modern historiography differs from its almost exclusively important role in the historiography of the ancient world. In the final part of Dennis Nineham's three-part article on "Eyewitness Testimony and the Gospel Tradition,"[24] an article that probably exercised considerable influence in persuading English-speaking Gospels scholars to set little store by the role of the eyewitnesses in the transmission of Gospel traditions, Nineham turned to precisely this issue of the difference between ancient and modern historiography in their treatment of testimony. His account of the difference led him to conclude:

> Even if the gospels consisted exclusively of eye-witness testimony, they would still have to abide the historian's question. They would still only be for him what basically [in the light of form criticism] they are now, crude

23. Quoted in S. Byrskog, *Story as History — History as Story* (WUNT 123; Tübingen: Mohr, 2000; reprinted Leiden: Brill, 2002) 179.

24. D. E. Nineham, "Eyewitness Testimony and the Gospel Tradition. III," *JTS* 11 (1960) 253-64.

ore to which he must apply his proper, rigorous techniques before he can extract the precious metal of historical truth.[25]

Nineham's understanding of the much diminished value of eyewitness testimony for the modern historian relies on a classic of historical method[26] — that of the French historian Marc Bloch, one of the founder members of the *Annales* school of historians — and on a classic of the philosophy of history: *The Idea of History,* by R. G. Collingwood.[27]

There are certainly some very valid distinctions to be made between the ancient and the modern ways of practicing history. The difference is not essentially a matter of the evaluation of sources. It is true that, from the early modern period onward, there was a significant movement away from the general credulity with which historical sources had often been treated in the medieval period and the development of systematic examination of the relative reliability of sources. Paul Ricoeur locates the "birth of historical criticism" in Lorenzo Valla's exposure of the Donation of Constantine as an imposture.[28] But the stark contrast is with the historiography of the late Roman and medieval periods rather than with the great historians of the Greco-Roman world, who were able to assess their sources with some degree of rigor because (at least when they were following best practice) there were eyewitnesses whom they met and questioned in person. For this very reason, as we have frequently emphasized, they restricted themselves to such history as was accessible in this way. What promoted the development of what Collingwood calls "scissors-and-paste historical method" was the desire to break out of these bounds and to write the kind of world history that could be achieved only by compiling the accounts of historians of the past, whose reliability went generally unquestioned.[29] When in the modern period more critical attitudes and methods developed, they were needed primarily for the study of history that, like most history, was not accessible to the historian through living eyewitness testimony.

Another development in historical method in the modern period was the increasing use of non-literary sources, such as have become very extensive with the growth of the systematic discipline of archaeology. But this merely accompanied the truly revolutionary development, which consisted in asking

25. Nineham, "Eyewitness Testimony and the Gospel Tradition. III," 259.

26. The English version is M. Bloch, *The Historian's Craft* (tr. P. Putnam; Manchester: Manchester University Press, 1954).

27. R. G. Collingwood, *The Idea of History* (Oxford: Oxford University Press, 1946).

28. Ricoeur, *Memory,* 172.

29. Collingwood, *The Idea of History,* 33, cf. 257-59.

and answering questions about the past that the sources were not designed to answer. This is virtually the only way in which non-literary sources can speak to us, but it is also a dominant way in which modern historians make use of testimony, that is, of literary sources whose authors wrote for the sake of communicating something to their readers. Such sources can be used to yield historical data on all kinds of topics and issues that their authors never contemplated their readers considering. From this perspective texts that, as historical accounts, must be judged quite unreliable, can be no less valuable as historical evidence than reasonably trustworthy accounts would be. Many Gospels scholars, for example, have thought that, even if the writers of the Gospels intended primarily to tell their readers about Jesus, and even if the Gospels are quite unreliable as sources for historical knowledge of Jesus, they are nevertheless valuable evidence about the Christian communities in and for which the Gospel writers wrote. But one could easily gather a very large number of less controversial examples.

In this connection Bloch speaks of both literary and non-literary sources being "witnesses in spite of themselves":

> [T]he narrative sources . . . that is, the accounts which are consciously intended to inform their readers, still continue to provide valuable assistance to the scholar. Among their other advantages, they are ordinarily the only ones which furnish a chronological framework. . . . Nevertheless, there can be no doubt that, in the course of its development, historical research has gradually been led to place more and more confidence in the second category of evidence, in the evidence of witnesses in spite of themselves.[30]

There are many "traces" of the past, as Bloch calls them, that only constitute evidence by witnessing "in spite of themselves," but even in the case of the "intentional" witnesses, even those

> most anxious to bear witness, that which the text tells us expressly has ceased to be the primary object of our attention today. . . . At least three fourths of the lives of the saints of the high Middle Ages can teach us nothing concrete about those pious personages whose careers they pretend to describe. If, on the other hand, we consult them as to the way of life or thought peculiar to the epoch in which they were written (all things which the biographer of the saint had not the least intention of revealing), we shall find them invaluable. Despite our inevitable subordina-

---

30. Bloch, *The Historian's Craft,* 61.

tion to the past, we have freed ourselves at least to the extent that, eternally condemned to know only by means of its "traces,"[31] we are nevertheless successful in knowing far more of the past than the past itself had thought good to tell us. Properly speaking, it is a glorious victory of mind over its material.[32]

This account of the way historical "traces" inform us "in spite of themselves" is accurate and important. We have practiced this kind of historical method frequently in this book (for example, no ancient writer intended to tell us about the relative popularity of various names in first-century Jewish Palestine). It is virtually second nature to any modern practitioner of history. But we should also note that nothing about modern historical method prohibits us from reading the explicit testimonies of the past for the sake of what they were intended to recount and reveal. It depends what questions we ask.

In playing down to the extent that he does the modern historian's interest in what the explicit testimonies from the past intentionally relate, Bloch perhaps displays an element of modernist arrogance with respect to the past. In the medieval period scholars could think of themselves as dwarves standing on the shoulders of giants, able to see further than the ancients only by virtue of depending on the ancients. The more characteristic modern attitude is to celebrate, as Bloch does, a kind of triumph over the past, liberated from dependence on it to the extent that we can know "far more of the past than the past itself had thought good to tell us." The modern historian is the autonomous thinker liberated from the entail of tradition and producing, just like the scientist, knowledge that no one has had before. This celebration of the historian's autonomy vis-à-vis "the past" (rather oddly personified in Bloch's words) appears even more triumphalistically in Collingwood.

Collingwood compares the truly scientific historian to the natural scientist as described by Francis Bacon. He even takes over Bacon's metaphor of interrogation by torture, a metaphor Bacon himself drew from the real practice of torturing accused persons and witnesses — compelling them to witness "in spite of themselves"! — with which Bacon was shamefully involved in his legal and political career. Collingwood treats this surely at the very least very distasteful metaphor merely as a "memorable phrase":

31. I have changed the word "tracks" in the English translation of Bloch's text to "traces" because the latter is more common in English usage for this originally French term for historical evidence.

32. Bloch, *The Historian's Craft*, 61-62.

Francis Bacon, lawyer and philosopher, laid it down in one of his memorable phrases that the natural scientist must "put Nature to the question." What he was denying, when he wrote this, was that the scientist's attitude towards nature should be one of respectful attentiveness, waiting upon her utterances and building his theories on the basis of what she chose to vouchsafe him. What he was asserting was two things at once: first, that the scientist must take the initiative, deciding for himself what he wants to know and formulating this in his own mind in the shape of a question; and secondly, that he must find means of compelling nature to answer, devising tortures under which she can no longer hold her tongue. Here, in a single brief epigram, Bacon laid down once for all the true theory of experimental science. It is also, though Bacon did not know this, the true theory of historical method.[33]

As an image of the scientific approach to nature, Bacon's metaphor of judicial torture now seems altogether too redolent of the modern project of domination of nature and the lack of "respectful attentiveness" to nature that has led to ecological disaster.[34] This should give us pause before accepting too readily Collingwood's reapplication of the metaphor to "scientific" history.

Why the violent image of forcibly extracting information? It seems to be part of Collingwood's notion of the modern historian's intellectual autonomy. He is concerned to deny that the past voluntarily "gives" the historian anything, as would be the case if the historian accepted answers to her questions offered "ready-made" in the testimony of witnesses in the past:

> Like every science, history is autonomous. The historian has the right, and is under an obligation, to make up his own mind by the methods proper to his own science as to the correct solution of every problem that arises for him in the pursuit of that science. He can never be under any obligation, or have the right, to let someone else make up his mind for him. If anyone else, . . . even a very learned historian, or an eyewitness, or a person in the confidence of the man who did the thing he is inquiring into, or even the man who did it himself, hands him on a plate a ready-

33. Collingwood, *The Idea of History*, 269. Without reference to Bacon, Bloch, *The Historian's Craft*, 64, says: "from the moment when we are no longer resigned to purely and simply recording the words of our witnesses, from the moment we decide to force them to speak, even against their will, cross-examination becomes more necessary than ever." Why "force"? Cross-examination alone does not use force, only cross-examination assisted by torture.

34. See, e.g., P. Marshall, *Nature's Web: An Exploration of Ecological Thinking* (London: Simon and Schuster, 1992) 182-86; R. Bauckham, *God and the Crisis of Freedom* (Louisville: Westminster John Knox, 2002) 159-65.

made answer to his question, all he can do is reject it: not because he thinks his informant is trying to deceive him, or is himself deceived, but because if he accepts it he is giving up his autonomy as an historian.[35]

Collingwood fully admits that in everyday life we "constantly and rightly" accept the testimony of others, but denies that knowledge acquired by accepting testimony can ever be historical knowledge:

> [I]t can never be historical knowledge, because it can never be scientific knowledge. It is not scientific knowledge because it cannot be vindicated by appeal to the grounds on which it is based. As soon as there are such grounds, the case is no longer one of testimony. When testimony is reinforced by evidence, our acceptance of it is no longer the acceptance of testimony as such; it is the affirmation of something based upon evidence, that is, historical knowledge.[36]

The individualist epistemology of the Enlightenment cannot, Collingwood concedes, be practiced in everyday life, but in truly rigorous — "scientific" — disciplines it comes into its own, requiring the scholar not to depend on testimony at all. Whatever testimony may tell her, she should believe it only when she has independently established its truth for herself. Thus, whereas in everyday life we treat testimony as reliable unless or until we find reason to doubt it, in scientific history testimony is suspicious from the outset and can be believed only when it is independently verified, at which point it ceases to be testimony.

This claim to the historian's complete independence of testimony is unsustainable. Coady's refutation of it[37] need not be repeated here. Testimony is as fundamental to the historian's knowledge of the past as it is to human knowledge in general. This does not mean that the historian does not require a certain kind of independence of the testimonies from the past. The historian does not put blind faith in testimony, but, as in ordinary life, can think independently only through a more basic dependence on testimony. Only because the historian accepts some testimony can she doubt other testimony.[38] Comprehensive doubt is impossible.

Just as no one lives their everyday life by means of a purely individualist epistemology, so no historian really does history without extensive depen-

35. Collingwood, *The Idea of History*, 256.
36. Collingwood, *The Idea of History*, 257.
37. Coady, *Testimony*, chapter 13.
38. Ricoeur, *Memory*, 180-81.

dence on testimony. Collingwood's account of historiographic epistemology has seemed plausible to some historians, as well as to other readers, because it is not completely wrong. It is really a considerable exaggeration of the undoubted fact that modern historical work has not only developed more searching critical methods of assessing the reliability of testimony but has also come to depend greatly on asking questions the sources do not profess to answer and on enabling the sources to give evidence "in spite of themselves." This can make the historian feel in control of her material rather than dependent on it. Intelligibly, perhaps, this exaggerated sense of the historian's independence of the past has now been challenged by a postmodern view of historiography that finds it barely distinguishable from fiction freely created by the historian.[39] As in other fields, Enlightenment individualism has led to postmodern skepticism.

In its attempt to cut loose from testimony altogether Collingwood's theory does not correspond to what historians generally do. However, it — or the kind of extreme individualist epistemology it embraces — can lead historians to an overly skeptical approach particularly to those sources that were intended to recount and inform about events of the past, that is, testimony in this restricted sense. Particularly in Gospels scholarship there is an attitude abroad that approaches the sources with a fundamental skepticism, rather than trust, and therefore requires that anything the sources claim be accepted only if historians can independently verify it. This is probably a combination of, on the one hand, the exclusively individualist epistemological attitude thought by Collingwood to be necessary if history is to be scientific with, on the other hand, the special features of Gospels scholarship that make many scholars anxious above all to avoid dogmatically influenced credulity. Most scholars in this field have little or no experience of working as historians in other areas of history. So it is easy for Gospels scholarship itself to develop its own conventions for gauging the reliability of sources. These do not necessarily correspond well to the way evidence is treated in other historical fields. Young scholars, learning their historical method from Gospels scholars, often treat it as self-evident that the more skeptical they are toward their sources, the more rigorous will be their historical method. It has to be said, over and over, that historical rigor does not consist in fundamental skepticism toward historical testimony but in fundamental trust along with testing by critical questioning. Testimony may be mistaken and may mislead, but this is not to be generally presumed but must be established in each case. Testimony should be treated as reliable until proved otherwise. "First, trust the word of

39. As in the works of Hayden White and Keith Jenkins.

others, then doubt if there are good reasons for doing so."[40] This general rule for everyday life applies also to the historian in relation to her sources.[41] Naturally, in the case of Gospels scholarship, the particular nature of specifically these testimonies must be understood if their reliability is to be plausibly evaluated, and this book has been a contribution to that task.

Ricoeur on Testimony and History

For a more adequate philosophical account of historiography than Collingwood's, we may turn to Paul Ricoeur's major recent work *Memory, History, Forgetting*.[42] Ricoeur's view of the place of testimony in history is rather different from Collingwood's.[43] He distinguishes three "phases" of the historian's work. These are intended as methodological moments and do not necessarily occur in chronological sequence.[44] They are: (1) the documentary phase, (2) explanation and/or understanding, and (3) the historian's representation. The documents the historian works with in the first phase are what Ricoeur, following Bloch, calls the "traces" left by the past in the present. They include testimonies and also other (non-literary) "vestiges" of the past. Testimonies he distinguishes as "voluntary," intended for posterity, and "involuntary," those that witness "in spite of themselves."[45] All these become historical documents when they are archived, that is, preserved and collected for the historian's use. The documentary phase of historical research is the process of evaluating them as historical evidence and of establishing the facts[46] to which they reliably attest. This can only occur when the historian puts questions to

40. Ricoeur, *Memory*, 165.

41. I. A. Provan, "Knowing and Believing," in C. Bartholomew, C. S. Evans, M. Healy, and M. Rae, eds., *"Behind" the Text: History and Biblical Interpretation* (Scripture and Hermeneutics Series 4; Grand Rapids: Zondervan, 2003) 229-66, also counters the neglect of the category of testimony in modern scientific history, vindicating the ancient reliance on testimony on the grounds that "we know about the past *primarily* . . . through the testimony of others and *not* through other avenues" (230); "we 'know' by listening to testimony and interpretation, and by making choices about whom to believe" (231). His article applies this emphasis on the indispensability of testimony in historical knowledge to Old Testament studies and current work on the history of Israel in particular.

42. Ricoeur, *Memory*.

43. Ricoeur does not explicitly refer to or criticize this aspect of Collingwood's work.

44. Ricoeur, *Memory*, 137.

45. Ricoeur, *Memory*, 170-71.

46. Ricoeur defines a historical "fact" not as the event itself but as "the contents of a statement made to represent it" (*Memory*, 178-79).

the documents: "The documents do not speak unless someone asks them to verify, that is, to make true, some hypothesis."[47] The second phase involves the interconnections among the facts for which documentary proof has been established. It is the phase in which the historian asks and answers the large interpretative questions, the "why" of historical events to which the answers may be causal or teleological explanations of events. The last phase is the composition of a literary text for readers of history, called "representation" in that it "stands for" the historical events.[48] Testimony reappears in Ricoeur's scheme in this third phase, its contents incorporated into the historian's account.[49] Though Ricoeur does not spell this out in detail, it is clear that he does not think that testimony is something of which the historian ever becomes independent.

One of Ricoeur's concerns throughout (in dialogue especially with Hayden White) is to distinguish history from narrative fiction by insisting that at every stage there is deliberate reference — whether by the witness or the historian — to what happened in the past.[50] This specific kind of referentiality in historiography can be discerned only by taking account of the relationship between all three phases of historiographic work. At the root of the whole enterprise is memory,[51] which has reference to the past as its distinguishing characteristic. Memory is declared in testimony, which when recorded and deposited in an archive becomes a document for the historian to study. Documents are therefore "archived memory."[52] It is the relationship of testimony to memory that for Ricoeur distinguishes testimony from other traces of the past. The latter are like the "clues" that feature in detective work, where they can be valuable for corroborating testimony.[53] But it is clear that Ricoeur makes testimony as the record of memory indispensable for historiography. Only through testimony is the historian's representation of the past connected to the events themselves:

47. Ricoeur, *Memory*, 177.

48. Thus historical narrative can have "the mode of truth proper to 'standing for'" (Ricoeur, *Memory*, 279).

49. Ricoeur, *Memory*, 161.

50. G. J. Laughery, "Ricoeur on History, Fiction, and Biblical Hermeneutics," in Bartholomew, Evans, Healy, and Rae, eds., *"Behind" the Text*, 339-62, gives an introduction to Ricoeur's thinking on history from this point of view especially.

51. Cf. Ricoeur, *Memory*, 87: "this book is a plea on behalf of memory as the womb of history, inasmuch as memory remains the guardian of the entire problem of the representative relation of the present to the past."

52. Ricoeur, *Memory*, 178.

53. Ricoeur, *Memory*, 173-74.

It would be futile to seek a direct tie between the narrative form [supplied by the historian] and the events as they actually occurred; the tie can only be indirect by way of explanation and, short of this, by way of the documentary phase, which refers back in turn to *testimony and the trust placed in the word of another.*[54]

Confronted with the postmodern claim that "facts" have only a linguistic existence, Ricoeur proposes a critical realism that must revert from the historian's narrative to the testimony in which it has its roots. Documentary proof — whereby the historian establishes the "facts" — has testimony at its very heart. In the end, testimony is all we have. For the historian, the testament, as a record of memory, is bedrock:

I have said that we have nothing better than our memory to assure us of the reality of our memories — we have nothing better than testimony and the criticism of testimony to accredit the historian's representation of the past.[55]

As this quotation makes clear it is not a case of uncritical acceptance of testimony. But testimony asks to be trusted. The witness says not only "I was there" but also "believe me." When questioned, the witness can only say "If you don't believe me, ask someone else."[56] Ricoeur affirms the intersubjective epistemology that we have already seen justifies our reliance on testimony.[57] But he observes that something happens when we move from the everyday situation of dialogical testimony to the archived testimony, which is "orphaned," deprived of its testifier, and no longer has designated addressees.[58] In this situation it becomes the object of critical questioning by historians who have no other access to its origins and may be set alongside other, discordant testimonies. The archives include false testimonies alongside true. Hence modern critical history "has had to blaze a difficult trail between spontaneous credulity and Pyrrhonian skepticism in principle."[59] Trust in the word of another, spontaneous and essential in everyday life, must in historiography coexist in dialectic with the kind of critical questioning that the archived testimony evokes. Here the need for trust is too easily overlooked be-

54. Ricoeur, *Memory,* 244 (italics added).
55. Ricoeur, *Memory,* 278; cf. 147.
56. This "triple declaration" of the witness occurs several times in the work: *Memory,* 164-65, 278, 497.
57. Ricoeur, *Memory,* 165.
58. Ricoeur, *Memory,* 169.
59. Ricoeur, *Memory,* 172.

cause the testimony has been removed from the immediacy of the dialogical context of everyday life, where the dimension of trust in the word of another is obvious, but for testimony archived as a historical document trust is no less required, complicated but not at all replaced by critical assessment.

So far we have made no reference to a feature of the historiographic process that belongs inseparably with the "factual" character of historical claims: interpretation. For Ricoeur this is not to be limited to any of the three phases, but occurs at all three levels. Even at the stage of forming archives, the selection of traces to include is an act of interpretation. We cannot separate out uninterpreted "brute facts," but neither should we wish to, since interpretation, "the subjective side correlative to the objective side of historical knowledge,"[60] is integral to the historian's quest for truth: "Interpretation is a component of the very intending of truth in all historiographic operations."[61] Ricoeur follows Bloch in seeing that historiography involves both the understanding of the past in the light of the present and the understanding of the present in the light of the past. At the heart of this movement between past and present is testimony, the most important form of trace left by the past in the present.[62] Interpretation of testimony is the historian's primary mode of seeking historical truth.

Testimony and Its Reception

To repeat, trusting testimony is indispensable to historiography. This trust need not be blind faith. In the "critical realist" historian's reception and use of testimony there is a dialectic of trust and critical assessment. But the assessment is precisely an assessment of the testimony as trustworthy or not. What is not possible is independent verification or falsification of everything the testimony relates such that reliance on testimony would no longer be needed. Testimony shares the fragility of memory, which is testimony's sole access to the past, while also, when it predates living memory, existing only as archived memory, cut off from the dialogical context of contemporary testimony. But, for most purposes, testimony is all we have. There are, indeed, other traces of the past in the present (such as archaeological finds), which can to a degree corroborate or discredit testimony, but they cannot, in most cases, suffice for the study and writing of history. They cannot replace testimony. In the end, testimony is all we have.

However, most modern historiography does not make use of testimony

60. Ricoeur, *Memory*, 337.
61. Ricoeur, *Memory*, 185.
62. Ricoeur, *Memory*, 170.

in quite the same way as the historians of the ancient world did. The latter very often substantially incorporated testimony into their own writing, making the eyewitness's story part of their own meta-story. Modern historians typically operate at a greater distance from testimony, for these reasons: (1) They are not usually in dialogue with living eyewitnesses. (2) More often than not, the questions they put to testimony are not the questions the testimony was designed to answer. They require the testimony to witness "in spite of itself." (3) Their resulting historical account, what Ricoeur calls "representation," is *based on* testimony but usually does not incorporate testimony. Readers typically encounter what the historian has done with testimony rather than becoming themselves recipients of the testimony.

That said, whatever modern historians do with testimony, the need either to trust or, as a result of criticism, to distrust testimony remains. Moreover, among the many ways of interrogating testimony, modern historians cannot neglect the understanding and the acceptance or rejection of what the testimony was designed to tell its readers. This is presupposed by the other approaches to the evidence, even though distrusting the testimony's explicit witness need not disable it as a witness "in spite of itself."

The special importance the historians of Greco-Roman antiquity attached to *participant* eyewitness testimony also retains its validity. It is true that the modernist prejudice against interested and therefore biased parties in favor of disinterested and so allegedly neutral observers has played an important part in modern historiography (and not least in biblical studies). But, however downplayed, the perspective of the involved participant still offers unique access to the lived interior of events. Readers of history still want to know how participants experienced the events. For such readers the historian can frame such testimony with a wider context and explanatory comment, thereby promoting better understanding of the testimony. But she must still substantially repeat the testimony, retelling if not reproducing it. This kind of testimony is irreplaceable because it takes us inside the events in a way that is rivaled only by semi-fictional imaginative reconstructions. But, unlike the latter, testimony can bring us up against the radically unfamiliar that we could not have imagined without it. (From her experience of reading with students a variety of texts that convey testimony, Shoshana Felman writes that "the texts that testify do not simply *report facts* but, in different ways, encounter — and make us encounter — *strangeness*."[63]) We shall return to this point shortly.

63. S. Felman, "Education and Crisis, or the Vicissitudes of Teaching," in S. Felman and D. Laub, *Testimony: Crises of Witnessing in Literature, Psychoanalysis, and History* (New York: Routledge, 1992) 7.

As a modern parallel to the practice of the Greco-Roman historians Samuel Byrskog adduces the relatively recent discipline of oral history.[64] In oral history the oral testimony of participants is recorded and valued for its own sake, not merely as the raw material for a historian's large-scale reconstruction and not in a way that sets aside the particular perspectives of the witnesses. Byrskog says that a

> fundamental tenet of the oral history approach is the notion that the participants of history are to be permitted to shape our understanding of the past. The "objects" of history become "subjects"; they create history.[65]

This does not mean that the oral historian does nothing but reproduce oral testimonies. The wider historical perspective of the historian should be brought into dialogue with the particularity of the witnesses' stories. The stories need evaluation (for example, by cross-checking with other evidence) and interpretation and can be brought together fruitfully in a variety of ways. But the work of the oral historian is fundamentally directed to enabling the witnesses themselves to speak and the social meaning they found in their experiences to become part of history.[66]

Participant eyewitness testimony has a special role when it comes to events that transcend the common experience of historians and their readers. The more exceptional the event, the more historical imagination alone is liable to lead us seriously astray. Without the participant witness that confronts us with the sheer otherness of the event, we will reduce it to the measure of our own experience. In such cases, insider testimony may puzzle us or provoke disbelief, but, for the sake of maintaining the quest for the truth of history, we must allow the testimony to resist the limiting pressure of our own experiences and expectations.

As the paradigmatic case in modern history of an exceptional event[67] of this kind, the Holocaust comes necessarily to mind. Ricoeur speaks of an event "at the limits" of experience and representation,[68] a phrase he borrows from Saul Friedlander.[69] (Previously Ricoeur used the term "uniquely

---

64. Byrskog, *Story as History,* chapter 1.

65. Byrskog, *Story,* 153; cf. 27 (quotation from Paul Thompson).

66. Byrskog, *Story,* 30.

67. On the idea of "exceptionality" in history, see J. Milbank, *Being Reconciled: Ontology and Pardon* (New York: Routledge, 2003) 84-86.

68. Ricoeur, *Memory,* 175, 254, 255, 258, 498.

69. S. Friedlander, "Introduction," in idem, ed., *Probing the Limits of Representation: Nazism and the "Final Solution"* (Cambridge: Harvard University Press, 1992) 8.

unique events."[70]) Holocaust testimonies, he says, "pose a problem of reception":

> This has to do with such literally extraordinary limit experiences — which make for a difficult pathway in encountering the ordinary, limited capacities for reception of auditors educated on the basis of a shared comprehension. The comprehension is built on the basis of a sense of human resemblance at the level of situations, feelings, thoughts, and actions. But the experience to be transmitted is that of an inhumanity with no common measure with the experience of the average person. It is in this sense that it is a question of limit experiences.[71]

Holocaust testimonies are not easily appropriated by the historian, since they are prima facie scarcely credible and since they defy the usual categories of historical explanation. (Charlotte Delbo said of new arrivals in Auschwitz what is also true of any who read Holocaust testimonies: "They expect the worst — they do not expect the unthinkable."[72]) This is why the testimonies of survivors of the Holocaust are in the highest degree necessary to any attempt to understand what happened. The Holocaust is an event whose reality we could scarcely begin to imagine if we had not the testimonies of survivors.

In the Gospels, if we believe them, we also have to do with an event "at the limits." The comparison is hazardous. In almost everything except the sheer historical exceptionality of the event, the Holocaust and the history of Jesus have nothing in common. Our argument is in no way intended to detract from the particular uniqueness of the Holocaust. On the contrary, we have to appreciate this uniqueness if the case of the Holocaust is to teach us anything about the role of testimony in other cases of exceptionality in history. With the uniqueness of the Holocaust clearly in mind, therefore, we turn to consider some examples of the testimony of its survivors.

Holocaust Testimonies

The following testimony is from one of the survivors of Auschwitz, not from one of the written accounts by survivors, but from one of the many hundreds

---

70. P. Ricoeur, *Time and Narrative,* vol. 3 (tr. K. Blamey and D. Pellauer; Chicago: University of Chicago Press, 1988) 188.

71. Ricoeur, *Memory,* 175.

72. Quoted in L. L. Langer, *The Age of Atrocity: Death in Modern Literature* (Boston: Beacon, 1978) 202.

of videotaped interviews with survivors. (These are the surely most remarkable case of oral history research.) This testimony is an unrehearsed oral remembering, a particular testimony we might easily not have had. It takes place in a situation typical for Holocaust victims: travel in a crowded cattle-car. In this case, the travel is not *to* Auschwitz, where the witness, Edith P., had already spent some time, but from Auschwitz to a labor site:

> One morning, I think it was morning or early afternoon, we arrived. The train stopped for an hour; why, we don't know. And a friend of mine said, "Why don't you stand up?" There was just a little window, with bars. And I said, "I can't. I don't have enough energy to climb up." And she said, "I'm going to sit down and you're going to stand on my shoulders." And I did; and I looked out. And . . . I . . . saw . . . Paradise! The sun was bright and vivid. There was cleanliness all over. It was a station somewhere in Germany. There were three or four people there. One woman had a child, nicely dressed up; the child was crying. People were people, not animals. And I thought: "Paradise must look like this!" I forgot already how normal people look like, how they act, how they speak, how they dress. I saw the sun in Auschwitz, I saw the sun come up, because we had to get up at four in the morning. But it was never beautiful to me. I never saw it shine. It was just the beginning of a horrible day. And in the evening, the end — of what? But here there was *life,* and I had such yearning, I still feel it in my bones. I had such yearning, to live, to run, to just run away and never come back — to run to the end where there is no way back. And I told the girls, I said, "Girls, you have no idea how beautiful the sun is, and I saw a baby crying, and a woman was kissing that baby — is there such a thing as love?"[73]

The most accomplished Holocaust novel could not equal the effectiveness of that story in conveying the horrifying otherness of the world of Auschwitz, in which people were not people but animals, in which existence was not life but already death, in which the beauty of creation could not be experienced as such, in which even memory of what the normal world, our world, is like, had died, the possibility of freedom forgotten and the possibility of love annihilated. The witness's glimpse of our world, which is surreal to her, to her an epiphany of another world she could no longer have imagined, discloses to us her world, the Nazis' kingdom of night, in a way that no novel-

73. Quoted in L. L. Langer, *Holocaust Testimonies: The Ruins of Memory* (New Haven: Yale University Press, 1991) 54-55, from the Fortunoff Video Archive for Holocaust Testimonies, Yale University.

ist could surpass and no regular historian even approach. This is truth that only testimony can give us.

The testimony draws on what Charlotte Delbo, herself a survivor of Auschwitz, calls "deep memory." Edith P. is able, very painfully no doubt, to live in her memory, to feel still the surge of unsought yearning for escape that came to her, quite hopelessly. In Delbo's words, she sees herself "again, *me*, yes *me*, just as I know I was."[74] At the same time, however unconsciously, the words come from what Delbo calls "intellectual memory, reflective memory."[75] They must, because she is not just living her memory for herself, but communicating it. She is enabling us to imagine that extraordinary reality of her, herself, as she was, and the world that she knew, but that we cannot know. She chooses words that belong to our world and make the connection that she is able to make because she too now lives in our world as well as in her memory. Many of the Holocaust survivors testifying in videotaped interviews struggle with this. The deep memory always threatens to destroy communication: its reality is so *other* that they know words betray it. But Edith P.'s story is astonishingly successful: the deep memory reaches us and we are stunned by its otherness.

The story's method is apophatic. It is powerful because it invites us to see the world of Auschwitz as a complete negation of what we take to be unremarkable and ordinary in our world. But there is nothing at all contrived about this: it is the very essence of this narrative moment. Again, we must surely recognize — and it is no detriment at all to Edith P.'s testimony — that she has cast it, whether or not with conscious deliberation, in a very effective narrative form. Notice how the detail of the woman *kissing* the baby is withheld until the last sentence, enhancing the effect of this saying as a conclusion that both encapsulates the meaning of the whole incident and also brings it to full expression with the addition of an element of the normal world — love — that goes beyond what the story up till then has portrayed. I know nothing of Edith P. except for this story and other parts of her testimony quoted by Lawrence Langer, and so I do not know whether she is one of those videotaped survivors who recounted memories they had never or rarely recounted to anyone before or even had never brought to conscious expression before. But I doubt it. This is surely a story honed in the memory or the telling. In this respect it is somewhat like the oft-told tales of an oral culture, but, on the other hand, it has lost none of its personal voice or its evident immediacy in the memory of the teller.

74. For a particularly clear example of deep memory, see Langer, *Holocaust Testimonies*, 17-18.

75. Quoted in Langer, *Holocaust Testimonies*, 6-7.

What is important to notice is that its narrative skill in no way detracts from its authenticity as testimony. There are no typically literary embellishments, such as we do find in written memoirs by survivors and which can, unless skillfully employed, seem to get in the way of our contact with the truth of the testimony. In Edith P.'s story there are no standard narrative motifs, no literary clichés. The language is direct and straightforward. The scene is vivid, but there is no redundant description, only what needs to be said. We are aware that the speaker is reflecting on her memory ("I forgot already how normal people look like . . ." is a retrospective explanation for the benefit of hearers), but what she remembers, in its visual and emotional clarity, we hear as an authentic moment of epiphany, interpreted for us to some degree, but not contaminated by its manner of telling.

Lawrence Langer, from whose study of the oral testimonies of Holocaust survivors I have taken Edith P.'s testimony, finds distinctive value in the oral testimonies by comparison with literary memoirs by Holocaust survivors. His main point is that in the oral testimonies we witness the irreconcilable collision between the other world of the extermination camps and the normal world in which survivors now live along with the rest of us. The literary accounts, by their strategies of communication, their use of familiar literary genres and devices, their intertextual relationships with other literary works, obscure the uniqueness of Auschwitz, reducing its otherness by connecting it with the normal world of experience and most literature.[76] No doubt Langer is right in some cases. But not, I think, in all, and I would like to contest one of his examples.

It is the most famous Holocaust memoir of all, Elie Wiesel's first book, *Night*.[77] We should remember both that after this book Wiesel wrote many successful novels that explore the reality of the Holocaust in fictional ways, but also that *Night* is not a novel but a memoir in which, Wiesel himself insists, he told the historical truth. Not surprisingly, however, its narrative is told with novelistic features and literary strategies that the oral testimonies generally lack.[78] The

76. See, e.g., Langer, *Holocaust Testimonies*, 18-19, 42-46.

77. First published in Yiddish as *Un Di Velt Hot Geshvign* (And the world has remained silent) (Buenos Aires: Y el Mundo Callaba, Central Farbond Fun Poylishe Yidn in Argentina, 1956) and then in French as *La Nuit* (Paris: Minuit, 1958).

78. Cf. B. Foley, "Fact, Fiction, Fascism: Testimony and Mimesis in Holocaust Narratives," *Comparative Literature* 34 (1982) 341: "Perhaps it is Wiesel's *Night* that most effectively combines the immediacy of autobiographical statement with the patterning and ethical distance of fiction, for Wiesel grafts onto his narrative not one but a series of novelistic devices. . . . [W]ithout relinquishing his foundation in factuality, Wiesel invests his memoir with some of the symbolic dimensions of a full-fledged fiction."

point that Langer picks up is an allusion to words of Ivan Karamazov in Dostoyevsky's *The Brothers Karamazov.* "A part of Auschwitz's uniqueness," he complains, "is thus inadvertently modified by a literary precedent."[79] I want to take a different example of allusion to the same "literary precedent": Ivan Karamazov.

The passage concerns perhaps the most unbelievably inhuman feature of the destruction of Jews in Auschwitz: the cremation of small children alive. I quote first another report of this before turning to Wiesel's account:

> The other gas chambers were full of the adults and therefore the children were not gassed, but just burned alive. There were several thousand of them. When one of the SS sort of had pity upon the children, he would take a child and beat the head against a stone before putting it on the pile of fire and wood, so that the child lost consciousness. However, the regular way they did it was by just throwing the children onto the pile. They would put a sheet of wood there, then sprinkle the whole thing with petrol, then wood again, and petrol and wood, and petrol — then they placed the children there. Then the whole thing was lighted.[80]

Wiesel's reference to this way of killing children[81] is in one of the most famous passages of *Night.* The young Wiesel and his father arrive in Auschwitz:

> Not far from us, flames were leaping up from a ditch, gigantic flames. They were burning something. A lorry drew up at the pit and delivered its load — little children. Babies! Yes, I saw it — saw it with my own eyes ... those children in the flames. (Is it not surprising that I could not sleep after that? Sleep had fled from my eyes.) ...
>
> I pinched my face. Was I still alive? Was I awake? I could not believe it. How could it be possible for them to burn people, children, and for the world to keep silent? It was a nightmare. ...
>
> My father's voice drew me from my thoughts:

79. Langer, *Holocaust Testimonies,* 43.

80. I have taken this account from A. R. Eckardt, "The Recantation of the Covenant?" in A. H. Rosenfeld and I. Greenberg, eds., *Confronting the Holocaust: The Impact of Elie Wiesel* (Bloomington: Indiana University Press, 1978) 163. Eckardt says that "it is adapted, with some changes, from a representation in an unpublished paper by Irving Greenberg" (234 n. 7).

81. When I first read *Night,* I assumed Wiesel was describing the cremating of corpses, not of living children, but it is clear from his autobiography that he intended the latter: E. Wiesel, *All Rivers Run to the Sea: Memoirs,* vol. 1, *1928-1969* (New York: HarperCollins, 1996) 77-78.

"It's a shame . . . a shame that you couldn't have gone with your mother. . . . I saw several boys of your age going with their mothers. . . ."

His voice was terribly sad. I realized that he did not want to see what they were going to do with me. He did not want to see the burning of his only son.

My forehead was bathed in cold sweat. But I told him that I did not believe that they could burn people in our age, that humanity would never tolerate it. . . .

"Humanity? Humanity is not concerned with us. Today anything is allowed. Anything is possible, even these crematories. . . ."[82]

The father's words here echo the catchphrase of Ivan Karamazov in Dostoyevsky's novel: "everything is permitted."[83] Ivan reasoned that, once a religious basis for respecting human dignity is lost, "everything would be permitted,"[84] and Albert Camus, in the book he was writing when Wiesel knew him in Paris after the War, commented that, "With this 'all is permitted' the history of contemporary nihilism really begins."[85] Wiesel is not here simply alluding to a literary precedent. He is identifying Auschwitz as the nihilistic world beyond morality that Dostoyevsky's Ivan Karamazov hypothesized.[86] This is certainly a way of evoking the significance of the burning of children to death, but not one that necessarily compromises the uniqueness of the Holocaust or assimilates it to normality. On the other hand, Wiesel's account is very different from the chilling account of the burning of the children that I cited before his. That account leaves the rather detailed facts to speak for themselves, whereas Wiesel's comparatively minimal account of the facts goes on to highlight their significance. (Did his father, as a matter of historical fact, take words out of the mouth of Ivan Karamazov? I imagine not.) Wiesel's is a different kind of testimony, one which incorporates interpretative reflection in a particularly literary way — through intertextual al-

82. E. Wiesel, *Night; Dawn; The Accident: Three Tales* (London: Robson, 1974) 41-42. (The translation is by S. Rodway.)

83. I discussed this allusion in R. Bauckham, *The Theology of Jürgen Moltmann* (Edinburgh: Clark, 1995) 78-79.

84. F. Dostoyevsky, *The Brothers Karamazov* (tr. D. Magarshack; Harmondsworth: Penguin, 1982) 77.

85. A. Camus, *The Rebel* (tr. A. Bower; Harmondsworth: Penguin, 1971) 52.

86. Note also that Ivan Karamazov's evidence against the possibility of theodicy consists of stories of cruelty inflicted on children by their parents. The climax of these tales tells how a landowner had an eight-year-old serf boy hunted like an animal, with huntsmen, whips, and hounds, who tore the boy in pieces before the eyes of his mother: Dostoyevsky, *The Brothers Karamazov*, 284.

lusion — but not one that obscures the searing memory.[87] This too is "deep memory" that he relives in remembering it but that also drives him to an endless attempt to understand what cannot be understood. Neither in Edith P.'s nor in Elie Wiesel's testimony do we have "deep memory" unmediated, because in that case there would be no communication. Each has found, over many years, different narrative ways of conveying without distorting the truth they witnessed.

Holocaust Testimony and Gospel Testimony

The testimony of Holocaust survivors is the modern context in which we most readily recognize that authentic testimony from participants is completely indispensable to acquiring real understanding of historical events, at least events of such exceptionality. Apart from this the cases of the Holocaust and the history of Jesus are vastly different. But their exceptionality and the role of testimony in conveying this, insofar as it can be conveyed, are common to both. In what follows I draw out some of the implications of this correspondence in exceptionality, with a view to highlighting some aspects of the Gospel testimonies to Jesus.

(1) Both the Holocaust and the history of Jesus, understood in the way the Gospels understand it, require Ricoeur's category of "uniquely unique events," even though it must be stressed again that what qualifies each for such a description is utterly different. Yet in each case analogy fails us much more seriously than it does in respect to the unique particularity of every historical event, and this failure of analogy is closely connected with the way in which each of these two events has the character of disclosure, though again in very different ways. The Holocaust discloses what we could not otherwise know about the nature of evil and atrocity and the human situation in the modern world, but only to those who attend to the testimony of the witnesses.[88] ("Our stories . . . are they not themselves stories of a new Bible?" asks

---

87. Cf. Wiesel, *Night*, 43: "Never shall I forget the little faces of the children, whose bodies I saw turned into wreaths of smoke beneath a silent blue sky." Returning to these events in his autobiography, he writes: "I who rarely weep am in tears. I see the flames again, and the children, and yet again I tell myself that it is not enough to weep. . . . I didn't understand, though I wanted to. Ask any survivor and you will hear the same thing: above all, we tried to understand. Why all these deaths? . . . Perhaps there was nothing to understand" (Wiesel, *All Rivers*, 78-79).

88. The idea of the Holocaust as revelation is associated especially with the Jewish theologian Emil Fackenheim, but what I suggest here is quite different from Fackenheim's famous idea of a 614th commandment given to Israel.

Primo Levi.[89]) The history of Jesus discloses God's definitive action for human salvation, but only to those who attend to the testimony of the witnesses.

When Ricoeur first discussed "uniquely unique events," he compared and contrasted positive and negative kinds. In the paradigmatic case of Auschwitz ("The victims of Auschwitz are, par excellence, the representatives in our memory of all history's victims"[90]) we are dealing with an event that evokes horror. Horror is the response that recognizes such an event, individuates it in our consciousness of history not just in terms of the unique particularity of all events, but in a way that defies the historian's attempt to make particular events understandable by tracing their interconnections with other events:

> [H]orror isolates events by making them incomparable, incomparably unique, uniquely unique. If I persist in associating horror with admiration [taken to be the opposite of horror], it is because horror inverts the feeling with which we go forth to be all that seems to us to be generative, creative. Horror is inverted veneration. It is in this sense that the Holocaust has been considered a negative revelation, an Anti-Sinai.[91]

What is it then that isolates the history of Jesus as exceptional in its positive disclosure of God? In place of "admiration" and "veneration," the terms Ricoeur offers here, we should perhaps speak of wonder and thanksgiving in the presence of incomparable "wonder-fulness." Just as it is horror (though the term seems too weak) that would be diminished by leveling the Holocaust down to the non-exceptional horrors of history, as, without the testimonies, we might well do, so it is wonder that would be lost were we deprived of the Gospel testimonies that evoke the theophanic character of the history of Jesus. (We cannot pursue here the way in which the Gospels relate the horror of the cross to this "wonder-ful" exceptionality of the history of Jesus.) Is it not this wonder that we lose when we turn from the Gospel testimonies themselves to the inevitably reductive reconstructions of some kind of "real" historical Jesus?

(2) The qualitative uniqueness of each of these two events creates a problem of communication, as we have already seen in the case of the Holocaust.[92] All too easily the attempt to connect what happened with the experi-

89. Quoted in A. H. Rosenfeld, "The Problematics of Holocaust Literature," in Rosenfeld and Greenberg, eds., *Confronting the Holocaust*, 25.

90. Ricoeur, *Time*, 187.

91. Ricoeur, *Time*, 188.

92. See also M. D. Lagerway, *Reading Auschwitz* (Walnut Creek: AltaMira, 1998) 141-47.

ences and understanding of our ordinary world makes for easy intelligibility at the cost of the uniqueness of the event and therefore also of its power to disclose. When the quest of the historical Jesus discounts what the witnesses claim in the interests of what is readily credible by the standards of historical analogy, that is, ordinary experience, it reduces revelation to the triviality of what we knew or could know anyway.

(3) Despite the difficulty of communication, participant witnesses in both events have felt the imperative to communicate, to bear witness.[93] Not all Holocaust survivors felt impelled to testify, but many did, especially those who wrote memoirs. Indeed, many who died in the Holocaust left behind their testimonies. Wiesel, paradoxically in view of his own statement that "By its uniqueness the Holocaust defies literature,"[94] also thought the uniqueness of the Holocaust actually created a new literature:

> If the Greeks invented tragedy, the Romans the epistle, and the Renaissance the sonnet, our generation [i.e., Jews who witnessed the Holocaust] invented a new literature, that of testimony. We have all been witnesses and we all feel we have to bear testimony for the future. And that became an obsession, the single most powerful obsession that permeated all the lives, all the dreams, all the work of those people. One minute before they died they thought that was what they had to do.[95]

The sense (not a properly generic one) in which the witnesses of the Holocaust created a new literature of testimony, is much the same sense as that in which the witnesses of the history of Jesus created the Gospels. Those witnesses understood the imperative to witness as a command of the risen Christ, but the parallel is sufficient to be suggestive. In both cases, the uniqueness required precisely witness as the only means by which the events could be adequately known.

(4) In both cases, the exceptionality of the event means that only the testimony of participant witnesses can give us anything approaching access to the truth of the event. In the case of the Holocaust, again Wiesel puts it famously: "the truth of Auschwitz is hidden in its ashes. Only those who lived it in their

---

93. Cf. T. Des Pres, *The Survivors: An Anatomy of Life in the Death Camps* (Oxford: Oxford University Press, 1976) 29-50. He writes of the way witness could be a motive for survival.

94. Quoted in Robert McAfee Brown, *Elie Wiesel: Messenger to All Humanity* (Notre Dame: University of Notre Dame Press, 1983) 24.

95. E. Wiesel, "The Holocaust as Literary Inspiration," in E. Wiesel, L. S. Dawidowicz, D. Rabinowitz, and R. M. Brown, *Dimensions of the Holocaust: Lectures at Northwestern University* (Evanston: Northwestern University, 1977) 9.

flesh and in their minds can possibly transform it into knowledge."[96] But the point is made over and again by survivors.[97] Taken as a privileged claim to unsharable knowledge that no one may question, this assertion rouses the professional objection of a sympathetic historian, Inga Clendinnen, who protests that, to the historian, "no part of the human record can be declared off-limits. . . . [T]he doing of history, our ongoing conversation with the dead, rests on the critical evaluation of all the voices coming from the past."[98] She makes her point by engaging in a critical assessment of the testimony of Filip Müller, whose account of his service as a *Sonderkommando* in Auschwitz is precious evidence of much that would not otherwise be known.[99] The assessment is reasonable. There are tests of coherence and consistency with other testimony that the historian may rightly apply.[100] But in Clendinnen's own admission that "Extraordinary events happened in Auschwitz, as in every camp"[101] there is recognition that assessment has to respect the exceptionality that inheres in the events to which testimony is given.

In this and other cases, including the Gospels, testimony asks to be trusted. It does not consist in the presentation of evidence and argument for what only the witness, the involved insider, can tell us. In all cases, including even the law courts, testimony can be checked and assessed in appropriate ways but nevertheless has to be trusted. In the uniquely unique events we are considering, this is all the more true. To insist, with some Gospel critics, that the historicity of each and every Gospel pericope must be established, one by one, with arguments for each, is not to recognize testimony for what it necessarily is. It is to suppose that we can extract individual facts from testimony and build our own reconstruction of events that is no longer dependent on the witness. It is to refuse that privileged access to truth that precisely participant testimony can give us. Ancient historiography rightly valued such testimony as essential to good history, and the Holocaust shows us how indispensable it can be when the events we confront are "at the limits."

96. Quoted in I. Clendinnen, *Reading the Holocaust* (Cambridge: Cambridge University Press, 1999) 20.

97. See, for example, the videotaped testimony of Chaim E. in Langer, *Holocaust Testimonies,* 62-63.

98. Clendinnen, *Reading the Holocaust,* 21.

99. Clendinnen, *Reading the Holocaust,* 21-24.

100. R. Kearney, *On Stories* (New York: Routledge, 2002) 68-69, suggests "the necessary conditions for a narrative counting as historically true — for example consistency of memories, coherence of testimonies, credibility of witnesses, confirmation of referential evidence, public sharing of truth-claims, appropriateness of narrative genres, effectiveness of account, moral persuasiveness of justice claims, etc."

101. Clendinnen, *Reading the Holocaust,* 24.

Testimonial Form

Our two examples of Holocaust testimony — Edith P.'s and Elie Wiesel's — may help us to appreciate something about the Gospels that has formed the central argument of this book. Form criticism encouraged us to think of the various pericopes in the Synoptic Gospels as having been formed through a process of community formation, adapted to the *Sitz im Leben*. More recently literary criticism has made us think more of the literary artifice with which the Evangelist has molded the material into narrative shape. In this book I have argued, without denying the role of the Evangelists in shaping their sources, that in many Gospel pericopes we are much closer to the form the eyewitnesses themselves gave to their stories than is usually credited in modern Gospels scholarship.

We noticed the narrative skill of Edith P.'s oral testimony and that it does not owe this to literary models, standard narrative motifs, or literary embellishments. The language is direct and straightforward. The scene is vivid, but there is no redundant description. In this it resembles many a pericope in the Synoptic Gospels. In the Gospel stories, as in Edith P.'s story, we find the vividness of sight concisely evoked (the four men making a hole in the roof to get their paralyzed friend into Jesus' presence [Mark 2:3-4]) or the aural impact of words spoken ("people like trees, walking," says the blind man healed [Mark 8:24]). True, we do not often hear the deep memory of the witness's feeling returning as the story is told, but there are some cases where this may be happening (e.g., Mark 9:6; 14:72; 16:8; Luke 24:32). We have to reckon with the difference that the Gospel stories, though close, in my judgment, to the way the eyewitnesses told them, are nevertheless in the Synoptic Gospels actually retold by others, for whom the fact of eyewitness testimony to what happened usually mattered more than the emotional experience of the witness (an obvious exception, however, is the story of Peter's denials of Jesus). We are also dealing with a style of narration (such as we find also, for example, in Genesis) in which subjective states are less often made explicit, more often suggested by the outward occurrences.

I supposed that Edith P.'s testimony must have been honed in remembering or telling. We can be more sure of this in the case of Gospel stories, which were surely told from the earliest days of the Christian movement and not for the first time several decades later. The witnesses themselves, like anyone who tells a story of what they have witnessed, had to make a story out of what they remembered, choosing what to include, shaping the narrative, and they would be likely to tell the story again and again in the form they themselves had given it. Instinctively such a teller of a story responds to audience

reaction, shapes the story so as to appeal and to communicate, and a more effective narrative form may develop.[102] But Edith P.'s example shows us that
the skilful narration of a story is entirely consistent with its immediacy to the
memory of the witness.

The passage from Elie Wiesel on which I commented is more literary,
not just in its forms of expression, but more importantly in the intertextual
allusion to Dostoyevsky, which gives the story an explicit direction toward interpretation. The interpretation is not an author's comment external to the
story but given within the story by the formulation of Wiesel's father's words.
For comparison with the Synoptic Gospels we might turn to Mark's story of
the stilling of the storm (Mark 4:35-41). This is more than direct memory in
that Jesus' pacification of the storm is couched in terms that allude to passages in the Hebrew Bible about God's subjugation of the waters of chaos (Jesus "rebuked" the wind and said to the sea "Peace! Be still!"). These allusions
(Pss 89:9-10; 104:7; 107:25-29; Job 26:11-12) place the story in a wider symbolic
field of resonance, identifying Jesus' command of the destructive power of
nature as that of God the Creator, and it is this associative significance of
what Jesus does that prompts the disciples' question at the end of the
pericope: "Who then is this that even the wind and the sea obey him?" The
question parallels the interpretative function of Wiesel's father's final remarks
in the passage we quoted. Moreover, as in Wiesel's story, the interpretation is
not artificially imposed on the Markan miracle: for Mark's contemporaries
the danger of a storm at sea really was an instantiation of the destructive
forces of nature symbolized by the waters of chaos in Jewish cosmology. Concrete experience and mythic resonance here converge naturally. So the interpretation does not come in between us and the realistic character of the story,
as interpretation can. The authenticity of the eyewitness memory, if that is
what it is, is not compromised or obscured by literary contrivance. Deep
memory may still be at work in the disciples' fear of death while Jesus sleeps
and in their even greater fear of the one who commands the storm.

The distinction between plain narratives and narratives that embody
interpretation through literary devices such as intertextual allusions may
bring to light an interesting difference between the narratives of the crucifixion and those of the resurrection. It is well recognized that the narratives of
the passion and especially the crucifixion itself constantly quote or allude to
the Old Testament, especially to the words of righteous sufferers in the

102. Of Holocaust testimonies, H. Greenspan, *On Listening to Holocaust Survivors*
(Westport, 1998) 31, writes: "Certain forms of recounting tend to evolve that are, simultaneously, more or less tellable by survivors and more or less hearable by others."

Psalms. There is an intertextual network that serves to interpret the passion of Jesus by setting it within the experience and the expectation of Israel. But when we read on to the accounts of the empty tomb and the resurrection appearances there are hardly any such allusions. The stories show little sign of following literary precedents, and standard narrative motifs, the building blocks of many an ancient story, are rare. For all the ingenuity of scholars these stories remain strangely *sui generis* and lacking theological interpretation. None of the standard Jewish formulas or images of resurrection occur. We seem to be shown the extraordinary *novum*, the otherness of resurrection, through the eyes of those whose ordinary reality it invaded. The perplexity, the doubt, the fear, the joy, the recognition are those of deep memory, mediated, to be sure, by literary means, but not entirely hidden behind the text.

Testimony as Historical and Theological Category

The burden of this book is that the category of testimony is the one that does most justice to the Gospels both as history and as theology. As a form of historiography testimony offers a unique access to historical reality that cannot be had without an element of trust in the credibility of the witness and what he or she has to report. Testimony is irreducible; we cannot, at least in some of its most distinctive and valuable claims, go behind it and make our own autonomous verification of them; we cannot establish the truth of testimony for ourselves as though we stood where the witnesses uniquely stood. Eyewitness testimony offers us insider knowledge from involved participants. It also offers us engaged interpretation, for in testimony fact and meaning coinhere, and witnesses who give testimony do so with the conviction of significance that requires to be told. Witnesses of truly significant events speak out of their own ongoing attempts to understand. Paul Ricoeur, in an early essay on the hermeneutics of testimony, speaks of the two inseparable aspects of testimony: on the one hand, its quasi-empirical aspect, the testimony of the senses, the report of the eyewitness as to facts, and, on the other hand, the interiority of testimony, the engagement of the witness with what he or she attests.[103] The faithful witness, in this sense, is not merely accurate but faithful to the meaning and demands of what is attested. And in the most truly significant cases this is where bearing witness becomes a costly commitment of life, and the Greek

---

103. P. Ricoeur, "The Hermeneutics of Testimony," in Ricoeur, *Essays on Biblical Interpretation*, 123-30. In this essay Ricoeur approaches the theological significance of testimony, writing explicitly about "testimony of the absolute."

word *martus,* from meaning simply "witness," takes in Christian Greek usage the sense that its English derivative, "martyr," has in English.[104]

Reading the Gospels as eyewitness testimony differs therefore from attempts at historical reconstruction behind the texts. It takes the Gospels seriously as they are; it acknowledges the uniqueness of what we can know only in this testimonial form. It honors the form of historiography they are. From a historiographic perspective, radical suspicion of testimony is a kind of epistemological suicide. It is no more practicable in history than it is in ordinary life. Gospels scholarship must free itself from the grip of the skeptical paradigm that presumes the Gospels to be unreliable unless, in every particular case of story or saying, the historian succeeds in providing independent verification. For such a suspicious approach the Gospels are not believable until and unless the historian can verify each claim that they make to recount history. But this approach is seriously faulty precisely as a historical method. It can only result in a misleadingly minimal collection of uninteresting facts about a historical figure stripped of any real significance. Neither in this nor in countless other cases of historical testimony can the historian verify everything. Testimony asks to be trusted. This does not mean that historians must trust testimony uncritically, but rather that testimony is to be assessed *as testimony.* The question is whether it is trustworthy, and this is open to tests of internal consistency and coherence, and consistency and coherence with whatever other relevant historical evidence we have and whatever else we know about the historical context. This is one context in which it is appropriate to hear what testimony can tell us "in spite of itself."

Historical assessment of this testimony must also take seriously the testimony's claim to the radical exceptionality of the event. The claim must not be disqualified as though it were, so to speak, against the rules of the historiographic game. We must beware of a historical methodology that prejudices inquiry against exceptionality in history and is biased toward the leveling down of the extraordinary to the ordinary. Exceptional events in history are, almost by definition, exceptional in very different ways. We must be careful not to reduce the exceptionality of each even by using a category of exceptional events or, in Ricoeur's phrase, "uniquely unique" events. Such events are a category only in a negative sense: in that they all resist reduction to "business as usual" in history and, by virtue of their difference from common human experience, pose particular issues about the continuity of the historical process, the credibility of testimony, and the possibility of gaining real understanding of such events. It is in this sense that the Holocaust, with no det-

104. Ricoeur, "The Hermeneutics of Testimony," 129.

riment to its own "unique uniqueness," can enlighten us about other events that testimony seems to isolate as exceptional.

The testimony of involved participants is especially valuable in the case of exceptional events. It is the only way in which we can expect to approach the inner reality of such events. There is risk involved in trusting testimony that, by the standards of the average person's experience in the culture to which we belong, may seem scarcely credible. But the risk is required by the quest for truth — both historical and theological. The degree of commitment to their testimony such witnesses usually have should not in itself arouse our suspicions: in more ordinary cases we usually take such commitment as a reason for taking especially seriously what a witness has to say. It is by no means irrational to take the risk of crediting the testimony of involved and committed participants to the extraordinary and the exceptional in history.

Of at least some "uniquely unique" events, including the Holocaust, one could understand the exceptionality as a *disclosure* of what can be known only to firsthand witnesses and by means of their testimony. For readers of the Gospels this aspect of disclosure is what makes testimony not only the appropriate category for the kind of history the Gospels are but also the theologically appropriate category for understanding the Gospels. I do not mean that there is any straightforward or necessary step from the mere historian's consideration of the Gospels to the believer's appropriation of their message.[105] Nonetheless the historical and the theological are intimately connected in these testimonies. In a believing response to the Gospels they must come together and, from the perspective of the Gospels' own message, it is entirely appropriate that they do. For in the case of the history of Jesus, as these witnesses perceived it, the "unique uniqueness" of the events is properly theological. That is, it demands reference to God. There is no adequate way of telling the story without reference to God, for the uniqueness of what God does in this history is what makes it the unique and particular history it is. The testimony is to a unique disclosure in the sense of a revelation of God. This uniqueness of the events gives itself to be understood and interpreted by witnesses. Unlike the mere historian, the witness can testify to transcendental meaning and speak of God, not merely as a factor in Jesus' belief or intention or even experience, but as the one to whom the witness cannot but give testimony.

In the immediate testimony of the witness, that which lives on in deep memory, the witness "sees" what is disclosed in what happens, the empirical

---

105. Note also that the Gospels incorporate, even if only to refute them, the perspectives on Jesus adopted by his contemporaries who did not believe in him. (I owe this point to Colin Brown.) Jesus is represented as a highly controversial figure.

event requiring to be seen as the revelation of God, fact and meaning coinhering. But memory is also remembered and understanding grows. In what is no doubt the most reflective Gospel testimony we have, that of John, the immediacy of memory is by no means lost. Rather, the ongoing process of remembering interpretation ponders and works to yield its fullest meaning. Reflective witness is reflective *remembering*, as this Gospel makes quite explicit (e.g., 2:22; 12:16; 14:26). Therefore, as Ricoeur also points out, it cannot without losing its true identity cease to be *narrating*.[106] We cannot, as he puts it, have the "prophetic moment" without the "historical moment."[107] Testimony, we might say, authorizes theology only as theologically understood history.

Francis Watson, who also takes up Ricoeur's idea of a "uniquely unique" event,[108] speaks of the event of God's revelation in Jesus as an event that includes its own reception. Revelation as God's communicative action does not reach its goal until it evokes recognition and understanding. Therefore, according to Watson, the "believing reception of the event of Jesus as the Christ belongs to the story that is told, and the telling of the story therefore reflects both the event and its reception; for event itself includes its own reception."[109] This is yet another angle on the appropriateness of testimony as the historical and theological category for appreciating the Gospels. On the one side, we may say that revelation is the event that includes testimony as its own reception; and on the other side, we may say that testimony is the kind of telling that the disclosure of God in historical signs requires.

In summary, if the interests of Christian faith and theology in the Jesus who really lived are to recognize the disclosure of God in this history of Jesus, then testimony is the theologically appropriate, indeed the theologically necessary way of access to the history of Jesus, just as testimony is also the historically appropriate, indeed the historically necessary way of access to this "uniquely unique" historical event. It is in the Jesus of testimony that history and theology meet.

106. Ricoeur, "The Hermeneutics of Testimony," 133-34: "There is therefore no witness of the absolute who is not a witness of historic signs, no confessor of absolute meaning who is not a narrator of the acts of deliverance."

107. Ricoeur, "The Hermeneutics of Testimony," 133. Cf. also: "A theology of testimony which is not just another name for the theology of the confession of faith is only possible if a certain narrative kernel is preserved in strict union with the confession of faith" (133).

108. F. Watson, *Text and Truth: Redefining Biblical Theology* (Grand Rapids: Eerdmans, 1997) 61. Note also the contention of J. D. G. Dunn, *Jesus Remembered* (Grand Rapids: Eerdmans, 2003) 132-33, that the Gospel traditions embody the faith of the disciples even before Easter.

109. Watson, *Text and Truth*, 165.

Index of Ancient Persons

Aaron, 104, 445, 446, 447
Abraham, 77, 96
Adaiah, 88
Addan, 109
Adelphius, 153
Aelian, 124
Aelius Theon. *See* Theon
Agabus, 298
Agrippa, 120
Ajax, 174
Alexander,
    Jannaeus, 42, 149, 446, 452
    of Abonoteichus, 132-37, 141, 218
    son of Simon of Cyrene, 52, 65
Alphaeus, 42, 56, 59, 65, 79, 87, 97, 108,
    110, 111, 113
Amelius Gentilianus, 138, 139, 140, 141,
    142, 143, 144, 151-54, 401
Ammaeus, 370
Ammonius
    Saccas, 138, 140, 151, 152, 154
    the Peripatetic, 154
Amphiclea, 138, 152
Ananias, 85, 298
Ananus
    (II), high priest, 187
    other, 86
Andrew, 16, 17, 20, 33, 56, 58, 61, 63, 98,

107, 113, 124, 126, 127, 148, 159, 165, 166,
168, 171, 181, 182, 206, 226, 294, 391, 397,
403, 409, 413, 414, 417, 418, 421, 424,
426, 429, 430, 431, 432, 460
Andronicus, 298
Anicetus, 456
Anna, 58, 66
Annan, 109
Annas, high priest, 40, 58, 60, 63, 186, 397,
    450, 451, 452
Annius, 154
Antigone, 174
Antigonus of Soko, 270
Antoninus Pius, 238
Antonius, 151
Apollo, 141
Apollonius,
    of Ephesus, 439, 444
    of Tyana, 145
Apollos, 130
Aquilinus, 153
Archelaus, 61
Aristion (also Ariston), 16, 17, 18, 19, 21,
    28, 29, 32, 33, 34, 294, 417, 419, 420, 429,
    430, 440, 457, 460
Ariston, son of Iamblichus, 152
Aristobolus, 224
Aristotle, 270

509

Josephus, 8, 9, 25, 36, 37, 68, 71, 87, 119,
120, 122, 206, 209, 210, 270, 296, 372,
385, 393, 445, 447, 457
Joses (Joseph),
brother of Jesus, 56, 62, 65, 78, 297
son of Mary, 42, 49, 50, 52, 57, 62, 65
Joshua, 75, 270
Judas (Judah),
Addan/Annan, 109
brother of Jesus (Jude), 56, 62, 65, 297,
413, 451
called Barsabbas, 81
Iscariot, 56, 61, 62, 63, 65, 96, 97, 98, 99,
101, 106, 107, 113, 114, 148, 149, 189,
192, 193, 196, 403, 413, 469
Maccabeus, 110
of Damascus, 85, 451
son of James, 63, 85, 99, 101, 102, 104,
107, 113, 414, 417
son of the druggist, 84
the Galilean, 77, 82
Thomas, 105. See also Thomas
Julius Caesar, 393
Junia, 298
Justin Martyr, 212, 213, 235, 466, 467
Justus,
also called Joseph Barsabbas, 81
of Tiberias, 385

Lazarus,
in parable, 85
of Bethany, 40, 43, 46, 63, 66, 195, 196,
200, 387, 403, 405, 413, 414
Lepidus, 150
Levi,
chief priest, 44
other, 86
son of Alphaeus, 42, 46, 56, 58, 65, 79,
87, 99, 108-12, 148
Linus, 451
Longinus, 143, 144, 152, 153
Lucian of Samosata, 25, 26, 118, 132-37,
141, 146, 150, 218, 219, 220, 232, 300, 409
Luke, 30, 118, 426, 468
Lysanias, 58
Lysimachus, 151, 154

Malchus, 40, 43, 44, 46, 63, 66, 194, 195
Marcellus, 138, 152, 153. See also Orontius
Marcus (Emperor), 150
Mariosa, 43
Mark, 52, 69, 197-201, 205-10, 211, 212, 271,
298, 410, 427, 435, 436, 453, 468
Martha, 43, 46, 59, 63, 66, 194, 195, 403,
405, 414
Mary,
mother of James and Joses, 42, 49, 50,
52, 57, 60, 62, 65, 80, 131, 149, 298
mother of Jesus, 56, 57, 58, 61, 63, 65,
148, 298
mother of John Mark, 298
of Magdala, 34, 42, 46, 49, 50, 51, 53, 57,
59, 62, 64, 65, 66, 81, 131, 149, 298,
395, 406, 441
sister of Martha of Bethany, 40, 43, 46,
59, 63, 66, 194, 195, 196, 197, 403, 414,
441
wife of Clopas, 43, 46, 47, 64, 66, 80,
414
Matthew, 16, 56, 59, 61, 98, 99, 107, 108-12,
113, 236, 288, 294, 417, 420, 421, 424, 453,
454, 461, 464, 469
Matthias,
disciple, 107, 130, 297
high priest, 450
the Hunchback, 81
Medius, 154
Melito, 32, 439
Menahem, 77
Miriam, 75
Mnason, 86, 130, 298
Mordecai, 109, 110
Moses, 75, 78, 127, 270, 387, 446
Musonius, 154

Nathanael, 20, 21, 43, 46, 63, 66, 81, 103,
110, 226, 395, 403, 414, 415, 417, 418, 464,
470
Neves, 43
Nicanor, the Alexandrian, 82
Nicodemus, 43, 46, 63, 66, 87, 88, 101, 378,
379, 403, 414

Oedipus, 174

Index of Modern Authors

Head, P. M., 11
Healy, M., 487-88
Hengel, M., 7, 13, 17, 21, 29-30, 95, 111, 125,
178, 203, 214, 221, 225-26, 238-39, 266-
67, 284, 289, 297, 302-3, 369, 371-72, 413-
14, 416-20, 422, 441-42, 444, 448
Henne, P., 426
Hennecke, E., 451, 460, 463
Henry, P., 137
Héring, J., 266
Hertel, P., 332
Heuer, F., 332
Hezser, C., 288
Hickling, C., 246
Hill, C. E., 16, 110, 213, 227, 421, 423, 426,
433-37, 440, 443-44, 455-56, 463-64, 466
Hirst, W., 311, 314, 337-38
Hitchcock, F. R. M., 360-61
Hobsbawm, E., 316
Hock, R. F., 216
Holmberg, B., 34
Holmes, M. W., 12-14, 16, 18, 26, 214, 226,
294, 417, 419, 429
Holtz, T., 282
Hooker, M., 246
Horbury, W., 73, 83, 95, 426
Hornschuh, M., 464
Horsley, R. A., 95, 191
Hoskyns, E. C., 369, 378
Houlden, J. L., 377
Hume, D., 474-75
Hyldahl, N., 212

Ilan, T., 67-70, 72-83, 85-89, 100, 102-7,
109
Inowlocki, S., 209, 224

Jackson, H. M., 198, 371, 373, 375-76, 393,
401-2
Jaffee, M. S., 251-52, 264, 288
Jenkins, K., 486
Jeremias, J., 101, 450
Jones, C. P., 134-35
Jungmann, J. A., 44
Junod, E., 460, 463

Kaestli, J.-D., 460, 463

Kane, J. P., 82
Kearney, R., 503
Keener, C. S., 288, 363, 365, 369, 381, 393,
401, 413, 416, 420
Kelber, W. H., 176, 248, 273, 283, 310, 316
Kennedy, G., 224, 228
Kiley, M., 111
Kilpatrick, G. D., 111
Kittel, G., 278, 360
Klassen, W., 106
Koch, K., 349
Koester, H., 276-77, 302-3
Kokkinos, N., 441
Körtner, U. H. J., 14, 17, 214, 225
Köstenberger, A. J., 363, 390, 413
Kozin, M., 334
Kraft, R. A., 238
Krodel, G., 238
Kruse, C. G., 413
Kuhn, K. A., 121-22
Kürzinger, J., 13-15, 25-27, 204, 207, 211,
215, 220-23, 225-27, 419, 429

Lagerway, M. D., 500
Lake, K., 434
Lalleman, P. J., 463-64
Lambers-Petry, D., 224
Lane, W. L., 109
Langer, L. L., 493-97, 502
Laub, D., 491
Laughery, G. J., 488
Lawlor, H. J., 434-35, 439
Lawrence, L., 173, 175
Layton, B., 460
Légasse, S., 45
Lemcio, E. F., 275-77
Leo, F., 220
Levi, P., 500
Levine, A.-J., 130-31
Lieberman, D. A., 326, 328
Lieu, J., 374
Lifshitz, B., 80
Lightfoot, J. B., 12-14, 16, 18, 26, 214, 225-
26, 294, 413, 417, 419, 425, 427-29, 431
Lightfoot, R. H., 244
Lincoln, A. T., 361, 378-79, 386-87, 398,
404-6

Index of Places

Index of Scriptures and Other Ancient Writings

24:6	131	1:43-46	403, 414	7:37-39	352
24:6-7	126, 130	1:44	403, 414	8:14	379, 383
24:9	30, 130	1:45	63, 66, 81, 110	8:18	379, 383
24:10	46, 48, 60, 65, 66,	1:45-48	103	8:21-28	353
	80, 130, 131, 138,	1:45-51	403	8:25	389
	298	2–12	402	8:26	383
24:13-35	55	2:3	63	8:44	389
24:18	47, 60, 66, 87	2:8	63	8:57	430-31
24:32	503	2:11	116, 366, 405, 427	9:1	63
24:33	30, 129, 130	2:12	63	9:4	379
24:34	125, 127, 131	2:19-20	353	9:6	343
24:46-49	390	2:22	352, 508	9:18	63
		3:1	63, 66	10:11	396
John	14, 20, 21, 29, 30,	3:2	378	10:15	396
	144, 145, 146, 343-	3:10-13	377-79	11–12	85
	44, 352, 358-474	3:11	370, 376-80, 383,	11:1	63, 66
1	407-8		387	11:16	63, 105, 403, 414,
1:1	364	3:12	378-79		417
1:1-18	364	3:31-32	378	11:40	405
1:6-7	462	3:32	376, 380, 383	11:44	343
1:7	366, 387	3:34	383	11:45-53	196
1:7-8	367	4:7	63	11:49	63
1:14	145, 364, 380-82,	4:39	387	12:1-8	196
	403-4, 406-8	4:46	63	12:3	43, 194, 197
1:14-16	380-81	4:54	427	12:10	196
1:15	63, 367, 380, 388	5:5	63	12:12-19	196
1:16	380-81, 404	5:19-20	378	12:14-16	352
1:18	364, 400	5:31	379, 383	12:16	508
1:29	397	5:32	373, 387	12:17	387
1:29-30	393	5:36	387	12:21-22	206, 403, 414
1:32	376, 380, 406	5:37	380	12:22	391, 403
1:34	376, 380, 406	5:39	387	12:27-33	353
1:35	127, 391, 397, 402	6:1-15	344	12:33	396
1:35-39	418	6:5-7	403, 414	12:38-40	382
1:35-40	391-93, 396-97	6:5-9	414	12:44-46	405
1:35-42	391-92, 395	6:8	391	12:49	383
1:35-51	418	6:8-9	403	13–21	395
1:37	128, 391	6:9	63	13:1	401
1:38	128, 391-92	6:36	405	13:2	106
1:39	128, 392, 398	6:42	65, 66	13:5	343
1:40	63, 127, 417	6:64	389	13:6-9	396
1:40-42	392, 403, 414	6:67-71	403, 414	13:6-10	177
1:40-44	20, 226	6:68	403	13:7	352, 396
1:41	417	6:68-69	177	13:20	285
1:41-42	127, 129	6:71	63, 106, 403	13:23	63, 128, 400-402,
1:42	63, 85, 87, 103, 104	7:7	379, 383		418
1:43	63, 417	7:16	383	13:23-26	393, 395, 397

531